Crystal Clear

The Selected Prose of John Jordan

Crystal Clear

The Selected Prose of John Jordan

Edited, with an Introduction, by Hugh McFadden

The Lilliput Press
Dublin

 First published 2006 by

THE LILLIPUT PRESS

62–63 Sitric Road
Arbour Hill
Dublin 7
Ireland
www.lilliputpress.ie

ISBN 1 84351 066 9

A CIP record for this title is available
from The British Library

Set in Perpetua by Planman I: TES India Ltd
Printed in Dublin by ColourBooks, Baldoyle

Contents

II: Blood, Poetry, P.K., K.O'B. and Heaney

III: Irish and European Perspectives

IV: Poetry Ireland and Literary Erudition

Editor's Acknowledgments

I should like to express my gratitude to the following:

John Jordan's brother, James Jordan, and his sister, Kathleen Jordan (Sr Grace, of the St Louis Order), for entrusting me with the task of being Executor of the Literary Estate of their brother and agreeing to my editing his *Selected Prose*; Antony Farrell and The Lilliput Press for proffering enthusiastic support for this book and for patience while I edited it; An Chomhairle Ealaíon/Arts Council of Ireland for assistance under their Title-by-Title scheme. Dardis Clarke for information on the date of a profile of his father, Austin Clarke, in *Hibernia*; Gerald Dawe, Maurice Harmon and Brian Lynch for furnishing testimonials of support to The Arts Council; Gerald Dawe, Paul Durcan, Seamus Heaney and Pearse Hutchinson for supplying the quotes used on the back cover; also Seamus Heaney for information on reviews of his collections of poetry; Finola Graham for permission to use letters of her late husband, Francis Stuart, and a poem; Maurice Harmon for information on *University Review* and *Irish University Review*; The Jordan Family, Marie-Louise Colbert, the late Maurice Henry, Pearse Hutchinson, John O'Neill and Vincent Woods for permission to reproduce photographs in the book; Maureen Gillespie, Picture Editor of *The Sunday Tribune*, for the photograph of Gainor Crist; Ben and Frances Kiely for information on reviews of Ben Kiely's work; The private owner of the portrait of John Jordan by Edward McGuire for permision to use a photographic reproduction on the cover; my thanks also to Sally McGuire; John Mulcahy and Nuala O'Farrell for their co-operation and information on *Hibernia*; Hayden Murphy, of *Broadsheet* fame, for sending me 'Silence', and for information on 'Untitled Diary of a Festival', and for sharing memories of John's visit to Edinburgh; Donough O'Brien and Eibhear Walshe for information on the papers of Kate O'Brien; Daniel Reardon for information on some John Jordan scripts broadcast by RTÉ; Stephen Ryan for permission to reproduce the portrait of John Jordan by Pauline Bewick; Jonathan Williams for giving me his opinion of an early draft of the material.

The editors of the various magazines and newspapers in which some of these essays, articles and reviews were published; the staff of the Dublin City Library and Archive at Pearse Street, Dublin (The Gilbert Collection) for all their professional help and courtesy, particularly in accessing newspapers and periodicals; Valerie Lang, who keyed-in much of the material, without whose help it would have taken much longer to prepare a typescript; finally, my thanks to all the members of my family for patience while the editing of this work was being done at home.

Hugh McFadden

Crystal Clear

The Selected Prose of John Jordan

Introduction

When Antony Farrell of The Lilliput Press asked me to write this introduction, he said something that rather shocked me: he said it would be necessary to explain to the younger reader who John Jordan was. The idea that a literate reader interested in literature or the theatre might not be very familiar with the life and work of John Jordan was a somewhat startling one for somebody like myself, who entered University College Dublin at a time when John's work as a literary critic and reviewer of drama was appearing regularly in newspapers, magazines and academic journals, and his very distinctive voice could be heard frequently on the radio, on arts magazine programmes and in the Thomas Davis Lecture Series. 'The man Jordan', to use a Jordanian expression, seemed ubiquitous. As a former actor on the stage of the Gate Theatre and elsewhere, he wrote with the authority and insight of a Thespian on contemporary drama; he was an outstanding and charismatic lecturer in English at UCD, who did with considerable charm what few other lecturers could do – both enlighten and entertain his students; he edited a literary magazine, *Poetry Ireland*, which was ground-clearing as well as ground-breaking, and reviewed books widely, most notably in *Hibernia* magazine, where he also wrote a stylish column once described by a UCD-graduate friend as the source of much of his education. He was well known, even by the unbookish, for his broadcasts on all manner of topics on the popular RTÉ Radio show, *Sunday Miscellany*. Later, he proved to be a mesmeric interviewee on such TV shows as *Folio*, hosted by Patrick Gallagher.

Besides, he was a 'legendary' figure (to use a current expression) by the time I first got to know him in the early 1960s. He was a close friend of Patrick Kavanagh, who valued his intellect very highly. The two of them could be found together quite frequently in that by-now mythical establishment, McDaid's of Harry Street, sometimes in the company of other writers such as Pearse Hutchinson, Anthony Cronin, or the editor/proprietor of *Envoy*, John Ryan (later proprietor of The Bailey bar and restaurant). Surprisingly, for someone who was so close to Patrick Kavanagh, he was also a good friend of Brendan Behan. And, perhaps more unusually in Dublin literary circles at that time, he championed the work of Austin Clarke as well as that of Patrick Kavanagh. He was even, *mirabile dictu*, on reasonably good working terms with Flann O'Brien/Brian Ó Nualláin/Brian Nolan/Myles na Gopaleen. . . in all that remarkable individual's nomenclative or nomenclatural guises. (See 'A Letter to Myles' [q.v.], and 'Untitled Essay on Flann O'Brien'[q.v.].)

And part of the legend or myth was that he was a friend of Gainor Crist, so wildly caricatured by J.P. Donleavy in his novel *The Ginger Man*. Tales of bohemian days in the Dublin of the fifties were told with some relish in the sixties, sometimes by people who had never set foot in The Catacombs, that subterranean haunt in the basement of 13 Fitzwilliam Place which often served as an after-hours annex to McDaid's. And, of course, John Jordan was a friend of Hilton Edwards and Micheál Mac Liammóir; moreover, he was a regular guest at the Dublin townhouse home of Edward Packenham, Lord Longford, and his wife Christine, Lady Longford, whose Longford Productions Company staged plays at the Gate for six months of every year at this time.

He was also a close friend of Kate O'Brien, the novelist, and two other formidable women of her circle, Enid Starkie, the Oxford don and biographer of Baudelaire, and Lorna Reynolds, an academic colleague at UCD. Yet, despite these creative, bohemian, even radical friends, he was highly regarded by somebody as mainstream and conservative as Jeremiah J. Hogan, later President of UCD. He could maintain cordial relations with persons who 'had the ear of the Archbishop of Dublin', the eminent John Charles McQuaid, as well as with those who 'caught the eye' of Paddy O'Brien, the celebrated and much-loved manager of that famous, even infamous, bar in Harry Street.

So, it is not an easy task to encapsulate in a few thousand words the remarkable career and personality of John Edward Jordan (1930–88), actor, poet, storywriter, academic lecturer, literary and dramatic critic, broadcaster, renowned editor, ranconteur and faithful friend who had a genius for friendship. He was an unusual person who moved in a variety of circles with equal ease and decorum, whether it was in the groves of academe or among the clientele of McDaid's, with its strange mix of writers, artists, ageing 'revolutionaries', self-proclaimed anarchists, actors, flower-sellers, solicitors, clerks, bank officials, musicians, bookiesrunners, students, house-painters, scholars, eccentrics, chancers and 'go-be-thewall' characters ... not to mention the occasional innocent abroad who just happened to wander in.

But to begin, in the traditional manner ... John Edward Jordan was born in the Rotunda Hospital, Dublin, on 8 April 1930, the eldest child of John Anthony Jordan and his wife, Mary Agnes (*née*) Byrne. His father worked at the Guinness Brewery in James's Street, Dublin. His mother Mary was born in Jarrow, England, of Irish parents. The family, which later included his sister Kathleen (Sr Grace) and his brother, James, lived in Park View Avenue, Harold's Cross.

John was educated firstly at Donore Avenue CBS and then at the Christian Brothers' School, Synge Street, both schools situated off the South Circular Road in Dublin. He was a pupil at Synge Street when the novelist and broadcaster Francis MacManus and Noel Barry taught there, quickly demonstrating his intellectual ability. As Ben Kiely observed much later in a tribute, great teachers such as these two men were entitled to expect great results from a pupil as talented as John Jordan. He really was a prodigy and his precocity can be seen clearly in his astonishing letters [q.v.] to James Agate, the distinguished English drama critic who worked for *The Sunday Times* and the BBC. At the age of fourteen John Jordan was writing regularly to Agate and his assistant, Leo Pavia. Agate included this correspondence in his *Ego* diaries, published in book form in the *Ego* volumes 7, 8 and 9 (London 1945–8).

In May 1945 Agate lunched at The Ivy in London with Hilton Edwards and recommended that the Gate Theatre director, who was looking for an assistant stage manager, should take on 'the boy Jordan'. At the age of fifteen 'the boy' began working for Edwards and Mac Liammóir at the Gate . . . after school hours, of course. A year later John was a script-reader for the Gate directors and was not slow in advising them about the plays they should be putting on. From the letters to Agate it can be seen that the teenage prodigy had already read much of the great literature in English and the scripts of an astonishingly wide range of dramatic works. He had scoured the shelves of the public libraries of the city, particularly the one nearest to his home, Rathmines Public Library at the end of Leinster Road, just around the corner from Park View Avenue.

At Synge Street his companions in the secondary school included Patrick Swift, later to become a distinguished artist; Pearse Hutchinson, now equally distinguised as a poet, who was in a class a couple of years ahead of him; and Ronnie Walsh, afterwards a noted broadcaster with RTÉ and presenter of the long-running programme *Sunday Miscellany*, on which John Jordan broadcast frequently in the 1960s, '70s and '80s. He demonstrated his early interest in literature when with these friends he set up the Synge Street Literary Society. Even before he left school he had begun to tread the boards at the Gate. When he gained a scholarship to UCD on the results of his Leaving Certificate, he faced the dilemma of whether to enter college and begin to follow his head along an academic path that would lead on to Oxford University and then back to UCD as a lecturer, or to follow his heart and throw himself into an acting career at the Gate Theatre.

It was a dilemma that he never entirely resolved to his own satisfaction, though he chose the cerebral and academic path and took up the Entrance Scholarship to University College, Dublin. There he quickly made a mark, becoming auditor of the English Literary Society. His guests as speakers at his inaugural meeting were the novelist Ben Kiely and Lennox Robinson, the playwright and former Abbey Theatre stage-manager.

He continued to act at the Gate during the late forties and early fifties, most notably in their production of *Hamlet* on location at Kronborg Castle, Elsinore,

Denmark, in which he played Bernardo and Lucianus. The programme for *Hamlet* notes that Jordan came to the Gate from university theatre, where 'he had most success as Synge's *Playboy [of the Western World]* at the Arts Theatre, Cambridge, and at The Playhouse, Oxford, in 1950, and as 'Creon' in the Dublin Arts Theatre's *Antigone* in 1951'. He also acted with Longford Productions, the company run by Edward and Christine Longford.

John Jordan took a Double First in English and French in his BA degree at UCD and won the Laforcade Medal and Cup after a nation-wide public contest in French in 1951, *concours oratoire et littéraire*, and was presented with these prizes by the then French Ambassador, Count Ostrogog. (The runner-up in this contest was John Montague, the poet.) In 1952 he won the prestigious National University of Ireland Travelling Scholarship; later, he was awarded an MA for a dissertation entitled 'Samuel Daniel: An Appreciation'. Early in 1953 he became a scholar at Pembroke College, Oxford, where he chaired the Arts Committee, was President of the Johnson Society, and was a noted player with the Oxford University Dramatic Society.

At the same time, under the pen name John Renehan, he contributed verse that was sophisticated for his age to the Oxford college journal, *Trio*. In 1955 he took a B. Litt from Oxford for a thesis entitled 'A Study of the familiar verse-epistle in English, 1590–1640, from printed works' (Oxford University 1955) [see an abridged version of part of this thesis as 'The Early Verse-Letters of John Donne' (*University Review*, vol. 2, no. 1)]. His tutor at Pembroke College, Oxford, was Helen Gardiner, a Hopkins' scholar, who had a reputation in some quarters of being temperamentally inimical to Irish Catholicism (seemingly paradoxical this, given her interest in Gerard Manley Hopkins). In any event, for whatever reason, John Jordan decided not to pursue any further postgraduate study at Oxford, leaving Pembroke College in 1955 and returning to Dublin as Assistant in the English Department at UCD. Later, in 1959, he was appointed Assistant Lecturer in English and then in 1964 he became College Lecturer.

This writer remembers how good he was as a lecturer, recalls the extraordinary intensity with which he recited lines from Shakespeare's *Richard III*, on the miniature stage of the Physics Theatre in Earlsfort Terrace; how he brought Chaucer's *Canterbury Tales* to life, and gave really memorable lectures such as the one on Johnson's 'On the Death of Dr Robert Levet'. There was a good deal of the actor's art in these performances, married with the acute sensibility of an exceptional critic and close reader of texts.

In 1962 he began editing *Poetry Ireland*, that seminal sixties magazine that continues to influence contemporary Irish poetry in a line that proceeds through other such magazines which it influenced; from James Liddy's *Arena* (co-edited with the late Michael Hartnett), to the short-lived *The Holy Door*, to *The Lace Curtain*, *Cyphers* and the current successor to *Poetry Ireland*, the *Poetry Ireland Review*, the first eight issues of which John Jordan edited in the 1980s.

But, back to the future: in 1962 he contributed a short story (by no means the first he had written, but the first one I recall reading), called 'First Draft', to *The Dolmen Miscellany of Irish Writing*, introducing us to that wonderfully exotic dame, Mrs Rose McMenamin (who proposed 'to give up the drink'), and to other colourful characters. In the editorial of the first number of *Poetry Ireland* [q.v.] he set out his policy: 'We are committed to no school, no fashion, no ideology. But we abhor mere opinion. We would wish, in the humblest of ways, to contribute towards the recreation of Dublin as a centre of letters. We hope we have the blinds up and the door on the latch.'

So he had ... and so he and his *Poetry Ireland* magazine did. And it was very much his magazine, bearing the stamp of his sharp, stylish and critical judgment. Yes, he had an advisory board of James Liddy, James J. McAuley and Richard Weber, but it was he who made the editorial judgments. In this journal he published the best of the established poets, including Clarke, Colum, Hewitt, Kavanagh, Donagh MacDonagh; near co-evals whose stars were on the rise, such as Thomas Kinsella and John Montague; and he 'discovered' some important new poets, including Paul Durcan, Michael Hartnett (Harnett) and Seamus Heaney. The magazine set the hallmark standard for all of the other poetry journals in Dublin that followed it throughout the next three decades.

By the beginning of the sixties John Jordan had already begun to establish a growing reputation as an astute literary critic and a fine dramatic critic. As early as 1955, in *University Review* he wrote an incisive essay on Sean O'Casey, challenging the received idea of O'Casey as the 'Dublin labourer of genius' [who] wrote three great plays for the Abbey but went astray when he left for exile in England after the unfortunate contretemps with W.B. Yeats over the rejection by the Abbey Board (in fact by Yeats) of *The Silver Tassie*. The essay, 'A World in Chassis' [q.v.], took apart this cosy thesis, the notion of 'the two Seáns' – the first one he described as 'Our Seán', who 'recorded passionately and sympathetically the slum-world of the 1920s, and in so doing came upon the mystery of tragic suffering'. 'Our Seán', in fact, was 'a man we could all be proud of'. Then there was the other Seán, to quote the then Bishop of Meath, 'Poor Old Seán', who 'was an affront to Faith and Fatherland, an elderly corner boy who does not care for priests or nuns, and who seems forever to be holding his thumb to his nose'. But, wrote John Jordan, it is doubtful if the first Seán ever really existed, outside the mis-readings by Irish commentators and 'mis-hearings of the early masterpieces'. This was a theme developed by him over the years, as he courageously championed the later O'Casey. [See, also, 'Illusion and Actuality in the Later O'Casey', in the John Jordan Papers, NLI List no. 45, 35,056/6(1–2); also 'Seán O'Casey 1880–1980' [q.v.] (*Hibernia* 27–03–1980), and 'The Passionate Autodidact' ... [q.v.] (*Irish University Review*, vol. x, no.1), and 'Dublin's Prometheus-Autolycus' [q.v.] (*The Irish Press*, 12–11–1981).

With equal valour and perspicacity he championed James Joyce, at a time when it was 'neither popular nor profitable' (to paraphrase Myles). This editor recalls that as late as 1962 one could not find a copy of Joyce's *Ulysses* displayed on the open shelves of any bookshop in the centre of Dublin. The only book-shop whose staff admitted, on being asked, to having *Ulysses* among its stocks was George Webb's old establishment on the southside quay near the Ha'penny Bridge. It was possible to purchase a copy there, on request, if one seemed to have reached the age of majority, provided one made the request in a suitably quiet and grave voice. It would be retrieved from a backroom and furnished in a brown-paper bag, rather like a 'carry-out' reluctantly slipped by a 'curate' to a regular at the side-door of McDaid's after-hours, it having been ascertained first by the tetchy 'curate' that the coast was clear.

This dog-in-the-manger attitude towards Joyce did not daunt John Jordan when, at the age of twenty-six, shortly after he had just taken up a lecturing post at UCD, he reviewed Hugh Kenner's book *Dublin's Joyce* [q.v.], once again in *University Review* (vol. 1, no. 12, Winter 1956), and Richard Ellmann's monumental *Life, James Joyce* (see, 'Joyce: One of the Boys' [q.v.], in *Hibernia* in October 1959). Meanwhile, the Alma Mater of both J.J.s studiously avoided any acknowledgment that Mr Joyce had ever graced its academic groves or corridors ... not a plaque, plinth or bust of Shem the Penman was to found anywhere near Earlsfort Terrace or the Green ('Stephen's, that is, my Green'). Nor, as far as I recall, was there any piece by Joyce on the English course when this editor began reading outside that course *c.* 1962–6. Jordan chided those of his countrymen who had a supercilious attitude towards the Joyce scholarship being carried out by foreign writers, especially Americans.

So the wider atmosphere in which John Jordan worked as a critic and an academic at this time was stolidly conservative, socially and politically very cautious, even among some Establishment elements a little reactionary. In this milieu that was so 'safe' and middle class, the essentially radical free spirit that was John Jordan. attempted to carve out a body of critical work in journals and magazines that took in the best of Modernist writing, from Pound and Eliot (see 'Jottings on the Use of the Grail Motif ... in *The Waste Land* [q.v.]), to Joyce and D.H. Lawrence (see 'On D.H. Lawrence' [q.v.]). He made the case for O'Casey and Synge as major playwrights in world literature, and examined both the work and tragic legend of Oscar Wilde, again at a time when it was anything but safe to dwell very long on Oscar (Micheál might get away with it, but he was different ... besides, he spoke Irish and was some kind of adopted patriot, of sorts!). John Jordan cherished the Irish language and its great literature (see, 'Aogán Ó Rathaille' [q.v.] and '*Deoraiocht*, le Pádraic Ó Conaire' [q.v.]. He had apronounced European, even internationalist, outlook. He had much regard for the best French, Spanish and Russian literature, in particular he cherished such French poets as Villon (whose *Les Regrets de*

la Belle Hëaumiere he linked, for the purpose of demonstrating an apt correspon-
dance, to the Gaelic masterpiece *The Hag of Beare*); Ronsard, Joachim du Bellay,
Jodelle, Rémy de Belleau, Louise Labé, but most especially the great French poets
of the nineteenth century, Gautier, Rimbaud, Baudelaire; and, in the twentieth century, Apollinaire, Paul Valéry, Jules Laforgue, Paul Éluard and Louis Aragon (see
'*J'ai Lu Tous Le Livres*' [q.v.], and 'Perfect Thoughts' [q.v.]). Among Spanish writers
he cherished such different, even disparate, souls as St John of the Cross, St Térèsa
of Avila, Lope de Vega, Calderon de la Barca, Antonio Machado, Cervantes and
Federico Garcia Lorca. And, of course, he had a special love for Avila, which he visited on a number of occasions, walking in the footsteps of Térèsa (see 'For Avila
with Love' [q.v.], and 'Kate O'Brien: *The Stony Thursday Book*' [q.v.]).

Of the Russian writers he admired Turgenev, Dostoevsky, Gogol and Tolstoy;
yet he chose to highlight in a radio broadcast a Russian writer who might appear to
have been a lesser luminary, Ivan Goncharov, whose marvellous novel *Oblomov* he
identified as being strangely modern, if not postmodern, in spirit (could Beckett
have been quite influenced by the peculiar anti-hero of this novel, the forerunner
perhaps of a line of supine, somnivolent, do-nothing Murphys, Molloys and
Malones?). He was acutely aware also of contemporary developments in European
theatre (see, '*Ùbu Roi*' [q.v.] and the three pieces on Beckett – 'Man's Last Dignity'
[q.v.], 'What Does It Mean?'[q.v.], and '*Il Rit Donc Il Vit*'[q.v.] – whose work he
almost instinctively understood).

So, the record shows that Mr Jordan was a man with a developed European
sensibility, one who from his late teens onwards began to visit the great cities and
cultural centres of the Continent, not alone the expected metropolis nearest our
shores, London, but also Paris, Monte Carlo (for the ballet), Salzburg, Florence,
Verona, Venice, Rome, Madrid, Barcelona and, later, Granada. This, at a time when
most people in Ireland were struggling to emerge from the grey soup of 'The
Emergency', long before the advent of the dreaded 'package tours', and before the
setting up of the EEC and the European Movement. As Ben Kiely recalled in a tribute he gave at the Requiem Mass for John Jordan in 1988, the Dromore novelist
and ranconteur was astonished at their first meeting around 1948 to hear the eighteen-year-old Jordan discuss the latest novel by Sartre with Pearse Hutchinson,
who introduced Ben to the prodigy in the Ritz Café near Independent House in
Abbey Street.

His idea of the kind of cultural milieu towards which he wished to see his people move was an inclusive one that would take full account of the cultural riches of
European traditions, in a variety of languages. He abhorred Irish national exclusiv-
ity (see 'Three Faces of Ireland'[q.v.], '*Collected Poems* by Thomas McGreevy'[q.v.],
'*Ireland and the Classical Tradition*'[q.v.] and 'Irish Catholicism' [*The Crane Bag*, vol. 7,
no. 2, 1983], among other pieces).

Oddly enough (as Jordan himself was wont to say), although he was temperamentally a cosmopolitan reformist and wrote in *Hibernia* in support of Irish writers who once were ostracised in polite society, including Wilde, Joyce and, more recently, Brendan Behan [q.v], he found himself criticized by a letter-writer in *Hibernia* who mis-read a piece that John Jordan wrote called 'Censorship. What Peter Lennon Said: John Jordan Comments' (*Hibernia*, February 1964). The rash would-be barricade-stormer accused Mr Jordan of not being sufficiently liberal because he took issue with some of the criticisms of Irish society by a journalist from *The Guardian*, in particular an attack on the President of UCD, Dr Michael Tierney, which John Jordan described as a 'ludicrous inflation of the President of UCD into some kind of Caudillo figure'. Mr Jordan was brave enough, as a still relatively young lecturer, to state in *Hibernia* that 'I am totally out of sympathy with most of the president's disciplinary actions against student activities' [the first stirrings of what later became a strong student demand for university reform – the 'Velvet Revolution' – had begun to make itself felt]. For his pains, he was still criticized by a letter-writer, Denis Harte, who rounded on 'people like John Jordan …' Mr Jordan replied: 'Since 1959, with a five-month break in 1963, I have been exposing myself in the columns of *Hibernia* to attacks from "the people" Mr Harte thinks I'm like.'

It was not an easy task in Dublin to be a critic with a popular audience and a high profile. In a 'Report on Thomas Kinsella'[q.v.] (John Jordan Papers, NLI List 45) John Jordan wrote: 'If what follows has any value, it will be due partly to the fact that my judgments are not likely to be slavered by personal affection or dislike, by awe or envy. Dublin's literary jungle is probably no better or worse ultimately than that of any other city. The aggravating hazard, however, lies in the fact that the jungle is miniature and the beasts keep on running into each other.' In 'Off the Barricade'[q.v.], in *The Dolmen Miscellany*, he wrote:

> Only in Dublin, perhaps, is it necessary to announce that there can be such a thing as criticism unloaded with personal animus. But Dublin … is so ingrown in its literary alliances that the little verse-reviewing which is done is often pocked with timidity, and non-committal. There is, indeed, in the whole Irish literary world, a tendency towards the formation of Protection Societies. I, too, have lived in Arcadia.

But John Jordan is the exception who proves the rule. For an example of studied objectivity in the criticism of a friend's book, have a look at 'Mr Kavanagh's Progress' [q.v.], published originally in *Studies* (Autumn 1960), which is one of the many gems in this *Selected Prose* and a case study in clinical dissection of both the strengths and weaknesses of Patrick Kavanagh's poetry up to and including *Come Dance With Kitty Stobling*. He also demonstrated his lack of bias in giving due credit to the importance of the work of Austin Clarke (see 'Austin Clarke' [q.v.] and 'The Clarke Canon'[q.v.]), despite the fact that Dublin at that time was divided into two camps, the Clarke and the Kavanagh camps, and generally speaking ne'er the twain did meet. For insight, see also his reviews of the novels of his friend, Francis Stuart: 'Spiritual Odyssey' [q.v.], 'Things to Live For'[q.v], and 'Small and Threatened Places'[q.v.].

As a critic he championed a number of women writers, most notably Kate O'Brien [q.v.], but also Elizabeth Bowen (see 'Jamesian Novelist'[q.v]), Molly Keane and the Abbey playwright Teresa Deevy, long before a feminist critique had developed. It is one of my regrets regarding this volume that demand on space prevented me from including John's lengthy essay entitled 'Teresa Deevy: An Introduction', which was published in *University Review* (Spring 1956). He described her in his essay, 'The Irish Theatre – Retrospect and Premonition', in the journal *Contemporary Theatre: Stratford Upon Avon Studies 4*, as 'the only genuine new voice of the Thirties' [in the Irish theatre]. Further, he said, 'Teresa Deevy in two plays, the unpublished *Temporal Powers* (1932) and *Katie Roche* (1936), treated with extreme delicacy the intangibles of human contact. Much influenced by Chekhov and perhaps by Jean-Jacques Bernard, she showed herself a mistress of silence and pause as expressive means of communication, and wrote dialogue that plays and reads as if quotidian words had never been uttered before.' He would have been very pleased that the Abbey revived one of her plays some years ago.

Throughout the sixties and seventies his reviews, both of books and plays, in *Hibernia* were particularly valuable. At such times as during the Dublin Theatre Festival it almost seemed as though there was only one drama critic in the country, so ubiquitous were his reviews. (The only other one worth mentioning at the time was Seamus Kelly, a.k.a. *Quidnunc*, of *The Irish Times*.) Space allowed only a sample selection of the most interesting play reviews (see, for example, *Murder in the Cathedral* [q.v.], *Othello* [q.v.], *Long Day's Journey Into Night* [q.v.], 'Theatre Reviews, 1964'[q.v.], *The Quare Fellow* [q.v.]: See, also, 'Untitled Diary of a Festival, Edinburgh 1979' (John Jordan Papers, no. 45, 35056/6[12]).

But among the more significant pieces in this collection are the long considered essays on the Irish theatre, such as those already mentioned on O'Casey, on 'Oscar Wilde' [q.v.], the marvellous take on Irish attitudes towards death as revealed by playwrights such as Synge, and other writers, called 'Amor Fati Sive Contemptus Mundi' [q.v.], and the *pièce de résistance* written for *The Irish Mind* (edited by Richard Kearney), entitled 'Shaw, Wilde, Synge and Yeats: Ideas, Epigrams, Blackberries and Chassis' [q.v.]. Another *tour de force* of criticism is the Thomas Davis Lecture Series essay on Goldsmith, 'The Startled Hare: Goldsmith as Literary Journalist' [q.v.]. Other notable long essays include his examination in *The Crane Bag* (Forum Issue) of religious attitudes among Catholics here, the day before yesterday and the deluge, called 'Irish Catholicism' (unfortunately too long to include in this selection). On the other side of the fence, as it were, there is a fascinating dissection of the writing and editing of the Northern dissenter (if one may call him that) Tom Paulin, in which John Jordan demonstrates a rigour of investigation and acute questioning that would be the envy of any Protestant sensibility (see 'Chapter and Verse' [q.v]).

The years from the mid-sixties to the end of that decade were difficult ones for John Jordan, as a succession of friends died during that time. In 1964 Gainor Crist died suddenly while on a sea voyage to the Canary Islands, allegedly after 'going on a spree' with the captain of the boat. In March of that year, Brendan Behan gave up the ghost, due to a collapse brought on by diabetes aggravated by alcoholism. He was only one month into his forty-first year. On 6 May 1966 his friend the painter Robert Mac Bryde, who shared a house in Upper Leeson Street with Patrick Kavanagh (and Dr Richard Riordan and Frank Henry), was knocked down by a car and killed not far from the house. On 1 April that year, also in Dublin, the novelist and columnist Flann O'Brien died.

John Jordan had experienced health problems himself. A bout of TB in 1962 had left his constitution fragile. On holiday at Christmas 1963 from his post in UCD he took ill early in the New Year of 1964 while on a visit to Gainor Crist and Pamela O'Malley in Barcelona (see, 'The Haemmorhage' [q.v]). By 1966 his life in Dublin seemed to have closed in on him: the strain of lecturing, writing and reviewing and much 'socialising' with his friends in McDaid's had begun to take its toll. He took leave of absence from his staff post at UCD and took up a position as Associate Professor of English at the Memorial University of Newfoundland in St John's. (The farewell party for him in The Bailey was memorable: it being the time of 'flower power', the poet Paul Durcan purchased red roses from a stall at the corner of Grafton Street and bedecked the tables and those [including this editor] sitting at them with these regal flowers.)

It was while he was lecturing at the Memorial University in Newfoundland late the following year that John Jordan heard the sad news of the death in Dublin of Patrick Kavanagh. It profoundly affected him (see, 'Obituary for Patrick Kavanagh' [q.v.] and 'To Kill a Mockingbird' [q.v.]). Resigning from his professorship in St John's he returned to Dublin to mourn his close friend. In 1969 he also resigned his post at UCD, in what he called 'an amicable settlement', in order to concentrate on his own creative writing. The seventies produced a flurry of books in a few years. He had been hospitalized in 1969, not long after a trip to North Africa at the end of 1968. Out of this stay as 'a guest of the Dean's' off James's Street, Dublin, came the startling poems in *Patrician Stations* (New Writers Press 1971). The volume was dedicated to Austin Clarke, whose fine long poem, *Mnemosyne Lay in Dust*, was echoed by the equally fine, if shorter, verse, *A Guest of the Dean's*. It was praised by the critics, but later some commentators expressed regret that Jordan's earlier poems had not been collected and published first. In 1975 Gallery Press did publish early work (including the brilliant 'Second Letter to P.S.'), together with later verses, in *A Raft from Flotsam*. His publishing history was further confused in 1976 when Gallery issued *Blood and Stations*, which contained two prose pieces, including 'The Haemorrhage', along with an expanded *Patrician Stations*. (For a discussion of Jordan's publishing history and how it may have affected his career, see Macdara Woods' Introduction to *The Collected Poems* [Dedalus Press 1991].)

In 1980 a limited edition of new verse, entitled *With Whom Did I Share the Crystal?*, appeared. Its short poems are acute aperçus: they include antic pieces (e.g., 'For Julius Henry Marx') and elegantly restrained elegies for Kate O' Brien ('Without Her Cloak') and Micheál Mac Liammóir ('Micheál').

In 1977 Poolbeg Press published a collection of short stories, modestly entitled *Yarns*, culled from work done since the end of the forties up to the sixties. Many had appeared in literary magazines, a few in David Marcus's 'New Irish Writing' in *The Irish Press*. (Jordan's *Collected Stories* edited by myself were published by Poolbeg Press in 1991.) Most are set in Bohemian Dublin and capture the era of McDaid's at its zenith, with echoes of The Catacombs, Baggot Street and 'Low' Leeson Street and environs. This *mise-en-scène* is the backdrop to tales of outsiders, dreamers and social misfits in an alternative city, 'exiles on Main Street', compassionately portrayed with humour and native Dublin wit.

The closure of the magazine *Hibernia* at the beginning of the 1980s was a great loss to its readers, especially those who looked forward to its review pages and, in particular, the reviews and columns written by Mr Jordan. (A short-lived successor, *New Hibernia*, did appear later for a couple of years. Now his main outlet for book reviewing, if not theatre reviews, was *The Irish Press* [of mixed memory!].) Here for some years he continued to produce very fine reviews of books, but no longer had he an outlet for regular theatre reviews – which accounts for the lack of material on two of that decade's most significant playwrights, Brian Friel and Tom Murphy. It is my personal knowledge that John Jordan admired at least two of Friel's plays from that time, *Faith Healer* and *Translations*. I also know, because I accompanied him to the play, that he was much taken by Murphy's *The Gigli Concert*, and that he considered it to be a major drama. It is regrettable that he did not get an opportunity to review these plays in a newspaper or magazine.

Somewhat surprisingly (but not really to those who knew him well), he began to write a Crime Column for *The Irish Press* Book Page in the early eighties. He had always liked to relax with such lighter stuff and was an enthusiast of the writings of Raymond Chandler and Dashell Hammett and their ilk. Some of these reviews are very good (a review of Graham Greene springs to mind), but part of me wishes he had continued to concentrate solely on more highbrow literature (he rebukes O'Casey, the autodidact, for being a literary snob for looking down his nose at some of the books on the tables of Yeats and Lady Gregory ... see 'The Passionate Autodidact: The Importance of *Litera Scripta*').

By the mid-eighties his physical health had begun to decline. He had had several bouts of illness over the years, no doubt exacerbated by his 'lifestyle' – he was a heavy smoker of untipped cigarettes and he had developed a growing dependence on alcohol. When he was not working, that is writing or broadcasting for RTÉ, he spent more time in the pub than was good for his health. Remarkably, though his physical strength began to wane, he retained a very good memory (he used to say that he had 'total recall'). And his spiritual well-being seemed to be unaffected by his lifestyle. But he began to look ten years older than his age ... 'when you get to my age'. In 1986 he suffered a relatively mild stroke and was hospitalized briefly in St Steeven's in Dublin. He made a recovery and went back to work. His critical faculty had not been noticeably affected (the following year he wrote the excellent piece which concludes this book, 'Chapter and Verse'). At the beginning of June, 1988, he went to Cardiff to attend the Cumann Merriman Summer School, which had gone on location there. He died suddenly in his hotel in Cardiff on the morning of 6 June 1988. He was only fifty-eight He was buried in Mount Jerome Cemetery near Harold's Cross Green, not far from his home in Park View Avenue, after Requiem Mass concelebrated by F.X. Martin OSA, in the parish church. His friends and fellow writers Ben Kiely and Francis Stuart delivered tributes in the church. Other writer friends – Paul Durcan, Pearse Hutchinson, Macdara Woods and the present editor – read poems at the graveside in honour of his memory. The late theatre director and actor Jim Fitzgerald recited lines from Shakespeare's *Cymbeline*:

> *Fear no more the heat o' the sun,*
> *Nor the furious winter's rages;*
> *Thou thy worldly task has done,*
> *Home art gone, and ta'en thy wages.*

In a special memorial section of *Irish University Review* in the autumn of 1988 F.X. Martin, the historian and a colleague at UCD, who had also attended the Cumann Merriman School in Cardiff, was one of the contributors who paid tribute to John Jordan. He wrote, *inter alia*:

> It is important that figures such as John Jordan, who have played a stimulating role in Irish cultural life during the past three decades, should not go unrecorded ... Much of his output was expressed first in university lectures, later in radio and television talks, also in a multitude of articles in journals, magazines and newspapers. Nearly all of them were *ad hoc*. By contrast, the ponderous tomes of other Irish scholars, once in print, are certain to have a major impact on later historians of Irish cultural development ... Who is willing to locate the elusive spread of John's newspaper and magazine articles?

This was said in hope, perhaps, but it was more of a rhetorical question than a real expectation. F.X. was more than a little surprised when I told him shortly afterwards that I intended to do it.

This book has been a long time coming. In the early nineties, after editing John's *Collected Stories* and his *Collected Poems*, I began work on collecting and collating 'the elusive spread' of his literary articles. At that time the publisher Colin Smythe expressed an interest in publishing such a volume. Unfortunately, as a journalist with the late lamented *Irish Press* (should that read, *benighted?*), which was then in a perpetual 'state o' chassis', the project had to be postponed. But the seed of the idea of the book was planted much earlier than that. Sometime, either at the very end of the seventies or in the early eighties, John Jordan asked me whether I would consider editing a selection of his prose, perhaps a selection from his *Hibernia* columns and reviews over nearly three decades. It wasn't possible then: the demands of working the late shifts on the City Desk or City Stone in Burgh Quay ruled it out.

And now it is done ... at last. Here is a book that I hope will do justice to the talents and memory of a remarkable man and a fine and stylish critic. It is a long text, but it had to be so, because John Jordan was a very prolific critic and an important one in the literary life of this country. The volume could have been nearly twice the size it is. One hopes that it will entertain and enlighen readers over many an evening's reading sessions. As for methodology in arranging the text, I have combined an element of chronological arrangement with a thematic one: so that, for instance, the pieces on Joyce, or O'Casey, or Kavanagh, are grouped together in the order of composition of the articles on these writers. Some reviews of drama and of poetry are also grouped together, where possible. Otherwise a chronological sequence is followed.

'The man Jordan' is still much missed by his friends. He was a truly singular individual and one of the most lovable persons that I had the privilege to know. He taught this writer, one of his former students, a very great deal. He used to say to me on occasion: 'You know, Hugh, you and I have a spiritual relationship.' The first time he said it, I was slightly taken aback at the seriousness of the remark. Although he had a tremendous sense of humour and at times an antic wit, he was essentially a serious and moral person. And he had a genius for friendship. The artist Michael Kane, whom I met at the commemoration of Patrick Kavanagh at the canal-bank seat at Baggot Street last St Patrick's Day, was surprised and very much taken when I told him that John Jordan, who was God-father to my daughter Catherine, never forgot the anniversary of her baptism, Easter Sunday, and her birthday on New Year's Eve, when he would arrive at our house bearing gifts for his God-child. It was a very different image for the artist to ponder, he who knew him as a man-about-town, and a bohemian area of town at that.

He was a complex man, gentle of nature, spiritual by nature. Politically he was always on the side of the underdog. No doubt his sexuality gave him an understanding of the outsider in society, but his Christian compassion already gave him that gift of empathy and fellow sympathy. Lest it be thought he was unduly grave, it must be said that normally his company was full of humour and fun. Everybody who knew him well has a charming, quaint or hilarious story to tell. Hayden Murphy, the poet-editor, recalled recently a trip to the theatre in Edinburgh when John addressed the cast of a theatre Company from Georgia in the then Soviet Union before they took the stage for a performance in their own language of *Richard III*. The cast was bewildered as John Jordan addressed them in French and Irish: and then told them, 'Don't mind me. I understand.' Indeed, he did.

My good memories of him are legion: from Terrace to Avenue, from the Physics Theatre in Earlsfort Terrace, or salad days around Leeson Street and St Stephen's Green, to 'vendible days' off Grafton Street. A trip to the theatre or the opera in his company was an adventure. Overhearing his amazing conversation sometimes caused unwary souls to turn and stare. One such unfortunate who did so in The Gaiety must still be blushing at the response. There were many hilarious trips in 'motoring cars'. One taxi-man got the response, 'Don't be absurd', when he had the temerity to ask him, 'Mr, do you mind me asking you, how do you earn your crust?' John pronounced the 's' of absurd as though it were 'z'.

And, of course, I remember him 'resting on my dreaming sofa'. In fact, he was very complex, but there was a sense in which he had a spiritual simplicity of soul. He could see correspondances everywhere: such as the time we sheltered together in a doorway near Grogan's pub during a heavy thunder-shower that flooded the gutter underneath the lamplight beside us. The light running through the water reminded him of lines from Rimbaud's 'Le Bateau Ivre', which he then recited: '*Comme je descendais des Fleuvres impassibles ...*'

And days in Harold's Cross ... and his going home. Allow me to end with a few lines composed at my home (near his own family's house) in Harold's Cross, after his funeral in Mount Jerome, near the park, or Green, which he loved.

The verse is entitled 'J.J.' (*for John Jordan*):

We spent a long evening talking
about you, sometimes as though
you had gone no further than
on holiday. Hours later, alone,
as the house settled into silence,
I re-read your lines for Mees Katie,
the real threnody. And I recalled
you resting on my dreaming sofa

listening to Broonzy and the Blues:
when, as we went deeper south
to Mississippi and to Lady Day,
you said: 'For the love of God
will you play me some Mozart.
You know, I'm a simple man.'
Then you smiled, beatifically.

I

FROM AVENUE TO SPIRES TO TERRACE

Letters to Leo Pavia and James Agate[1]

[Agate's entry in his diary:]

'Leo came in this morning (December 22nd, 1944) with two letters and saying: "I think you'll have to print this kid in *Ego* 7. You and I can afford to wait a couple of years, but to a boy of his age, it's an eternity". Here's the first letter.'

> 18 Park View Avenue,
> Harold's Cross,
> Dublin.
> December 2nd, 1944[2]

Dear Leo Pavia,

I have gathered in the past from *Ego* that, despite those barbed, cynical witticisms to which you give vent, there is no one in James's circle possessed of a heart like yours! That your heart is of the finest part of pure gold is proved by the fact that you deigned to answer my absurd guff. I was as glad of your signature as I was of James Evershed Agate's when I received a little, very patient note from him in July. I was sorry he didn't include the Evershed part of his name. You may be interested to know why a person of my tender years – I'm fifteen in April[3] – should lavish his devotion on a critic of James's eccentricity. Well, Mr A. opens for me the door of a new and brilliant world – a world of culture and, to a certain degree, refinement. If ever I have any pretensions to literary culture, I may thank James. He alone is responsible for my love of Shakespeare. I thank him from the bottom of my poor schoolboy's heart. With my first introduction to J(ames) A(gate) my love of reading grew to a love of good reading. He made me realize the glory of the stage as compared with the cinema. He introduced me to, and made me familiar with, the divine Sarah. She stands like a glittering ornament in a corner of my brain – oh pooh! I suppose you're thinking that this is just another example of my particular kind of nonsense. Well, believe me, it's not. I'd be obliged if you let James read this effusion. Tell him that despite his almost Ben Jonsonish coarseness I think he is one of the finest writers in the English of today.

> Sincerely,
> J.E. Jordan.

'Leo replied, saying that I hoped to find room for his letter in *Ego 8*,⁴ and would he mind being referred to as "a talented little beast". Today comes this:'

Second Ego Letter

18 Park View Avenue,
Harold's Cross,
Dublin 6w.
December 17ᵗʰ, 1944.

Mr P.!!!,

Despite your Heart of Gold, you can be deuced malicious! I don't for a minute credit your story of my letter being printed in *Ego 8*. Why? Because I know well that James can't be further than *Ego 7*. Like our Mr Shaw (what a mature ego I have!) I'm a 'hopeless duffer at mathematics', but I know the fundamental rules of addition and subtraction. According to my calculations *Ego 8* won't be started till 1946! Of course I may be wrong, but I think you're pulling my leg. Anyhow, thanks for replying. At this point a happy thought strikes me. James should publish a book called *Agatian Nights*, containing all the witty things said by you and that extraordinary Mr Dent during the past twenty years. But to return to *Ego*, I'd adore having my letter printed in *Ego 7*, but not in *Ego 8*. I don't object to being called a 'talented little beast'. However, I'd rather it was 'ingenious' than 'talented'. 'Talented' is rather hard to believe, especially from Mr A. I have decided in future to refer to Mr A. as the high-priest of the goddess Sarah. Oh, Mr P.! I also play the piano atrociously. Through experience I've discovered that anyone who plays the piano is talented! My tastes in music are terribly lowbrow-hackneyed things like Rimsky-Korsakov's *Spanish Caprice*, the Prelude to Act 3 of *Lohengrin*, and the Grieg *Piano Concerto in A minor*. But I'm getting prosy, so I finish.

As ever, yours sincerely,
J.E. Jordan.

Third Ego Letter¹

18 Park View Avenue,
Harold's Cross,
Dublin

29–3–1945.

Dear Ogre,

I'm afraid you're an ogre with a tendency to be naughty. Why? For letting J.A. waste his leisure moments in replying to me. I know James, dear fellow that he is, can't restrain these kind but rash impulses. But you ought to have more sense. Indeed, your letters would seem far too skittish, to some people. However, I enjoy people of advanced years with a youthful sense of humour. As Elia says, 'I hate people who meet Time half-way; I am for no compromise with that inevitable spoiler.' You see, I suppose, that I'm writing this letter simply for the sake of getting a reply. A letter from you now and again would keep me alive. I'm bored to death. There is nothing so boring as a conventional childhood for one who knows that there is such a thing as an unconventional childhood. People in my circle don't read anything worthwhile, don't say anything witty, and for a young prig like me that's unbearable. I'm in the mood at this point for giving a highly emotional outburst, but I know what effect that would have on a hardened old cynic like you. But I'm boring you now, and I'd hate to think that. Spare a few moments and reply, like a nice kind ogre.

> All the best
> From your clever child,
> J.E. Jordan.

Fourth Ego Letter[1]

> 1 8 Park View Avenue,
> Harold's Cross,
> Dublin 6w.
> 20–4–1945.

Ave Dulcissime Leo!

I shall attempt to deal with your charming letter in the same logical, businesslike manner that you dealt with mine.

Firstly, 'J.E.' stands for John Edward.

Re my not getting an opportunity to talk, I meant that there is no one to talk to. At least, not in an intelligent manner. You may, Leo, go over to your desk and deliver a magnificent speech on 'Art for Art's sake'. But the desk remains dumb. You can get no satisfaction out of making your magnificent speech …

I hope you weren't expecting a witty letter bubbling over with Noelisms,[2] and Irish humour as typified by our Mr Shaw. You bemoan the fact that the English have never heard of anybody. Well, they can't be worse than the Dubliners. Earthly bliss for them is realised in some awful blonde showing her hideous legs in some film, or some horrible he-man doing vulgar gyrations in a private cop's tailor-made. *Othello*, running for ten performances, broke all records. A ham thing like *Irish Eyes Are Smiling* ran for nearly a month at one of Dublin's biggest cinemas. No wonder the late Mrs Shaw[3] left her fortune for the advancement of culture in Dublin!

You must forgive my dulness [sic] today. There's a heat wave here and my latest short story hasn't turned out so well. Perhaps some day in the starry future I will send James one of my efforts.

There are no existing photos of me at my present ripe old age. Any at earlier ages show me as an odiously stupid child (which is exactly what I was). Here is a rough description of me at present:

Body. Long, thin, and awkward. Lots of leg.

Hair. Once fair, now mousey, and has distinct aversion to restraining influences.

Nose. Sir Hook and Sir Bulbous fight a bloody battle.

Eyes. In colour – blue. In quality – like the last drop of very weak tea. In expression – 'Insipid with veracity', as Henry James's father said about Swedenborg

Mouth. Thick, sensual upper lip and ordinary, unremarkable lower lip.

Altogether I'm like an embarrassed horse. Reply if you get time. Love to James.

Vale, carissime Leo!
J.E. Jordan.

[Agate's entry in his diary:]

'Lunching at the Ivy, by a stroke of luck I fell in with Hilton Edwards, the Director of the Gate Theatre, Dublin. I told him about the boy, and Edwards very graciously said that if Jordan would call he would see whether he could find something for him at the theatre. He said he badly wanted an assistant stage – manager, and I suggested his starting the lad as call-boy with a view to his learning the theatre from the beginning. Nobody can make careers for other people, but a push at the start does no harm.'

May 16
Wednesday. 'Another letter from our little Irish friend.'

Fifth Ego Letter

18 Park View Avenue,
Harold's Cross,
Dublin.
Saturday, 12th May, 1945.

Mr Dear James
My Dear Leo,

First let me thank you, James, for your very thoughtful introduction. I won't embarrass either you or myself with a surfeit of sugary nonsense. Suffice to say that I am immensely grateful. I expected the interview with Mr Edwards to last a quarter of a minute – after which I would be heaved out on my egotistical ear

Actually we talked from seven till a quarter to nine! About what? About everything concerning the theatre, from sex appeal to sentiment. At first I informed Mr Edwards (whose affability and condescension would have won the heart of Mr Collins) that I desired to become one of that 'fine body of men' – as Max Beerbohm called the critics – but I'd better not repeat what Mr Edwards said. We discussed acting, Sarah, Rachel, and other things about which I know practically nothing. Mr Edwards invited me to come round after each show and talk with him. (Magic words, O James and O Leo!) His partner, Mr Mac Liammoir, whom I used to plague with my unasked-for criticisms, drifted in, presssed my hand, swore eternal friendship, and drifted out again.

And now, dear James, please forgive me if I address the rest of the bombast to Leo. Thank you, Leo, for such a charming letter. Such taste! I'm afraid I'm like Lady Teazle at the time of her marriage – I have no taste. Well, if you really want to know: (a) My favourite dramatists are Shakespeare, Shaw, Synge, O'Casey, and Tchehov [sic]. I also burrow in Marlowe, Kyd, Jonson, Webster, Ford, and Tourneur. And, if you're of my way of thinking, you may throw in Eugene O'Neill with the last three! (b) Favourite poets are Tennyson and Yeats – why, I don't know. (c) Favourite essayists, Lamb and G.K. Chesterton. (e) Favourite annoyances, Wilde and Maugham!

Thine and James for aye,
J.E. Jordan.

Sixth Ego Letter

June 16

Saturday 'J.A. is a believer in taking his good where he finds it. In other people's correspondence, perdy! Here is another letter to Leo from his and my little Dublin friend.'

18 Park View Avenue,
Harold's Cross,
Dublin.
June 12th, '45.

Mon cher Papa Pavia,

What has this *enfant terrible* done to offend you? Has he said something unusually stupid? Has his spelling been more insulting than ever? In brief, my sweet lion, why the stony silence? I don't mind waiting two or even three weeks for a reply, but it is exactly four weeks since I wrote to you, telling of my perilous adventures in Harcourt Terrace.[1] Or have the wretched postal authorities mucked about with my fragrant murmurings?

Sir, you are cruel! Each morning for the past three weeks have I patiently awaited the postman. My heart has pounded eagerly each morning: my dreams have been coloured by gloriously witty notes in your distinctive typewriting. But alas, I have been so very sadly disappointed. My anxiety has been such that from a Paycockish state of 'chassis' I have advanced into a Pepysian condition of 'with child'. I am afraid, gentle beast, that you are a 'prevaricator and a procrastinator'. So, please, don't postpone answering this effusion. Answer it now and be doubly witty.

My blood boils at the thought of those vulgar persons who write to James reminding him that he isn't as young as he used to be; the person whom James answered in *The Sunday Times* a week ago was the subject of much vitriolic abuse from my faithful tongue. Personally, I dislike most persons under thirty-five. This includes actors and actresses. I like my actresses to be about thirty-nine or forty. There isn't a single movie actress under thirty, with the exception of Jennifer Jones, whom I would pay to see. Among my chief aversions are women under twenty-five who smoke. This oddity of mine has caused me much embarrassment in the past. But I shall enlarge when I am writing my memoirs. These will be Agatian and very sentimental. Sentimentality has caused me much unhappiness in my fifteen years. My sentimentality is not that of dear Sir James Barrie and his fragrant creations, drenched with the odour of spring flowers, 'dewy with nature's teardrops'. It is a sticky, sludgy, sweaty sentimentality, which has drained me of moral courage and the ability to defend myself. I have received countless little injuries in the past. I have for a while nourished 'slaughterous thoughts', but soon I have forgotten, to be injured yet again.

But this is all drivel, and I must not risk offending you. Were you a brilliant mathematician in your youth? I am quite absurd in the face of the simplest geometrical problem. Probably because I am forever thinking of other matters. You see, I am not what the lower-middle classes call a 'healthy-minded boy'. I often wish I were. James seems to have been aggressively healthy in mind. What about you? Please tell me more about yourself. (Even at present I'm thinking about something totally unconnected with this letter – Lady Longford's voice. Though I have never spoken to this brilliant creature,[2] I very often 'tail' her and her husband, simply to hear their voices.)

Now please reply and be intensely witty, and earn the unlimited gratitude of

Thy,
In a state of anxiety,
Very lone,
Very lorn,
J.E. Gummidge-Jordan.

Ps. As usual, my best wishes to the other J.E.[3] Does the poor lamb still suffer from asthma?

Seventh Ego Letter

Saturday,
June 23, 1945. 'Again from our little Irish friend – this time to me.'

You want to know about my family? There's nothing remarkable. None of my great-aunts comforted Parnell in his hour of tribulation. Nobody gambled away the family fortune. I had a great-uncle, who was kicked out of the navy for drinking, and I believe my grandfather also drank. But no man can be sober for ever, and we must be satisfied.[1] My great-grandmother was killed in an earthquake somewhere. Which is all the piquancy in an incredibly prosaic family. Are my parents clever? Dear people, of course. My mother wallows in the philosophy of life propounded by Ethel M. Dell, Ruby Ayres, Berta Ruck, and the rest of the talented ladies who fool all the female public all the time. My father reads the newspapers. Harold's Cross has gone to the dogs altogether.[2] The place reeks of poor imitations of the Captain – O'Casey's, not Strindberg's – and old-age pensioners who spit tobacco all over the place. Gentility is confined to a few back avenues where everybody is as snobbish as can be, and the word 'common' echoes all through the day. When I was small I wasn't allowed to play with 'common' children. You will be interested to know that the cook and the second footman have given notice. At the rate things are going, the mater will have to clean the brasses herself. I asked Lady L. about lending us a butler, but she said she had murdered the last one some time ago.

[Entry in Agate's diary, op. cit., p. 159]
'Note from my little Irish friend, with his photograph, in which I trace something of the spirituality of Stephen Haggard combined with the truculence of the Irish navvy.[3] He writes: 'I am so glad you and Leo don't quarrel. There is something so poetic about two old gentlemen passing their days together in peace and harmony ...''

Eight Ego Letter[1]

Wednesday,
October 10. 'Letter from Leo's and my little Irish friend.'

> 18 Park View Avenue,
> Harold's Cross,
> Dublin.
> 6th October, 1945.

Dear James,

I am desperately sorry.[2] Like Harold Skimpole I am a 'mere child' and my emotions are usually false. But I am genuinely sorry. Leo was always very kind to me in his letters, and I don't think that I ever fully realised that he was seventy and ill. It seems incredible that a sick man could write with such unfailing cheerfulness, but I might have known from passages such as this:

'I grow serious. And if you had a heat-wave and then a week of freezing cold, rain, snow, sleet *and* a cold in the head so violent that when you sneeze the houses on the other side of the road commence to wobble ... you would be in a grave state of mind. I was so grave I thought for a whole day of nothing *but* the grave. And about the Sting. Sting, do I say? Not at all; at the worst, only a mighty clout on the head.'

Again:

'I was a cynical child, bitter-tongued and ruthless. That I have grown so sweet and benevolent in later years is just the mellowing of a vintage wine. Oh, John, pray that the dust and cobwebs may not cover the bottle all too soon!'

I've nothing more to say. I can't be flippant in the realisation that Leo won't answer me. But this is awful! I shall shed tears in a moment. You are very lucky to have had a brother like Edward Agate and a friend like Isidore Leo Pavia.

Sincerely,
J.E. Jordan.

Ninth Ego Letter[1]

December,
1945.

Dear James,

Many, many thanks for *Ego* 7, in which I am engrossed. You really can't realise what a pleasure it is to be able to have at least one of your books in my possession. Of the 27 books of yours which I have read, *Ego* 7 is the first I have owned.[2] The book seems to me a great deal less vulgar than *Ego*s 1 to 5 (I haven't read 6). I believe *Ego* will become, after some preliminary ups-and-downs, a classic. A few years after your death, people will cease to read *Ego*. Then, after a century or so, some clever young man will 'discover' you. Whereupon, people will read the *Ego*s, and then write books about them. Then, essays will be written about your 'circle', and enquiries will be made ...

I'm very interested in what you say about Oscar's plays. I myself can only bear *The Importance*, and *Salomé*. The others creak and are exceedingly dull. Recently, in this God-forsaken city, Mr Edwards produced *An Ideal Husband*. As soon as I heard it was to be done I started a campaign against it. I besieged Mr Edwards (who, by the way, has grown tired of me; the novelty of being told your business by a child wears off) with complaints. But it was produced, I was bored to death, and everything was a great success. Not that I object to artificiality. I adore Congreve and Sheridan. But two-hundred years have not yet tarnished the gold of the characters of *The Way of the World*, and *The School for Scandal*. Fifty years have sadly chipped the gilt-paint of Oscar's creations.

George Moore. Once, when I was more priggish than I am now, I thought George Moore an odious character. Careful reading and re-reading of *Ave*, *Salve*, and *Vale* taught me how wrong I was. He had, I think, a singularly fresh and unspoiled mind. I, a schoolboy, take myself very seriously. I take my views on sex, religion, and politics, all very seriously. George Moore was another schoolboy who did much the same. A proof of his eager, schoolboy-eager mind is the perfect gravity with which he related his expedition with Æ on bicycles in search of the ancient Irish gods. He was always credulous and always absurd in a manner startlingly like mine. The 'sinning' of G.M. can be taken just as seriously as the 'sinning' of a schoolboy. Susan Mitchell, in her very good book on George, wrote, 'Mr Moore is no Rabelais, his Irish nature forbids it'. And again, 'Perhaps the Latins can sin gracefully, the Irish cannot'. Which hits the nail on the head. G.M. was a very great literary craftsman, but he never grew out of his callousness.

In case you're interested, Dublin is getting crazier and crazier, vulgarer and vulgarer. If things continue as they are, Dublin will become the stronghold of Philistinism. The latest UNFORGIVEABLE eccentricity has been to present *A Midsummer's Night's Dream* in Persian settings and costumes. Everybody (except Sybil Thorndike's son, Christopher Casson, who played Oberon) seemed to have his mouth full of half-masticated buns.

I beg and implore you for a picture of Leo! He himself promised me one 'when I get back all the things I have given to various people to take care of'.

My very best wishes, dear James,
J.E. Jordan.

Tenth Ego Letter[1]

(21 August 1946)

Dear James,

My friend Miss Wood has written me of her visit to your flat. 'A little before noon a near-petrified young person crept up the stairs at Queen Alexandra Mansions and rang the bell with trembling hand. There was a short silence, then a discreet fluttering among some long curtains which could be glimpsed through the frosted glass door. A hurried conference inside, then the door was opened by a quiet, shy, very gentle young man in a dark suit, and wearing an oddly tired, peaceful look ... At the end of the dark hall there hovers for an instant a Vision, some Sage of the Lower Ganges, wrapped in many a billowy shirt (none of which covers its dainty ankles), white hair standing straight up, large horn-rimmed spectacles terrifyingly directed towards me. The Vision disappears.'

Mr Agate says will the boy please write to him. The boy would be very pleased to spend his nights and days writing to Mr A., if Mr A. ever replied. Indeeed, the boy's admiration for Mr A. has been revivified by hearing him broadcast two or three times of late. The boy agrees that no poet living can write as Tennyson *did at his best*. The boy agrees that all modern composers, except Sibelius, can't hold a match to Beethoven, or for that matter poor, dear, unappreciated Haydn. The boy would give all modern music – always with the glorious, soul-ravishing exception of that tremendous genius Sibelius – for Beethoven's *Violin Concerto*, or indeed Tschaikowsky's *Symphony No. 5*. (However much people sneer at T., the fact remains that his melodies are still lovely and infinitely better than anything done by contemporary composers.) The boy would give all books published by intellectuals today for one volume of Dickens or Jane. (He likes, however, Kate O'Brien and Elizabeth Bowen, Evelyn Waugh, Graham Greene, Seán O'Faoláin, and one or two others.) The boy still likes Mr A. better than any other critic, despite his lapses into nonsense, his jaundiced eye, his bourgeois complacency, and his rather boring vulgarity.

The boy signs himself Mr Agate's devoted servant.

J.E. Jordan.

Eleventh Ego Letter[1]

December 1946

'In remembering my dear Rebecca's enchanting letter after Brother Mycroft had called her 'odious' (*Ego 2*, p. 105), I have no hesitation in including part of the latest from my little Dublin friend, J.E. Jordan.'

Browsing in *Ego 2*, my back against the hard library shelves,[2] my chest heaving with joy, I was delighted to see how much your nice Brother Mycroft dislikes that awful Rebecca West. The woman is intolerable. For me, her one redeeming quality is her genuine love for you. God knows I'm no Virginia Woolf fan, but I infinitely prefer her 'meandering' novels, which you find intolerable and unreadable, to the gibberings and mouthings of *la* West! I grunted in satisfaction when I saw in your January 2nd *Tatler* article mention of Théodore de Banville and his foreseeing of the cinema. I wondered when you were going to use that; I was amazed that a man of your perspicacity had not noticed the startling common sense of Baring's essay on 'Punch and Judy', in which he quotes Théodore. But now you *have* used it, and I'm glad. Baring's death shocked me. Only Shaw (90 this year), Wells (80 this year), Belloc (76 this year), and you (69 this year) remain of my literary gods. Enough. I'm gibbering in a singularly Rebecca-ish manner.

Sincerely,
J.E. Jordan.

Twelfth Ego Letter[1]

1947
March 26,

Wednesday. 'In a letter from my, and Leo's, little Dublin friend, J.E. Jordan, now official play-reader to the Gate Theatre:'

I sometimes wish I'd never read a line of you, that I'd never, out of curiosity, taken down from the library shelves the bulky first two volumes of *Ego*; then I should never have acquired, perhaps, a taste for the past, its people and its art, far exceeding in intensity my taste for the present and the future. I should then have developed in the normal fashion of the modern youth, and cultivated a passion for poetry about lavatories and copulation, and novels about lavatories and copulation, and (dare I say it?) music about lavatories and copulation. I should then have acquired a healthy contempt for doddering dramatic critics dribbling about an old barnstormer called Irving and a French cow called Bernhardt. I suppose it's possible to retire into one's own intellectual and spiritual planet and gaze only occasionally and with complacency on the worlds of one's fellows. But it comes with age, I imagine. At fifty it may be that I shall be able to write in perfect sincerity, like Edward Agate: 'What do I care for anything that can happen to me at Thomson's Cross so long as I have the surge and surf of the Great Pandemonium in my ears?' But not at seventeen.[2]

Dublin's Joyce[1]

(University Review, Winter 1956)

A glance at Magalaner and Kain's *Joyce, the Man, the Work, the Reputation* (New York 1956), with its elaborate notes and bibliography, is enough to dismay any non-Joycean specialist. (It, also, by the way, is sufficient reminder that the vast bulk of serious work on the subject is the fruit of transmarine students.) Joyce, whether, as in this country, he is approached with kindly, slightly deprecatory scepticism, superstitious mistrust, or adolescent self-identification, is already, within twenty years of his death, part of our literary heritage. He may no more be ignored than Homer, Virgil or Shakespeare.

And it is the outstanding merit of Professor Kenner's massive examination of the canon that for the first time, so far as I know, a wholehearted attempt has been made to establish Joyce's position, not in terms of a specifically twentieth-century phenomenon, but in relation to the whole history of Western culture. Nothing could be further from Kenner's approach than that, say, of Mr Sean O'Faolain, in his *The Vanishing Hero*: a fresh contribution to the old 'romantic' view of Joyce as rebel angel, Joyce as interchangeable, allowing for the inevitable re-orientations of the creative act, with Stephen Dedalus. Professor Kenner's bias is traditional and classical; it is also veered by acquaintance (one cannot say how profound) with modern neo-Thomist thought, by distrust of both nineteenth-century introspection and nineteenth-century liberalism, and (it seeps from the whole book for this reader) by a general dissatisfaction with post-Renaissance man. Certainly, Professor Kenner appears committed to the view that post-Kantian man underwent a kind of Second Fall: the backbone of his book is the thesis that Joyce must be seen as critic, in the most serious sense, of nineteenth and twentieth-century civilization. On the title page, we find an epigraph from Oedipus's speech to the Thebans: '*I grieve for the City, and for myself and you ... and walk through endless ways of thought.*' In one context, Kenner's Joyce is an enlightened Oedipus, and his Dublin a Thebes, stricken by no physical plague, but by intellectual and spiritual petrifaction. '*The Dublin from which he was exiled, even when he felt its stones beneath his feet, was the paralysed form of the historic City.*' There is no sneer intended when I observe that the very tone of this sentence, sonorous, evocative, is an index of the extent to which Professor

Kenner's imagination is engaged with Joyce as a type of the classical hero, his work the testimony of a lucid, coolheaded scapegoat.

By the 'historic City', Professor Kenner, I gather, wishes to indicate the civil manifestation – ultimately, perhaps, no more than a blueprint of the imagination – of Western culture, before the advent of Romanticism, and of its consequent tendencies towards the psychic displacement of the individual and the flying apart of intelligible reality. In Dublin, Joyce found to hand the fossilized skills of Europe, the Trivium – Grammar, Logic and Rhetoric – preserved by his Jesuit teachers. The spirit of those skills, he found fugitive and corrupted in the modes of Dublin speech and the unconscious *personae* of his contemporaries. Hence the grammarian, Stephen, a *'reader of signatures'*, the logician Mulligan *'a master of ironic disputation'*, and the rhetorician Bloom, *'a frustrated doctus orator.'* It is typical of Professor Kenner's commitment to thesis that he finds it necessary to place Bloom as a Senecan, as distinct from Ciceronian rhetorician, and go still further, with the statement that Bloom's rhetoric is *'a parody of the Enlightenment, which was itself a slicking-up of the idealized Seneca.'*

Like his subject, Professor Kenner's work has ramifications, back-corridors, niches and crannies: the central thesis of Joyce as critic of civilization has all manner of subsidiary theses, maintained with dazzle and craft, but weakened in impact by the relentlessly authoritative fashion in which they are set down. No reasonable reader should object to Professor Kenner's parallel between, on the one hand, Sherlock Holmes (aesthete, decadent, reader of clues) and Stephen Dedalus, and on the other, the 'Watsonian Conan Doyle' and Leopold Bloom. But Professor Kenner writes without a single tentative breath, so that even the most sympathetic reader must wish to cry out for some relaxation in the unvarying assumption that the world constructed here for Joyce's putative critique, is necessarily the *only* one. The trouble – and it is not wholly to be unthankful for – with Professor Kenner's approach is that it involves a multiplicity of specialist skills: that of the philosopher, of the sociologist, of the cultural historian, of the statistician, even, as well as of the numerous branches of 'literary criticism.' It results, this approach, in a gigantic superstructure on the texts which bears almost as great a relationship to what Professor Kenner's reading has encompassed, as it does to Joyce. One must admire the inventive use Professor Kenner makes of allusion and cross-reference from pre-and-contemporary - with - Joyce literature: he offers numerous bright starting-points for critical chases. One must respect the imaginative intensity with which he invests his hero with completely conscious awareness of his work's direction. And one must be grateful for the attempt to see Joyce in a worthwhile perspective. (The book should be required reading for young men in this country, interested in contemporary literature, be it academically or otherwise.) A definitive work on a giant cannot be expected. But anyone who ever presumes to write about Joyce must take cognizance of this heroic exegesis

Joyce: One of the Boys[1]

(Hibernia, 30 October 1959)

From 41 Brighton Square West, Dublin, February 2, 1882, to the Fluntern Cemetery, Zurich, January 15, 1941,[2] Mr Richard Ellmann details with exemplary scholarship and tact the progress of James Joyce, apostate and man of genius. It is a monumental achievement and will for decades be a happy hunting-ground alike for Joycean specialists and casual students.

And before going on to discuss some aspects of the book, let me protest against a fashionable tendency to sneer at American scholarship on the grounds of its weight (avoir du pois). Someone has to undertake the patient headaching business of collecting the facts and collating the testimonies of a man's life.

I trust that our many Irish pundits, who have not yet grown out of the habit of regarding Joyce as one of the boys and consequently not to be taken seriously, will pay due attention and respect to Mr Ellmann's seven hundred and forty-six pages of text and some hundred more of apparatus.

Clongowes Wood, Belvedere, the old Jesuit-run University College, Paris, Pola, Trieste, Zurich, Trieste again, Paris again and Zurich, Mr Ellmann has filled in numerous gaps, always with an eye for his subject's human frailties and with discretion, his many considerable virtues.

The only other biography is Herbert Gorman's, published in 1941, a vulgar and flashy piece of Joyce-doctored hero-worship, even allowing for the difficulties under which Gorman worked. It can have done no good for Joyce's reputation.

But Mr Ellmann's surely will, though [it is] no spraying job, and motivated by a deep love of Joyce as one of the greatest Christian writers of our time, rather than, as some well-meaning people would have him, a great 'Catholic writer'.

I must not, however, fall into the journalist's temptation of attempting capsule-form literary criticism. I will merely add that for many Catholics, lay and clerical, throughout the English-speaking world, *Ulysses* is the greatest attempt ever to render the condition of man, when he lives in a world where the Word has become words, the Verb become gestures. Leopold Bloom is Adam in the nets of evening, the evening of Western civilization. To deny him is to deny our humanity and our common plight.

But back to base. It is hard to distinguish in Joyce's life between that part of it which was geared by genuine feeling, and that fashioned consciously towards the fulfilment of a myth. From the evidence it is difficult to avoid the conclusion that he sought the slights and unkindnesses which he built into the language of betrayal and persecution.

The young Joyce was excessively precocious and hopelessly out of line with (as time has shown) the highly pitched, but insecurely founded, enthusiasms of his generation.

While his contemporaries at University College (a 'tragic generation' that would repay study as a group – Dr C.P. Curran might or may have done the work) were engaged in learning Irish, he was learning Dano-Norwegian. While they were getting up protests against *The Countess Cathleen*, he was pondering the relationship between Drama and Life, steeping himself in the literature of Europe, writing little verses which owed more to Campion than the school of old Æ, studying Dante and D'Annunzio, sprouting the wings that would bring him to the mainland of Europe.

And this precocity, this intellectual and temperamental isolation, combined towards the creation of a *persona*: the Rebel, the Outsider, the Aristocrat, Parnell, Wilde, and with the years, the whole boiling of those who found themselves out of tune with the official or popular baying.

I am inclined to think that as a private man (the writer is always public – his safeguard and his cross), Joyce never fully succeeded in disengaging the fact and fiction of his own mind and heart. In his role of [the] persecuted, some of his actions and his letters are distressingly reminiscent of Frederick Rolfe (Corvo) and his megalomaniac heroes.

His behaviour is sometimes justified, as in the case of *Dubliners* and George Roberts (whom I knew when he was too old and I was too young; but whose personal kindness I must record). At other times, it shows signs of an almost psychotic self-dramatization.

And it is interesting to note that Carl Jung professed to find in Joyce ('not easily freudened') signs of the malady that erupted catastrophically in his daughter Lucia.

Quite arbitrarily, I would single out from Mr Ellmann's thesaurus the information he has brought together on the subjects of Joyce's Galway Héloise, Nora Barnacle, his common-law wife for twenty-seven years, and afterwards in civil law, and his gifted daughter, Lucia, whom he was to watch growing steadily madder for over ten years.

Mr Ellmann confirms what we have always known from the testimonies of friends: that Joyce was more faithful to his semi-literate and wholly unintellectual Nora than many a husband strengthened with the graces of Matrimony. And she repaid him in like fashion.

Mr Ellmann quotes a narrative dictated by Mary O'Holleran, Nora's girlhood friend, to Kathleen Barnacle, her sister: 'she was the straightest pal I ever had'. This testimony from an old woman, 'not good at writing', might serve for Nora's epitaph in her relations with 'Jim'.

On the delicate subject of Lucia, Mr Ellmann is both revelatory and decorous. She is still living in a mental home. Many of those who attended her tragedy (she might have been the Ophelia in Joyce's, or Dedalus's, reconstruction of *Hamlet*), are alive also. It is to the lasting honour of Mr Samuel Beckett that he has allowed his part in the tragedy to be recorded. And, incidentally, Mr Ellmann supplies a picture of Joyce and Beckett together, which may well be the best starting-point for an investigation of the genesis of *Waiting for Godot*.

No one can claim that Joyce had not his share of the world's normal suffering, hunger, humiliation, remorse. He had more than his share of exceptional suffering: recurrent periods of blindness, frequent intense agony, the horror of his child going mad in her twenties. A man I knew once said to me, 'Such are the wages of sin'. One could look at it in another way.

My shrivelled pedant's soul will this time restrain from pointing out one or two misspellings, and the re-christening of the Registrar of N.V.I. (*sic*). But surely 'T.G. Keller' should be 'Thomas G. Keohler', one of Æ's singing birds? The context (p. 208) suggests so. The Catholic University was founded in 1854, not 1853.

But more important than these slips are certain statements impugning the veracity of a contributor to *Hibernia*: Mr Michael J. Lennon (16/10/59) has stated that in the autumn of 1929 he 'had no direct contact with Joyce'. In March 1931 Mr Lennon wrote an article for *The Catholic World*, on Joyce and his family.

Mr Ellman (p. 655) describes Mr Lennon as one 'with whom he [Joyce] had been friendly for several years'; later (p. 656) he identifies Mr Lennon with 'people to whom I had done nothing but friendly acts', a reference in a letter to T.S. Eliot, written on January 1, 1932, and finally (p. 737) he records Joyce as describing Mr Lennon as one who 'had accepted favours from him and his family'.

Does all this talk of friendship and favours refer to the drink Joyce gave Mr Lennon in the Euston Hotel in August 1930 (*Hibernia* 16/10/59) and the meal the same night (do. 23/10/59) Incidentally, Mr Lennon's articles provide a valuable supplement to Mr Ellmann's account of Joyce's efforts for John Sullivan between July 1930 and March 1931.

But in the interests of truth it would be well to clear up the details I have listed. No one will be surprised if Joyce has distorted the facts.

Joyce Without Fears: A Personal Journey

(from A Bash in the Tunnel: James Joyce by the Irish)[1]

There still exists in Ireland a body of opinion which tends towards reductive comment on the labours of foreign Joyce scholars. I have heard derisive comment even on Richard Ellmann's by now classic biography. These people pride themselves on their first-hand information on, and intimacy with, Ireland, with Dublin, with the Roman Catholic Church. Yet only three full-length studies of any aspect of Joyce have been written by Irish people to date: J. F. Byrne's *The Silent Years: An Autobiography with Memoirs of James Joyce* (1953): *Our Friend James Joyce*, by Padraic and Mary Colum (1959), and Constantine P. Curran's *James Joyce Remembered*, (1968).[2]

The acknowledged Irish Joycean mandarins, Niall Montgomery and 'Andrew Cass', have not found it worth their while to assemble their findings in book form. It would be comic, if it were not disgraceful, that Maurice Harmon has had to say recently, 'It is … significant that the two Irish contributors to this collection of essays take Joyce seriously, concerned as scholars everywhere are with the literary achievement, its modes, relationships and sources'.[3] Now, admittedly, there is a considerable quantity of shale in the Joycean academic machine. But on the native side there is also, I suggest, a burden of resentment that good American dollars, especially, should be lavished on a local who started off little better than many another middle-class Irish boy, an education by the Jesuits and a B.A. from University College Dublin as his equipment. My countrymen veer between extravagant praise and snide depreciation of those of their fellows who have been successful by international standards. And a fair share of the depreciation goes to the intellectual and the artist.

In fairness, half-baked attitudes to Joyce and his monument more lasting than gall have diminished, and diminished rapidly, over the last fifteen to twenty years. In 1947, I recall, my lay schoolmaster in English at the Christian Brothers, an estimable man on many counts, spoke briefly of Joyce in hushed tones. I will never forget the sepulchral, monitory, tone of his last words: 'He died blind.' One had to resist the impulse to chirp, 'So did Milton.' Book One of *Paradise Lost* was part of our curriculum.

Nineteen forty-seven, that was the year I first read *Ulysses* and what follows is an account of how it was possible for an Irish boy to become acquainted with and grow to love Joyce, before ever he had heard of Homeric parallels or had read even a paperback translation of the *Odyssey*. In some particulars my experience may have been singular, but I believe that on the whole many of my generation (late twenties, early thirties) whether or not they had the good or ill fortune to take a university degree, followed comparable paths. For all my grateful acknowledgement of foreign scholarship I never read a book about Joyce, not even Herbert Gorman's biography, until I had graduated. As for Homeric parallels and analogues, I knew nothing of them until I began my training as a university lecturer.

In the years immediately after puberty (1945–6) Joyce, for me, was only one of a stellar system waiting to be explored. But as a Dubliner and a Catholic, and disposed to literature, I was ready for him. At least for *Dubliners* and *Portrait*. Reading *Dubliners* at fifteen, Emerson's phrase about seeing our own thoughts reflected back in alienated majesty, which I had picked up somewhere like the jackdaw I was, came back to me. But it was not 'thoughts' that were reflected, but objects, details of living, the fabric of my life. A few examples will suffice to show how easily the book could find a slot in my mind. And perhaps, after all, the Dubliner in terms of sense-experience, and if exposed to Joyce at an early age, must have a *kind* of pleasure that can only be acquired by an imaginative extension on the part of foreigners (and to the true Dubliner, I am afraid the historic Pale is still in some measure a reality). For me, forty years after *Dubliners* was written, the idiom of my childhood sprang out on the page bright as fresh paint. In the first story 'The Sister', the narrator's uncle remarks of their lodger: 'Mr Cotter might take a pick of that leg of mutton now'[4] I recognized immediately the language of shabby genteel euphemism. Like the narrator of 'An Encounter', I 'miched' (the Elizabethan word is still current as we move into the Seventies), but it was not far from my own home and out of school-hours that I encountered a local tramp who talked to me of what I later learned to be perversion. And 'An Encounter' synthesized innumerable incidents in my school-life from eight onwards: for instance, the jovial Christian Brother who slapped the bottoms of little boys as they were changing into ducks for the Annual Drill Display at Iveagh Grounds. It has always been a source of wonder to me that children can retain their innocence so long in such matters.

'Two Gallants' came alive for me because one of the heroes pretended he had worked in Pim's, a now extinct emporium,[5] and for years I had gone there with my mother or aunt to see Santa Claus and receive from him a bauble costing one shilling. I could still pass it every day on my way downtown and reflect, 'That's where Corley chose to have been employed.' Pim's was regarded as a very respectable firm, and that is why Corley picked it to deceive the poor 'slavey' (the term is virtually gone now, but in 1945 was still quite common) from Baggot Street. And Joyce's 'gay Lothario' used to go with 'girls off the South Circular Road'. This was the territory of all my schooldays, from five to eighteen, when all of Joyce except *Finnegans Wake* (but for fragments) would have become part of my mind. The poetry of urban street names Joyce taught to me, Nassau Street where I tried to buy and sell second-hand books; Kildare Street, where I was mortified in the National Library when the Assistant Librarian, these days a Professor in the Institute of Higher Studies, looked me up and down disdainfully and refused to issue me a Reader's Ticket;[6] Hume Street, where a mysterious body known as 'The Department' functioned, and had final control of our destinies; Stephen's Green, Grafton Street, Rutland Square, Capel Street, Dame Street, Westmoreland Street: they were all in 'Two Gallants', and surely no normal boy could fail to be electrified at finding his own city, the setting of his works and days, enshrined in a book peopled by familiar persons speaking in a familiar idiom.

But if the topography of *Dubliners* was mine, so also were the forms of its dialogue, whether direct or reported, and of course its peculiar phraseology. It took a Vatican Council to eliminate from Dublin speech that popular institution known as 'the short twelve'. In 'The Boarding House', Mrs Mooney intends to catch this convenient Mass at Marlborough Street the Sunday morning she decides to have it out with Mr Doran. I have not, that I recall, seen any reference in the Joyce critical literature pointing to Mrs Mooney's exemplary Sunday morning: half-an-hour spent in settling the destiny of her daughter and Mr Doran, and twenty minutes of mandatory worship. In 'Clay', I found infinite poignancy in one particular fragment of indirect speech. Maria, the laundress, is duped while blindfolded, into putting her finger into a saucer of clay. 'There was a pause for a few seconds; and then a great deal of scuffling and whispering. Somebody said something about the garden, and at last Mrs Donnelly said something very cross to one of the next-door girls and told her to throw it out at once: that was no play.' In the speech of my childhood the word 'angry' was never used, it was always '*cross*'. And every phrase at that Christmas party given by Aunt Julia and Aunt Kate, which was to lead to the anguish of Gabriel Conroy, had the authenticity not only of brilliantly selected speech but of *heard* speech. This, of course, is not really surprising when I realize that Joyce had died only four years before this year, 1945, and the idiom of Dublin is tenacious, though fading fast. It should be remembered, of course, that the idiom of 'The Dead' is itself a sub-species: the idiom of gentility, of a class that in Joyce's time was still vigorous, and even in my own. Consider this summation of the mode of life of the Miss Morkans and their niece, Mary Jane: 'Though their life was modest, they believed in eating well; the best of everything; diamond-bone sirloins, three-shilling tea and the best bottled stout.' How exquisitely Joyce indicates the line between frugality and luxury. Balanced quality-buying is here more than a token of good housekeeping. It is a banner of class. So long as at they can afford three-shilling teas, the Misses Morkan can claim their status.

But, of course, it was years later before I learnt the true greatness of 'The Dead'. The story that made most impact on me was, 'Ivy Day in the Committee Room'. The extraordinary fact is that I managed to get through ten years of schooling without ever hearing the name of Parnell. (Even more surprising is the fact that my teachers gave up teaching Irish history altogether after the age of twelve.) Anyway, I first learnt of the reality of that monument by Gaudens at the end of O'Connell Street from Joyce's chancers and codgers drooling over a dozen of stout sent in from the 'Black Eagle'. It was many years later that I read the words Joyce wrote about Parnell in the Triestine paper: *Il Piccolo della Sera*:

> In his final desperate appeal to his countrymen, he begged them not to throw him as a sop to the English wolves howling around them. It redounds to their honour that they did not fail this appeal. They did not throw him to the English wolves; they tore him to pieces themselves.[7]

Nor had I read at that time Yeats's *Last Poems* (1939). 'Ivy Day', however, had done the job: at fifteen, Parnell was, for me, the very type in Irish politics of the tragic hero. The Chief, as he was known to the cronies of John Aloysius Joyce and their contemporaries, came before, and for long overshadowed, the signatories of the document proclaiming the Irish Republic, and Sir Roger Casement.

By Holy Week of 1946 I was reading *A Portrait of the Artist As a Young Man* for the second time. I will always associate it with the elaborate and dirgeful ceremonies of Holy Week. Three great sections of the book struck immediate and plangent chords, and indeed they form almost the whole of it.

My pre-university education was wholly given by the Christian Brothers (Joyce had them for a few months when the cupboard was bare),[8] while Joyce had the Jesuits at Clongowes and Belvedere. Nonetheless, I could identify. The education provided by the Christian Brothers had, by my time, reached an unquestionably high level. I would even say that little nuggets of Jesuitical lore had found their way into the Brothers' classrooms. For instance, somewhere along the line I had picked up the solemn pronouncement overhead by Stephen in his last year at Belvedere: 'I believe that Lord Macaulay was a man who probably never committed a mortal sin in his life, that is to say, a deliberate mortal sin.'[9] It may well be that one of my teachers had actually read *A Portrait*, but even the youngest of the Brothers, good souls with a taste for the 'Leather', did not appear to have progressed beyond the Chesterbelloc. (This, of course, was over twenty years ago.)[10]

What I may call the school identification went further, of course. Stephen's Retreat Sermon is still, I know, the common experience of Irish Catholic schoolboys, perhaps even schoolgirls. 'Hell lay about them in their infancy', wrote Graham Greene of his classmates, in sombre parody of Wordsworth.[11] What Stephen heard, my fellows and I heard, not only at Retreats, but in the daily half-hour of what purported to be 'religious instruction'. I have it on unimpeachable evidence that as recently as the early sixties the baroque tropes of Joyce's sermon were in use in one of the most progressive of the Christian Brothers' schools, as my informant put it, 'the time-span of Hell measured in terms of the sands of the desert and the drops of the ocean'.[12]

A second section I was prepared for was, of course, the 'Christmas' dinner scene, where the *passio* of Parnell is re-enacted. And when the next year I finally came to *Ulysses,* what I was later to know as the '*Hades*' episode was to pivot about the Parnell exchange between Hynes and Mr Power.[13]

At sixteen, I never dreamed that two years later I would be entering University College Dublin, the lineal descendant of Joyce's Jesuit-run University College, nor that I would spend much time in the rooms where Joyce had been lectured, now known as Newman House and the students' recreation centre.[14] Nonetheless, I followed closely, in *A Portrait*, the moves of Stephen and Cranly and Davin and the others, because I knew the outside of the building and had envied these seemingly carefree students as they came down the steps, scarves flying in the wind. As it happened, I was not to see them on the steps of the National Library until I became a student myself, for that Assistant Librarian had made it for me a place of shame.[15]

In point of direct influence, the ruminations and conversations of Stephen bore odd fruit for me. It will be recalled that in his interchange with the Dean, an English convert, he reflects:

– The language in which we are speaking is his before it is mine. How different are the words home, Christ, ale, master, on his lips and mine! I cannot speak or write these words without unrest of spirit. His language, so familiar and so foreign, will always be for me an acquired speech ...[16]

Later Stephen explicitly rejects the Irish language. Now whether I felt about English what Stephen felt, *before* I read *A Portrait*, is not relevant. The fact is that Joyce planted in me his particular kind of 'unrest of spirit'. And I began to read Irish outside my school curriculum and I owe it, in fact, to Stephen that I can read modern Irish with genuine pleasure, and when necessary speak and write it with moderate proficiency. I often wonder whether this experience of mine through Joyce has been uncommon.

* * * *

Foiled by the Assistant Librarian of the National Library, my extra-mural education continued weekly at the tea-table of Lady Longford, who lived around the corner from me at 123, Leinster Road.[17] It was she who lent me *Ulysses*, at the beginning of my last year at school. I began it in a quite preposterously romantic setting. A friend's parents had taken a farmhouse in Woodenbridge, County Wicklow, for the month of September. My friend, Donal O'Farrell, invited myself and two others, one of them the painter, Patrick Swift – who now lives in the Algarve,[18] but was then twenty and a clerk in the Dublin Gas Company – to camp in the garden of the farmhouse. I came armed with Christine's *Ulysses* and a little book of translations from Lorca by J.H. Gili and Stephen Spender. Swift, who was to influence me until our ways parted and I went to the university, had already familiarized himself with extracts from *Finnegans Wake* and had worked up an uncanny rendition of Joyce's own recording of the best pages of Part II. If anything, I found this recital more moving than Joyce's, when at the drop of a hat, he would begin, in a high, clear voice, and an accent which though like Joyce's, was also reminiscent of Shaw's: '*Ah, but she was the queer old skeowsha anyhow, Anna Livia trinkettoes!*'[19] He had also by heart the last pages of the novel, and I too committed them to memory one time, but I have not read them aloud since asked to do so by one of my lecturers in English, for his own pleasure and that of the Professor of Greek. That was twenty years ago and little did I know then that the same lecturer would, many years later, become my implacable enemy.[20] For I know little of '*their little warm tricks*' and '*their mean cosy turns*'.[21]

But to return to *Ulysses*. By the light of oil lamps, and sitting about a great deal table, we pored over the precious text. We all knew the Tower, of course, and we had all walked along Sandymount Strand. We knew beforehand also that 'stately, plump Buck Mulligan' was derived from Oliver St John Gogarty, whose delicate neo-classical and neo-Elizabethan lyrics we cherished, and I certainly still do. I can recall being shocked by Mulligan's parody of the Mass, but unlike some of my elders, I was sensible enough to recognize that the blasphemy was Mulligan's, not Stephen's, and that Joyce was the tenacious recorder. What came home to the heart most in the section I was to learn years later to call 'Telemachus' was Stephen's bitter comment on Mulligan's shaving-mirror: 'It is a symbol of Irish art. The cracked looking-glass of a servant.'[22] Mulligan's recalled comment, '*O, it's only Dedalus whose mother is beastly dead*'[23] and, above all, that extraordinary interchange between Haines and Stephen:

> – I am the servant of two masters, Stephen said, an English and an Italian.
> – Italian? Haines said. A crazy queen, old and jealous, kneel down before me.
> – And a third, Stephen said, there is who wants me for odd jobs.
> – Italian? Haines said again. What do you mean?
> – The imperial British state, Stephen answered, his colour rising, and the Holy Roman Catholic and Apostolic church.[24]
> The 'third' is the 'crazy queen, old and jealous'.

Commentators have not noted the abnormal emotiveness of that description of Ireland, for the Irish at least. I have indicated that Stephen's attitude drove me to – rather than from – the Irish language. At this stage, I saw more than Yeats's Cathleen Ni Houlihan behind the image of the 'crazed queen'. I was aware of a thousand

JOYCE WITHOUT FEARS: A PERSONAL JOURNEY

years of Gaelic literature and all its innumerable personifications of Ireland. At this time I was reading the Irish Texts Society's edition of Aogán Ó Rathaille, and at school we were inundated with Gaelic Jacobite verse. I knew the dark centuries' dream of a queen rescued by the Stuarts or by the progeny of the exiled Earls of Ulster. Joyce, of course, knew Mangan's 'Dark Rosaleen',[25] and must have been aware of the long tradition of Ireland personified by her poets as a queenly beauty. Did he know the ninth-century poem 'The Hag of Beare'? Whatever, his 'crazed queen' cut to the bone. It must be realized that my generation came to puberty in a neutral Ireland. At seventeen, I had already seen the bombsites of London. I had known guilt over neutrality, since the Brothers had failed to infect me with their singularly unpoetic brand of Nationalism.

Donal O'Farrell slept in the farmhouse that weekend. We others adjourned to a tent in the garden and read by torchlight from *Ulysses*. I have mentioned the Gili-Spender volume of Lorca. We read from that also. And one of those nights I pondered bitterly Buck Mulligan's contemptuous 'snotgreen sea' and the 'green' of Lorca. *Green, how much I want you green.*[26]

The imaginative engulfment of *Ulysses* had been well and truly initiated. When we got back to Dublin, Swift and I finished the book in a few weeks. It did not strike us that it was a very difficult book. We knew and recognized the kind of superstitious anti-Semitism evinced by Dr Deasy in 'Nestor'. And we knew the poor Jews of Dublin who lived on the South Circular Road. Coming from school during Yom Kippur, I would be accosted by poorly dressed Orthodox Jews who would offer me a penny, or maybe even a threepenny bit, to light their fire or their gas-stove.

We knew intimately the setting of 'Proteus'. As for '*A hater of his kind ... his mane foaming in the moon, his eyeballs stars*', one had lived all one's life less than a mile from St Patrick's Cathedral and the immanence of Swift was in all that area.

It would require a much weightier essay than this to itemize the points of contact between my experience and the experience of *Ulysses*. But there are some responses I would single out. The kind of jumbled and pinchbeck erudition possessed by Leopold Bloom was not unlike that we ourselves possessed as schoolboys. A reflection such as Bloom's on the woman outside the Grosvenor Hotel, '*The honourable Mrs and Brutus is an honourable man*', struck home immediately, for *Julius Ceasar* was one of the first Shakespeare plays we read on entering secondary school. Though we knew little or nothing of the Victorian theatre in Dublin, at school we had sung '*The Croppy Boy*' and got the effect of Martin Cunningham's 'pompous' comment on Ben Dollard's singing of the ballad. We knew the funeral trains and the funereal gossip of Glasnevin and Mount Jerome, for members of our families lay in those cemeteries. For me, one passage in *Hades* had a peculiar poignancy. '*A tiny coffin flashed by*'. '*Sad*', said Martin Cunningham. '*A child.*' '*Poor little thing*', Mr Dedalus said. '*It's well out of it*'. At four or five, I had overheard my mother speak of an infant sister: 'Yes. Baptized and buried in Mount Jerome.'

'Aeolus' and 'The Lestrygonians' were plain sailing, and also a revelation. We found that we were living in a work of art. The familiar treat of Lemon's Sweets, even, was now a detail in the vast tapestry. We followed Bloom up Grafton Street[27] and knew nothing of the vast research machine that was cranking into action. Yeates and Son, and Brown Thomas were and are still there,[28] and Combridge's the booksellers', but by then Davy Byrne's 'Moral pub' in Duke Street had changed character completely.[29] And we were with him when he led the 'blind stripling' across Dawson Street to Molesworth Street, and when he turned into Kildare Street and turned into the Museum to avoid Blazes Boylan.[30] For reasons I have given, I did not follow him into the Library. O, if I had known that the episode in the Library had been described as 'Scylla and Charybdis'! But I did fancy that I had been humiliated a year or so previously in the very room where Stephen is closeted with Æ, John Eglinton and the Librarian, T.W. Lyster.[31] But 'Scylla and Charybdis' is an education in itself for a boy of seventeen: Goethe, Milton, Shakespeare, Ben Jonson, Shelley, Aristotle, Plato, Hyde's *Love Songs of Connacht*, Mallarmé, the minor Elizabethan Robert Greene, Villiers de l'Isle Adam,[32] Padraic Colum, James Starkey ('Seamus O'Sullivan'), George Moore, Edward Martyn, George Sigerson, James Stephens, Brunetto Latini, Drummond of Hawthornden, Ernest Renan, Sir Philip Sidney, Coleridge, Boccaccio, Meredith, Dumas *pére et fils*, Maeterlinck, Oscar Wilde, not to mention Professors Georg Brandes, Sidney Lee, Edward Dowden and Mesdames Marie Corelli and Helena Blavatsky. Of all those then living, I was to meet only Seamus O'Sullivan, who quoted Verlaine to me when I proclaimed the greatness of Patrick Kavanagh, and later Padraic Colum. And one other. 'George Roberts is doing the commercial part.' This was the Roberts of Maunsel and Roberts, whom Joyce was to regard as his enemy, and lampoon in 'The Holy Office'. When I met Roberts in London in December 1948, he looked like a leprechaun, tiny, rubicund, whitewhiskered and bearded. He was more than kind to me and although he spoke with reverence of Æ, who he published in *New Songs*, the volume discussed in 'Scylla and Charybdis', he would never speak of Joyce.

I must jump ahead to *Circe*, the episode in *Ulysses* furthest removed from my experience, except in so far as Dublin was, and still is, a city of picturesque and foul-mouthed speech. As one who might be described then, superficially at any rate, as a devout Catholic, 'Circe' of course shocked me. It also left in me a profound sense of the piteousness of unsatisfied sexual desire. When the Bawd in 'Nighttown' spits after Stephen and Lynch, 'Trinity medicals. Fallopian tube. All prick and no pence', I was less shocked by the moral squalor of commercial sex than by the fact that people have to seek it out. Strangely, I was moved too by the wrangle between Stephen and the two English private soldiers, Compton the *provocateur* and Carr the poor dumb ox with his blind loyalty to Edward VII: 'I'll wring the neck of any fucking bastard says a word against my bleeding fucking king.' For all Carr's bravado and brutality, he has pathos when faced with the cocksure Dedalus. Stephen is struck down, but does he not deserve it?

After the nightmare of *Circe*, Part III of *Ulysses* was easy going, except, very naturally I think for someone without academic assistance, the catechetical interrogation of the second last episode *Ithaca*. And what of Molly Bloom's soliloquy? So far as I was concerned, for exact literal meaning one needed only the addition of punctuation and some conjunctions. I was less dazzled by its technical virtuosity than by its gross and poignant poetry. I cannot recall the approximate date of my first acquaintance with Yeats's *Last Poems* (1939). But for me Molly's soliloquy was epitomized in Yeats's phrase '*the foul rag and bone shop of the heart*'.[33] Molly is often 'foul', her reflections are miscellaneous junk, but 'the heart' was there as surely as in *Hamlet* or the *Odes* of Keats. And I had to begin to read Villon after D.B. Wyndham Lewis's biography had impressed me.[34] Poor Molly's fantasies could not shock me with *La Belle Heaulmié*re in mind. If anything, I was most moved by the singular sweetness of Molly's novelettish notions of high Romance. I failed to understand how a great prose poem could be disedifying.

I will leave *Ulysses* there and my garnerings of how it affected me twenty-two years ago. About 1949 Patrick Kavanagh told me he had read *Ulysses* twenty times. I disbelieved him. But I will give him the third last word; he is writing about 'that readjusting of one's values which is common in regard to one's enthusiasms'. He says 'It often happens in the case of a person with whom we were in love.' The second last word to Graham Greene on discovering *Ulysses* in 1923: it was *comme une bible et aussi riche que-elle*.[35] And the last word to P.S. O'Hegarty:

> Ireland is all through him and in him and of him; and Dublin, its streets and its buildings and its people, he loves with the wholehearted affection of the artist … he may live out of Dublin, but he will never get away from it.

Leopold Bloom: *Ulysses*

(John Jordan Papers)[1]

J.J. Joyce's *Ulysses*, once regarded as a most scandalous book in some quarters, is now 55-years-old. It has been written about by Jesuits and Marxists, poets and civil servants, by men of all religious persuasions and none. It has laid the basis of a flourishing academic industry, so flourishing that the trees often take precedence over the wood; and by the wood I mean the book's abundant humanity; a humanity which, in the opinion of some readers, places it in the class of Chaucer and Dickens, if not of Shakespeare.

And the humanity of *Ulysses* is not reduced by the book's duration and locale: one day, from about 8 a.m. on June 16, 1904, and a few hours of the beginning of the next, June 17, in the ancient city of Dublin and environs. The environs, chiefly Glasnevin, and the coastline from Sandymount to Dalkey, are as important as the centre of the city. Appreciation of this book – which immortalizes a single day in the life of a city as experienced by two very different men, Stephen Dedalus, a 22-year-old part-time school-teacher educated by the Jesuits, and Leopold Bloom, a 38-year-old adver-tisement canvasser, son of a Jewish father and a mother Christian on the mother's side, educated at the High School in Harcourt Street – apprecia-tion of this book does not require keeping an eye open for Homeric paral-lels. For my purpose it is sufficient to recall that Leopold Bloom may be seen as a type of the Odysseus figure; and his wife Molly, born Marion Tweedy, may be taken as a type of the Penelope figure; but of course, on a carnal plane, incorrigibly faithless.

I wish to put before you a Leopold Bloom who, while being a Dublin Jew, yet like no character in the book, clings to the tattered mantle of Christian chivalry in all his relationships, with men, with women, with all animals, from the domestic cat to the stray dog. I use the verb 'to cling' and the adjective 'tattered' advisedly. Bloom is a commonplace, vulgar, lubri-cious man. So, if we are honest, are most of us. But most of us also try to be polite to our friends and even to those we know are our enemies; we try to be respectful to women, even if we know or suspect that they are worthless or wanton; we try to reverence the mysteries of childbirth and death; we may have broken marriages, but we hold to the idea of the family; we try not to turn away from the needy and the handicapped and the socially embarrassing. We try, in brief, to be gentlemen. So does Leopold Bloom. We meet him about 8 a.m. in the kitchen of his home at 7 Eccles Street. He talks to his cat while considering preparations for breakfast.

L.B.   – *Mihgnao!*

– o, there you are, Mr Bloom said, turning from the fire ...

He bent down to her, his hands on his knees.

– Milk for the pussens, he said.

– *Mihgnao!* The cat cried.

They call them stupid. They understand what we say better than we understand them. She understands all she wants to ...

J.J.   We will find that Bloom's routine tenderness extends beyond the domestic cat to all manner of creatures outside the human domain. He disapproves, for instance, of animal acts in the circus, on the not uncommon presumption that the beasts are doped. He is, after his fashion, Franciscan in his attitudes. We will see him later buying Banbury cakes to crumble for the gulls as he crosses over O'Connell Bridge. Late that night, he hands over victuals he has bought for himself to a smelly retriever in Nighttown. This action is, of course, misinterpreted by two constables on night-watch:

Watch Caught in the act. Commit no nuisance.

L.B.   (STAMMERS) I am doing good to others.

J.J.   A covey of gulls rises at this point, with fragments of Bloom's Banbury cakes in their beaks. They caw approval, it would seem, and Bloom says:

L.B.   The friend of man. Trained by kindness.

J.J.   The second watch observes:

Watch Prevention of cruelty to animals.

J.J.   This at once sets off Bloom on one of his hobby horses:

L.B.   (ENTHUSIASTICALLY) A noble work: I scolded that tramdriver on Harold's Cross bridge for ill-using the poor horse with his harness scab. Bad French I got for my pains. Of course it was frosty and the last tram.

J.J.   It is symptomatic of Bloom's consideration for human beings that while abusive of the tram driver's cruelty, he tempers his indignation with an excuse for the man's behaviour, the last tram on a frosty night. Of course, it could be argued that Bloom's weakness in anger, his lack of stamina in hatred, are signatures of his mediocrity. Yet this consistent effort to see the other man's point of view might also be taken as evidence of the kind of compassion one asssociates with holy people, with them rather than heroes. But to come back to the morning and Eccles Street, it is one of the hallmarks of Bloom's quotidian mediocrity that he is forever speculating, putting things on the long finger. Thus he is a model gardener in his dreams. As he makes his way to the outhouse after breakfast, he pauses to consider his back garden, his mind a vague swirl of projects. 'He bent down to regard a lean file of spearmint growing by the wall':

L.B.   Make a summerhouse here. Scarlet runners. Virginia creepers. Want to manure the whole place over, scabby soil. A coat of liver of sulphate. All soil like that without dung. Household slops. Loam, what is this that is. The hens in the next garden: their droppings are very good top dressing. Best of all though are the cattle, especially when they are fed on those oilcakes. Mulch of dung. Best thing to clean ladies' kid gloves. Dirty cleans. Ashes too. Reclaim the whole place. Grow peas in that corner there. Lettuce. Always have fresh greens then. Still gardens have their drawbacks. That bee or blue-bottle here Whit Monday.

J.J.   Bloom is heartbreakingly ordinary in his ability to rationalise inactivity how-ever desirable or profitable. His cottage garden is at the mercy of his fear of bluebottles or bees: the imprecision is, of course, quite in character. And so, after his own breakfast and serving breakfast in bed to his wife, defecation and sundry pseudo-philosophical reveries, Bloom sets out on his Odyssey. He leaves Eccles Street in the knowledge that his wife later that day will receive her current lover, a flash artist – this is an expression still used in Dublin – known as 'Blazes' Boylan, a real Micky Dazzler.

      Bloom's main business of the day is attendance at the funeral of one Paddy Dignam and the transaction of some advertising chores, apart from the collection of a letter *post restante* from a lady called Martha Clifford, with whom he is conducting an epistolary flirtation under the name 'Henry Flower'. His first port of call is to the Post Office in Westland Row. On the way, he continues his observations on the human condition, commonplace, confused, but always lit by a kind of aborted compassion. Outside some poor cottages in Lime Street, 'a boy for the skins lolled, his bucket of offal linked, smoking a chewed fagbutt':

L.B.   A smaller girl with scars of eczema on her forehead eyed him, listlessly holding her battered caskhoop. Tell him if he smokes he won't grow. O let him! His life isn't such a bed of roses! Waiting outside pubs to bring Da home. Come home to Ma, Da.

J.J.   Before doing his business at the Post Office, he has a reverie about the Far East inspired by the shop window of a tea merchants. After collecting his letter – his one concrete testimony to the world of Romance – he is pestered by C.P. McCoy, who wants to borrow a high-class valise for his wife, also in the singing business like Molly; he reads his letter and destroys the envelope under the Loop Line Bridge; visits All Hallow's Church, where he attends part of the Mass and speculates on the guile and acumen of the Catholic Church; and is pestered again by one Bantam Lyons, who wants to look up the racing lists for a horse in the Ascot Gold Cup. He inadvertently gives Bantam a tip for a horse called '*Throwaway*', and reflects on the evils of gambling.

L.B.   Silly lips of that chap. Betting. Regular hotbed of it lately. Messenger boys stealing to put on sixpence. Raffle for large tender turkey. Your Christmas dinner for threepence. Jack Fleming embezzling to gamble then smuggled off to America. Keeps a hotel now. They never come back. Fleshpots of Egypt.

J.J.   Bloom proceeds towards his own Egypt, 'the mosque of the baths' in Leinster Street near the back entrance of Trinity College. It will soon be time, eleven o'clock, to embark on the journey to Glasnevin. Bloom occupies a coach with several others, including Stephen Dedalus's father, Simon. Bloom points out Stephen to Simon. Simon launches into a magnificent tirade against his son's low company, including Malachi 'Buck' Mulligan. Bloom's reactions are mixed.

L.B.   Noisy selfwilled man. Full of his son. He is right. Something to hand on. If little Rudy had lived. See him grow up. Hear his voice in the house. Walking beside Molly in an Eton suit. My son. Me in his eyes. From me. Just a chance.

J.J.   And, since Rudy was conceived in far from romantic circumstances, he is driven to ponder the mystery of desire and procreation.

L.B.   Got big then. Had to refuse the Greystones concert. My son inside her. I could have helped him on in life. I could. Make him independent. Learn German too.

J.J.   Where his carnal desires are concerned, Bloom is as base as any man. But in that passage just cited, and the one before, we see in him an awareness more than usual in the average sensual man, of the glory of fatherhood. Of course, we can take for granted that Joyce appreciated the Jewish concern for family life, a concern perhaps heightened by the circumstances of Bloom's Jewry: one of a tiny minority from which he has cut himself off by his marriage to a Christian.

One of his more ignoble traits is his willingness on the way to Glasnevin to share in, indeed tell, jokes about his fellow Jews, and stay silent in the face of Simon Dedalus's vituperative anti-Semitism. His flexibility is, no doubt, understandable. Bloom is on sufferance with his Christian acquaintances – we can hardly call them friends. At this stage of Bloomsday, as June 16, 1904, is now universally known, Bloom's acquaintances do not show openly their disdain for the Jews. All he has to put up with are unanswered comments and questions, or frozen looks, as when he attempts to ingratiate himself with the solicitor John Henry Menton, by pointing out a dent in his mourner's top hat. Late in the book, Menton is listed among Molly Bloom's swains, if not her lovers.

Bloom's status as an unheroic outsider is compounded by the tradition-al absurdity attaching to the cuckold, *le cocu*, the man with horns, a figure of fun in all the great writers of Western Europe, Shakespeare, Cervantes, Molière. Paradoxically, Bloom as cuckold is not a figure of fun for us, if we attach any value to the virtues of courtesy, diffidence motivated by charity, even that virtue which Edmund Spenser derived from Aristotle and called Magnificence, and which we may call 'magnaminity'.

In the mighty Glasnevin scene, commonly called 'Hades', Bloom is not impressed by the burial service, nor by the myriad tombstones. A Jew who, we will learn, has been baptised twice – first in the Protestant Church of St Nicholas Without, the Coombe, and secondly (presumably before his mar-riage to Molly) in the Church of the Three Patrons, Rathgar – Bloom has no links with any established religion, and his approach towards religion is pragmatic and morbid in the same breath.

But he is touchingly sentimental inasfar as the graveyard and the funeral strike chords of memory, notably of his son Rudy, the fruit of concupis-cence, who died aged eleven days, and of his father Rudolf, who died from an overdose of aconite in a hotel room in Ennis, Co. Clare. Bloom is most genuinely touched when he notices:

L.B. A bird sat tamely perched on a poplar branch. Like stuffed. Like the wed-ding present Alderman Hooper gave us. Hu! Not a budge out of him. Knows there are no catapults to let fly at him. Dead animal even sadder. Silly Milly burying the little dead bird in the kitchen matchbox, a daisychain and bits of broken chainies on the grave.

J.J. Let us not dismiss this as undiluted sentimentality on Bloom's part, granti-ng that he is a sentimental man. Joyce would expect his readers to remem-ber that there is special providence in the fall of a sparrow. All dead things are worthy of reverence, since once they were living. Not for nothing does he allow us to perceive through Bloom's consciousness our perishability and ultimate putresence:

L.B. How many! All these here once walked round Dublin. Faithful departed. As you are now so once were we.

J.J. We next see Bloom in the offices of *The Freeman's Journal* and *The Evening Telegraph*. As he waits for attention from Councillor Nannetti, the *Freeman's* foreman printer, he reflects:

L.B. Strange he never saw his real country. Ireland my country. Member for College Green. He boomed that workaday worker tack for all it was worth.

J.J. Nannetti's Italian origins have not precluded him from election to the City Council. And, unlike Bloom, he has the common touch, can be hail-fellow-well-met with the workers. His attitude to Bloom is distant. Even among deracines, among Italians and Jews, there are gulfs. Later in the day we will

find Bloom on even steeper precipices. In the newspaper offices and outside, Bloom suffers various small indignities, not least being mocked in his
gait by the urchin newsboys. But part of his business is done: he now has to
traverse the centre of the city to look up an ad in the National Library. He
just misses meeting Stephen Dedalus, who meditates on his day-long ben-
der with the newspaper man and cronies.

Bloom's walk to the National Library, with his pause in Duke Street for
a snack consisting of a glass of burgundy and a cheese sandwich, can be followed to this day. So many have made that walk that few, perhaps, have pondered the immense significance of Bloom's interior reflexions insofar as he
compassionates the misery of others. At this point, I make no bones about
saying that Bloom, this anti-hero, cuckold, this sentimentalist who is neither
fish nor flesh in religion, shows an heroic awareness of the quotidian suffering. In a city where the springs of feeling appear to have dried up, he alone
cares. Before he steps on to O'Connell Bridge, he notices a young girl
standing outside Dillon's Auction Rooms on Bachelor's Walk. He recognises her as one of Simon Dedalus's daughters.

L.B.   Good Lord, that poor child's dress is in flitters. Underfed she looks too.
Potatoes and marge, marge and potatoes. It's after they feel it. Proof of the
pudding. Undermines the constitution.

J.J.   In Westmoreland Street, Bloom bumps into a friend of his and Molly's
youth, Mrs Breen, who tells him about her husband's latest stroke of luna-
cy. He observes:

L.B.   Same blue serge dress she had two years ago, the nap bleaching. Seen its best
days. Wispish hair over her ears. And that dowdy toque, three old grapes to
take the harm out of it. Shabby genteel. She used to be a tasty dresser. Lines
round her mouth. Only a year or so older than Molly.

J.J.   To change the subject, he asks her about a common friend, Mrs Mina
Purefoy, and learns that she is in a lying-in hospital in Holles Street, having
been in labour for three days. Bloom is genuinely grieved. Already he has
lamented the late Mrs Dedalus, who had to bear fifteen children to Simon.
They were Catholics. Now he bewails the fate of Mina Purefoy:

L.B.   Poor Mrs Purefoy! Methodist husband. Method in his madness. Saffron bun
and milk and soda lunch in the educational dairy ... Poor thing! Then having to give the breast year after year all hours of the night. Selfish those t.t's
are. Dog in the manger. Only one lump of sugar in my tea, if you please.

J.J.   Bloom continues to be pre-occupied with the sufferings of women in childbirth, until his attention is drawn to a squad of constables making for their
dinners. Bloom's attitude to the police is ambivalent: he credits tales of their
brutality; but, on the other hand, he grants that they have a lot to put up
with. At Tom Moore's statue, he reflects on the suitability of its site: over a

gents' public lavatory. He also deplores the lack of such facilites in Dublin for women. 'Ought to be places for women. Running into cakeshops.' Perhaps, in these words, Flann O'Brien found the inspiration for the grand design of Mr Collopy in *The Hard Life*.

Bloom finally reaches Duke Street, is sickened by the eating habits of the men in the Burton Restaurant (we know it as The Bailey), and walks across the road to Davy Byrne's for his snack of burgundy and cheese. While he is in the gents, an acquaintance, Nosey Flynn, intimates to the proprietor, Davy Byrne, that Bloom is a Freemason (which he is not), but grants that he has his good points. That is, I reckon, one of the very few compliments paid to Bloom, and never to his face. A few hours later, one Lenihan remarks to his crony, McCoy: 'He's a cultured allroundman, Bloom is. He's not one of your common or garden, you know. There's a touch of the artist about old Bloom.'

After his collation in Davy Byrne's, Bloom has an important encounter with a blind youth who wishes to cross from Dawson Street to Molesworth Street. As and after Bloom guides him across, he becomes imaginatively involved in the experience of blindness. Here is one of his reflections:

L.B. Poor fellow! Quite a boy. Terrible. Really terrible. What dreams would he have, not seeing? Life a dream for him. Where is the justice being born that way? All those women and children excursion beanfeast burned and drowned in New York. Holocaust …

J.J. Bloom spots Blazes Boylan as he reaches Kildare Street, and takes refuge in the Museum, where he has a prurient mission. He next pops up in the National Library, where the librarian T.W. Lyster is called out to attend to him. Through the half-door of Lyster's inner sanctum, Buck Mulligan recognizes him. 'The sheeny', he cries, and goes on to tell how when he went to the Museum to pay homage to Venus (a cult, by the way, introduced to Dublin by George Moore, at whose house Oliver Gogarty [or Buck Mulligan] was a frequent guest), he found Bloom squinting indecently at the statue. Dedalus and Mulligan bump into Bloom on the way out. Quite gratuitously, Mulligan accuses Bloom of unnatural lusts. It is he also who calls Bloom, 'the wandering Jew'; which is true in that Bloom does wander over Dublin, but false in its imputation of collective guilt.

That afternoon, Bloom finds himself having a meal with Simon Dedalus's brother-in-law, Richie Golding, in the Ormond Hotel. In the bar parlour an impromptu concert is being held, which is climaxed by Ben Dollard's rendition of 'The Croppy Boy'. The words of the ballad, sweet and maudlin, touch Bloom. The Croppy Boy is the last of his name and race:

L.B. I too, last my race. Milly young student. Well, my fault perhaps. No son. Rudy. Too late now. Or if not? If not? If still?

J.J. It is in the section of the book that we call 'Cyclops' that Bloom is goaded into assertion of his dignity as a Jew, and indeed as an Irishman.

L.B. – Mendelssohn was a jew and Karl Marx and Mercadente and Spinoza. And the Saviour was a jew and His father was a jew. Your God .... Christ was a Jew like me ...

Simon Gob, the Citizen made a plunge back into the shop.

– 'By Jesus', says he, 'I'll brain that bloody jewman for using the holy name. By Jesus, I'll crucify him, so I will. Give us that biscuit-box here.'

J.J. Bloom departs on the jaunting car amid a howling mob, with Garryowen, the Citizen's mongrel, in hot pursuit, the Citizen still threatening murder.

We next meet Bloom on Sandymount Strand, where there occurs the sordid little episode which perhaps has shocked certain readers: when he releases himself carnally at a distance from the girl Gertie McDowell. I have neither time nor inclination to dwell on it. But I would point out that when Gertie ventures a glance at Bloom, 'the face that met her gaze there in the twilight, wan and strangely drawn, seemed to her the saddest she had ever seen'. Poor Gertie's head is full of nonsense from novelettes, but perhaps here her perceptions are sound.

That evening, Bloom betakes himself to Holles Street to enquire after Mrs Mina Purefoy. Over and over again, Joyce uses stylistic parody to stress Bloom's essential compassion for the weak and the suffering. 'Of Israel's folk was that man that on earth wandering far had fared. Stark ruth of man his errand that him lone led till that house.' He is inveigled into a party being held by the interns, at which Stephen Dedalus is a guest. There is a good deal of bawdy talk about procreation and birth, and sex in general.

'Thereat laughed they all right jocundly only young Stephen and Sir Leopold which never durst laugh too open by reason of a strange humour which he would not bewray and also for that he rued for her that bare whoso she might be or wheresoever.'

J.J. Well we all know, or have heard, how at this not altogether untypical medical get-together, Bloom establishes a bond of sympathy with Stephen. All the other participants, including Buck Mulligan who, it seems, has come from George Moore's house in Ely Place, profess a frenetic lightheadedness in the face of both cofinlation and death. Bloom recognises an element of high seriousness in Dedalus. After the phantasmagoric adventures of the pair in Nighttown, where they adjourn from Holles Street, adventures in which both their psyches are laid bare, it is Bloom who takes upon himself the welfare of Stephen, saving him from arrest and dangerous injury, sobering him up, guiding him to his own house in Eccles Street, where he offers to put him up for the rest of the night.

It has been suggested by some critics that the final conjunction of Bloom and Stephen is an anti-climax, that the elaborate but fundamentally tedious interchanges between the two in the cabman's shelter and in 7 Eccles Street are so much wasted effort. There are some who, after the Nighttown episode, known as 'Circe', prefer to skip on to the concluding section known as 'Penelope', in which Molly Bloom has her monstrous and beautiful interior monologue. But it is only when one tries to leap from 'Circe' to 'Penelope' that one realizes the necessity of the two long sections in between. Perhaps if we look again at Bloom we will see that his hopes for involving Stephen in his life as a surrogate son, even as a controllable lover for Molly, for setting him up as a teacher of Italian, a really toney protégé, his ambitions for participation in what he conceives as the intellectual life, all this is moonshine. He is unsalvageable, the little man. Stephen is Hero. His few hours with Bloom may be seen as his creator's education in humanity, taken in parvo. Bloom is anti-hero, if you like.

Yet there is glory in his quiet desperation, only futile anguish in Stephen's posed triumphalism. And when they, both men, look up at the sky at the rere of 7 Eccles Street, alike they see '*the heaventree of stars hung with humid nightblue fruit*'.

Joyce's Triestene Library

(Hibernia, 18 February 1977)

It is always a pleasure to read anything by Professor Richard Ellmann[1]: over the years the urbanity of Oxbridge has judiciously been brought to bear on the unengaging tortuousness of American academic prose (my adjective has its function, for it is possible to delight in mind-boggling styles, the Sir Thomas Browne of *Urn Burial* for instance, or the later Henry James). A friend from Vassar College has just sent me Ellmann's essay on Washington Irving's *Rip Van Winkle,* called 'Love in the Catskills', an excellent instance of literary detection, humane and magisterial.

It may be seen then that if I do not get into a state of elation about Professor Ellmann's new book on Joyce, it is not from ill-will: I still keep the letter he wrote to me when I did the first review of his *James Joyce* in 1959, in *Hibernia*. But *The Consciousness of James Joyce* seems to be to be a quite shameless piece of bookmaking. The text proper is a mere ninety-five pages, amplified by a most valuable Appendix, listing the books in Joyce's possession, plus some others, before he left Trieste in 1920. Some of the items are surprising, given Joyce's lack of sympathy for the Irish Dramatic Movement: three plays by William Boyle, almost the entire dramatic output of Colum to–date, T.C. Murray's *Maurice Harte*, Lennox Robinson's *Patriots*, Joseph Campbell's single play *Judgement*, and, of course, most of Synge, but only a couple of plays by Yeats. To me the most interesting item of all is Brinsley MacNamara's *The Valley of the Squinting Windows* (1918). How did Joyce come so quickly on the first novel to achieve *a succès de scandale*?

Also in his library were pamphlets by Kropotkin and Bakunin, both anarchists, and the social reformer Proudhon. I am afraid I am not convinced by Professor Ellmann's wispy demonstration of their influence on Joyce's presentation of Bloom and Stephen. The subject is too large to be disposed of in a few elegant sentences which demand an act of faith from the reader, hard enough when Professor Ellmann himself is far from clinching.

After decades in which Parnell has been given a second and more heroic life, by Joyce, Yeats, Robinson, Francis Hackett (*The Green Lion*), Sean O'Faolain *(Bird Alone)* and others, this mythologized figure, as we learn more of him, tends to shrink in charisma. Professor Ellmann is uncomfortably aware of this, and just as uncomfortably presents Arthur Griffith, the non-violent separatist, as Joyce's political hero. There are considerable difficulties in accepting this, though I am not ashamed to admit admiration for Griffith's services to this State. Joyce must have been aware of Griffith's friendship with the execrable Gogarty. 'Buck Mulligan' is represented as being coarsely 'anti-Semite'. I put the phrase in inverted commas, because the virus, always hateful, differs in degree and provenance. In Mulligan's case, it is a form of snobbery rather than an ideological polyp. Now we know that Joyce abhorred anti-Semitism. We know that he read Griffith's *United Irishman* and his political pamphlets. I would like to know if ever he read Griffith's Preface to John Mitchel's *Jail Journal*, in which, following Mitchel himself, Griffith dismisses any equation between Irish vassalage and negro slavery. Griffith, like many another Irish Nationalist, was selective in his advocation of freedom for other races.

On the other hand, Griffith was Joyce's ally in his newspaper campaign against the suppression of *Dubliners*. Professor Ellmann does not reveal whether Griffith knew the contents of the book. It is hard to see it being approved by the man who made such an unsavoury fuss over Synge's *In the Shadow of the Glen*. Joyce's passion for correspondences found one in the fact that Valery Larbaud's pre-publication lecture on *Ulysses* was delivered on the day the Treaty was signed, 7th December 1921, and further than on 8th January 1922, Griffith assumed the Presidency. Hence the references to Griffith in Molly Bloom's soliloquy. But even if Griffith were not a chauvinist, and almost certainly a racialist, I cannot treat him as Joyce's successor to Parnell, that great fictional creation of Irish genius.

Another useful item in Joyce's Triestine library was a little book of popularized scholarship by May Byron, under the pseudonym 'Maurice Clare') called *A Day with William Shakespeare*, which provided materials for sentences like the matchless '*In Gerard's rosery of Fetter lane he walks, greyed–auburn*'. This is a pleasant but costly hour's reading.

Stan Was No 'Mute Inglorious Joyce'[1]

(Hibernia, December 1962)

Within a few days of the publication of Stanislaus Joyce's *Dublin Diary* (this volume is misnamed, by the way, since it is not the only Dublin diary composed by S. Joyce) I had heard and read several subscriptions to a new nonsense. They were to the effect that Stan, a 'mute inglorious Joyce', was the real man of genius in the family, and not James.

This rubbish may well gain greater currency, especially in Dublin; for any stick, even his own brother, is good enough with which to chastise James. We may concede James's genius on the grounds of his acute observation of Dublin manners and morals, grant him pious laurels on the count of his supersaturation with Catholicism, but we have still some way to go before we accept the full implications of his comedy, that glory of laughter which blows off all our pretensions and leaves us naked to the mercy of God.

Only God could love the cods and wastrels and fly-boys who posture in the niches of that cathedral of fiction, *Ulysses*. God and James Joyce. For *Ulysses* is what Mr Patrick Kavanagh might call a 'love-act'.

It is chiefly the sense of comedy and its concomitant, the tragic sense, which distinguish James Joyce from his two creations Stephen Daedalus (*Stephen Hero*) and Stephen Dedalus (*Portrait of the Artist as a Young Man*). And it is chiefly the absence of the sense of comedy, and a debased version of the sense of tragedy, which couple Stephen (pre-*Ulysses*), and Stanislaus Joyce, as he reveals himself in this diary.

At this point it is essential to stress that Professor Healey has not done a very good job on the editing. He damns himself in the Preface with the admission that '*A few passages, marked by dots* (…) *have been omitted, most of them because they lacked interest, the rest because they were libellous or otherwise offensive.*' The only justification of the editorial side of the academic industry, is the provision of full and accurate texts. Otherwise editing under the umbrella of an academic title is mere self-pushing.

Professor Healey talks about 'a few passages' but then goes on to suggest that the passages in question are numerous enough to (1) lack interest, (2) be libellous, (3) be otherwise offensive. Which means, in effect, that some other editor will have to do Professor Healey's work. Professor Healey's procedure is justifiable only if he indicates *which* omissions 'lack interest' (a purely subjective judgment by Professor Healey is here implied), *which* are libellous, and *which* are, and in what way, otherwise offensive.

But Professor Healey's sins as an editor are not limited to abiding the questions of any alert student of Joyceana. His notes are quite inadequate. One of the things that emerges in this diary is that Stanislaus Joyce, barely twenty, had the makings of a superb, if arrogant, polemicist and critic.

It is a mark of any original critical intelligence that it refuses to accept the fashionable cliché (on any given work and works upward from honest and not merely received impressions). This is particularly striking in the case of Stanislaus Joyce. He is very good on the subject of Synge's *In the Shadow of the Glen* and the attacks that it provoked in the Nationalist press:

> They seemed to assume – I don't know why – that it was a portrayal of typical Irish peasants, and though they admit adulteries have been committed in Ireland – O thank you Mr Griffiths! (*sic*) – they deny indignantly that adultery is typical. Leaving aside the question as to whether it is more or less typical of Ireland than of Scotland or England or Norway or Germany, do they intend that nothing should be portrayed but statistically observed types?

Surely this passage, with its perversions of Arthur Griffith's surname ('Griffiths') requires a note. Three questions arise: did Stanislaus Joyce make a slip? Did Professor Healey transcribe incorrectly Joyce's 'tiny hand'? Or does Professor Healey not know who was meant by 'Mr Griffiths'?

Again some eleven pages of the diary are devoted to a comparative study of George Meredith and Henry James, pages full of acute perceptions and judgments. For instance, 'James writes quietly and without haste and seems to write not what he is thinking about but what he has thought. He does not grasp at a thought when it is presented to him, but waits until it has settled itself in his mind's perspective and then arranges it with easy lucidity, writing clearly, minutely, and consequently.'

In these pages Joyce refers to several novels by James and Meridith, and many of their characters, but Professor Healey refuses a single note. This, although he provides notes on several passages, which would hardly be required by even the casual reader of Joyce.

A shrewd, powerful, limited critical intelligence is what we find in Stanislaus Joyce, and a dour, distrustful, hyper-introspective temperament. There is an astonishing resemblance to the character of the early Stephen in James Joyce's novels. James Joyce the creator, we are told, made use of his brother's diary, to such an extent that certain episodes recorded by Stanislaus may be found transmuted, alchemized, in *Dubliners*. (It is less significant that certain personages, mainly friends of the Joyces' father, should appear in both the diary and the novels.)

It seems obvious from his diary that James Joyce also transmuted Stanislaus. Consider their statements, how they seem to prefigure the mental stance of Stephen: 'I loathe my father. I loathe him because he is himself, and I loathe him because he is Irish – *Irish* – that word that epitomizes all that is loathsome to me' (p. 28). 'I would like to be revenged on my country for giving me the character I have,' and, 'I am tempted seven times a day to play a part, and others encourage me by playing up to me. Let me guard against this and I may become someone worth knowing' (p. 34). And the passage on the *bourgeoisie* (p. 66) is worthy of the later Stephen, but also of Joyce himself.

We are moving, in fact, in the genuine Joyce country, that of the man and of the novelist, but there is one factor absent, James Joyce's compassionate and sanative laughter.

Buck Mulligan

The diary has two leading anti-heroes: James and the father. Stanislaus is obsessed with both, and if not with them, with their friends. About his brother's friends he is mordant and, one suspects, perceptive. As in the figure of Buck Mulligan in *Ulysses*, Oliver St John Gogarty emerges as the villain, even as an image of corruption: a snob, a materialist, a flirter with heresy, a blasphemer, an unsteady clown, a purveyor of smut. The following passage seems to sum up the Gogarty of 1904, and perhaps of later years:

At present he (Jim) is staying on sufferance with Gogarty in the Tower at Sandycove. Gogarty wants to put Jim out, but he is afraid that if Jim made a name someday it would be remembered against him (Gogarty) that though he pretended to be a bohemian friend of Jim's, he put him out.

That has the ring of truth, for Stanislaus couldn't know that nearly sixty years later the Tower at Sandycove would become an official shrine to the memory of James Joyce and that Gogarty's name would survive only as that of 'a great talker' and of course as an accomplished scatologist. (I know all about Gogarty's 'exquisite lyrics', but no man can be reading those forever.)

The portrait of 'Pappie' is painful and, one fears, true in the light of a hurt and angry boy's experience of deprivation and ignominy. It is valuable as a first-hand account of the home-life of the Joyces, a home-life which was not altogether unique in the palmy days of late Victorian and Edwardian Dublin. Stanislaus's feelings for his father veered between hatred and cold dislike, and significantly he is exercised by his brother's ambiguous attitude of respect and loyalty, tempered by mockery.

Already in 1903–4 James must have been seeing his atrocious father as the matter of art. Stanislaus could only see him as part of the matter with living. But let him have the last word in the terrible closing sentences of the diary, sentences which establish beyond dispute Stanislaus Joyce's natural gifts as a writer:

After ten Pappie came in with few pence left. We – and the children – had fast-
ed 14 hours. I heard his drunken intonations in the dark downstairs, and then
the saddening flow. This is a true portrait of my progenitor: the leading one a
dance and then the disappointing, baffling, baulking and turning up – drunk –
the business of breaking hearts.[2]

*   *   *   *

I have called Stanislaus Joyce 'a hurt and angry boy' as he shows himself in this
diary. About a decade ago, the British press began to call Mr John Wain, novelist, critic, and now autobiographer, 'an angry young man', in company with a
much inferior writer, Mr Kingsley Amis. The label was, of course, ridiculous,
and the grouping even more so, an excellent instance of how the journalistic
mind seizes on superficial similarities and not on profound differences.

This 'part of an autobiography'[3] should kill the angry young man myth so far
as Mr Wain is concerned. As for the Wain–Amis grouping, it is no longer tenable
even as critical telegraphese. Mr Wain is honest, courteous, industrious, a little
vain, and perhaps in danger of becoming a little dull. What may save him, and this
transpires in his new book, is his sense of the pitiful in human destiny.

This of course is only to be expected from a man who as an undergraduate read
Johnson, not Boswell's *Johnson*, but the great seer and tragic visionary himself. No
one who has read Johnson in his youth, with an open mind, can ever after fail to be
touched by the great and necessary misfortunes that man, the angelic beast, is heir
to. And it is perhaps from Johnson that Mr Wain learnt the art of treating with candour and compassion difficult human material.

The best thing in his book is his study of E.H.W. Meyerstein, whom he knew
as neighbour, friend, and mentor, during his undergraduate days in wartime
Oxford. (Mr Wain, by the way, was *not* a scholarship boy.)[4] This is a magisterial
instance of a young man's attempt, in reason and affection, to grapple with and
understand an elder's quirks and manias and absurdities.

The Oxford chapter makes much the best reading. Unlike, for instance, the
earlier chapters on his Staffordshire childhood, and the later ones on Russia and
America, it has an air of unforced nostalgia, a flowing quality which is lacking in
the book as a whole.

Mr Wain comes from an unimpassioned Nonconformist background, but he
found himself at Oxford in the thick of Anglican and to a lesser extent, Roman
Catholic feeling. He gives friendly glimpses of C.S. Lewis and the late Charles
Williams. I wish he had said more about Professors Tolkien and Coghill and that
amiable man John Heath-Stubbs. Nothing could be less angry than his evocation of
the little group of Oxford Christian conservatives, who during the war provided an
oasis of order and hierarchy for a young and dislocated mind.

But *Sprightly Running* is a disappointment. Mr Wain decided to write about his first thirty-five years, quite arbitrarily. He may be sixty or even seventy before he knows, or begins to know, what was really worth writing about in the years 1925–60. This book indicates a desire to 'department' life, which is surprising in a post-Proustian.

A Printing House That Fosters Poets

(Hibernia, April 1959)

Where may an Irish poet look for book publication in the Republic of Ireland? If he is a serious artist and not merely a spinner of patriotic or even pious jingles, and if he does not write in Irish, then there is, virtually, only one firm likely to consider his volume – The Dolmen Press.

That fact alone makes the Dolmen experience one of the few important events in the history of Irish publishing since the inauguration of the Free State. A good deal of the work issued by the Press is esoteric in appeal, and I am afraid that many of the items are valuable as collectors' pieces rather than for intrinsic literary merit. Fine printing has gone, frequently, with vapid text, and indeed the printing experiments have not always been successful.

But the venture has been brave and dignified. At least one young Irish poet, Mr Thomas Kinsella, who needs no boost from me, is the Press's child, and his success in Ireland and England is the result, in some measure, of careful nurture and timing on the part of his publishers.

And now the Press introduces another young Irish poet, Mr John Montague (*Forms of Exile*). I doubt whether Mr Montague's collection of twenty-four poems will bring him immediate acclaim, critical or popular. But I am certain that he is a poet, as distinct from a writer of occasional verses.

In any first book of verse one is charmed by unity, or even the materials for unity, of feeling and vision. Despite an admirable variety of themes, Mr Montague manages to convey an impression of such a unity. The Montague of the first poem, 'Dirge of the Mad Priest', is essentially the Montague of the last, 'The Destructive Element', and this though the first is trite and derivative, and the last original and penetrative.

All the poems describe 'forms of exile', not exile in the narrow geographical sense, but in the sense of spiritual or intellectual or social dislocation. Mr Montague is himself an 'exile' from contemporary Ireland, as may be seen from the brief sequence, 'Rhetorical Meditations in Time of Peace', an 'exile' from the Irish political scene as he sees it, an 'exile' from 'the last flowering sweet garden of prayer and pretence', an 'exile' even among Irish pilgrims in Rome, with his passionate awareness, so reminiscent of Mr Denis Devlin, of the European context of Catholicism.

Like Mr Austin Clarke, Mr Montague appears to hunger for a spirituality of non-compromise, as in 'A Footnote on Monasticism: Dingle Peninsula', where he avoids, successfully, a parody of Mr Clarke's tone:

> *Breaking the stubborn*
> *Structure of flesh*
> *With routine of vigil and fast,*
> *Till water-cress stirred on the palate*
> *Like the movement of a ghost*

Perhaps the most successful poem is 'The Quest', a profound miniature allegory of the human condition as experienced by the truth-hunters. The last lines have extraordinary evocative power:

> *And came at last with*
> *Harsh surprise*
> *To where in breathing*
> *Darkness lay*
> *A lonely monster with*
> *Almost human terror*
> *In its lilac eyes*

I expect much from Mr Montague, if only because in his first volume he has told us nothing of his private heart, and I suspect this is so because of a self-imposed discipline, in the interests of unity.

Dolmen have also issued recently two further numbers of their *Dolmen Chapbook, Irish Elegies,* by Padraic Colum (no. 9, 3/6), and *Angel Sons,* translated from Rilke, by Rhoda Coghill (no. 10, 3/6).

Dr Colum's memorabilia, as he calls them, deal with Casement, Kuno Meyer, John Butler Yeats, Dudley Digges, Seamus O'Sullivan and Arthur Griffith. They are not an important part of of Dr Colum's creative work, but illustrate a breadth of sympathy in the face of gifted men, unusual in his own or any subsequent Irish generation.

Miss Coghill's Rilke versions strike me as more important in the context of her own poetry than as contributions to the Rilke cult. Only the first is successful, and perhaps I find it moving because of memories of certain poems in Miss Coghill's *The Bright Hillside.*

Oscar Wilde [1]

(John Jordan Papers)

One of Wilde's early fairy tales, 'The Devoted Friend', in the volume called *The Happy Prince*, consists largely of a cautionary tale told by a linnet to a water-rat. The Water- rat is extremely annoyed at the end and swims away. The Duck asks the Linnet what she thinks of the Water-rat, and the story ends:

'I am rather afraid that I have annoyed him', answered the Linnet. 'The fact is that I told him a story with a moral.' 'Ah! That is always a very dangerous thing to do,' said the Duck. And I quite agree with her.

That last comment is Wilde's own and it might seem quite in line with some of his later comments on the confusion of art and morality, of aesthetics and homiletics. The fact is, however, that in his prose writings – I exclude the critical pieces, of course – Oscar Wilde very nearly ruined himself as an artist in his attempts to tell stories with morals. There is, of course, one great exception, *The Importance of Being Earnest*, which in effect is the only true fairy-tale Wilde ever wrote, as well as being the most perfectly constructed comedy in the language. Those stories of Wilde's called 'fairy tales', 'The Happy Prince' and 'A House of Pomegranates', are of a very special kind. They have little to do with the world of Cinderella and Red Riding Hood and Puss in Boots. Wilde's fairy tales posit the vigilant presence of God, supernatural love, even heroic sanctity. They posit good and evil, rather than right and wrong.

But this is to anticipate my argument, which is that Wilde's complex nature had in it an element blending curiously nostalgia for and revolt against moral norms. No artist, of course, can be described like an auction item or a book bargain: Morality slightly scratched, Artistic Faculties in sterling condition, or, Moral Sense slightly warped, Artistic Achievement as new. And as Wilde himself said, 'cheap editions of great men are absolutely detestable'. I have no wish to be a purveyor of cheap editions. But I think it is possible to demonstrate that Wilde, on the evidence of his writings alone, was as much a reformer as an iconoclast, as much an evangelist as a tempter, and as much a Christian as a Greek. For all through his life and work Oscar Wilde exhibits the tension between Bethlehem and Helicon, between Calvary and Parnassus. The tragic comedian was also the giddy aspirant to suffering. The man whose work in part I am going to discuss was almost a paradigm of humanity itself: *ni ange ni bête*, neither angel nor animal. Society, nineteenth-century English society, decided to brand him as an animal. And even now, sixty years after his death, his name has an irrelevant aura of sinister notoriety, though we should all know by now that Oscar Wilde is a classic instance of the scapegoat or the whipping-boy. There is no question but that his years in prison and in exile hastened his death, and that death was, in a manner of speaking, a burnt offering.

Wilde was born in Westland Row [Dublin] on October 18th, 1854 – not 1856 – son of Sir William Wilde, eye and ear surgeon and antiquarian, and 'Speranza', the lady who contributed spirited verses to *The Nation*. He went to school at Portora Royal School [in] Enniskillen and proceeded to Trinity College, Dublin, and from there to Magdalen College, Oxford. He visited Italy in 1876, and Greece in 1877. He had begun to write and publish poems, and because even Wilde enthusiasts tend to neglect these early poems, I am going to say something about them. Many of the poems he wrote during his Italian visit of 1876 display a remarkable imaginative awareness of the Mysteries of Christianity, and an awareness with an explicitly Catholic bias. We may also see in these poems, even in the most devout of them, the churning of an imagination irretrievably committed to the lore and imagery of ancient Greece. Here is *'Ave Maria Gratia Plena'*,[2] written in Florence, and most probably on seeing Fra Angelica's pictures in the Convent of San Marco:

> Was this His coming! I had hoped to see
> A scene of wondrous glory, as was told
> Of some great God who in a rain of gold
> Broke open bars and fell on Danae:
> Or a dread vision as when Semele,
> Sickening for love and unappeased desire,
> Prayed to see God's clear body, and the fire
> Caught her white limbs and slew her utterly:
> With such glad dreams I sought this holy place,
> And now with wondering eyes and heart I stand
> Before this supreme mystery of Love:
> A kneeling girl with passionless pale face,
> An angel with a lily in his hand,
> And over both with outstretched wings the Dove.

This sonnet, with its juxtaposition of legendary accounts of the visitations of Greek gods and the Annunciation to Our Lady, pinpoints at an early stage Wilde's self-awareness in the matter of conflicting allegiances in the soul. Another sonnet, written during Holy Week at Genoa, clinches this self-awareness:

Written in Holy Week at Genoa

I wandered in Scoglietto's green retreat,
The oranges on each o'erhanging spray
Burned as bright lamps of gold to shame the day;
Some startled bird with fluttering wings and fleet
Made snow of all the blossoms, at my feet
Like silver moons the pale narcissi lay:
And the curved waves that streaked the sapphire bay
Laughed i' the sun, and life seemed very sweet.
Outside the young boy-priest passed singing clear,
'Jesus the son of Mary has been slain,
O come and fill his sepulchre with flowers.'
Ah, God! Ah, God! those dear Hellenic hours
Had drowned all memory of Thy bitter pain,
The Cross, the Crown, the Soldiers and the Spear.

'Those dear Hellenic hours': Why 'Hellenic' or 'Grecian' to describe a perfectly innocent walk in a grove? It would seem that Wilde now, and later, tended towards a view of all pleasure, sensuous and sensual, as being Greek, of all suffering, of all moral urgency as being Christian. He further tended to react against Catholicism when surrounded by external magnificence. This may be seen in the sonnet written 'On Hearing the *Dies* [*Irae*] Sung in the Sistine Chapel', which also rejects Hell, and the Sonnet called 'Easter Day'. Before leaving these Italian poems I may as well quote the curious sonnet called 'E Tenebris'.

On Hearing the Dies Irae Sung in the Sistine Chapel

Nay, Lord, not thus! white lilies in the spring,
Sad olive-groves, or silver-breasted dove,
Teach me more clearly of Thy life and love
Than terrors of red flame and thundering.
The empurpled vines dear memories of Thee bring:
A bird at evening flying to its nest
Tells me of One who had no place of rest:
I think it is of Thee the sparrows sing.
Come rather on some autumn afternoon,
When red and brown are burnished on the leaves.
And the fields echo to the gleaner's song,
Come when the splendid fulness of the moon
Looks down upon the rows of golden sheaves,
And reap Thy harvest: we have waited long.

It cannot as yet be established definitely whether this poem figures a genuine spiritual crisis, or whether it is a mere exercise in the convention of repentance.

What concerns me here is that in his very early twenties Wilde was deeply preoccupied with the figure of Christ and more especially Christ the Crucified.

Several of the poems written soon after his return to Oxford from Italy show a violent reaction against Italy and Catholicism The long piece, 'The Burden of Itys', celebrates Greece and the landscape of Matthew Arnold's 'The Scholar Gypsy', to the disadvantage of his Italian impressions:

> This English Thames is holier far than Rome, ...
> Is not yon lingering orange afterglow
> That stays to vex the moon more fair than all
> Rome's lordliest pageants! Strange, a year ago
> I knelt before some crimson Cardinal
> Who bare the Host across the Esquiline,
> And now — those common poppies in the wheat seem twice
> As fine.

We must remember, of course, that although the tension in Wilde was, as I believe, perfectly genuine, allowance must be made for certain great influences from the literature of his time, more particularly from Swinburne. Swinburne and Keats are all over Wilde's early verse and that simplification of Wilde's I spoke of, of the differences between 'Greek' and 'Christian', may legitimately be interpreted as a literary attitude taken over from Swinburne. But as Wilde might, possibly, have said, 'We are all the sum of our literary attitudes.'

I have drawn on some of the early verse of Oscar Wilde not because it is very good, nor because I wish to depict him as a hare in the Hound of Heaven stakes, but we cannot afford to forget this part of Wilde, and go bang in to his Society Period, when he began to create the well-substantiated legend of his brilliant conversational powers. Incidentally, one wonders if Wilde husbanded his conversational gems as carefully he did his written ones. I will have the task of pointing out that in many ways Wilde was curiously uninventive, not least in the minting of new epigrams, or as I prefer to call them, jokes.

By 1883, when he was not yet thirty, he had published his collected *Poems* and a blank-verse tragedy, called *The Duchess of Padua* (which I have not had the time to discuss), and had another play (of which, ditto) called *Vera* unsuccessfully produced in New York. The previous year, 1882, he had toured triumphantly in America, where he also made a number of very good jokes. In 1884 he married Constance Lloyd; and his two sons Cyril and Vivian [Vyvyan] were born in the two succeeding years. In 1887 he published his first stories, 'The Canterville Ghost', 'The Sphinx Without a Secret', and 'Lord Arthur Savile's Crime'. Four years later in 1891 these stories were collected along with 'The Model Millionaire'. In the interval he published the essays collected in 1891 as *Intentions*, the first book of fairy tales, *The Happy Prince*, the fantasy on Shakespeare's sonnets called *The Portrait of*

Mr W.H, and *The Soul of Man Under Socialism*, and of course *The Picture of Dorian Gray*, of which the complete version in book form appeared in 1891. Later that year the second book of 'fairy tales', *A House of Pomegranates*, appeared.

Leaving aside the critical works, the centrepiece of this activity is unquestionably *Dorian Gray*. Almost all the other stories may be referred to it, and it has one character, Lord Henry Wotton, who follows Wilde's career right up to 1895 and to what some may call downfall and others apotheosis. *Dorian Gray* is an extraordinary mixture: one part mediaeval fable, one part Victorian melodrama, one part dining out or taking tea with Oscar. Jack the Ripper's London lies around the corner from the Athenaeum, a young Faust walks through Covent Garden, male friend reproaches male friend in the accents, thrilling but faintly ludicrous, of Marie Corelli and over it all there is the odour of lilac and roses, of fog and of gas. It all has the quality of nightmare, relieved only by the jokes of Lord Henry and some others. But if one goes through that nightmare too often, the quips of Lord Henry seem to fall with the ghastly precision of water-drops from a leaking tap. And soon one realizes that the fog and the gaslight are more real than the perfume of roses and lilacs, and it is precisely that which gives the book the rank of – I will not say 'masterpiece' – but the 'irreplaceable'.

The plot of *Dorian Gray* is so well known that I will not inflict a direct *précis* on you. But, for a beginning, let us recall that the book has three principal male figures: Basil Hallward, a successful portrait painter, Dorian Gray, a wealthy young man of great personal beauty and [with] nothing much to do, and Lord Henry Wotton, a dandy and connoisseur who, at the age of thirty, appears to have loved much and learnt everything. He makes the kind of joke accredited to Wilde in his conversation. Is Wilde Lord Henry Wotton? I am inclined to believe that he is, but no more so than Basil Hallward, unquestionably no more so than Dorian Gray. The whole book reads to me as a projection of Wilde's own fears, dreams, remorses, perhaps even of his sins. But for the moment let me point to the analogy between the book and the Faust legend. (Wilde handled the Faust theme also, by the way, in his fairy tale 'The Fisherman and His Soul'.)

Basil Hallward's portrait of Dorian Gray so entrances the sitter that at one point he cries out, 'I am in love with it', and immediately we have introduced a theme never far from Wilde's brain, that of Narcissus and his love for his own pool-reflected beauty. Later, Dorian reflects on the portrait and says, 'It will never be older than this particular day of June ... If it were only the other way! If it were I who was always to be young, and the picture that was to grow old! For that – for that – I would give everything! Yes, there is nothing in the whole world I would not give! I would give my soul for that.'

Now it has been Lord Henry who has, so to speak, prepared Dorian's mind for such a reaction – in that sense he may be described as a Mephistophelian character. But that would be too easy a simplification. Lord Henry does not really exist in the world of good, or evil. He lives entirely in the fashionable 'nineties limbo of delicate sensations and exquisite emotions. His wit is the thrown-off glitter of an angel who has lacked sufficient passion to fall completely, and who has entirely forgotten about both Heaven and Hell. If guilt is to be imputed to him as a moral being, it is the guilt of selfishness, of reducing the world and humanity to the dimensions of an epigram. Later Dorian, before he is finally committed to degradation, reproaches Lord Henry, 'You cut life to pieces with your epigrams.' And even Lord Henry's friendship for Dorian is based on the pleasures to be derived from observing the development of a young and beautiful creature, an artless if pampered boy, turning into a tasteful, narcissistic, completely useless dandy. On the level of dandyism, and of the pleasure-cult, Dorian may be a victim of Lord Henry, but it is clear that Wilde did not intend Lord Henry to be taken as a direct agent for Dorian's damnation.

Later, after Dorian's first major offence against charity and honour – I mean his ultimate behaviour towards Sybil Vane – Lord Henry, it is true, gives Dorian a book which is afterwards described as having 'poisoned' him. The book is generally supposed to have been *À Rebours*, by Joris-Karl Huysman. It is with the hero of this book in mind, Des Esseintes, that Wilde traces Dorian Gray's fantastic experiments in the decadence of the senses. Nowadays the book is tiring rather than titivating to read, and it is hard to credit that it could ever have poisoned anybody. I don't think Wilde seriously intended us to believe that the book was responsible for Dorian's downfall: he introduced it *after* the death of Sybil Vane, just as it is after his behaviour to Sybil that his wish is fulfilled and the picture begins to change, while he remains immaculate physically. And anyway, it provided him [Wilde] with material for several pages of his own book.

In the light of medieval fable Basil Hallward has the role of Good Angel, and also he represents a side of Wilde which is often forgotten in the din of the jokes. Hallward may be sententious, but he is passionately sincere. Here he is addressing Lord Henry [in reference to his portrait of Dorian Gray]:

> 'You don't understand me, Harry', answered the artist. 'Of course I am not like him [Dorian]. I know that perfectly well. Indeed, I should be sorry to look like him. You shrug your shoulders? I am telling you the truth. There is a fatality about all physical and intellectual distinction, the sort of fatality that seems to dog through history the faltering steps of kings. It is better not to be different from one's fellows. The ugly and the stupid have the best of it in this world. They can sit at their ease and gape at the play. If they know nothing of victory, they are at least spared the knowledge of defeat. They live as we all should live, undisturbed, indifferent, and without disquiet. They neither bring ruin upon others, nor ever receive it from alien hands. Your rank and wealth, Harry; my brains, such as they are – my art, whatever it may be worth; Dorian Gray's good looks – we shall all suffer for what the gods have given us, suffer terribly.'

How prophetic that passage is, not alone of the outcome of the book but of Wilde's own life. Basil Hallward, of course, may be written off as a timid attempt to suggest sublimated romantic love for Dorian, but time and again he voices moral sentiments which Wilde explicitly commends elsewhere. It is also significant that Hallward, the Good Angel, should be killed by Dorian once he has viewed the abominably corrupted portrait. And Dorian … let us leave aside Lord Alfred Douglas and see what he tells us of Wilde himself. I cannot believe that it is not Oscar who as Dorian Gray wanders through the streets of London after he has hurt Sybil Vane so monstrously.

> Where he went to he hardly knew. He remembered wandering through dimly-lit streets, past gaunt black-shadowed archways and evil-looking houses. Women with hoarse voices and harsh laughter had called after him. Drunkards had reeled by cursing, and chattering to themselves like monstrous apes. He had seen grotesque children huddled upon doorsteps, and heard shrieks and oaths from gloomy courts.
>
> As the dawn was just breaking he found himself close to Covent Garden. The darkness lifted, and, flushed with faint fires, the sky hollowed itself into a perfect pearl. Huge carts filled with nodding lilies rumbled slowly down the polished empty street. The air was heavy with the perfume of the flowers, and their beauty seemed to bring him an anodyne for his pain. He followed into the market, and watched the men unloading their wagons. A white-smocked carter offered him some cherries. He thanked him, and wondered why he refused to accept any money for them, and began to eat them listlessly. They had been plucked at midnight, and the coldness of the moon had entered into them … After a little while, he hailed a hansom, and drove home. For a few moments he loitered upon the door – step, looking round at the silent Square with its blank, close – shuttered windows and its staring blinds. The sky was pure opal now, and the roofs of the houses glistened like silver against it. From some chimney opposite a thin wreath of smoke was rising. It curled, a violet riband, through the nacre-coloured air.

Earlier Wilde had published *Lord Arthur Savile's Crime*. Lord Arthur has been convinced by a palm-reader that he must, inevitably, commit murder. He, too, wanders through the streets of London, and:

> After a time he found himself in front of Marylebone Church. The silent roadway looked like a long riband of polished silver, flecked here and there by the dark arabesques of waving shadows. Far into the distance curved the line of flickering gas-lamps … He walked hastily in the direction of Portland Place, now and then looking round, as though he feared that he was being followed. At the corner of Rich Street stood two men, reading a small bill upon a hoarding. An odd feeling of curiosity stirred him, and he crossed over. As he came near, the word '**Murder**', printed in

black letters, met his eye. He started, and a deep flush came into his cheek. It was an advertisement offering a reward for any information leading to the arrest of a man of medium height, between thirty and forty years of age, wearing a billycock hat, a black coat, and check trousers, and with a scar upon his right cheek. He read it over and over again, and wondered if the wretched man would be caught, and how he had been scarred. Perhaps, some day, his own name might be placarded on the walls of London. Some day, perhaps, a price would be set on his head also.

The thought made him sick with horror. He turned on his heel and hurried into the night.

Where he went he hardly knew. He had a dim memory of wandering through a labyrinth of sordid houses, and it was bright dawn when he found himself at last in Piccadilly Circus. As he strolled home towards Belgrave Square, he met the great waggons on their way to Covent Garden. The white-smocked carters, with their pleasant sunburnt faces and coarse curly hair, strode sturdily on ... and the great piles of vegetables looked like masses of jade against the morning sky, like masses of green jade against the pink petals of some marvellous rose. Lord Arthur felt curiosly affected, he could not tell why. There was something in the dawn's delicate loveliness that seemed to him inexpressibly pathetic, and he thought of all the days that break in beauty, and that set in storm. These rustics, too, with their rough, good-humoured voices, and their nonchalant ways, what a strange London they saw! A London free from the sin of night and the smoke of day, a pallid, ghost-like city, a desolate town of tombs! ... By the time he had reached Belgrave Square the sky was a faint blue, and the birds were beginning to twitter in the gardens.

For what it's worth, the lady whom Lord Arthur is to marry is called Sybil Merton; as the lady whom Dorian rejected was called Sybil Vane. Maybe I am setting an unexistent literary puzzle, for I have already mentioned Wilde's laziness in invention. But there is a further link between the two passages.

Here is how Dorian describes Sybil Vane: 'She had all the delicate grace of that Tanagra figurine that you have in your studio, Basil. Her hair clustered round her face like dark leaves round a pale rose.' And we are told of Lord Arthur's betrothed that 'she looked like one of those delicate little figures men find in the olive woods near Tanagra'. For the record, Mabel Chiltern in *An Ideal Husband* will be described as 'really like a Tanagra statuette'.

What am I suggesting? Merely that there may have been an episode in Wilde's life, an episode that aroused violent emotions of some kind and which he associated with roaming the streets of London at night, finding some refreshment only with the dawn and the advent of the country folk bringing their wares to Covent Garden. And Sybil, or rather the two Sybils? It may be, simply, that he liked the name, or it may be that the episode in question had relevance to his relations with a single woman. Both his Sybils are models of constancy. Wilde's wife was called Constance.

The triple reference to the Tanagra statuette may indicate no more than Wilde's taste in female beauty. Or, as is not unlikely in the case of Oscar the aesthete, it may simply be that he liked the word 'Tanagra'.

I submit, then, that the three principal figures of the novel [Dorian Gray] are all aspects of Wilde himself and his personal predicament. Dorian Gray, once dead and damned, is not revived. But Basil Hallward is, and Lord Henry. Wilde's four West End plays give us several versions of them, and at one point they seem to coalesce in the person of Lord Goring in *An Ideal Husband*.

Time precludes a thorough-going establishment of my contention that all Wilde's other stories may be referred to *Dorian Gray*. But I must make some esssential points. There is a distinction to be drawn between the stories in *The Happy Prince* and *A House of Pomegranates*. The first book, for all its verbal craft, has a quality of innocence which is completely lacking in the second, except perhaps in the last story, 'The Star-Child'. The first story of *A House of Pomengranates*, called 'The Young King', is uncomfortably close in its first sections to the world of the corrupted Dorian Gray. 'Many curious stories were related about him at this period.' That sentence might have been written about Dorian, just as Wilde wrote of him, 'Curious stories became current about him after he had passed his twenty-fifth year.' But it was written about the Young King, a hunter of pleasure and worshipper of beauty saved by visions. And in 'The Fisherman and His Soul' it is clear that evocation of curiously artificial beauty is at least as important as the moral. For the tension in Wilde between Grecian and Christian, between Eros and Agape, was further complicated by this time, by the attraction towards the French so-called Decadents, whom Wilde seems to have read without much critical discrimination.

But now he had reached his period of triumph as a successful dramatist. His early plays had been unsuccessful, and I do not think our time warrants considering them. Nor will I say much about *Salomé*, which he wrote for Sarah Bernhardt. I find it, in French or in English, turgid and unsavoury.[3] That last rather prim adjective means merely that I cannot take an analysis of human passion couched in a mixture of pseudo-biblical and pseudo-Huysmanesque language.

Back now to Lord Henry Wotton. He reappears as Lord Darlington in Wilde's first stage success, *Lady Windermere's Fan*. He even quotes (without acknowledgement) some of Lord Henry's best jokes. When I said that Wilde was uninventive or thrifty in the coining of epigrams, I wished merely to indicate that he was a most industrious self-plagiarist. The charge of lack of invention is more serious on the grounds of theatrical interest. But this, I hope, will emerge.

Lady Windermere is a 'good woman' who is led to believe that her husband is carrying on with a notorious Mrs Erlynne. In her high-minded fury she allows herself to be compromised with the suave home-breaker (Lord Henry put in his place)

Lord Darlington. Her honour is saved by the intervention of Mrs Erlynne, who in fact is her mother, who abandoned her as a baby for a lover. The play ends happily without Lady Windermere ever learning the truth about Mrs Erlynne. Now, whether we like it or not, this play is a moral tract. Lady Windermere describes herself as a 'Puritan' with a capital P. She believes in non-forgiveness for the fallen, especially if the fallen rear their ugly heads on the domestic hearth. This does not prevent her being half-deceived by the blandishments of the serpent, Lord Darlington. Her moral, rigidity is shaken by the immense (as she thinks) sacrifice of Mrs Erlynne, and so she can declaim to her frightful stick of a husband:

> (Lady W.): You will never speak against Mrs Erlynne again, Arthur, will you?
> (Lord W., *gravely*): She is better than one thought her.
> (Lady W.): She is better than I am.
> (Lord W., *smiling as he strokes her hair*): Child, you and she belong to different worlds. Into your world evil has never entered.
> (Lady W.): Don't say that, Arthur. There is the same world for all of us, and good and evil, sin and innocence, go through it hand in hand. To shut one's eyes to half of life that one may live securely is as though one blinded oneself that one might walk with more safety in a land of pit and precipice.

In *A Woman of No Importance* Wilde juggles a little with the situations of the earlier play, and instead of a mother who has abandoned her child, gives us a mother who has been abandoned with an illegitimate child who does not know the secret of his origins. Mrs Arbuthnot, as she has been known, has brought up a clean-living but rather gormless son who is taken up by the second version of Lord Henry, Lord Illingworth. Mrs Arbuthnot recognizes Lord Illingworth as her seducer and the father of her son. She violently opposes her son taking employment with his father. The son, by the way, is in love with an American heiress who describes herself as a 'Puritan', and has views on fallen women similar to those of Lady Windermere. Mrs Arbuthnot herself accepts her punishment, but calls upon [sic] a similar degradation for male offenders.

The truth finally emerges and everything is resolved satisfactorily, except for Lord Illingworth. Rather surprisingly Mrs Arbuthnot and her former lover are not reconciled, in a marriage of convenience, and we leave her on the brink of emigrating to America with her son and his prospective bride, who like Lady Windermere has learnt that the fallen are not untouchables.

It is interesting to note that Lord Illingworth, who turns out to be a ruffian, has a high proportion of excellent quips and that most of them are pillaged from Lord Henry in *Dorian Gray*. One begins to wonder if Wilde is not exorcising the image of Lord Henry by equating his verbal brilliance with his moral turpitude.

And in the next play, *An Ideal Husband*, Lord Henry emerges, in the person of Lord Goring, not alone as wit, but as moralist and Good Angel. And in him we see, too, the outline of Algernon Moncrieff in *The Importance of Being Earnest*, just as in the Tanagra statuette, Mabel Chiltern, there is the forerunner of Gwendolen and Cecily in the same play.

It is Lord Goring, who in between his scherzos of nonsense, straightens out the personal problems of Sir Robert and Lady Chiltern. In him are fused the best of Lord Henry and Basil Hallward, and the whole play first produced in 1895, the year of Wilde's trial, seems an exquisite balancing of his instinct towards a generous moral rectitude and his relish for the daintily affected, the − here at any rate − innocuously dandyesque, and for a world perhaps where the pressures of time and flesh, of conscience and desire, do not exist.

It is such a world we find in his last play, *The Importance of Being Earnest*, produced on 14th February 1895. To attempt to outline the plot of this play would be absurd: as well try to catch a moonbeam in one's fist. But let me remind you that Algernon Moncrieff is Lord Henry finally purged and refined, just as his friend John Worthing is a kind of zany Basil Hallward. And the old theme of the abandoned child turns up. John Worthing does not find a parent, but he finds an aunt and mother-in-law in the shape of that deplorable and adorable dragon, Lady Bracknell.

In this play Wilde has turned his back on the actual world, but if we recall that the composition was going on in 1894−95, it is possible to see at least one pathetically ironic parallel between the situations in the play and in Wilde's own life. Both Algy Moncrieff and John Worthing lead, on a frivolous level for frivolous purposes, what may be called 'double lives'. And, whenever I see or read the play, I cannot help contrasting the harmless fantastical deceptions which make up the 'double lives' of Algy and John, and that reflection of Dorian Gray's on 'the terrible pleasure of a double life'.

Within a few months after the opening of *The Importance*, the harlots were dancing in the streets, and Oscar Wilde was in gaol. I have chosen not to discuss the last five years of his life, but you may care to be reminded that he died on 30th November 1900 in Paris, after he had been received into the Catholic Church by a Passionist priest, Fr Cuthbert Dunne. That this actually happened is proven by the publication in *The London Magazine* last year of the relevant extracts from Fr Dunne's papers. Until contrary evidence appears, we may take it that Oscar Wilde died a member of the Roman Communion, and I like to think that he is in Purgatory making jokes about people who didn't [die as members of the Church].

I seem to have gone on for a long time[4] about Oscar Wilde and yet to have said very little about him. But I hope I've suggested something of the fascination which his work can offer. I believe that when one can say of any writer's work that it is, however multifarious, somehow 'all of a piece', it becomes worthy of serious attention. And Wilde's work *is* all of a piece. Viewed as a whole it is not merely a series of isolated works, but rather a pattern in which there are recurring figures. The work, like the life, has its own internal terms of reference, its own peculiar logic.

I have made no cut-and-dried pronouncements on the total value of Wilde's work, because I do not know what that value is. As I have tried to show, and although I have said very little about Wilde's life, the development of Wilde the artist and Wilde the man seem inextricably linked. That, of course, is a truism valid for many artists. But with Wilde there is a special difficulty. So much that he wrote has an almost prophetic significance for his later life. And so the work is rendered more fascinating by the life, and the life by the work.

I can't think he will ever lose his fascination as a man and as a writer. And both life and work exist within one of the more durable preservatives: his supreme, his valiant, his finally so edifying gaiety. Wilde knew the hights and the ditches, the flattery of dowagers and the spittle of prostitutes, the acclamation of audiences and the opprobrium of friends; and we may think of him in any or all of these connections. For myself, I like most to think of him passing into eternity with a joke on his lips. Laughter, said the philosopher Hobbes, is 'a sudden glory'. Like sunlight in these islands. Oscar Wilde never lost the gift of bringing 'sudden glory'. In the final reckoning perhaps that is his message for us. 5

Life Is a Limitation

(Hibernia, 26 July 1979)

In 1962 Sir Rupert Hart-Davis produced *The Letters of Oscar Wilde*, a Herculean labour characterised by exact scholarship and an unobtrusive affection, but no *parti pris*, for his subject. That great volume is now out of print, and even if it were not, would be beyond the pocket of the average reader.

The present volume is based on the 1962 *Letters* and its reduction in size and content does not mean a diminution of scholarship. In fact it includes six new letters, of which one to Lily (should it not be 'Lillie'?) Langtry, written in January 1884, in which he announced his engagement to Constance Lloyd, is of special interest. (H. Montgomery Hyde used part of it in his *OscarWilde* [1976].) In reprints of *Selected Letters* no doubt room will be found for the remarkable letter to R.B. Cunninghame Graham, part of which Messrs Watts and Davies cite in their recent book on Graham (v. *Hibernia*, 12 July 1979). Graham had written responsively to *The Ballad of Reading Gaol*, and Wilde in his reply wished

> We could meet to talk over the many prisons of life – prisons of stone, prisons
> of passion, prisons of intellect, prisons of morality and the rest – all limitations,
> external or internal, are prison-walls – and life is a limitation.

Some of Wilde's best writing, over and above *The Ballad* (itself immeasurably superior to the rest of his verse), had its origins in the conditions of prison life. That is why the long letter to Lord Alfred Douglas, written January-March 1897 in Reading Gaol, is given here in its entirety, although perhaps it unbalances the book; on the other hand, this text, usually known as *De Profundis,* a title suggested by E.V. Lucas to Robert Ross for the extract he edited from the letter in 1905, was not published as Wilde wrote it until 1962, in Sir Rupert's *Letters,* and thus not easily accessible. It is essential that it be read as a whole if we are to understand Wilde's awareness of his own folly in allowing himself to be imprisoned by his passion for Douglas, which led to the 'absurd and silly perjuries' of what came to be known as 'The First Trial', Wilde's libel action against Douglas's half-mad father, the Marquess of Queensbury. I think myself there are some absurdities in this long letter to Douglas, e.g. *'There is something so unique about Christ'*, but it remains a document that lacerates the heart, not least because we know that after his release from prison in 1897 Wilde continued to hanker for his 'own darling boy'.

But Sir Rupert gives us also from Wilde's prison experience his letters to the Press on the prison conditions of the time as he himself had known them. Barely a week after his release he wrote a long and impassioned, but perfectly reasonable, letter to *The Daily Chronicle*, occasioned by a report that a warder at Reading, one Thomas Martin, 'had been dismissed by the Prison Commissioners for having given some sweet biscuits to a little hungry child'. Wilde had known himself the humane approach to prison rules of Martin (a native of Belfast). But in his letter to the *Chronicle* he is more concerned with his own memories of children in prison and of a particularly frightful case of an adult prisoner, A.2.11, who was repeatedly flogged 'on the report of the doctor' although clearly going insane. Consider this terrible passage and recall that it was written little more than two years after *The Importance of Being Earnest*:

> It was my Sunday in prison, a perfectly lovely day, the finest day we had had the whole year and there, in the beautiful sunlight, walked this poor creature – made once in the image of God – grinning like an ape, and making with his hands the most fantastic gestures, as though he were playing in the air on some invisible stringed instrument or arranging and dealing counters in some curious game.

For most of this review I have concentrated on 'Wilde' rather than 'Oscar'. But I am not insensitive to 'Oscar' and that incorrigible, some might say unforgivable, gaiety of spirit that sustained him even to the gates of death. Oscar's gaiety is, of course, amply demonstrated in these letters. It is hard to define the quality of Oscar's gaiety. Sometimes it is what I would call meritorious flippancy, as when he writes to Robert Ross in April 1900 about Leo XIII:

> I have seen nothing like the extraordinary grace of his gesture, as he rose, from moment to moment, to bless – possibly the pilgrims, but certainly me.

But I like as much another kind of flippancy in a passage about photographing cows in the Borghese Gardens, also in a letter to Ross:

> Cows are very fond of being photographed, and, unlike architecture, don't move.

Some of these letters, of course, may shock those who like to think of Oscar Wilde as progressing consciously to that famous deathbed reception into the Catholic Church. Perhaps Joyce had the truth of it when he wrote over seventy years ago in a Triestine paper that at the very base of Wilde's 'subjective interpretations of Aristotle ... is the truth inherent in the soul of Catholicism: that man cannot reach the divine heart except through that sense of separation and loss which is called sin'. So be it.

One of the Saddest Books Ever to Come Out of Ireland[1]

(Hibernia, 5 August 1960)

The literary reputation of Mr Brian Nolan (or is it O'Nolan?), as distinct from any legendary accretions – for like the other few men of distinction who live most of the time in Dublin, he is the victim of popular myth-mongering – is based chiefly on the following work: in Irish, *An Beal Bocht*, which is hard to classify; in Irish and English, his contributions to *The Irish Times*, for which he uses a splendidly traditional pen-name 'Myles na Gopaleen' (see Gerald Griffin's *The Collegians* and Boucicault's masterpiece *The Colleen Bawn*) and which are even harder to classify; and in English, and quite unclassifiable, *At Swim-Two-Birds*, now republished on its twenty-first birthday (MacGibbon & Kee, 21/-).

There are also several minor works, including the play *Faustus Kelly*, and a rewarding anecdote called 'The Martyr's Crown' published originally in *Envoy*. But the above works are Mr Nolan's chief call on our attention.

I have often been asked by members of that large and motley crew who affect disdain for the Irish language why, if it's so good, so acute etc., *An Beal Bocht* has not been translated.[2] The answer is simple. It is a bookish book. Appreciation of it requires some familiarity with the spate of autobiographical treatises that form a very large part of the literature produced by the movement for the revival and preservation of the Irish language. Some of these books have literary merit, some have not. Even the best are a bit dubious.

To savour *An Beal Bocht* you need to have savoured the threnodic and complacent elements of, say, *Peig* or *An t-Oileánach*, and perceived that they can harden into clichés.

I've called it 'bookish', but then Mr Nolan is a very 'bookish' man. He once called himself, in his horse-dealer's capacity, (see Griffin's *The Collegians*)[3] a 'spoiled Proust'. He might more properly be called (I'm not up to an equivalent splendour in punning) a foiled scholar. Every other day in *The Irish Times* he demands from his readers a range of literary and historical reference not unlike that required by the more allusive kind of academic. He also requires some knowledge of Latin, Irish and the major European tongues. What then does he do in *The Irish Times*? This is best answered perhaps by considering the *persona*, not always *grata*, of 'Myles na Gopaleen'.

First of all, this individual seems to live in Bantry. He has a house there, a housekeeper and a well-stocked cellar. Though he is of extreme age and often incapacitated, these disabilities are offset by the possession of gifts normally attributed to Merlin (and to others less and more respectable). He has a bird's-eye view of everything that's going on everywhere. This faculty is accompanied by the gift of multi-location.

How, and for what purpose, does he employ these gifts? Well, they enable him to send out bulletins to the Plain People of Ireland (one of his few weaknesses) on every conceivable (or printable) subject at home or abroad, and to direct their wandering attention to folly in high places, local or universal codology, cant (in Dr Johnson's sense), mis-prints, mis-translations, mis-appropriations, and many other serious things in which the Plain People have not the slightest interest.

Why does he undertake this most thankless of tasks? For it would seem that he would be happier with his buddies Keats and Chapman, of whom he occasionally records charming anecdotes and boutades.

I think the answer to this final question is that the creator of 'Myles', Mr Nolan, as well as being a foiled scholar, is a spiritual disciple of Savonarola, diverted from martyrdom by two facts: (a) martyrs, unless political, are out of fashion in Ireland; (b) no-one takes him seriously. He might do better in Russia, or even in America. Even as the bard of the strange and complex workings of the Dublin Mind, he is largely underestimated.

'Did you read Myles this morning?'

'God, yes, he's a gas man.'

To be a little graver: it seems to me that behind the Gopaleen mission of bad tidings, there is a genuinely sombre, even bitter mind, and that to call him a 'humourist', thus placing him in the category of D.B. Wyndham Lewis or J.B. Morton, is both insulting and foolish.

And perhaps that mind is at its most melancholy in the book I'm supposed to be reviewing, *At Swim-Two-Birds*. Of course it is a very funny book, and technically a tower of strength. Of course it is linguistically a triumph. But whether or not he intended it to be so, it is one of the sadddest books ever to come out of Ireland.

Consider the narrator. This is a young student in his final year at an easily identifiable 'College'. The greater part of his time is spent either in bed or in some easily identifiable pubs. He lodges with his uncle, a brilliantly realised figure of unimpeachable authenticity. He is writing a book about a publican (who spends even more time in bed) who himself is writing a book about a marvellous collection of Dublin Men (and others) who come alive while he is sleeping and write a book about him (the publican). I haven't the space to examine the virtuosity of execution in this complicated scheme.

What strikes me as important is the way in which so cerebral a plot seems to figure the exact mental condition of the narrator. It is the kind of plot we might expect from Oblomov, that character of Goncharov who, it will be remembered, spent his life in bed until overtaken by nothing more dignified than ejection and a pathetic end.

And the narrator himself might well stand for a symbol of the terrible Irish vices of talking and not doing, of planning and not completing, of scoffing and not contributing, of dreaming, dreaming, dreaming. This boy is better evidence than any actual data why Joyce found it necessary to leave Dublin, and his creator has invested him with the tragic significance of the Irish intellectual, of every age group and every degree of talent, who fails to fight off lethargy and canalize bitterness into creation.

I have touched only on one aspect of the book, and on that one in particular because it is likely to be overlooked. But on the symbolic level, the book is immeasurably rich. For instance, the fate allotted to the publican Trellis by his characters, while verbally very funny, is in fact peculiarly horrible in its brutality and sadistic intensity: here we might see a fable of the fate of Irish writers in their own country. And in Mr Nolan's use of the story of Mad Sweeny, we might see a parable of the relationship in Ireland between the writer and the Church.

But *At Swim-Two-Birds* is the kind of book in which it is possible for each reader to find his own level, and I would not deny that there are many passages which are quite crazily funny. Mr Nolan knows, to every inflexion and turn of phrase, the idiom of spoken English in Dublin; and in that, and in his linguistic virtuosity, he is the only true heir of Joyce. 'Tell me, do you ever open a book at all?' is the recurrent question of the student-narrator's uncle. All our young men should open *At Swim-Two-Birds*, and it would not do some of the older ones any harm at all to re-open it.

A Letter To Myles

(Hibernia, October 1964)

Dear Myles: I can't keep it in. I've just been reading a book I think you'd like —
though with reservations. It's called *The Dalkey Archive,* by Flann O'Brien, published
by MacGibbon & Kee at 2 1 /– s

(I learned this arduous phraseology through assiduous reading of Cathal
O'Shannon *pere*). What may interest you primarily is that this fellow O'Brien has
very obviously been influenced by you. I saw something of the kind in his last book,
The Hard Life, and indeed I got a kind of prenatal whiff of you in his first book,
At Swim-Two-Birds. The brutal truth is that the chap is what they call out here an *afi-
cionado* of yours.

Consider the situation. Two lads, Mick Shaughnessy and one called Hackett, a
kind of jukebox age Mulligan–Gogarty, act as Samaritans to a gent who has hurt his
toe in a bathing place at Dalkey. (Said village and environs described very well in
the manner of eighteenth-century [late] guidebooks). The gent, who has a play-
with-words *a la* Gopaleen on his front gate, turns out to be a creature out of that
grand old writer, H.G. Wells. This gentleman has a secret weapon which can
destroy all living things when used to unproper advantage. When used for the most
exciting kind of parlour game, the weapon can call down vasty spirits from the
heights. (I happen, d'you know, to be reading *The Tempest* in an atrocious but jolly
Spanish translation). Among them are the damnably eclectic Fathers of the Church,
but as Mick and Hackett discover to their slightly befuddled cost, the arch *revenant*
is that dubiously orthodox Christian, Augustine, Bishop of Hippo.

Now you, dear Myles, are on record as having pronounced blasphemous the
second act of *The Silver Tassie* by Mr Sean O'Casey. Thus you may flinch at the gay
irreverence of the dialogue between H.G. De Selby and St Augustine. You may, with
your particular cult of the mother, be shocked at Augustine's reference to Monica
as 'the mammy'. But you, like all intelligent sinners, will perceive that Mr
O'Brien's intention, though deflatory, is also salutary. One is really sick to death of
the fraternalist version of Augustine, a fifth-hand redaction of an excellent if con-
ceited writer who has served as an *apologia* for countless *cafe-au-cathedral* purvey-
ors of questionable beauty. (I don't question the beauty in question myself, but I

must take into account the opinion of ninety-nine per cent of your beloved Plain People). At all events, the passage at arms between De Selby and Augustine is erudite, funny and graceful. It is also disgraceful reading for mothers of growing lads.

The situation is only the first for our hero, Mick. For he discovers the whereabouts, not as a cadaver in Zurich, of James Augustine Joyce, in of all humble places, the delightful watering-place of Skerries. I will not spoil your fun by describing in detail Mick's quest for Joyce. Suffice it to say that he turns out to be a humble fellow who has written *gratis* for the Catholic Truth Society (C.T.S.), and who has no higher aim in life than to become a purifier, a kind of incarnated *aggiornamento*, of the Society of Jesus. We leave this latter-day Savonarola (surely Dominicans, Augustinians and Jesuits are brothers in the Lord?) in no. 35, presumably to unveil to Father Cobble, S.J., the story of his soul.

I think, dear Myles, this might have been a gayer and more serious book, if the fellow O'Brien had essayed the supreme effrontery, an encounter between the Bishop of Hippo and Mr Joyce of Skerries, aspirant to orders within the Society of Jesus. And I think you will agree when and if you get round to reading the book, that poor Mick needs a little amplification. After all, his carryings-on with De Selby and Mr Joyce involve him in the discovery and loss of a priestly vocation, and an unhappy ending with a foolish culture-monger who debits him with a child, fathered presumably by the atrocious Hackett. Mick could have been a Candide of our ghastly Dublin: he is, as he stands, a scrap of a lad manipulated by a devastating intelligence; Mr O'Brien, whom hitherto I have considered a gent of commendable bravery (albeit influenced by you) has on this occasion failed in nerve. This is at once forgivable and deplorable.

I will not bore you with the old French tag. But there is no question but that elder writers like Mr O'Brien must, in a country such as ours, 'give a lead' (Baden Powell had a point) to the very young, the young, and the youngish.

In the meantime, dear Myles, I hope that your body and soul are moderately tranquil and that you will continue to exercise on Flann O'Brien an influence more stringent, but no less benevolent. – Yours, etc.,

John Jordan
Casa del Maestro,
Toleda,
5 September 1964

(Untitled essay on) Flann O'Brien

(John Jordan Papers)

There is on exhibit[1] a letter from B.O'N.[2] to me, dated 30 April 1965, which requires an amount of exegesis. By the beginning of April 1965, I had been on friendly but not intimate terms for about a decade with Myles. Perhaps because he had appreciated what I had written about *At Swim-Two Birds* in 1960 and *The Hard Life* in 1961, he had taken the trouble to visit me when I was ill in 1962[3] and given me a preview of his work-in-progress, which was *The Dalkey Archive*.

But in the third week of April 1965, in what was then a class of literary pub, McDaid's of Harry Street[4], I landed myself in the most absurd of rows with Myles – over the exact form of an early pseudonym of Bernard Shaw, used by him in 1888 and 1889 when he began his career as a music critic in T.P. O'Connor's journal *The Star*. I was, of course, an idiot to pit myself against a master of pseudonymery, who was also a man of considerable musical culture – any hack can waffle about Beethoven or Chopin, but only a man of high taste would have De Selby improvising on César Franck's *Sonata for Violin and Piano*, in the opening pages of *The Dalkey Archive* – and also, though I did not know it then, had, only three months earlier, as Flann O'Brien, published an article on 'George Bernard Shaw on Language'. Before returning to that infernal Shavian pseudonym, I'd observe that Shaw seems to have been one of the few so-called Anglo-Irish writers in this century for whom Myles had time. He was contemptuous of Synge, as I knew from a conversation in the summer of 1955. From an earlier *Cruiskeen Lawn* column I recalled his curiously conventional reactions to O'Casey's play *The Silver Tassie*: he considered the expressionistic Second Act blasphemous. Years later I came to realize that he might have been influenced by his oldest literary friend, the novelist and dramatist, Brinsley MacNamara, twenty-one years his senior. In 1935, when finally The Abbey put on *The Tassie*, Brinsley had in protest resigned from the Board of Directors. Incidentally, in 1953 Myles, as Brian Ua Nualláin, published a Gaelic translation of his friend's best play, the tragedy, *Margaret Gillan*, which he may have seen at The Abbey twenty-one years earlier.

But I must return to the Shavian pseudonym, which was of course 'Corno di Bassetto', which is the Italian form of the 'basset-horn', an instrument lower in pitch than the clarinet; hence the 'basset-hound' for that animal's low voice. I am sure that Myles knew all that, although he did not include it in the unquotably abusive letter he wrote to me when he had checked his own correctness about 'Corno di Bassetto'.

You will understand that when in 1967, the year after his death, *The Third Policeman* was published, I was moved to see that among the many commentators from many countries on De Selby and his writings – Le Fourniers du Garbandier, Klaus, Le Clerque, and so on – the man Bassett emerges with most credit, even above the heroic Hatchjaw.

But back to April 1965. I had the temerity to reply to the abusive letter about 'Corno di Bassetto'. And by return of post came the broadside:

> Dear John,
> Strange reason for replying to your letter of 29 April is that it arrived beside my bed with other mail, but with the stamp not cancelled. How is that for automation of the Post Office? The stamp is on the envelope of this note.
>
> You say '... of course you are aware that correspondence, even when typed by a secretary, can constitute libel ...'
>
> I am not so aware, and beg you to stop using words you do not understand. Libel does not and cannot exist in the absence of publication. The root of the Eng. word libel is LIBELLUS (dim. of L. *liber*) 'a little book', and that gives the clue. I can send by closed post to you at a known address every day of the year the most derogatory appraisal of yourself and your behaviour, and there is no libel. I wd. be libellous to do so by open envelope or on a postcard, or through any other medium that brings in a third person – and just one individual third party is sufficient. Similarly, I can snarl at you face to face and, provided we are alone, there is no slander.
>
> Too late now, alas, but you should have gone to the CBS where they inculcate Latin through not Irish but corium.
>
> B. O'N.
> 30–4–65.

There are, I believe, three points of interest in this letter, in relation to Myles. First, his glee in having scored over a Government Department, or officialdom, to the extent of a five-penny stamp. Second, his thorough grasp of what are the circumstances that are required for libel or slander. Third, his extraordinary reference to the Christian Brothers' School and their methods of teaching. The last word of the letter, 'corium', by the way, is Latin for 'a leather whip, thong or strap'. Myles himself attended the Christian Brothers in Synge Street, Dublin, for a time when his family settled in Dublin in 1923, when he was about twelve. The boy Manus in *The Hard Life* seems rather younger when he enters what he calls 'the sinister portals of Synge Street School' and got to know the 'leather, the 'corium', of which he gives a blood-curdling description. Oddly enough, I myself entered the 'sinister portals' aged thirteen and learnt Latin through the medium of the 'cori-um', although Myles appeared to think I learnt it through Irish and at a superior establishment.

Myles's inference I find odd, because unless he is wishing that I had undergone his alleged torments (which, in fact, I had) he is revealing a secret admiration for the system of teaching he elsewhere savages, especially in *The Hard Life*. But then, in some respects, he was like the Third Policeman – 'an uncontestable character and a man of ungovernable inexactitudes'.

For Avila with Love

(Hibernia, November 1960)

I came to Avila late in September, attracted chiefly by its associations with Saint Teresa of Jesus, and to a lesser extent, with Saint John of the Cross. I knew I was about to walk on holy ground, but I've done that before and, humanly speaking, felt none the better for it. Five days in Avila left me refreshed in mind and spirit.

Perhaps it was the high clear air: the little walled city is four thousand feet above sea-level. Perhaps it was the people of Avila, aloof mentors of what is really meant by the phrase 'Castilian courtesy' – a complex attitude towards people, especially strangers, which at first impression may strike one as being sheer bad manners. Perhaps it was the prevalent Teresian ambiance and the sympathy one brought to it. (Mr Arland Ussher is lukewarm about Avila largely, I think, because, on his own gallant confession, he can't take nuns, not even great nuns).

But it might simply have been the fact that I came at a time when tourists were rare birds. I counted eight in all in the first four days, and on the last day talked in a macaronic confusion of Spanish and Italian with a Venetian: it is a grace to be the thankful for, that in this exquisite and palpably sacred city, I was alone and away from the English language. The strength of Avila is best drawn in solitude and silence.

For despite what Mr Ussher or Mr V.S. Pritchett may say, Avila is no dead town, no mere monument. It is living and life-giving, and, of course, miraculously un-tainted by the current international passion for obscuring identity in the interests of tourism. Avila offers itself, not a little more, and if the tourist is not satisfied, he may be sure that Avila does not care.

Though in summer day-trips are the usual thing (French tourists, or pilgrims, spend up to a week, at Christmas and Easter), Avila cannot be experienced in a day. Nor, I should say, in a month. When I left I had just begun to grasp the nature of the city's special boon; its unfathomable air of incorruptibility. This would be explicable if it were only a question of immunity from the commercialism of the average tourist centre. But Avila seems to breathe a kind of defiance in the face of time and change, to carry itself with an integrity that mocks the temporal and inessential.

Within and without its marvellous walls it is possible to believe that here, if only for a little time, one can entertain the illusion of a whiff of eternity. This fortress of a city, isolated in a landscape of rock and scrub-grass, may indeed be the essence of Castile. It is also an austere, but withal passionate, reminder of how relatively absurd are our preoccupations with getting and spending, how arrogant our aspirations to fortune and success. And believers will grant me that whereas Avila nurtured Teresa, she in turn may be sustaining Avila, keeping inviolate its message of everlastingness.

I do not know if many Irish people, apart from some of my acquaintance, make a point of visiting Avila. I do not even know (but would be glad to) if Teresa has a cult in this country. I should think not. There are fashions even in devotion to the Saints. And I think that for most Irish people, 'Teresa' means the indomitable little girl from Lisieux. Avila's Teresa indeed has tended to become the exclusive property of the intellectuals, who in turn tend to cast a cold eye on the Little Flower if only because her prose is so atrocious when set beside Mother Teresa's[1]. But it was Mother Teresa who said 'the Lord walks among the pots and pans', which contains, surely, the term of the Little Flower's teaching on 'the little way'.

It seems a pity that we in Ireland, who could so well appreciate Mother Teresa's immense human virtues of resilience and forthrightness and gaiety of heart, should not know her better. I do not propose a mass invasion of Avila by Irish tourists (after all, I want to go back there myself, and have no desire to hear complaints about the cooking). But I wish to record that the Teresian pilgrimage – which may be done in a day – cannot fail to move, at least on the purely human level.

Avila is small enough to be encompassed on an afternoon and intricate enough to upset a scheduled tour. I had intended to visit the chief Teresian landmarks in their relation to Teresa's own development. But one afternoon while tracking down a hermitage called Vuestra Senora de la Cabeza, which may without irreverence be translated as 'Our Lady of the Head-Cases', I found myself on the way to the Convent of the Incarnation. Here Teresa took her habit, suffered agonies in mind and body, uneasily triumphed, and became prioress. Here she made her confession to St John of the Cross – the spot is marked. Here she was advised on her spiritual problems by St Francis Borgia;, and, later, on these and the more mundane problems of her Reform, by St Peter Alcántara. Here, over a period of several days, she had that unique vision of the Transverberation. That day I saw the first of my few tourists, and I will remember them because a dandyish young Catalan wiped away the tears from his mother's eyes.

Having found myself by accident mid-way in the Teresian pilgrimage, I decided to go forward rather than go back. I was quite alone, apart from the old woman who unlocked the doors and babbled a liquid but intelligible commentary, when I visited Teresa's first foundation of the Discalced Reform of the Order of Carmel. The Convent of San José (or locally '*de las Madres*') was, in effect, the forcing-house of Teresa's ascetic ideal. It might even be said that this utterly tucked-away convent deserves to be known as one of the caryatides of the monastic ideal of Western Europe. Here Teresa wrote and prayed and meditated and at the age of fifty set out on her great journeys of Reform.

Her cell has been turned into a chapel and there is a display of curious and homely relics. Perversely, I was less stirred by her collar-bone (one remembers the mutilations to which her body was subjected after death) than by the oddments which she handled in her daily life: the jug from which she drank, the whistles (pitos) and drum with which she raised up her heart. And may all her children forgive me when I say that Mother Teresa's drum is not unlike the contemporary bongo drum.

The chapel as it stood in her time has been restored, but the original structure is intact. Much of Teresa's life is reflected in the worn lettering of the tombs: her brother lies here and her confessor Gaspar Daza, her biographer Julian of Avila, her friend Catalina Daz, Gaspar's sister, and his mother Dona Francisca. In many ways, San José is the richest of the Teresian shrines in Avila and, from a sentimental point of view, more satisfying than the church and convent built on the site of her birth.

Here again I was alone, even in the chapel built on the site of the very room where she was born, where there stands on the altar the crucifix she embraced when dying. In a little room off the entrance to the convent there are further relics to be seen, including her finger in a phial and her discipline. For the first and only time I was impressed by a slight vulgarity, an air of contrivance. Teresa was presented, it seemed, as if on show. Whereas in the Incarnation and San José her presence seemed to inform and justify the unpretentious little displays of her material existence. Perhaps my meaning will be clearer if I say that at the Convent of St Teresa, a chief exhibit is a large crucifix described as 'made from wood of the room in which St Teresa was born'. One jibs at manufactured relics. There is also a visitors' book, which I did not sign.

In a sense then, I missed a good deal in not doing the pilgrimage the right way round. It would have been better to have ended at San José, to have moved from the posthumous veneration to the contemporary witness. But in all it was, as the Spaniards say, 'of a glory'.

I have not mentioned the other splendours of Avila – the cathedral, the Church of San Vincente, the monastery of Santo Tomás, for instance – because I am not attempting a guide, merely a testimony of gratitude.

And on my last evening, as I sat in the main square watching the Marian blue of the sky deepen into old gold and crimson and then into night, my head full of Spanish journalistic rhetoric about U.N.O. and the Chief of the Soviet State, and war and disarmament, and the Lord knows what else, it occurred to me that Teresa of Avila, eagle and dove, soldier and peace-maker, intellect and love, might well be the ideal servant to intercede with 'His Majesty'

The Irish Novelists[1]

(Studies, Spring 1961)

Some half-a-century ago, Thomas MacDonagh, in one of his 'frankly experimental studies' in Anglo-Irish literature gathered together and published in 1916 as *Literature in Ireland* (and never, so far as I know, re-published and edited), asked, 'what then will the historian of Anglo-Irish literature have to deal with?' And MacDonagh was categorically excluding what he called the 'Hiberno-English writers': Swift, Goldsmith, Sheridan and so on (we may add Wilde).

His answers are interesting, even if his examples, or some of them, demonstrate the shattering parochialism which could infect even a man of MacDonagh's European culture in a period of nationalist aspiration. What is to the point here is that MacDonagh, although a passionate student of the Gaelic literary tradition, recognized the importance of the nineteenth-century Irish novelists: Maria Edgeworth, Charles Maturin, William Carleton, Charles Lever, Samuel Glover, Gerald Griffin, J. Sheridan Le Fanu, the Banims, and some more recent writers. A long tradition of commentary, good, bad and indifferent, on Irish life, provided a rich if uneven quarry for the critic and scholar, more especially, one would think, for Irish critics and scholars. And yet, in our own time, the only significant contribution to a study of those novelists made by an Irishman is Mr Benedict Kiely's book on Carleton, *Poor Scholar*.

Now, as has been the case with Joyce, with Yeats to a large extent, and more recently with O'Casey, it has been left to an American, Professor Thomas Flanagan of Columbia, to tackle the job seriously and with scholarship. To adapt a complaint Gide used to make about Claudel, the Americans have more talent, more libraries, more money. They also have more energy and more enthusiasm. Their scholars of taste and balance more than compensate for their sloggers and assemblers.

Prof. Flanagan studies at length four of the novelists listed by MacDonagh; Maria Edgeworth, John Banim, Gerald Griffin and William Carleton, plus Lady Morgan. As we might expect from a pupil of Lionel Trilling and Jacques Barzun, Mr Flanagan is concerned with literary values in the widest sense. He places his subjects fairly and squarely in their political, social and historical contexts, realising, for instance, that to try to understand Carleton outside 'the world of the cabins, the lost, splendid, terrible world of the Celtic peasantry were as fruitless as to try to understand Blake outside the industrial revolution, or Lawrence outside the scarred hills and blackened terraces of its later monstrous blossoming'. Mr Flanagan is never better than in his first section, an 'Introduction' to the world from which these Irish novelists wrote, and I would recommend this part of the book alone, even to professional historians, as an instance of how to convey the 'feel' of a cataclysm and surge in the events of history. I certainly have never found a comparable imaginative grasp of what lies behind the sentence, 'the issues of race, religion, and politics became hopelessly entangled'.

Let me quote, not only to illustrate Mr Flanagan's unsentimental awareness of the issues involved, but also how well he can write. He remarks about the oratory of Grattan's Patriot Party that it 'was a prized accomplishment in eighteenth-century Ireland, the glittering, posed, language of public men who had modelled themselves upon the heroes of Plutarch' (MacDonagh advised the study of, among others, Grattan, Flood and Curran). But he qualifies, 'Set against the stench and misery of Irish life, it marks the measure of their political failure'.

Again, on Lecky's great history, and the fact that 'the loyalist professor of history at Trinity College' should write a 'stirring celebration of independent Ireland':

> It was the tragedy of the nineteenth-century Ascendancy, which none felt more keenly than did Lecky himself, that the national cause had passed out of their hands and into those of men who gave it a new shape and new passions. The press of events would force upon the descendants of the Volunteers a position which was staunchly Unionist. Yet over the fireplace of many a great house would hang, in honor [sic], the sword of a grandfather who had served in the Volunteers, and his uniform would be carefully preserved. The sword and the uniform may serve to remind us how rich in paradox was the culture of nineteenth-century Ireland, and how embittered.

Mr Flanagan's book, then, is as well as being a critical evaluation of five novelists, a study of paradoxical and embittered culture. But in his treatment of individual writers he shows equal perception, and a rare gift in those whose task it is to brush away the cobwebs from forgotten books and, in at least three cases, largely forgotten writers. He can give us a précis of a novel without ever losing freshness of style and command of our interest.

Maria, of course (why not 'Maria', if the Austenites can get away with 'Jane'?), is not forgotten. But most of us never go further than *Castle Rackrent*, which Mr Flanagan describes as 'as final and as damning a judgment as English fiction has ever passed on the abuse of power and the failure of responsibility', and again as 'that rare event, an almost perfect work of fiction'. Mr Flanagan takes us through the other relevant novels, being especially good on *The Absentee*, to my mind a greater book than *Castle Rackrent*, if only because of its larger canvas and complexity of interest. No one who has ever read that marvellous evocation of a world in which nobility of motive (in Lord Colombre) burgeons out of contact with half- a-dozen cultures, amoebic, vestigal, or miscarried, can ever doubt that Maria was a major novelist in her time – and I will go further; by any standard.

Sydney Owenson, Lady Morgan, is, I think, forgotten. I knew only *The Wild Irish Girl*, which has something of the elegiac sweetness, the Ossianic melancholy, of Moore's *Melodies*. Indeed, Mr Flanagan sees Lady Morgan as maintaining with Moore, Macpherson's tradition. More importantly, from a cultural standpoint, he argues that 'for several generations the issues of Irish politics would be argued out in the terms of Sydney Owenson's rhetoric'. He discusses, with uncommon lucidity and (I suspect) a degree of over-generosity, Lady Morgan's other novels, pinpointing the precise strand of opinion-cum-sentiment *vis-à-vis* Ireland which she represented, 'caught as she was between her bright, secular, Whiggishness and her hankering after a glamorous and immemorial past'.

Maria and Lady Morgan were, in their very different ways, of the Ascendancy. John and Michael Banim were Ireland's 'first Catholic novelists', Catholic that is by virtue of stock, upbringing and allegiance. For, of course, in a strictly literary sense, Joyce was Ireland's 'first Catholic novelist', perhaps the only important one to-date. Mr Flanagan's discussion centres on John Banim as 'the controlling genius' of the partnership, a conscious explicator of the Irish peasant to the English market and, as he concludes, 'one who could not bring himself to admit how much he cherished the one and detested the other'. He also reminds us that Banim was the first to shed light on 'the secret, strangely self-sufficient, Gaelic world'. And as I read through Mr Flanagan's analysis of *Crohoore of the Bill-Hook*, Banim's novel of the Whiteboy period, I had the oddest fancy. There is one terrible scene depicting the torture and mutilation of a tithe-proctor. I know nothing quite like it in English fiction of the age – such things, apparently, did not happen. But in later French fiction, yes: that gruesome episode in Zola's *Germinal* where a mining-town gombeen-man is murdered and even more frightfully mutilated. Banim is *better,* not because his talent in any way equalled Zola's, but because his violence is observed experience, not the product of a superbly efficient mental laboratory.

So odd a juxtaposition reminds us of one important fact about the history of the Anglo-Irish novel. Irish life in the eighteenth and the nineteenth centuries was sufficiently bloody and brutalized to provide material for a dozen Zolas. But the Irish novelists were also children of the British Lion, and the British Lion was their biggest customer, a Lion in high prosperity, suddenly become ever so careful about the areas of human experience to be explored by the novelist. The days of Fielding, Richardson and Smollett had gone, and there had never been their Irish equivalents. Vast tracts of Irish life were, perforce, left unexplored. It is instructive to think what the Irish novelist might have written about, if the country had not been so closely linked with one which could afford artistically to shut its eyes to the murkier aspects of human nature, secure in her *Tom Jones*, her *Moll Flanders*, and her *Lovelace*. As it is, it is surprising that so much physical violence got set down, especially by a man like John Banim, who finally decided that he had written too much about 'the dark side of the Irish character'. It will not do to neglect Banim when it comes to writing a history of the Irish Catholic mind, with all its pieties and sophistries, at grips with the novel.

That also applies to Gerald Griffin, treated by Mr Flanagan with something like love. *The Collegians*, of course, is as much part of a now fading sub-branch of our culture as is Tom Moore. Its most substantial echo, however, is heard in the pseudonym of Mr Brian O'Nolan. The only person I have ever met who has read the book is Mr Kiely (but then he has read almost everything ever written by Irish novelists). I love it, but might have gone no further in critical enthusiasm than does Dr Colum in his Introduction to the edition available. But Mr Flanagan has opened my eyes to Griffin's sense of symmetry and design with his special approach, he is able to show with what skill Griffin revealed the gradations in the society he depicted, and to bring home, too, the comparative boldness of his subject. We have no *Lovelace* and *Pamela*, but we have Hardress Cregan and Eily O'Connor. As an exercise in the best kind of close reading, Mr Flanagan's exposition could not be bettered. He is also particularly illuminating about *Tracy's Ambition*, illustrating further Griffin's peculiar power over the significant image.

But the greatest of them all was, as Yeats recognized, Carleton: Carleton the apostate, the hired hack, the unquiet pilgrim, the visionary. When he died, the Protestant rector of his parish and a 'nearby Jesuit' (according to O'Donoghue's *Life*) disputed the possesion of his soul. The episode, if it ever happened, is symbolic of the life and work of this curiously schizo-phrenic [sic] genius. He *had* genius, more especially that power of rendering the life of his peasant people apocalyptic, which in lesser degree is possesesd by a not dissimilar writer, Mr Liam O'Flaherty. And far more than Banim, he tried, as Mr Flanagan puts it, 'by main force, to bring the Gaelic world into the orbit of English letters'. My own knowledge of Carleton (and the basis of the foregoing) is confined to the *Traits and Stories*, and two novels, *Valentine M'Clutchy*, and *The Black Prophet*, the beginnings of an attempt to cover the canon, inspired by Mr Kiely's book, *Poor Scholar: A Study of the Works and Days of William Carleton*.

Mr Flanagan re-whets the appetite for illumination. I use the word advisedly. Carleton is the only writer in English who can take us back beyond the Famine, to where so many of us, through our forefathers, incurred an eradicable wound of the spirit. The fact that Carleton's books should not be in print is an indictment of all Irish publishers. But then, nor are Banim's, and Griffin is not well served by the pious maintenance of a single.

I have touched on only a few, necesssarily selected, points in this rich book. Mr Flanagan represents the very best of American scholarship. He is lucid, unfussily accurate, gracefully allusive, and obviously no book-maker. I will conclude with a recommendation that this seminal work be read by all graduate students of Anglo-Irish letters, and a final question:

To understand the Ireland which shaped two such different men as Yeats and Joyce, one must move back, as we have done, beyond the thronging murmurs of the Dublin streets, beyond the waste of the empty decades, beyond the fields and valleys swept bare of all life, beyond the final delirium of the brave.

Poetry Ireland

The name *Poetry Ireland* will already be familiar to many readers of verse in Ireland and abroad. It may be useful to summarize its previous publishing history. The first *Poetry Ireland* appeared in April, 1948, edited by David Marcus, then co-editor with Terence Smith of *Irish Writing.* In this series there were nineteen numbers, the last being in October, 1952. *Poetry Ireland* then appeared as a supplement to *Irish Writing,* numbers 22 to 28, there being seven issues in this new form, the last in September, 1954. *Irish Writing* 29 to 37 (the last issue) was edited by S. J. White, and numbers 30 and 33 had *Poetry Ireland* supplements, the last being devoted to 'Gaelic Poetry Today', and edited by Valentin Iremonger. There were then, in all, including supplements, twenty-eight numbers of *Poetry Ireland* in the decade 1948–58.[1]

In offering this new series of *Poetry Ireland* at the rate, initially, of two issues yearly, but in a much enlarged form, we are not showing excessive timidity. There are many signs that the supply of verse in Ireland and from Irishmen abroad, is greater in quality and quantity than ever before since the thirties and early forties. It remains to be seen whether the demand is commensurate. This means, in effect, not merely a public ready to read the verse, but one which cares enough about verse to wish to buy it.

We are concerned with the publication of the best available verse by Irish poets or of special Irish interest, but we will attempt to include verse outside these categories, including translations. We are committed to no school, no fashion, no ideology. But we abhor mere opinion. We would wish, in the humblest of ways, to contribute towards the recreation of Dublin as a centre of letters. We hope we have the blinds up and the door on the latch.

John Jordan.[2]

Report on Thomas Kinsella[1]

(John Jordan Papers)

Of the poets under forty who have lived in Dublin all or part of their adult lives, Thomas Kinsella is, if the best known, the one I know least well personally. I cannot remember what of significance, if anything, I have written about him in reviews or in the course of articles. If what follows has any value, it will be due partly to the fact that my judgments are not likely to be slavered by personal affection or dislike, by awe or envy.[2] Dublin's literary jungle is probably no better or worse ultimately than that of any other city. The aggravating hazard, however, lies in the fact that the jungle is miniature and the beasts keep on running into each other.

I

I have never been an unqualified lover of Kinsella's verse. In the first place, I thought I detected in some of his earlier poems, 'Death of a Queen', 'Test Case', for instance, a factitious, though most elegant, attempt at a heroic note for our time.[3] And though I found the bated tenderness of the early love poems as touching as any other reader [did], I was vexed by a certain liquidity of tone, an absence of the hard identifiable pain which was clearly struggling to surface. (But 'Who Is My Proper Art' remains for me a poem of exceptional thrust into the consciousness of the lover who is also artist.)[4] The persona's love managed to seem, for me, unsatisfyingly easy, and the debt to Yeats and Auden was not concealed by the poet's craft. For the record, I have come to terms with the Guinness Poetry Award-winning 'Thinking of Mr D', which once annoyed me because it was and was not a poetic analysis of Austin Clarke, but which now excites me because of its glimpse into an area of Kinsella's mind which is not recognised and could scarcely have been shared by the people who hold him up as an example of the adjusted, respectable, salaried, verse-maker: Ireland's Own Answer to the *poète maudit*. The area may conveniently be described as Hell. The Kinsella that interests me is not the elusively sentimental poet of 'Dick King', or 'The Laundress', or 'Cover Her Face'.[5] It is the Kinsella that has looked into the abyss and realized that the private agony is part of the aboriginal catastrophe: he may be found almost exclusively in the volumes *Downstream*, and *Wormwood* (Dolmen Press, 1966, published the month of the poet's thirty-eighth birthday).

II

To my mind, any claim Kinsella has to status as an Irish poet who has definitively crossed the barriers of region, centre about the long poem *'Downstream'*. I have been living with it off and on for the last couple of months, and I have come to the conclusion that it will one day be recognized as a major poem: as qualitatively important as Devlin's *'Lough Derg'*, Kavanagh's *'The Great Hunger'*, or Clarke's *'The Loss of Strength'*. *'Downstream'* describes a boating journey by river. But the journey is also one into the hinterland of the narrator's consciousness, and by extension into the consciousness of a country whose inhabitants have, like Devlin's pilgrims on Lough Derg, been untouched by the primal shame of our century.

Not the least remarkable thing about this poem is the wholly decorous fusion of verse-form and subject-matter: both the physical stream and the stream of the narrator's awareness. The fluvial triplets from beginning to journey's end are never, over 154 lines, either soporific or ostensibly contrived to alert.

Three Faces of Ireland

(Hibernia, July 1962)

The Hard Road to Klondike. By Michael MacGowan. Trans., Valentine Iremonger. (Routledge & Kegan Paul, 1962)
James O'Mara: A Staunch Sinn Féiner. By Patricia Lavelle. (Dublin & London, 1962)
Ag Scaoileadh Sceoil. By Seosamh Ó Duibhginn. (An Clóchomhar Tta., 1962)

Michael MacGowan and James O'Mara died within a week of each other in November 1948. They were both Irish Catholics and they were both materially successful: there their resemblance ends. Their stories are widely and most informatively different and to read MacGowan's reminiscences in conjunction with Mrs Lavelle's biography of her father is to realize the astonishing and co-existing diversity of human experience which lies behind that stirring but tragically lofty phrase, 'the common name of Irishmen'.

I see red whenever I read or hear guff about '*our* Irish heritage', or '*our* Irish culture', or even '*our* Irish boys and girls', when it is clear that the writer or speaker is inspired only by *his* notion of what is 'ours', and is clearly unaware of the experiences and memories and ways of life of all those others who have been born to our island.

And I thank God that Ireland is so rich in varieties of experience, and not made in the image of countless possessive parochialists. Ireland is a country singularly varied in its social stratifications and its cultural epiphanies. If it were not, it would be very dull.

MacGowan was a Donegal peasant born in 1865. He had little formal school-ing and his real education was in the lore of his Gaelic-speaking people. At nine he was being hired out to Lagan farmers, and at fifteen he was a seasonal worker in Scotland. On the brink of manhood he went to America, and *via* the steel-works of Pennsylvania and the silvermines of Montana arrived in Klondike, where he struck gold, enough to return to Donegal in 1902, and eventually to settle down in a 'big house' in Gortahork.

It is a story of frugal living and immense tenacity rewarded romantically. It is also a story of a man's *pietas*, for MacGowan could have gone back to America and grown a great deal more wealthy, but he did not, it seems, suffer from Virgil's *sacra auri fames* and chose to remain and found a family in Donegal. He tells us nothing of the last forty years of his life beyond the fact that he derived pleasure and some amusement from the attentions of visiting scholars, folklorists and antiquarians. He had kept his Gaelic through the years of toil and hardship in America, and it is clear that for him the language was a vital part of his being, an untainted expression of his social and cultural environment.

MacGowan's was one of the last of a series of generations that managed to escape the curse of self-consciousness, despite the inherited ritual of migration and its consequent dangers of mongrelization. He was not typical in so far as he made money and returned to spend and enjoy it in Ireland while still a young man, and he was not perhaps typical in the unexpected range of his insights as revealed in this book. But *The Hard Road to Klondike* is a most valuable social document, and in Mr Iremonger's translation (less thin in texture I think than the Gaelic original, *Rotha Mór an tSaoil*) it is often touching, always interesting, and at times shafted with a simple naked beauty.

As MacGowan and his companions travelled up the Yukon, he tells us, 'We saw thousands of wild geese flying south also and cranes that sang with the sweetness of harps as they flew south'. I find enormously moving such memories, preserved for half-a-century in the consciousness of an old man who could have known nothing of the artifice of remembrance this century has taught us.

James O'Mara was born in Limerick in 1873, the son and grandson of prosperous bacon-curers, founders of a famous mercantile dynasty. At the age when Michael MacGowan was was tramping out of Glasgow in search of work, James O'Mara was entering Clongowes Wood College. He grew up to be a successful businessman and an ardent Home Ruler, representing South Kilkenny at Westminster until his resignation in 1907. He was a disillusioned parliamentarian and later in the years immediately before and after the Treaty he was to be a disillusioned Republican and Sinn Féiner.

Mrs Lavelle has not handled well the mass of private correspondence at her disposal, and it is not clear precisely what caused the rift between de Valera and O'Mara while the latter was directing the Bond Drive in America.[1] As she presents the material however, there would seem to be a link between the disharmony and O'Mara's subsequent support of the Provisional Government. I am not suggesting that O'Mara's allegiance was in any way directed by personal animosity to de Valera. But it may not be unfair to repeat an old contention of de Valera's opponents that personal magnetism combined in him [de Valera] with seemingly unaccountable shifts in policy, and James O'Mara, as his daughter presents him, was not a man likely to be patient with the inscrutable.

In his public life O'Mara was not a particularly sympathetic man. He was, Mrs Lavelle tells us, 'an absolute capitalist', and he held out as long as he could against trade unionism. He was managing in London when the Lock-Out Strike of 1913 came to Dublin, and Mrs Lavelle tells us nothing of his reactions to it. One suspects that they would not awaken agreeable responses.

O'Mara gave money, time and labour to the Independence Movement, but within a few years of the establishment of the Free State he was politically a back number. One wonders if he realized the extent to which, in his non-political capacity he was a symbol of a new and powerful Irish Catholic mercantile *bourgeoisie,* as much the product of history as Michael MacGowan. Certainly he would never concede that he was less Irish than the Gaelic-speaking peasant who struck gold.

Part of the charm of Mrs Lavelle's book lies in her personal memories of home life and holidays. She is an exact contemporary of her father's sister-in-law, Kate O'Brien (Miss O'Brien's sister is the widow of O'Mara's younger brother Stephen) and her book is in part a valuable gloss on Miss O'Brien's novel *Without My Cloak.* And Mrs Lavelle, like Miss O'Brien, has luminous memories of Kilkee in West Clare, the playground of well-off Limerick families in *la belle époque.*

Mr Seosamh Ó Duibhginn's story begins with a brisk account of how he outwitted the Liverpool police in the course of his activities as an I.R.A. saboteur. He is an unrepentant bomb-planter of the 1939–40 period who returned to Ireland in July 1939. He was interned in the Curragh Camp in February 1940, and was released in November 1943. The bulk of his book deals with what happened to him from his release until his appointment as secretary to the newly-founded *Feasta*[2] in 1948, of which he later became editor. *Ag Scaoileadh Sceoil* then is the story of five years in Mr Ó Duibhginn's life, years of hunger, ignominy and precarious employment. He obviously loves Irish passionately and his love rewarded him in a sense, for it helped to lift him from a slavish rut to a post where his natural gifts could find expression. He reveals himself as a remarkably independent and clear-sighted man, never for long bamboozled by revivalist bureaucracy or official cant. He has a gift for sardonic observation and is not afraid to make strictures on Gaelic personalites, nor is he beyond sudden flares of passionate indignation before the hypocrisy and small-mindedness of some reputedly Christian Irishmen.

He shares with Mr Brendan Behan, another former I.R.A. activist, an embittered impatience with the failure of nationalism on a social level. But if his views of the problems of poverty and unemployment are left-wing (in a loose, popular sense) he also shows a certain disquieting tendency towards sympathy with Nazi Germany. He is righteously indignant about R.A.F. bombing of Berlin, but does not mention Coventry. He goes overboard about the Nurembourg Trials,[3] but appears to be ignorant of attempted genocide and the racial doctrine which were perhaps the most positive evil in the Nazi cult. His silence on these matters diminishes the authority of his indictment of the Allies as 'revengeful and unChristian'. I suspect that Mr Ó Duibhginn is, despite his abhorrence of codology, infected with that grimmest of codologies, Anglophobia (grimmest, that is, for Irishmen, as Germanophobia is for Frenchmen).

Mr Ó Duibhginn writes well with a practised eye for the poetry of
incongruity: himself, for instance, sitting in a mice-invaded basement flat, before
him the haven of the National Library where he spent evenings collating and
transcribing texts of Brian Merriman's *Cúirt an Mheán Oíche*, entirely for his own
pleasure. We get glimpses too of the Glún na Buaidhe movement, of *Aiséirí* and its
curious editor Gearóid Ó Cuinneagáin, of Cumann na Scríbhneoirí (a meeting is
described with something of the malice of George Moore) and later of some of the
mandarins of the Gaelic League ... I find this book fascinating, even in its details of
Government subsidies to Gaelic periodicals. But the author has a great deal more
to tell us about his life in the Curragh for instance and, as he himself says, his
editorship of *Feasta*, which coincided with the beginnings of a new literary
movement in Irish. May he be soon and indiscreet in the telling.

These three books are required reading for those who wish to acquire an
adequate knowledge of Ireland and her immediate past. The more we know of
Ireland the better we are prepared to join with Europe.[4] The old peasant dreaming
of the Yukon in Gortahork, the disillusioned capitalist who opted out of political
power, the editor of a Gaelic monthly who braved imprisonment and possible
execution, and tramped the streets of Dublin for work, all represent elements of
'our Irish heritage', and must be reckoned with under the heading of 'the common
name of Irishmen'.

A Testimony: Some Irish Verse in English Since 1945

(Irish Hibernia, 1962)

The term 'Anglo-Irish' was never satisfactory. Today it is misleading and tendentious in its implications. It posits the lie that Irishmen who write in English are in some way dissociated from Irish 'tradition', and it suggests a barrier between those who choose to write in English and who choose to write in Irish. The brief survey that follows is partial and to a certain extent arbitrary. I make no claim whatever to presenting a complete picture of Irish poetic activity in the last seventeen years. For that would involve discussing Gaelic poets such as Máire Mhac an tSaoi (Máire MacEntee), Seán O Riordáin, and Máirtín Ó Díreán. It would also involve considering the work of a whole batch of non-resident poets who have worked in an English poetic tradition: Robert Graves, Cecil Day-Lewis, Louis MacNeice, W.R. Rodgers[1]. If I exclude them it is not because of any silly 'Anglo-Irish' criteria, but because they may be considered more conveniently in the context of modern English verse. The poets I have chosen to write about have not as yet been absorbed, and seem unlikely to be.

The amount of worthwhile verse published in book-form since the Second [World] War, by poets normally resident in Ireland, is very small. And in many cases there is a substantial interval between the periods of composition and collection. Apart from less than a dozen volumes, the chief sources are the magazines extant within the period, *The Bell, The Dublin Magazine, Envoy, Irish Writing, Poetry Ireland,* and more recently, *Threshold* and *The Kilkenny Magazine.* There are two important anthologies, *Contemporary Irish Verse,* edited by Robert Greacen and Valentin Iremonger, and *New Irish Poets,* edited by Devin A. Garrity, both published in 1948.

Where a few of the volumes are concerned there may be a little cheating in relation to time, I hope justifiably. To begin with, all or the bulk of Patrick Kavanagh's *A Soul for Sale* (1947) was written in 1946 or the five years immediately before. This includes the long poem *The Great Hunger,* which appeared first in the Cuala Press edition of 1942. But until 1947 Kavanagh's important poem was known only to a few, though many knew it by hearsay, as a scandalous document in which the Irish peasantry were exposed as sexually frustrated aboriginals. But of course the poem is no essay in which some of our Dublin newspaper critics call 'sordid realism'. Instead it is a great howl of lamentation over the tragedy and blasphemy of a man's failure to love, a Jeremiad on the inversion and distortion of values in a supposedly Christian community. And perhaps for the first time since the death of Yeats, the poem reveals a *recognizable* poetic presence, rivalled only in authority by that of Austin Clarke.

Since 1947 Kavanagh has emerged as a biting verse satirist, with an entrancing gift for Byronic rhyme and a deadly ear for the inflexions of Irish rural and urban speech. But little of this satiric bent is seen in his latest book, *Come Dance With Kitty Stobling* (1960), which is largely a testimony of light after darkness, faith after despair, reverence for life after having dwelt in the valley of the shadow. Above all there is communicated the restoration of the sense of wonder before the common objects of life, as in 'The Hospital', of which I give an earlier version, and I think a better one, printed in *Nimbus* (Winter, 1956):

> *A year ago I feel in love with the functional ward*
> *Of a chest hospital: square cubicles in a row,*
> *Plain concrete wash-basin — an art lover's woe*
> *Not counting how the fellow in the next bed snored.*
> *But nothing whatever is by love debarred*
> *From opening windows on a creative show —*
> *The corridor leads to a staircase, and down below*
> *Was the inexhaustible adventure of gravelled yard.*
> *This is what love does to things: the Rialto Bridge,*
> *The main gate that was bent by a heavy lorry,*
> *The seat at the back of a shed that was a suntrap.*
> *Naming these things is the love act and its pledge,*
> *For we must set in words the mystery without claptrap*
> *Experience so lighthearted appears transitory.*

This sonnet, both technically and spiritually, is not a wholly inadequate instance of the new and more exciting Kavanagh, silent alas at the moment

The late Denis Devlin's *Lough Derg and Other Poems,* published in America in 1946, is little known in Ireland or England. His work will have no appeal for those who require of a poem that it be 'simple and straightforward' (as if *any* worthwhile poem was like that, including the one just quoted). Devlin's imagination worked in an exceedingly intricate fashion, perhaps over-anxious to encompass and control an abundance of perceptions and associations. Accordingly, at first, or even at later readings, his verse is, not partially, but in its totality annoyingly obscure. But a little patience reveals that Devlin is obscure only through the density of his meaning. This is especially true of *Lough Derg,* an impassioned meditation on the apartness of Ireland in relation to Christian Europe. The poem's fluidity through nineteen sestets makes comprehensible quotation difficult, but these lines may help to illustrate Devlin's control over initially complex subject matter. They form the conclusion of *Lough Derg*, and are a return to an earlier theme of 'Clan Jansen'.

> Then to see less, look little, let heart's hunger
> Feed on water and berries. The pilgrims sing:
> Life will fare well from elder to younger,
> Though courage fail in a world-end rosary ring.
> Courage kills its practitioners and we live,
> Nothing forgotten, nothing to forgive,
> We pray to ourself. The metal moon, unspent
> Virgin eternity sleeping in the mind,
> Excites the form of prayer without content;
> Whitethorn lightens, delicate and blind,
> The negro mountain, and so, knelt on her sod,
> This woman beside me murmuring, My God! My God!

Devlin's most important poem after *Lough Derg* (that I know of) was 'The Heavenly Foreigner' (*Poetry Ireland*, 10 July 1950). Sections of this poem still puzzle me, but I think I am safe in describing it as a record of the rediscovery of guilt and innocence in the business of love, and as a meditation on the tensions and confusions of the lover's experience. Devlin is untypical of modern Catholic Irishmen in his recognition of the existence of love as a serious emotion, and his consequent awareness of its labyrinthine ways of torment and recompense. The poem is rich in stylistic versatility, and in an un-Anglo-Saxon gift for surreal imagery, as when he writes of 'spires, firm on their monster feet'. The passage I quote may be faulted rhythmically, but it may indicate the nature of Devlin's preoccupations:

> Last night on the gilded Bourbon bridge
> The doom of Adam brought me down to earth
> While the houses with their worn freight
> Filed down the flowing muttering river.
> I was not guilty had I but known it.
> But now and then the royal pall of peace
> Falls without prayer, without need,
> Love's earnest gift being frivolously given;
> And as the lucid pagan music
> Blows with brown leaves over the asphalt,
> Guilt slips off like a wet coat in the hall.

The publication of Austin Clarke's *Ancient Lights* in 1955 was as close to being a major event in Irish letters as there had been since the War. For some seventeen years Clarke had been occupied with verse-drama, and the pundits might have been forgiven for thinking the poet was silent for good. Far from it, for *Ancient Lights* was followed in 1957 by *Too Great a Vine* and in 1960 by *The Horse-Eaters*. The three little books together with some earlier work were collected in *Later Poems* (1961).

No honest discussion of Clarke's verse can fail to take into account its recurrent and not always comforting obsessions. Clarke is a somewhat old-fashioned anti-clerical, with his own puritan programme for the clergy, and a programme of sexual freedom for the laity. He is fascinated, enraged and amused by real or imagined clashes between human impulse and passion and the Church's rulings on morality. It is irrelevant whether or not Clarke is justified in his inflation of these clashes. The point is that they make a powerful poetic subject, and Clarke has risen to it magnificently. And there is more to the little poems, in which a bleak and oppressive religion is envisaged as at war with the 'natural flow' of the unfortunate Irish people, than a subtle kind of Voltairean satire (though the voice sounds, frequently, Voltairean). There is the weighty factor of compassion to be considered, whether Clarke and his critics know about it or not. Here is the last verse of 'The Envy of Poor Lovers':

> *Think, children, of institutions mured above*
> *Your ignorance where every look is veiled,*
> *State-paid to snatch away the folly of poor lovers*
> *For whom, it seems, the sacraments have failed.*

The very cadence of the last line suggests that the satiric impulse has yielded to 'pity' in its pure sense. And while I'm at it, I may as well point out that even in this apparently simple poem, language is used with an awareness of enriching ambiguity, astonishing in a poet who in his capacity as a literary journalist is forever harking back to the Georgians.

It is not explicit in the lines quoted, for instance, whether the description of the 'institutions' for illegitimate children, run by nuns ('where every look is veiled'), is addressed to 'children' literally, or to 'children' as a collective description of 'lovers'. But surely both meanings are involved, when we examine the phrase '*mured above/Your ignorance*', walling in or enclosing, that is, both things that children do not know about and the fruits of ignorant or guilty lovers.

Of the longer latest poems of Austin Clarke, perhaps *The Loss of Strength* is the most accomplished.

For myself it is one of the great Irish poems, and I would go so far as to say that it is one of the major poems of our time. It is difficult, though not impenetrable: dense in local and historical allusions and demanding a working knowledge of the poet's biography. On one level it is the story of Clarke's life from his teens to his sixties. On another it is an account of Ireland, ancient and modern, as seen by one of her more informed and disillusioned victims. Its tight, sometimes crabbed idiom makes satisfactory quotation impossible, but if only to make it a little more widely known I cite one passage:

> *Beloved strength*
> *Springs past me, three to one. Hall door*

> *Keeps open, estimates the length*
> *To which I go: a mile to tire-a.*
> *But I knew the stone beds of Ireland.*

The extraordinary poignancy of these lines owes nothing to easy sentiment, but rather to the perfect balance of nostalgia and intellectual toughness. 'Beloved strength' combines a reference to the lost strength of the title, and the youth and vigour of his three sons, while the jaunty 'three to one' conveys, in the racing sense, that the boys are 'favourites', but also presents the more general image of youth outstripping age. The reference in the second last line to Autolycus's song (*The Winter's Tale*, IV, II) and its conclusion, '*A merry heart goes all the day / Your sad tires in a mile-a*', is not merely clever literary allusion. Clarke himself was a kind of Autolycus in his youth, wandering on his bicycle over Ireland in search of the sacred places of mythology. And the reference leads beautifully to the triumphal proclamation of the last line: '*But I knew the stone beds of Ireland*'. Not all of the poem is as simple, comparatively, as the lines I have quoted. Only prolonged reading will reveal its 'unknottable power'.

It is in reckoning with the work of Kavanagh, Devlin and Clarke that one realises how at last the balance of poetic achievement has been restored, as between the so-called 'native' Irish and the so-called 'Anglo' Irish, or if I may say so, between predominantly Catholic and predominantly Protestant stock. This is to utter no sectarian war-cry, merely to record an observation pertinent to Irish literary history.

Donagh MacDonagh attracted and deserved attention when his *The Hungry Grass* appeared in 1947. 'The Veterans' is a poem that may, among others, endure:

> *And with their youth has shrunk their singular mystery*
> *Which for one week set them in the pulse of the age,*
> *Their spring adventure petrified in history,*
> *A line on a page.*
> *Betrayed into the hands of students who question*
> *Oppressed and oppressor's rage.*

Since 1947 MacDonagh has devoted himself to verse drama of a more popular type than Austin Clarke's, and has shown himself to be an adroit adapter of the less intricate kinds of Gaelic verse. He has done an immense disservice to Irish letters with his *Oxford Book of Irish Verse*, produced in collaboration with the late Lennox Robinson.

In all surveys of Irish verse, the late Patrick MacDonogh is given a kind word for his lyrics, especially 'She Walked Unaware'. But in his last years he wrote verse of unexpected power and a ferocious poignancy. These poems were gathered in MacDonogh's only substantial collection, *One Landscape Still* (1958), and perhaps the most remarkable is 'Escape to Love', a treatment of the theme of absence of love and loving, equated with living death: '*Years of this heart held no month but December*'. Here is part of the opening:

> *A dead hand silenced the glistening house,*
> *And then, like a mouse in the gut, It moved, like a breath,*
> *A flower opening, a whispered malice, a four — month sin*
> *In a woman's frightened flesh, softly, but certain within.*
> *Softly It moved, nosing inside him, softly withdrew.*
> *Then returned with a confident tooth, or a claw, and he knew*
> *That the thing living and growing inside him was Death.*

Pádraic Fallon has published no volume that I know of, but he has been publishing in periodicals since long before my time, and I can remember when I was eighteen hearing the poet Anthony Cronin tell a younger poet, Pearse Hutchinson, how he had met Pádraic Fallon, in a tone compounded of suppressed price and ill-hid awe. For Fallon has always commanded an admiring audience not only among the young, but among the undying generations who find a comprehensible image of poetry and the poet in the work of the late Pádraic Ó Conaire (a gifted slovenly writer in Gaelic who was encouraged to drink too much by men with fixed abodes and regular hot meals), the late F.R. Higgins, a minor poet even within his minor mode, and Pádraic Fallon's own jazzed-up Synge-lined versions from the Gaelic. I have heard praise for Fallon lavished on every side. Because of his representative position, not even my arbitrary selection can exclude reference to him. But I had better say nothing explicit about his verse, and confess that in moments of depression over my failure in sympathy with this much-loved poet, I am further hag-ridden by the recollection that Anthony Cronin, a critic accoladed before a largely academic audience by Patrick Kavanagh, has said of Fallon's 'Raftery and the Whiskey' that it will last as long as the English tongue.

And now to turn away a little and comment briefly on a curious current in the history of Irish letters. Shortly after the War and for the first time in quantity since the Revival began, Irish emerged as a valid contemporary literary medium, a language which might be used for the communication of unanachronistic adventures of the imagination. What is immediately relevant to my subject is that the new pulse in Gaelic verse did not go unheeded by some of the young poets whose chief preoccupation was verse in English. Valentin Iremonger and Pearse Hutchinson will be stupefied when and if they read this article and find themselves linked. But they had initially, not parity of years (for Iremonger is considerably the elder), not parity of temperament, but a similar unapologetic awareness of Irish, as well as an interest in and knowledge of modern European verse. In a decadent society (for the late forties and early fifties of this century will surely go down as Dublin's most accomplished charlatan period) where serious and informed attitudes to Irish did not prevail among what Mr Robert Briscoe has described in a curious figure of speech as 'the young men coming up', Iremonger and Hutchinson represented the possibility of a unique fusion of 'Gaelic' and 'Anglo-Irish' streams. But only a minimal and devious fusion has occurred, and Iremonger and Hutchinson are the names that are still relevant, especially the latter. Iremonger has translated Rilke into Irish, while Hutchinson has translated into Irish both Spanish and Catalan verse[3]. He has also written many poems in Irish during the last decade and while this work may displease traditionalists it is comparable only with that of the better Gaelic poets, at least to my mind, which lacks interest in the correctness of idiom.

This divagation I can justify by pointing out that the fusion which did not take place could yet come about. Young poets are far less cock-a-hoop about their ignorance of Irish, and no longer does it seem odd for a writer devoted to English to be seen with a copy of a Gaelic magazine. Maybe it is the fantasy of a tired mind, but I dream of a bi-lingual literary culture in Ireland, and such a culture would enrich both Ireland and Europe.

Iremonger's *Reservations* (1950) is the garnering of at least six years' work. It is one of the best books of Irish verse, and it is also profoundly uninsular in mood and content, a relevant consideration since it came out of neutral Ireland's enviable snugness. Almost every poem is distinguished by an absence of verbal and emotional stridency and the presence of a sad ordering wit: 'wit' as one thinks of the term in connection with Allen Tait and John Crowe Ransome rather than in the context of F.R. Leavis's famous 'line'. The ending of 'A Marriage has been Arranged' will perhaps make my point: '*so I wish her, my dear, / As much happiness as she can conveniently bear*'. Iremonger has published little verse since 1950, but he is still a young man as poets go and also one hears encouraging rumours about new productivity.

I have neither the space nor the inclination to more than mention the work of poets who have come to some stature during the Fifties. Iremonger's work is sufficiently isolated to justify mentioning him among the older men. It would be indecorous, merely for the sake of completeness, to cram in observations on the younger poets within the present context. I am not writing a history of contemporary Irish verse. But for those who are not in touch with the latest developments of Irish verse, I will say that three poets in their early or mid-thirties seem to me to have exciting talent. They are Pearse Hutchinson, already referred to in another context, born in 1927, Thomas Kinsella born in 1928, and John Montague born in 1929. There are, of course, others somewhat younger who have impressed, but only the three I have mentioned will I bet on. But I cannot discuss them together on an adequate basis, for Hutchinson has not yet published a book (one is promised for Autumn 1962 from the Dolmen Press, Dublin[4]) and I am unable to collect from periodicals what I want for my purpose[5]. Perhaps my three names are an obvious choice, but in fact it is one that involves the rejection of names that certainly command more attention in the fashionable London world. (One would be a fool to ignore London opinion, but where the Irish are concerned, London adores gimmickry). So let it be recorded that I, John Jordan, a teacher by profession and an amateur of verse by some unfathomable doom, do hereby commit myself to the poetic fortunes of three people[6]. It is after twenty-two hours on the first day of May 1962. The night is calm and starless and so far as I know I am in full possession of my faculties.[7]

Off the Barricade: A Note on Three Irish Poets

(The Dolmen Miscellany of Irish Writing)

In the bad old days when Yeats was in his Mediterranean grave and the singing birds of Æ and their melodic progeny were accepted as the chief representatives of indigenous Irish verse, Valentin Iremonger, Robert Greacan and Bruce Williamson published a little book of their own poems called *On the Barricade*. It was by way of being a protest against their elders' easy assumption that *après eux, le déluge*. Or rather that they, the elders, were official custodians of the Anglo-Irish Falls.

That was in 1944. Eighteen years later I do not believe that young Irish poets feel a similar sense of psychic oppression. It is true of course that they have few worthwhile or effective elders to exercise malevolent paternalism: the indisputable big men of Irish verse, Kavanagh and Clarke *redivivus*, command more respect as artists than they inflict annoyance as critics. And ultimately these two poets are solitary birds who are untrammelled by adherence to dubious traditions. No one in his senses could place either of them in a school, beyond of course the common poetic gymnasium, 'the foul rag and bone shop of the heart'.

In 1961 appeared three books of verse of special interest interest, though of varying quality, by young Irish poets. The best-known name is that of Thomas Kinsella. Before going into the quality and kind of his achievements in *Poems and Translations*[1] (Atheneum: New York) it might be useful to point out that Kinsella's publishing history is of prime importance in the general history of Irish publishing since 1922. For his reputation has waxed in unbroken association with an Irish publishing house[2] and this American volume is made up of work most of which appeared first in book-form from that firm. The importance of this will be recognised by all who appreciate the dependency of Irish writers on English or American publishers, and more particularly the dependence of poets.

Poems and Translations consists of Kinsella's 1958 volume, *Another September*, re-arranged and with additions, the chapbook *Moralities* (1960), also re-arranged but with omissions, and his translations from

Early Irish. Of the last I am totally unqualified to speak, beyond saying that they read well, especially 'The Breastplate of St Patrick'; though I cannot suppress an entirely unwarranted suspicion that lines like the following may be better than the original:

> *I call these Powers*
> *to take my part*
> *against every warped, implacable power*
> *that would stray my soul and body.*

But it is possible that Kinsella's translations may be less important in themselves than as evidence of a guileful self-discipline. As Pound knew well, translation, if it is to be more than literal, forces the mind to aim at precision, and what matters as much, taste and judgment are driven into decision as to the peculiar rightness of one out of a dozen potential equivalents. A further point and then no more: translation of verse or of fashioned prose tones up, in some cases may even awaken, the writer's responses to cadence and pause. Whether or no this has been the case in Kinsella's development, he has from the first shown remarkable grace and coherence in the unfolding of difficult themes, as in 'Who Is My Proper Art', and 'Ulysses'. Those who know these poems superficially may jib at the attribution of coherence. But the final criterion of a poem's success is the sum of its virtues, not the lucidity or obscurity of its components, and working from there, these poems are coherent, they mean something, they add up to significant expansion of their theme. But Kinsella, taking another approach, may also be described, not, God forbid, as a writer of *poésie pure*, but as a delighter in sheer texture. Here are some lines from 'Who Is My Proper Art', which might be described loosely as a poem mirroring its own making:

> *White horses, twice*
> *Glimpsed, she made already*
> *A legend in a glade, pounding*
> *Harnessed in a green dream, rounding*
> *With manes streaming side*
> *By side a field she travelled past*
> *To come here that day.*

Here the communication of a fact esssential for the poem's meaning is lovingly and delicately dwelt on for its pictorial qualities. The effect is of seemingly-animated tapestry, but there is nothing extraneous to the poem's purpose. The decoration, if I may use the word without dishonourable connotations, is functional as well as intrinsically fine.

No one, I believe, has as yet stressed a salient factor in Kinsella's earlier verse: his cool and elegant version of romantic passion, as in poems such as 'Soft to Your Places', and 'A Lady of Quality'. If we except Yeats and Denis Devlin, Irish poets have shown no particular interest in the heart of a man with a maid.[3] Kinsella, although he has paid his toll to Deirdre and the general notion of high-born death-and-glory heroines, is more convincingly interested in unheroic woman, possibly a particular woman. He has re-asserted a basic presumption of the Romantics proper, that we may be interested in a man's intimate and particularized experiences of the heart. But Kinsella's romanticism is not always of an effective kind. 'Baggot Street Deserta' is marred by a fundamentally sentimental approach to the self and to the self as poet:

> Compassionate
> I add my call of exile, half-
> Buried longing, half-serious
> Anger and the rueful laugh.
> We fly into our risk, the spurious.

Kinsella does not escape the spurious in this poem, but I believe he is sufficiently aware of the enormous difficulty of presenting the personal 'I' (as distinct from the assumed 'I') out of brackets as it were, whether they be of self-pity or of self-love.

Kinsella's later verse, while retaining the pressure of intelligence and an unfussy care for form, is on the whole more impersonal and more mordant than his earlier work. I propose in this connection to make a bold statement. Kinsella's 'Old Harry' is a runner for the title of being the best poem (in English) about the major catastrophe of our time: Harry S. Truman's decision to drop the atom-bomb. He has avoided all the pitfalls inherent in the treatment of a public theme, more marvellously since the theme has as yet not fully penetrated the Western consciousness. He has even managed to lead a kind of Puritan sub-nobility to the human instrument of unimaginable horror:

> He raved softly and struggled for righteousness,
> Then chose in loneliness near the blurred curtains
> The greater terror for the lesser number.
>
> Jaw jutting with power for good, he inclined
> Rounded cheeks, eyes like coins, to the toy Arctic
> And Boreas blew his dreadful moral blast.

The short series of poems called '*Moralities*' does not dispense with the treacherous 'I', as distinct from the 'I' of the most successful dramatic lyrics. But the 'I's' potentially garish effulgence is contained and shaded by the taut and epigrammatic form which Kinsella has carefully mastered, as in 'The Beer Drinkers' and 'Handclasp at Euston'. *Moralities*[4] has at least one poem which posits Kinsella's full awareness of the way he is going.

> Love's doubts enrich my word; I stroke them out.
> To each felicity, once. He must progress
> Who fabricates a path, though all about
> Death, Woman, Spring, repeat their first success.

As a whole, *Poems and Translations* has authority and the excitement of measured growth. It lacks the excitement of passion, a quality almost inseparable from severity of language and simplicity of trope. If Kinsella has a fault to beware of, it is over-indulgence or unwarranted indulgence of his allusive faculty. But the poems of *Moralities* already point to tautening of diction and pruning of excrescence.

Thomas Kinsella is a Dubliner. But there is little or nothing in his verse ('Baggot Street Deserta' could as well be 'King's Road Deserta') to suggest involvement with the city. Nor indeed is there much in his verse to suggest the imaginative claim of any of the numerous masks of Ireland. He looks back, it is true, to late-medieval Ireland and finds material for cameos. But so far he has shown no signs of participation in the immemorial struggle between sow and farrow.

This could not be said of John Montague in his first English selection, *Poisoned Lands* (Macgibbon & Kee), which contains many revised poems from his 1959 Dolmen Press volume, *Forms of Exile*, and several new poems in a noticeably different mode. To-date Ireland seems to have mattered to Montague:

> *Ancient Ireland indeed! I was reared by her bedside,*
> *The rune and the chant, evil eye and averted head,*
> *Formorian fierceness of family and local feud.*
> *Gaunt figures of fear and of friendliness,*
> *For years they trespassed on my dreams,*
> *Until once, in a standing circle of stones,*
> *I felt their shadows pass*
> *Into that dark permanence of ancient forms.*

The poem from which this is taken was written about 1960 and it would seem to mark at least a working resolution of the tension between the pull of roots and the questioning of knowledge. But Montague's erstwhile or resolved *irisch-angst* is not objectionably egocentric. It is chastened by awareness of humanity, both in the country itself and beyond the great divide of the English Channel. Of 'Murphy in Manchester' he writes:

> *Passing a vegetable stall*
> *With exposed fruits, he halts*
> *To contemplate a knobbly potato*
> *With excitement akin to love.*

These lines of course reveal one of Montague's weaknesses, his tendency to graft on to his observed people an expected response encountered before in literature. 'Murphy' [*sic*] is not Mr Patrick Kavanagh and to suggest that he is, even fleetingly, is sentimental. But the poem as a whole mirrors Montague's sense of the Irish calamity. And elsewhere in one of the poems in the sequence 'The Sheltered Edge' he describes emigrants as:

> *Poor subjects for prose or verse,*
> *In their grief, as animals, most piteous.*

The more personal aspects of the Irish dilemma are calmly touched on in the slickly-titled 'Auschwitz, Mon Amour':

> *To be always at the periphery of incident*
> *Gave my childhood its Irish dimension; drama of unevent:*
> *Yet doves of mercy, as doves of air,*
> *Can tumble here as anywhere.*

And again, in 'Rome, Anno Santo', he conveys the smart of conscious detachment from the unyielding pattern of Irish Catholocism, with its supreme disdain for humanism and its indomitable complacency. This is not a good poem, for it makes its points as if the poet were writing for dunderheads.

But Montague must not be projected as solely a poet of peculiarly Irish themes.

I have stressed that part of his work because it is time that someone reasserted that 'Irish' themes as such are not aesthetically or morally unjustifiable, though they have been condemned outright by Mr Patrick Kavanagh and his London branch, Mr Anthony Cronin, and by implication in the supercilious brutalities of Dr Donald Davie when reviewing *Poisoned Lands*.

Montague's later poems, I've already suggested, indicate a change of direction. He is now far more interested, on the one hand, in the truth of landscape and object, and on the other, in the fable value for our time of disparate fragments of erudition. 'The First Invasion of Ireland', based on a story in the *Leabhar Gabhála*, fuses an interest in the peculiarities of the Irish sexual temperament with the satirist's pleasure in incongruity, but there are lines which offer promise of development as a kind of compassionate *Pasquin* with romantic allegiances.

> *Division of damsels they did there,*
> *The slender, the tender, the dimpled, the round,*
> *It was the first just bargain in Ireland,*
> *There was enough to go round.*

I think, though, that Montague missed a trick in not writing 'last' for 'first', just as I believe he should eliminate literary allusions of doubtful efficacy. In this poem 'all passion spent' jars as a cliché – quoted long before it invokes a parallel between the plight of Milton's Samson and that of an ancient Irish lover. Far worse, in another poem, is the description of an old peasant woman as 'a well of gossip defiled'. Cleverality has ousted decorum. Another kind of cleverality is evident in 'Walking the Dog', where a pseudo-Gallic earthiness scarcely becomes him. The poem has also a brazen echo, from Thomas Kettle this time, who of course is unknown to most foreigners, but for better or for worse forms part of our glorious heritage.

These minor irritants in Montague's verse are part of a general leak-through of the poet's social and educational background. This of course is neither a good nor a bad thing. I note it for the purpose of making an elementary distinction between kinds of verse. Kinsella's later verse I have described as 'more impersona'. But while his earlier verse might be described as revelatory of intimate feeling, it yet can be called reticent. He tells us nothing about his childhood, his education, his social mileau, whether he has travelled or speaks foreign languages or goes to picture galleries, though he seems interested in architecture. Montague, on the other hand, reveals a good deal about himself. Without any prior knowledge one can deduce that he has travelled, is a university man, is familiar with French and German, is interested in painting and is a Catholic Ulsterman. It is possible to see in him a recognizable image, whereas Kinsella's poetic *persona* is elusive, even chameleon.

If Kinsella has his own protective colouring and Montague his very human generosity in self-exposure, it is only fair to say that Desmond O'Grady has something of both. But his *Reilly* (Phoenix Press) is a depressing and suety book where almost every poem, including those of the 'Reilly' sequence, is a stroke for the portrait of a *poète maudit*, with the addition of some hints towards recognion of the literary wild goose. Reilly, we are told, will take refuge from his neighbours in 'the allied security of silence, exile and cunning'. What grand notions some of our Irish lads possess. But, as laid down by a forgotten Edwardian writer, J. Williams Butcher, 'unfortunately brag often commits a boy to a false position'. O'Grady is such a boy:

> *The change is protection from further intrusion*
> *By those who have claimed*
> *So much through their vulgar suburban*
> *Ways _ that provincial success-minded*
> *Crowd in the town.*

This is not a Reilly poem, but it mimes a Reilly stance. Elsewhere O'Grady writes of Reilly:

> *The horrible part of this going out*
> *Is the people you meet outside;*
> *With their mean little minds full of shrewdness and pride*
> *And their frightening rushing about.*

'Vulgar suburban ways' and 'mean little minds' are of course legitimate, if drearily described, objects of attack. O'Grady's implied 'brag' is that he, the poet, is outside all that. But he says so without authority or passion or savage indignation. So far as his verse is concerned, his revolt is commonplace.

The first third of the 'Reilly' sequence consists of character sketches of Irish oddities. Some of them are effective, none unmarked by glaring faults. Plump in the middle of reported country speech of 'The Father' comes the metaphysical notion (what else can it be?) of 'he began being strangely'. In 'The Mother' we are faced with the sham Gaelic syntax of 'great was the hate that was at her on him'. In 'The Son' a deserted husband is 'like a scratching post in a far field' (why 'far'?), but the walls and furniture are 'darkly around him like guards at a hanging'. 'The Daughter' shows an ignorance of the procedure for admission to convents astonishing in one who is described on the book's jacket as 'educated by the Jesuits and the Cistercians'. I have not had O'Grady's advantages, but I do know that kind neighbours cannot simply arrange for an indigent spinster to be admitted as 'a kind of nun'. The story itself is a bald *résumé* of what might have provided Joyce, or even Frank O'Connor, with a challenge to their creative powers at their very highest voltage.

O'Grady as *poète maudit* and as a Columban (i.e. as a poetic son of rare Pádraic Colum) of the sixties, is not a success. But he has moments of feeling, truly and unpretentiously expressed, as when he writes of 'Reilly and Child':

> *Here*
> *Now in this home-strong hour*
> *Of your very own day*
> *On the roof's top of your year,*
> *He watches you out of his penitent eyes*
> *Seeing you damned by the sin of his making you*
> *Blond child of a bombed generation.*

I have known and liked Desmond O'Grady, and only in Dublin perhaps is it necessary to announce that there can be such a thing as criticism unloaded with personal animus. But Dublin, in this respect curiously like London, is so ingrown in its literary alliances that the little verse-reviewing which is done is often pocked with timidity and non-committal. There is, indeed, in the whole Irish literary world, a tendency towards the formation of Protection Societies. I, too, have lived in Arcadia.

There they are then: Kinsella, Montague, O'Grady, all under thirty-five. They are not the whole of young Irish verse. The picture will be more complete when we have volumes from Pearse Hutchinson, Richard Weber and James Liddy. They are the generation which succeeds that of which Valentin Iremonger in the South and Roy McFadden in the North were the most distinguished. Somewhere in between came Anthony Cronin – a curious evidence of how late Auden came to Ireland. Our poets nowadays are far more hep, and they deserve critics less kindly and more rigorous than myself.

On D.H. Lawrence

(John Jordan Papers, untitled MS)[1]

We may take it, I think, that the reputation of D.H. Lawrence, who died just thirty years ago, is unassailable for the next few decades at least; and probably for as long as we have time to ponder the destiny of Spiritual Man, Acquisitive Man, Industrial Man, and all those other facets of Lear's 'poor, bare, forked animal' that Lawrence studied with such visionary intensity and occasional absurdity. The Establishment has taken him under its ample wing, and gallantly rising to the occasion, Penguin Books have added six new volumes of his work to their existing selection, of which I am concerned with five.

This is not the place, nor have I the time, to deal with Lawrence's significance as a prophet, or as a symptom of the age. But one can recall that more than any other writer of his time – his writing time of 1910–30 – and apart perhaps from Joyce and Mr Eliot, he was aware of the cancer in the body of Europe. He was one of those few who truly suffered imaginatively from the hangover of the Industrial Revolution and the rack of increased mechanization. Much may be said for and against Lawrence, but we can surely grant him his anguish over, not Fallen Man, but Forgetful Man, forgetful not only of an immortal soul, but of a mortal dignity, of what he called 'otherness', that marvellous factor of 'difference' which for Lawrence meant far more than 'equality'.

But whether or not we accept the messianic elements in Lawrence, we are left with the phenomenon of a very great storyteller of unequalled range and power within his time. This is almost sufficiently illustrated by the novel *Women in Love* (Penguin), first published in 1921 (and which, ideally, should be read in conjunction with *The Rainbow*, of 1915). We say so easily in praise of a classic that it seems so modern. Here is a case where a forty-year-old book seems not only 'modern', which is to say timely or specially relevant, but seems also to look back to the nineteenth century and the great age of solid, rounded novels. Odd as it may sound, Lawrence for all his lack of inhibition (though he is rarely indecent in the accepted sense of the word) yet has links with the Victorians. He can furnish a world as well as project its inhabitants. And in this novel there is all that generosity of imagination which sends us back to writers as different as George Eliot and Dickens. The burden of the story is the working out of the love-life of two men and two women, and it is superbly done. But of course we have at times to bear with the overflow of Lawrence's peculiar vision of the relations between the sexes – and I use that prim phrase advisedly, because many people still think that Lawrence was interested in sex, which is quite another matter. And this overflow, I think, is tolerable only because it has the authority of a splendidly imagined world behind it. We accept Lawrence's occasional incoherence, his more than occasional lapses into the idiom of women's magazines, because he has, so to speak, so many other cards on the table. A novel like *Women in Love* convinces us that he can do almost anything. When describing a raffish café-set, or a definitely sinister house party of the twenties, for instance, we see all that Aldous Huxley must have learned from him.

But Lawrence's successes here strike me as being quite effortless, the result of no *special* satiric gift, but rather part of what his conception required, and which was, therefore, carried out. For it is his greatness as an artist that nothing in his work has the impact of being inorganic, even when we least understand him. The comprehensiveness of his genius may be seen as early as *The Trespasser*, his second novel, published in 1912 (Penguin). The greater part of this story of adultery fading from romantic ecstasy to squalor and guilt, might be described as immature 'swoon', to use one of Lawrence's key-words: but how finely he leads his loves out of swoon into the drab light of their suburban London homes. Even in this minor work the 'overflow', as I've called it, has the authority of a world observed with almost painful precision. Here I would note yet another aspect of Lawrence's comprehensiveness. He seems at home anywhere: in city, mining town or country, in Continental resort or mountain fastness, on an English Green or among the glittering Alpine snows.

In the volume called *The Ladybird*, published in 1923 (Penguin), which contains three short novels, *The Ladybird*, *The Fox*, and *The Captain's Doll*, we move from fashionable London to a south of England farm, and from there to occupied Germany and an Austrian resort after the First World War. That in itself is no great feat, where three separate stories are concerned. What dazzles is Lawrence's complete absence of sleight of hand, and the ease with which totally different sets of circumstances and people are made, without monotony, to project his vision of the sheer mystery of human beings, of their ultimately irreducible 'otherness'. Other novels enchant or repel us because they tell us so much and so convincingly about their people. Lawrence rivets us with the fact that people, like the moon, must always have a dark side, and must thus be unpredictable. It is this fact which gives such dignity and occasional splendour to his depiction of love. And it is his unfailing recognition of this fact that enables him to plot the graph of such a relationship as that between Ellen March and Henry in *The Fox*, or the Captain and the Countess in *The Captain's Doll*, relationships to which the maxims of a Rochefoucauld or the jottings of a Stendhal have as much relevance as an X-Ray to a cave drawing.

This capacity for respecting and conserving mystery in human beings is well illustrated, on a smaller scale, in the volume of short stories, *England, My England*, published in 1922 (Penguin). One (or at least I am) is inclined to forget what a master of this form Lawrence was. The title story fails, perhaps through constriction of form – the opening pages read like a précis of an unwritten novel. But 'Monkey Nuts', 'Wintry Peacock', 'You Touched Me', and some others, are almost perfect glimpses of unclassifiable human misery.

Not surprisingly, the little book of travel sketches, *Twilight in Italy* (Penguin) impresses as much by its human snapshots as by its erratically vivid descriptions of landscape. And it is interesting to note that in the opening essay, 'The Crucifix Across the Mountains', we meet the fallen Tyrolean Christus, later to be present at the physical death – for spiritually he died earlier – of Gerald Crich, the Instrumental Man of *Women in Love*, Lawrence's symbol of Adam Irredeemable.

Ùbu Roi

(John Jordan Papers)

On December 10, 1896, W.B. Yeats went to the Theâtre de L'Oeuvre in Paris to see the first professional production of *Ùbu Roi* by atwenty-three -year-old poet and fantasist, Alfred Jarry. Afterwards, Yeats recorded his impressions at the end of *The Tragic Generation:* 'The audience shake their fists at one another and the rhymer (almost certainly Arthur Symons) whispers to me: 'there are often duels after these performances', and he explains to me what is happening on the stage. The players are supposed to be dolls, toys, marionettes, and now they are all hopping like wooden frogs, and I can see for myself that the chief personage, who is some kind of king, carries for sceptre a brush of the kind we use to clean a closet. Feeling bound to support the most spirited party, we have shouted for the play.'

Yeats could not have known that Jarry's play – directed by the illustrious Lugné-Poe, with décors and masks by, among others, Pierre Bonnard, Vuillard and Toulouse-Lautrec – had begun as a puppet-play when Jarry was still a schoolboy at the Lyceé of Rennes. A schoolmate, Henri Morin, gave Jarry the text of *Les Polonais*, a lampoon by Morin's elder brother on a teacher at the lyceé – called Hebert. Jarry told his audience they would find in *Ùbu* whatever satanic symbols they liked, or simply a skit by a schoolboy 'on one of his teachers who represented for him all that was grotesque in the world'. This was disingenious on Jarry's part, for he had worked and reworked on *Ùbu* to the point where he himself had *become Ùbu*. Indeed, he wrote four more 'cycles' on *Ùbu*, drawing heavily on an elaborate private mythology, quite as elaborate as Yeats's own.

Even amateurs of theatrical history must have gathered that Jarry may have been the father of the Theatre of the Absurd; that his progeny are Artaud, to some extent Beckett (it's a wise child, etc.), Adamov, Ionesco, Pinget, Arrabal *et al*. For myself, I suspect that Yeats may have been – consciously or otherwise – influenced by Jarry's use of masks, and I find a trace of Jarry in Yeats's *The Player Queen*.

King *Ùbu*, a savage poltroon with yet a dash of Neronic artistry, may be seen as a travesty of the *Tamburlaine* of Christopher Marlowe, with whose work Jarry was familiar. But *Ùbu* is also curiously prophetic of trends in twentieth-century Heads of State: for instance, the late 'Papa Doc' of Haiti, and General Amin. Indeed, in his comic aspects he prefigures Chaplin's *Great Dictator*.

But more serious questions apart, *Ùbu* in 1896 faced fairly and squarely the matter of four-letter words and such-like in the theatre. It begins with *Père Ùbu* exclaiming '*Merdre!*' – the Old French spelling for the more familiar *merde*. From then on, this word is seldom absent from the mouths of the *Ùbus*, man and wife. But this is the least of the 'obscenities' in the dialogue, and the names of certain characters, e.g. the King of Poland's son is called 'Bongrelas'.

A World in Chassis

(University Review, Spring 1955)

IRISH opinion of Sean O'Casey to-date may be summed up, without unfairness I believe, as follows. In the years 1923–5, a Dublin labourer of genius wrote three plays, which were produced by the Abbey Theatre, and which, although one of them (*The Plough and the Stars*) caused riots on account of its offensiveness to Irish National sentiment, have since been accepted as an enduring contribution to the Irish Theatre's classic heritage.

In 1928, after he had left Dublin for England, the Dublin labourer wrote a fourth major play, *The Silver Tassie*, which was rejected by the Abbey Directorate, on the grounds that it was a bad play. Productions of the play in Dublin in 1935, 1947 and 1951, appear to have confirmed for Irish critics the judgment of Yeats and his distinguished colleagues (though that judgment was not unanimous).

Since the publication of *The Silver Tassie* in 1928, O'Casey has published six more full-length plays, and recently Dublin saw the first production of his tenth full-length play, *The Bishop's Bonfire*. The reactions of Irish critics to this play and their methods of expressing them suggest that, on the whole, the belief is held among them that thirty years' exile has turned a dramatist of genius into an embittered and vulgar old man.

But no one has, in the recent controversy, gone so far as to suggest that O'Casey, as a middle-aged man, and at the time of the composition of the early 'masterpieces', was also embittered and vulgar. If I were attempting a more than preliminary approach to O'Casey's dramatic writings, it would be necessary to devote considerable space to his autobiographical writings, to that astoundingly vital and savage record of an inflamed mind. It would be necessary, also, to attempt to recreate the conditions and atmosphere of the life O'Casey knew before he left Ireland. Some day, when O'Casey has gone among the angels, such a complete study will be necessary. In this article I propose only to indicate what I believe to be the essentials of his vision. And it is the vision of a man of genius, if it is any part of genius to grasp with unequalled intensity any one aspect of life.

For us then there are two Seáns. They may be described as Our Seán, and if I may borrow a phrase from the Bishop of Meath, Poor Old Seán. They would appear to be different men. Our Seán portrayed a gallery of zanies and grotesques without rival since the death of Charles Dickens. Our Seán recorded passionately and sympathetically the slum-world of the nineteen-twenties, and in so doing came upon the mystery of tragic suffering. Our Scán, in fact, was a man we could all be proud of, a feather in Ireland's cap.

Poor Old Seán, on the other hand, is an affront to Faith and Fatherland, an elderly corner boy who does not care for priests or nuns, and who seems forever to be holding his thumb to his nose. So far as I can make out, the most expected from Poor Old Seán is that he will be re-born as Our Seán. But if we really hope for that, we are crying for the moon. Indeed it is doubtful if Our Seán ever really existed, outside our mis-readings and mis-hearings of the early 'masterpieces'.

They are bitter pills, these early 'masterpieces', once we have seen the jam of the zanies for what it is. The zanies themselves are mean, cowardly, hypocritical, vainglorious and lazy. Their blather is, of course, more immediately sympathetic than the stilted heartfelt rhetoric of a Donal Davoren, or the whimpering of Nora Clitheroe. But it remains blather, the window-dressing of the unsalvageable. The early plays, like everything O'Casey has since written (I except some of the one-act plays and *Purple Dust*), are about suffering. But it is not the zanies and grotesques who suffer. O'Casey's early world, like the later one, is sharply divided. On the one hand, there are the unredeemable scurf of life; the Paycocks and Uncle Peters and Séamus Shields, the blatherers; on the other, the vaguely aspiring and inevitably hurt: Minnie Powell and Davoren, Mary Boyle, the Clitheroes. Juno and Bessie Burgess do not fit into this pattern, of course. They are outside and above it, great exceptions and significantly enough, both middle-aged women. For when O'Casey is not occupied with his blatherers and his young idealists, his mind goes back to the only human glory he appears to have known in his childhood, the courage and gaiety of his mother. Outside the *Autobiographies*, his last tribute to her is in the character of Mrs Breydon in *Red Roses For Me* (1942). Juno and Bessie Burgess are not mere 'tributes', but they embody that flame of charity which is the one brightness in the appalling world of the early plays, and in his memories of childhood. They have not been embittered and they still care for human beings. Who are the sufferers, apart from these two middle-aged women? They are the young people whom we rarely think of and, when we do, find somewhat tiresome. They are his marred sketches for a Utopia of the imagination, a pleasure-world opposed to the world of chassis which he has seen with such disturbing intensity.

It has to be admitted that this Utopia is the least satisfying part of O'Casey's imaginative vision. His alternative to the stupidity and ignorance and cowardice consequent upon the human condition, would require the gifts of a very great lyric poet to be at all convincing. In O'Casey's Utopia, the workers are all fine handsome young lads and lasses, who enjoy love and wine and song and art. Mary Boyle is typical, because of her pretty figure and a taste for Ibsen. With a little more spine and some regard for the people, Donal Davoren would get into the pleasure-world. He reads Shelley. In later plays, the Dreamer and the Young Whore (*Within the Gates,* 1933), O'Killigain (*Purple Dust,* 1940), Drishogue O'Morrigun (*Oak Leaves and Lavender,* 1946) – he reads Shakespeare, Milton and Darwin, Ayamonn Breydon (*Red Roses For Me,* 1942 – he reads Shakespeare and Ruskin and yet is so insensitive as to attack a girl because she insists upon attending a Retreat), Loreleen Marthraun (*Cock-a-Doodle Dandy,* 1949 – she reads *Ulysses* and 'a book about Voltaire') – all these would be successful applicants. And these for the most part paste-board people are the progeny of an imagination entirely in revolt against the actual world, the dream children of an autodidact.

There is a certain kind of mind which will never be content with anything short of perfection. Sometimes this kind of mind is gifted with the grace to adapt the yearning for perfection to practical use. I do not need to point out the saints in whom this may be instanced. At other times, and just as rarely, this kind of mind is graced, or cursed, with the genius for recording its profound dissatisfaction with the world as it is, always has been, and seems likely to remain. Swift, [as well as] the author of *Piers Plowman,* and certain Elizabethan satirists, had this kind of mind and genius. We have to think in terms of vision in which each mote is a beam, each barren tree a wilderness of desolation. Sometimes, O'Casey has looked at people and situations where the most inflamed vision could hardly distort the horror of what was to be seen. That is why *The Silver Tassie* and *Within the Gates* are the most satisfying, for me, of the later plays. In them there is nothing to suggest a disproportionate expenditure of bitterness or ferocity. The catastrophe has happened and O'Casey has had the courage to see it and set it down. When people talk about O'Casey as a 'religious' dramatist (and Mr Cusack was no pioneer in the matter) they mean, I think, that he has a most extraordinary awareness of some great catastrophe at work in human affairs. He has seen that the texture of life is forever being tusked by the forces of darkness. In Ireland, we cannot forgive him because we believe that, for O'Casey, protest against imperfection means only protest and even blasphemy against the Christian religion. We forget that at no point in his career has O'Casey denied Christ, though whether he accepts His divinity I do not know. Nor is it any of my business. Here is the girl Julia in *The Star Turns Red* (1940):

> Against you, dear one, we have no grudge; but those of your ministers who sit like gobbling cormorants in the market-place shall fall and shall be dust, and shall be priests no longer.

It is the accent of the Protestant reformer, and we shall not get very far if we forget that O'Casey is a Protestant, one of a minority in a predominantly Catholic country, and accordingly doomed to prejudice over and above that of a naturally bitter temperament. In fairness to him it should be said that his anti-clericalism does not exist *in vacuo.* There are two priests in *The Star Turns Red,* the 'Purple Priest of the politicians' and the 'Brown Priest of the poor'. The first is a monster of pomposity and stupidity, and the other kindly but ineffectual. But perhaps O'Casey leaves us to judge whether the Brown Priest can be other than ineffectual when he has parishioners like the Old Man, who at one stage tells his wife:

> And it's near time the Brown Priest of the poor should be harnessed to common-sense, and from spouting queer and dangerous *Rerum Novarum Quadrig-essimo Anno* nonsense, trying to make the people uneasy in the state of life they live in.

On sentiments like these, Communist states are built. But I will return later to the question of O'Casey's anti-clericalism. First I think it may be worthwhile to look at the two plays that I regard as the peaks of O'Casey's later achievement in the theatre.

War, of some kind or another, had been the background of the Abbey O'Casey plays. But it was war made tolerable by intimations of human grandeur: Juno with her abounding charity and patience, Minnie Powell 'shot through the buzzom' for a pair of weaklings, Bessie Burgess dying, with Christ on her lips, for a mad girl. *The Silver Tassie* is war without any anaesthetic. There are no heroics, no fine sentiments, no ennoble-ments through suffering. Instead we have recorded the mood of Ezra Pound's lines:

> *frankness as never before,*
> *disillusions as never told in the old days,*
> *hysterias, trench confessions,*
> *laughter out of dead bellies.*

The first act, with its picture of human meanness and frailty in the shadow of war, is the most terrible thing in the English-speaking theatre of our time. O'Casey uses the scalpel ruthlessly on the characters of his early plays. Mrs Heegan, the mother of the young soldier Harry, is in dread lest her son endanger her Government Allowance by failing to leave in time for the Front. Chassis is certainly come again when the tenderness of mother for child is lost in worry about a pension. Sylvester Heegan, her husband, is a paler version of the Paycock, with all Boyle's meanness of soul, but with a thinner top-dressing of blather. This entire First Act is a fantasia on the ironic contrast between the two utterly different levels lived on by civilian and combatant. But neither has any conception of what war means, of its misery and dirt and spiritual loneliness. the curtain-line is given to Mrs Heegan: 'Thanks be to Christ that we're after managin' to get the three of them away safely.'

By the time the play has passed through the symbolic Second Act to the hos-pital ward of the Third, where all the chief characters of the First Act are brought together again, we know the intense savagery which led O'Casey to write that curtain-line. For it means that parents have with an easy conscience packed off children to hell. There are no overt indictments of the Heegans.

Their failure of imagination is part only of a world accused of blasphemy. After a fashion, there is blasphemy in Harry Heegan's great speech of the third Act:

> I'll say to the pine 'Give me the grace and beauty of the beech': I'll say to the beech 'Give me the strength and stature of the pine.' In a net I'll catch butterflies in bunches; twist and mangle them between my fingers and fix them wriggling unto Mercy's banner. I'll make my chair a Juggernaut, and wheel it over the neck and spine of every daffodil that looks at me, and strew them dead to manifest the mercy of God and the justice of men.

Blasphemy this may be; but it is also the authentic howl of intolerable pain. It is all the more terrifying since it comes after a bout of stratospheric clowning from Sylvester and his butty Simon Norton. Here the technique of the earlier plays is brought to a triumphant success. Craft and vision are wholly at one. The fools clown on, the blather cascades like porter, and the young suffer. In the Fourth Act again, there is the quick transition from foolery to anguish. Most ghastly of all is the effort to cheer up Harry, by getting him to sing his favourite negro spiritual, 'Just as he used to do ... Behind the trenches ... In the Rest Camps ... Out in France.' The failure of imagination continues. In peace as in war, human beings remain cut off from one another. And there are no surer indications of a world in chassis.

Harry Heegan is a symbol of one of the kinds of suffering implicit in O'Casey's broken world. But Harry's suffering is due partly to impersonal forces. Even more disturbing as a symbol is the Young Whore of *Within the Gates*. She is a Magdalen who has managed to find Christ neither in cleric or layman. But she has retained spiritual vitality. She knows that there is something wrong with the world, and is, literally, worried to death by her apprehension of chaos. From her come some of O'Casey's most passionate indictments of contemporary civilization. She comes upon four men reading newspapers marked 'Murder', 'Rape', 'Suicide' and 'Divorce' and cries out:

> Let every sound be hushed, for the oblate fathers are busy reading the gospel of
> the day. Furnishing their minds with holy thoughts and storing wisdom there.

Here she is acting as a chorus. Elsewhere, in her conversation with the Bishop, she is the protagonist in another tragedy of human beings cut off from one another. She attacks the Bishop because she senses in him the presence of a simulacrum of virtue, safe, respectable, unapproachable.

> A tired Christ would be afraid to lean on your arm. Your Christ wears a bowler
> hat, carries a cane, twiddles his lavender gloves, an' sends out gilt-edged cards
> of thanks to callers.

The Bishop is obscurely Anglican, and so in this case we are spared the embarrassment of detecting hostility to the Catholic Church. But whether or not, the Bishop is meant to be a symbol of a certain kind of churchman common to all persuasions, there is no good reason for refusing to recognize the validity of O'Casey's moral passion. On the subject of the Young Whore, it may be added that O'Casey, the Dublin Protestant, the agnostic-cum-pantheist-cum-early Christian, is not far distant from a French Catholic like M. Mauriac, or an English Catholic like Mr Greene. Like them be believes that the sinner who retains generosity of spirit is liable to be of greater account than the man or woman in whom virtue has become a kind of premium laid down in return for salvation. Should *Within the Gates* ever find a production in Dublin, there is no doubt that we would sympathize with, for instance, O'Casey's attack on the popular British Press. But we might fail to see that in the Young Whore O'Casey is dramatizing one of the great Christian paradoxes: that the poor and the outcast, bruised by the world, the flesh and the devil, may be among the first to enter the Kingdom of Heaven.

Within the Gates is a religious play. That is to say, it is about salvation, how it is lost and how it is found. When the Bishop and the Young Whore finally come together, it is almost too late. She is dying, and in him the well of feeling cannot burst through. But her death, it is implied, is his salvation, just as the death of Rose in Mr Green's *The Living Room* is the salvation of a family in which religion has become a sapless limb.

Nothing that O'Casey has since written for the theatre can equal *Within the Gates* in poignancy or weight of moral passion. *The Star Turns Red* I have referred to. Although moving by dint of a kind of desperate, willed sincerity it fails to rise above its propaganda content. *Purple Dust* is a romp, alternately airy and ponderous, in which two caricature Englishmen are gulled by witty romantic virile Irishmen. It is the only full-length play of O'Casey's in which his brilliant talent for cornerboyism (I use the term to describe a certain bawdy, ruthless one-dimensional humour) is given a field-day. Stoke and Poges have no defence against this kind of humour. *Purple Dust* has no parallel in the modern theatre, and it is unlikely to have successors, since it is unlikely that cornerboyism will ever again be backed by O'Casey's verve.

Red Roses For Me (1942) is a heavily nostalgic return to Dublin of O'Casey's young manhood. It concerns the death in a strike-demonstration of Ayamonn Breydon, a fine young Protestant Socialist. Although I am sure such a thing was not O'Casey's conscious intention, what most clearly emerges from the play is his inherent sectarian prejudice. All the sympathetic characters in *Red Roses* are Protestants: Ayamonn, Mrs Breydon, the Rev. Mr Clinton, Brennan o' the Moor. The dice are too heavily loaded against the Catholics. Sheila Moorneen is represented as a willing victim to the tyranny of a sodality. The flower-seller and the inhabitants of the tenement are shown as creatures who have abandoned all hope, but retained a superstitious veneration for the Blessed Virgin. What is really distressing is that O'Casey shows a tolerant kindliness towards the Catholics and their 'superstition', rather like the attitude of certain Englishmen towards the native Irish. This is the only play of O'Casey's that I personally find offensive.

Oak Leaves and Lavender (1946) is O'Casey's tribute to the county of his exile, Devon, during war-time, as well as a Socialist gloss on the passing of Big Houses. O'Casey, the singer of a 'just war', is a less convincing figure than the savage vision-ary of *The Silver Tassie*. But the play is interesting for the light it throws on O'Casey's capacity for irrational loyalty. England was fighting for her life and O'Casey was liv-ing in England. He saw gallantry and suffering. That was enough to attract his sym-pathies. Nor is the play unmoving in its mixture of jingoism and Communist rhetoric, the defiant mixture of an unreasoning and passionate nature.

Cock-a-Doodle Dandy (1949) is, like its successor *The Bishop's Bonfire*, an extrav-aganza motivated by the old vision of chassis. With the years, O'Casey has grown more and more fond of the alternation of farce and melodrama. But the function-al tension between the two remains. The Cock of the play is a symbolic bird who creates the most glorious confusion in an Irish village. He is O'Casey's symbol of what he believes to be lacking in Irish life: liberality, gaiety, charity, and all the humane virtues that cement a community. The leading characters are old men and young women. And the young women pack up at the end of the play, and leave, presumably, for that Utopia I have mentioned. For three 'scenes' the foolery goes on and at the end an old hypocrite, Michael Marthraun, is left alone on the stage. He has just asked the Messenger: 'What, Messenger, would you advise me to do?' The Messenger answers: 'Die. There is little else left useful for the likes of you to do.' But if I read O'Casey rightly, Michael's death will not repair the damage of three young women driven away by stupidity and ignorance. They have gone as a result of a series of melodramatic instances, but in the real Ireland from which O'Casey has fashioned his extravaganza, they would have gone because they could not find husbands under fifty, or because tattling tongues had corroded their repu-tations, or because their employers could not give them a living wage.

Cock-a-Doodle Dandy is in many ways an unjust, even a cruel play. But we must think of it as the work of the same man who wrote our beloved early 'master-pieces', the work of a 'convicted' imagination goaded into extravagance by the intu-ition, if not the first-hand experience, of wasted lives, and broken hearts. If O'Casey had stopped writing with *Cock-a-Doodle Dandy*, we might not have had the opportunity to air all our grievances against him and at the same time perhaps, attempt to reassess his achievement before it was too late.

Now, six years later, has come *The Bishop's Bonfire* and all the grievances have been aired and all the advice given and all the nonsense talked. I understand from two leading Irish newspapers that favourable comment on the new play is liable to be interpreted as 'bowing to Devon'. What there is to gain from flattering an iras-cible and notoriously ungrateful old man is hard to imagine. This writer would pre-fer to wait until he has seen the published text before going very much further than this: he was intensely moved by *The Bishop's Bonfire* and found in it what he expect-ed to find in O'Casey, the passion, the heroic bitterness, the unfailing awareness of the texture of living. And he found something more: some signs of a possibility of bridging chassis, if only from the elderly dream-child babble of Codger Sleehaun or the rhetoric of Father Boheroe.

I suspect that, in the last analysis, O'Casey's new play is his greatest since *Within the Gates*.

Sean O'Casey: 1880–1980[1]

(*Hibernia, 27 March 1980*)

In the fifth volume of his Autobiographies, *Rose and Crown* (1952), O'Casey tells of a dinner and conversation with Yeats in 1935, in which the poet in the course of a spoken meditation on the later Elizabethan (more properly, Jacobean) dramatists, murmured, 'We are afraid of sadness ... we have it in life, but we fear it in the theatre. You mustn't be afraid of it, O'Casey.' But O'Casey had never been afraid of it, least of all in the play which Yeats, Lady Gregory and Lennox Robinson had rejected seven years before, *The Silver Tassie*. *Tassie* did eventually get its Abbey premiere in 1935, and it will be remembered that, in the ensuing rumpus, Brinsley Mac-Namara resigned from the Directorate.

But lest we forget, men who might have been expected to know better, Liam O'Flaherty and Austin Clarke, had been hostile to the earliest O'Casey. In fact, if an overall view were to be taken of Irish critical reaction, from *The Shadow of a Gunman* (1923) to *Behind the Green Curtains* (1961), the bulk of it would be found to be hostile and/or dismissive.

I take a little pride in the fact that, almost exactly twenty-five years ago, I may have been the first in this country to attempt a sympathetic approach to the O'Casey canon as it then stood, from 1923 to the publication of *The Bishop's Bonfire* ('A World in Chassis', *University Review,* Spring 1955). At that time it was safe and almost *de rigueur* in Ireland to admire the trilogy of the early twenties. But *The Tassie*, despite two complete revivals (both by Ria Mooney: at the Gaiety in 1947 and at the Abbey-Queens in 1951) was still regarded as a botch and a freak. Not until Tomás MacAnna's revival at the Abbey in September 1972 did our journalists (and audiences) seem to recognize the greatness of the play whose rejection by Yeats amounted to taking back from O'Casey what he had given him in his Jovian defence of *The Plough and the Stars* (1926).

What I felt about *The Tassie* in 1955 I still feel, but more strongly and advisedly. O'Casey's concern from the beginning was 'sadness' or, more precisely, 'sorrow': the sorrow wrought by men upon each other because of greed, apathy, constricture of the imagination, the cowardice of half-blinkered souls. Yes, of course this abiding moral defectiveness often went hand-in-hand with likeable oddity, hilarious quaintness, great gusts of entrancing foolery. It might even be said that in the early trilogy we are purged less by pity and terror than by laughter. Unless handled by a sensitive director and players, the comedic element in the trilogy is so great that the increasingly sombre vision of the dramatist is squinted. For my money any production of *Juno* on which the curtain does not descend in silence is ultimately a failure.

There are no unbridled Paycocks nor Fluthers to squint the vision in *The Tassie*. The unquestionably glorious *braggadocio* has been cut down to size. The naked wound gapes at us. The curtain of *The Shadow* comes down on Seamas Shield's solemn, 'I knew something ud come of the tappin' on the wall!' *Juno* ends with Boyle's 'I'm telling you ... Joxer ... the' whole worl's ... in a terr ...ible state o' chassis!' *The Plough* ends with the British soldiers, Tilney and Stoddart, singing '*Keep the 'owme fires burning ... Till the boys come 'owme!*' (I've often wondered if O'Casey at that stage knew that Ivor Novello, of all people, was the author of that circumstantially heart-twinging ditty). *The Tassie*, on one level, is a play about what happens till and after 'the boys come home'. It ends with Mrs Foran's 'It's a terrible pitty Harry was too weak to stay an sing his song, for there's nothing I love more than the ukulele's tinkle, tinkle in the night-time.' All four endings clinch O'Casey's indictment of the short circuit in feeling, but Mrs Foran's, since it tempts neither to laughter nor to tears, but merely boggles us, is perhaps the most awesome.

O'Casey broke down the tenement walls in *Tassie*: that in itself would have thrown Dubliners into disarray. His next play, *Within the Gates* (1933), takes us away altogether from Ireland, where it has never been produced professionally (The Sundrive Players gave it in May 1977). It was conceived originally as a film scenario for treatment by Alfred Hitchcock, who had filmed *Juno* in 1929. After one prelimi-nary discussion Hitchcock dropped the project wordlessly (O'Casey lambasts him in *Rose and Crown*) and the scenario was worked out as a play. In fairness to Hitchcock, unless as a young director he had the massive insouciance of an Orson Welles and the same ability to conjure up cash, O'Casey's Morality Play on English Life seen from Hyde Park and against the background of the Four Seasons might have toppled him for good from the stellar ladder. *Within the Gates*, besides imaging a sexual morality hardly likely to appeal to the British public, is also the first of O'Casey's plays in which he posits social revolution. The central male figure, The Dreamer, prototype of many O'Casey young men to follow, intones towards the end of the play: '*Way for the strong and the swift and the fearless; / Life that is weak with the terror of life let it die; / Let it sink down, let it die and pass from our vision forever!*'

The next six years were relatively barren dramatically. But in 1940 came *The Star Turns Red* (seen, eventually, at the Abbey in 1978) and *Purple Dust* (at the Abbey in 1975) and, in 1942, *Red Roses For Me* (premiered by Shelagh Richards at the Olympia in 1943). *Oak Leaves and Lavender* followed in 1946, the only O'Casey play, apart from *Within the Gates*, set outside Ireland and, like it, still awaiting production in Ireland. *Cock-a-Doodle Dandy* came in 1949 (first seen at the Abbey in 1977) and, in 1955, *The Bishop's Bonfire* was premiered at the Gaiety by Cyril Cusack. This was the occasion when *The Standard* began a pre-production campaign against the play and Mr Cusack's contention in a curtain-speech that O'Casey was essentially a 'religious' dramatist was received with some derision. It also fuelled the updating of an article published in *Irish Writing*, 'Tender Tears for Poor O'Casey', in 1947, and reprinted in *The Green Crow* (1956), which castigates, with some justice, the Irish 'notice-writers' on the grounds that they expected him to, miraculously, journey back in time and produce duplicates of the early 'masterpieces'.

By 1955 O'Casey had completed the massive six-volume autobiography: *I Knock at the Door* (1939), *Pictures in the Hallway* (1942), *Drums under the Windows* (1945), *Inishfallen, Fare Thee Well* (1949), *Rose and Crown* (1952), and *Sunset and Evening Star* (1954). The first four volumes, which take us up to O'Casey's departure for London in 1926 ('It was time for Sean to go. He had had enough of it. He would be no more of an exile in another land than he was in his own') are a rich record of four decades of Dublin life as seen by an impassioned and acerb visionary. The last two volumes are more diffuse and shriller in tone but, to the last word of *Sunset*, 'Hurrah!', full of tetchy vigour.

Nineteen-fifty-eight saw the now seventy-eight-year-old dramatist in the Irish headlines again when, following the refusal of the Archbishop to say an inaugural Mass for the Dublin Theatre Festival, and as an ill-judged placatory gesture, the production of Allan McClelland's *Bloomsday*, an adaptation of *Ulysses*, was withdrawn, O'Casey withdrew his new play *The Drums of Father Ned* (published in 1960 and seen in Ireland at the Olympia in 1966, two years after O'Casey's death). His last plays, *Behind the Green Curtains* (seen in 1975 at the Project), *Figuro in the Night* (seen in 1975 at the Peacock) and *The Moon Shines on Kylenamoe* (premiered on RTÉ in 1962 and seen at the Peacock in 1975), were published together in 1961. O'Casey's last book before his death in 1964 was the 1963 collection of miscellaneous essays, *Under a Colored Cap*. In 1967 Ronald Ayling collected more essays in *Blasts and Benedictions*. Included are O'Casey's defence of *The Silver Tassie*, in 1935, when the clerical attack was led by the late Fr M.H. Gaffney O.P., whose shade must have been a little uneasy when the Catholic Archbishop of Dublin attended the 1972 revival, and of *Within the Gates,* also in 1935, when at initial Jesuit instigation performances were banned by the Mayor of Boston.

It cannot be denied that O'Casey took a good deal of abuse from the Catholic clergy. He experienced at first-hand, more than any other Irish writer perhaps, over uninformed clerical power in the domain of the arts. But, as indicated, he had also, throughout his creative lifetime, to withstand attacks from fellow Irish writers: from

Liam O'Flaherty in 1926 to Patrick Galvin in 1953. I pick these two instances since both Mr O'Flaherty and Mr Galvin would have described themselves as Socialists.

Now, fifty-four years after *The Plough*, forty-five after Fr Gaffney fulminated against *The Tassie*, twenty-two after the non-sensical rumpus over *The Drums*, all seems quiet on the homefront where O'Casey is concerned. The Green Crow, as he liked to call himself in later years, is at full liberty to caw. On 30 March his centenary year begins and I for one will be a little disappointed if somewhere along the line, from beyond the grave, that loquacious and unmeditative man does not raise a handful of green dust.

The Passionate Autodidact: The Importance of *Litera Scripta* for Sean O'Casey

(Irish University Review, Spring 1980)

He took the Reading Lesson-book out of his pocket, opened it, and recited:

> *I chatther, chatther as I flow*
> *To join the brimming river,*
> *For men may come and men may go,*
> *But I go on for ever.*

Well, he'd learned poethry and kissed a girl. If he hadn' gone to school, he'd met the scholars; if he hadn' gone into the house, he had knocked at the door.[1]

I

Sean O'Casey is the most bookish of all Irish dramatists.[2] From *The Shadow of a Gunman* (1923) to the last three plays, published together, *Behind the Green Curtains, Figuro in the Night* and *The Moon Shines on Kylenamoe* (1961), quotations from and references to the books he had read, or at the least was aware of (and chiefly from his protracted incubatory period), play an important part in his dramaturgy. The importance of the Book, for that child who preened himself on being able to read Tennyson's '*The Brook*', is nowhere better attested than in certain passages from the third and fourth volumes of his autobiography, where something like moral judgment enters into his observations of the literary taste of others. Cultural snobbery is not uncommonly an acrid fruit of autodidacticism. Here is a magnificent passage from *Drums Under the Windows* (1946) which, while it has imaginative truth, is yet wrong-headed about individuals, certainly about Thomas MacDonagh, Joseph Mary Plunkett and John Francis (later 'Seán') MacEntee:

> Pity, though, few of them cared a thraneen about art, literature, or science. In this respect, even, they weren't International. A few of them, one of the Plunkets, MacDonagh, and McEntee, paddled in the summertime in the dull waters of poor verse; but gave hardly any sign that they had ever plunged into the waters that kept the world green. No mention of art, science, or music

appeared in *Sinn Féin* or *Irish Freedom* To them, no book existed save ones like *The Resurrection of Hungary* or the *Sinn Féin Year Book*. None of them ever seemed to go to a play, bar one that made them crow in pain and anger. A great many of them were ignorant of the finest things of the mind, as the onslaught on Synge showed. Even Mangan was beyond them. All of them knew his 'Dark Rosaleen' by heart; sang it so often that one got tired of her sighing and weeping, longing to hear her roar out vulgar words with the vigour of a Pegeen Mike. But Mangan's splendid 'Ode to The Maguire' was known to hardly any of them, or, if known, never mentioned. In all the years of his sojourn in Irish-Ireland, he never once heard it mentioned. Thomas Davis was their pattern and their pride. He sang for them every hour of the day, and, if he happened to tire, ... William Rooney, Griffith's great butty, sang instead. In a literary sense, they could have chosen a king in Mitchel; instead they put a heavy gilded crown on the pauper Davis. Almost all of them feared the singing of Yeats, and many were openly hostile to him, though few of them could quote a line from a poem of his. All they treasured of him was the dream which fashioned the little play about Cathleen Ní Houlihan, a tiny bubble, iridescent with a green tinge ... Apart from Pearse, Seumas Deakin, and Tom Clarke, few of the others showed any liking for book, play, poem, or picture. (*A*, I, 616 – 17)

But if O'Casey makes an almost blanket indictment of Irish-Ireland's cultural poverty, he makes a comparable indictment of the impunity of Anglo-Irish Ireland's literary taste. Yeats, Lady Gregory, Oliver St John Gogarty and James Stephens are rapped on the knuckles with varying degrees of severity in *Inishfallen, Fare Thee Well* (1949). He tells of how, knowing from Lady Gregory that she had just given Yeats *The Idiot,* and *The Brothers Karamazov*, the poet had had the effrontery to hail him, O'Casey, as 'the Irish Dostoevsky'.

Another Dostoevsky! An Irish one, this time! And Yeats only after reading the man's book for the first time the night before ... Yeats was trying to impress Seán with his knowledge of Dostoevsky. That was a weakness in the poet. But why hadn't Seán the courage to tell Yeats that he knew damn all about the Russian writer? That was a weakness in Seán. (*A*. II, 163)

Clearly Yeats's ignorance at sixty of Dostoevsky is as culpable for O'Casey as his attempt to conceal it. And he goes on to expose 'weakness' in other established figures in the Anglo-Irish Pantheon. At Coole, Lady Gregory read to him from Hardy's *The Dynasts*, *Moby-Dick* and W.H. Hudson's *The Purple Land* (*A*, II, 115). But on the station at Athenry he came upon her 'sitting on a bench, her head lovingly close to a book'. He approached her and 'Catching in her dulling ear a sound of his movement, she snapped her book shut, but not before he had seen that the book was called *Peg o' My Heart*'. Seeing 'the look of bewilderment in his eye', she said: 'Ah, dat book? I fordet who dave it to me. I just wanted to see what tort it was.'[3]

At Æ's house he catches Stephens out 'suddenly and hurriedly asking Æ, author of the *Homeward Songs*, for a Blood-and-Thunder novel, and Æ had fished one out from his books, without a search; he had plunged a hand in among the books and out came the Blood-and-Thunder novel' (*A*, II, 163). Æ's literary taste is further castigated in a stylized conversation between O'Casey and two companions in a Dublin pub: says O'Casey, 'But then he couldn't stand Shakespeare's *Sonnets*, didn't like his plays and no wonder, for Alexandre Dumas, Zane Grey, and others like them were the literary nectar his gods gave him' (*A*, II, 178). This manifest injustice concerns me here less than O'Casey's insistence on the importance of the top-drawer Book. But perhaps the most telling evidence of O'Casey's absolutism in literary taste deals with Gogarty and, again, Yeats.

> Long afterwards, when Oliver Gogarty came on a visit to him in London, what he had known before was confirmed again. Gogarty had entered on a whirlwind of restlessness. He had flung down his suitcase, the impact had burst it open, and a book fell out on to the floor. Seán's wife and Oliver had made a dive together to get it, but Gogarty was a second too late; and Seán saw the title of one of Edgar Wallace's rich and rare inventions. (*A*, II, 166)

The spectacle of Gogarty and Eileen O'Hare 'diving' for the 'rich and rare', with its echoes from *The Tempest* (I.ii.399) and Thomas Moore ('Rich and Rare Were the Gems She Wore'), is mildly comic: more disturbing is the surprisingly sharp-eyed Sherlock O'Casey, who goes on to recount a visit to Yeats when the poet was 'busy with his last anthology of modern poetry'. In the course of a wide-ranging conversation, 'Seán's eyes kept turning to glance at a disordered pile of books strewing the marble mantelshelf.' Yeats noticed 'and cocked one of his own eyes towards them – for the other was covered with thick green shade – and remarked that they were Wild Western Tales and Detective Stories. Yeats made no bones about it' (*A*, II, 166). He turned 'for shelter and rest to Zane Grey and Dorothy Sayers'. O'Casey's reaction is decidedly a moral one. 'Dope, thought Sean. He uses them as dope to lull the mind to sleep, just as the one-two, one-two, mind of a Roman Catholic keeps awake by reading the tuppenny booklets of the Catholic Truth Society'. He has referred to the 'weakness' of Yeats and also of Stephens (*A*, II, 163). The moral tone of his strictures on bad taste in literature is clinched in the following:

> Aye indeed; even the greater gods of Dublin had their frailties and their faults. They could sometimes build their little cocks of antic hay, and try to tumble about in them. The lordly ones weren't always quite so lordly with literature as they generally posed to be. (*A*, II, 166)

I should add that Aldous Huxley's novel *Antic Hay* was published in 1923, but Oliver St John Gogarty's autobiography of his early days, *Tumbling in the Hay*, did not appear until 1939, three years after Yeats's *Oxford Book of Modern Verse*, on which he was at work when O'Casey visited him at Lancaster Gate.

II

When his father, Michael Casey, was dying, 'Johnny Casside', the *persona* O'Casey created for himself as a child, records: 'There was one comfort, that if he died, he would die in the midst of his books' (*A*, I, 27). There were, it seems, alongside 'a regiment of theological controversial books', including Merle D'Aubigné's *History of the Reformation*, the *English Bible*, the *Latin Vulgate*, the *Douai Testament* and Cruden's *Concordance* (a book essential, by the way, for all or most O'Casey exegesis), the novels of Dickens, Scott, George Eliot, Meredith and Thackeray, the poetry of Burns, Keats, Milton, Gray and Pope, *The Decline and Fall of the Roman Empire* and Locke's *Essay on the Human Understanding* (*A*, I, 27 – 8). It may be noticed that O'Casey's listing has no pedantic regard for chronology: e.g. Dickens before Scott, Burns and Keats before Milton. And, of course, there was Shakespeare. From the remnants of 'her father's fine store' Ella (Isabella), O'Casey's married elder sister, unearthed some 'unsaleable books, from which to give her brother some elementary education' (*A*, I, 172). Thus O'Casey learned to read 'Poethry' as indicated above. It is possible to chart from the volumes after *I Knock at the Door* (1939) a laborious self-education and the effect it had on his life and the effect, as I hope to show further, on his dramatic canon.

O'Casey was scarcely into his teens when he became involved in rehearsals for a charity concert at the Coffee Palace in Townshend Street. 'Johnny Casside' was to play Henry VI to his brother Archie's Gloucester in *Henry VI*, V.iii. (*A*, I, 191). He 'learned the part from one of three volumes of the *Works of Shakespeare* won as a prize by Ella when she was a student in Marlborough House Teachers' Training College' (*A*, I, 192). But, at this stage 'Johnny Casside' is more for Dion Boucicault than Shakespeare. 'What a pity they hadn't chosen a bit outa *Conn the Shaughraun* instead of pouncin' on Shakespeare's stiff stuff. If they only knew, Boucicault was the boy to choose' (*A*, I, 195). He fancies himself as Father Dolan in Boucicault's *The Shaughraun* (1874). A passage from Act I, Scene I, is quoted, I would say from memory, since it diverges slightly from the printed text.[4] Because of the death of the Duke of Clarence the Coffee House concert was cancelled, but at fifteen he did indeed play Father Dolan, at the Mechanics' Institute, later converted into the Abbey Theatre (*A*, I, 305–8). But before that he had acted for the Townshend Dramatic Society in scenes from *3 Henry VI*, *Julius Caesar* and *Henry VIII*, as well as from Boucicault, including *The Octoroon* (1859) and 'lots of others in Dick's little orange-coloured books of Standard Plays' (*A*, I, 298).

At the Mechanics' Institute he had free passes for the shows of a former Boucicault star, Charlie Sullivan, in whose company his brother Archie had small parts (*A*, I, 299). But this familiarity with a decidedly non-literary theatre was not enjoyed *in vacuo*. He was reading Shakespeare outside the range of the snippets provided by the Townshend Dramatic Society. He was buying books and reading them, as well as poring over what remained of his father's old books, including Merle d'Aubigné. He torments his mates, senior and junior, in the emporium where he works, with his superior general knowledge and especially his catechumen's knowledge of Shakespeare. 'Settin' aside the Chronicle Plays, name ten of the others. No answer? Yous couldn't. What's th' name o' th' play containin' the quarrel between th' two celebrated families, an' what was the city where they lived called? No answer? Verona, Verona, th' city; Montague and Capulet, th' families.' He baits his superior, Dyke, with allusions to 'fiery Tybalt' and *Romeo and Juliet* I.i., lines 4, 50–7 (the dialogue between the servants of Capulet and Montague). I cannot trace 'dismantled messengers' to which he refers (*A*, I, 276).

The books he was buying included novels by Balzac, Scott, Dickens, Hugo, Fenimore Cooper and Dumas (presumably, his respect for Dumas had diminished by the time he met Æ) and, in poetry, 'the works of Byron, Shelley, Keats, Goldsmith, Tennyson, Eliza Cook – a terrible waste of sixpence – Gray and the *Golden Treasury*, with the glorious Globe edition of Shakespeare falling to bits.' (*A*, I, 289) In 1966, Jack Lindsay wrote: 'I should like incidentally to stress the debt I feel he owed to Ruskin for helping him as a young man to gain a broad, subtle, and unsectarian sense of the issues.'[5] Ruskin indeed bulked large in the young O'Casey's library. He had *The Seven Lamps of Architecture, Sesame and Lilies, Ethics of the Dust, Unto This Last,* and *The Crown of Wild Olive* (*A,* I, 289). The last-named, being four lectures, on Work, War, Traffic and the Future of England, published in 1882, is of special importance. Literally, he burned the midnight oil over grammar, geography and history. 'Whenever he got tired of these things, he read some bit from the *Deserted Village* or from Ruskin's *Crown of Wild Olives*' (*sic*). His dwindling paraffin's 'last few inches were giving a flickering salute to the glories of Goldsmith, Ruskin and Marlowe' (*A,*I, 348–9). When a zealous Nationalist friend, Ayamonn O'Farrel, calls on him, bringing *Speeches from the Dock* and the *Life of Wolfe Tone* (*A*, I, 354–7), Johnny Casside spouts *The Crown of Wild Olive* at him, and how far O'Casey was steeped in this book may be judged from the fact that in *Pictures in the Hallway* he appears to be writing from memory; the texts quoted (from 'War' and 'Traffic') vary significantly from Ruskin's. One of the more important variations is O'Casey's anticipation of Ruskin's 'Goddess of Getting-on', which in fact occurs a page later in the original.[6]

O'Casey also makes much, writing of Johnny Casside's teens, of his adventures in the acquirement of a *Collected Milton*. In the context he quotes *Paradise Lost* (VI, 207–19), 'from a book on Elocution, left behind by his father' (*A*, I, 286). In the event, he steals the Milton from Hanna's bookshop on Bachelor's Walk, thus giving ammunition to a self-righteous Dublin journalist who denounced him, as recently as 1975, as 'a self-confessed thief and cheat'.[7] But clearly, 'buyin' a book was a serious thing' for the young autodidact.

Untypically, *Drums Under the Windows* (1946) has a formal literary epigraph, but unacknowledged: 'Study that house/ I think about its jokes and stories.' This of course is from Yeats's second-last play.[8] There are many Yeats references in *Drums*, of which I cite the more important. At a Connolly meeting 'Seán' (as 'Johnny Casside' becomes as an adult) reflects in fantastic terms on Griffith who is present, and on varying attitudes to Yeats, specifically in relation to his receipt of a pension from the British Crown. (His name was put on the Civil List at the end of 1910.)[9]

> We have too few, too few such men to spare a one like Yeats the poet, and the Gaelic Leaguers who heard him grew silent. Devil a much you fellows do to keep a few shillings jingling in the poet's pocket. What about the Israelites who took gold, silver, and jewels from the Egyptians before they left them? If England pays the man's rent, then let it be counted unto righteousness for her. None of you know a single poem by Yeats, not even *The Ballad of Father Gilligan*. And the poor oul' gaum, Cardinal Logue, condemning *Countess Cathleen* though he hadn't read a line of it. We were paying a deep price for that sort of thing since Parnell went away from us. He himself had read the ballad only. (*A.* I, 416)

That last is an extraordinary admission if, in fact, it refers to 1911, when Yeats's pension became public knowledge. Elsewhere, we learn that in 1907 he had never seen *Cathleen Ní Houlihan*, 'a shilling was too much for him to spare for a play', and wished he could see 'this play by Singe or Sinje' (*A*, I, 519), (*The Playboy*). He will tell us in *Inishfallen, Fare Thee Well* (1949) that when he began to submit plays to the Abbey in the twenties he had only twice been to the theatre: in December 1917 to see *Blight* by Gogarty (and, apparently, it was accompanied by Lady Gregory's *The Jackdaw*), and, most likely, in August 1920, to see Shaw's *Androcles and the Lion* accompanied by James Stephens's *The Wooing of Julia Elizabeth* (*A*, I, 96). Later, after his Abbey successes, when Lennox Robinson was entertaining him to dinner at the Thirteen Club, he discovered that he was ignorant of writers that 'were common names in the mouths of those who sat beside him'. He had never seen or read Andreiev or Giacosa or Maeterlinck or Benavente or Pirandello:

> ... while Seán whispered the names of Shaw and Strindberg which they didn't seem to catch, though he instinctively kept firm silence about Dion Boucicault, whose work he knew as well as Shakespeare's; afterwards provoking an agonized My Gawd! from Mr Robinson, when he stammered the names of Webster, Ford, and Massinger. (*A*, II, 105)

Here again, is the slightly priggish tone of the autodidact, who believes that he has acquired a gravamen of solid literary culture, as distinct from others with more formal education (neither Yeats nor Robinson had much of that) and a cosmopolitan background, but with a questionable enthusiasm for the exotic and modish. In fact before 1926 when O'Casey left Ireland, Robinson's Dublin Drama League had produced plays by Andreiev, Benavente and Pirandello, and indeed his beloved

Shaw and Strindberg.[10] O'Casey must or should have known this. But, for better or worse, he sniffed a gilded rat in the Thirteen Club.

III

Almost from the beginning of his career as a published writer, O'Casey tended to air his hard-won learning. The title-page of *The Story of Thomas Ashe* (1917) bore lines from Browning. The following year a second edition re-titled *The Sacrifice of Thomas Ashe* had lines from Pope on the cover, and on the title-page Shakespeare and Pope again.[11] Pope and Browning seem indecorous in the context of the hunger-striker Ashe and the great Glasnevin funeral in 1917. Antony's lines on the dead Brutus (*Julius Caesar*, V.v. 73–5) are little more congruous.

In the first staged play, *The Shadow of a Gunman* (1923), O'Casey left the hallmark of his self-conscious literary culture on his hero (or anti-hero), the would-be poet and player gunman, Donal Davoren. In the stage directions we are told that he has '*an inherited and self-developed devotion to "the might of design, the mystery of colour, and the belief in the redemption of all things by beauty everlasting"* '.[12] Davoren echoes Dubedat, from whose dying speech in Shaw's *The Doctor's Dilemma* O'Casey's quotation is taken, when in Act II he attacks the People: 'To them the might of design is a three-roomed house or a capacious bed' (*CP*, I, 127). But Davoren's chief contact with the more 'poetic' aspects of literature is through Shelley's great unactable verse-play *Prometheus Unbound*, from which three times in Act I and again towards the curtain he quotes Prometheus's refrain 'Ah me! pain, pain ever, forever!'[13] As an index to character or type, the line is viable: Davoren's anguish, at least initially, is factitious and so requires for sustenance incommensurate statements. At the beginning of Act II he quotes ii. 281–4 from *Epipsychidion*:

> The cold chaste Moon, the Queen of Heaven's bright isles,
> Who makes all beautiful on which she smiles;
> That wandering shrine of soft yet icy flame,
> Which ever is transformed, but still the same.   (*CP*, I, 125)

The full-stop is O'Casey's, for the line runs on in a half-line, 'And warms not, but illumines.' Should the Shelley quotations seem obtrusive, a case may be made for them as suggested above. I do not think that the same might be said for Davoren's reply to his room-mate Seumas Shield's query as to the time: 'The village cock hath thrice done salutation to the morn.' The pedlar Shields's quick response need not seem odd in a man of the kind who as a boy may have frequented the Mechanics' Institute: 'Shakespeare, *Richard the III*, Act Five, Scene III. It was Ratcliffe said that to Richard just before the battle of Bosworth' (*CP*, I, 131). What is odd is that while Shields's location of the line is exact, Davoren's quotation is not.

It should be 'the early village cock', though 'twice' instead of 'thrice' may be Davoren's essay at a feeble donnish joke. Elsewhere (*CP*, I, 93) Davoren laces his conversation with familiar quotations from *The Rubai'yat of Omar Khayam* and Milton's Sonnet XIX ('*When I consider how my light is spent*'). But none of his quotations has the effect of his incorporation into his last speech of *Ecclesiastes* 12.6 in part: '*Or ever the silver cord be loosed, or the golden bowl be broken*' (*CP*, I, 156–7). In later plays O'Casey will be bolder in his use of the Old Testament.

In his first full-length play, *Juno and the Paycock* (1924), O'Casey almost certainly used books as symbols. Mary Boyle is an enlightened Minnie Powell. She reads above her station. Her father 'Jackie' Boyle, the Captain, has caught her reading a volume of Ibsen: 'three stories, *The Doll's House*, *Ghosts*, an' *The Wild Duck* – buks only fit for chiselurs'! To which, 'Joxer' Daly rejoins: 'Didja ever rade *Elizabeth, or Th' Exile o' Sibayria?*'[14] This is not Joxer's only favourite book. He has also a stock of mediocre verse of which the following are two samples (I have de-Joxerized them.):

> And how can man die better
> Than facing fearful odds
> For the ashes of his fathers
> And the temples of his Gods? (*CP*, I, 27)

This is from Horatius, XXVIII, in Macaulay's *Lays of Ancient Rome* (1867). The provenance of the second on Joxer's lips is rather mysterious.

> Tender-hearted stroke a nettle
> And it stings you for your pains.
> Grasp it like a man of mettle
> And it soft as silk remains (*CP*, I, 27)

The author of those sublimely trite lines was Aaron Hill (1685–1750), who wrote tragedies and farces, some for Drury Lane. Joxer has two other favourite books, whose titles are introduced at crucial moments. He observes of Father Farrell, 'I wondher did he ever read the Story o' Irelan'. And Boyle replies: 'Be J.L. Sullivan? Don't you know he didn't' (*CP*, I. 38). It seems unlikely that the audiences of 1924 (or since) got the joke. *The Story of Ireland or a Narrative of Irish History written for Irish Youth* was written and published by Alexander Martin Sullivan (Dublin 1886). 'J.L. Sullivan' is Boyle's conflation of this Sullivan and the Irish-American boxer. At the end of the play the drunken Joxer has the penultimate speech: 'D'jever rade Willie … Reilly … an' his own … Colleen … Bawn? It's a darlin' story, a daarlin' story!' (*CP*, I, 89). William Carleton's novel *Willy Reilly and His Dear Colleen Bawn* was published in 1850–1, and a revised version in 1855. Just eleven years before the historical time of *Juno*, James Duffy of Dublin brought out an edition (1909). The novel, by the way, has nothing to do with Gerald Griffin's *The Collegians* (1829), from which Dion Boucicault took material for his play *The Colleen Bawn* (1860).[15]

If Mary Boyle and Ibsen represent an attempt to escape from a washed-out popular culture, then Joxer with his 'darlin' stories, *Elizabeth or the Exiles of Siberia,* Sullivan's *The Story of Ireland* and Carleton's *Willy Reilly*, his snatches from Macauley, Hill and others may be said to represent that culture at its nadir. And Boyle's reaction to the news of his daughter's pregnancy pre-figures venomous attacks on the Book in plays written many years later:

> Her an' her readin'! That's more o' th' blasted nonsense that has the house fallin'
> down on top of us! What did th' likes of her, born in a tenement house, want
> with readin'? Her readin's afther bringin' her to a nice pass – oh, it's madnin',
> madnin', madnin'! (*CP* I, 75)

But there is a reference in *Juno* which goes further back than Mary Boyle's explorations of continental drama, which may be taken as a reflection of O'Casey's own. Curiously it occurs in a speech from 'Captain' Boyle. 'An', as it blowed an' blowed, I ofen looked up at the sky an' assed meself the question – what is the stars, what is the stars? ... An' then, I'd have another look, an' I'd ass meself – what is the moon?' (*CP*, I, 26) This may be compared with this from *Pictures in the Hallway:* 'Johnny glanced up at a sickle moon hanging in the sky among a throng of stars. What was it and what were they? He had looked in the pages of Ball's *Story of the Heavens* and at the pictures, but it was all too hard for him yet' (*A*, I, 256). Sir Robert Stawell Ball's *The Story of the Heavens* was published (London: Cassell) in 1885, and reissued in 1886 and 1891. The coincidence of the adolescent Johnny's and the middle-aged Boyle's reflections suggests, I submit, some investigation into how far O'Casey *distributed* his actual experience among his characters.

The Plough and the Stars (1926) is the first play in which O'Casey makes use of the Old Testament as a stroke in stage-portraiture. This he can do without loss of verisimilitude, since Bessie Burgess is at least the remains of an Evangelical Protestant. O'Casey has her quote the Bible inexactly, as when she castigates Mrs Gogan none too obliquely: '... a middle-aged married woman makin' herself th' centre of a circle of men is as a woman that is loud an' stubborn whose feet abideth not in her own house' (*CP*, I, 202). The verse, *Proverbs* 7.11, 'She is loud and stubborn; her feet abide not in her house', is more insulting than it might appear to the non-Bible reader, for it is preceded in *Proverbs* by 'And, behold, there met him a woman with the attire of a harlot, and subtil of heart' and succeeded by 'Now she is without, now in the streets, and lieth in wait at every corner.' O'Casey in 1926 may have enjoyed airing his knowledge of the Old Testament before a largely Roman Catholic audience. Few Catholics, I hazard, would have been able to place Bessie's prayer at the end of Act III: 'Oh, God, be Thou my help in time o' throuble. An' shelter me safely in th' shadow of Thy Wings!' (*CP*, I, 238) In fact, Bessie, characteristically, garbles *Psalms* 36.7, 46.1, 61.4, and 63.7, to make her sublime appeal.

If O'Casey appeals to us through his use of biblical language, so also does he through the rhetoric of P.H. Pearse which also, of course, is an integral in the structure of Act II. Pearse's writings had appeared in collected book-form 1917–22 and so were easily available to O'Casey when he was writing *The Plough*. The extracts from Pearse's speech at the graveside of O'Donovan Rossa are not all that is heard of him in Act II (*CP*, I, 213). We also hear him quoting from an article he published in *Spark* in December 1915, 'Peace and the Gael', an article which 'went too far even for Connolly'.[16] From it O'Casey culled the passage in which Pearse declares:

> The old heart of the earth needed to be warmed with the red wine of the battlefields … Such august homage was never [before] offered to God as this: the homage of millions of lives given gladly for love of country. (*CP*, I, 196)

This statement by Pearse, derived from print, is more crucial to the significance of Act II than the passages from the Rossa oration, since it attempts to glorify *all* war, 'for love of country' as 'homage' to God. Act II in effect is, on one level, O'Casey's first major pacifist statement (he will exhibit a rather different stance towards the Second World War). We may with hindsight see that, having made that statement, it was not unlikely that he would go on to write a play like *The Silver Tassie* (1928).

Davoren's quoted *Ecclesiastes*, Bessie Burgess quoted *Proverbs* and *Psalms*, The Croucher, who opens Act II of *Tassie*, paraphrases and adapts verses from *Ezekiel* 37, which, I would say, would be unfamiliar to the vast majority of audiences. But the provenance of The Croucher's speeches is crucial. Thus *Ezekiel* 37.9, runs 'Prophesy unto the wind, prophesy, son of man, and say to the wind, Thus saith the Lord God, O breath, and breathe upon these slain, that they live', but becomes from The Croucher 'And he said, prophesy, and say unto the wind, come from the four winds a breath and breathe upon these living that they may die' (*CP*, II, 36). The Croucher reverses the sense of the Lord's message to the preacher, just as the warlords have reversed the Gospels.

IV

The Silver Tassie, though rejected by the Abbey, had been intended for that theatre. *Within the Gates* (1933) was the first of eight full-length plays which were not (as well as two near full-length and four one-act[17] plays). The explicitly bookish content of this play is not great. The Atheist, adoptive father of The Young Woman, established her (after a fashion), in the line of Mary Boyle. He boasts to The Dreamer, 'D'ye know, one time, the lass near knew the whole of Pine's [Paine's] *Age of Reason* off by 'eart!' (*CP*, II, 124) That line is from the Stage Version, which appeared in *Collected Plays;* it does not appear in the original printed text of 1933. But an amusing exchange, between the Bishop and the Bishop's Sister after he has made something of an ass of himself blessing babies in the park, is not carried over to the Stage Version from the text of 1933:

> *Bishop's Sister.* Shall we go somewhere dear, and read a little of Tennyson?
> *Bishop (snappily).* Oh, damn old Tennyson.[18]

The Star Turns Red (1940), O'Casey's apocalyptic version of Irish Labour's past
and future, is remarkably pure from the bookishness one might expect from
O'Casey's treatment of such a subject. There is perhaps an echo from the first lines
of Yeat's 'Sailing to Byzantium' in Jack's speech in Act III which begins, 'The young
in each other's arms shall go on confirming the vigour of life' (*CP*, II, 319).

In *Purple Dust* (1940) O'Casey pillages well-known English verse not to laud it,
but to satirize the cultural pretentions of his two English refugees from the War:
Basil Stoke and Cyril Poges. The fact that Stoke Poges is a village associated with
the composition of Gray's 'Elegy in a Country Churchyard' suggests that O'Casey,
temporarily at least, has had his surfeit of official English culture. In the space of a
few pages, Poges, romanticizing over his Irish mansion and the joys of country
seclusion, hesitates over schoolbook lines from Wordsworth's 'The Solitary
Reaper'; attempts to paraphrase his sonnet The World is Too Much with Us; Late
and Soon'; misquotes Poe's 'To Helen' ('the glory that was Rome and the grandeur
that was Greece'), and maintains that 'Shakespeare knew what he was talking about
when he said that'; hits on [Wordsworth's] 'the primrose by the river's brim, a yellow primrose was to him, but it was nothing more', as one of 'the wild flowers that
Shakespeare loved' (*CP*, III, 21–5). Clearly Poges is the produce of a culture in
which all other poets have been, as it were, strained through Wordsworth. Space
considerations preclude full quotations of the stonemason O'Killigain's onslaught
on 'good old Wordsworth'. It is inordinately vicious (*CP*, III, 21–2). In line with
O'Killigain's perfervid deflation of Wordsworth in his description of Oxford, as,
parodying James Thomson, 'The city of dissolute might!' (*CP*, III, 103). When
O'Killigain bids Avril, Poges's lady, be ready to leave when the river rises, Poges
surpasses himself in trite quotations: 'Come with me and be my love! Come into
the garden Maud' (*CP*, III, 109). Marlowe, of course, he gets wrong. He closes the
play, however, with his first *conscious* misquotations: from Browning's 'Home
Thoughts, From Abroad' he distils: 'Would to God I were in England, now that
winter's here!' (*CP*, III, 119).

If Poges (and Stoke) represent the superficies of public-school culture, Ayamonn Breydon in *Red Roses for Me* (1942) represents the genuineness of enlightened
working-class culture. When the play opens we find him rehearsing Gloucester in
3 Henry VI, V.vi. for a concern in the local Temperance Hall. Ayamonn says of the
audiences: '... they're afraid of Shakespeare out of all that's been said of him. They
think he's beyond them, while all the time he's part of the kingdom of heaven in
the nature of everyman' (*CP*, III, 131). Later (p. 136) we hear that one Mullcanny

will be bringing Ayamonn Haeckel's *The Riddle of the Universe*. Later again in Act I, Ayamonn offers to lend an Irish Irelander Ruskin's *The Crown of Wild Olive* and there follows a conversation that resembles Johnny Casside's with the tram conductor and includes the self-same quotation from Ruskin.[19] In Act II Ayamonn reads out *Hamlet*, I.ii, 613–4, and cries, 'Oh, Will, you were a boyo; a brave boyo, though, and a beautiful one!' (p. 163). In Act IV (p. 208), Ayamonn's friend, the Rev. Mr Clinton, defends the young man's cross of daffodils for Easter, to his verger, with Shakespeare: *The Winter's Tale*, IV.iv.118–20. The verger's reply typifies the response already indicated by Ayamonn: 'Altogether too high up for poor me, sir.'

Ayamonn Breydon with his Shakespeare, his Ruskin, his Haeckel, his reproductions of Fra Angelico and Constable, is of course an idealized image of O'Casey himself. But he is something more: Everyman redeeming himself from the depths by the power of the Book, of *litera scripta*. The importance of *litera scripta* is seen even in his often jingoistic play about wartime England, *Oak Leaves and Lavender* (1946). The ghostly Dancers who return to the blacked-out manorial house maintain that 'Goldsmith, Berkeley, Boyle, Addison, Hone, Swift, and Sheridan still bear flaming torches through the streets of life' (*CP*, IV, 9). The Irish leftist Drishogue bids his English friend Edgar fight and perhaps die for all the Englands: 'For all of them in the greatness of England's mighty human soul set forth in what Shakespeare, Shelley, Keats, and Milton sang ...' (*CP*, IV, 29). The Land Girl Jennie larks about with tags from Gray and Fitzgerald (p. 33). Drishogue's father, the butler Feelim, shows off to the pacifist Pobjoy about his knowledge of both the birth-place and grave of Milton (p. 95). Even in bouts of farcical comedy, we are never allowed to forget the mighty dead of literature.

The Book has an important place also in the last five plays to be discussed here. In *Cock-a-Doodle Dandy* (1949) Father Domineer, come to exorcize the house of Michael Marthraun, hears that Michael's daughter Loreleen has 'evil books', gets into a frenzy not dissimilar from Jackie Boyle's in *Juno*: 'Bring them out, bring them out! How often have I to warn you against books! Hell's bells tolling people away from th' truth!' (*CP*, IV, 200–1) Books are brought out for his inspection. They are 'A book about Voltaire', which Father Domineer maintains has been banned,[20] and 'Ullisississies, or something' (p. 201). The books are sent to the Presbytery to be burned, another apparent victory for the pressure groups of anti-intellectualism. Loreleen, of course, is another variation on Minnie Powell/Mary Boyle. Robert Hogan has noted that 'Of the late plays *The Drums of Father Ned* and *Behind the Green Curtains* are probably the most allusive, and *The Bishop's Bonfire* is probably the least.'[21] But possibly that gorgeous prop, the 'buckineeno', later 'bookneeno', a horn or cornet blown at inauspicious moments by the statue of the Bishop's patron, St Tremolo, has its origins in O'Casey's literary experience. 'St Tremolo', we are told, was 'the fella ... who played a buck, a buckineeno, in the old Roman Army'.[22]

O'Casey would have perhaps encountered 'the bucina, the Roman war-trumpet' in Act I of Shaw's *Caesar and Cleopatra*, where it is described as making a 'terrible bellowing note'.[23] If we see 'St Tremolo' as a commander-in-chief of Ballyoonagh's Roman legions, there is an added comic dimension to the fatuous gesture of the *Bishop's Bonfire* in which 'piles of bad books an' evil pictures ... are to go away in flames' (p. 29). A priest-writer who loved books is alluded to in the liberal young Father Boheroe's speech to Foorawn, who has asked him if he is going to watch the Bishop's Bonfire: 'my road goes in an opposite direction, where, though there be no cedars, at least, I shall walk under the stars' (p. 113). The allusion to Canon Sheehan,[24] I fear, is lost on most of those who read O'Casey.

The Drums of Father Ned (1960) gives us a development of Father Boheroe, but Father Ned does not appear. Under his influence Doonavale ('Shut his mouth') is waking up, and the young people are preparing a Boucicault-type play for An Tóstal.[25] In this springtime for Donnavale, literary allusions are rife. Johnny Casside and Jackie Boyle creep into the mind when young Michael and Nora look at the stars (p. 82) and Nora completes Michael's quotation from Tennyson's *Locksley Hall* (ll. 9–10). The nouveaux-riches Binningtons try to impress guests with a story about Yeats and Gogarty in Gogarty's *As I was Going Down Sackville Street*, but never get to tell it (p. 88). Michael scandalizes all by stating that God 'may be but a shout in th' street' (p. 92) echoing Joyce.[26] Nora quotes Eliot in reverse when she says that the question of Red timber in Doonavale will be answered 'not with a whimper, but with a bang!'[27] Binnington and McGilligan, in dishevelled mayoral robes, in feeble bravado quote (p. 101) from Blake's *Milton* inaccurately ('burnished gold' and 'arras of desire). The local allusions in *Behind the Green Curtains* (1961), a play set in Dublin and a town outside called Ballybeedhost ('Bally-Be-Quiet': compare Doonavale), are numerous, but the purely literary allusions are thin on the ground. The enlightened industrialist Chatastray has Renan's *Life of Jesus* in his library: the journalist McGeelish takes it for 'some cod book o' devotions'.[28] The progressive worker, Beoman quotes Burns ('Wee, sleekit, cow'rin, tim'rous beastie') (p. 81), when Chatastray yields to ecclesiastical pressure (*Le chat* has become a mouse, perhaps).

Figuro in the Night (1961) bristles with an old man's literary jokes. It is an Old Woman who introduces Eliot's 'Sweeney Agonistes' when she asks if Adam and Eve could sit forever 'undher a bread-fruit, undher a banyan, undher a bamboo tree, in a garden, eatin' grapes'.[29] It is an Old Man who counters with Thomas Edward Brown's 'A garden is a lovesome thing, God wot', and precipitates lovely nonsense (p. 99). Another Old Man misquotes *The Ancient Mariner* (ll. 115–16) and is complemented by yet another greybeard (p. 106) misquoting ll. 117–18. The first of these two Old Men plays on *Hamlet* III.iv.103 (and possibly *The Mikado)* when he describes how his clothes have become 'a thing o' shreds and patches' (p. 107). He also asks 'Oh who'll call for th' robin an' th' wren' for protection against 'all kinds of evil things' (p. 111), in the wake of the notorious Brussels 'Figuro' set down overnight in Dublin, thus recalling Cornelia's lament for Marcello in Webster's *The White Devil,* V.iv. This bookish joke is perhaps one of O'Casey's most bitter and effective: an echo from Renaissance tragedy in life and theatre introduced into the manic prurience of contemporary Ireland as he saw it.

I have by no means covered all the ground in this article, which has attempted to establish not merely the weight of literary reference in O'Casey's plays, but also his life-long love and respect for books. He throve on them, and often his imagination was fired by *litera scripta*. The autobiographies and the plays in a manner complement each other up to 1955 and provide one of many O'Casey portraits: the passionate autodidact.

Dublin's Prometheus-Autolycus[1]

(The Irish Press, 12 November 1981)

The first volume of the O'Casey letters covered the years 1910–11. The third and final volume will cover the years 1955–64. On the strength of this second volume I am certain that the three taken together will constitute a monument not alone to O'Casey, but to over half-a-century of political and social change in these islands. I am willing to go further and say that taken with the six-volume Autobiography (1939–54) – a work which is no more fanciful than George Moore's *Hail & Farewell*, though with comparable longueurs – they will constitute a non-dramatic achievement demanding as much attention as O'Casey's work for the theatre.

Certain Irish responses to O'Casey's work might be taken as indices to the cultural climate during the fearful forties and early fifties. (I would, if a cultural historian, date the presentation of *The Bishop's Bonfire* in Dublin in 1955 as the first major open, as distinct from occult or elitist, breach of the Emerald and Purple tapestry: *The Bell, Irish Writing, Envoy* had not, for all their varying forms of dissent, more than ruffled the literate general public.) For instance, we learn here of Walter Macken presenting a Gaelic translation of *The Plough* at the Taibhdhearc in November 1942, while the same play was rejected as an entry from a Kerry Group by the Cork Drama Festival in December 1946, and as an entry by a Tipperary group at the Father Mathew Féis at some later year. (O'Casey writing in March 1950, says 'recently': Professor Krause, uncharacteristically, has not checked this.) The play, which of course had caused uproar of a limited extent in 1926, had certainly become respectable by 1940; yet there were still pockets of ferocious resistance and at that point of time what was deemed fit for audiences at amateur festivals signified mightily. Needless to say, such instances, which could be paralleled in other graver fields, were all fuel for O'Casey's smouldering imagination. But, while it is true that a large share of these letters is devoted to official obscurantism, bigotry, and scarcely conceivable (except that O'Casey provides the evidence) instances of inhumanity, it is not these that nestle in the mind; which, since perhaps they should, may indicate a weakness in O'Casey's epistolary rhetoric. He himself, contrary to received opinion, was quite capable of admitting rents in his jersey but maintained the right to wear it: in June 1954, aged seventy-four, he writes to an American professor: 'The foolish things I've done, said, or written, are part of the living man, and should not be concealed so as to suggest infallibility – which God forbid!, or make a mask to cause a man to look more like an angel – which God has already forbidden.' That same month he had written to Francis MacManus (d. 1963) whom he had met on his last visit to Dublin in 1935 and corresponded with ever since: 'Oh, these troubles! They smite all those who hope in God as deeply as those who don't. That is one reason why I have ever been fighting to unite all in rebellion against a stupidity and a carelessness that bring a lot of them into existence. Trouble at least unites us in one family.' O'Casey, professed unbeliever and Communist (who puzzled his Soviet correspondents with defences of T.S. Eliot and Picasso), is at his most humanly sympathetic in letters to MacManus, a practising and intellectually convinced Catholic. Through him he kept in touch with Irish writing in English and Irish. In 1946 he is lavishing praise on Seosamh MacGrianna and lamenting his mental breakdown: '... (he) should try to take care of himself, for as a writer, he owes it to man to live as long as he can, and write as often as he feels he must.' In February 1950 he is urging MacManus to use his influence to secure an Irish Academy of Letters award for Séamus O'Neill (d. 1981) whose *Tonn Tuile* (1947) he admired.

In January 1948 he tried, in vain, to persuade Patrick Kavanagh to contact Professor David H. Greene of New York University, who was compiling material on contemporary Irish writing. He records to MacManus the interesting detail that Kavanagh put 'S.A.G.' on the back of his letters. But O'Casey was tireless in his efforts for fellow Irishmen (above all). In August 1948 he used his good offices with Shaw (then ninety-two) to try to procure, at Peadar O'Donnell's request, a Preface to Tom Barry's *Guerrilla Days in Ireland*. In March 1949 he was advising Roger McHugh on how to get his Abbey prize-winning play, *Rossa*, produced in Britain and America. But perhaps the most poignant evidence of O'Casey's sincere interest in other Irish writers, especially the young, may be seen in his solicitude for the feelings of twenty-five-year-old Maurice Meldon when, in February 1951, his *A House Under Green Shadows* flopped and *Juno* had to be rushed on. O'Casey lavished praise on him for years after his performance as Brennan o' the Moor in Ria Mooney's 1946 London production of *Red Roses for Me*.

In April 1945 an Irish Catholic factory girl, designated here simply as 'Sheila' (at her own request: she may, from internal evidence, have been an O'Donnell or an O'Neill), initiated with O'Casey an extraordinary correspondence in which he is seen at his fierce, exasperated best as a polemicist against power and privilege, and since 'Sheila' had connections (unexplained) with the Jesuits and the family of one of them, who had helped to 'place' Cardinal Hinsley in the See of Westminster, it is English Catholic power and privilege that he flails (I have little doubt in my own mind as to the identity of this family). I use the adjective 'extraordinary' advisedly:

the ageing Communist unbeliever giving counsel, practical and cultural, often spiritual, to the girl who has taken a vow of chastity, alternately reviles and flatters him
– and discusses him with her disapproving rich Catholic friends. I find O'Casey's
letters to 'Sheila' among the most moving in the book. On May 7, 1945, he wrote
to her: 'Whether you ever become a Communist or no, be true to your comrade
workers. You will never offend The Sacred Heart by being loyal to your class.'

O'Casey, it must be recalled, was a late Irish Victorian, and he retained some of
the priggishness of his age and class. As a committed self-improver, he had no time
for detective fiction and the like. He used Æ's weakness for such trivia as a stick
to beat him. Did he know that his 'very dear' George Nathan (1882–1958), the
doyen of New York drama critics, had founded in 1920 with H.L. Mencken the pulp
detective magazine *Black Mask*? He had an unhealthy aversion to homosexuals and an
obsession with 'Cissies' in the theatre. But did he know that one of his demi-gods,
Walt Whitman, was a 'Cissie'? (And, for that matter, T.E. Lawrence, who raved over
both *The Silver Tassie* and *Within the Gates*, to O'C's gratification.)

Through the forties he wrote passionately for Irish causes: for Irish neutrality
against St John Ervine (in a *Time and Tide* correspondence initiated in February
1944 by a familiar name in Dublin nowadays, Hilary Boyle); for the release of IRA
prisoners in Parkhurst, in 1947, in the campaign initiated by the late Eoin O'Mah-
ony; for the Lane pictures' return to Ireland, in 1948, an old cause he had taken up
with Lady Gregory more than twenty years earlier: he was always our chevalier, if
imperfect man.

In a compilation of this magnitude, there are bound to be editorial slips. Giving
Miss Horniman's first name as 'Alice' instead of 'Annie' is an unusual one. Patrick
Kavanagh was born in 1904, not 1906.[2] There is no book by Austin Clarke called
Past and Present: a section of *Collected Poems* (1936) is so-called, and the name of the
poem O'Casey refers to is 'The Fair at Windgap', not 'Windygap'. Since Professor
Krause knows, for instance, that the drama-critic Seamus Kelly died as recently as
1979, he should know that the Cork writer Con O'Leary has been dead since
1958, and 'Thomas Hogan' (the pseudonym of Thomas Woods) since 1962.

But Volume II of *The Letters* is on the whole as fearless a joy as its predecessor,
though without the magnificent period photographs. I look forward to Volume III:
what will Seán have to say about the conversion to Catholicism of his 'very dear'
George Jean, about the accession of Pope John XXIII, about the assassination of
President Kennedy? Whatever it may be, we can be sure that Professor Krause,
meticulously loving, will do Dublin's Prometheus-Autolycus more than proud.

Murder in the Cathedral

(Hibernia, November 1962)

Miss Nora Lever's production of T.S. Eliot's *Murder in the Cathedral* must be cherished on several different counts. In the first place the performance was given in St Patrick's Cathedral, which is the principal place of worship of the Church of Ireland, which though in close communion with the Church of England has not had a comparable history of dalliance with Rome. And one of the dominating ideas of Eliot's play is that the state must not usurp the authority of the Church, and the Church means, explicitly, the Church of Rome. Thomas à Becket represents the authority of the Pope. It is, therefore, an occasion for Christians of all denominations to thank the authorities of St Patrick's for a noble example of toleration and magnaminity.[1]

Eliot's play on one level, then, is about the supremacy of papal authority in matters spiritual. On another, it is about the psychology of martyrdom. On yet another, it posits the teaching that only in God and with God can man be truly 'living'. Otherwise he is 'partly living'. This is part of the message of the chorus, who fear not merely natural disaster, but the disaster of contact with a crime that will pierce their hearts with the sword of reality. And 'Human kind cannot bear very much reality.'

The central message of Christianity is the reality of life in Christ; and very very few among the Christian millions can support the full apprehension of that reality. In Eliot's play, Thomas à Becket represents humanity in touch with that life in Christ that devastates and refreshes, splits the heart and makes it holy. It is a very terrible play, and it is nonsense to disdain it on the grounds that it is not as good as Shakespeare. Only foolish and vulgar fellows who pretend to live on Parnassus all the time can afford to despise Eliot.

I am not sure that all the above emerged clearly from Miss Lever's production. But Mr Ray McAnally's Thomas was, from the Christmas Morning sermon onwards, very fine. What a very good actor he is. I've said that before and I'll say it again. Some day he may be a great actor, and that will happen when he ceases to please us with his intelligence and electrifies us with passion. Mr McAnally must play Shakespeare.

Jottings on the Use of the Grail motif in T.S.Eliot's *The Waste Land*

(John Jordan Papers)

Any discussion of the use to which Eliot has put the Grail legend in *The Waste Land* must be tempered by the extent of his debt to Jessie L. Weston's *From Ritual to Romance*; this debt is obviously a considerable one, as Eliot acknowledges in his notes, but it is open to doubt whether Miss Weston's book has any real relevance to the Grail legend as it is found in the Arthurian cycle. *From Ritual to Romance*, inspired by Frazer's *The Golden Bough*, another source acknowledged by Eliot, is basically an anthropological study of various vegetation, fertility, and folk myths, which attempts to interpret the Grail tradition in the light of these myths. The argument is very plausible, since there can be little doubt that the vegetation myths and their attendant mystery cults were very widespread in the Middle East and in the Roman world, but no evidence is forthcoming to establish any definite connection with the Arthurian Grail quest, or to bridge the gap between the Gnostic sects, which tried to combine the mystery cults with Christianity, and the Grail romances of the twelfth century. We may agree that the Smyrna merchants spread Gnostic ideas throughout Europe, that mumming plays and morris dancing have their roots in some vegetation rite, but there is still no visible proof that the strange Gnostic mixture of Christian and pagan belief took lasting root, or that British and Celtic vegetation rites had a Roman or Eastern origin, or were encouraged by gypsies. Nor is it good enough to explain this lack of evidence by claiming that mystery cults are by definition mysterious, and secret societies secret, as Miss Weston does, because mystery and secrecy have not preventd the accumulation of a vast amount of data concerning witchcraft and freemasonry. Indeed, Miss Weston is inclined to cut corners when faced with such matters, and thereby casts doubt on the validity of her arguments. Perhaps it is not inopportune to quote an example of her sometimes unscholarly approach:

> Some years ago, in the course of my reading, I came across a passage in which certain knights of Arthur's court, riding through a forest, came upon a herb 'which belonged to the Grail'. Unfortunately, the reference, at the time I met with it, though it struck me as curious, did not possess any special significance, and either I omitted to make a note of it, or entered it in a book which, with sundry others, went mysteriously astray in the process of moving furniture.[1]

It is difficult not to be of the opinion that Miss Weston is here going mysteriously astray, for, even putting the best possible construction on this sad little story, it's not evidence. Nor is her critical judgment always above suspicion:

> Probably the four best romances, in the opinion of literary scholars, would be reckoned to be the *Chanson de Roland, Renaud de Montauban, Huon de Bordeaux,* and *Aliscans*; but not one of these could bear comparison, as a piece of literature, with any one of the masterpieces of Arthurian romance.[2]

Further instances of vague, unsupported generalizations are to be found in her reference to the Knights Templar, and to the higher Masonic degrees, but above all one might be permitted to wonder about the identity of the literary scholars who think so poorly of the *Chanson de Roland* as to demote it from its place as one of the masterpieces of European literature; no matter whether such scholars existed only in the mind of Miss Weston or not, such over-statement of the Arthurian case can do nothing but damage her reputation as a critic, and cast doubt on the validity of her other theories. It is noteworthy that subsequent criticism has developed in such a way as to place her outside the mainstream of Arthurian criticism, and to make her book an interesting curiosity.

However, although the validity of Miss Weston's theories may be open to question, there is no doubt that Eliot derived his background material from *From Ritual to Romance*, and used such Grail lore as he found in it, whether the interpretation of this material was correct or not; Eliot presumably accepted it. He seems to have been fascinated by the fertility rituals and by the examples of sympathetic magic quoted by Miss Weston from classical sources, especially the resurrection theme. It is possible that Eliot was attracted because of the extent of his own reading of classical and oriental authors, and because of his ideas concerning the universality of classical and medieval philosophy and culture.

The acceptance of the Grail motif is implicit in the title of the poem, but Eliot begins the 'Burial of the Dead' with a statement of the resurrection theme contained in a reference to the vegetation cycle which starts with germination in the Spring; the seeds have lain dormant, but now they must die to bring forth new life. However, this fertility is not always welcome:

> *April is the cruellest month, breeding*
> *Lilacs out of the dead land, mixing*
> *Memory and desire, stirring*
> *Dull roots with Spring rain.*
> *Winter kept us warm, covering*
> *Earth in forgetful snow, feeding*
> *A little life with dried tubers.*

This is, of course, a theme which became so recurrent in Eliot's work that it is almost a commonplace; a most obvious re-statement is made by the chorus of the women of Canterbury:

> *We do not wish anything to happen.*
> *Seven years we have lived quietly,*
> *Succeeded in avoiding notice,*
> *Living and partly living.*

It is this 'Living and partly living', this death-in-life or life-in-death, this hollow existence that constitutes a sort of moral and intellectual gelding, which is the curse on *The Waste Land*.

The structure of the poem is dominated by the almost cinematographic cutting from one scene or aspect to another.[3] The various themes are introduced in symphonic progression, stated, developed, thrust aside only to return sometimes in a major key, sometimes in a minor one, the whole somewhat disconnected at first, but gradually taking on a cohesion apparent only if the poem is accepted on Eliot's terms. The second theme is introduced in line 8, a déraciné theme involving an individual who lacks any worthwhile background save for a sterile social whirl. This scene fades into the *Waste Land* theme, stated in biblical terms, which in its turn fades to a scrap of song from *Tristan ünd Isolde* which combines within itself love, life, and death, and suggests a betrayal. Cut once again to the hyacinth girl in the hyacinth garden, possibly a reference to lost innocence, although we should remember that Hyacinth was a fertility goddess. Faced with this innocence/fertility which must needs be the 'heart of light', the narrator is very conscious of his half-life, and perhaps yearns for rebirth. Unfortunately, the Tarot pack, the means of foretelling the coming of the life-restoring waters, has itself been perverted and is used only by such as Madame Sosostris who doesn't even know the mysteries symbolised in the blank card; nevertheless, the drowned Phoenician sailor is turned up, which, with its embodiment of the Osiris resurrection myth, foreshadows some slight hope. Madame Sosostris, however, warns against a watery death, once again perverting the use of the Tarot, and expresses her own degradation by an allusion to the interest that the police have in her activities. She fades to be replaced by the waste land of the modern city peopled by dead or, even worse, half-living beings,[4] which in its turn leads to a reprise of the resurrection theme in the references to the burial of the corn god and to Osiris in the form of a dog.

A 'Game of Chess' opens with Cleopatra who, no matter what failures she may have brought about on the historical plane, at least opted for love and fertility. Soon, however, the parody of Enobarbus' words gives place to a description of the modern (? 1920) boudoir with all its '*strange synthetic perfumes*'[5]; this artificial atmosphere in all its unreality and infertility is mocked by the picture above the mantel.[6] The '*withered stumps of time*' silently comment, for although 'her hair', a fertility symbol, is '*spread out*', it is in '*fiery points*', burning with a sterile lust. Various fertility themes appear, '*the wind* under the door', 'my hair down', even the sea change in 'Those are pearls that were his eyes', but they all come to nothing since the rain is kept well away by the 'closed car at four'; the whole thing is a rather nasty charade whose sole *raison d'etre* is the game of chess. The satisfying of lust which seeks no fertility, and probably goes to endless lengths to prevent it, is reinforced by the abortion theme set in the pub, an abortion which has caused a loss of youth, which is regarded as a normal topic of conversation, and which is endlessly related despite the call to rebirth implicit in the publican's 'Hurry up please it's time', a call eventually silenced by Ophelia's good-night, the goodnight of yet another doomed to unfruitfullness and self-inflicted death, a good-night very reminiscent of a popular ditty.

The Fire Sermon begins with the river (water) motif. The river holds promise of salvation, but has been befouled; at the narrator's back is the waste land which manifests itself in the rat (*'we are in rat's alley'*), which disturbs the fisherman who combines in himself several manifestations of the lost leader theme, Coriolanus/ King of Naples/Fisher King. The sounds of civilization intrude, motor cars, Sweeney, Mrs Porter, and the ribald ballad mocks hope of salvation, since *'they wash their feet in soda water'*.[7] The cry of the nightingale leads to *'Mr Eugenides, the Smyrna merchant unshaven'*, one of Miss Weston's Gnostic Syrian merchants who spread knowledge of mystery cults; Mr Eugenides has lost his true purpose, although his ambiguos invitation seems to imply that he is still dealing in hidden mysteries of some different sort.

The bivalency of the situation is stressed by the development of the narrator who becomes Tiresias, the hermaphrodite, who watches over the seduction of the typist like a weary voyeur; neither of the two parties involved in the seduction is interested in the possibility of fertility, one being passive, the other full of wild and rather clumsy lust. There springs to mind the anecdote of the whore who always used to eat fish and chips.

A life/fertility theme is introduced by the *Tempest* quotation (1.257), which leads to the evocation of the living city – 'O City, city' etc. – the fishermen, traditionally close to the life-giving water and to the fish, symbol of eternal wisdom, preserve some vestiges of a life worth living with all its essential gaiety, and their church reflects the magnificence of their life and, by standing as a silent witness to the risen Christ, enriches the life of the surrounding community. Unfortunately, Magnus Martyr seems to be scheduled for demolition.

The description of the Thames is obviously derived from Wagner's *Götterdämmerung*. Some hope is evident as the tide turns – reference to the Isle of Dogs – but is cancelled out by the red sails.[8] The Elizabethan scene, Elizabeth and Leicester's relationship was rather sterile, cuts in: '*A gilded shell Red and gold.*' This is magnificent, but dead, since they are only going through the motions, and the 'gilded shell' gives the clue to the hollowness of it all, besides being somewhat reminiscent of 'whited sepulchres'. Each of the Thames maidens is seduced in her own way, and the river is polluted and seems to have become synonymous with the Styx. Finally, the shades of St Augustine and of Buddha are invoked to introduce the burning theme, burning (red?) with sin.

'Death by Water' introduces the Adonis/Attis/Osiris resurrection cult, derived from Miss Weston. The Phoenician is supposedly Mr Eugenides, according to several critics, but one wonders why this should be so. At least, someone is in the water and liable to be plucked out to general rejoicing. However, perhaps the resurrection is more in the category of serving up material used in 'Dans le restaurant'.

'What the Thunder Said' opens with a death theme – '*After the torchlight red on sweaty faces*' – but also announces the death which foreshadows new life. Thunder is heard in distant mountains, the lost leader seems to have managed to die, and 'We who were living are now dying with a little patience'. The approach to the Chapel Perilous introduces a Grail/J.L. Weston influence; all is barren and dead: '*But red sullen faces sneer and snarl*'. There is no water and the narrator longs for water, the '*hermit-thrush sings in the pine trees*' and lets his droppings fall (l. 357) (cf.6). At the limit of endurance, a shadowy figure appears (ll. 359–65). Is it the lost leader?

The European theme is blended into the approach to the Chapel Perilous, and still '*voices sing out of empty cisterns and exhausted wells*'. There seems confusion between the Chapel Perilous and the Cemetery Perilous (ll. 385–90), possibly due to Eliot's confusing them together after reading Miss Weston's book; they never occur together in Arthurian manuscripts, but either appears depending on the whim or source of the authors of the manuscripts.

Is the initiation ceremony (pure J.L. Weston) or surrender successful? It would appear so – '*Then a damp gust bringing rain*' heralds the storm which will bring a renewal of life, but still '*the limp leaves wanted for rain*'. The Thunder speaks as a result of the initiation/ surrender/ sacrifice: '*Datta, Dayadhvam, Damyata*'; Coriolanus revives for a moment – will the lost leader return? The boat responds, presumably to Coriolanus' '*hand expert with sail and oar*'.

Flashback to the narrator/Fisher King who now has the plain (*Waste Land*) behind him as he sits on the shore in touch with the water. The fact that he can even consider setting his lands in order suggests at least partial recovery of his fertility/virility. It is also suggested that there is need for speed, for he must act quickly before London Bridge does fall down. Various images are suggested; '*e Prince d'Aquitaine à la tour aboli*' is reminiscent of '*Child Roland to the dark tower came*'. At least something is left: 'These fragments I have shored against my ruins'; possibly these are the remnants of a lost culture.

Decision is taken; '*Why then, Ile fit you, Hieronymo's mad againe.*'[9] Like Hamlet, Hieronymo is only mad 'nor' nor' west', and is incapable of action while sane. He too presented his play, to reveal the vile secret of his son's death, and distributed the parts which are meaningless to the actors and to most of the spectators, but have hidden meaning – *Datta, Ddayadhvam, Damyata. Shantih, Shantih, Shantih.*

Perhaps the narrator (Eliot?) has passed through his personal dark night of the soul, his night in the Chapel Perilous, and has indeed found the progression which brings the peace which passeth all understanding, or perhaps he thought that he had.

No doubt, there is a possibility of the original version, free from Pound's editing, turning up in Eliot's papers; if so, it might throw some light with which to interpret more clearly his message, if any.

It is implicit in the poem that the poet himself is journeying on a quest through a waste land. It would be hard to establish it as fact in the case of every line, but there seems to be little that is original in the poem, save for the arrangement, and even that may be Pound's. Various debts are acknowledged in the notes, but many remain unacknowledged; one notices the Chaucerian derivations (ll. 1–2), the childhood trip to the archduke's (ll. 8–18),[10] even the conversation in the pub could have been reported second-hand. Granted that there may be original material, the poem, nevertheless, gives an impression of what Wavell called 'other men's flowers', a collage of other men's lines, plagiarized, imitated, parodied. If this were so, it would mark the culmination of disillusionment in Eliot, and the ending of the poem would foreshadow the profound change in attitude seen in his later work.

Othello

(Hibernia, November 1962)

So seldom is W. Shakespeare played in Dublin these days that one may tend to over-rate Mr Edwards' new production of *Othello* at the Gaiety.[1] But for me over-praise is less abhorrent than under-praise. And this production, though with many faults, shines with intelligence (to be expected of Mr Edwards), and with a feeling for the conflict between good and evil, which is rather less expected.

I have never subscribed to the view that the 'noble Moor' is wholly noble, in the sense, that is, that he is initially a phenomenon embodying all the virtues, who is then got at by the nasty Iago. I agree with Mr William Marshall's[2] decision to play Othello as a decent, kindly, rather childish fellow whose initial weakness is his acceptance of the ridiculous white Christian contention that his colour is something to be excused only on the grounds of his military prowess.

Early in the text, and in this production, it is established that Othello's wooing and winning of Desdemona is not merely the stock situation in which the lover carries off his lady in the face of parental opposition. It is made clear that the important issue, both for Othello and Brabantio, is Othello's colour. And so in marrying Desdemona, Othello is winning not alone a lover's victory but a racial victory. If we remember that Othello *himself* recognizes the oddity of the situation, concedes in fact that the palpably absurd and wicked notions of Brabantio have some validity, then it is not surprising that he should be so vulnerable when Iago sets about his devilry. Othello's real weakness is his concession to racialism. That established, Iago's work is easy. Let no one say that W. Shakespeare knew nothing about racialism. So far as I know he knew nothing about Sigmund Freud, but in *Hamlet* he presents, as well as much else, a classic case of mother-fixation. (The work of psychologists would be made easier if their patients were as articulate as Hamlet.) Certainly, in *Othello,* Shakespeare hammers home the fact of his hero's colour, and if we remember that Othello's hold on Desdemona has for him the quality of dream, it is all the more credible that he should batten on threats to that dream.

I should add that I am willing, if anyone cares enough to ask me, to support this reading of the play by direct references to the text. I should also add that

Mr Marshall's performance has helped me to it. He is, as yet, not a great Othello, but unlike others, I am not distressed by his sometimes eccentric pronunciations and rhythms. His '*cold, cold, my girl*' will go into my private anthology of unforgettable fragments of stage utterance. I say he is not yet a great Othello because he misses some of the agony of the final scenes, but that will come.

Mr Mac Liammóir's Iago is, except for some face-pulling and other nonsense, magnificently coherent. His Iago is clearly a third-rate con-man and crook in the grip of an illimitable evil which, at odd moments, he himself half understands. Iago's bewildering diversity of motives for villainy becomes understandable only if we grasp that, as Mr Mac Liammóir shows us, he himself does not know why he is engendering a 'monstrous birth'. Satan has taken possession of a trivial gangster and the fool must obey.

I might add that Mr Mac Liammóir's performance is finely unselfish and that the only occasion, at the end of Part Two, when he might seem to be hogging the stage, is perfectly justified in the context of his interpretation. He sits then at Othello's desk, like an exhausted medium, or more aptly, a debased Faustus, waiting for the next satanic infusion.

Of the other performances the most true, the least imitating, is Miss Eithne Dunne's Emilia, warm, shrewd, kindly. The Desdemona is blighted by ladylikeness, which is unfortunate since she has moments of pathos. The Cassio and the Roderigo differ little; which is enough said. I found the Carpaccio costumes and wigs enchanting. Mr Mac Liammóir's tights, however, were not skillfully designed.

Long Day's Journey into Night

(Hibernia, November 1962)

Aesthetically it is irrelevant as to whether or not a theatre festival shows a leaning one way or another religiously or philosophically. The fact remains that the first week of the Dublin Theatre Festival[1] was dominated by the Christian, even the Catholic, point of view.

To qualify: the first five plays I saw could only be appreciated by persons at least in touch with Christianity and, in three cases, with Catholicism. All five demonstrated that the absence or presence of religious faith is possibly the most exciting dramatic subject in the world. Without faith there is nothing. With it there may also be nothing.[2]

This reviewer has so often written abusively about the Abbey and its vulgar mendacity that it is a pleasure to be able to praise the new production of Eugene O'Neill's *Long Day's Journey into Night*, so much better than that of 1959 that it would be a waste of time to make sustained comparisons. With the same cast, almost the same set, and not quite the same audience, Mr Proinnsias MacDiarmada has achieved a reading of O'Neill's great play (yes, I've written 'great') which I, for one, do not hope to see bettered.

For one thing, he has brought out the play's inherent tautness and classic structure, has shown us that this play, far more than O'Neill's avowed attempts to imitate Greek tragedy, induces in a responsive audience that rare cathartic experience that purists refuse to recognize as occuring after the seventeenth century. O'Neill grounds and pulverizes four human hearts, and miraculously, when the long agonizing process is over, they seem more whole, less frail, brightened by suffering.

A drug-addict mother going mad, a selfish, miserly, vainglorious lout of a father, two sons, the one an alcholic womanizer, the other a dying consumptive: not, you might say, the likeliest matter for the workings of Grace (no, dear, she's *not* a character in the play).

But the beginning of redemption is honesty, and this sad family tortures itself into honesty, and the anaesthetic that makes the surgery possible is love, blood-love, the love which like sexual love can both destroy and make whole. The Tyrones are not made whole, but they have attained honesty, even in the case of the lunatic mother who in her final ravings apprehends what exactly has gone wrong with her life.

The blind and disgraced Oedipus, Lear reduced to babbling and blasphemy (what is more blasphemous than his condemnation of the generative act?), the Tyrones waiting on their own dissolution, but transfigured by their love for and dependence on each other: these are, for me, equally valid aspects of the central human predicament, which I take to be man's possesion of free-will and his bondage to the frailties within him. To keep the discussion in the Christian context, Lear and Hamlet are permitted by Elizabethan convention to die as soon as they attain Grace. The Tyrones are not. But I think anyone in touch with the Christian message must agree, that when the curtain falls on their blighted and soiled lives, they may not be going into night, but into the first pale light of dawn. They are waiting on Grace.

The piece is very finely acted. Miss Ria Mooney's performance I have praised before. It is better this time only because she is in better voice. Mr Philib O Floinn's Father is now quite remarkable. All his natural deficiencies as a player he has turned into assets. As the two sons Jamie and Edmund, Messrs T.P. MacCionnáith and Uinseann Ó Dubhlainn are, again given their natural limitations, equally impressive. Mr Ó Dubhlainn especially has improved beyond recognition. Behind this whole production I sense hard work and humility, and if only twice a year we had productions like this one, the long dark vigil of Mr Ernest Blythe might be justified (by a very lenient judge, of course).

Theatre Reviews

(Hibernia, December 1964)

The Lady of Belmont

First, a modest but well-intended posy to the Directors of the Abbey. Presumably they were responsible for the selection of St John Ervine's *The Lady of Belmont*, and though I'm quite prepared to swallow my words, this production may be the first breath of a change of wind in policy.

It is not that the play is of any great importance in itself. The dialogue lacks the distinction and poetic insight which alone can justify academic surmise about what happens to the characters in a play – in this case *The Merchant of Venice* – after the curtain falls. Very dated academic surmise it is too. (How many children had Lady Macbeth? What was that young pup Laertes up to in Paris? Where was Iago when the light went out?)

Nor are the situations, though adroitly contrived, either unexpected or inevitable. The moral, that the Jew may be more Christian than the professional believer, is lammed home without either style or conviction. I am as likely to be moved to passion as any man, by anti-Semitism, but the man who invented the word 'Eirish' lacks the intensity of vision, and in this play certainly lacks the satiric blade to deal other than in platitudes with a complex, and infinitely horrible manifestation of the Beast. (And I don't mean Alastair Crowley. I mean you and me and ours, *hypocrite lecteur*.)

Why then the bouquet? Because a large section of the Abbey Players are given for once an opportunity to spread their wings, to experiment with conventions of acting radically different from those most of them are used to, to speak for minutes at a time in standard English, and in all to extend their range as actors, even if it be only a trivial play.

They acquitted themselves in most cases tolerably, and Mr Rae Mac an Áilli's Shylock had, as one might expect from this most equipped actor, moments of grave pathos and a consistent patriarch's authority. Among the better performances were Mr Pilib O Flionn's Balthasar, a cunningly minor-key Malvolio, Mr Eamon Guailli's brash and well-spoken Bassanio, and Miss Bríd Ní Loinsigh's warm (if vocally stilted) Portia. Tomás Mac Anna's sets had colour (some gimcrack seats could have done with a lick of paint) and the costumes were worn with aplomb, considering that in many cases they were not built to measure.

I, a chicken among the Foxes, a page among the Paiges, yea, a 'J' amongst the 'Ks' (I can hardly say a snake among the Finnegans), have a suggestion to make. The Abbey might, with profit for all concerned, devote a month of its eleven-month season to the classics of the Anglo-Irish theatre, as we know it from 1700 to 1900. And, dare I say it, to Shakespeare? There are the precedents of a *Lear* (1928) and a *Coriolanus* (1936), in rather special circumstances, of a *Macbeth* (1934). But I am thinking of the comedies. What about Mr Guailli and Miss Máire Ni Chathain in the *Shrew*? I dream.

A Moon for the Misbegotten

Eugene O'Neill's last plays are intractable in the face of the conventional yard-sticks. They defy our usual notions about verbosity and sentimentality and construction and so on. And they demand from audiences an initial sympathy with all human wrack which knows love and mercy only in frail visitations, but knows them then with a passion that shames us.

The three chief characters of *A Moon for the Misbegotten* (Longford Productions and '37' Theatre, at the Gate), a trash Irish emigrant farmer, his would-be trollop of a daughter and their guilt-and-booze soaked landlord, are none of them the kind of people most of us care to have in our lives. They live in a twilit world where the normal beacons are loud talk and frenzied ribaldry: it seems at times as if O'Neill's people have only self-explanation and reciprocal scourging to enable them to hold on to sanity, and to the minimal decency required for continued existence.

But the sheer gusto of their rage against the dark endows them with a dignity not to be found in the safe 'good' people of lesser dramatists. O'Neill was a dramatist not by virtue of language, nor of a capacity to dominate harsh – and sometimes sentimentally – construed material, nor of an ability to hew pleasing shapes from the jagged stuff that fed his dominantly sombre imagination. He was great because he loved the misbegotten and managed to put that love on the stage. An incomparable intensity of feeling with his characters, even when they are most despicable, is the crucible that refines the over-plus of dross in language and situation and sentiment. We forgive the corn for the love.

This present play has the usual abundance of faults, notably in the language of sentiment. (How often O'Neill falls back on scraps of well-known verse in order to create mood!) But Miss Nora Lever's production takes them gamely, and she has drawn two admirable performances from Mr Arthur O'Sullivan as the shanty farmer, and Miss Anna Manahan as his daughter – the latter a marvellous demonstration of variety in unity, child, vixen, lover, madonna. All actors, of necessity, must play to the audience, otherwise they might as well stop at home and look at the mirror.

But watching Mr O'Sullivan and Miss Manahan, I was reminded of how seldom actors really play to each other. This couple do so, and are at moments almost unbearably touching. I am less happy about Mr Barry Cassin's playboy-drunk. A certain tone of whinge is certainly in character, but Mr Cassin, the night I saw him, had not yet solved the problem of sustaining interest in maudlinity.

Miss Lever handled the composite set of Messrs Noel McMahon and Fergal McCabe with great skill, except during a long passage when Mr O'Sullivan was divided vertically by a doorpost.

Brendan Behan's *The Hostage*

The first night of *The Hostage*, Mr Brendan Behan's new (to Ireland) version of *An Giall*, passed off quietly at the Olympia, in a production by Avis Bunnage (in association with Alan Brett). The name of Miss Joan Littlewood did not, in any connection, appear on the programme, and a good thing for her reputation that it did not. For this production of an interesting play was slack, gapped, groping and nervous (the players may have been intimidated by the prospects of Demonstrations).

With three exceptions, the playing was inadequate, with two exceptions, the singing amateurish and with no exception, the dancing painful. Mr Behan was not done proud, and it is a tribute to his play that it survived at all.

What then does survive? Mr Behan is by temperament an anarchist. His tactics are ridicule and half-truth, employed, it must be said, against the ridiculous and half-truthful. His bug-bear is humbug, his hatred of it his strength, and his complicity seen more clearly than in the slabs of processed 'history' with which we are regaled, as we watch the assembled grotesques and lay-abouts cavorting about a doomed English soldier. Against that is Mr Behan's unerring flair for cod. And there is its obverse; tenderness and respect for the pure in heart.

To my mind, *The Hostage* is more important than *An Giall* because it highlights innocence – two kinds of innocence, the hostage's and the skivvy's – against a more solid background of opportunism and knowingness.

It is a pity that Dublin should not have seen a better production of this sad, so very much alive, play. But Miss Peggy Marshall's madam, Miss Rhona Woodcock's skivvy, and Mr Brian Hewlett's soldier were rewarding.

Behan

(Hibernia, April 1964)

A few days before Brendan went on the Way of Truth, I had occasion to quote the first half of Act II, Scene iii of *Henry V*, that great passage in which Pistol announces the death of Falstaff to some of his old drinking companions:

> Bardolph, be blithe; Nym,
> rouse thy vaunting veins;
> Boy, bristle thy courage up;
>   for Falstaff he is dead,
> And we must yearn therefore.

The night of his death, five minutes after its announcement, those lines came back to me and I quoted them to an old and common friend. We both realized that in a sense Brendan was a Falstaffian character, heroic in his faults, heroic in his virtues. More than that, we realized that he was part of the fabric of our lives, someone to love and hate, to cherish and abuse, as inevitable and as permanent as the weather. It did not ever seem possible that, in one's own time, he would go on a one-way journey. His illnesses, though grave, were carried off with such self-mocking panache that they acquired, for most of us, an air of fantasy. We knew of course that he was, and for years had been, seriously ill. But his spirit seemed so indomitable, his physical resistance so infinite, that when finally the news came, it seemed cataclysmic, like a breach of the natural order.

Brendan would have laughed – is laughing – at so solemn a reaction of how I and others have felt at his passing. For he was an irreverent child where solemnity was concerned, in most of the matters of life. But he was a child, too, in his instinctive reactions against cruelty, meanness and injustice, and the various faces of humbug. So tenacious was he in his reactions, that shallow-minded persons, attributed humbug to him. They could not see that his external *persona* did not necessarily belie the legendary genuineness of his heart.

And this external *persona*: how harmless it was, except perhaps where he himself was concerned. This roistering, brazen-tongued public entertainer was merely the defensive obverse of the warm-hearted, generous, slightly unsure friend. And the generosity did not suddenly descend upon him with fame and success. It was with him as a grace even in those years of the late forties when I first knew him. He loved to give and he was not, even in recent years, ashamed to ask when he had temporary need. These are all generalizations about him. The particularities I have to offer are mainly too personal, and I would rather yearn for Brendan than contribute to the stockpile of anecdotes about his drinking adventures. But this detail may serve to illustrate an abiding aspect of his character. Five or six days before Brendan went to his last hospital, I met him by chance. He was not well, and so quiet. Suddenly he said, 'John, do you remember the time I brought you home?' I said I did. And then with that marvellous courtesy of his which never allowed him to forget the ramifications of family, he asked, 'How's the mother?'

When he'd gone, I suppose I knew subconsciously that this time he was truly ill and I asked the opinion of the doctor who was with me. He said, 'He looks like a man who has not slept for years.' Now he sleeps the sleep of peace, *somnium pacis*.

Lest We Forget

(Hibernia, 21 January 1977)

We are all anecdotal now. Two of my near coaevals have published books recently, which while they cannot be considered of the same genre, do depend to a great extent on anecdote. Mr John Ryan and Mr Anthony Cronin[1] might consider this a disdainful comment, but they have illustrious progenitors in George Moore and Yeats. Both of them deal with Brendan Behan, the first with affection and a sense of joyful living, the second with acerbity and a perhaps undue stress on Brendan's streak of sadism.

I can claim to have known Brendan intimately before his international success, though my introduction was a proxy one from the now famous American novelist, Terry Southern, who was astonished that I did not, as a Dubliner, know very much about him. In my next piece I'll say a little about Brendan as I knew him.

But it was at least three years before I met Brendan and two before I heard his name, '*Jimmy Bourke*', from Christine Longford, who lived around the corner from me, in a somewhat larger house.[2] Not until 1949, the year of my first encounter with B.B., did I learn that his maternal uncle, Peadar Kearney (also Séamus de Burca's), was the author of the National Anthem ... And I had been ten years with the Christian Brothers. Brendan was intensely proud of his Uncle Peadar's authorship and of his friendship with Michael Collins. The Behan reverence for Collins is carried on by Brendan's mother, the indestructible, incorrigible Mrs Kathleen Behan. It is worth remembering that complex loyalties survived the insanity of the Civil War.

Brendan was also very proud of his maternal aunt's marriage into the Bourke theatrical family.[3] I cannot recall meeting any Bourkes on a memorable Christmas/New Year spree, '49-'50, when Brendan took me the rounds of his eccentric family circle. Quite frankly, this rumbustious, grand design of disorder was novel to me. At nineteen my experience of high living and uninhibited thinking was limited to the *salons* held in 'the Catacombs',[4] a den of iniquity invented by Brendan in his *Confessions of an Irish Rebel*, and perpetuated by Mr Ulick O'Connor: I could name two well-known academics who, if 'not available for comment', could testify as to the innocence of the proceedings.

So at nineteen I was on the rim of the milling Behans, of which more later. At the moment I am concerned with Seamus de Burca's[5] latest publication, a collection of letters written by Peadar Kearney to his wife, Eva O'Flanagan, from Ballykinlar Internment Camp, in the period April–November, 1921.[6] It would be cant to hail these letters as of high literary merit. They are pallid and repetitive and pious to the point of being pietistic. But there are other merits than the purely 'literary'. Because of censorship regulations and Peadar's own conviction that it was best to write only 'domestic' letters, they contain no startling revelations, and scant information about fellow-internees.

Peadar Kearney was clearly not an 'ordinary' man, if the word means anything, but he was an ordinary man in that he pined for his Eva and his two young children, Pearse and Conn, and was not above some petulance when parcels arrived late or letters were too short or too infrequent. Next to his wife, he seems to have been closest to his sister, Máire, and his brother-in-law, Michael Slater. But artless and often naive as some of the letters are, there are occasions when he is moving, simply *because* he is writing hastily and from the heart with no premeditated effect.

The passages in question are not easily quotable, unless one can divine the writer's curiously faded Dublin idiom. There is the slightly genteel reference to his bowel movements: '*I had been without butter for some time, as I think I have been going more bread and butter lately than usual*' (almost every second letter has a reference to butter: the Kearneys evidently did not live by bread and dripping, the staple of many poor Dublin families, but then Peadar was a house-painter by trade, like his second brother-in-law, Stephen Behan, and Brendan).

Peadar took over as Camp Librarian from Henry Dixon, but although 'books' are often mentioned, the only volumes he writes of are O'Neill's *Irish Music*, 'a little book of Scotch airs', a prayer-book in Irish, and *Duanaire na Gaeilge*. The only writers he mentions are Henley and W.S. Gilbert. Was it that 'Dear Eva' was simply not interested in books?

More About Brendan

(Hibernia, 4 February 1977)

In his biography of Brendan Behan[1], which though factually not impeccable and with understandable indecorum, is a valuable book, Ulick O'Connor records how, in the last days of his life in the Meath Hospital, a bottle of brandy was acquired by Brendan. The name of the culprit is well known. Yet in November 1968, in Tripoli, Libya, an Irish poet told me he had heard from another Irish poet that I was the idiot responsible. I think it is time thirteen years after his death, and within weeks of what would have been his fifty-fourth birthday, to nail that cruel slander.

But association with Brendan tended to breed misunderstandings and lies. This particular slander might have its origins in the fact that less than two years before, when Brendan was in Baggot Street Hospital, his wife Beatrice told me not to give him a glass of brandy. Nor did I. My visit was not comfortable. I had, a couple of months before seen the Renaud-Barrault production of the version made of *The Hostage* by Georges Wilson. I began to talk about *L'Orage* (which of course is a play by Paul Claudel), but Brendan roared, '*Un Otage*', though he knew perfectly well I had made an understandable slip. This gave him the cue to attack me for being a friend of Patrick Kavanagh, which was true, but also of 'sitting up in McDaids' abusing him, which was quite untrue. I discovered that the source of this lie was an Irish composer who for many years had had for Brendan what used to be called a 'crush'. This is the composer mentioned, but not named, in Mr O'Connor's book.

O'Connor is, by the way, incorrect in saying that Kavanagh hated Behan even after his death. I can recall him enjoying *Hold Your Own and Have Another*,[2] and saying, 'Poor fellow, he had some talent', a statement that in Kavanagh's idiom was not ungenerous.

I have told in my obituary, 'Brendan', in *Hibernia*, the circumstances of our last meeting, which was in McDaids the week before he entered hospital. (This fact makes nonsense of the allegations by Ulick O'Connor and by Beatrice Behan that no-one could wear him in his old haunts.) He spoke, disconnectedly, about his infant daughter and about events of 1950, known only to myself and him. As I said in the last issue, I met him first months after I had been quizzed about him in Paris by Terry Southern. In the late spring or early summer of 1950, he would call at my home, always, I was told, perfectly sober, tidily dressed, although without a tie. My late father described him as seeming to be 'an ordinary Dublin working-man'. I was a twenty-year-old student with scarcely more money than himself. On the few occasions I was in, we would go to a pub on the canal near Portobello Barracks, and drink glasses of Smithwick.

So many people have been afraid to raise their voices when Brendan has been branded as a sexual glutton that I prefer now not to be counted among them. Yes, he had what he called a 'shine' for me. It can hurt only me to say this now, but I doubt it. At the time some people suspected this, and resented me for it. Brendan had the knack, and the curse, of making his friends, male and female, unhealthily acquisitive. Self-inflation is the occupational risk of those who reminisce about the notorious. But I can do some service to Brendan by recording that, although I saw him behave brutally and loutishly in various circumstances (I saw him smash the glasses of a friend of ours when he knew he would be half-blind without them), where his affections were concerned he was different and utterly unsophisticated. Perhaps the truest index to his confused emotional nature is the short story, 'After the Wake' which appeared in Sinbad Vail's Paris magazine, *Points.*

My brief sketch of my relationship with Brendan is justified only in so far as anything about any artist worth considering is of interest. To me, Brendan is interesting as much as a social phenomenon as he is as a writer. I have little patience with the 'If only' school of criticism.

If Brendan, this school says, had not been an alcoholic, if he had not been sexually bent, if he had not been a jailbird, if he had not been a Republican, and so on, he would have been a great writer. A great writer of what? I suggest that he is not a great writer, but only a very good one, with glaring faults. But the work of any writer is what it is because of the nature of the man. Dismiss Behan completely, rather than dream up an hypothesis.

The Quare Fellow[1]

(Hibernia, 31 August 1978)

Behan's status as a dramatist has not yet been resolved, fourteen years after his death. There is so much in his plays that is slapdash, inchoate, and struggling, there are so many fleetingly topical allusions, that the printed texts give sparse testimony to the excitement, the wildness, they can engender in performance.

At once we must consider the camp that holds Miss Joan Littlewood responsible for the perversion of Behan's genius (a term I use in the loosest possible sense). Mr Simpson, who with Ms Carolyn Swift created the first production of *The Quare Fellow* at their Pike Theatre in 1954, deals with this question sensibly in his introduction (*erratum*, dear Alan: P.J. Bourke was Brendan's uncle by marriage, not his cousin). Though he does not say so, Behan owed as much to him and Ms Swift for their mounting of *The Q.F.* as he owed to Ms Littlewood for the creation of *The Hostage* in 1958. I must be personal here: there is nothing in the printed texts of either play nor, for that matter, Mr Simpson's masterly reconstruction of *Richard's Cork Leg* in 1972, which I do not recognize as if not literally authentic Behan, something as important: imaginatively authentic Behan.

Brendan's mind was like a stock-pot. In it, literature and many cultures and sub-cultures, including the sub-culture of blue innuendos and dirty stories indigenous to Dublin, Northside and Southside (an indecent story not used by Mr Simpson for *Cork Leg*, but included here in an appendix of rejected passages, involving nuns and a castrated donkey I heard thirty-five years ago on the Southside), were stirred up with intuitions, sometimes sound, sometimes jaundiced in expression, of all classes of Irish society.

Some Irish have taken exception to the expansion and 'distortion' of *An Giall* (1958) (Pádraig Ó Siochrú's translation should have been included here) into *The Hostage*. The chief objection would appear to be to 'Rio Rita' and 'Princess Grace'. But Brendan knew well Dublin's gay underworld (as well as its more classy counterparts in 'respectable' society). He probably saw the film *Rio Rita* with Bebe Daniels when he was a child. And it was totally true to form that he should have called a black homosexual 'Princess Grace'. In doing so he was cocking his snook at those Irish who thought that the sun shone out of the Irish-American film-star's firmament.

I had thought both *Q.F.* and *Hostage* might have dated. Capital punishment does remain on the statute books, but we don't practise it. But *Q.F.* retains its power and its priceless gallows humour, as well as some characters who have earned their place in the long gallery of Irish theatrical portraits of the off-beat and the zany. Behan, who certainly owed much to O'Casey's early plays, was also steeped in Dickens, the great master in English of splendid and enriching low life. He also owed much to Joyce, as may be seen from the discussion on the physical effects of hanging in Act One of *Q.F.* Though the political situation in the North has changed radically in twenty years, *Hostage* is still close enough to the situation that has existed since 1922 to be relevant on a national level, and broad enough in its sweep of sympathies to matter on an international level.

Mr Simpson describes *Cork Leg*, which he created at the Peacock just six years ago, as the writer's 'theatrical last will and testament' (thought he does not mention it was (allegedly) envisaged as a play in Irish, *Lá Breá sa Roilig*). He is right. There is, if not all Behan here, a good deal of him. He loved Dublin malapropisms (his are better than Sheridan's) and he loved the godlike – as when Chesterton talks of Dickens's *'godlike horseplay - confusion of moonstruck illiteracy'*. Almost my favourite line in Irish theatre is Maria Concepta's *'Blessed Evelyn Waugh. She was a young girl that wouldn't marry Henry the Eighth because he turned Protestant.'* (But how many Irish or English would catch the reference to the Jesuit martyr Edmund Campion – now canonized – about whom Waugh wrote a classic book?)

The remaining plays are three short sketches: *Moving Out* and *The Garden Party*, commissioned by RTÉ in 1952, and *The Big House*, commissioned by the BBC Third in 1957, of which the published text first appeared, not, as stated here, in the *Evergreen Review* in 1961, but in Sean J. White's *Irish Writing* (no. 37, 1957). The first two, clearly autobiographical, are far beyond the run of domestic comedies we get on our beloved Home Station, and the third has a note of gut in his portrayal of the Dublin spiv 'Chuckles Genockey' which offsets the caricature of his landed victims, the 'Baldcocks'. There is a tinge of sadism in his treatment of this pair, not unlike that often found in *'Blessed Evelyn Waugh'*. There was more nor a smack of Basil Seal in Brending Behing.

I do not think that he was a 'great' dramatist, even within the context of the twentieth century. Yet there were nuggets of greatness in him. From the brambles and the dung shines the light of his splintered *persona*, joyous, naive, melancholic, permeated with the sense of living's acid and Turkish Delight. Excellent value at the price, the book has also a Select Bibliography by the indomitable Professor E.H. Mikhail.

II
BLOOD, POETRY, P.K., K.O'B.
AND HEANEY

The Haemorrhage

(i.m. Gainoris Cristi 1922–1964)[1]
(from Blood and Stations)[2]

Sticky scarlet stuff that one read about in thrillers and war books and had heard about as a child from conversations between childbearing women who thought that this child, so bloody a child on this gay and squalid Christmas Day, was too young to understand. And I'd heard about it too in the sanatorium but never had seen it, for I was, supposedly, at any rate, a simple cure.

And now I was seeing it gush out of my own scrawny throat, something between tomato sauce and the purple of cardinals, on Christmas Day in the comparatively luxurious bathroom of a comparatively luxurious flat high above the indifferent plane trees of a Barcelona square. Gainor, I offer you this fragment of nightmare because you were in at the near-kill as it were, when the first spasm took me in San Fernando over Christmas dinner and you gave me your snowy handkerchief and I promised to have it washed and returned, and I never did, and now you are dead, and perhaps as I write, disputing varieties of nectar with Brendan and Seán.[3]

You remember we were listening to the Clancy Brothers, you and I and Pamela[4] and the Captain's Daughter and a Young Englishman, when the call came from the Square of the Plane Trees, and I went, joyous in the transition from one cherished company to another.

The cardinal's sauce happened in the bathroom. I tried to conceal the evidence with a bath-towel and went back to the others and I don't know what they were talking about because, like the man in Mairtín Ó Cadhain's great story 'An Pionta', I had seen the blood… but unlike him, my own. I can't honestly say that worse was to happen, because for me there couldn't have been. But the second time there were three witnesses to the maroon torrents that fouled carpets and chair-covers and bespattered Pearse Hutchinson[5] and Séamus Ó Fearghail who were mercifully and mercilessly present.

So in the small hours they drove me from clinic to clinic and doctor to doctor, but the clinics had no room and the doctors were not in. San Esteban was not praying for me, and my godson Stephen Ryan[6] was still in his cradle. We carried with us a pot of my blood, and hysteria was relieved by blasphemy. And at last to a great Barcelona hospital. For the first time I was to be a patient in a teaching hospital and not a night-guest in the residencies of interns. Ah, Rotunda and Holles Street and St Vincent's – had you seen me then! I have, thank God, been a figure of farce many times in my life, but never more so than then when, after the interns, taking time off from their seasonal refreshments, had subjected me to an amusingly speculative examination, I was lifted into a bath-chair and wheeled through the stony arcades of the Hospital to death or worse.

Alone in the darkness of a huge ward which was wrongly, unhumanly, silent, no grunts, no groans, no snores, no eerie intimations of where you are now, Gainor, I was afraid. And I wanted to urinate. Downstairs and back along the stony corridors I stumbled in my bare feet, and there the intern called Bach found me and chided me for risking pneumonia and told me where to go. What an ignoble piece of work is man, that the passing of filthy water should allay briefly all anxiety, all memories, all hopes of future joy. Too briefly. No sleep. And I woke trembling to what seemed the most extraordinary sound I had ever heard. A hard monotonous woman's voice chanting mysterious words and the distant growl of male voices in response. Dear God, it was Sister Someone giving out the Rosary to sleepy, disgruntled, reluctant men, and giving it to them up the banks and down the braes. Up and down through the intercommunicating wards of the Stomach Unit she went and she seemed to be knelling my doom. As she progressed from 'my' ward out of sight, a little monkey of an Andalusian made mocking faces and gestures and then the ritual ended and life began. I was to love Sister Someone.

I was in my shirt, of course, and my jacket and trousers and overcoat and glamorous new scarf and dressy tie were piled higgledy-piggledy on the floor beside the bed. There was also a basin. The last of the cardinal's sauce went into it. At this stage it had taken on the comparatively innocuous appearance of vomited red wine. That's what it is, I told myself, that's what it is. I suddenly had a desert thirst. An anonymously uniformed man whom I took to be an orderly was passing through carrying in either maw a glass vessel of a shape I was to become familiar with. It looked like a monster *porrón,* the narrow-spouted jar from which Spaniards drink wine. The right maw had a *porrón* of amber-yellow wine which, I decided, must surely be urine, and the left carried a *porrón* of dark red wine, which was to fox me for a few days until I learnt of the technicalities of kidney diseases. Needless to say I began to cheer up and called for a glass of water. I got it, and it was the last for several days.

Eight, nine, ten o'clock – I had no watch – the intern Bach came, a comfortable chubby young man who gave me an injection in the bottom (no terror this for an old hand like me), told me I could have no natural nourishment liquid or solid, until further orders, of course must not smoke, and that *los amigos* had come to see me. He also said something about *how* I would be fed which I did not grasp.

So in they came, *los amigos,* Pearse and Séamus, and trooper that I am, I tried to perk up. They, like me, were highly tickled by the giant *porrónes* of wine and looked as if they could do with a drop of the real thing. For all they knew, they had an imminent corpse on their hands, and there is little question but that contacting consulates, who contact embassies, who contact relatives, who in turn make contact with stunned families, is a dreary and traumatic experience. Knowing their thoughts, I expressed preference for dandelions, a favourite of Pearse's, although I am not at all sure that dandelions grow in Spain. I also asked for my luggage to be brought from my hotel. I might as well make a clean and gay death, like Mabel Beardsley as recreated by Yeats. Then Bach came in again, and Pearse dazzled him with his Catalan. From this magnificent demonstration of the solidarity of small nationalities, there emerged one solid fact – that I would be fed intravenously. And after the dear ones had gone, I was: through an ugly contraption to which I was attached by a homely body with whom I exchanged nonsenses about the beauty of Spain and the splendour of Barcelona. (*Nuestra Señora de la Merced* tonight!)

It took about forty minutes for the huge jar of pale yellow liquid, which was my food, to drip through the puncture-slit in my arm. And since it was still, so to speak, Christmas Day in the Workhouse, the other patients, who appeared to have nothing at all wrong with them, were served veal cutlets and oranges. Oranges. A good orange. A character in a story of mine claims that there's nothing she likes better than a good orange. As I watched the steady drip of my food, the world seemed to contract into a good orange. I looked yearningly at the Andalusian monkey who was into his second, and no doubt my eyes said, 'There is all Jaffa and her charms in the cusp of your hand.'

The needle was removed and the beast was fed. Then Bach again, now with Sister Someone. This splendid woman, whose congregation and name in Religion I was not to know until the day I left, was to all outward appearances a nun. But the starch-framed woman within had brilliant black eyes and a coppery skin, and like the solitary artistic treasure in a mendicant community: one fulgent gold tooth in an indifferent denture. And her voice was gentle, not that fearsome rattle of the Morning Rosary. She nodded approvingly as Bach told me in French that they were moving me to a private room 'where I would be more comfortable'. So I dressed and feeling all of a sudden overwhelmed with hysterical and tearful gratitude I went into a solitude which never, in the week that followed, was absolute, except in the mid of night, for dear ones, and less dear but no less welcome ones, were to come, and I have always adored doing the gallant soldier act.

I think it was before my first blood transfusion that Pearse came back with my suitcase and my first after-the-kill visitor, whom I will call Omar, because although he did not bring me a jug of wine, he did bring me a book – no, two books – and one of his true names *was* Omar. He was a gentle American, as you were, are, and will be for all eternity, dear Gainor, not all platinum perhaps, but not your distorted image as reflected, supposedly, in a notorious best-seller.[7]

From then until I left, the memories are jumbled. Doctors, bigwigs and interns, came and went and came again and this almost bare forked animal was palped, pummelled, often pulverised by all shapes and weights of fingers poking at its abdomen. A good deal of fun was had by all, even me. Pearse was almost always there, even when 'clinics' were being held over my body. He and various specialists were apt to digress into Catalan discussions which seemed to have little to do with My Body. But It got more than a fair share of attention. It seems that they did not know what it was that was wrong with It. And you, Gainor, who before the kaleidoscope to be described sank into my fantasy, had gone back to Madrid, will be interested in the clinical concern as to the colour of my body-waste. Because, like most intelligent men, you had a cloacal imagination and treasured the aesthetic, spiritual, and corporeal aspects of a good 'poop'. To cut a long – sometimes it seemed *so* long – story short, they pressed me continually about the colour of my *caca*. You remember the old yarn about Matisse, how his magistral last statement was supposed to have been '*Je veux du rouge et du vert*'. And how the wit said, he really meant, '*Je veux un verre de rouge*'. Well, I'm no Matisse, but I often longed for a glass of red wine while I discussed with these lads the colours of my *caca*. Since they had only my word for it, I could range the spectrum (within reason), always, and truthfully, stopping short of the sinister black. They were specially happy the day I announced *amarillo*, and I knew that even on what was by then a milk diet, *amarillo* meant substantial progress. A major victory was gained when I rang the changes on chocolate.

There was also a colour problem based on my own somewhat incoherent account of what had come up. Each visiting team was a further goad to my desire for absolute descriptive accuracy. But this form of inquisition got boring, and I resorted to the colour of my pyjamas, which happened to be a kind of orangey tomato. I'm inclined now to think that those grave dark heads would have been just as satisfied, in the early stages, if I had said sky-blue pink.

All this was part of the lighter side of things. One couldn't really take seriously the colour of filth now condemned by the body to the sewers of Barcelona. And even if it were one's own blood that was concerned, the body had disowned that too.

But if it had, it needed replenishment. And being like its owner, somewhat peculiar, it needed one of the rarer kinds of replenishment. The hospital had it handy for the first transfusion. Then there was a class of a panic. The Dear Ones were all summoned and asked if they had my blood group. Most of them didn't know, and, God bless them, volunteered to be tested. In the end I think only one was tested, and she big with child. I found this touching and valiant, and in the event futile. I will have to confess that the thought of passing out for want of a drop of blood depressed me more than somewhat. But as various persons were assisting at my bedside, they also suitably depressed, the adorable Bach burst in, rosy cheeks triumphant, his black eyes back-lit with celestial radiance, his baby jowl a-quiver with import, and '*Nous avons trouvé un prêtre catalan!*'

Tell me this and tell me no more, Gainor, wouldn't you be startled by such an announcement? In the first gust of disbelief I stupidly failed to see that if I were in *articulo mortis*, it wouldn't have mattered if the priest were a Martian, let alone a Catalan. I also failed to see that Bach, comfortable well-fleshed Bach, was hardly likely to be a cheerful harbinger of the Four Last Things.

Nor was he. Later that day the blood of a Catalan priest ran in my veins, I think, Gainor, it was pumping in when you first came with Pamela. I think, too, you had fortified yourself with the kind of courage wholly congruous to an American of Dutch extraction. Ah, the angels by my bedside, the doctors in the morning, the Dear Ones in the afternoon, even one or two of them in the evening, and like the saint she was, is, and forever will be, Sister Someone glided in periodically and said, if I happened to be getting my serum or having blood put in, 'He is good, very good.' It is notorious that the very weak cry easily. Each visit of Sister Someone left my eyes pricking, but happily my salad tears were soon quenched by some bout of nonsense, usually precipitated by the homely body who first serum-fed me. She had a bedside manner of excessive absurdity and I fear that she was not efficient in her insertions – the needle was always coming unstuck. But what could all that matter with a woman who described the German nation as *Muy filharmonico*?

I cannot say that the hospital was harmonious in its total workings. Everyone did his or her job, but there was a notable tendency towards what I began to think of as crash-courses. For instance, it was surely not necessary that while I was being serum-fed and unable to move one arm, or for that matter my whole body, some bright young Miss should bounce in and roguishly brandish an obscene test-tube for the purposes of a urine analysis. Heavens, when I think of the day when there were four females in the room, one wanting my urine, one wanting my blood, one wanting to stick a needle in my rump, and the philharmonic lady setting up my feeding apparatus. *Nessun maggior dolor* ... I must reverse that old Dante tag. For there is no greater pleasure than to remember in happiness, past misery. And it was truly miserable to have driven home to one the frailty, the sheer bloody worthlessness of the body. I had no beautiful physique to be wrecked in a week. I had no golden tan to glow away into pallor. But it wouldn't have mattered if I had been the David of Michaelangelo. And to think people can fall in love with a little crudded milk, fantastical puff-paste.

The Sunday you and Pamela drove back to Madrid, almost the first thing you must have done, Gainor, was to send me a card, telling me to take care of myself and get well, and signed 'S.D.' – Sebastian Dangerfield, that early alias of yours which was later purloined for a work of fiction: perhaps, fundamentally, fiction is immoral, an affront to the totality of a human being. That book about you knew nothing of your gentleness, of your courtesy, of your sedate wildness. The other day I spoke about you to an Irish boy, told of your card, and God bless us and save us only a monstrous fear of being dubbed unmanly held back the salt from my eyes. And it was salt dredged up from the heart, Gainor, and not distilled from alcohol. (I was always a bit weak on chemistry.) O, they didn't do you proud in that city where you made and confounded myths! They didn't even spell your name right. Though not quite as bad as the English wench who thought your name was 'Gaiter'.

What strange conjunction of stars was it, Gainor, that on the feast of St Stephen, your other first name, I should bleed? Ah well, I got better and took a little care. The body was found to be medically sane, no lesions, no ulcers, no diagnosis at all, except that maybe something had burst in the oesophagus. God was very good to me and I am intellectually grateful. But I tasted my own blood and so I will never be the same again.

So from serum and milk to meagre solids and the furtive fag. The injection three times a day and often the third was given after midnight, when I was just about to drift with that blessed tide that only insomniacs can truly fathom. One night a handsome lady looking like a female doctor in a television serial gave me two injections. I asked why two, and I declare to my God, she replied (in Spanish), 'So make you look more beautiful.' It would seem that the nursing jargon is international, like love.

After a few days I forgot to worry about health and began to worry about money. Drugs, X-rays a private room – surely a small fortune? Several persons separately interviewed Sister Someone, Bach and others. Only you, Gainor, ascertained from Sister Someone the incredible truth. For, of course, they charged me nothing. Back in dirty Dublin my enemies were attempting to confound me. In Barcelona, that city of the blind, as I once called it some ten years ago, I felt perfect security in the last twenty-four hours of my hospitalization. I think were it not for the necessity of earning my living, and of course of concealing my haemorrhage, I would have accepted their invitation to stay on for further 'tests'. You and Pamela had gone, Gainor, but I knew there would always be Pearse and Séamus and Patricia and the Captain's Daughter and Cionnait Ó Liatháin and Antonio and María Antonia and the exquisite Turull. And I could go on reading detective stories in French and dipping occasionally into harder matter, and there would be letters from the Dear Ones keeping me in touch with the mushroom City of Dublin, the goings-on of the young poets, the peregrinations of various hearts with whom I have nothing in common but possession of a similar organ. Something similar.

The last day broke. The last *porrón* of urine was removed and, feeling splendidly rich, I gave the orderly 75 *pesetas*. It was like leaving a hotel, and he asked me if I had been content during my stay.

Pearse came to fetch me, and Sister Someone was about like a great bird in snow. She seemed anxious, perhaps was, either to hold on to me or to see the last of me. I thanked her, she said 'for nothing', and then through Pearse I asked for her name in Religion and the name of her Order. She was, she said, and her coppery face seemed gold, of the Sisters of Charity of St Anne, and her name was Purificación. And Purificación asked if in Ireland there were hospitals with such services, and in this she was truly Spanish. She meant, of course, if sick foreigners received such exemplary treatment. I had to admit that I didn't know, and I didn't think so. Dear Gainor, you will remember Purificación, and I trust that as you lay dying into our hearts and memories, the Religious that held you was of the warmth of Purificación.

So then to the taxi and the wonderful crisp January sunlight, and the last *rendezvous* and the first cup of coffee since Christmas Day. Of course, Toni Turull drove me to the airport, and that night I was back among the snide faces with their mean tricks and their unimpassioned jealousies, and their ignorance of purification.

I do not know very much about love, Gainor, but I think I must have loved you. I give you this, and to Pamela, but only in the next dimension of eternity can I return your snowy handkerchief.

Playa Rabasada,
25th September/ 1st October 1964.

Mr Kavanagh's Progress

(Studies, Autumn 1960)

'The people didn't want a poet, but a fool:
Yes, they could be doing with one of those.' *The Green Fool* (1938)

'The story of the heifer that came back is nearly symbolic of my life. I have failed
many times to get my cattle to the fair.'

– Ibid.

It would be foolish for the present writer to pretend that he is not personally
acquainted with Mr Patrick Kavanagh. It would be even more foolish to write
about him as if his slight acquaintance gave any right to attempt an authoritative
interpretation of a small but very difficult body of work, on the grounds of
extraneous assumptions as to character or personality.[1] What follows, it is
hoped, is based on nothing other than the evidence of texts, and as far as is
humanly possible, the estimate offered will be uninfluenced by that folk-lore
which is Dublin's special contribution to the misunderstanding of genius,
whether or not the genius be comprehensive (as with Yeats) or fragmentary and
erratic (as with Kavanagh).

Patrick Kavanagh's first volume of poems was *Ploughman and Other Poems* (Macmillan, 1936). He was thirty-one and still living in Monaghan, where he
practised the craft of cobbler and farmer. *Ploughman* shows evidence of a small but
pure talent, remarkably unclogged by the mists (fairy and mental) which, together
with stage-winds, property moons and stars, and synthetic twilights, make the
going and the visibility so difficult in the bulk of minor Irish verse he might as a
neophyte well have imitated. He does, admittedly, in one poem see Thomas Aquinas
in the wind-spaces, but that in itself is a healthy sign, when he might have been
seeing one of the amoral ladies of our Saga literature, or even, under Æ's
influence, the Earth Mother. (Mother Earth and the Earth Mother embody two
vastly different efforts of the imagination.) The chief significant of Mr Kavanagh in
1936 – and in 1960 for a good many foolish people – was that he was an autodidact (so far as poetry was concerned) who worked on the land and wrote verses. I
hazard, in humility, the guess that for some years Mr Kavanagh was immature

enough to play up to a drawing-room conception of the primitive. In *The Green Fool*
he tells us of 'a couple of villainous journalists': 'The latter never missed an opportunity of putting a lurid paragraph in the Sunday newspapers about me. I must be
an interesting character, I thought. So I decided that in future if I was to be exploit-
ed I should do the exploiting myself.'

I should not be surprised if Mr Kavanagh flinches at a bare reference to, let
alone quotation from, *The Green Fool*. Much of it makes painful reading, especially
those pages in which he records his opinions of Irish contemporaries. The Kavanagh
of 1960 can scarcely wish to recall that he was once an admirer of F.R. Higgins,
'one of the best of the young Irish poets'.

But *The Green Fool* cannot be written off as a young man's aberration. It is Mr
Kavanagh's most successful attempt at sustained prose narrative, to my mind of
greater merit than the novel *Tarry Flynn* (The Pilot Press, 1948) which covers a deal
of the same ground. The latter book has perhaps more cohesion, but it is rather more
self-regarding, and lacks the bright and clear transfer effects of *The Green Fool*. And in
this openly autobiographical book there are laid bare the elements of Kavanagh, the
pieties and predispositions that have been the sustenance of his talent and the architecture of its products. In his later verse Mr Kavanagh has not been afraid of walking
naked, as in the beautiful poem 'I Had a Future', of which more later. The chief value
of *The Green Fool* may be the revelation, almost embarrassingly authentic, of a mind at
once cunning and naïve, suspicious and trusting. I suppose the unsatisfactory term
'peasant' has to be brought in, sooner or later. *The Green Fool* demonstrates how devious the mind of the peasant can be, and yet how simple when it is released from traditional bondages of land and cattle and family. But it is Mr Kavanagh's mind I am trying to write about, and only quotation and commentary can illustrate that.

Even in this early book there are inklings of his later strengths as a poet. Here
he is on the subject of a pig-killing: 'It was a memorable morning; the blood of
dawn was being poured over the hills and of that other blood we only thought how
much black-pudding it would make. Our talk had the romantic beauty of reality.
We were as close to life and death as we could be.'

I can think of no other writer who could get away with a phrase like 'the
romantic beauty of reality'. But in no other writer would so flabby a phrase have
the backing of a red sky at morning juxtaposed with the blood of stuck-pigs. It will
be seen, I hope, that Mr Kavanagh has adhered, increasingly through the years, to
the extreme form of the doctrine of 'meanest flower' as subject-matter for the
imagination. Much of this essay will be given to demonstration of his growing
awareness of his own inmost preoccupation, and of his attempts, sometimes
successful, to create poems, emblematic or discursive, on the theme of ripening
consciousness. It might be said as a general proposition of any worthwhile poet,
that he struggles to establish to his own satisfaction the nature of reality. Mr

Kavanagh's peculiar status as a poet depends very largely on the freshness of his rediscovery of an axiom. He is archetypical.

*   *   *

Mr Kavanagh, I believe, is not favourably disposed to the book by which he is best known, *A Soul for Sale* (London 1947). This volume includes the long poem *The Great Hunger*, originally published by the Cuala Press in 1942, and the occasion of a mild scandal. It may be worthwhile to indicate the virtues and oddities of what must remain an important part of the skimpy contribution, outside Joyce and George Moore, made by Irish Catholics to the literature of the English-speaking world.

Despite its adventures with authority, *The Great Hunger* is, in substance as well as in structure, a morality. It is about the perversion of the Catholic teaching on sex and marriage, as portrayed in the life of a small farmer Patrick Maguire. The first line '*Clay is the word and clay is the flesh*' announces this perversion in a complex way, which I have not seen noted. Mr Kavanagh may dislike the critical method known as explication, but I'm afraid his own work needs a good deal of it. The fact that the Word was, and forever is being made Flesh, is the central truth of the Christian Revelation. It is also the prototype of the act of love. Mr Kavanagh's farming community have substituted for love, marriage and birth (which may be allowed to be divine in so far as they mirror the love of the Trinity) 'the passion that never needs a wife', and their symbol, Patrick Maguire, is 'the man who made a field a bride'.

> He lives that his little fields may stay fertile when his own body
> Is spread in the bottom of a ditch under two coulters crossed in
> Christ's Name.

In short, this poem is the analysis of an extended blasphemy against Creation. The analysis is not carried out on a consistently high level of relevance and the verse is too often slack, but perhaps Mr Kavanagh has come closer than any other writer outside Joyce to the problem of religion, when it curdles, in Catholic Ireland, and unlike Joyce he attempts to understand the phenomenon, and to treat it with compassion. I also suspect that, if such a paradox is possible, he is an instinctive theologian:

> Once one day in June when he was walking
> Among his cattle in the Yellow Meadow
> He met a girl carrying a basket —
> And he was then a young and heated fellow
> Too earnest, too earnest! He rushed beyond the thing
> To the unreal. And he saw Sin
> Written in letters larger than John Bunyan dreamt of.
> For the strangled impulse there is no redemption.

The quasi-theological bent of Mr Kavanagh's mind may be seen in the line '*He rushed beyond the thing / To the unreal*'. The sense of sin when over-active passes easily enough into sin itself. And this over-active sense of sin is part and parcel of the general spiritual condition of Patrick Maguire's community. It might even be concluded that it is almost the sole thing which is truly alive, were it not that Mr Kavanagh's peasants are allowed intimations of glory:

> *Yet sometimes when the sun comes through a gap*
> *These men know God the Father in a tree:*
> *The Holy Spirit is the rising sap,*
> *And Christ will be the green leaves that will come*
> *At Easter from the sealed and guarded tomb.*

This is the place to note that Mr Kavanagh's mystique is a little unorthodox: It is difficult to detect at what point a traditional use of analogy shades into an older cult of nature-worship. His Catholic admirers may find it distasteful, but there are indications here and elsewhere in *The Great Hunger* that the only spiritual illumination these male peasants receive comes not from their devotional practices (which he describes with something closer to tenderness than to irony) but from their Wordsworthian contacts with an imperfectly manifested Nature.

But Mr Kavanagh's vaguely pantheistic (but perhaps Franciscan) approach in this context does not take from the central importance of *The Great Hunger* as the only major poem of our time by an Irish Catholic (Denis Devlin's *Lough Derg* might be an exception) to examine the rôle or the subsidence of religion in life. I've harped on this aspect of his poem because what to me seems so obvious has never, to my knowledge, been stated.

The remaining poems of *A Soul for Sale* are of varying quality. 'Father Mat' is an accomplished exercise in decent religious sentiment, chiefly remarkable for an early statement of the Kavanagh doctrine of common things. A curate is described (as against the old priest Father Mat — Mr Kavanagh has a weakness for old priests) as

> *One who was not afraid when the sun opened a flower,*
> *Who was never astonished*
> *At a stick carried down a stream*
> *Or at the undying difference in the corner of a field.*

'Pegasus', much admired by young men ten years ago, does not wear well. The parable of the soul for sale to Church or State or 'meanest trade' is marred by romantic complacency. The famous 'Stony Grey Soil' will always be of interest as evidence of how far Mr Kavanagh has advanced, from a belated condition of rebellion, to acceptance of at least part of his past — he has not yet learned to look with serenity on the rebellion itself. In the context of his later development, the most relevant poem is 'Spraying the Potatoes' with its tight if weepy final stanza:

> *And poet lost to potato-fields,*
> *Remembering the lime and copper smell*
> *Of the spraying barrels he is not lost*
> *Or till blossomed stalks cannot weave a spell.*

I call these lines 'weepy' because they pre-suppose unconvincingly a lost paradise. The mature Kavanagh carries the paradise about within him.

*   *   *

Since 1947 Mr Kavanagh, initially through his Journal in *Envoy*, and later through his own paper *Kavanagh's Weekly*, has become the object of an unhealthy cult, based largely on his wild, uninformed and deliberately provocative generalizations, rather than on a few perceptions of Coleridgian brilliance. He has been vocal also in periodicals such as the *Farmers' Journal* and the *National Observer*, to note only his series of regular contributions.

It is since 1947 also that he has emerged as a considerable verse satirist, with a gift for Byronic rhyme and an equally impressive gift for catching the inflexions of Irish rural and urban speech. The longest of his verse satires are 'The Wake of the Books' (*The Bell*, November 1947), a gay laceration of Censors and Censored, in the form of a semi-expressionistic playlet; 'The Paddiad' (*Horizon*, August 1949), a dissection of Dublin literary cliques, in which the tone is growing more savage, and 'The Christmas Mummers' (*Nimbus*, Winter 1954), another episode in the war of Kavanagh versus the New Bourgeoisie. Of these, he has reprinted 'The Paddiad' in his latest book, *Come Dance with Kitty Stobling*.[2] Four other satirical pieces may be found in what is practically a small book, the nineteen poems printed in *Nimbus* (Winter, 1956). Somewhat dishonestly, the editors of *Nimbus* failed to point out that these were not new poems, but a gleaning of what the poet had published over the previous eight or nine years. More than half of these nineteen poems appear again in the new book. Of those omitted, the most important is 'I Had a Future'.

'I Had a Future' is symptomatic of Mr Kavanagh's new and imaginatively enriching acceptance of the past and what it has done to him, a fragment of naked autobiography contained in self-knowledge. There can be no more difficult task for the writer than to see himself as he once was, blurred neither by self-pity nor self-abhorrence:

> *Show me the stretcher-bed I slept on*
> *In a room on Drumcondra Road*
> *Let John Betjeman call for me in a car.*

The present writer was a very young man when he first read this poem, and can remember feeling that the reference to Mr Betjeman was over-revelatory. The feeling was, of course, wrong. The mood of the poem is not one of nostalia, but of wonder over a former self, a self with 'quarter-seeing eyes' and 'animal-remembering mind', and the concrete details about Mr Betjeman and the Drumcondra Road, the stretcher-bed and the car, a hint of luxury against a background of Bohemian frugality, nail down the poet's passionate desire to understand that former self. This is Mr Kavanagh's earliest attempt, perhaps, to use verse as an instrument towards the comprehension of his own experience.

Almost all the most recent poems of quality in *Kitty Stobling* are further, more complex attempts to attain a kind of passing self-knowledge. In the superbly jazzy 'Auditors In' he writes,

> From the sour soil of a town where all roots canker
> I turn away to where the Self reposes
> The placeless Heaven that's under all our noses
> Where we're shut from all the barren anger,
> No time for self-pitying melodrama ...

Leading to the wry gravity of the conclusion:

> I am so glad
> To come so accidentally upon
> My Self at the end of a tortuous road
> And have learned with surprise that God
> Unworshipped withers to the Futile One.

Mr Kavanagh's Self is a very different one from that in *A Soul for Sale*, but he still has links with the man who praised 'the undying difference in the corner of a field'. This is best illustrated from the sonnet 'The Hospital', appearing here with some, to my mind, dubious revisions. I quote the sestet as it appeared in *Nimbus*.

> This is what love does to things: the Rialto Bridge,
> The main gate that was bent by a heavy lorry,
> The seat at the back of a shed that was a suntrap.
> Naming these things is the love-act and its pledge;
> For we must set in words the mystery without claptrap,
> Experience so light-hearted appears transitory.

In 'Kitty Stobling' the last two lines run,

> For we must record love's mystery without claptrap,
> Snatch out of time the passionate transitory.

The first emendation is acceptable, the second disastrous. For a rediscovered truth – that experience appears transitory to the outgoing heart – is substituted the cliché of art eternizing the moment. But even in its new version the sonnet is not alone masterly in its control of speech-rhythms, but most moving as a declaration of faith in life.[3]

There are others in this book:

Gather the bits of road that were
Not gravel to the traveller
But eternal lanes of joy
On which no man who walks can die.
Bring in the particular trees
That caught you in their mysteries,
And love again the weeds that grew
Somewhere specially for you.
Collect the river and the stream
That flashed upon a pensive theme,
And a positive world make,
A world man's world cannot shake,
And do not lose love's resolution
Though face to face with destitution.   ('Prelude')

Love is the theme of this book ultimately, love for life as it is, not as it might have been, or ought to be, or might well be in the near future. And how many fruitful statements Mr Kavanagh makes in naming his great discovery:

To look on is enough
In the business of love
('Is')

and again,

I will have love, have love
From anything made of,
And a life with a shapely form
With gaiety and charm
And capable of receiving
With grace the grace of living
And wild moments too
Self when freed from you.
('The Self-slaved')

Kitty Stobling contains several botched poems – 'In Memory of My Mother' collapses one word from the end – but as a whole it stands out as that rarest of achievements, a book of verse which manifestly indicates an integrated personality, rather than an album of shots from various angles. This is Kavanagh, nor are we out of him.

As against this, there are some suggestions that Mr Kavanagh has not yet expunged from his thinking and his writing certain gritty elements. I am not thinking of the enchanting 'House Party to Celebrate the Destruction of the Roman Catholic Church in Ireland', a lampoon in the grand style rising to the final searing indictment of pinch-beck liberalism:

In far off parishes of Cork and Kerry
Old priests walked homeless in the winter air
As Séamus poured another pale dry sherry.

What I have called the 'gritty elements' in the poet's thinking are best seen at their clogging process, whenever he writes about his vision of the Eternal Feminine. I'm afraid that Mr Kavanagh collapses irremediably into sentimentality when he proclaims his image of woman as warm, intuitive, uncomplicated, comprehensive of the poet, as distinct from calculating, shallow man. The image is as valid potentially as any other, but he has not as yet succeeded in presenting it satisfactorily. It is seen at its lachrymose worst in a poem not reprinted in the new book, 'God in Woman':

While men the poet's tragic light resented,
The spirit that is woman caressed his soul.

It mars an already uneasily poised poem, 'Intimate Parnassus':

It is not cold on the mountain, human women
Fall like ripe fruit, while mere men
Are climbing out on dangerous branches
Of banking, insurance and shops; ...

The convenient, over-cosy dichotomy suggests a temperamental fixation, the kind of fixation which makes for bad verse unless chastened by the discipline of self-knowledge. This dichotomy may be seen in a less explicit form in 'If Ever You Go To Dublin Town', an inferior ballad in which Mr Kavanagh refurbishes an old fustian icon of the poet as solitary, eccentric, head-in-the-air, but withal tenderhearted:

He had the knack of making men feel
As small as they really were
Which meant as great as God had made them
But as males they disliked his air.

Why male, wherefore base? This kind of implied dogma is, of course, one of the varieties of sentimentality and such a disrupter of poetry.

I will just touch on another variety of sentimentality to which Mr Kavanagh is prone, a kind which might be traced to one of his chief strengths, the re-burnishing of the banal.

The sonnet 'Lines Written on a Seat on the Grand Canal, Dublin' is a beautifully spikey tribute to his ravishment by the ordinary – until the last two lines:

O commemorate me with no hero-courageous
Tomb – just a canal-bank seat for the passer-by.

There is here, I submit, a double failure of language and feeling. That infernal world 'just' cheapens the poet's wish into a wheedling petition – 'just' a song at twilight, or a penny for a poor blind man. But it is the 'passer-by' that does the real harm. Between the poet and the object-experience falls the shadow of a cliché sentiment, posthumous contact with the undying generations. Yet, apart from the exigencies of rhyme, it is fairly obvious that Mr Kavanagh was aiming at no more than the kind of tentacular simplicity he achieves through 'naming' objects; but to adapt from the book's title poem, he is here ceasing to be 'namer' and becoming 'the beloved'.

Mr Kavanagh's defects are grave. A catalogue of them would include over-reliance on portentous abstractions, the mandarin platitude (see, for both, 'The One'), an uneasy acquaintance with Greek mythology (he must never again mention Parnassus, in any form), and a habit of trailing his coat unnecessarily – this mars the sonnet 'Dear Folks' ('*the laughter-smothered courage, / The Poet's*').[4] But for me the defects are often in themselves contributory to the success of individual poems, breaking up the light and refracting it. And he can make high capital out of jagged verbal effects, out of a kind of shrewd and tender clumsiness:

> *Leafy-with-love banks and the green waters of the canal*
> *Pouring redemption for me, that I do*
> *The Will of God, wallow in the habitual, the banal,*
> *Grow with nature again as before I grew.*

And again:

> *The gravel in the yard was pensive, annoyed to be crunched*
> *As people with problems in their faces drove in in cars*
> *Yet I with such solemnity around me refused to be bunched*
> *In fact was inclined to give the go-by to bars.*

Mr Kavanagh now speaks in a manner that leads us to await, constantly, surprises of language and rhythm, and no-one with an ear for rhyme can fail to be enchanted by his skill in breaking down cliché associations. In fact he is a major craftsman in words. As for his substantive values, it is sufficient for the time being to recognize that he is, first and foremost, a celebrant of life.

*   *   *

Strictly speaking, a man has to be dead before we can detect a pattern, or pronounce a chaos in his life. Rimbaud stopped writing before he was twenty but he did not, in the context of meaningful pattern, waste the long years in Abyssinia nor, humanly speaking, did he fail to triumph by that squalid death in Marseilles. A poet, or any imaginative writer of quality, is the sum of speech and silence, of fruitfulness and waste, of integrity and cowardice.

But their interim patterns may be established, and with the groping prescience of the natural artist, Mr Kavanagh has so ordered his life that at least one pattern may be detected: not dissimilar, in terms of the imaginative life, from that recorded by Wordsworth in his great Ode on 'Intimations of Immortality'. The pattern is roughly one of departure, disillusion and bewilderment, enrichment and return. So *The Green Fool* set out, with his faggot of useful memories, burnt them up, wandered in the wilderness, and found them again, marvellously restored. Yet being no longer a fool, being in fact a Poet, a maker, he saw that they were not necessarily good in themselves, but only in so far as he loved, or might love, them with intensity.

Come Dance With Kitty Stobling is the first full report of the illumined return. It remains, of course, to be seen whether the return ends up, finally, in a cul-de-sac of reiteration, or whether Mr Kavanagh will employ his dazzling new skills n the wider exploration of his, so far, very moving affair with life. He has many years yet in which to get a prize herd to the affair – one envisages, for instance, a long poem in praise of life and love and Creation equivalent in weight to, but denser in texture, than the centre-piece of his early period, *The Great Hunger*. He might yet be the first poet to come out of Ireland with great love from little room. On the evidence of *Kitty Stobling* he has never before had such an abundance of vitality and purpose. We could be doing with such a poet.

Obituary for Patrick Kavanagh

(John Jordan Papers)

The news was phoned to me at noon today.[1] Congruously, I was marking at the time an essay on Molière's *Le Misanthrope*, that great play about a man who loved humanity so much that its postures and poutings and pandering to the world of received opinion acted on him like a hair-shirt. Indeed, there was so much of Alceste in Patrick, the impatience with bores, the ill-advised locations, the peremptory dismissal of the pseudo in however elegant or accomplished a guise.

I could, I suppose, go on writing in this falsely urbane manner, but Patrick would not wish it. I will try to write about him as my heart dictates and my memory permits. By the time these words are published he will, no doubt, have had a reasonable share of praise as the important poet he was, and is, and will be for as long as there are readers of English with gaiety in their hearts, and [as long as] the tragic sense of life be that sixth one essential for decent living. But those who knew him well cannot at this moment be preoccupied with his literary achievement or reputation. They can only feel as I do, the day of his death, a sense of utter desolation, the kind of desolation, I believe, that can only be analysed after one has sought for a qualitatively comparable experience in one's life. I was genuinely grieved when Edward Longford died in 1961. I was saddened when Anew McMaster went in 1962. When 1964 took toll of Brendan Behan, who was one of my earliest friends, I was torn between rage and distress. Seán O'Sullivan followed him that year, but there was no shock in my sadness. There have been others. But ransacking my memory I can come up with only the painter Robert MacBryde, who was killed in 1966,[2] and, yes, I have it, my father, who died in 1954.

The texture of the grief one feels for the loss of one's family and the loss of one's friends must perforce be different. MacBryde's death hurt me deeply, but the world seemed no smaller. But Patrick's death is a bereavement of almost familial intensity. I risk offending his dear wife, my friend, Katherine, by so intimate an incursion into the territory of mourning, but I trust she will understand.

I forget the exact circumstances of my first meeting with Patrick in the summer of 1948. At the time there was some talk of having me introduced to him by Miss Deirdre MacDonagh, who once ran the Contemporary Pictures Gallery in

Baggot Street (I imagine Patrick had first come to know Miss MacDonagh in his capacity as Art Critic for a Dublin newspaper: he was great fun on how he made an ass of himself over Matisse). But, anyway, meet him I did, and from the first year's acquaintance I retain one heart-breaking memory. The scene was the Pearl Bar, and Patrick was having drinks with myself and a boy called Donal O'Farrell (whose parents had known Patrick in his earliest London days) and a girl called Róisín. A slight argument arose, and suddenly Patrick fixed his blue eye on me, and in a voice that wonderfully blended mischief and canniness, said: 'I'd better mind what I'm saying. That fellow Joordan (sic) will be writing about me in twenty years.' And so it turns out that nearly twenty years after, I am writing about him, desolate that I cannot cross the Atlantic and pay honour to his shell. [3]

The acquaintance waxed and waned in the following five or six years. His friendship was always jealously sought by my elders and no doubt betters. In the almost passionate vying for his attention, personal loyalties frequently got hard knocks, and though I am now on moderately good terms with the contenders of those days, I cannot help feeling that they failed to perceive in Patrick what I knew by the grace of God: his basic distrust of discipleship. I know I have in certain respectable and morally despicable circles the reputation of being a Patrician. But in other circles less respectable, but morally viable, it is known that I loved the man, the solitary soul, the stranger and pilgrim in an unredeemed world.

That love grew from 1955 onwards. It had little or nothing to do with Patrick's Points of View, which were, as often as not, distasteful to me. Nor had it anything to do with what the world knows as getting and spending. In the years up to 1966, whenever it happened that both of us were in Dublin at the same time (which was not, at any point, for more than a few months at a stretch), I saw him every second day,[4] and when I think of the sheer fun of those meetings, when I realize that all that gaiety has been eclipsed, that never again will I hear him sing, for instance, a ballad by Richard D'Alton Williams, or 'Lord Ullin's Daughter', never again quote with alarming accuracy Pope or Johnson or Goldsmith or Edward Martyn trying to get George Moore to go to Mass, my eyes wetten and I feel I can write no more.

His conversation was of a very extraordinary kind, conducted on several intersecting planes. He was capable of interrupting his own denounciations of Mr Wilson's government[5] on the grounds that its economics were not Keynesian, with a question on the source of some quotation, usually abstruse, he could not place. Discussion of Carleton, George Moore or Joyce, whom he loved most of well-known Irish writers, could be terminated by the intrusion of some worry about the best place to purchase underwear, or where to have a snack. For he was, like most sensible men who have suffered severe illnesses, a strong believer in eating. Years ago I spent the night in a house where he was staying, and I slept it out. At about eleven he returned festooned, as always in the mornings, with every available newspaper, and, when questioned, he announced, with an immeasurable gusto: 'The — – Café'. (In recent years, he used the term 'kafe'.) The point was he had found a place where it was possible to have a cheap edible breakfast in privacy. He had lived in Dublin for years, but he never ceased to wonder at the mystery of minimum comfort as *he* wanted it. Patrick asked for so very little in the way of material comfort, less than any lung-whole[6] man I have ever known.

Ah, those years of fantasy. At noon today, reading about Alceste in my comfortable office in the capital of the Land of Fish,[7] the last of my youth guttered out. Some day, when all our hearts are less raw, I will write about them. For the moment, I will only set down what I remember of Patrick as I last saw him, in the summer of 1967. A sixty-year-old smiling public man, so relaxed and confident with his bride, so innocently happy about the successful dramatization of his novel, *Tarry Flynn*, so generous to the players, who in turn so loved him, so content with 'laughter and the love of friends', as the author of those words can never have been. Yes, the last memory is the best for the time being. With his publisher, but not talking about himself or about his friend, Myles na Gopaleen, who preceeded him in 1966,[8] and whose *The Third Policeman* had just come out, but pressing the wares of a very young poet who I know will remember that meeting through all the days of his life.[9]

It is given to few men to have brushed against the hem of genius. I believe it is given to fewer still to have known the very quintessence of gaiety in advertisy, of wisdom in folly, of abounding mental health in physical sickness. Let then his friends and lovers mourn the extinction of their source of gaiety, their fount of wisdom, their corrective to the sick fancies of melancholy.

I have not attempted to polish or sophisticate this script: I would be a fool for Patrick's sake.

From a small townland in Monaghan …

(Irish Independent, 6 November 1971)

It would be useless to speculate on Kavanagh's progress had not Oliver St John Gogarty caused this book[1] to be withdrawn when it was first published, in 1938, by Michael Joseph. But no more useless than speculation on O'Casey's progress had not Yeats and his colleagues (but primarily Yeats) rejected *The Silver Tassie* in 1927. For myself, I believe that Gogarty's reaction to a single corner-boy's jest may unwittingly have both re-directed and retarded, and ultimately enriched, the development of an Irish poet of international stature.

Kavanagh was thirty-four when *The Green Fool* was first published. In later years he affected to despise the book, maintaining that it was 'all lies'. I have seen the book described as an 'autobiographical novel'. It is, of course, nothing of the kind.

It is not hindsight for me now to claim that *The Green Fool* is a cameo masterpiece, for I first read it, in a rare copy, in 1947, at an age when one perhaps lacks critical sense but the imagination is fresh, and unpolluted by the crucial but not always pleasant knowledge of evil that comes with age.

The Green Fool, a quarter of a century after first reading, strikes me as a genuinely innocent book, and if anyone thinks fit to argue that the 'innocence' is merely contrived naïveté then, Kavanagh at thirty-three, when he wrote the book, was a considerable literary artist.

Maybe he told a few '*lies*' about his childhood, adolescence and early manhood in a small townland in Co. Monaghan, but I know for a fact, from non-literary sources, that he told enough of the truth to infuriate some of his neighours.[2] Kavanagh's story is not one of 'rags to riches', but how from an unlikely background of respectable peasant frugality and industry, in a community that rarely looked beyond the neighbouring fields, there emerged a talent of violent yet delicate beauty.

In many a sentence, some of these qualities are marvellously encapsulated, for instance: 'In my own district the goat and donkey were passing out; they were too spiritual animals for a people who had begun to take their gospel from the daily newspapers.'

How much of the mature poet was seeded in this community may be seen in a passage like this: 'I looked across at the sun-flecked plains of Louth and Meath and knew how fine a thing it was to be alive. The green fields and the same simple homes and the twisty primitive folk told me of the unchanging beauty of Ireland. 'At my feet were primroses and violets, a magic carpet on which I could journey over the Baghdads of dreamland.'

Read this hilarious, tender, and devastatingly shrewd prentice work of a major poet.

To Kill a Mockingbird

(Hibernia, 30 November 1973)

Six years ago to the day, November 30, 1967, a cable was phoned through to me in St John's, Newfoundland, from Katherine Kavanagh and a doctor friend:[1] Patrick Kavanagh had died that morning in his sixty-fourth year. I have never made the slightest capital out of a friendship which during the last decade of his life was fairly close,[2] and I had known him for nearly twenty years. Recently, however, I gave for charitable purposes a lecture on Patrick Kavanagh, and the rudimentary research and memory required brought me up again against the phenomenon of the non- conformist in Irish society, especially the non-conformist writer.

Preparing my talk, I realized that I myself as a boy had been conditioned by the media into accepting a potential version of Kavanagh the man. For instance, in March 1948, a few months before I met him, there appeared in *The Bell* an extraordinary piece called 'Meet Mr Patrick Kavanagh', by the late Larry Morrow, writing under the pseudonym 'The Bellman'. The following is typical of this dreadful piece's content: 'Mr Kavanagh has been described, by those who pretend to dislike him, as a Consommé of a Boy; by others (who don't pretend so hard, perhaps) as The Last of Lever's Gossoons.' I am afraid that, pushing eighteen, I found this kind of stuff amusing. Patrick was in his forty-fourth year when 'The Bellman's' article appeared.

Patrick enjoyed some local glory with his *Envoy* diaries in 1950–51; and after *Envoy* had closed down, he edited with his brother thirteen numbers of the by-now legendary *Kavanagh's Weekly*, most of which he wrote himself. After this sheet had folded, after he had augmented his generous stock of enemies, and swollen the choler of the snide and the cosy, there appeared in *The Leader* in October 1952 an anonymous Profile. It should be noted that, under the editorship of D.P. Moran, *The Leader* had built up a fine, manly, tradition of Catholic Right-Wing scurrility. Under the editorship of Nuala Moran it had been relatively civil. Now a band of 'New Liberals' from TCD[3] and UCD[4] had taken over, and part of their new-look policy was the *Profile* series.

A condensed version of the coverage given to the case of *Kavanagh* v. *The Leader* appears in *Collected Pruse* (1967). For myself, I think Patrick over-reacted. I have suggested that *The Bell* article was offensive and also why Patrick could not act. Mr John A. Costello invoked *The Bell* article, but so far as I can make out, neither the defence nor Patrick's counsel[5] recognized that *The Bell* article did *not* infer what the Profile did: that Patrick Kavanagh was a compulsive drinker, a sponger on the young; weak-minded and gullible, and something of a charlatan. The damning inferences of the *Profile* far outweighed the fulsome and patronizing praise.[6]

Whatever, I see the trial as having a larger significance even than the catastrophic effects it had on Patrick Kavanagh.[7] There is, first, the fact that an honourable man like John A. Costello should, in the practice of his profession, have to reduce a hyper-sensitive man to the point of breakdown. Second, the trial revealed that there were elements in the Dublin intellectual establishment malevolent or thick-headed enough to *allow The Leader* to defend the Profile. Those who put the caricature together knew Patrick Kavanagh's state of health and his state of pocket. It was a classic case of moral and intellectual sadism. For, how could a peculiar poet hope to win against an institutional organ long associated with Faith and Fatherland? In 1954 no Irish jury might be expected to find in favour of a 'mere poet', who also had the reputation of being something of a clown. In the spring of 1955 Patrick Kavanagh's cancerous lung was removed. He left hospital to enjoy, too late, over a decade of comparative prosperity, but also a new, exciting, creative season.

The morning the cable came from Dublin, the bleak, cold sunlight was like a lotion on the cheek. I packed up my brief case as early as possible and went home to grieve and dream and remember, and late in the night to write a tribute which I guessed the editor of *Hibernia*[8] would ask for: I did not say then, nor for years will I ever say, how much his passing troubled me.[9]

By Night Unstarred

(Hibernia, 23 December 1977)

Since his brother's death in November 1967, Dr Peter Kavanagh has been engaged in a massive campaign of rehabilitation, which has involved three large volumes edited and published by himself: *Lapped Furrows* (1969) being correspondence between the two brothers and 'other documents', *November Haggard* (1971) being 'uncollected prose and verse', and an expanded *Collected Poems* (1972) which I have not seen. All of which is commendable and pious. Unfortunately, this industry has been accompanied by undignified tilting at windmills and a tone of rancour unredeemed by the wit and lovable cunning that characterized many of Patrick Kavanagh's utterances.

The rancour sings (or rasps) out again in the Introduction and Epilogue to his conflation of two unfinished novels whose provenance is, to put it mildly, mysterious. It will be recalled that Kavanagh's autobiography *The Green Fool* was published in 1938 and was withdrawn almost immediately by the publisher Michael Joseph when Oliver Gogarty sued for libel on the flimsiest grounds. It did not become available again for over thirty years. Now hear Dr Kavanagh: 'It was a juvenile mistake he was not allowed to forget. In later years those who could not abide his prophetic message responded by praising *The Green Fool*. Something had to be done about it and in 1950 I urged him to write his true autobiography.'

The result was two novels, both incomplete. The first part of this book (more than half) is not about Patrick Kavanagh at all, but about the rise of one Peter Devine, son of a small farmer, from peasant squalor to bourgeois affluence. The story begins in the last century in what is clearly the poet's own townland, and if the society described here bears any relation to that in which he grew up, then it is miraculous that Patrick Kavanagh survived in it as long as he did. *The Green Fool* offended more than Gogarty (I have been told that at one stage copies in the area were kept under lock and key). The first part of *By Night Unstarred*, if it is supposed to be a corrective, must, by analogy, be described as an exorcism. In its indictment of greed, superstition, hypocrisy, general spiritual mouldiness, it is quite as terrible as *The Great Hunger*. Peter Divine is depicted with hatred. 'There was something in Peter's vicious mentality that compelled his enemies to help him forward.' This reluctant admiration for the mediocre and unscrupulous is understandable in a society where romantic love is seen as a weakness that 'went with insanity and consumption', where Peter Divine looks on the body of his prospective bride and 'every part of the girl was a symbol of her farm', and 'The right way to break a neighbour's heart was to succeed oneself.'

There is, too, a slashing attack on cosy notions about peasant culture:

> In all that countryside, in the whole parish of Ballyrush, which numbered more than a thousand families, there was not one who had ever dreamt of the world of education. There was, it is true, what was called traditional learning and the love of learning, but this was for the most part mere sentimentality. It was – even when it repeated the old poems – nothing better than the hunger for useless information which is satisfied by the popular press. The same was true of the hedge schools where pedantic Greek and Latin were taught parrot-like and in the same way the dictionary devoured.

I hazard that this passage was written during Kavanagh's *Envoy* days (1950) where he was in his most violent reaction against romantic concepts of vestigial Gaelic Ireland. But, as a whole, the passage conveys a personal disgust with his native surroundings, and must be seen as a tile in the erratic mosaic that Kavanagh made out of his memories.

'He didn't belong to Inniskeen', writes Dr Kavanagh, who also believes that his brother should never have come to Dublin. The question to be asked here, and not theoretically, is whether he would have written anything at all of importance if he had stayed in Inniskeen, or in London after his first visit. (Yet in the latter case, he might, conceivably, have made great verse out of life in wartime London.)

Certainly his life in Dublin during and after the War, as described in the second part of this 'novel', makes painful reading. The Devines of Ballyrush in the first part have become the De Vines in Dublin, with powerful clerical and medical connections, and that mysterious 'pull' in the job-allotment area which has broken the heart of many a man less insecure, less touchy, than Kavanagh. The De Vine family is connected with the Bishop of Dublin (clearly Archbishop McQuaid, who was to say, when Kavanagh died, that they had been friends for twenty-five years). It is the Bishop and the De Vines that Patrick must court to get a job as PRO, or something of the kind, in a plastics company.

Patrick emerges almost as a Raskolnikov figure – innocent, gauche, arrogant and doomed. It might have been better if Dr Kavanagh had published this fragment separately and in its entirety, for there are fine things in it: the interview with the Bishop where close observation vies with ancestral awe – 'His grey long face was the face of an ascetic, or of a dealing man from some mountainy district in the county Leitrim' – the frightful musical *soiree* at the De Vines: 'The night was looking in from the garden and the trees; the rosebushes became terrifying spectres in the imagination.' No one who has ever experienced the stupor and fear induced by remote ecclesiastics, the bewilderment and shame of patient merit in the face of well-heeled insiders, can doubt the authenticity of these passages.

While it is possible to identify the Bishop, R.M. Smyllie and some others, it would be dangerous to try identifying the De Vines and their cronies. They are, of course, conglomerates, but only frugally so. Nothing that Patrick Kavanagh wrote can be quite without interest. Dr Kavanagh has done us and his brother a service in revealing the existence of these texts. He has done both a disservice by trying to impose a shape on materials which defy any chronological pattern I can discern. All those who knew him have their own Patrick Kavanagh. But to present him, as does his brother, as being at all times in Dublin a hounded and friendless reject comes dangerously close to novelistic invention by Peter Kavanagh himself.

Sacred Keeper

(University Review, Spring 1979)

'When I write about Patrick Kavanagh', says Dr Kavanagh, 'I write as a partisan, as his alter ego, almost as his evangelist.' The qualification of the last phrase is supererogatory. He does write as an evangelist, but a somewhat confused one. 'While it would be wrong to over-emphasise the religious element in Patrick's character, it would be more wrong to ignore it. He was a Christian mystic, with the spiritual element dominant.' I will try to sort out this congeries of misapprehension and misassumptions. What is clear is that by 'the religious element' Dr Kavanagh has in mind the practices and behaviour of Irish Catholic orthodoxy quite as much as what may be called the religious sense: an awareness and acknowledgment of the supernatural which may or may not govern the conduct of life. He appears to believe that deficiency in orthodox adherence and a seeming failure of the religious sense in the conduct of life may, as it were, be transcended by 'the Christian mystic' with 'the spiritual element dominant'. How a man or woman could be a Christian or any other kind of mystic without a dominance of the spiritual element is beyond me.

But I question if Dr Kavanagh knows the meaning of the term 'Christian mystic', as lesser mortals understand it, even from cursory reading of Térèsa of Avila or John of the Cross. True, one may use the term legitimately in the case of poets, by way of analogy: George Herbert and Gerard Manley Hopkins may serve to illustrate the point. I fear, though, that Dr Kavanagh has not thought out the implications of his statement. If Patrick was, metaphorically, a mystic, he was one in the Wordsworthian sense, and that is not specifically Christian. Indeed, one of the most interesting aspects of Patrick's verse (I write 'Patrick' since as such I always addressed him in his lifetime) is the intertwining of traditional – as they call it nowadays – Irish Catholicism and a transcendentalism not dissimilar from that of Thoreau. If I had to label Patrick as a poet I would call him an Irish Catholic transcendentalist, and of course in doing so would be offending his shade: for in life it was impossible to label him, dear chameleon that he was.

Dr Kavanagh, in his evangelical piety, finds it necessary to engage in quite unnecessary whitewashing of his brother. 'He never blasphemed, never said By God or By Christ because for him poetry and God were the same thing and it would be unthinkable for him to insult the poetic fire, his most sacred possession and the reason for his being.' Not content with attributing mysticism to Patrick, he endows him with a restraint of speech very rarely encountered by those who work on the land or congregate in taverns. Since Dr Kavanagh has chosen the tack, I have no compunction in recording that Patrick was capable of the most hair-raising maledictions, which might justly be termed blasphemies against the human person and also of turns-of-phrase which only hair-splitting would consider non-blasphemies. There is a 'traditional' Marian hymn, '*I'll sing a hymn to Mary, the Mother of my God*', which contains the lines '*When wicked men blaspheme Thee, I'll love and bless Thy name*'. Patrick's version was '*When fuckin' bastards blaspheme Thee ...* '. No doubt Dr Kavanagh would maintain that this is an invention, or argue that I am making his point for him, an obsessional point, it seems, for in the Kavanagh household, 'Cursing or taking the name of God in vain was never part of any conversation or row and this interdiction on cursing remained permanently as part of our style of expression up to this moment of writing.'

   Dr Kavanagh's remembrances of his brother at home, before the family dispersed, are vivid and touching. There was twelve years between them and so this vignette has an unadorned poignancy: 'He was always home for the Rosary. Then up to bed, checking my shirt before going to sleep to make sure the top button was open and there was no danger of my choking.' This memory of nearly sixty years ago (Dr Kavanagh is sixty-four this year) pinpoints as nothing else the intensity of the more agreeable aspects of Peter's love for Patrick. A less agreeable aspect is that fierce protectiveness which often shades into ugly possessiveness. After his account of Patrick's athletic activities, he goes on, 'Yet all this time he was writing verse and I had become his sole audience and literary critic. I held that position almost until his death forty years later.' I cannot follow what he means by 'sole audience and literary critic', other than that he, Peter Kavanagh, and he alone was, and is, capable of understanding and criticizing Patrick's work. (It should be recalled that when Æ accepted three poems from Patrick for *The Irish Statesman* in 1929, Peter was thirteen: a precocious 'literary critic'.) But I believe that the 'ugly possessiveness', as I have called it, extends and extended beyond Patrick's literary soul, and nowhere may it be seen more clearly than in Dr Kavanagh's attitude to Patrick's marriage to Katherine Moloney on 19 April 1967, at the Roman Catholic Church of the Three Patrons, Rathgar, Dublin. His reference to it in this book is even more distasteful than that in his compendium of letters and other documents, *Lapped Furrows*, published by the Peter Kavanagh Hand Press, New York, in 1969. In that volume he writes (p.55):

   Shortly before he died in November 1967 – months as it turned out – Patrick
   married. Many were astonished at this move, especially those who knew how

sick he was, suffering from alcoholic poisoning, heart, liver, and kidney disease, not to mention the one lung. Ten years earlier he had been warding off marriage proposals. He did not want to marry at that time. As he wrote me 6 July 1957: 'Married you cannot go to the U.S. without the woman's consent.'

That is all. I can say, however, that the two 'proposals' referred to in the letter quoted did not involve the widow of Patrick Kavanagh. At least, however, Dr Kavanagh in *Lapped Furrows* grants that Patrick 'married'. The tone hardens in *Sacred Keeper*. Having quoted from Patrick's last letter to him, Dr Kavanagh goes on: 'Exactly two months later I received a letter from one of his Dublin acquaintances informing me that Patrick had just gone through a marriage ceremony in Dublin. Nothing came directly from Patrick.' Who was this acquaintance who, Dr Kavanagh would have us believe, did not inform him of Patrick's bride's name and the fact that Patrick did not choose to inform him of his marriage, or, perhaps, more wounding to his sense of possession, did not enter into preliminary discussions.

The last letter, as indicated, was written on 24 February 1967. Dr Kavanagh goes on: 'Seven months later, on 30 November, the Irish police phoned my apartment in New York to say Patrick was dead. Of those intervening nine months I have no memory.' The sacred keeper had lost charge of his possession, as he deemed, and I suppose it is no more than human that he should blame the woman who stepped in, and seek his vengeance by insult through disdainful and misleading silence. But, of course, perhaps Mrs Katherine Kavanagh is as well off. Professor Patrick Rafroidi in his review of *By Night Unstarred* (*Études Françaises,* December 1978), Patrick's unfinished novel, completed by Dr Kavanagh and published by The Goldsmith Press in 1977, comments about the Introduction: *On connaissait les veuves abusif, il fallait encore découvrir les frères.* Overwhelmingly, Dr Kavanagh is a *frère abusif.* Only rarely, and then never directly, has he a good word to say about anybody with whom Patrick was friendly or had any dealings. Christopher Fitz-Simon and Adrian Cronin, responsible for Irish television's 1966 documentary on Patrick, are among the few to escape censure.

Publishers, patrons, former friends, not to mention, naturally, institutions and governmental departments, are all out of step, and always on Patrick's notoriously unreliable evidence. Except where his own interests are concerned, as in the matter of the sale of the evidence. Except where his own interests are concerned, as in the matter of the sale of the farm at Shancoduff ('I had as much right to the place as he had'), and the banking of his – Peter's – salary cheques while he was first in America, he accepts Patrick's account of everything, including his dealings with the firms of Macmillan, Longmans and MacGibbon & Kee. Truly he is partisan to the point of absurdity. He would have us believe that Patrick did not know who was responsible – 'someone from Ireland, who was utterly distasteful to Patrick' – for editing the

Collected Poems (1964). I am almost certain that Timothy O'Keeffe, then of MacGibbon & Kee, told me it was John Montague[1] – and he would hardly have done so if he had wished to keep the name from Patrick. In another context, while he records the fact that Patrick was not invited to the President of Ireland's reception for Robert Frost in June 1957, Dr Kavanagh fails to record that Patrick *did* meet Frost, on a far less impersonal basis, at a reception given by the President of University College, Dublin. But then, Dr Kavanagh has little use for research where Patrick is concerned, and on that account his biography is largely *disjecta membra*, no more and no less than *materials* of a biography. Future scholars may well have a hell of a time elucidating references which Dr Kavanagh refuses to clarify, though he may, in some cases at least, be uninformed. I fear, though, that often he is reluctant even to name people who at any time were close to Patrick, even for the purposes of abuse. This goes as far as omitting to identify Anthony Cronin as Patrick's companion on the cab facing the Bailey Restaurant in Dublin on Bloomsday, 1954 (facing page 166). Beyond the fact that I am a Dubliner, I do not think Dr Kavanagh has any particular *animus* against myself. But, for the record, I am the *'young lecturer from U.C.D.'* asked by the President of the College to go through a manuscript of Patrick's lectures (p. 310). In a letter of 3 April 1961, Patrick refers to two articles in '*Studies* for last Autumn'. One of those articles was written by me, the other by Basil Payne. I make these points not to puff my ego, but to indicate the kind of problem a serious and scholarly biographer will have to face.

But if *Sacred Keeper* may not be accepted as any way near to being an authoritative biography, it has the merit of being a literary document in its own right. It might be called the story of a love affair, though the participants are two brothers. There is a certain harsh, crude, sadness attaching to Dr Kavanagh's love for and unconditional loyalty to Patrick, even pathos in his empathy.[2] It is an unjust and in many ways a cruel book. Yet I have to confess that I found it eminently readable, despite the thorns and briars of Dr Kavanagh's style.

Sacred Keeper: A Biography of Patrick Kavanagh by Peter Kavanagh. (Goldsmith Press, The Curragh, 1979)

Hopkins Annotated[1]

(Irish Independent, 14 June 1969)

It is arguable that heroic sanctity does not constitute the ideal matter of great tragedy as we know it in Sophocles or Shakespeare. Likewise, it may be argued that the process of sanctification rendered articulate, precisely because it is so very rare, is not the matter of great poetry. The kind of spiritual illumination attained by Hamlet or Lear is qualitatively different from that reached by Blessed Edmund Campion or St John of the Cross (both considerable poets). The sufferings of saints are, as it were, fire-transfigured by their imminent glorification. Tragic heroes are left at peace, but suspended in an inter-penetration of the natural and supernatural worlds.

Holy people, who are recalled primarily for their poetry, like George Herbert or Hopkins, run the risk of being labelled self-indulgent in matters of the spirit and limited, humanly speaking, in breadth of vision. That hateful 'I' that Pascal cried out against, so dangerous in its careless use by imprudent poets, in any field, is particularly mischievous in 'religious' verse.

Hopkins ran great risks in the 'Sonnet of Desolation' written in Dublin, probably in 1885. He was then in his second year as Professor of Greek at UCD. In 'Carrion Comfort', he writes, *'I am in Ireland now;/ now I am at a third/Remove.'* He was, as Mr McChesney reminds, isolated from his family, his Anglican faith (he was converted at twenty-two in 1868), and his country.

In Retreat notes of January 1888 he writes: 'Five wasted years almost have passed in Ireland … I am like a straining eunuch', and in a poem written two months before his death, he is *'Time's eunuch'*. But Hopkins, miraculously, hammered his turmoil into concrete universal signatures of that condition described by William James (Mr Chesney tells us) as 'anhedonia'. These sonnets are difficult at first reading, though not so [much] as are the earlier 'The Wreck of the Deutschland' or 'The Loss of the Eurydice'.

The first of these is considerd a major poem, but this reader, unworried, as elsewhere in Hopkins, by his rhythms, syntax, compound adjectives, omission of relative pronouns, eccentric coinages, etc., finds distasteful (and diminishing) the poem's rigidity in matters of 'Salvation outside the Church'. There is nothing grand or heart-lifting about Hopkins' Ultramontanism so evident in 'Deutschland' or 'Eurydice', or 'Spelt from Sybil's Leaves', or 'Henry Purcell'.

His dazzling techniques, his pied vocabulary, his undoubted capacity for the wry, and even the feline (seen in his correspondence) cannot dispel his air of Jansenism, in which the strain of genuine passion has been crossed by Victorian fundamentalism. Mr McChesney makes no bones about his subject's adherence to this point of view.

Mr McChesney has drawn heavily on the correspondence, the journal and the notebooks, the sermons, and Robert Bridges's notes to the first edition of 1918,[2] almost thirty years after Hopkins's death. For the common reader he has provided an ample guide to the major poems. Yet he does refer casually to 'a Dorset poet called Barnes', and to think that Joyce's last book is called '*Finnegan's Wake*' (sic) is unpardonable at this stage. Trivia when set against his loving but initial restoration of Hopkins's 'self'.

And it is no 'common comfort' to follow Hopkins again from Oxford via Lancashire and Stoneyhurst to that grave in Glasnevin, where he kept his 'elected silence' till the agnostic poet Robert Bridges gashed the Georgian gentility of word and mood with his First Edition of 1918.[3]

Oblomov

(John Jordan Papers)

I suppose that for most of us any reference to the nineteenth-century Russian novel evokes the names of Turgenev, Dostoevsky and Tolstoy, especially the Tolstoy of *War and Peace*. Yet the nineteenth century in Russia was, perhaps, as rich in the art of the novel as it was in France and England. And if most of us tend to forget this fact, so also we tend to think of Russian literature as one pervaded with gloom, saturated with confessional melancholy. Yet we have only to remember Gogol's *The Inspector General*, which once provided a film vehicle for Mr Danny Kaye, to realize that the Russians may be quite as pithily humorous, as bitingly satirical as, for instance, Dickens or Balzac.

In the first rank of the lesser luminaries, and also one of the great humorists is Ivan Goncharov, who was born in 1812 and died at the age of seventy-nine. He wrote only three novels: *An Ordinary Story*, *Oblomov*, and *The Precipice*. It is the second of these, *Oblomov*, published in 1859 that I am going to talk about.[1] It is not only the author's greatest work but also, I reckon, one of the great novels of the nineteenth century.

Goncharov achieved the extraordinary feat, for his time, of writing a novel without a hero – for the man who gives the book its title, Oblomov, known to his intimates as Ilya, almost literally does nothing. He is a substantial landowner – and that of course meant, since it was before the emancipation of the serfs in 1861, he was also a substantial serf-owner – and he has, like many of his kind, come to St Petersburg and attempted to make a career in the Civil Service.

Sensitive, intelligent, cultured in an amorphous fashion, he has soon tired of what to him are the fatuous bumblings and prescribed sycophancy of his colleagues and superiors. When he has a chance of anticipating dismissal, he opts out. He tries then the diversions of Society; good-looking and well-off, he should have been a success. But Oblomov carries within him the seed of a malignancy of the spirit: and by the time the novel opens, that seed has become a monstrous blossom – the disease which Oblomov's boyhood friend, Stolz, who is half-German, will diagnose as 'Oblomovitis'. What is 'Oblomovitis'?

Well, let's look at our non-hero on a typical morning. He is in bed:

(Reader) – 'Lying down was not for Oblomov a necessity as it is for a sick man, or a man who is sleepy; or a matter of chance, as it is for a man who is tired; or a pleasure, as it is for a lazy man; it was his normal condition. When he was at home – and he was almost *always* at home – he lay down all the time, and always in the same room …which served him as a bedroom, study, and reception room. He had three more rooms, but he seldom looked into them, except perhaps in the morning, and that, too, not every day, but only when his man-servant swept his study, which did not happen every day. In those rooms the furniture was covered with dust sheets and the curtains were drawn.'

(J.J.) – In his musty, delapidated flat Oblomov does little but eat, drink, sleep, and dream. From his bed he receives a motley riff-raff of parasites, the most notable of whom is one Tarantyev who will in the event contribute to Oblomov's almost total degradation. Not all of his visitors are quite contemptible. One of them is Penkin, a writer of what sometime later in the century would be called the slice-of-life school. He elicits an outburst from Oblomov, which testifies to the element of Franciscan – perhaps Christ-like – compassion in this too easily dismissed sluggard.

(Reader) – 'Depict a thief, a prostitute, a defrauded fool, but don't forget that they too are human beings. Where's your feeling for humanity? You want to write with your head only! Do you think that to express ideas one doesn't need a heart? One *does* need it – ideas are rendered fruitful by love; stretch out a helping hand to the fallen man to raise him, or shed bitter tears over him, but do not jeer at him. Love him…'

(J.J.) – We might here be listening to the voice of Dostoevsky himself who, though nine younger than Goncharov, had begun to publish earlier. Not all of the first section of *Oblomov* is as highly pitched as the interchange with the writer Penkin. Much of it is very funny, especially the ructions between Oblomov and his serf-valet, Zakhar, a singular portrait of the privileged serf, and indirectly an indictment of the system: for Zakhar is lazy, mendacious and occupationally vindictive. His sole virtue is the dubious one of loyalty to his Master and memories of the family's hey-day.

On the day the novel opens, the half-German Stolz, go-ahead, clear-eyed, the antithesis of his dreaming vegetable of a friend, comes to rescue Oblomov from his torpor. He succeeds, up to a point, in restoring Oblomov to Society. For a brief and idyllic season, the sluggard is re-animated by love for and from Olga, a girl of twenty. But this physically chaste affair begins on a false note: Olga's rendition of the aria 'Casta Diva' (which means, of course, 'Chaste Goddess') from Bellini's opera *Norma,* of which Oblomov is inordinately fond. Olga sees herself as a redemptrix, destined to rescue Oblomov from the slough of indifferentism. At this stage she does not realize that her beloved Ilya's apathy, his inability to identify the name of action, are not of an ordinary kind. She makes him read, she makes him diet and cut out post-prandial naps, she makes him take physical exercise. But the book is not, of course, concerned with anything so simple as the salvation of a blacksheep through the love of a good woman. Although T-bone sex scarcely raises its appetizing head, we are made aware of a magnetic attraction between two utterly disparate natures. Oblomov comes forth from the tomb for a certain time, and Olga is set inexorably on the track of emotional and intellectual maturity.

The contained passion of this couple, female eaglet and male dove, has some pretty, romantic, even novelettish trappings – sprays of lilac, the aria 'Casta Diva' and the like – but it is genuine so long as Oblomov remains within the sphere of Olga's influence. It is now that the abominable tout and parasite Tarantyev, whom I mentioned earlier, comes again to the foreground. Before leaving for the country to be near Olga, Oblomov, passive under Tarantyev's influence, had signed a lease for a flat he had not even seen. Since funds have not arrived from an estate he has not visited for eleven years, he has perforce to live in a ramshackle house in a depressed area, alongside Agafya, a widow who is also his landlady, her two children, an old granny who coughs night and day, and the widow's brother Ivan, an obscure figure initially, but later to prove daemonic as only the invincibly petty and mediocre can be. The sole, but important, consolation for Oblomov is that the widow Agafya is a superlative cook and housekeeper. She is, though on the surface almost moronic, attractive in an earthy way and this Oblomov cannot help but recognize. But she is dominated by her brother Ivan, a corrupt minor functionary, who detects the moral weakness in Oblomov, and with the connivance of his drinking companion, who turns out to be Tarantyev, manages to gain control, through a middleman, of the revenues of Oblomov's estates.

While Oblomov is being stripped both of financial assets and his recently patched-up personal dignity, he is fencing with Olga. Never does he lie directly about his state of bondage – indeed, he himself barely recognizes it as such – nor does he lie about his gradual reversion to sloth, gluttony and intellectual constipation. But the showdown must come, and when it does, in the flat of Olga's aunt, it is agonizing. Olga finally grasps that Oblomov will never marry her. And she realizes that even if they had married, nothing would have changed.

(Reader) – 'You would sink deeper and deeper into sleep every day, wouldn't you? And I? You see the sort of person I am, don't you? I shall never grow old or tire of life. But with you I should be living from day to day, waiting for Christmas, then for Shrovetide, go visiting, dancing, and not thinking of anything. We'd go to bed and thank God that the day had passed so quickly, and in the morning we'd wake up wishing that today would be like yesterday. *That* would be our future, wouldn't it? Is that life? I'd pine away and die – what for, Ilya? Would *you* be happy?'

(J.J.) – Later in this lacerating encounter, realizing that she has no longer any weapons to combat a mysterious malady of the soul, she asks:

(Reader) – 'Why has is all been ruined? ... Who laid a curse on you? What have

you done? You are kind, intelligent, tender, honourable, and – you are going to
wrack and ruin! What has ruined you? There is no name for that evil …'

(J.J.) – And Oblomov remembers the semi-jocular diagnosis of his friend Stolz,
and whispers, 'There is a name – Oblomovitis.'

Oblomov goes home to be nursed through grave illness by the widow Agafya, and
Olga goes abroad, where in Paris, the novelist, rather facilely, contrives a meeting
between herself and Stolz. This is not, however, a case, in the idiom of our childhood,
of the chap's pal getting the girl, thus betraying the chap. Although Stolz and Olga
marry, they both continue to love, even to revere, Oblomov. In the meantime he has
been tricked into further so-called 'legal transactions' by Agafya's brother Ivan. The
fruits of the 'transactions' enable Ivan to move out, get married and, to preserve
appearances, dole out a frugal allowance to Agafya. She, great simple heart, is put to
the pin of her collar to provide Oblomov, her 'gentleman', with even a semblance of
luxury. To do this she pawns and re-pawns all her valuables – and one day we are told:

(Reader) – 'Oblomov, without suspecting anything, drank the currant vodka,
following it up with some excellent smoked salmon, his favourite dish of giblets,
and a fresh white hazel hen. Agafya and the children had the servants' cabbage,
soup and porridge, and it was only to keep Oblomov company that she drank two
cups of coffee.'

(J.J.) – But matters are even worse when once again Stolz descends upon
Oblomov. From the decrepit condition of the apartment, and the deplorable dinner that is all Agafya can rustle up for him, Stolz detects something rotten. Loyal as
ever and from no sense of guilt in having annexed Olga, he sets about disentangling
Oblomov's financial affairs. He himself takes over Oblomov's *affairs*, having exposed
brother Ivan and his crony Tarantyev. Oblomov, for once quite out of character,
slaps Tarantyev's face, when he comes boorishly claiming intercession on behalf of
Ivan. But this blow is purely symbolic, for despite Stolz's pleadings, Oblomov
refuses to budge from the house of Agafya, who has been to him nurse and mother and perhaps lover, and who, as Stolz discovers years later, will have become his
wife and borne him a son.

Before that final visit Stolz and Olga discuss the mystery of Oblomov as Stolz de-
livers an astonishing panegyric on the sluggard, the sybarite, the socially expendable:

(Reader) – 'People knocked him down, he grew indifferent and, at last,
dropped asleep, crushed, disappointed, having lost the strength to live; but he has
not lost his honesty and his faithfulness. His heart has never struck a single false
note; there is no stain on his character … A regular ocean of evil and baseness may
be surging around him, the entire world may be poisoned and turned upside down
… Oblomov will never bow down to the idol of falsehood, and his soul will always
be pure, noble, honest … His soul is translucent, clear as crystal. Such people are
rare; – they are like pearls in a crowd! His heart cannot be bribed: he can be relied
on always and everwhere.

I have known lots of people possessing high qualites, but never have I met a heart more pure, more noble, and more simple. I have loved many people, but no one so warmly and so firmly as Oblomov. Once you know him you can not help loving him.'

(J.J.) – Clearly, Agafya, herself a simple heart, recognizes all this. She nurses Oblomov through his last illness with the utmost devotion, and when he dies, she surrenders their son to Stolz, refusing to touch a kopeck of the revenue of the estate which is legally hers. Soltz and Olga try to persuade her to come and live with them in the country, but always she replies:

(Reader) – 'Where one was born and bred, there one must die.'

(J.J.) – But the meetings in St Petersburg between Stolz, Olga, and the Oblomov child and Agafya have an almost ritual burden of emotion. 'They were all bound by the same feeling, by the same memory of the crystal – clear soul of their dead friend.' As for Oblomov himself:

(Reader) – 'His body is resting under a modest urn, surrounded by shrubs, in a lonely corner of the nearest graveyard. Branches of lilac, planted by a friendly hand, slumber over his grave, and the wormwood spreads its scent in the still air. The angel of peace himself seems to be guarding his sleep.'

(J.J.) – For years after the publication of *Oblomov*, Russian critics debated the question, 'What is Oblomovitis?' Well, clearly, it is the flaw in the crystal. But it is surely something more. It is perhaps that element in all of us which, if uncontrolled, will allow us to drift without rudder across the ocean of life, until we meet shipwreck. Maybe it is the simple death-wish, or an innate distaste for the world as we find it. It is a measure of Goncharov's greatness as an artist that he can lend a wry, even a tragic, dignity to a figure whom we first meet as a semi-grotesque nincumpoop, but whom we end by, if not loving, certainly not despising. The novel *Oblomov* tests the stamina of our hearts.

Austin Clarke

(Hibernia, 18 July 1969)

In 1962 the Oxford University Press produced a very odd volume called *Six Irish Poets,* edited by Robin Skelton. The oddness consisted in the fact that all of the poets but Austin Clarke were under forty. Clarke at the time was nearly seventy. A couple of years later, Oxford brought out a paperback featuring Clarke, Charles Tomlinson and Tony Connor. Now, this kind of bridging the generations is excellent, but let there be no mistake about it, it is also unusual. How does it come about that a seventy-year-old, and not invariably smiling, public man should be associated with the most forward-thrusting of young Irish poets?

One must go back a little. In 1917 Yeats was nearing the height of his power. Æ's 'nest of singing birds' had been quenched. Yet Yeats, being like all great men excessively human, needed disciples. Clarke was not one that he chose, but he did bestow the laurel on a far lesser poet, Clarke's boyhood friend, F.R. Higgins. God forgive me, but there are times when I think Yeats was a blockhead.

At all events, Clarke, with the instinct of a lone wolf, made off to London in 1922. He had to his credit an M.A., three or four years teaching at University College, Dublin, an unhappy marriage (to 'Margaret' of the Autobiographies), and three volumes of verse: *The Vengeance of Fionn* (1917), *The Fires of Baal* (1922) and *The Sword of the West* (1922).

For fifteen years he earned his living as a reviewer – 'professional reviewer', he is careful to stress. Some of these years may have been lean, but there is little evidence in the Autobiographies that the sustenance of the Clarkes (he had re-married) was confined to bread and cheese. The real leanness lay in the grind of reviewing and the subsequent hacking of review copies. Yet, for all the hackwork, he could produce *The Cattle Drive at Cuailgne* (1924), his first verseplay, *The Son of Learning* (1927) *Pilgrimage and Other Poems* (1929), and his first prose romance, *The Bright Temptation* (1932). Despite the fact that this latter was banned in Ireland, as was his magisterial successor, *The Singing Men at Cashel* (1936), he returned to Ireland in 1937. It is well to note that Clarke is steeped in *pietas,* not only the *pietas* of his country but of his clearly beloved native city. And family *pietas,* too, is there. He is proud of his ancestors, the Brownes, and he has gone so far as to call his third son 'Dardis' after his maternal grandmother, Ellen Dardis, of County Meath.

But after his return to Ireland in 1937, for all the prestigious achievement of the two prose romances, he might well have taken his place as a slightly a-diapasonal note in the Irish Literary Establishment. He was only forty-one but already a man with a 'niche'. In 1938 appeared another thin volume of verse, *Night and Morning*, and I think I can say safely without contradiction that this cold, lucidly passionate booklet struck my contemporaries growing up in the early fifties as the last cry of an extinct bird.

There were, of course, the plays, some of them very nearly popular successes (*The Plot Succeeds*, for instance). And in *The Flame, Silver Eucharia, Black Fast, The Moment Next to Nothing*, one perceived that imagination eternally mortified (and tormented?) by the battles between the subtleties of conscience and the subtleties of the flesh.

But for all this, how did Austin Clarke in the space of fourteen years (1955–69) become undisputedly the greatest living Irish poet?[1] And how can it be that of the younger poets of my friendship or acquaintance – I could list many names, but Kinsella, Montague, Hutchinson, O'Grady, must suffice – regard him as Elder Statesman?

Well, in the first place, a minor miracle occurred with *Ancient Lights* (1955), verse both local and corrosive, both topographical and penetrative. In quick succession followed *Too Great a Vine* and *The Horse Eaters*. These three little volumes were collected with *Pilgrimage* and *Night and Morning* as *Later Poems* (1961).

Much of this verse may seem esoteric, or hoity-toity. The fact remains that except for certain long autobiographical excursus, these poems are about the probems of the Dublin poor, as Clarke understands them, and also that they reveal a blazing candour and, if I may be pardoned a poor 'clerks' pun, Augustinian honesty. No other poet in hand has dared to tackle the problems of foundlings, illegitimacy, contraception, not to mention hyprocrisy in high places, purple and green. In the second place, Clark's juniors, quite apart from the substantial values of his verse, have rejoiced in the flexing of muscles within chains. As every schoolboy knows, Edmund Gosse said of Racine, that his ' verse was in silver chains'. Clarke's verse strains at the chains and leaves them intact.

But the *Late Poems* of 1961 was not to be Clarke's *dimittis*. In 1963 came *Flight to Africa*. In 1966, on the occasion of Clarke's seventieth birthday, the formidable *Mnemosyne Lay in Dust*. To explore the history of a mental illness requires not merely self-knowledge but also considerable moral courage. To explore it in the fixed context of a fixed locale, while at the same time rendering a testimony of universal relevance, is surely a mark of genius. Clarke's hero, 'Maurice Devan', has his habitat in St Patrick's Hospital.[2] But he is also Everyman in the jungle of the modern world. The local details about the Liffey and Guinness barges and Steeven's Hospital[3] serve to point up the poem's central plea.

> When sleep has shut the bolt and bar,
> And reason fails at midnight,
> Dreading that every thought at last
> Must stand in our own light
> Forever, sinning without end:
> O pity in their pride
> And agony of wrong, the men
> In whom God's image died.

Old Fashioned Pilgrimage which followed in 1967 is, for this reader, of less urgency than some earlier volumes. The 'pilgrimage' embraces much of Clarke's American tour, and the Americans have so much money that they can afford to restore even what they have destroyed.[4] (A childish argument, superfiscal (*sic*), but worth pondering.) It's quite another matter with *The Echo at Coole* (1968), which is for the first thirty pages a sustained and incontrovertible attack on Barbarism in all sections of the community, in so far as reverence for the past is concerned.

> Of Thomas Moore, no longer any sign,
> Only a public-house with a new sign.

In the second part of this book, the satire is both ferocious and pertinent (the two do not always go together). The poem on the President of the State is nearly virulent. But we must remember that in the twenties Clarke wrote stirring lines against the Provisional Government of the Irish Free State. One poem, 'New Liberty Hall', indicates how in touch with ordinary people a great poet can be. So also 'In O'Connell Street' and the extraordinary 'The Subjection of Women'. Lesser men might have praised Maud Gonne and Con Markievicz. Only Clarke would have remembered Helena Molony and Louie Bennett and Dr Kathleen Lynn. It is a small point, but indicative of how deeply Clarke is in touch with his people and their past. Indeed his interest in Dublin may be compared only with that of Joyce. The three undisputed Dubliners in contemporary literature are Joyce, O'Casey, and Clarke, and Clarke's Dublin is immediate and palpable.

I have earlier mentioned his preoccupation with Swift in his capacity as founder of St Patrick's Hospital. I have also hinted that *Mnemosyne Lay In Dust* is a great poem. But perhaps *A Sermon On Swift* (in the volume of the same name) is even greater. For it is a rare literary achievement – we must look back to Persius or Pope to find an equivalent. It is at once an important poem and an important human and critical evaluation.

> Tympana, maddened by inner terror, celled
> A man who did not know himself from Cain.

And again, and these lines harmonize with Clarke's burning sense of social justice.

> *Swift gave his savings*
> *To mumbling hand, to tatters. Bare kibes ran after*
> *Hoof as he rode beside the Liffey to sup*
> *At Celbridge.*

Most moving of all are the lines that bring us back to *Mnemosyne*.

> *Last gift of an unwilling patriot, Swift willed*
> *To us a mansion of forgetfulness. I lodged*
> *There for a year until Errata led me*
> *Beyond the high-walled garden of Memory,*
> *The Fountain of Hope, to the rewarding Gate,*
> *Reviled but no longer defiled by harpies. And there*
> *In Thomas Street, nigh to the busy stalls,*
> *Divine Abstraction smiled.*

I have touched on only a few facets of Austin Clarke's work. He is, for instance, an assiduous scholar: he has edited Joseph Campbell and George Fitzmaurice, and even as I write, I have the jacket of his UCD Lectures, *The Celtic Twilight and the Nineties*, with a foreword by Roger McHugh.

But no portrait of this seventy-three-year-old man, so kindly, indeed so avuncular to the young, must omit the essential tenderness beneath so many of his satirical poems. Let me translate from his French translator, Claude Esteban: 'and under the mordant tone and the bitterness of the propositions, one will easily detect the voice of a tenderness that has been wounded, perpetually trembling, but always contained'. The week this appears, Mr Clarke will represent Ireland at the Poetry International organized by the Arts Council of Great Britain.

The Clarke Canon[1]

(The Irish Press, 26 March 1981)

SEVEN years after his death (on 19th March 1974, at the age of seventy-seven) the scenario of Austin Clarke's writing life has been pretty dogmatized. In this country at least one of the orthodoxies is that of a great divide in Clarke's achievements dating from 1955, when at the age of fifty-nine he published *Ancient Lights, Poems and Satires*, followed by *Too Great a Vine in 1957*, and *The Horse Eaters* in 1960. Not unfairly, I believe, a simplistic version of this orthodoxy is that at about the age of sixty Clarke became a modern, even an ultra-modern poet. (So it was that in 1962 Clarke figured in Robin Skelton's *Six Irish Poets*, at the age of sixty-six, with confrères of whom the oldest were only 35 and one of the others only thirty.)

Another received opinion is that if Clarke had not had his astonishing rejuvenation and, in a sense, metamorphosis in 1955, he would not count for much in Irish letters, because of his attachment to outmoded and/or outworn forms. Even as sympathetic a commentator as Thomas Kinsella (in several places apart from his Introduction to his selection from *The Collected Poems* [of Clarke] now reprinted) tends, if only by force of emphasis, to reduce the achievement of pre-1955 Clarke. Some of my contemporaries have shorter memories than mine.[2] We did not foresee *Ancient Lights* when we revered the chilly lyricism of *Pilgrimage* (1929) and the bone-dry anguish of *Night and Morning* (1938). And some of us had read the banned prose romances *The Bright Temptation* (1932), *The Singing Men at Cashel* (1936) and *The Sun Dances at Easter* (1952), and seen some of the eleven verse plays he wrote between 1927 and 1955. I think our respect wavered only when we read his neo-Georgian reviews in *The Irish Times*.

So grateful am I to Dr Tapping for covering the entire canon that my caveats will seem ungracious, even to myself. He deals with the whole *Collected Poems* (1974); with the whole *Collected Plays* (1963) – which contains not twelve but eleven items – and those uncollected, being the *The Two Interludes* from Cervantes (1968) and *The Impuritans* (1973) and the posthumous *The Third Kiss* (1976) and *Liberty Lane* (1978), and with the three prose romances which he prefers to call novels, though Clarke did not. Oddly, he has no reference to an important later play, *The Visitation*, which appeared in *Irish University Review*, Spring 1974. I suspect, but cannot prove, that he did not check *Two Interludes* with their originals; Clarke is much more ribald than Cervantes.

Particularly valuable for Irish people will be Dr Tapping's account of the three prose romances, since only *The Bright Temptation* is in print, and *The Sun Dances at Easter* remains banned, I believe.[3] But what he has to say about the first of these is somewhat weakened in power by the misprint 'Cile-na-gCich as Irish for 'Sheila-of-the-Paps', taken over wholesale from the Dolmen Press 1965 edition. That Dr Tapping should not have detected this gross misprint is disquieting: as a Canadian he might be pardoned, but surely someone in the Academy Press knows a little Irish?

And in his spirited account of *The Singing Men at Cashel*, as well as in his discussion of the poem 'The Confession of Queen Gormlai', from *Pilgrimage*, he might have looked at Maire Cruise O'Brien's essay 'The Two Languages' (in *Conor Cruise O'Brien Introduces Ireland*, ed. Owen Dudley Edwards, 1969), in which she expands Clarke's imaginative achievement, 'In effect his novel ... actually fills a lacuna in our repertory of medieval romances. It is the lost tale of Queen Gormley of Cashel ... of which only the lyric interludes survive from the Irish original.' He also ignores Clarke's own signpost to Máire MacNeill a propos *The Sun Dances* and the play *The Moment Next to Nothing* (1953).

If, as I have indicated, the pre-1955 Clarke is not to be written off in the national minor league, the 'great' Clarke is perhaps too various in kind and technique and temperament to be contained in a single book. In that sense, Dr Tapping is right in maintaining that his subject is the other 'great Irish poet'. But I think that he overlooks a disturbing weakness in Clarke: the man who could produce masterpieces like 'The Loss of Strength', and 'Martha Blake at Fifty-One', and who could work and brood over 'Mnemosyne Lay in Dust' for over forty years, who could in one volume contain the antithetical loveliness of 'Orphide' and 'The Healing of Mis', was also vain (or innocent) enough to publish bitty word-games. Unlike Yeats, he never (except towards the very end) in his 'great' period seemed to be aware of the gravel in the rapidly tumbling volumes. Future scholars will have to decide whether the volumes from *Flight to Africa* (1968) to *A Sermon on Swift* (1968) – four in all, excluding, of course, *Mnemosyne* (1966) – required the discipline of an editorial hand.[4]

For all I've written here for and against Dr Tapping's book, only the begrudging will have the gall to withhold respect for this marathon pioneer achievement.

The Irish Dimension[1]

(Hibernia, 13 July 1978)

This weighty volume based on, but not exclusively, the lectures delivered at the Sixth Annual Conference of the Canadian Association for Irish Studies held at McGill University, Montreal, in March 1973, has, despite its follies, much to commend it. The editor is hard put to it to defend the volume's title, which, as he admits, could cover almost everything in Irish literature. Indeed 'myth and reality' might be a useful starting point for the study of *any* literature or *all* literature. The panel discussion chaired by Ann Saddlemyer, in which the participants were David Greene, Thomas Kinsella, Jay Macpherson and Kevin B. Nolan (sic), was a non-discussion, with some interest from what the speakers revealed of themselves as they gave forth on '*Ancient Myth and Poetry*'. Kevin B. Nowlan of U.C.D.'s History Department (I am deliberately chucking academic styles for the review), for instance, quite clearly is in the vanguard of the demythogizers of Irish history. Since presumably his contribution was taped, it is not his fault that 'Pearse' should appear as 'Pierce'.

What pleases me about this volume, chiefly, is the quality of the contributions from native Irish writers: to put it bluntly, with one or two exceptions the Irish contribution is clean, free of provincial verdigris. One of the exceptions might be Leonard Boyle O.P. who, in seeking to vindicate the tradition of Irish as 'Island of Saints and Scholars', finds it necessary to be claimant of his nationality ('As an Irishman, however, I have no intention of embracing an English cause ...') and tonally contemptuous ('innocent foreigner'). Fr Boyle writes very well on his enormous theme, but it does not seem to occur to him that there is a vast difference between solid achievements in scholarship and piety, and picturesque apocrypha like the delicious tale of the seventh-century abbot Ailbe and the three saintly nuns Tallulah (Halleluia!), Tallitha and Squiatha. I should add, in fairness, that I have gone off Dominicans.

Denis Donoghue continues to intrigue me by his wholly personal combination of massive cerebral activity and awareness of the relationship between art and life. Writing about Yeats and 'The Question of Symbolism', he is at once human (to the dangerous extent of 'a stolen kiss') and clinical, passing elegantly from laboratory to garden.

Thomas Kilroy[2] (nb, should this not be Kinsella?) is one of a new Irish breed, the creative academic. Here he takes the unicorn by the horn and makes illuminating comparisons between the theatres of Yeats and Beckett. We do learn something when he, for instance, analogizes Yeats's orchestration of myth and Beckett's use of music hall routines: the poetry of *reprise*. Mr Kilroy[3] rides high but skilfully on Antonin Artaud and the theatre where the primacy of language is not absolute. He is valuable on *The Herne's Egg,* the most scathing of Yeats's plays.

J.R.R. Mays[4] I take to be Irish, though I am puzzled when he writes 'admirers of Clarke's work who have read *Murphy* have seemed oblivious of the identification (that between Clarke and the poetaster 'Ticklepenny'). In the Dublin of my youth, the identification was accepted with distress, but without question. But Mr Mays's treatment of *Murphy* and other of its identifications with contemporaries, more shadowy, less obtrusive than the Clarke-Ticklepenny one, is admirable. Here is the kind of scholarship which makes us want to re-read *for pleasure*. And Mr Mays has exonerated the *Mauvais Gout* of Clarke's intrusion into *Murphy:* 'The coupling of commitment and indecision, which Clarke reflects *in only the most obvious way,* is an aberration integral to this early fiction.'

Alec Reid's succinct piece on Beckett seen on screen, and the immense and lustrous contribution made by the late Jack MacGowran to the revelation of Beckett theatre in English, may seem lightweight in its learned (and often prolix) company, but it is essential as an Irish theatre critic's view. I remember the shame I felt when MacGowran played his *From Beginning to End*, his evocation of the Beckett Man, in Dublin, to paltry audiences.

Denis Johnston figures both as subject and talker in this volume. Veronica O'Reilly (whom I take to be Irish-Canadian) takes us along Mr Johnston's intellectual trail right up to 1976, using his unpublished diaries, face-to-face interviews, and *The Brazen Horn* (1976). Mr Johnston, although he communicates some misinformation – e.g. Graham Greene praised *At Swim - Two-Birds* when it was first published in 1939, not when it was reissued in 1968 – is sprightly about Myles na Gopaleen, which means 'Myles of the Little Horses', not 'Myles the Litter Horse'.

The late Kate O'Brien (1897–1974) was seventy-five and none too well when she gave her Canadian address on '*Imaginative Prose by the Irish, 1820–1970*'. Presumably she did not oversee her script (she died in August, 1974); otherwise she would not be so misrepresented, shamefully so. 'I have been very much moved by what one must call 'National' passion – I mean that the idea of being Irish rather than any other breed is important'. What the context makes clear is that in fact she wrote 'I have *never* been very much moved ...'. For 'being Irish' in an elitist context was not for her important, 'but to be free, to be able to say when you mean, that is vital'. Purely as a personal document this address/essay is most moving: full of that generous enthusiasm so offensive to our strict younger critics.

[Ann Saddlemyer]⁵ ... closes the volume with a hard, shrewd look at some of the myths which, willynilly, have stuck to us from Yeats, and the manner in which Joyce proceeded, through the 'mediation of Bloom in particular', to repudiate the mythologizations of the Irish Literary Revival.

In mentioning only the Irish contributors to this volume, I may be accused of something worse than 'provincial verdigris'. My stratagem has been deliberate; far too seldom do we hear what the Irish themselves think about the Irish, in a serious context. The report is grossly insufficient given the consummate folly of the book's title.

Five Voices

(Irish Independent, 6 September 1969)

Poems. By Jorge Luis Borges. Trans. Anthony Kerrigan. (Dublin 1969)
The Hag of Beare. A rendition from the Old Irish. By Michael Hartnett. (Ibid.)
Homage to James Thomson (B. V.). At Portobello. By Michael Smith. (Ibid.)
Watches. By Trevor Joyce (Ibid.)

Mr Kerrigan has brought together some translations from the eminent Argentinian writer, Borges. A splendidly baroque form of dedication includes *'The Re-created and Re-enacted Sinn Féin and I.R.A. of the Future.'*

Very often, a foreigner may understand a country better than a native, and, anyway, I have been assured that I am not a characteristic 'native'. But I doubt if the bodies mentioned in Mr Kerrigan's dedication will be pleased by association with these magnificent poems, especially 'Tango' and 'Allusion to a Ghost of the Eighteen-Nineties'. Here are some lines from the first:

> *What obscure alleyways or*
> *wasteland*
> *Of heaven is darkened by*
> *the hard*
> *Shade of the man who was*
> *shadow,*
> *Muraña that Knife of*
> *Palermo?*

Mr Hartnett's version of 'The Hag' will, perhaps, give offence to senior poets and the quite remarkable number of people who are never heard to speak Irish, but who somehow give the impression of having divined its riches. For myself, this version is more than an accomplished instance of its kind.

What is rare in translation, it has a note of the poet's own voice, as I know it from his earlier poems and his version of *Tao*.

> *the three floods*
> *in which I would dream to*
> *drown:*

> *A flood of loves, of horses*
> *and of gentle slim grey*
> *hounds.*

Michael Hartnett never raises his voice, but he can articulate passion. He is not wholly successful, as when the Hag spurns the ninth-century equivalent of counter-jumpers:

> *today you claim all, yet you*
> *grant none nothing: if you*
> *give*
> *you shame the given, with*
> *great*
> *boasting of a little gift.*

The English language will not take 'grant none nothing'.

Mr Smith's poem in homage to James Thomson (B.V.), 1834–1922, is scarcely of a stature to warrant separate publication, but it is to me, who lives not far from Portobello and the Paul Smith country, very interesting.

I sense in this poem the seed of a much more important one. The fact that Mr Smith is attracted to the author of 'The City of Dreadful Night' suggests that his imagination is toying with the horrors of our own city, themes not treated yet in verse. His philosopher-vagrant's vision is one of ultimate darkness.

Readers may be puzzled by 'B.V.', as I was myself, until another young poet, younger even than Mr Smith, Hayden Murphy, told me that Thomson signed himself so, signifying 'Bysshe-Volanis', the first being Shelley's middle name, and the second an anagram of the German Romantic Novalis's name.

Trevor Joyce is twenty-two, and has published already a booklet I do not know. I can conceive that many of my own contemporaries would have little time for these icy, unrelentingly hopeless poems, with their bleak cityscapes and unblinkered view of human forms. It would be facile, though, to dub these verses the postured stances of youth's modish pessimism.

I cannot, myself, recall any other young Irish poet writing like this at the moment. Mr Joyce forewords his poems with a text from Francis Bacon (the Anglo-Irish painter, not the philosopher):

'The existence of a rose is a violence.' There are no roses in Trevor Joyce. His Dublin may have affinities with that of his Brobdingnian namesake, but it resembles more Baudelaire's Paris of the 1850s.

> *All forms are savaged as they*
> *come!*
> *maimed men who limp on*
> *club-leg,*
> *garrotted men with meths-*

> *blue faces*
> *women whose secret hangs*
> *like flesh upon a stunted*
> *fang,*
> *and all the ashen faces of*
> *the dead.*

I will burn my boats: these few poems have impressed me more than any young poet's seen for the first time, since Michael Hartnett sent me verses for *Poetry Ireland* in 1962. But let him not be parsimonious with his bleak utterance.

Collected Poems: by Thomas MacGreevy

(The Irish Press, 13 November, 1971)

With a cover drawing of the author by Jack B. Yeats, and a Foreword by Samuel Beckett, which is a reprint of his review of MacGreevy's *Poems* (1934), this elegantly got-up book is bound to become a collector's item. It may without prejudice be argued that MacGreevy was a collector's poet. But here I must introduce a personal and indeed a confessional note.

About 1949, before ever I had read Eliot's *The Waste Land* in its entirety I was familiar with the MacGreevy *Poems* of 1934, as were some of my slightly older friends. I even began an 'Homage to MacGreevy', of which three lines survive:

Thomas MacGreevy / Heard unearthly music / Passing westwards over Stephen's Green.

What was it that attracted myself and my contemporaries, barely literate by today's student standards, to a poet whose obscurity was not of the then currently fashionable kind, and for whose proper comprehension one needed some acquaintance with at least seven cultures?

Looking back to 1949, four years after the War and during its aftermath of uneasiness about our country's abstention from Europe's agony, I think MacGreevy satisfied our subconscious yearning for the ideal of a thoroughly Europeanized Irishman. Of course the poem most often on our lips was his 'Áodh Ruadh Ó Domhnaill', even though it required some knowledge of Spanish. But the scrap of verse of my own was based on lines from his 'Homage to Hieronymus Bosch', and now, after over twenty years, reading these poems again (only five other poems complete the canon), I am astonished and touched to find how many of them have remained, like sunken treasure in my consciousness. And because one is older and presumably better educated, few of them seem obscure, even if few of them may be styled easy.

What I had forgotten was how, even as a young and iconoclastic European, MacGreevy clung to a kind of aristocratic Catholic Nationalism. In a poem such as 'The Other Dublin', from *Poems*, right down to 'Homage to Vircingetorix (1950), he is writing as an 'Irish-Irishman' with disdain for what he calls a 'Norman-Irishman'. I think he got an impious pleasure from knowing that he, the Kerry Catholic, was so much more instructed in all the arts than his Anglo-Irish culture-dabbling acquaintances. I use the last term advisedly, for Beckett and Jack Yeats were his friends and if my memory does not trick me, he once shared a flat with Lennox Robinson. In his last years, despite several invitations, I refused to meet him. Old man subconscious must have warned me that he would have hated my inclusive concept of the Irish nation.

But what a fine poet! Look at 'Homage to Li Po':

> *I fought the fever*
> *I thought I had got this too*
> *adolescent heart in hand —*
> *One must be classical.*
> *Then I set out, serene,*
> *To enjoy the bright day,*
> *But I met you again,*
> *I am a sick man again.*

Kate O'Brien: First Lady of Irish Letters

(Hibernia, 11 May 1973)

PROFILE

Kate O'Brien has been in town, among other things recording for RTÉ's 'Rich and Strange' series a talk on the great Spanish novelist, Benito Pérez Galdoós. Before that, she had been to Montreal, where, at McGill University, she had spoken on the tradition of Anglo-Irish prose to a Conference of Irish Studies.

She was seventy-five last December. She jokes about her age, her physical slowness, her occasional lapse of memory. But this writer has known her for twenty-five years, has heard many of her stories, personal and public, and can aver that, for all her protestations, her mind is as keen and luminous as ever and mercifully has escaped that last affliction of noble minds, repetitiveness.

This lovely girl – and her early beauty is almost legendary – came to UCD shortly after the 1916 Rising., when Dublin was, as she puts it, 'a smoking ruin'. Her favourite story concerns her first-year Latin class, held 'in an old tin shed', and her lecturer, Michael Tierney, later to be a President of UCD She was one of a pack of 'giggling girls' whose Latin was nugatory and who, when asked to construe Livy, read straight from *Kelly's Key*. Kate O'Brien, being clever, 'and I was', also used the *Key*, but to achieve an effect of honest labour, she 'hummed and hawed', until one day the then Mr Tierney (in his early twenties himself) announced: 'Miss O'Brien, you are the cleverest reader of *Kelly's Key* I've ever known.'

Whatever about her Latin, she took a good B.A. in 1919, with First Class Honours in French and Second in English. And then, because of straitened family circumstances, it was the emigrants' boat. She answered an advertisement in the *New Statesman* for a job as translator on the Foreign News page of the *Manchester Guardian*. And she got it. I asked her whether her beauty might have influenced her Fleet Street interviews in the selection of an untried young Irish woman graduate. 'It might have, but I didn't know – I wasn't aware of it.' So she began her journalistic career at the then princely salary of 5 a week. 'Everybody was very kind to me; I found that my French was good enough, my German wasn't, and anyhow, I couldn't translate things like "Russian rolling-stock".' But the Foreign Page folded and Kate O'Brien found herself teaching in a Hampstead school run by 'some awful snob nuns'. One compensation was the nuns' 'sideline', a branch for refugee Russian, Polish and Hungarian children, 'by far the most intelligent'.

I was aware of Miss O'Brien's progress up to this point, in a vague way. What I did not know was that in 1921 she went to Washington to act as 'a kind of secretary' to Stephen O'Mara, who, in June of that year, had taken over from his brother James as co-ordinator of de Valera's Bonds Drive. It was there that she met Harry Boland, an intimate of both Michael Collins and de Valera and a prominent member of the I.R.B. I think only when she was speaking of Harry Boland did I detect a slight glistening of the eyes. 'Whenever he took me to New York with him, we'd go to see Sophie Tucker – you know, the Red Hot Momma – he loved her'. Sophie Tucker will appear again, but only after the Treaty was signed, 6 December 1921.

Miss O'Brien's brief comments form a not unmoving footnote to the official histories. I hope I summarize her memories without inaccuracy or prejudice. Boland wanted to return to Ireland to take part in the Treaty Debates. De Valera cabled back to the effect that he had 'better stay where he was'. It is possible the 'Chief' feared that Boland, because of his friendship with Collins and his I.R.B. connection, might take the pro-Treaty side. But Boland insisted on his wish to return and finally de Valera yielded and cabled back, beginning 'Mo ghrá thú ...'

In the event, Boland voted against the Treaty. On a July evening in 1922, Kate O'Brien saw the name of Sophie Tucker in lights in the West End and, in a spontaneous gesture of nostalgic affection, wired to Harry Boland. She learned later that at about 2 a.m. that night, or rather morning, Boland was mortally wounded in a swoop by Free State forces on the Grand Hotel in Skerries. At this point, without any prompting from me, Miss O'Brien said 'I have always been a-political'. Indeed, in previous conversations I have heard her speak with emotion about the gunning down of Kevin O'Higgins.

Then came the beginning of the long love affair with Spain, when she went as a governess to the Alreiza family, outside Bilbao, for a period of ten months. She came back to London to marry a young Dutchman, Gustaaf Renier, once famous for his book, *Are the English Really Human?* The marriage was not a success.

In 1926 her friend from Dublin days, the actress Veronica Turleigh, bet her a pound she could not write a play in a month. 'I did, and she paid the pound.' This was *Distinguished Villa*. In this connection she has some wry stories. On the first night she received a telegram from Sean O'Casey: 'Dublin salutes Limerick ...' and he asked if he could come to see her. He did, and she remembers him saying: 'I never sit in the stalls before the curtain goes up without wishing it'll be a damn bad play.'

Distinguished Villa, while not a great success in London, did well enough to tour to allow her to take a cottage near Tonbridge Wells in Kent.[1] There, at the suggestion of her agent, she began to write a novel. It was accepted by Heinemann on the strength of the first few chapters. 'It seems incredible these days, but they kept me while I finished it.' *Without My Cloak* was published in 1931, and won the Hawthornden Prize.[2] Some of the characters from that book re-appear in *The Ante-Room* (1934), which remains one of her own favourites, although she is less enthusiastic than she was, say, ten or fifteen years ago. In 1936 came two books that mirrored her Spanish experience, the novel, *Mary Lavelle*, which was banned immediately,[3] and the travel book, *Farewell Spain*. She would not be drawn on the question of the interdict on the novel, and also *The Land of Spices* (1941)[4] (which Irish University Press are re-issuing soon in paperback).[5]

As regards the title of the travel book, it is *not* to be taken as an overt comment on the issues of the Civil War. She would have gone back to Spain had she had a sponsor. To jump forward a decade, when she did try to return to Spain in 1947, she was refused entry on the grounds that Generalissimo Franco had taken exception to her treatment of Philip II in her novel *That Lady* (1946).[6] Eventually, through the intervention of the Irish Ambassador to Spain ('who had to tell a lot of lies – I was a Reformed Character, a High-Class Convent Girl') she returned to Spain in 1957. Since then she has returned off and on to Madrid and her beloved Avila, birthplace of her special, if not quite orthodox cult, Santa Térèsa. (She published a little book on the saint in 1951.)

By 1957 she had been settled over seven years in Roundstone, Co. Galway, where 'the quality of the light, the courtesy of the people, the grace of the children' enchanted her, as they continue to do. Her house there was a perhaps over-hospitable centre for personal friends, transient writers and painters and (it is I who am saying this) nuisances. This lovely place she was able to acquire from the success of *That Lady* and the play she made of it, in which Katherine Connell played on Broadway. (Shelah Richards did it in Dublin.) But after eleven years, she was compelled to give up Roundstone. She chose finally to live again in Kent, where, so to speak, her first ladder started, to adapt Yeats.

I am not writing either a biography or a critique of Kate O'Brien. She is at present writing her own *Memoirs*: I hope she will enlarge on how she and the late Poet Laureate (Cecil Day-Lewis, one of her keenest admirers, as I recall) scandalized Stephen Spender by singing Moore's *Melodies* and '*Credo in Unum Deum*' in the Piazza San Marco in Venice by moonlight. That's the kind of story which, as told by her, brings out the high-spirited girl who still lives in this 'old lady' (her own expression) of seventy-five.

Her seventies brought her a new public through radio. Harold Pinter's associate, Guy Vaesen, has adapted *Without My Cloak* and *Pray for the Wanderer* (1938) for the B.B.C. This link between O'Brien and Pinter through Vaesen may seem odd. But there are many other odd connections in Kate O'Brien's life. She was one of the first to acclaim Samuel Beckett's first novel *Murphy*, in 1938. It was she who first mentioned the name of the late Arthur Adamov, a pioneer of the Theatre of the Absurd, as far back as 1949.

It is now eleven years since Miss O'Brien has published a book – or rather two books, *My Ireland,* and *Presentation Parlour*, in 1962. Her last novel was *As Music and Splendour*, which came in 1958. Now in between completing her *Memoirs*, she is working on a new novel, her tenth, which is called, provisionally, *Constancy*, set in France and Spain. 'I hope to finish it – but at my age...'

Neither of our universities has chosen to honour Kate O'Brien. Her offence may have been that she wrote at least two bestsellers. It would be fitting to recognize her when *Constancy* is published, not alone for her personal achievement, but for her intransigent commitment to European culture.[7]

A Passionate Talent

(Hibernia, 30 August 1974)

The last time I saw Kate O'Brien was in May 1973. The meeting is recorded in an issue of *Hibernia* for that month. The first time I saw her, as distinct from meeting her, was in the summer of 1945, when on the stage of the Dublin Gaiety she was taking the bow after the ovation given her play *The Last of Summer*, dramatized from her 1943 novel of the same name. There she was: from the heights of the gallery a tiny figure, but one of ineffable dignity in her black cloak.

I met her personally in the Shelbourne Hotel in December 1948, two days after her fifty-first birthday. She was then at the crest of her career. Her 1946 novel had been dramatized (by herself) and the result, though not a great commercial success, at least put her name in lights on Broadway. It may also, I surmise, have slowed down her industriousness, for there were only two more novels, *The Flower of May* (1958) and *As Music and Splendour* (1958).

I am not saying that the bright lights corrupted her. For rather more than most people she was incorruptible, in that she cared for, and sometimes loved, all manner of human beings. In a phrase, she was a natural aristocrat. Such a breed cannot be made, but it can be brought to something near perfection. And perhaps the nuns of Laurel Hill Convent did that for Kate O'Brien.

Her memories of that convent are lovingly evoked in *The Land of Spices* (1941), which our censors thought unsuitable, as they did *Mary Lavelle* (1936). There is tragic irony in the fact that *The Land of Spices* should have appeared openly in Irish bookshops just weeks before her death.

As I said on RTÉ the other morning, I do not think this is the time to make a critical assessment of her novels. For myself, I feel that to speak of her as a one-book writer would be folly. In all her books, there are passages of grave and lovely prose, and that applies to the last time she published, non-fictional, both in 1962, *Presentation Parlour* and *My Ireland*. Those (and there were some) who questioned Kate O'Brien's deep love for her own country can never have read the latter book, indeed can never have known her. But that love was a controlled passion. Sometimes in her human relationships she could give way to tears, but in judgment, in the texture of her affections for art and nature, she was consistently unsentimental.

I may sound as if I knew the woman intimately. I did not. But I knew her as well as any Irishman of my generation. And this I can aver: only under extreme provocation did I ever see her lose her temper. Maybe the regime of Laurel Hill had much to do with this. She suffered nimcompoops if not gladly, yet with patience. They included people who were attracted by her personality, but who could never have read her books. I remember a lady discoursing artlessly on the works of Vicki Baum. Kate said nothing, merely smiled and winked at me. And as this lady rambled on about the glory of '*Grand Hotel*', I thought of that great tapestry of family life *Without My Cloak* (1931), of its sequel, Racinian in its perfection, *The Ante-Room* (1934), and all those others, even the slightest, *Pray for the Wanderer* (1938), which bore the imprint of austere, yet passionate talent. And in that phrase, I find myself passing an interim judgment. But then someone else should be writing about her, for my eyes dim when I think of how much more she could have achieved.

Kate O'Brien

(The Stony Thursday Book 3, Summer 1976)

Towards an appreciation, by John Jordan

IT is difficult to write dispassionately about the work of someone one has known well, and cared for greatly. I might do that one day about Kate O'Brien. I might even have done it in her lifetime. But I am haunted by my last meeting with her in the Spring of 1973, when she was in her seventy-sixth year and yet seemed older. I am not implying a diminution of intellect nor of courage nor of generosity, nor, above all, of gaiety. Merely, and sadly, that within a few years she had become an old woman. Even as late as 1970, she had retained the magic of youth, if in fact, exuberant girlhood.

But perhaps in 1973 I was sad because I had known her since 1948, and if she was now an old woman, then I must be middle-aged. Perhaps it was for my own youth I was grieving.

I will not attempt serious critical judgment, only a few pointers that may inform the young and infuriate the old. The most important influences in Kate's youth, outside her family, may have been her convent upbringing, her spell as a governess in Spain in the twenties, and her unsuccessful marriage. How she alchemized these influences is part of her achievement. After she graduated from UCD in 1919, there came spells of working as journalist (with *The Manchester Guardian*), as teacher in a Hampstead Convent school, as Harry Boland's secretary in America, as governess in Spain, as wife of G.H. Renier (who wrote a famous book called *Are the English Human?*). Her career as a writer proper did not begin until 1926 when she wrote a play, *Distinguished Villa*, which to her surprise was produced not without success. (The text of this play, published in 1927, is very rare: I have never seen a copy.)

On the strength of her play's success and a stipend from Heinemann (who was to publish all her novels) she set about the book by which, perhaps, she is best known, her classic saga of 'Mellick' or Limerick, *Without My Cloak*, which was published in 1931, and won her the Hawthornden Prize. I am told that, in 1931, *Without My Cloak* did not win Kate many friends in Limerick. Apart from putative identification of real and fictional characters, she had the courage to explore certain intensities of love not expected to be within the comprehension of a well-brought-up convent girl. Nowadays such comprehension is commonplace: Certainly not in the Limerick of 1931, for that matter in the Ireland of 1931. I believe that had it been published in 1932 it might have got the chopper, along with, say, Seán O'Faoláin's *Midsummer Night Madness*. But it survived and has been dramatized for R.T.É. Radio. If *Without My Cloak* has a fault, it is a certain shapelessness arising out of an attempt to compress too much material. And Kate once told me that the book was originally much longer, that 'certain material had been cut'. I did not press her on the nature of the 'certain material'. She chose a lesser group of characters from *Without My Cloak* as the *Dramatis Personae* for her second novel, *The Ante-Room*, published in 1934. As I recall, this was Kate's favourite among her own novels. One can see why: this almost intrusively classical presentation of romantic passion is as close as anything in English to the French tradition. She, of course, knew her Racine and in later years was to praise Mauriac. Incidentally, I suspect that had it not been for its rigidly Catholic framework, *The Ante-Room* might have been proscribed.

No such luck attended the third novel, the first book with a Spanish subject, *Mary Lavelle*, published in 1936. Every schoolgirl by now knows why five years later *The Land of Spices was* banned. I'll come to that. But, quite apart from the governess Mary Lavelle's brief, but explicitly passionate, affair with her employer's son, there is introduced another Irish governess, Agatha Conlan. And Agatha confesses to Mary that she likes her own sex. That is about as far as she goes and the scene in question is written with the utmost tact and gentleness. Perhaps it was the gentleness that offended. There is certainly no *apologia* for lesbianism; merely a recognition that Agatha is a human being with human problems. Forty years later, in this country and elsewhere, such a fact is being disputed. Shortly after this novel came the second Spanish book, travel sketches entitled *Farewell Spain*. The title, Kate told me, had not necessarily anything to do with the new political situation in Spain. The book, by the way, indicates the extent of Kate's involvement with Castile. She showed no interest in the South.

Many have seen the next novel, *Pray for the Wanderer*, published in 1938, as Kate's attempt to come to terms with her native country and native city, after the débâcle of *Mary Lavelle*. It's a plausible theory, supported by the book's title and even the book's theme: Matt Costello returns from London to his native city, Mellick. But he goes away again, and there is no indication that he will ever come back. There is quite enough in Kate's work that might be called 'sentimental' without adding to the measure. But the allegedly 'penitent' Kate was out of whatever favour she had managed to pick up. In 1941, her touchingly nostalgic, exquisitely written evocation of convent boarding-school life, *The Land of Spices*, was banned. People, of Kate's coevals who survive, seem to believe that the book was banned because of a 'single sentence'. But the famous 'single sentence' was only part of the matter: even without it, one cannot gainsay the fact that the theme of 'the love that dare not speak its name', this time among men, has been introduced. And another kind of sex, perhaps more distasteful, appears in the character known as 'the judge' who figures in the chapter, 'Summer with Charlie'.

It has always seemed to me that it is a weakness in the construction of the character of the Reverend Mother, formerly Helen Archer, that her entry into religion should have been motivated so *directly* by discovery of her father's pederasty. That is the only flaw I can at present detect in a book which, quite apart from the qualities I have indicated briefly, mirrors without fleck several strata of Edwardian Ireland. I have not space to go into the major theme of the book: the education of the child Anna by Reverend Mother, which, though Anna cannot know it, is reciprocal, for Reverend Mother learns from the child.

I will pass over the next novel, *The Last of Summer,* published in 1943, as it is many years since I read it. But it was from the very top of the old Gaiety in Dublin in September 1945 that I first saw in person the figure of Kate O'Brien as she came forward to take her bow after the first night of the play she and John Perry had made of *The Last of Summer.*

In June 1946, for the first time, I was reading an O'Brien book hot from the press, her novel *That Lady.* (Kate has written somewhere that it was in the correspondence of Saint Térèsa of Avila that she first found a reference to Aña de Mendoza, Princess of Eboli, and was moved to follow her into history.) In a sense, but not in the sense of the last word, *That Lady* marks the apex of Kate's career. There were to be during the next sixteen years, that is up to and including the year 1962, a little book on Térèsa in 1951, two more novels, *The Flower of May* in 1953, *As Music and Splendour* in 1959, and finally in 1962, her book of early reminiscences, *Presentation Parlour*, and what I consider one of her finest achievements, the travel book *My Ireland.*

At the height of her career, even from critics who otherwise might sniff a little, came acclamation of Kate's prose. Let me cite two passages, an acute pleasure to transcribe. The first is from the 1941 novel *The Land of Spices.* Anna Murphy is leaving school. One of her most vivid impressions is of seeing the Spanish girl Pilar as 'a motive in art'.

> So Anna beheld her; something that life can be about, something with power to make life compose around it. She stared at her in wonder, hardly seeing her any more, but realising her lustrous potentiality, and feeling, that for her, the watcher, this moment was a long awaited, blessed gift; that in seeing this transience, this grace, this volatility, flung in a sweet summer hour against great ilex trees, against the evening star, she was encountering alone and in terms of her secret need, a passage of beauty as revelatory and true as any verse of the great elegy (Lycidas).

This is from the 1951 *Térèsa of Avila.* Térèsa is dying.

She may have been lonely for Avila of her childhood, and known that she would not see its towers and walls again. But it is not far from Alba — she would have thought nothing of the mule-ride. And the Salamancan landscape that her dying eyes perceived was gold and tawny in those September days as was the high Paramera of home, and the sky was Castile's immaculate blue, that she had known and suffered under in sixty-seven years. She was not far from home, in those last hours, if she still acknowledged in her affectionate but purified heart that earthly word ...

No one who knew Kate O'Brien without prejudice would deny that a few lines from Térèsa are congruous in any tribute. [1]

Kate O'Brien

(New Hibernia, May 1987)

Oddly it was mid-way through and towards the end of my first term at Oxford[1] that my admiration and affection for Kate O'Brien (1897–1974) was dinted slightly, even if temporarily. In Michaelmas term 1953, through K.O'B., I was introduced to the Reader in French Literature, another Irish woman, Enid Starkie (1897–1970), and was slightly shocked when she jested affectionately about K.O'B.'s 'sentimentality' in her third novel, *Mary Lavelle* (1936).

But I was more shocked when a few weeks later a very distinguished Spanish novelist – in exile from Franco's Spain since 1939 – Arturo Barea (1897–1957) came on a day's visit to Oxford with his Australian-born wife Ilsa and the latter referred flippantly to K.O'B.'s 'sugary' novels, while admitting she had read them. The implication was that this was a forgiveable weakness.

These and other memories surfaced as I was reading Lorna Reynolds' *Kate O'Brien: A Literary Portrait*. I had not realized that Professor Reynolds' friendship with K.O'B. had begun barely two years before I first made the acquaintance of the novelist on 5 December 1948. I was not able to attend the party given later that month by K.O'B. in the Shelbourne in honour of the American actress Katherine Cornell and her director husband Guthrie McClintic, who the following year were to present on Broadway her dramatization of her 1946 novel set in sixteenth-century Spain, *That Lady*: the invitation was conveyed to me by Professor Reynolds but (this sounds barely credible) I had to play in Kilcock in T.C. Murray's *Maurice Harte* the same evening . Incidentally, McClintic had directed in London in 1936 a dramatization of K.O'B.'s second novel, *The Ante-Room* (1934). Professor Reynolds attributes this version to John Perry; my records indicate that the adapters were G. Gower and W.A. Carot. But *The Last of Summer* (1943) was put on stage by K.O'B. and John Perry in 1944, and had its Dublin premiere at The Gaiety, presented by Cyril Cusack, on 16 July 1945. The Dublin premiere of *That Lady* was at The Gaiety also, on 11 June 1951.

I must agree with Professor Reynolds 's memories of that production: 'I saw the play when it was put on in Dublin, and thought it was too discursive and failed to reach a dramatic climax: the material probably needed much more drastic re-shaping than it had been given.' I think it may be concluded that K.O'B.'s only real success as a dramatist, given her fame as a novelist in the years 1931-46 (from *Without My Cloak* to *That Lady*), was with her quickly written play *DistinguishedVilla* produced in the summer of 1926, before she was twenty-nine, and about two years after the collapse of her marriage to the exiled Dutch writer, Gustaaf Renier, in 1924.

We may have to wait for years to know the factual reasons for the brevity of that marriage, which took place in May 1923. Before it she had her first experience of Spain, as governess to the children of the 'wealthy de Areilza family' in a village outside the Basque Nationalist centre, Bilbao. Mary O'Neill, in her introduction to the new edition of *Farewell Spain*, 1985 (the original published in 1937, led Franco to ban K.O'B. for some twenty years from entering Spain, which may explain why, at sixty, her Spanish had ceased to be fluent), quotes a letter from José de Areilza within thirty years after K.O'B. had left Bilbao in 1923, in which he addresses her as 'Miss Kitty' and reveals his discovery of *Mary Lavelle*: 'Thank you, Miss Kitty, for bringing to life the dear shadows of my youth! ...' Was Señor de Areilza aware that Mary Lavelle had been banned in Ireland?

K.O'B.'s first and longest novel, *Without My Cloak*, 1931 (she once told me that originally it was even longer but was 'purged'), Professor Reynolds hails for its 'overall theme... the necessity of love for the development and well-being of every human creature, adult as well as child, and as a concomitant of this, the necessity for the freedom which true love allows to the beloved'. I accept, with distant memories of Fr Martin d'Arcy, her conclusion that 'true love embodies *agape* as well as *eros*, when it is a question of love between the sexes, and is totally *agape* where other relationships are concerned'.

On *The Ante-Room*, 1934, Professor Reynolds is cogent and classical in the restraint of her admiration of what, quintessentially, is K.O'B.'s most perfectly shaped novel. She notes that over All Hallows Eve, All Saints and All Souls, 'the author can turn her searchlight on the workings of the internal world, the movements of the loving heart and the intelligent mind in a condition of agonising conflict'. K.O'B. had much reverence for the novels of Francois Mauriac. Perhaps Professor Reynolds had him in mind when she writes about K.O'B., 'Catholic teaching is not just given mouth-service, merely acknowledged, but is understood and accepted as an inescapable part of life. But love too is inescapable.'

The banning of *Mary Lavelle* in 1934 was not, of course, an isolated affront to Irish writers. The same year Francis Hackett's *The Green Lion*, Seán O'Faoláin's *Bird Alone* and Austin Clarke's *The Singing Men at Cashel* were chopped. Nineteen-thirty-six was a vintage year for the Censorship of Publications Board. I believe, myself, that *Mary Lavelle*, so much admired by José de Areilza, may have been banned as much for the sexual disposition of Agatha Conlon, warned by her confessor of 'a very ancient terrible vice', as for Mary Lavelle's culpable, because clear-headed, adultery with her employer's son.

Professor Reynolds makes the valid point that *Pray for the Wanderer* (1938) and *The Last of Summer* (1943), written after the banning of *The Land of Spices* (1941), represent 'a time of stocktaking for the author and of comment on Irish society'. Certainly they are slight works in comparison with the intervening *The Land of Spices*. At the moment of writing I recall that during a Jesuit-conducted Retreat at Rathfarnham Castle[2] (when the novel was still officially proscribed) I was surprised that when I mentioned it to the Spiritual Director he gave a little *moue* of distaste and changed the subject. When I re-read of the spiritual travail of Mère Marie-Helene Archer and the progress from six to sixteen of her protégé Anna Murphy – a quarter of a century later – I was even more touched and amused and, something more, astonished by the book's purity of motive.

Christine Longford lent me *That Lady* almost as soon as it came out in June 1946. At the time, the story of the Princess of Eboli, her lover Antonio Pérez and the manically pseudo-pious Philip II of Spain, its convolutions and its dying fall, ravished me. In later years, I was better able to appreciate the sombre loveliness of the prose, of a kind I found afterwards only in her 'personal portrait' *Térèsa of Avila* (1951), which I cannot resist quoting, even if Dr Reynolds does not mention the book, although of course she is fully aware of K.O'B.'s attachment to Térèsa: '*She may have been lonely for Avila of her childhood and known that she would not see its towers and walls again. But it is not far from Alba ...*'[3]

Her second-last novel, *The Flower of May*, came out in 1953; her last, *As Music and Splendour*, in 1958. Professor Reynolds is cool about *The Flower of May*: 'It is a book of considerable charm, but of nostalgic charm.' The friendship between the Irish girl, Fanny Morrow, and the French girl, Lucile de Saint Mellin, who have been at school together in Brussels at the beginning of the century, seems factitious, while the villain of the tale, André-Marie, Lucile's brother, belongs to another canon. K.O'B.'s male sinners are all of them, with this one exception, rounded and credible.

She is almost as cool about *As Music and Splendour*, of which the principal characters, Rose Lennane and Clare Halvey, are two Irish girls of the 1880s who attain operatic success in Rome with what seems unnatural rapidity. Professor Reynolds has no doubt that the model for Rose was Margaret Burke-Sheridan, and suggests that the model for Clare may be a contemporary of Burke-Sheridan's, Margaret Lydon.

I find *As Music* far more compelling than *The Flower*, but it is only fair to quote Professor Reynolds's tentative judgment on the decline, as she sees it, in K.O'B.'s creativity: 'Life in Connemara was not turning out to be the ideal it had seemed at first. The place was too isolated, offered too few engagements for the active intellect. It was easy to fall into a routine of good fellowship which involved the too frequent and too long-continued lifting of the elbow.' K.O'B.'s last novel was published when she was still only in her sixty-first year. Her last two books, *My Ireland*

and *Presentation Parlour*, an idiosyncratic travel book, and family reminiscences, respectively, were published in 1962 and 1963.

When I met her last in May 1973 she was talking about a novel she had in hand, entitled *Constancy*. She died on the 13th of August 1974, in her seventy-seventh year, reconciled to the Church, I learn from Professor Reynolds's stylish, reticent, and fundamentally poignant book.

Chatelaine of an Age[1]

(Hibernia, 30 November 1978)

On 2 March 1919 Augusta Gregory, canvassing English parliamentarians for support for Dublin's claim to her nephew Hugh Lane's collection of modern
pictures, relaxed in the evening over a book about *China Under the Empress Dowager*
– of whom she comments, 'an amazing woman, an energy moving in the wrong
direction'. If we substitute 'right' for 'wrong' that judgment might be applied to
Lady Gregory herself.

Most people will know her name in connection with the foundation of the Irish
Literary Theatre, along with Yeats, Edward Martyn and, more dubiously, George
Moore. They might be less aware that without her tireless energy and indomitable
spirit (as well, of course, as her considerable dramatic talent, which achieved
popularity without sacrificing purity of taste) the Abbey might never have survived
into the twenties and the coming of O'Casey.

Many might be even less aware that, after Hugh Lane was drowned in 1915,
when the *Lusitania* was torpedoed, and the disputed legality of the unwitnessed
Codicil to his Will, right up to her death at eighty in 1932, it was she who was the
dynamo in the battle for Dublin's right to such pictures as Renoir's *'Les Parapluies'*
and the two Manets , *Le Concert aux Tuileries* and *Portrait de Mlle. Eva Gonzales*.
(Twenty-seven years after her death, the battle was half-won by a compromise
between Dublin and London.)

Of course she had many helpers, of all shades of political opinion, and all degrees of enthusiasm. She was not above importuning Edward Carson, whose
politics were to her anathema, nor a minor Nationalist M.P. like Alderman Alfred
Byrne (who for most of my childhood seems to have been Lord Mayor of Dublin).

This fat first volume, however, covers only the period from 10 October 1916
to February 1925, just before her seventy-third birthday. The *Journals* cover a great
deal of her activity as a worker for the restoration of the Lane pictures to Ireland
and her travail in the Abbey Theatre. We would have to look to her many formal
prose works for her achievement as a folklorist, and popularizer of both the Red
Branch and Fenian sagas. She was not by modern standards a Gaelic scholar – Maud
Gonne used to say, maliciously, as if she could possibly know, that she cogged from

French versions by D'Arbois de Joubainville in the *Revue Celtique* – but she was a tremendous worker and a genuine lover of the stimulating mixture of aristocratic and peasant Gaelic culture which she found at her doorstep and which, if she did not master, could absorb in a way Yeats never could.

She must not, in her personal relationships, be confined to that long partnership in which she was both nurse and cosseting elder sister to the great poet who was thirteen years her junior. She had a genius for friendship with remarkable men close to her own age, even when their world-views differed vastly from her own. She, a deeply religious woman who read the Bible and Book of Common Prayer for far other than the aesthetic value of their prose, could enjoy trusting relationships with a liberal agnostic like Shaw and the erratically (and erotically) Catholic Wilfred Scawen Blunt, her conversations with whom she records plainly and convincingly, as she might those with an old piper or fisherman: '*Oscar Wilde, he says, overshadowed every other talker where he was. I asked if he was put out if not allowed to talk as much as he wished, but he says he never went to any house where he was not.*'

Politically, she was a separatist, but of an almost incredible kind in the Ireland of her time. If anything, before the Civil War, she was republican in sympathy. But even during the Civil War, when she accepted the Free State status as a step towards Dominionhood and thence towards the Republic, she could grieve both for the assassination of Michael Collins and the judicial murder of Erskine Childers. But what else might we expect from a woman who, during the long agony of Terence MacSwiney, saw nothing incongruous in reciting the '*Prayer for a Sick Person*' from her beloved Book of Common Prayer? Her more general prayer before and during the Civil War was for '*the coming of Thy Kingdom – in Coole – in Kiltartan – in Ireland*'.

It is not commonly known that Lady Gregory held Coole in trust for her son Robert, and that, after his death in an air crash on active service in Italy in 1918, she stayed on in Coole only with the intermittent good-will of her daughter-in-law Margaret. These *Journals* reveal that this 'amazing woman', one of the great chatelaines of her time, was, after 1918, in effect a sublime landlady.

A Growing Monster

(Irish Independent, 23 July 1977)

Judy Garland & the Cold War, by James Simmons. (Belfast 1977)
Poisoned Lands, by John Montague. (Dolmen/Oxford, 1977)
A State of Justice, by Tom Paulin. (London 1977)
Time Enough, by John Hewitt. (Belfast 1977)

At the moment the poet in English closest to Dr Simmons that I can think of is the Canadian, Irving Layton: they are both deliberately slangy (I doubt if either would acknowledge the validity of this term), cock-snooking, keen on bawdiness, but not averse to throwing tenderness in sexual affairs, resolutely in arms against a monster which day-by-day grows less easy to corral and identify – the Establishment.

They both like to sing their poems. A major difference is that Dr Simmons is an Establishment figure himself, paid to instruct the young in English literature.

I have never heard Simmons sing, but would love to now, having read, for instance, 'The Dawning of the Day', and the quite lovely 'For Thomas Moore', and several others in this collection, the spume of a mind undaunted by the categories of academe. The title poem should be read on several levels; the rag-time verses are deceptively simple. Before starting 'No Land is Waste', I was wary. Parodies of Eliot are not my cup of coffee. But this is not a parody. It is a series of poems united by rather more than Simmons' claims : viz. a reaction against 'refined anti-life', a feeling most famously exemplified by Eliot's *The Waste Land*. Simmons uses the Eliotic structure for a funny and poignant autobiographical sequence.

In 1958 Dolmen published Mr Montague's first book, *Forms of Exile*, which contains twenty poems. Of these only twelve re-appeared in *Poisoned Lands* (London 1961). Of the remaining eight, almost all are restored to the new edition of the latter, which also contains several so far uncollected. We may say that the book now represents what Mr Montague wants to keep of his verse for the decade 1950–60.

We are given no biographical details about Tom Paulin. From internal evidence we can deduce that he is a Northern Irelander of recent Scottish extraction, who knows at least Donegal across the border, that he went to Oxford and that he has spent time in Iceland and Scandinavia. His is a bleak, taut voice. His ironies, such as they are, are so controlled as to be almost impalpable, eg 'In Antrim'. His poems about the Northern 'situation' are perhaps the most terrible I've read, since they wince no feeling, other than clinically-disciplined distaste. It is possible that I am not yet up to Mr Paulin, and that my response of intense admiration and great dislike derives from incomprehension.

Mr Hewitt is the most scrupulous of Irish poets. He is the only man among them to whom I would apply the adjective 'moral'. He is concerned, as indeed we all should be, with the nature of his responses to ambigous situations, as for instance in 'Strangers and Neighbours' when he has to accommodate childhood impressions of Jews in Belfast with middle-aged visits to Auschwitz and other memories of genocide, or in 'As You Like It', when he has to define an attitude for himself when two homosexual youths turn up at a Law Reform meeting. Mr Hewitt is seventy this year. Who or what is honouring this moral man?

Man's Last Dignity [1]

(Hibernia, July / August 1964)

It is common chat among Christians, Humanists and Agnostics alike, that the theatre of Samuel Beckett is 'depressing', 'sordid', 'hopeless', and so on. Some otherwise rational human beings go so far as to say that Sam is a humbug or a leg-puller. With none of this do I hold.

Beckett's *Godot, Endgame*, and *Happy Days* are all plays that come out of a post-Christian world, but which have not accepted the jolly values of scientific humanism. They are the most moving and quintessentially poetic expressions in the theatre of man reduced to his last dignity, his consciousness that he is man. Beckett, like most major artists, is a poetic extremist: the plights of Vladimir and Estragon, of Hamm and Clov, of Winnie and Willie, are surreal intensifications of the common human plight in a world where deistic values are no longer operative as defence or attack.

One of Mr Beckett's glories is his genius in ennobling common speech. I noticed in *Happy Days* that he was relying more and more on cliché, stock quotation, conversational fatuity as matter for his theatrical lyricism. I see a further development of this in a comparatively slight work, *Play*. But first I had better point out that this work is the most extreme of Beckett's stage experiments. On a bare darkened stage, there are three actors, a man and two women, all encased up to the head in yard-high urns. They face front undeviatingly and when they speak it is always at the dictate of a spotlight, which has the effect of an examining counsel, or even of a lightning-quick third degree.

And from the urn-people (is there a terrible anti-Keatsian irony here?) comes an angle-by-angle account of a common-place triangular affair. Which brings me back to Beckett's heightening of the cliché. The affair for all its seediness is given a quality of ironic sadness because so often the protagonists lapse into, sometimes the jargon of the divorce court witness, and sometimes that of the high-society novelette. So we have the Second Woman: ' "Judge then of my astoundment when one fine morning, as I was sitting stricken in the morning room …" '

How it would play, I cannot conceive, but, in reading, *Play* is both funny and touching. *Play* is supplemented in this volume by a radio piece, *Words and Music*, broadcast by the BBC, and by another, *Cascando*, translated from the French by the author. I have caught glimmerings of the sense of these two excursions into the twilight of consciousness, but not having heard them in their prescribed radio medium, I'm unwilling to stick out my neck. Lest I be accused of critical cowardice, both of these pieces were written to be played with music, and as such might best be considered as tone-poems of the psyché.

End of *Play*. Hardly likely to titivate (titillate) all those nice chaps who believe that Truth is Beauty and Beauty is Truth.

What Does It Mean?

(Irish Independent, 15 August 1970)

Lessness, by Samuel Beckett. (Calder & Boyars, London, 1970)
Tributes in Prose and Verse to Shotaro Oshima. (Hokuseido Press, Tokyo).

This latest example of Mr Beckett's *residua* has already aroused derision in certain quarters, derision veiling unspoken insinuations of 'I told you so'. Now I am prepared to admit that this very brief and at first glance pretentiously arcane text is such as to make, for instance, *Imagination Dead Imagine*, another recent short text, seem a model of lucidity. But I will not admit that Mr Beckett is pulling our legs.

Formally the work consists of twenty-four prose poems united by the recurrence in various combinations and permutations of certain concrete images and metaphysical propositions. What does it all (or little) add up to? For the moment I have not worked out these Clementi exercises in despair in relation to an overall pattern, but each one *in itself* is open to approximately intelligible interpretation, as are certain phrases within the unit.

A review is no place for close exegesis, but I am determined to refute the charge of mountebank that has been levelled against Beckett.

I will take two easy 'notes' for example. Consider this: 'All sides endlessness earth sky as one no sound no stir.' This needs only two commas to be immediately intelligible as an apprehension of utterly desolate universe. Less easy is this: 'Figment dawn dispeller of figments and the other called dusk.'

What Beckett is saying is that both dawn and dusk are figments of the poetic imagination. In fact we live in a world where night and day no longer have a metaphysical validity.

Unless I am very much mistaken, this little text goes as far as Beckett has ever gone in intuiting not alone the absurdity of man's condition, but also the absurdity of the universe itself.

The little book from Japan is published by the Yeats Society of Japan in honour of their president, Shotaro Oshima, on the occasion of his seventieth birthday. It contains tributes in verse and prose, and since this is a private publication, it would be invidious to criticize the quality of the verse or question the contentions of the prose. But it is one of the most exquisitely produced books I have ever handled.

Il Rit Donc Il Vit

(Hibernia, 19 April 1979)

The Beckett phenomenon has manifested itself on five fronts: in the printed word, in the theatre, on radio, on television, and on film. But that elusive creature, the person in the street, will most probably know of him only for the title of his play *Waiting for Godot*, written October 1949-January 1950, published in 1952, and first produced in its original French in January 1953. I say 'only for the title', because it may be heard in colloquial speech from the most unexpected sources, rather as people quote the Bible and Shakespeare, 'as the saying goes'. Thus, on the most elementary level, Beckett is a classic, almost a museum-piece, in his lifetime. (He was born, with a frightful decorum, on Good Friday, 13 April 1906, a fact which his exegetes might well ponder.)

Another elusive creature, the person that knows what he/she likes, infected by journalese, will know about 'dust-bin' drama in the vocabulary of counterfeit thinkers after Beckett's second stage play *Endgame*, published in 1956 and first produced, again in its original French, in London in April 1957, in English in October 1958. (The radio play *All That Fall*, written in English for the BBC, was broadcast before *Endgame* was staged.)

So then, the popular icon of Beckett might be of a man waiting in a dustbin to be collected. And I wonder if this frail joke be quite unrelated to the imaginative truth about Beckett, though to pursue it would unquestionably lead into the trails of the shaggy dog. The point of departure is not the dustbin but the humanity contained in it. Hamm in *Endgame*, hearing from Chou that Vagg in his bin is crying, comments, *Il pleure donc il vit*. This seems to be a crucial epigraph for Beckett. But I suggest, in relation especially to his earlier work, whether it will be *Murphy* (1938) or *First Love*, which though not published (in its original French) until 1970, was written just after the war, a converse summation: *Il rit donc il vit*.

Man weeps and laughs in Beckett and that is why his appeal can transcend the very often self-defensive differences between believer and agnostic, between conservative and liberal, between pessimist and meliorist. We are faced with the paradox that the seemingly least penetrable of modern writers is also the one who best knows the plight of 'unaccommodated man'. Lear's speech on the almost naked

Edgar is, I opine, as useful a commentary as any on Beckett's man living while weeping. But the Fool is surely a primary Beckett germinal, for he disappears from the action when he can no longer laugh or cry. Ronald Hayman, in his excellent and disturbing book on anti-theatre, tells us that Peter Brook's 1962 *King Lear* was influenced by Beckett and especially by *Endgame*. I think myself that *Endgame* has its seedlings in Beckett's earliest youth. But to illustrate this even briefly would require an expertise in the sacramental rites of the Church of Ireland, which regrettably I do not possess. (For instance, the sacrament of Confirmation may be relevant here.)

Mr Hayman also lets drop that Harold Pinter, while still a touring actor, first encountered Beckett in an extract from the novel *Watt* (published in its original English in 1953), which appeared in *Irish Writing* (ed. David Marcus and Terence Smith). Pinter was touring with Anew McMaster in 1950–2 and I find charming this vignette of Pinter, a young actor in his twenties, fresh perhaps (or jaded) from one of Mac's legendary rehearsals, discovering Beckett in some Irish country town. Pinter, of course, was to owe a great deal to Beckett, though not in the obsessive reductionism which worries critics of the author of *Breath* and (since the latter is an extreme case) his later theatre-work in general. Nor is it, I believe, from Beckett that Pinter derives his special quality of terror, of ineffable menace, which, as in *The Caretaker*, freezes me as does Henry James's *The Turn of the Screw*.

Mr Hayman is less than convincing in allying Pinter's *No Man's Land* with another of his subjects, the Austrian Peter Handke, though he does not say Handke has influenced Pinter, rather the reverse. But enough said, since I am ignorant of the Austrian, as I am of the American Sam Shepard, and the directorial work of the Pole, Jerry Grotowski, and the American Joseph Chaikin who in 1963 founded the Open Theatre in dissatisfaction with the Living Theatre of Julian Beck and Judith Malina (which has been seen at the Dublin Theatre Festival to the consternation of the populace and strong men like Mr Con Houlihan).

But Mr Hayman writes most informatively about theatre matters beyond the ken of most people in this country, including the work of Peter Brook since his *Theatre of Cruelty* with Charles Monowitz in 1964. What disturbs me in his accounts of the experiments of Brook, Grotowski and Chaikin is less their attitude to the word, which is one of indifference rather than of hostility, than their negative example; the more than elephantine gestation of single productions (after the manner of, variously, Meyerhold and Piscator) which, if followed on by the national repertory theatres of the world, could bring theatre to the status of religion, fulfilling not merely the superficies of religion (i.e., its 'aesthetic' appeal, as for instance in High Anglicanism or ante-Vatican Council II Catholicism) but also its functions as revelator, guide, and consolator.

Behind all this of course is the wonderful man, Antonin Artaud, who invented the term 'Theatre of Cruelty' (which does *not* mean a theatre preoccupied with physical cruelty as such) having seen a performance of the Balinese dancers at the colonial Exhibition in Paris in 1931. (Those Balinese have a lot to answer for: they find their way even into Peter Steele's recent *Jonathan Swift: Preacher and Jester*, reviewed here 22 February 1979, by way of a footnote reference to an article on the *Balinese Cockfight* by Clifford Geertz.) Artaud's notions about ritual and sacrifice in the theatre reinforced Genet's natural dispositions when he came to write for the theatre: Genet who posited a theatre situated in a graveyard.

In one of the more engaging pieces in the Beckett *Critical Heritage* is the reminiscential essay by the Rumanian E.M. Cioran, who confirms what we might easily adduce: Beckett's fondness for cemeteries (cf. *First Love*: '*I set out in the morning, and was back by night, having lunched lightly in the graveyard*').

But he also states something 'most needful to be said': '*Beckett's (nature) is so impregnated with poetry that it becomes indistinguished from it.*' So far as 'poetry' in verse form is concerned, Donald Davie is less than fair to Beckett's original poems in English, but Richard Coe is just about his translations, not the least successful of which is his version of Apollinaire's *Zone*, published first separately in 1972 by the Dolmen Press.

As must be inevitable in such a compendium, certain items glitter, others plumb in the mind. Closing my eyes, I recall Kate O'Brien's joyous reception of *Murphy* (she and Vivian Mercier are the only Irish contributors), Hugh Kenner's clever (without cleveralilty) study of *How It Is* (1961) as also Jacques Mayoux's, Christopher Ricks on both the collection of shorter prose pieces *No's Knife* (1967) and Benedict Nightingale on *Not I* (1972) which provokes compassion '*more powerfully than anything I've yet seen by Beckett*'.

Amor Fati Sive Contemptus Mundi

(Crane Bag, Mythology Issue, Vol. 2, No.s 1&2, 1978)

'Michael has a clean burial in the far north, by the grace of God. Bartley will have a fine coffin out of the white boards, and a deep grave surely. What more can we want than that? No man at all can be living forever, and we must be satisfied.'—*(Riders to the Sea)*

'I buried two uncles last week.'—(Remark overheard in a Dublin tavern. The speaker, male, appeared proud of his achievement.)

There is a story that Sir Thomas Urquhart, the seventeenth-century translator of Rabelais, died from laughing when he heard of the return of Charles II. One (or rather this writer) could not conceive of an Irish person who would die laughing, though some, we are told, die roaring (Oscar Wilde's alleged death-bed remark about himself and the wallpaper merely tests the rule). But since we cannot possibly know what passes through the mind of an individual in the terminal moments, we must be content with the living attitudes towards death which, as it happens, writers are not only most fitted to set down, but the only people who care enough to do so in countries, like ours, where anthropology is in its gestatory stage (I would like to know otherwise).

Synge's Maurya, whom I quoted as first epigraph, I will return to. But a more useful point of departure might be Patsy Mac Cann in James Stephens's *The Demi-Gods* (1914),[1] of whom we are told, 'in despite of his apparent outlawry he was singularly secure; ambition waved no littlest lamp at him; the one ill which could overtake him was death ...' It is not, of course, for nothing that Stephens places the travelling-man in a timeless Ireland, [an] Ireland where 'it was also believed in ancient times, and the belief was world-wide, that the entrance to heaven, hell and purgatory yawned in the Isle of Saints'.[2] Perhaps the best paradigm of the relationship between Irish Life and Irish Death is, then, the phenomenon of St Patrick's Purgatory on Lough Derg. As such it has been taken, and within the same period, the Second World War, by two major Irish poets writing quite independently, Patrick Kavanagh and Denis Devlin. The testimony of two such different men, the peasant autodidact and the cultured diplomat, cannot be discounted. Devlin's *Lough Derg*, ('one of the great modern poems', Allen Tate called it to the present writer in 1959) should be well known:

> *The poor in spirit on their rosary rounds,*
> *The jobbers with their whiskey-angered eyes,*
> *The pink bank clerks, the tiphat papal counts*
> *And drab kind women with their tonsured mockery tries.*
> *Glad invalids on penitential feet*
> *Walk the Lord's majesty like their*
> *Village street.*[3]

Kavanagh's mini-epic *Lough Derg*, published posthumously,[4] has startling points of resemblace, among them his observations of St Patrick's clientele and that streak in the Irish character which seeks by temporary denial of life to hold death at bay: what we might call, irreverently, *contemptus mundi* on the installment plan.

But it would be both inaccurate and unjust to argue that the retreat from quotidian life exemplified by the unglamorous excesses of Lough Derg – which, of course, embody a scarcely articulate view of death and the afterlife – is merely a kind of inverted materialism. We Irish, even if we think ourselves unmanacled as compared with our forefathers, are all after our fashions monastics *manques*: perhaps bruised into violence and rapine in this life, precisely because something in the blood accuses us of not rejecting, despising, the temporal world. We tend to forget nowadays that our literature, in Irish and English, is in the main orchestrated by the consciousness that we are mortal. So what, asks the bright student. Of course, all European literature has been so orchestrated.

I suggest, tentatively, even fearfully, that the Irish notion of life as *questa tanto picciola vigilia*, in Dante's phrase, is complicated by superstition, irreverence, guilt (as I indicated above) and something very like rebellion. And, curiously, what Shaw in *John Bull's Other Island* calls 'a horrible, senseless, mishievous laughter'.

But more of Larry Doyle's speech is worth quoting: 'When you're young you exchange drinks with other young men; and you exchange vile stories with them … And all the time you laugh! laugh! laugh! Eternal derision, eternal envy, eternal folly, eternal fouling and staining and degrading …' This is an extreme summation of that quality in the Irish imagination which Dr Vivian Mercier has treated in his *The Irish Comic Tradition* (1962).

So, then, I write on the premise that one of the masks of the Irishman in the face of death is the mask of derision, or, alternatively, of contemptuous defiance. A familiar instance of it in English is Swift's *Verses on the Death of Dr Swift*. Less familiar might be Synge's *Queens*, the ending of which mocks both Death and the poet:

> *Queens who wasted the east by proxy,*
> *Or drove the ass-car, a tinker's doxy,*
> *Yet these are rotten – I ask their pardon –*

And we've the sun on rock and garden.
These are rotten, so you're the Queen
Of all are living, or have been.[5]

But it is in prose of this century that we must look for true instances of Shaw's diabolic laughter, and we need look no further than *Ulysses*. Shaw's play had appeared in 1906, and although Joyce's mighty book did not appear until 1922, it is set in 1904, in a Dublin that had changed little from the Dublin which Joyce's father would have known, and by extension the Ireland evoked by Shaw's Larry Doyle. The mask of derision is worn time and time again in *Ulysses*. I offer a few instances, the more telling because of their dreadful relevance to the book's schemata. In the first, Stephen is reproaching Buck Mulligan: *You said, Stephen answered, O, it's only Dedalus whose mother is beastly dead.*

And Mulligan attempts to justify himself: *You saw only your mother die. I see them pop off every day in the Mater and Richmond and cut up into tripes in the dissecting room. It's a beastly thing and nothing else. It simply doesn't matter.*[6]

In this context, Mulligan's gallows humour is punctured by Stephen. In the section of the book known as 'Hades' which pivots on the funeral of one Paddy Dignam, the gallows humour, which I have called 'the mask of derision', is not always immediately distinguisable from serious if commonplace meditation on mortality and the appurtenances of burial. We can recognize straight away as gallows humour the interchange between the Glasnevin caretaker and the cronies of Paddy Dignam, including Simon Dedalus, all of them clearly old hands at the funeral game. To John O'Connell, Simon says, *I am come to pay you another visit*, and the caretaker answers, *My dear Simon ... I don't want your custom at all.*

O'Connell then tells a story (still current, by the way) about two drunks who come on a foggy evening to look for a friend's grave. The story, even in 1904 a chestnut, we may take it is well received, and Martin Cunningham observes judiciously, *To cheer a fellow up ... it's pure goodheartedness: damn the thing else.*

But the ruminations of Leopold Bloom, while they have an element of the derisory, a touch even of the blue comedian, are flecked with compassion, as in the following, just before Dignam's coffin is lowered into the grave:

> Poor Dignam! His last lie on the earth in his box. When you think of them all it does seem a waste of wood. All gnawed through. They could invent a handsome bier with a kind of panel sliding let it down that way. Ay but they might object to be buried out of another fellow's. They're so particular. Lay me in my native earth. Bit of clay from the holy land. Only a mother and deadborn child ever buried in one coffin. I see what it means. I see. To protect him as long as possible even in the earth. The Irishman's house is his coffin. Embalming in catacombs, mummies, the same idea.[7]

In the 'Cyclops' section, which takes place in Barney Kiernan's pub, we find a blazing exemplum of what, quite literally this time, is gallows humour. But first I must return to Vivian Mercier's invaluable book, *The Irish Comic Tradition*. There he proposes a theory of 'grotesque humour as being inseparable from awe', and that it 'serves as a defence mechanism against the holy dread with which we face the mysteries of reproduction'.[8]

In Barney Kiernan's pub, Alf Bergan produces a clutch of letters from a person applying to the High Sheriff of Dublin for the job of hangman. Joe Hynes reads one of them aloud: it is illiterate, ingratiating, and sanctimonious. This leads to a discussion of the mechanics of hanging and the ethics of capital punishment. Then follows the gallows humour than the like no Dublin pub can ever have heard.

> There's one thing it hasn't a deterrent effect on, says Alf. What's that? says Joe. The poor bugger's tool that's being hanged, says Alf. That so? says Joe. God's truth, says Alf. I heard that from the head warder that was in Kilmainham when they hanged Joe Brady, the Invincible. He told me when they cut him down after the drop it was standing up in their faces like a poker.[9]

What more calculated to inspire awe and uneasy jocularity than the double ignominy of an assassin who was also a quasi-political hero?

Before discussing other aspects of the Irish stance before death than the humorous – whatever the nature of the humour – there is a modern text which needs some attention, the novel of Flann O'Brien perhaps least known to the general public, *The Hard Life* (1961). A respectable citizen, Mr Collopy, in Edwardian Dublin, is much exercised by the absence of public conveniences for females. (As momentarily was Bloom: '*Ought to be places for women. Running into cakeshops*'.)[10] Afflicted by rheumatism, he allows himself to be dosed with a preparation concocted by his half-nephews, and as a result gains inordinate weight. Stricken by remorse, the half-nephew arranges a pilgrimage to Rome for Mr Callopy and his confidant Fr Fahrt, a German Jesuit. So off they go, the gravid Collopy nursing his obsession about the provision in Dublin of public conveniences for females, but Fr Fahrt and the half-nephew hoping for a miracle which would readjust Mr Collopy's weight. There is a disastrous private audience with the Pope, Pius X, who concludes that Collopy is mad when he raises the question of ladies' conveniences in Dublin, a matter outside his province, nor of course is there any miracle. Instead, Mr Collopy, now well over 30 stone, crashes through a wooden landing to his death, and is buried hurriedly in the Campo Verano; hurriedly, since the corpse has decomposed with distressing rapidity. Mr Collopy's death and the circumstances which lead up to it are both macabre and grotesque, but scarcely more so than the interchange back in Dublin between the half-nephew and his younger brother, the narrator.

> I liked the poor old man. He wasn't the worst. All right. His death wasn't the happiest he could get. In fact, it was ridiculous. But look at it this way. In what bet-

ter place could a man die than in Rome, the Eternal City, by the side of St Peter. Yes, I said wryly. There was timber concerned in both cases. St Peter was crucified.[11]

Deaths in Beckett's fictions are multiple and metaphysical. One indubitable physical death is that of the eponymous hero of *Murphy* (1938), who had desiderated that his 'body, mind and soul' be burnt, placed in a paper bag, and flushed in 'the necessary house' of the Abbey Theatre's pit, 'if possible during the performance of a piece, the whole to be executed without ceremony or show of grief'.[12] But Murphy's plans go a-gley: his ashes end up, not in the Gents of the Abbey, but on the floor of an English saloon, '*the object of much dribbling, passing, trapping, shouting, punching, heading, even some recognition from the gentleman's code*'.[13]

Dedalus's mother who is 'beastly dead', Joe Brady shamelessly phallic even in death, a cadaver Dagda,[14] Mr Collopy betrayed by his own weight, and even a wooden floor in the City of Emperor and Pope, Murphy's ashes swept out '*with butts … the matches, the spit, the vomit*': none of these images are conducive to reverential thoughts of the body. Perhaps even Synge's '*stack of thigh-bones, jaws and shins*' in his poem 'In Kerry' is more reassuring, because the words recognize that the body has been, whereas those other images in their combination of the grotesque, the farcical, and the obscene, tend to diminish the body's existence in terms of the senses. They are so much less 'real' than '*the body of Bartley, laid out on a plank, with a bit of sail on it*', even if only as a stage direction.

This disdain, close to hatred, for the body, is an aspect of *contemptus mundi*: taken in isolation it smacks of the Manichee. The body, the flesh, if not positively evil, is disgusting or ludicrous, or both.

On the other hand, it is not possible to accept Maurya's last words as an expression of orthodox Christian belief. Ideally, I take it, Christianity is a religion of Hope. This does not square with the Sibylline utterances of Maurya, which amounts to *amor fati*. T.R. Henn put it succinctly and temperately:

'…the resolution of the play rests upon a resignation that is more stoic than Christian, a sense of relief that no further loss is possible when humanity confronts the ultimates of death …'[15] He quotes a telling passage from *The Aran Islands* (1907):

> As they talked to me and gave me a little poteen and a little bread when they thought I was hungry, I could not help feeling that I was talking with men who were under a judgment of death. I knew every one of them would be drowned in the sea in a few years and battered naked on the rocks, or would die in his own cottage and be buried with another fearful scene in the graveyard I had come from.[16]

As against the *amor fati* Synge found in Aran (his enemies might say he invented it), I would cite this from Tomás O Criomhtháin, as rendered by Robin Flower:

> Ten children were born to us, but they had no good fortune, God help us … All these things were a sore trouble to the poor mother, and she, too, was taken from

me ... She left a little babe, only I had a little girl grown up to take care of her; but she, too, was only just grown up when she heard the call like the rest. The girl who had brought her upmarried in Dunmore. She died, too, leaving seven children. I have only one boy left with me now. There is another in America. Such was the fate of my children. May God's blessing be with them – those of them that are in the grave – and with the poor woman whose heart broke for them.[17]

Even in this fairly conventional passage it is possible to highlight the difference between *amor fati* (I am aware of the several interpretations that may be given to this phrase) and Christian resignation. When Tomás writes of a daughter, '*When she heard the call like the rest*', he is thinking in the same mould as, of all people, Charlotte Bronte when she wrote of Emily and Anne that '*they both made haste to leave us*', or indeed Shakespeare when he has Kent say, after Lear's death,

> *I have a journey, sir, shortly to go:*
> *My Master calls me, I must not say no.*

Amor fati and contemptus mundi I have used in perhaps idiosyncratic senses. We should not forget that the first has its sweet Virgilian overtones, which Newman recognized when he wrote of 'his single words and phrases, his pathetic half-lines, giving utterance, as the voice of Nature herself, to that pain and weariness, yet hope of better things, which is the experience of her children in every time'.[18] It is precisely the absence of 'the hope of better things' that distinguishes *Riders to the Sea*. Strangely (and, from the biographical point of view, heartbreakingly) this Virgilian note is most poignant in Joyce's poem for his grandson and his father, 'Ecce Puer', where death is vanquished by birth:

> *A child is sleeping:*
> *An old man is gone.*
> *O, father forsaken*
> *Forgive your son.*

Nor should we forget the purer forms of *contemptus mundi*, which may be exemplified by texts, such as Yeats's '*Cast a cold eye...*', Pearse's '*Naked I saw you...*', Austin Clarke's flagellation of the mind and spirit, 'Tenebrae'. The supreme expression of *contemptus mundi* was written in Latin and set in the wall of St Patrick's Cathedral. Yeats paraphrased it, beginning, '*Swift has sailed into his rest*': unwittingly introducing a Virgilian note into that fierce and peremptory epitaph.

I have steered an unsteady course between embraced destiny and spat-upon world. I will leave the last words to Yeats in his essay on Berkeley. Of abstractions, he writes: '*Without them corporate life would be impossible. They are as serviceable as those leaf-like shapes of tin that mould the ornament for the apple-pie, and we give them belief, service, devotion.*'[19]

Classic Collection

(Irish Independent, 19 November 1977)

It seems only the other day that Michael Hartnett first came to Dublin, looking about seventeen, for the inception of *Poetry Ireland* (second series). In fact the year was 1962, and he was twenty-one.

Since then he has established himself as a poet of starkness, not always of language, but always of feeling: the stripped, honed ego, the unlustred eye, the familiar or ancestral memory like a bleached bone in a living landscape. In 1975 he published his best volume to-date, *A Farewell to English,* which by his own account meant precisely that: he would write all of his future verse in Irish.

At the time I thought that the use of the indefinite article in the title allowed him an option (if the public requires that poets be moral dogmatists). I still think that it does, despite the fact that as recently as October 9 [1977], at the North Cork Writers' Festival in Doneraile, he reaffirmed his commitment, total and poignant.

Poems in English (Dolmen, £6.00) is Mr Hartnett's selection of his work from about 1958 (in his *Selected Poems,* 1970, he so dates certain poems which were not published until 1962 in *Poetry Ireland*) to 1975. Ironically, the poems from *A Farewell to English* show him at his most powerful, and not least in the title poem.

> *I have made my choice*
> *and leave with little weeping:*
> *I have come with meagre voice*
> *to court the language of my people.*

Whether or no the courtship be fertile, this book, with its good reproductions (black and white) of the poet's superb portrait by Edward McGuire, must become a classic.

Poets native to the North of Ireland have had, this last decade, an intolerable burden or an incalculable blessing laid upon them. One of them who has managed to survive the lure of the bandwagon and the Mercutian posture, is Seamus Deane, as we saw in his first collection, *Gradual Wars* (1972). In his new book, *Rumours* (Dolmen Press, £2.50) he is less concerned with the physical manifestations of Northern disease than with the child who grew up into manhood, and escaped its grosser manifestations.

But if I read him correctly, in a poem such as 'Bonfire', he is struggling to convey the complexity of an emotional attitude which as a Derry Catholic he could not possibly be without. 'Bonfire' may not be the finest poem in the collection (although his imagery is powerfully sustained), but it goes far towards underpinning Mr Deane's polemical writing. I liked also his poems about his dead father and one called 'The Pleasure Principle', in which, God save us, he sends me back to Emily Dickinson. Above all, there is little trace of academic glibness in this book, and many memorable lines, for example, 'Poetry's a nearness felt as far'.

From the one or two reviews I'd seen of Aidan Carl Matthews's *Windfalls* (Dolmen, £2.50), which won the Patrick Kavanagh Poetry Award, I did not expect such confident and mature verses (Mr Matthews is now twenty-one). In fact, they are so finished that they prompt the unworthy desire for the imperfection that intrigues. I can see no sign of where Mr Matthews is likely to go. But he seems most himself in 'In Chartres Cathedral', and 'In Koln Cathedral', and what may be an early poem, 'Night', all with themes from orthodox religion. That at this age, and in this country, such things should bother him at all, is itself significant. We could be doing with a poet of orthodoxy.

A Requiem for Man Alone, by Christopher Daybell (published by the author, Dublin), is a hand-stapled sheaf of verses that read like very literary pub poems. The best of them, on Edinburgh, is 'Festival City'.

Cyphers (Summer 1977, No. 6) is edited by four poets – Leland Bardwell, Eiléan Ní Chuilleanáin, Pearse Hutchinson and Macdara Woods – and is, of course, our only verse magazine. The quality is high, and this edition has at least half-a-dozen poems in English that survive first reading, as well as Mr Hutchinson's translations from Catalan, and poems in Irish from Mairtín Ó Direain and Gabriel Rosenstock.

New Poetry

(Irish Independent, 3 February 1979)

Just over a year ago I noticed on this page[1] Michael Hartnett's *Poems in English* (Dolmen) which included a large part of *A Farewell to English and Other Poems* (Gallery, 1975), the volume he flung down, half as challenge, half as threnody, as he set out to 'court the language of my people'.

Now we have an Enlarged Edition of *A Farewell to English* (Gallery, £1.50) in which the editor, Peter Fallon, is at pains to point out that his poet has not cheated or reneged. Any new material was composed before the original *A Farewell*. As if, God help us, it mattered, especially in the light of Mr Hartnett's forthcoming versions of Daibhí Ó Bruadair, most difficult of seventeenth-century Irish poets. If these are any good at all (and from a broadcast talk in 1976, we know they will be), they will be good poems in English. What price, then, *Farewell*?

The new volume is, uncharacteristically of Gallery, disfigured by misprints and seems overpacked, Even so, it is good to have, for instance, 'The Retreat of Ita Cagney' (1975) in handy form. Presumably we may expect sometime to see the Gaelic version of this small-town mini-epic, so redolent of Hardy, in a collection. 'Cúlú Ide' was the beginning of the *Farewell*.

Desmond O'Grady's versions from the Irish [in] *A Limerick Rake* (Gallery £1.50) are, at the very least, intriguing. From what Fenian text, for instance, did Mr O'Grady derive a poem on 'Benn Aedar' with the following: *Free our fine fresh open / hills where gamesome Deirdre eloped / with fairheaded Gráinne.* This is to introduce an entirely novel element into our grand old love stories.

And on what grounds may 'Donncha Bán' be translated as Donncha White? As well translate 'Róisín Dubh' as Róisín Black.

He gives the misleading title 'Abandoned Love' to a version based, though he does not say so, on the Jacobite song-poem 'A Dhroimfhionn donn dílis'. Pádraig de Brún's 'Tháinig Long Ó Valparaiso' shines through 'Promised Land' which, he comments, 'I'm told, was originally written in German and translated into Irish.' I throw that to Gogartians, since a poem by Gogarty is supposed to have been the basis of Monsignor de Brún's.

I wish Mr O'Grady had been more generous about his sources; some of his early (in European terms) Renaissance versions of love poems are fine. But neither reviewer nor common reader should have to resort to homework to appreciate them.

Francis Harvey's *In the Light on the Stones* (Gallery, £1.20) is a first collection from a poet in his fifties. We might expect maturity, and certainly we get it; maturity of technique, of vision, of feeling. But there is a bonus. For all the preponderant pastoral quality of his verse, Mr Harvey does not rest on the laurels of his poems on his adopted Donegal, its landscape and its older natives. Here are good poems about Brendan Behan, Patrick MacGill, Patrick Kavanagh and Swift ('claw-marked prose' is masterly). And he sees the Donegal of the tourists in the context of emptied homes and drowned fishermen.

There are three poems on the Northern situation, of which one, 'Dorothy Wordsworth in Belfast', is quite perfect. What excites me in Mr Harvey's verse is no element of what usually constitutes excitement, but rather the sense of unrevealed strengths, of unflexed muscles, not unlike what we (or rather I) savour in John Hewitt.

Pilgrimages

(The Irish Press, 8 March 1979)

Lough Derg, by Patrick Kavanagh (Martin Brian & O'Keeffe, London, 1979)
Lough Derg, by Patrick Kavanagh (The Goldsmith Press, The Curragh, 1979)
Patrick Kavanagh Country, by Dr Peter Kavanagh (The Goldsmith Press, The Curragh, 1979)

The appearance of two editions of Patrick Kavanagh's long poem (some 639 lines, including half-lines) *Lough Derg*, written in 1942, the year of *The Great Hunger*, put on the market almost simultaneously, will intrigue biographers and has already titillated gossip columnists. The brouhaha, of course, has nothing to do with the considerable merits of Kavanagh's poem, which is at once more naked and more cagey than Denis Devlin's poem on the subject, one which goes back to Calderon and Dante.

But for the record, I give as I detect them the differences in the two texts. There is some disparity in the paragraphing of the verse. Quotations and dialogue are given single inversion in the first edition as cited above, but double inversion in the second. In the first, non-English words e.g., *Agnus Dei*, are given plain, in the second italicized. There are a few variants in punctuation, of which one is important for the verse's sense. For the first's *'This piety that hangs like a fool's unthought'* (p.17), the second has *'Their piety that hangs like a fool's, unthought'* (p.33). Other textual variants are more conspicuous. The first has *'the concrete stilts of the Basilica/That spread like a bullfrog's hind paws'* (p.3), whereas in the second the stilts spread *'like a bulldog's hind paws'*. The first has *'the dry bones in histories'* (p.14), from which the second omits the article. *'Old films that break the eyeballs ...'* in the first (p.20) is *'Old firms ...'* in the second (p.36). *'Where the heroic armies advance'* in the first (p.36) is *'Whether the heroic ...'* in the second (p.37). Finally, the second asterisks a word 'sic' (p.41), which the first leaves alone. I do not claim comprehensiveness in this examination.

It seems to me that both Paul Durcan in his *Introduction* to the first, and Peter Kavanagh in his to the second, make tactical errors. Mr Durcan with commendable forthrightness takes on the awesome Professor Denis Donoghue,[1] but weakens his case by a frivolous description of this Parnassian scholar-critic as 'a queen-bee of Anglo/American/Irish Academe'. If Professor Donoghue cannot see the merit of

Kavanagh, if he is deaf to all that delirium of the humble and despised heart on a conscious pilgrimage to the state of *simplicitas*, then that is his loss, and one of the failures of perception that may affect the most honourable of men. Nor does Mr Durcan help us by analogies with Eliot, Pound, Crane, (David) Jones, and Mac-Diarmid). He is on much surer ground when he writes of a 'completely passive inspiration such as is to be found in the work of the jazz masters'. But if Mr Durcan overloads his terms of reference, he gives every impression of knowing what he is talking about.

But (and this is a grievous thing to have to say about a devoted brother and memorialist) Dr Kavanagh faces us with near-nonsensical generalizations. (Patrick Kavanagh was not guiltless of the like, but in his case they as often as not were impatient reactions against the tyranny of received intellectual formulae.) Thus, we are told: 'Patrick Kavanagh was a Catholic with emphasis on the mystical element. He did not dismiss the penitential approach as wrong. He wanted to understand it.' What in the name of, say, St John of the Cross, or St Térèsa of Avila, or for that matter, Vaughan or Herbert, does he mean by 'the mystical element'? As to his brother not 'dismissing' the 'penitential approach', not even the poet's least enthusiastic readers would accuse him of 'dismissing' the practice and doctrine of nearly two thousand years.

And I doubt if Dr Kavanagh is in any way uneasy about the hedged bets of *Lough Derg*. The poet's pilgrimage does not resolve, to my mind, the tension in his marrow between the traditional pieties of his people and his own intuition of a Christianity more magnanimous, less exclusive, than any he found in Ireland. '*The sharp knife of Jansen/Cuts all the green branches...*' Lough Derg is naked in its disclosure, compassionate and wry, of the secret foolishness, and as secret anguish, of the Faithful. It is evasive in its side-stepping of an issue which Kavanagh, a natural believer, never tackled satisfactorily: the borderline between Faith and the keeping-up of premiums on the Salvation Policy. No sinner, if he thinks at all, can fail to ponder that wavering frontier. And *Lough Derg* is a notable contribution to the confessional verse of our time. We should be grateful to the publishers concerned (who each provide also hard-back editions which I have not seen).

Dr Kavanagh has provided a compact little history of the townlands and village of the parish of Inniskeen, and his brother's place there. I cull this on the occasion of the poet's protracted debut in the *Weekly Irish Independent*: 'The man was becoming a menace and Salamanca Barney predicted that he would end up in the Big House, a local term for the lunatic asylum.' 'Salamanca Barney' was the Parish Priest.[2]

Younger Poet

(Irish Independent, 14 June 1969)

Mr Heaney's second book[1] is a Choice of the Poetry Book Society. Readers of *Death of a Naturalist* (1966) will know that he is one of the best poets in Ireland, of the late twenties and early thirties group.

These age groups are useful. In 1962 I was describing Pearse Hutchinson, Thomas Kinsella and John Montague as the most interesting of the young Irish poets: seven years later they are forty and older, *ag tarraingt go teann ar na laethaibh liatha*, and in their idiosyncratic ways, part of the Literary Establishment.

Much is expected of Mr Heaney. I, for one, am somewhat disappointed. This is not to say that I do not recommend the book as required reading for [the] habitual verse-reader. But it is too early for Mr Heaney to allow himself the risk of being labelled as a 'genre' poet, as a 'ruralist' for instance, or 'a keen observer of the natural scene', which of course he undoubtedly is.

The best of these poems are not about the land-and-sea scapes he knows so well. Nor are they about slightly folksy figures like the thatcher and the blacksmith, emblems of a 'passing away of life'. They are those where he writes about the elemental mysteries of procreation, gestation and birth.

There are three poems as fine as anything he has, to my knowledge, published, and, to my mind, probably his best. 'The Mother' explores the sensations of a pregnant woman drawing water, a figure of biblical simplicity and touchimg brass-tackery:

> *I am tired of walking about*
> *with this plunger,*
> *Inside me, God, he plays like*
> *a young colt*
> *Gone wild on a rope,*
> *Lying or standing won't settle*
> *these capers,*
> *This gulp in my well.*

'Elegy for a Still-born Child' is a poem of exquisite conceits and controlled sentiment to assuage, one of the traditional functions of elegy:

> For six months you stayed
> cartographer,
> Charting my friend from hus-
> band towards father,
> He guessed a globe behind
> your steady mound,
> Then the pole fell, shooting
> star, into the ground.

Very powerful is 'Gallerus Oratory Revisited', a cry from the depths of claus-
trophobia spirituality, which I may have overread because of its echo from
Marlowe's *Dr Faustus*:

> Would leap up to his God
> no worshipper off this floor.

Mr Heaney cannot be forced to look into his heart or outside of his chosen
field. But I feel that one who uses language so carefully and sees so sharply with
so grave and tender a feeling for the cycles of nature, and the generating act
of love, might well move on to closer exploration of man clipped of his rural halo
and undwarfed by mountain, soil, lake or sea, or put in his place by animal or
fish or bird.

Heaney Re-visited

(Irish Independent, 26 July 1969)

Door Into the Dark[1] (London 1969)

On the 14ᵀᴴ June [1969] in this newspaper I reviewed Mr Heaney's second book, *Door Into the Dark*. It was not a hyperbolic notice and turned out even less so than intended, because of an unfortunate omission in the printed text.

I stated that the three best poems of Mr Heaney's that I knew of were in this book, 'Mother', and 'Elegy for a Still-born Child', got mention. The third, 'Cana Revisited', did not.

Quite improperly I claim the space to make an *amende honorable* and refer to it again. After one reads this poem, with all its theological, physiological and metaphysical implications, Coventry Patmore can go for his tea.

But as a whole book, I still prefer *Death of a Naturalist*. I think my preference stems from the book's greater generosity in the field of personal statement. It is possible to construe a whole personality from the book: Heaney the country lad, Heaney the schoolteacher (one of his pupils has told me he was a very good one), Heaney the lover, both guache and sophisticate, Heaney the observer of a mortally divided city.

Perhaps because I am a teacher of sorts myself, I am with him when he writes in 'The Play Way':

> *A silence charged with*
> *sweetness*
> *Breaks short on lost faces*
> *where I see new looks.*

Perhaps because I am a human being, I am with him when he writes in 'Gravities':

> *Loves with barrages of hot*
> *insult*
> *Often cut off their nose to*
> *spite their face,*
> *Endure a hopeless day,*

> *declare their guilt,*
> *Re-enter the native port of*
> *their embrace.*

Perhaps because I am an unenchanted (not disenchanted) Christian, I can sense the moral seriousness behind the last lines of 'Turkies':

> *Now, as I pass the bleak*
> *Christmas dazzle,*
> *I find him ranged with his*
> *cold squadrons*
> *The fuselage is bare, the*
> *proud wings snapped,*
> *The tail-fan stripped down to*
> *a shameful rudder.*

Only on re-reading it have I grasped the more solemn implications of this poem. The turkey stripped is 'just another poor forked thing (the echo, of course, is from *King Lear*). If I live to see the next 'bleak Christmas dazzle', I fear that the sight of those poor trussed birds will inevitably remind me of the archetypal 'poor forked thing' Who hung on a Cross, and Whose Birthday we will be supposed to be celebrating.

Mr Heaney would not wish that on me, I am sure. But, to adapt Shelley, poets are the unacknowledged legislators of our imagination.

An Inner Émigré

(Irish Independent, 7 June 1975)

North (London 1975)

This is Mr Heaney's fourth major collection. His books have come at three-year intervals since the first, *Death of a Naturalist* (1966). *Door into the Dark* (1969) and *Wintering Out* (1972) are the other two volumes. In this last, Mr Heaney revealed his preoccupation with the primeval, notably in the desperately poignant 'The Tollund Man':

> *Out there in Jutland*
> *In the old man-killing parishes*
> *I will feel lost,*
> *Unhappy and at home.*

He has told us that 'The Tollund Man' and 'Nerthus' originated from a reading of P.V. Glob's *The Bog People*, and in so doing has very considerably done some of the homework for his critics.

In the new book he returns to the theme of *The Bog People*, notably in 'Bog Queen' and 'The Grauballe Man', and quite terribly in 'Punishment', of which the last two stanzas, on certain ugly happenings in Belfast, show an honesty not always pervasive in verse about the North by Northerners (or Southerners).

They must be quoted:

> *I who have stood dumb*
> *when your betraying sisters,*
> *cauled in tar,*
> *wept by the railings,*
>
> *who would connive*
> *in civilized outrage*
> *yet understand the exact*
> *and tribal, intimate revenge*

Bogland is also the gravamen of 'Kinship', which in its sixth section directs us from evolution to the present: *'report us fairly, / how we slaughter / for the common good*

/ and shave the heads / of the notorious, / how the goddess swallows / our love and terror'.

In a poem like 'Ocean's Love to Ireland', Mr Heaney is dazzling: an adjective one may with justice use for the first time about a poet whose effects are more often achieved in half-light or autumn than in the full glare of summer conceits. Such is the conceit of Ireland as a maiden properly violated by her neighbour (here emblamatized by Sir Walter Raleigh) whereas '*The Spanish prince has spilled his gold*', and, '*Iambic drums / of English beat the woods where the poets / sink like Onan*'.

Not perhaps a popular, but certainly an audacious, view of post-Elizabethan Gaelic culture: the *aisling* as *somnium humidum*.

In a superb poem, 'Act of Union' transmutes into sexual terms the whole historical relationship between Britain and Ireland, and more specifically in the Ulster dimension: '*The Act sprouted an obstinate fifth column / Whose stance is growing unilateral*'.

While Mr Heaney in Part 1 of his book touches on Ulster only with passionate obliquity, in the shorter Part 2, much easier reading (in the sense that the responses come more quickly), he faces his home counties full square. (I avoid the term 'province', misused even by Northern politicians of a Nationalist dye.) There is wry fun in his 'The Unacknowledged Legislator's Dream', in which he takes the mickey out of Shelley's famous, and ultimately sad, aphorism about poets and society. In other poems he goes far towards illustrating Samayana's dictum that true genius is 'the imaginative dominion of experience' (*The Life of Reason*).

The Northern 'tragedy' as manifested to the outsider, the ignoramus, has nothing in it of the noble or enhancing. It is squalid, mean-minded and bloody. Some verse reactions to it have been querulous or narcissistic. Hitherto, I would have rated Seamus Deane's *Gradual Wars* as the high-water mark of the Northern experience imaginatively controlled.

Now his senior, Mr Heaney, has in this new book given us a clutch of poems whose nobility, of language and feeling, rises from the compost.

> *O land of password, handgrip, wink and nod,*
> *Of open minds as open as a trap,*
>
> *Where tongues lie coiled, as under flames lie wicks,*
> *Where half of us, as in a wooden horse,*
> *Were cabin'd and confined like wily Greeks,*
> *Besieged within the siege, whispering morse.*

The book's last poem, 'Exposure', written in County Wicklow, where the poet is, in a manner of speaking, in an Ovidian exile (the reference to *tristia* makes the point), is a marvellously succinct confessional-piece, honest, poignant, intensely self-aware but not self-pitying: *I am neither internee nor informer; / An inner émigré, grown long-haired / and thoughtful.*

This ability to use the first-person singular with authority, with no stench of bathos, marks Mr Heaney's accession to senior rank. And, when he declares that in each drop of the rain that falls through the alders he can perceive 'the diamond absolutes', we believe him.

North is the most difficult of Mr Heaney's books. It is not likely to appeal to some of his admirers, who go for his earlier Arcadianism or his links with English pastoralists like Edward Thomas. His diction has become at once more rich and more spare, as in the sequence 'Viking Dublin: Trial Pieces'. His mind has developed in subtle and exciting ways, and one can detect a closer relationship between his impulse to make poetry and his intellectual preoccupations. We are now in the presence of an organized sensibility.

III
IRISH AND EUROPEAN PERSPECTIVES

Deoraíocht, le Pádraic Ó Conaire (1882–1928)

(from The Pleasures of Gaelic Literature)[1]

'He belongs to the European kind', wrote Stephen MacKenna, journalist, linguist and maker of the mighty English version of Plotinus. Seosamh MacGrianna sensed this European quality in Pádraic Ó Conaire. He says, 'The English-speaking writers of Ireland were writing national literature or trying to write it.' Ó Conaire was not. About the time Joyce was writing the first stories of the volume that was to appear as *Dubliners*, in 1914, Ó Conaire was writing *An Chéad Chloch*, his third book of stories, which also appeared in 1914. But, in 1910, Ó Conaire published a book quite unique in its time, by an Irishman, or for that matter an Englishman, a short picaresque novel called Deoraíocht, or 'Exile'. Pádraic's twenties were spent as a civil servant in London. His hero Micil, from Galway city, finds himself in the city of London deprived of an arm and a leg as the result of a street accident. His story is told in a series of flashbacks which brings us to within a few hours of his ghastly death in the Great London park where first we find him. After he has been discharged from hospital, Micil has received two hundred and fifty pounds in compensation, paltry enough even by the standards of 1905. This he has insisted in collecting in gold sovereigns. The bag of gold becomes for him 'The little yellow bag'. In his room he plays with and almost dandles the sovereigns with 'the satisfaction of a mother'. He awakes in the morning to behold 'a cloth of gold on the table and the morning sun turning to gold everything in the room'. The sun shines especially on a picture of three young men drinking together. They seem to be happy, and Micil yearns for such companionship. The transition from gold to sunlight to boozy company is, of course, deliberate: Micil squanders real gold in the material sense, on the counterfeit gold of easy companionship oiled by drink.

After a spell as an Irish immigrant Timon, Micil realizes that his store of money is very considerably reduced and he hides out in the suburbs. The other occupants of the house where he finds a room appear to shun him: but one day, to his astonishment, he is presented with the miracle of a wheel-chair, self-propelled.

An April coming in with snow finds him reduced to half-a-sovereign. One snowy evening Micil rouses himself and goes out. By the riverside he is accosted by 'a strapping sailor', who persuades him to buy a silver-mounted pistol. In this dark night the gun has magic for him: we may be permitted to see in the gun a surrogate virility, especially when bought from *an mairnéalach groí*. (Specifically Pádraic refers here to London as 'Cathair an Dorchadais'.) The bargain sealed, they go drinking. Micil, fuddled on an empty stomach, brags about his adventures and without thinking lapses into his native Irish. When a low-sized yellow-complexioned man shows interest, the sailor is quite prepared to spin an elaborate yarn about Micil being a German who had once been mad, killed eight men, been incarcerated, released, gone to East Africa, and there armed only with a knife, slain a fierce old lion, who yet injured him so badly that an arm and a leg had to be amputated – and so on.

Micil enters into the fantasy and subscribes to the sailor's account of their journey through Spain, with Micil posing as a mad limbless wonder. Micil lets out a screech, which impresses everyone but a certain woman, memorably described the first of the two extraordinary women who will attach themselves to the embittered young cripple.

> Bean mhór a bhí inti, bean mhór mhillteach a raibh éadan uirthi mar a bheadh ar Impire na Rómhànach. Grua ar dhath an chaoir chaorthainnuirthi. A brollach scaoilte aice. Boladh an óil uaithi. A dá súil ar lasadh inaceann. (*Deoraíocht*, p. 18).

From now on we will know this woman as 'An Bhean Mhór Rua', an earth-goddess figure, full of compassion for the weak, but withal irascible, wayward and feckless. About a certain story in Pàdraic's second book of short stores, *An Scolàire Bocht agus Scéalta Eile,* Mícheál Mac Liammóir once said to me that he wondered if Pàdraic knew what he was writing about.

All through *Deoraíocht*, I get a similar impression immediately countered by the simple realization that Pàdraic may *not* have been the possessor of exceptional intuition alone, but an artist of the greatest deliberation. Certainly the bringing together of the Big Red-Haired Woman and the cripple is a masterstroke that pierces our sensibility: some forty years later or thereabouts we find such significant juxtapositions in writers of the American South, Carson McCullers for instance. The Big Red-Haired Woman has not been fooled: she comes from Cill Aodàin in Galway and understands Irish and foresees Micil's doom in the hands of the sailor and the Small Yellow Man, whose name we learn later is Alf Trott, a fraudulent travelling showman who will sign on Micil as a side-show freak. The woman's rage against the world and against the 'thieves' is expressed in the traditional clichés of drunken nationalism.

> Do chrochadar na sagairt. Do shladadar an pobal. Do dhíbríodar na manaigh agus na bràithre. Do bhànaíodar an tír.
>
>   'Fíor duit,' arsa mise.
>
>   'Chuireadar Wolfe Tone sa bpríosún,' ar sise, 'chuireadar Emmet sa bpríosún, chuireadar … chuireadar mé féin sa bpríosún … chuir …'

Micil concludes that she too had wished to strike a blow for her country and the torrent subsides, laughably and pitiably.

> 'Cheap, a mhuirnín … ach ní mar gheall air sin a cuireadh sa bpríosún mé.'
> 'What else?' Micil asks.
> 'An t-ól,' arsa an bhean mhór rua. (p. 19)

Then follows a silence. All the pathos of the drunken immigrant with his or her burden of racial memory is in this interchange.

The outcome of the evening is that Micil is signed on by the Small Yellow Man, gets an advance and goes out into the night to collect a small army of down-and-outs for coffee and food, and is rescued by the Big Red-Haired Woman, who wheels him home to her own lodging. 'And you would think', says Micil, 'that I was a child and she my mother.' Not alone does she wheel his chair but at her lodging she, almost literally, nurses him by the fire, humming a lullaby.

> *Seo mar a chuirinn mo leanbh a chodladh,*
> *I gcliabhán óir ar úrlar socair,*
> *Nó … agus an ghaoth á bogadh.* (p. 26)

So then, restored to health by the Big Red Woman, Micil sets off on his tour as a 'feic saolta' – a 'living sight', with the Small Yellow Man.

The tour brings them to Micil's native city of Galway. Curiously, Pádraic's evocation of Galway is minimal compared to the powerful impressions he gives of London: the Thames, the great parks, Hyde Park certainly, though it is not named, the London-Irish slums and doss houses. In Galway we are introduced to Micil's second improbable *femme fatale* – fatale in the literal sense – the circus's Fat Woman, who falls hopelessly in love with the cripple. After the customary parade through the town, Micil retires to his tent, casts off his great black wig and brass chains, his crazy man's trappings, but retains his make-up for the evening. The Fat Woman brings him a sumptuous meal for which he has no appetite. He is sick from humiliation and disgust. She takes up a book of verses she has been reading and gives forth:

> *Rise up, Willie Reilly, and come along with me,*
> *I'm goin' to leave my father's houses and quit this countiree,*
> *To leave my father's house, his dwellings and free lands,*
> *And go along with Reilly, as you may understand.* (p. 34)

No less than his night with the Big Red Woman is this encounter extraordinary. Micil tells the Fat Woman it's time for her to go. She demurs: '"Is anseo is sócúlaí agus is suaimhní a bheas mé", ar sise …'

And then she lays her head on his breast. It is after a particularly agonizing first night, as it were, when Micil recognizes in the audience the cousin he was to have married, with her husband, that he decides to sleep in the open air. Thus comes one of several passages in which Pádraic's description of the natural world may owe much to the bright detailed pictures of dawn and dusk to be found in Ivan Turgenev's *A Sportman's Sketches*.

> Féchaim anonn trasna an chuain ar sheanchnoic clochach' na Boirne. Táid gorm. Tá an spéir gorm. Ach féach an difríocht atá idir an dá ghorm úd. Shílfeá go raibh no cnoic ag bailiú chucu a raibh de dhubh i ngorm na spéire. Go raibh sé ag sileadh anuas orthu díreach is dá mbeadh sé níos troime ná an t-aer. Agus níl an fharraige ar aon dath le ceachtar díobh cé go dtabharfá form ar dhath na farraige, freisin. Tá an difréocht chéanna idir ghorm na farraige agus gorm na gcnoc is a bhíonn idir an duine nuair atá sé ciúin socair agus nuair a bhíonn cuthach air. Níl an fharraige feargach fíochmhar anocht – tá sí an-chiúin – ach go bhfuil dath feargach uirthi. Dúnaim mo dhá shúil agus déanaim iarracht ar na trí ghorm úd i gorm na farraige, gorm no gcnoc agus gorm na spéire a mheascadh ina chéile, agus aon dath gorm amháin a dhéanamh astu. Agus feictear dom nach bhfaca súil duine riamh aon dath a bhí chomh hálainn leis an dath sin. (p. 41)

I would argue that no writer in Irish in this century has written prose more exquisite than that. The King of Day is at hand and so is the Fat Woman. She brings him love and a little bottle of whiskey, 'warm from the heat of her body'. She begins hugging and kissing him. He is revolted, yet aware that she might be the one woman in the world not revolted by him. Pádraic, writing in 1910, even in the pseudo-decent obscurity of Irish, is on dangerous ground here. The kisses of the Big Red Woman might be adjudged maternal – but only just. The kisses of the Fat Woman are quite clearly an expression of passion. Passion got the knock in Ireland with the coming of Independence. I doubt if, in the twenties, Pádraic had produced *Deoraíocht*, that it would have been published.

The Galway fair ends in a debacle. The Small Yellow Man has devised the wonderful gimmick of betrothing the Crazy Man and the Fat Woman. At the be-throthal party, Micil the Crazy Man goaded beyond sufferance, casts off his trappings and reveals the extent of the fraud. Of course uproar follows. Micil with-draws from the mayhem. As his train steams out of Galway, he notices the Fat Woman in the lamplight pouring her eyes out. The stage is now set for the final catastrophe. The Small Yellow Man will be out for Micil's blood, the Fat Woman for his love, and Micil himself will begin his second and last exile in the City of Darkness.

> Londain arís! An chathair mhór uafásach úd atá ag síorshíneadh na ngéag leis na daoine atá i bhfoisceacht na gcéadta míle di á tharraingt chuici dá mbuíochas, agus lena ndéanamh ina cosúlacht féin, lena slogadh, lena n-alpadh, lena n-athchumadh. (p. 59)

Micil has reached the stage where he attributes his gross personal disfigure-ments to a malevolent power into whose hands he again puts himself. Crassly expecting to receive his back money from the Small Yellow Man, he is meanwhile reduced again to the point of starvation when he sucks a button to work up the illusory nutriment of saliva. His sole hope is in finding the Big Red Woman. When he goes to her former lodging, which is above a stable, he meets a stone-deaf ostler who augments the quality of his hunger-driven nightmare. But not before he has lain down and wept on the floor of the Big Red Woman's empty room. 'Like the children of Lir, I made a song – except that the words of it were my tears.' The Irish, of course, is more poignant: 'Fearacht Chlann Lir, chúmas dán – ach gurb iad mo dhe-ora na focail a bhí ann.' (pp. 75–6)

The ostler can tell him nothing. Back in the park that night he follows the crowd, all gravitating towards a great chemical factory which is on fire. On the scene there are two factions among the women who had been employed, those lamenting the loss of their jobs, and those rejoicing in the destruction of a dynamo powered by slave labour. And leading on the latter is the Big Red Woman, Madame Defarge or La Pasionaria, or erupted Erda herself. To attract her attention, Micil screeches out inflammatory slogans taken up by the women. The Big Red Woman rescues him from the mêlée, taking him up like a child, kissing him again and again. She carries him home in her arms, feeds him, compares him to her own dead small brother, puts him to bed, and after a few days back in the womb as it were, finds him lodgings in what is still called an 'Irish' house, run by and patronized by immigrants exclusively. The picture that Pádraic draws of an Irish ghetto in the early years of this century is familiar to the point of heart-break. The district in which Micil lodges was once known as 'Little Ireland'. But now there are no more than forty people left of those who came from Ireland after the Famine.

> Bhí cuid de na scéalaithe agus de na seanchaithe agus de na ceoltáirí orthu siúd.
> Ach bhí a ré beagnach thart. Bhí clann na scéalaithe agus na seanchaithe ann, bhí
> agus clann a gclainne, ach nár mhór an chreidiúnt dóibh iad. (p. 90)

It is while in the ghetto that we learn positively that Micil is writing his own story, while in the next room men are playing cards and drinking, swearing and blaspheming.

It is in the 'Irish' house that Micil meets the Fat Woman again. He learns now that the Small Yellow Man is her father and that his motive in contracting her to Micil was not then wholly mercenary. But she warns him that her father has sworn to kill him with the very knife he, Micil, had used as a prop: the knife supposed to have killed the lion in East Africa. The result of the exchanges between Micil and the Fat Woman is that she gets the impression he still wants to marry her. This comes to the ears of the Big Red Woman, who confronts them with the news. It is clear now that the Big Red Woman's feelings for Micil have ceased to be purely pro-tective or motherly. In all sexual jealousy there must be an element of sadism. The Big Red Woman's immediate instinct is to humiliate both Micil and the Fat Woman.

She compels the supposed lovers to kiss, then physically attacks the woman. Here is another instance, when one wonders if Pádraic knew just how far he was descending into the maelstrom. The climax of the sadistic scene is when the Big Red Woman goes, locking Micil and the Fat Woman alone together. This might be the stuff of high farce, were it not that the Fat Woman can tell why they have been locked in. Not surprisingly, Micil's kinsfolk from Galway have been on his track. The Big Red Woman, by way of revenge as much as by way of wakening up Micil to the realities of his supposed engagement to the Fat Woman, proposes to confront him with the girl he had long ago planned to marry, together with her father.

There follows then this exquisite interlude while Micil ponders his condition:

> Tá sé ag cur sneachta. Tá brat uasal bán ar na stráideanna salacha agus ar na sean-tithe atá ag titim ó chéile leis an aois. Níl torann dá laghad le clos sa teach lóistín. Tá na lóisteoirí uile go léir ag ól thall sa teach leanna. Mise i mo shuí cois fuinneoige ag féachaint anonn orthu agus ag fanacht le mo chairde gaoil. An bhean ina suí ar an leaba ag gol os Óseal. (p. 112)

But then the wretched Fat Woman reveals that she has a key: she will give it to him if he is ashamed to have his people see her. He is and brings the Fat Woman with him, out into the snow and the saturnalia of Saturday night. They make for the house of a shadowy figure called Seán Mac Donncadha, to whom Micil is supposedly indebted for the fluency of his Irish. This is a flimsy thread in the story, but useful perhaps for any serious student of Pádraic's London life. It is not out of keeping with the phantasmagoric nature of the novel that all the chief characters should be assembled in this hosting place of the London Irish: the Big Red woman and the Small Yellow Man, and the new element of Micil's kinsfolk, the girl Máire now widowed and her father. By now the demon is in Micil. He presents the Fat Woman as his bride-to-be, bringing in with him a rabble from the streets, loaded with drink, singing, swearing. He has his 'wedding-guests' make obeisance to the 'respectable' people, his kinsfolk. Chief among them is Cing Cang, supposed to be polylingual. 'You learnt French in the convent,' says Micil to the girl Máire who had been his sweetheart, but Cing Cang is too drunk to speak any language and so Máire, with her convent French, is saved one humiliation. To humiliate himself even further and others as much as possible, is Micil's intention. Music is struck up, the singing begins, and the pre-wedding party of Micil and the Fat Woman begins: it is not unlike something conceived by the Spanish film-maker, Luis Buñuel. In the midst of it all Micil slips out. As he moves through the streets he is stopped by a grisly sight: the man whose domestic happiness he had envied that morning, standing over his unconscious wife, and the dead child to which she has just given birth. There is a hammer lying nearby. It is with this epiphany of the blackness in the heart of man that we leave Micil, until the Spring comes again, and he has taken his place among the human debris in the parks. Again he is hungry. His sole hope is the prospect of a job as a nightwatchman; meanwhile he enjoys the delirium of dreams.

Dreams of fair women: Helen of Greece, Deirdre, Donna Elvira of Spain, Joan of
Arc on a white steed, Maeve and Cleopatra of Egypt:

> Na daoine móra a bhí ag dul thart ina gcóistí breátha gleoite, ní fhacadar na hion-
> tais seo sa spéir. Na truáin a bhí ina luí ar an talamh, ní fhacadar iad. An bacach
> agus an bacach amháin a chonaic ia. (p. 129)

For the last few pages the author, Pádraic, identifies himself with his creature
Micil, in some measure at least. When he bids Micil dispel his seductive visions and
set to work in the real world, I believe he is taxing 'himself'. But Micil does not get
his job: instead he is bid go to the workhouse. So he returns to his dreams and the
park. We learn of how for a fee of tuppence he has been able to buy some bread and
cheese and a glass of beer. In his last hours we see him sitting under an oak tree,
singing, new hope running in his veins. The author has the last word: 'The poor man
was found dead under an oak tree in the middle of a London park.' The weapon that
killed him was a blunt old gapped knife – the Crazy Man's prop – how could the
poor fellow know that the sailor's silver mounted pistol was a dud? But is not life
itself a dud?

We will need to know very much more about Pádraic Ó Conaire's life before
we say that *Deoraíocht,* published when he was only twenty-eight, was simply an unforced blossom of the imagination, or the objective correlative of a great spiritual
wound.

J'ai lu tous les livres

(Hibernia, 31 October 1975)

Chacun a deux pays, le sien et la belle France. I have a confession to make, for years I read more French and Gaelic verse than I did English (except Shakespeare – but that is another story). At university I was lucky. I was introduced to that great Protestant poet of the sixteenth century, Agrippa d'Aubigné, and thrilled to that great passage from his epic *Les Tragiques*: *'Prère a Dieu pour venger les Protestants'*, represented in Part Two of *The Penguin Book of French Verse*, a magnificent collection of four earlier volumes, edited respectively by Brian Woledge, Geoffrey Brereton and Anthony Hartley. Also I was introduced to that poor darling who kept a lobster on a string and then hanged himself, Gérard de Nerval : *Le Prince d'Aquitaine à la tour abolie* from *El Desdichado* is a line that has haunted me for twenty-five years.

I cannot confess great enthusiasm for the verse of the First Part, from *Le Chanson de Roland* (c. 1100) until we come to the fourteenth-century Charles d'Orleans, whose Ballads and Rondeaux are compressed Spring, and the fifteenth-century Villon: has some scholar linked the Hag of Beare with *Les Regrets de la Belle Hëaumiere?* And perhaps the greatest religious poem in the world is the *Ballade pour prier Nostre Dame*, with its earth-shaking affirmation of Faith: *En ceste foi je veuil vivre et mourir.*

Still in Part Two, before the Pléiade – such splendour, Ronsard himself, Joachim du Bellay, Jodelle, Rémy de Belleau – came the Neo-Platonic School of Lyons, led by Maurice Scève, and possibly the first known French female poets: Pernette Du Guillet, the human inspiration of his *Délie*, and the French poet who most reminds me of Emily Brontë, Louise Labé (c. 1524–66), though Emily could never have written 'Kiss me again, re-kiss me and kiss: give me one of your most delicious, give me one of your most amorous: I will give you back four, more hot than coals' (*plus chaude que braise*). The translation is faithful: Labé died before Donne was born. From the post-Pléiade period I cherish Robert Garnier's 'Élegy on the death of Ronsard' : *Adieu, mon cher Ronsard: l'abeille en votre tombe / Fasse toujours son miel.*

(English scholars will know of Garnier's influence on the Elizabethan poet and closet-dramatist, Samuel Daniel.)

If I pass on without comment on La Fontaine, the arch-classicists Malherbe and Boileau, both very good poets, and the pre-Romantic André Chénier, the passionately personal poet guillotined in the Revolution, it is not only for lack of space, but because the nineteenth century changed the course of French verse. Asked who was the greatest French poet, André Gide replied, 'Victor Hugo, *Hélas.*' I seldom look at Hugo nowadays, though his *Booz Endormi* seems still to me to be one of the most perfect French poems. Nor, except from memory, do I think of Lamartine, Vigny and Musset.

For me, modern French verse begins with Gautier: 'Carve, file and chisel: let your hazy dream be sealed in the hard block!' This is, of course, derived from Horace's *Exegi monumentum aere perennius.* Gautier was in many ways a scoundrel: but we must not forget the acknowledged debt of Baudelaire. How many times have I read *Les Fleurs du Mal* and the prose poems *Le Spleen de Paris.* And that cautionary tract, *Les Paradis Artificiels.*

We talk of 'Chatterton, the marvellous boy', but no boy was more marvellous than Arthur Rimbaud, who wrote his masterpieces between the ages of sixteen and twenty. His masterpiece, *Le Bateau Ivre,* is not included here: how often as boy and man have I drawn sustenance from those lines of the crouching child releasing boats frail as May butterflies into the cold dark puddle. And how thrilled I was at nineteen to hear the painter Patrick Hickey launch into *Le Coeur Volé.* To be candid, I have never taken to Verlaine, though recognizing him as a great poet; I baulk at the mood-swings between pietism and sensuality. I suspect Verlaine is a poet for old men who have come to realize that their whole lives have been spent on the trapezes of unctuous piety and gross desire. *Et o ces voix d'enfants chantant dans la coupole!* from *Parsifal* still floats back from time to time: it was a favourite line of my mentor in French verse, the late James Agate.

As one progressed with Eliot, one of course became acquainted with Tristan Corbier and Jules Laforgue. But before them I once knew, by heart, Stéphane Mallarmé's *Brise Marine: La Chair est triste, hélas! et j'ai lu tous les livres,* which expresses perfectly the world-weariness of others than mere book-reviewers.

The fourth part of the book has conspicuous omissions: the Comtesse de Noailles and Jean Cocteau. Whatever Cocteau's faults, his peacockery, his un abashed pederasty, his pathetic attempt to master all the media, *Plain-Chant* is a great sequence. Whatever about Anna de Noailles, I suspect Mr Anthony Hartley of prejudice in the case of Cocteau.

Mr Hartley is very good on Claudel, Péguy and the diplomat who wrote under the pseudonym of 'Saint-John Perse'. Despite the fact that Claudel and Péguy are intensely Catholic poets, they have never caught on in this intensely Catholic country. A performance of Claudel's *The Tidings Brought to Mary,* in the Bernadette Hall in the 1950s by Longford Productions, was not a success. Péguy, who died in the First World War, is hardly known in this country.

I can read Claudel and Péguy only in short stretches, but Claudel's play, *Partage de Midi,* ravished me when I saw it in Paris in 1962 with Edwige Feuillère, Pierre Brasseur and Jean-Louis Barrault. Mr Hartley includes the *Cantique de Mesa* from that play, as well as an extract from the first *Tête d'Or*. Mr Hartley is also generous with Valéry and Saint-John Perse, in many ways more hermetic than Mallarmé. And then we come to Guillaume Apollinaire, 'poet among painters' (Francis Steegmuller's excellent book on this aspect of Apollinaire is available in Pelican at 60p), poet and First World War hero (he died as a result of war injuries). Apollinaire is not an easy poet. In my youth, I preferred his semi-erotic novels like *Le Poète Assassiné*. Nowadays I rank him almost as high as Baudelaire and Rimbaud.

Among Apollinaire's circle was Max Jacob, a converted Jew who died in a Nazi concentration camp. All the holy water of the Jordan could not efface his ethnic origins in the eyes of his monstrous captors. Since Jacob (1876–1944) is so little known in this country, I give a few lines from his poem *Connaissez-vous Maître Eckart?*: 'We little know those we love, but I understand them well enough, being all those folk myself, who yet am only a baboon.' The 'baboon' may come into his own outside France during his centenary year, 1976. Jacob was the intimate not alone of Apollinaire but of Picasso, whom he met in 1905. The three were inseparable – the Breton Jew Jacob, the Catalan Picasso, and the Polish-Italian (?) Apollinaire.[1]

An alleged mistress of Pierre Reverdy introduced me to his work in 1949; shortly after the English painter Edward Wright put me on to the great Communist poet, Paul Éluard. Another Communist poet, Louis Aragon, I knew already from the Irish versions by the late Monsignor Pádraig de Brun in *The Bell*. For a whole summer the painter Patrick Swift and I feasted on Eithne Wilkins's translation of Aragon's *Aurélieu*.

This memoir-review is scarcely adequate for a book of nearly seven hundred pages. I would like especially to have gone on about Jules Supervielle, René Char and Yves Bonnefoy. But the book will remain by my bedside, as do Racine's play *Andromaque* and Henri Michaux's *Un Certain Plume*.[2]

Perfect Thoughts[1]

(Hibernia, 14 September 1978)

'We later civilizations ... we too now know that we are mortal ...' This great lapidary utterance seems so familiar that one might easily forget it is the opening of Valéry's essay 'The Crisis of the Spirit', written just after the end of the First World War. A little more, to convey the noble limpidity of his prose, (as distinct from the throbbing hermeticism of his greatest verse): 'Elam, Ninevah, Babylon, were but beautiful vague names, and the total ruin of those worlds had as little significance for us as their very existence. But France, England, Russia ... these too would be beautiful names. *Lusitania*, too, is a beautiful name. And we see now that the abyss of history is deep enough to hold us all ... The circumstances that could send the works of Keats and Baudelaire to join the works of Menander are no longer inconceivable; they are in the newspapers.'

This is the tone of the cultured Western humanist, of a Gide or Unamuno. But Valéry had other tones. At twenty-five, in 1896, he published his devastating fiction, *Monsieur Teste*, a chilling portrait of a man 'who commits himself without reservation to the frightening discipline of the free mind ...' In 1924, he added what purports to be a letter from Teste's wife, in which we find him lingering towards evening 'in a place worthy of the dead. It is a botanical ruin'.

In 1890 Valéry used bring his new friend, André Gide, to the ancient Botanical Garden in Montpelier, where, according to Henri Mondor in his *Les Premiers Temps d'une Amitié* (Monaco 1947), the two young men would stop by a marble tomb supposed to be that of Edward Young's stepdaughter, who appears as 'Narcissa' in his *Night Thoughts*. From this richly Gothic setting came Valéry's superb early poem, 'Narcissus Speaks', with an epigraph 'To please the shade of Narcissa', from the marble tomb in Montpelier. There was no reason why he should not have gone on to win glory from his verses which, despite the preposterous origins of 'Narcissus', owe healthily to Mallarmé and Racine.

But it was not until 1917 that the epochal *La Jeune Parque* ('The Young Fate') appeared: epochal because here was the first major manifestation of 'pure poetry'. What of Mallarmé? The author of *Hérodiade* and *L'Apres-Midi d'un Faune* never sloughed the confessional skin. As Professor Lawler points out in Introductory prose as elegant as Valéry's own, 'The Young Fate' was greeted with enthusiasm by Eliot, Ungaretti, Wallace Stevens, Jorge Guillén (and, the Professor might have added, the latter's brilliant generation, a Spanish Pléiade: Lorca, Cernuda, Alberti, the recent Nobelist, Vicente Aleixandre). Rilke wrote, 'I was alone. I was waiting, my whole heart was waiting. One day, I read Valéry. I knew my waiting was over.'

But most of us would, if honest, admit that whatever Valéry's theories about the elimination of the Self from poetry, about the poet being at best no more than a word-mason (the latter perilously near to the Ordinary Man's view of poetry), a miracle like 'The Young Fate' can reach us, if it reaches us at all, only in terms of mysteriously generated emotion, alien to Valéry's dictate that 'A poem must be a festivity of the intellect'.

The difficulties are less in his later and shorter *Le Cimetière Marin* ('The Graveyard by the Sea'), 1920, in which, taking his cue from Pindar, he essays to 'exhaust the realm of the possible'. Oddly, it is in this, the second most difficult of his poems, that we find his best-known line: '*Le vent se lève! ...Il faut tenter de vivre!*' ('The wind is rising! ...One must try to live!') The enigma of Valéry may be seen if we compare this line with the words of Monsieur Teste some twenty years earlier: 'I keep what I want. But that is not the difficulty. *It is rather to keep what I shall want tomorrow.*' I find echoes of this diabolic self-sufficiency in some wonderful pages of François Mauriac's *Interior Memoirs:* 'One of his last utterances was "I look only at the wall", Mondor recalls that he had written somewhere. "I am not turned towards the world. I keep my face to the wall. There is nothing of the surface of the *wall* that I do not know." '

This book, the distillation of Jackson Mathews's great fifteen-volume edition of the *Collected Works*, superbly well translated by various hands, has given me enormous pleasure. Says Socrates in Valéry's dialogue, 'Dance with the Soul': 'How lively and gracious an introduction of the most perfect thoughts!'

Francis Stuart's Spiritual Odyssey

(The Irish Press, 29 April 1972)[1]

Even before Francis Stuart left after the outbreak of the war to take up a lectureship at Berlin University, his life had been extraordinary. At seventeen he married Iseult Gonne, who was at least six years his senior, and probably eight. From the year of his marriage, 1919, to the year of his departure for Nazi Germany, a period of twenty years, his life was like a lyric-cum-grotesque version of what his early mentor Yeats had in mind, presumably, when he wrote of Robert Gregory being 'our Sidney and our perfect man'. But the mighty Yeats was an artificer of mythologies. Stuart's pied existence (I drop the 'Mr' since I know the man and hereby aver my bias) had more to do with 'the foul rag-and-bone shop of the heart' than with any image of a multi-facetted personality.

Yet, the proximate analogy is not absurd. Stuart wrote verse and was laurelled at the first Tailteann Games. He was a soldier of the Republic and suffered in the prisons and camps of the established State. He owned and ran horses. He flew planes. Intellectually he was a cosmopolitan. He steeped himself in mysticism and guzzled the flesh-pots. His homes were a lonely glen in Wicklow and the capitals of Europe.

All of this may be gleaned from his pre-war novels, beginning with *Women and God* (1929) and from other printed sources. Crucial to an understanding of his work is his autobiographical volume *Things to Live For* (1934),[2] written when he was barely thirty-two. In one passage he writes: 'I will remain with those on the coastline, on the frontiers. With the gamblers, wanderers … martyrs and mystics. With the champions of lost loves and lost causes, the storm-troops of life. With all who live dangerously, though not spectacularly, on the knife-edge between triumph and defeat.' This might be discounted as the rhetoric of a young man over-exposed to the perverse moral passion of Dostoevsky. But Stuart, when he set out for Berlin in 1940, began to live his own rhetoric. The bitter fruits may be found in the post-war novels (*The Pillars of Cloud*, 1948, was the first) and now, with so much else, in *Black List, Section H*, a book of breathtaking sweep and at times unbearable moral splendour. Given my bias, I use these grandiose phrases with the utmost intellectual precaution.

Stuart has re-incarnated that moribund expression, 'spiritual Odyssey'. Through the *persona* of H he recounts the journey of his soul. It is all there. And here one must tackle what for many may be an offensive aspect of the book. It is through his tutor for Trinity Entrance, one called 'G.O. Grimble' that H, on the strength of some verses, is brought to one of Æ's 'Sundays'. I deduced that 'Grimble' was the man who was to become the late Professor H.O. White, before ever the author made an oblique public reference to the fact last month. But why disguise 'H.O.', as he was affectionately known, and not Æ or Yeats, or Iseult Gonne or Helena Molony, or Joseph Campbell, and several others? It may be a question of who, or who did not, die before, say 1960, but I cannot work out a consistent pattern, especially since his old friend Liam O'Flaherty appears in all his hectic summer. The matter must be consigned to the Stuart scholars, who are growing in number.

At Æ's, H meets Iseult. He meets her again at her mother's. They elope. The odyssey begins with his arrival at Euston to join her. The harsh dry pain of these pages, and of those describing the early days of their marriage, the sense of doom which pervades the events leading to the conception of their first child, make a kind of emotional mosaic which is re-created in the more frightening context of the book's final stages. Of course, the book's patently autobiographical. But it is *fashioned* autobiography. Santyana has said that genius is 'imaginative dominion over circumstances'. H and Iseult clinging together in 1919 in the narrow bed of a cheap rooming-house in Soho prefigure H and Halka clinging together as the Allied bombs fall on Berlin. In between is a relentlessly honest account of a life that for better or worse, is wholly lived. Baudelaire has some great lines which, translated roughly, mean *'My youth was but a tenebrous storm / Penetrated by brilliant sunlight'*. H's youth includes nine months imprisonment during the Civil War, but it also includes the joy of the course, of eating and drinking, of travel and love-making, and it includes, too, extremes of religious and erotic ecstasy. I might have written here some nonsense about Eros and Agape. But it is only towards the very end of the book that H and Halka come close to the mystery of Agape.

I have not yet touched on what, for those who have not read the book, might be its most controversial aspect: H's decision to go to wartime Germany and his endurance there. At no point does H apologize for his decisions. Nor does he bewail his sufferings during the Twilight of the Gods, and afterwards at the hands of his Allied captors. In fact, H *returns* to imprisonment in vanquished Germany, from post-war Paris. But frankly, political, racial and ideological considerations in the case of H seem to me only peripherally relevant.

This book is a major work of art, as extraordinary as *Ulysses*, and if it has an ideological message, it is that certain human spirits live in a country beyond any ideology.[3]

On 12th of February, 1972, Francis Stuart wrote to John Jordan as follows:

> 2 Highfield Park,
> Dublin 14.

Dear John,

It was a relief to hear you would review my novel *[Black List]*. It has nothing to do with expecting something 'favourable'. I know you will say what you think, and, whatever that may be, need I tell you there could be no repercussions such as you mentioned in *Hibernia* lately. I think of the serious novel and critics in various ways, but one that recurs is of the imaginative fiction as a small animal, undomesticated, that has been captured and is shut in a room awaiting the investigators. The door is opened, a glare directed on it and an 'expert' wearing thick gloves enters and starts to examine it. How grateful the creature is when someone enters quietly and gently, without a blinding light, speaks to it in sounds not unfamiliar and touches it with his bare hand! What he reports about it, it cannot then resent …

> All good wishes,
> Francis

On 1 May 1972 Francis Stuart again wrote to John Jordan and said, in relation to John's review in *The Irish Press*, 'I see it not as a 'review' but as the deep response of someone so receptive to messages from these hinterlands of 'tenebrous stark and brilliant sunshine', because he himself is particularly exposed to them … I was glad to see your contribution in *'Festschrift'* [qv], which I was given in Derry on Saturday, with its intense evocation of the past. In affection, Francis.'

For the letters from Francis Stuart to John Jordan see John Jordan Papers, N.L.I. List 45, Correspondence IX.i., 35,109 (fifteen items). [Ed.]

Things to Live For

(from A Festschrift for Francis Stuart)[1]

Mauriac has written that, 'When I was a boy, a few lines from Maurice de Guerin's *Journal* could make me feel nearer to him than his Cayla is to my Malagar' (*Second Thoughts*, 1961). Despite Matthew Arnold's valiant campaign for Maurice and Eugenie Guerin, it is still difficult for non-natives to savour the spiritual bouquet of this unique brother and sister. But Mauriac's main contention of the probability of spiritual identification with one or more writers at an impressionable age is likely, if not inevitable. It is more than just a question of 'influence', it is a question of conceiving one's destiny in similar terms, or, as it were, taking on the skin of various writers.

Perhaps I was pre-conditioned to like Francis Stuart, whom I just read mainly because he was the son-in-law of Maud Gonne. Perhaps I was already even past what Stuart could give me, for, as an eighteen-year-old Irish Catholic boy, I was more than usually conversant with Villon and Racine, with Baudelaire, Verlaine and Rimbaud. Of course, I had already read what was available in Rathmines and Ballsbridge Public Libraries of the work of Mauriac and Bernanos and Julien Green. I had even read a little of Péguy and Francois Jammes and Léon Bloy. But Stuart was Irish and intensely unlike his fellow-Irish writers in his pre-occupation with the duality of flesh and spirit, the mud in the metaphysical, and the platinum in the physical. And unlike his generation, O'Flaherty, O'Faoláin, O'Connor, Kate O'Brien, he was rarely gratuitously anti-clerical. At eighteeen I was callow enough to be beginning to find anti-clericalism a bore, and I was also undergoing one of my many 'conversions'. However it was, it was not from writers in English that I learned of the mortal sweetness of the flesh, the drama of sin, the intermittent duel between God and the Soul. From the French I learnt that the human heart was the background of the gravest victories and the basest defeats. For weeks a single line from Racine's *Bernice* made Aragon's novel of that name a little bible. It is important to record that I had passed beyond the plays of Chekhov, and Turgenev's *A Sportman's Sketches*. I had read none of the great Russians, certainly not *The Brothers Karamazov,* which Stuart mentions several times in *Thing to Live For* (*sic*); [and] *Notes for an Autobiography* (1934), which he wrote when he was thirty-two. I find that I had read only five of Stuart's many pre-war novels: *Women and God* (1931), *Try the Sky* (1933), and *The Coloured Dome* (1932), *The White Hare* (1936), *The Bridge* (1937).

But there were factors that shielded me from Stuart, notably his passion for horses and horse-racing, and his cultus for (then) Blessed Bernadette and Ste. Thérèse of Lisieux (*The Little Flower*). Neither of these saints had much attraction for me and I was as sceptical about the Lourdes Miracle as I was disdainful of mineral-bottles of 'Lourdes water' and other Lourdes 'relics' which were frequently hauled around by Lourdes pilgrims.

What I read in Stuart's *Notes for an Autobiography* did not reassure me: 'I saw in Bernadette a beauty that I had never before seen in anyone', and, 'I knew the joy of the Quest of the Knights of the Round Table, for a love that is ever bright, everlasting, ever new; tender and sweet and yet demanding everything even to the last sacrifice.' It is clear that Stuart's experience as a francardier, some time during the twenties, affected him in a peculiarly personal way. He writes how he has listened to 'flights of tawdry rhetoric and clap-trap oratory from an Irish bishop preaching in the pulpit in front of the grotto. I have listened till I feel ill and have gone into the baths and helped the sick pilgrims to undress, stripping tortured bodies of filthy underclothes matted with blood and worse, and breathed fully again.'

It is notable that unlike Zola, or Huysmans, or even Mauriac, he was not repelled by the hideousness of Lourdes' art-works and the pervasive air of commercialism. He even embraces the notion of a soiled and disreputable Lourdes: 'The most tawdry and the most lovely, the most blatant and the most secret. You are like a woman dressed and painted as a prostitute who in reality is full only of a passionate innocence'. His later reference to the 'tawdry rhetoric and clap-trap oratory from an Irish bishop' is almost the sole reference in the book which might be termed 'anti-clerical'. By and large, Irish writers have been anti-clerical in one of three ways: presenting them as mirthless and inhumane authoritarians, or figures of fatuousness, or affectionately observed old grumpies with hearts of gold. The latter kind may still be observed, as in a recent tale by Seán O'Faoláin, '*Feed My Lambs*'.

For Stuart, Bernadette is more than an Inspiration. She is what more orthodox Catholics recognize as *The Word Made Flesh*. I did not realize it then, but Stuart was recording a period of what was theologically dangerous, far worse even than Mariolatry (to which the Irish race is much addicted), Bernadettology. What else is the following:

> All the things I admire most I feel to be but a pale reflection of the reality seen
> by Bernadette. What inspires me when I see horses like Miracle and Glegalach,
> in my little boy Ion, in Marlene Dietrich, in that Antrim bogland, in poems, in
> people, are sparks from that furnace.

He has tried to write of the 'white girl', he tells us, 'in a novel of mine called *Women and God*, but I was too near to it then. And now, perhaps, I am too far away.'

Re-reading it over twenty years later, I can see why I was taken with it. The narrator, Colin Sullivan, and several of the other characters, including Elizabeth who is miraculously cured, are Catholics. Those who are not are (except for Elizabeth's father, a rigidly orthodox behaviourist borrowed fron Ibsen's notebooks), indifferent, but not hostile. Frank is willing to become a Catholic to marry Laura, Colin as a Catholic cannot have an affair with Catherine, with whom she imagines he is in love. In terms of human happiness, Catherine's cure affects only herself, and the narrator suggests that Ste. Thérèse of Lisieux is the model for Elizabeth Bailey. The glorification of woman is, of course, very strong in Stuart's later work, but I don't believe that elsewhere he has so blatantly submitted women into his current favourite saints.

Colin finally returns to Wicklow with his wife and family; Anne, his wife, offers him a generalization of the Irish which is at least questionable:

> There is no sharp division between physical and emotional love for us. Life is a tragic blending of the physical and spiritual for us Irish. The physical and emotional is all so much one that you couldn't have an affair with a woman you didn't love, or, if you didn't to begin with, you would end by loving her in that deep, exclusive way.

It should be clear by now that one of the major strands of *Things To Live For* [2] is the idealization of woman, almost medieval in quality. But the book could not have attracted me on that dubious score. I was more taken by statements like these: 'I had started in search of that romance that cannot be counterfeited, that is stark and cold and harsh like the smell of water and the noise of leaves. But it was a long time before I learned, if I have even now learnt, that it cannot be counterfeited.' This was a doctrine fundamentally different from Gide's *Les Nourritures Terrestres*, but, like it, held out a challenge to young hearts ready for secular impregnation. But I was captured early on by the following passage which I had never before met the likes of in English:

> To love, that is all that matters, to lavish love even on objects unworthy of it is infinitely better than living a cold ordered life in a study, in an office, even in a garden tending flowers … Of all the strange varied people I have met it has not been the sinners, the degraded, the drunkards, the gamblers, the crooks, the harlots, who have made me shudder, but the dead, the respectable dead; cut off like a branch from the tree.

He speaks also of the waning of religious certitude, of the feeling of being outcast, damned, soiled and filthy. Of the failure and torture of human love. I knew of no Irish writer who had written like this, of no other writer in whom the Spirit of the Gospels as I read them seemed to breathe. For better or worse, I have led my life according to Stuart's declaration[3]

> I will remain with those on the coastline, on the frontiers. With the gamblers, wanderers, fighters, geniuses, martyrs, and mystics. With the champions of wild

loves and lost causes, the storm-troops of life. With all who live dangerously, though not necessarily spectacularly, on the knife edge between triumph and defeat.

Compton Mackenzie once said to Stuart: 'There are two great moments in life, falling in love and conversation.' As I have said, I was going through a process of re – conversion and I was seriously in what I took to be love. It was not Francis Stuart's fault that the mixture of musings on love and religious passion should have had so heady an effect on me. I wrote to him through his publishers to where he was still virtually a prisoner in the French Zone of Germany.[3] I had heard vaguely of his ambiguous relations with the Nazis. But these important things were not uppermost in my mind: only the injunction, 'To love, that is all that matters'. God alone knows what nonsense I wrote to Francis Stuart, but he replied, to my joy and wonderment. Here is the letter:

Schwarzwaldstr. 2,
Freiburg,
French Zone of Germany,
March 28, 1949.

Dear Mr Jordan,

Thank you for your letter, which I appreciated very much. It is an encouragement to me to get such a letter and to know that *Things to Live For* has been a help to you. Looking back, it seems to me I was very young when I wrote this book, but perhaps just because of that, there may be something in it that has reassurance for the especial pain of youth. I know what I myself went through at that time and earlier, and the book was an attempt to bring it all into coherence.

I have no doubt that with courage and honesty you will come through too.

With very best wishes,
Yours sincerely,
Francis Stuart.

The line about my 'courage and honesty' both embarasses and amuses me.

Dublin, December 1971.

Small and Threatened Places: *Memorial*[1]

(The Irish Press, 27 October 1973)

Last year, on this page, I reviewed the author's *Black List:* Section H, a powerful novel which dismayed some right-thinking reviewers and readers. These good people may be even more disquieted by Mr Stuart's twenty-first novel, which throws down the gauntlet to Irish Catholic morality in a manner both fervent and contemptuous. Faced with a charge of corrupting a teenage German girl, the elderly hero, Fintan Francis Sugrue, gives his occupation as 'Recorder of improbable but true fantasies with which I hope to forge better instruments of understanding and imagining'.

This must be kept in mind lest we think of F.F.S. as a kind of pinchbeck Humbert Humbert, and the girl Herra as a somewhat older Teutonic Lolita. For this is not the story of an ageing roue's passion for a nymphet, but of youth and age clinging together for mutual protection from a world which each, after different fashions, finds intolerable. The writer has for years lived as a hermit. The child-woman, if she had come from a poor family, would have been classed as a juvenile delinquent. She has attempted suicide, has finally managed to escape from the bondage of school, to seek refuge in the Ark of F.F.S. She is obsessed with the pain of dumb creatures and, especially in Ireland, the horrors of coursing.

There is no reference in the book, I think, to St Francis of Assisi. Herra's instinct for the agony of animal life comes from no sentimental indoctrination. At one point she says about the slaughter of hares, that if we think a few more or less do not matter, then 'It means that Christ didn't rise after all, that his body rotted in a ditch or was eaten by dogs like the hares. God sent him to speak to us and that's what was done to him, so perhaps God tried again and sent the weakest, most innocent creatures to speak in an even simpler language.'

This may be taken as the outburst of an hysterical child. But the image of the hare persists throughout the book to the very end and she is tempted to surmise that the hare is the crucified Christ, and by extension, mankind impaled by men.

F.F.S. consciously sees his cottage as an Ark. But not only he and Herra inhabit it. There is also Herra's 'governess', Liz Considine, who long since has spent her nights 'in her substitute, alcohol-induced rose garden. The only unsavoury note in the book, on a sheerly realistic level, is the strategy by which Herra and F.F.S.

for their own purposes pander to Liz's alcoholism. Yet, when in her stupor, she moans and calls out 'O God, O God', we realize that her betrayal by Herra and F.F.S. makes her a limb, an organ of the Body of Christ. If this be a strained reading, I have no compunction, for the book teems with biblical analogies and references.

But the elderly writer, Herra, the 'heart's hare' and the wine-sodden Liz, must flee the Ark. F.F.S. is invited by a militant Republican to establish a community centre in 'Laggan', described as a Northern 'ghetto'. No need here for exegesis. The trip North involves a visit to Dublin, where there are some scenes of ruthless moral observation. I will not easily forget the encounter with the sheep being led to the slaughter, nor the slaughterhouse 'assistant' who is also a skid-row alcoholic. These are the stuff of nightmare.

But to my mind the finest, and sharpest, writing in the book comes when the three 'less-than-respectable' people arrive in 'Laggan', the 'besieged city'. 'We were together and free for the first time, cast up together on a deserted island as the sun set over a wide ocean, come after a long and perilous trek to an uninhabited building in a wasteland where within ancient walls that kept out the encroaching sand we walked in the evening shadows through our rose garden.'

It is the task of F.F.S., and the strictly orthodox Catholic revolutionary Mullen, on behalf of the 'Committee of Five', to transform a disused station premises into no-one knows quite what. I have not the space to enlarge upon the often-hilarious misunderstandings that crop up in the course of the transformation. The community centre is to be called the 'Hall of Freedom', but it is quite clear that notions of 'freedom' are not uniform in Laggan.

But I do not think that Mr Stuart intends this community project to be taken on a purely naturalistic level: rather as a pattern of muddled thinking, of the baffling contradictions in the Irish psyche. Thus Mullen, who goes to Mass every day, quotes Sartre. The priest whose Mass he attends quotes Heidegger.

Meanwhile, the affair between F.F.S. and Herra draws to its grim and ambiguous end. I have not fathomed whether the British sergeant, who gets lifts in a laundry van, is to be taken as an agent provocateur. Like Herra, he has risked his life for a hare dying after the birth of leverets. Yet, perhaps significantly, he is named 'Hide'.

I have given but a skimpy account of a novel which moves and disturbs. Has it any 'message' for Mr Stuart's detractors? Well, 'I can't believe in, I mean I don't feel, any brotherhood of man that hasn't come very privately and mostly in small and threatened places.'

Editorial note: At about the time of John Jordan's review of *Black List, Section H*, April 1972, Francis Stuart wrote a poem to mark their friendship that was entitled ' The Botanic Gardens' (For John Jordan), dated 8 April, Jordan's birthday:

I've never been inside the Botanic Gardens,
Having lost the entrance ticket
Bequeathed me by a Welshman
(I'd meant 'wellwisher' but that's how it came out,
Best leave it)
On a windy day of debacle
In an eddy of dust at the corner of H street.
But at the angelic hour
When the slanted light reaches furthest through the gates
And touches ('touches' is two pounds overweight in the airy gleam)
A wet forget-me-not,
I sign on as weeder-in-exile,
Or, at times of vainglory,
As gardener-outside-the-walls.

Francis Stuart

The Patriot Game

(Hibernia, October 1977)

The ethos of reviewing for the general reader books executed by specialists for specialists is perhaps fragile. But the two handsomely printed books before me, being volumes Five and Six respectively of The Cadenus Press series, *Irish Writings from the Age of Swift*,[1] provoke some general reflections that may compensate for an absence of scholarly expertise.

I do not know how history is taught nowadays in the schools of the Republic. But when I was fifteen or sixteen, shortly after the war, it was customary to rope in anyone, but anyone, who could possibly be classified as an Irish Patriot. Molyneux was held up to us because, allegedly, his *The Case of Ireland's Being Bound by Acts of Parliament in England Stated* (1698) was ordered to be burned by the common hangman. Professor J.G. Simms now assures us that there is no evidence for such a story, though it was printed by 'patriots' as dissimilar as Grattan and Tone. There is plenty of evidence that Molyneux had the narrowest possible conception of what he called 'my own Poor Country'. Neither Dr Simms in his Introduction, nor Professor Denis Donoghue in his Afterword, the one concerned with History, the other with Rhetoric, finds it necessary to indicate the extent to which Molyneux was committed to what some call the Glorious Revolution, others the monstrous usurpation of saintly Billy.

The *Case* is dedicated to William III, in a style, and kind of sentiment, which would warm the blood of every God-fearing Loyalist of the Northern mode: 'The expedition Your Majesty undertook into *England*, to Rescue these Nations from Arbitrary Power, and those unjust invasions that were made on our Religion, Laws, Rights, and Liberties, was an Action in it Self so *Great*, and of such immense Benefit, to our Distressed Countries, that 'tis impossible to give it a Representation so Glorious as it Deserves.' And he goes on about the Kingdom of Ireland being raised 'from the Depth of Misery and Despair ... to a Prosperous and Flourishing Condition'.

The immediate cause of the *Case* was the proposed legislation in the English house of commons (I follow Dr Simms's lower case) prohibiting the export of Irish woollen cloth. In his Preface to the Reader, Molyneux avows that in his attempt to block external legislation, '*the* True Interest of England *is as Deeply Engaged, as the*

Protestant Interest of Ireland'. Rhetoric can cover a gallimaufry, one allows. What concerns me is that Molyneux must be one of the earliest voices to celebrate this island as a Protestant Nation. Certainly he ranks high in the rhetoric of religious enthusiasm. I wish I had space to transcribe the splendid passage in which he speaks of 'the Insolencies and Barbarities of the *Irish Papists'*. I do not think my masters can have read the *Case* at all.

Nor can they have read of Swift, whose patriotic laurels derived from *The Drapier Letters*. But the extent to which Swift was committed to Ireland, or even the Protestant Nation, is a huge topic. Certainly, in the text known as *Polite Conversation*, published in 1738, forty years after Molyneux's *Case*, Swift deploys one of his subtler modes of irony, a kind of acid-drop tone, both sweet and acrid, when it comes to Protestant Loyalism in general. He is at pains to assure his readers of his intention 'to install early the best Protestant loyal notions into (their) minds ...

It is to *Polite Conversation* that we may relate the two slender texts edited here with flabbergasting care by Professor Alan Bliss of University College, Dublin. [2] Indeed the editorial matter is what, the most of it, the general reader will find engaging if he be Irish. It includes a cogent essay on 'The English Language in Ireland in the Eighteenth Century'. Professor Bliss is an Englishman who, in the tradition of scholars in different disciplines from his country, such as Robin Flower and George Thomson, has studied living Irish. In this context, incidentally, he quotes Swift's advice against speaking Irish to 'gentlemen' who intend to visit England: 'For I do not remember to have heard of any one man that spoke Irish, who had not the accent upon his tongue, easily discernible to any English ear.'

Swift himself certainly knew more than a little Irish, whatever about speaking it. Professor Bliss states that his 'Description of an Irish Feast' is a translation (as distinct from a version of a prose translation) of Aodh Mac Gabhráin's[3] song 'Pléarácha na Ruarcach', which was set to music by Carolan. If Swift knew Mac Gabhráin, who lived in Dublin in the 1720s, he probably knew others of the twenty-six Irish scholars listed as living there at the time of Tadhg Ó Neachtain. This, and other insights, may be found if one pastures in Professor Bliss's copious Commentary.[4] So far as Swift's 'Irishness' is concerned, this jackeen is more interested in the Dublin amateur Gael than whether he deserves a pass as an Irish Patriot.

Pained and Free

(Hibernia, 22 March 1979)

Dr Steele's packed study of Swiftian procedures[1] is not for those not already reasonably well grounded in the canon (Herbert Davis's edition of the prose runs to fourteen volumes), nor is it for those whose interest in 'the doctrinaire entertainer' is exclusively Hibernian. The latter will find more to their taste in Clive Probyn's admirable compilation, which includes Angus Ross's *The Hibernian Patriot's Apprenticeship*, a short examination of some texts of Irish interest written before Swift's return to Ireland in 1714 as Dean of St Patrick's, and David Woolley's account of the famous, so-called, 'Armagh' *Gulliver* and its disputed Swiftian corrections. Mr Woolley comes down heavily on the side of those who believe the marginalia of the Armagh *Gulliver* to be Swift's hand (as, for instance, does Colin McKelvie, whose edition of *Gulliver*, Belfast 1976, was reviewed in *Hibernia*, by Dr Eileen McCarville). But it is still not clear how the *Gulliver* in question came to be in Primate Robinson's Public Library in Armagh. Did it come from that Canon Thomas Jordan whose father-in-law, Jonathan Osborne M.D., once owned it, and who was Treasurer of Armagh Cathedral from 1900 until his death in 1908?

The body of Dr Steele's book consists of four extended discussions of Swift's imaginative procedures, under the headings of 'Fools', 'Acting', 'Play', and 'The Grotesque and Dying Animal'. When I first had the book and flicked through the pages, I was a little dashed, for I lit on words like *'entropy'*, and *'dystopian'*. Was I to plough through another ponderous academic exercise in the modish Anglo-American non-style (Dr Steele is an Australian)? But my misgivings were allayed almost immediately when, on the second page of the Introduction, I read:

> There are in his life areas of mellowing and of amelioration. But, on the whole,
> Swift's attitude is that if he is answerable to anybody, it is to God alone.

Clearly, Dr Steele was to be my kind of critic, not afraid to be plain when occasion demanded. In the chapter on 'Fools', and in the context of the Grand Academy of Lagado depicted in 'A Voyage to Laputa', he hits on a pervasive Swiftian note, his *'savouring of the marvellous'*, even when the matter for astonishment be ludicrous, horrific, or merely disgusting, and this relish he associates with 'simplicity *of heart'*. Later he encapsulates his general thesis in a memorable sentence which may well become a signpost in Swiftian studies: 'The vigour of the pamphleteer is constantly being overhauled by the fascination of the visionary.'

Of Dr Steele's many *exempla* of this process at work, I pick out *A Short Character of Thomas Earl of Wharton,* of which the author writes, taking a clue from the eminent American Swiftian, Irvin Ehrenpreis, 'The dark fool Wharton is dismayingly potent in begetting other fools in deception.'

If Yeats could write, 'Swift haunts me: he is always just around the next corner', then, for Dr Steele, Yeats in the Swiftian context is always there, a tutelary ghost. So, in the chapter on *'Acting'*, we have this on Swift and Yeats: 'The remembered heroic – statuesque, almost heraldic – and its ludicrous equivalent are likely to merge almost anywhere in the writings of either of them.'

But of course Dr Steele has a broader notion of *'Acting'* than that implied by, say, Maud Gonne at Howth Station. Many of Swift's figures are, in fact, *pretenders*, from his 'Marlborough' to Lemuel Gulliver, so often reduced to the status of a mythical plain, honest, Englishman.

> The most famous of Swift's figures is indeed his most characteristic, in that he cannot attain the humanity he mimics.

(As Clive Probyn's essay, 'Swift and the Human Predicament',[2] in the second book noticed.)

Older Swiftians may look askance at Dr Steele's chapter on 'Play', in which he relates the categories of the French sociologist Roger Caillois (himself a descendant of Johan Huizinga, author of the small classic *Homo Ludens*) to the procedures of Swift. But, as a middle-aged dabbler, I found it entrancing, especially as Dr Steele's investigation can steer him to such a splendid conclusion as this:

> To the pains of the observing mind there answer, in his case, the pleasures and resources of the free mind: and the fortunes of utopia in his writings are the result of the full exercise of both.

(I have had to bypass the discussion of 'utopia' and 'dystopia'.)

The concluding chapter's title is ambiguous: for the matter here is *both* 'the grotesque' (as a mode of vision) *and* 'the dying animal', as Swift saw Man from the moment of his birth. As for 'the grotesque', Dr Steele posits that in Swift, 'If the dream of reason begets monsters ... the dream of monsters begets laughter.' He examines the functions of mortality, disease, madness and filth as agents of Swift's gigantic effort to project, *and* contain, what he sees about him. In the whole course of his book, Dr Steele only twice alludes to Pascal. But strangely, while he quotes approvingly Paul Fussell on the Augustan understanding of man – 'He both is and is not like an angel; he both is and is not like a brute' – he seems to have forgotten the classic utterance of Pascal: '*L'Homme n'est ni ange ni bette ...*' (*Pensees. 77*).

It is exemplary of Dr Steele's pleasing eclecticism that in seeking to pluck out the lacerated heart of Swift, he should turn to as unlikely a source as Ignazio Silone and an essay he wrote in 1954 about the large number of modern writers who have committed suicide. Silone suggested that 'some of them probably died as the victims of wretched anxiety precisely because they excluded it from their own doctrine and art. Inhibition is more deadly than honesty'. Dr Steele sees in Swift,

> The struggle to admit in the right measure, and exclude in the right measure, for doctrine and art, the 'wretched anxiety' which constantly threatens to well up.

This seems to me a wonderfully humane formulation, which yet does not trap Dr Steele in a subjective (that is to say, self-indulgent) view of the 'strenuous vindicator of human liberty', of 'that one mind ... pained and free', as he says finely.

Dr Steele's book is of that critical kind which both instructs and delights. It is replete with the latest Swiftian scholarship, of which he makes adroit and grateful use, and it is instinct with affection for his subject. I use the term 'affection' adviedly, and am grateful, as many other half-baked enthusiasts haunted by stereotypes must be, for an expansion of the imagination.

Aodhagán Ó Rathaille

(from The Pleasures of Gaelic Poetry)[1]

In any approach to the literary culture of the extraordinarily diverse island of Ireland, it is sometimes illuminating to consider certain curious coincidence of dates. When an Irishman recalls that 1856 saw the birth of Bernard Shaw in Dublin, and of Tomás Ó Criomhthain on the Great Blasket Island off the coast of Kerry, he may, or should, experience a *frisson*, a minor thrill, in the realization that he can embrace in his heritage the antipodes of *John Bull's Other Island* and *An tOileánach*.[2]

For myself, I take pleasure in the fact that Jonathan Swift was born in Dublin in 1667, only about three years before the birth of Aogán Ó Rathaille, in the Sliabh Luachra region of County Kerry, more precisely at Screathán an Mhíl – Scrahan-aveale – a mile north of Meentogues and ten miles east of Killarney. It is a sombre pleasure: the mighty Latin epitaph which Swift made for himself, and which may be read over his resting place in St Patrick's Cathedral in Dublin, would not be in-apposite on the grave of Ó Rathaille in Muckross Abbey near Killarney. I am not, of course, the first to link the *saeva indignatio* of Swift with Ó Rathaille's defiant ulu-lation. Most recently, John Montague did so in the Introduction to his *Faber Book of Irish Verse*, linking both with Daibhí Ó Bruadair, still alive when both were growing up: 'three angry men', he calls them.[3]

But the worlds of Swift and Ó Rathaille were vastly different. Swift, for large sections of his life, could look across the water, aspire even to the real and glittering spoils that lay on the other side. Ó Rathaille never left Munster and when he looked across the water it was to envisage the illusory rewards coming in the wake of an illusory saviour, the Old Pretender, son of that Catholic Stuart King, James II, whom other Irishmen called 'Séamus a' Chaca' – 'Messy James', with cloacal overtones – but who for Ó Rathaille had been the liege lord of the Brown family of Kenmare, who were his liege lords, as the great, dispossessed, MacCarthy clan had been the acknowledged masters of his forefathers.[4]

To appreciate the poignancy, and sometimes the theatrically savage power of Ó Rathaille's verse, it is necessary to accept certain facts perhaps unpalatable in democratic, nation-conscious, societies. Ó Rathaille had no notion of nationalism as such, not even as it may be seen emerging in, say, *The Faerie Queen* of Spenser some seventy years before his birth. Nor had he any notion of what used to be called egalitarianism; less so, indeed, than many of those, including Milton, who had thrown in their lot with the Cromwellian revolutionaries. By heritage and, I would say, by temperament, he was a monarchist, accepting in the order of things the principle of hierarchy; in cruder terms he believed, naturally and unquestioningly, in the caste system, in which he saw himself as occupying an honourable and honoured place. He was an *ollamh*, a bard.[5] Without that system, he could not fufil his vocation. If he could not practise his craft, he could not make a livelihood: he became a displaced person. Appreciation of Ó Rathaille's high and lonely utterance depends, largely, on acceptance of these factors. His first and only editor in full, the great Patrick S. Dinneen, tends to gloss over Ó Rathaille's dependence on and acceptance of the medieval system into which he had been born: 'The energies which other poets devoted to the praise of wine or women, he spent recounting the past glories and mourning over the present sorrows of his beloved land, whose history he had studied as few men have ever done ...'[6]

The comment of Fr Dinneen's sympathetic biographers, Prionnsias Ó Conluain and the late Donncha Ó Ceileachair, is apposite: 'Ó Rathaille is more of a poet and less of a patriot than Dinneen imputes to him.'[7] (My translation.) They instance a *marbhna*, or elegy, which Ó Rathaille wrote for John Blennerhasset of Ballyseedy, County Kerry. A decade or so before his death, Blennerhasset had been one of the prime movers in an attempt to plant Protestant settlers on the estates of Nicholas Brown, second Viscount of Kenmare, a Catholic attainted for his participation in the Williamite Wars. Ó Rathaille proclaimed allegiance to the Browns, but made no bones about later composing an elegy of 120 lines for Blennerhasset. And it should be remembered that he could mourn with equal intensity the MacCarthys, the Gaelic overlords of his forefathers, and the Anglo-Irish (or Hiberno-English) Browns who dispossessed them. Both families are associated with some of his most plangent verse.

Sometime between 1703 and 1708–9[8] he was compelled to move to Corcaguiny on the Dingle Peninsula, where the great wave of Tóim, Tonn Tóime, is said to be the tutelary spirit. One night, kept awake by the storm, he meditated on his present misery as against the putative comfort of life under the patronage of the MacCarthys. But he also laments Sir Nicholas Brown.[9] Seán Ó Tuama has noted the juxtaposition in this poem of the sea's rage and the poet's mental anguish.[10]

> *Is fada liom oíche fhír − fhliuch gan*
> *suan, gan srann*
> *Gan ceathra, gan maoin caoire ná*
> *buaibh na mbeann.*
> *Anfaithe ar toinn taoibh liom do*
> *bhuaidhir mo cheann.*
> *Is nár chleactas im naoidhin fíiogaigh ná*
> *ruacáin abhann.*[11]

From the last line of that first stanza, 'and I was unused in my childhood to dog-fish and periwinkles',[12] James Stephens took a hint for a proud little poem of his own in his *Reincarnations* (1918), called 'Egan Ó Rahilly'. Eavan Boland has made a fine free version of the whole poem, from which the following are the second, third, and final stanzas:

> *O if he lived, the prince who sheltered me*
> *And his company who gave me entry*
> *On the river of the Laune,*
> *Whose royalty stood sentry*
> *Over intricate harbours, I and my own*
> *Would not be desolate in*
> *Dermot's country.*
> *Fierce MacCarthy Mór whose friends were welcome,*
> *McCarthy of the Lee a slave of late,*
> *McCarthy of Kenturk whose blood*
> *Has dried underfoot:*
> *Of all my princes not a single word —*
> *Irrevocable silence ails my heart*
> *Take warning, wave, take warning, crown of the sea*
> *I, Ó Rahilly — witless from your discords —*
> *Were Spanish sails again afloat*
> *And rescue on our tides,*
> *Would force this outcry down your wild throat,*
> *Would make you swallow these*
> *Atlantic words.*[13]

But no translation can convey the outrageous splendour of Ó Rathaille's last line, which might be absurd were it not for the occult significance of Tonn Tóime, harbouring god or fairy: *'Do ghlam nach binn do dhingfinn féin it bhraghaid.'*[14]

In that poem he refers to 'the prince who sheltered me', Sir Nicholas Brown, but in a later poem he is at odds with Sir Nicholas's son, Valentine Brown. Never more bitterly has 'patient merit spurned' reacted in circumstances of misery and decrepitude:

> *Do leathnaigh an ciach diachrach fám*
>   *sheana — chríoi dúr*
> *Ar dtaisteal na ndiabhal iasachta i*
>   *bhfearann Chuinn chughainn;*
> *Scamall ar ghrian iarthair dár cheartas*
>   *ríoghacht Mumhan*
> *Fá deara dham triall riamh ort, a*
>   *Bhailintín Brún.*
> *Caiseal gan chliar, fiailteach na*
>   *macraidhe ar dtúis*

> That my old bitter heart was pierced
>   in this black doom
> That foreign devils have made our
>   land a tomb
> That the sun that was Munster's
>   glory has gone down
> Has made me a beggar before
>   you, Valentine Brown.
> That royal Cashel is bare of
>   house and guest.

Is beanna – bhruigh Bhriain ciar-thuilte
    'mhadraibh úisc,
	That Brian's turreted home is
	    the otter's nest

Ealla gan triair triaithe de mhacaibh
    riogh Mumhan
	That the kings of the land have
	    neither land nor crown

Fá deara dham triall riamh ort, a
    Bhailintín Brún.[15]
	Has made me a beggar before
	    you, Valentine Brown.[16]

While Frank O'Connor's translation of those first two stanzas from 'Bhailintín Brún' is in acceptable simple language, the language of the original is relatively baroque – 'and Brian's turreted mansions, black-flooded with otters'[17] – but Ó Rathaille, as we shall see, was capable of punitive starkness, and, while addicted in traditional mode to alliteration and imaginative compounds, was seldom an exemplar for the next major Munster poet, Eoghan Rua Ó Súilleabhain, who often expires in a morass of loveliness.

In so far as he was an *ollamh* or bard, Ó Rathaille – perforce almost – is a learned poet, presenting a peculiar difficulty as far as his allusions and nomenclatures are concerned. He draws on the mythology and history of Greece and Rome and from the Bible, but also, often to the bewilderment of even the Irish reader, from the more arcane Irish mythology and from the earliest Irish historical records. We must add to this load numerous references to townlands, villages, hills, dales, rivers and streams, not only in his native Kerry, but all over Ireland. He carried in his heart the outlines of a country most of which he had never seen.

Yet it is not, I believe, in his poems for patrons of whatever rank, in which he deploys the bardic armoury, that his personal genius is best articulated. This can find expression in what by the middle of the eighteenth century had become almost a folk-mode: I mean, of course, the *aisling* or vision-poem.

This form became widespread both in the North and South of Ireland in the eighteenth century as a mode of political allegory. In a vision, the poet meets a beautiful woman in distress – a *spéir-bhean*, or sky-woman – who is mourning a lost hero or lover. The poet either comforts the lady and promises redress, or is comforted by her. In the North of Ireland, the lost hero may be identified with one of the exiled O'Neills or O'Donnells, the great families who went into exile after the Battle of Kinsale (1603). In Munster, the lost hero and expected redeemer is identified with one or other of the Stuarts. In his lifetime, Ó Rathaille saw two dynasties as usurpers of the House of Stuart: the House of Orange and the House of Hanover. But, as did his patrons, Catholic and Protestant, he remained a Jacobite, and with one major exception his *aislingí* are geared to the Stuart cult. The exception (if in fact it be one) is '*Mac an Cheannaí*' (or The Merchant's Son), in which the poet meets a distressed maiden on the seashore awaiting the arrival of the merchant's son and the succour he will bring with him. The poet tells her that the saviour she is expecting has died in Spain. Here there is no evidence that any Stuart is in question: Seán Ó Tuama opines that the death in Spain may refer to the death of the young King, Luis I, in 1724 and the foundering of all hope of military aid from that source.[18] This *aisling* is slighter, certainly, than '*Gile na Gile*' (or 'Brightness of Brightness') or '*Maidin sul a smaoin Titan ...*' (or 'One Morning Before Titan Thought ...'), but there is a special Virgilian pathos in the picture it sketches of the lady gazing over the wave for the lover-hero who will never come.

There is no doubt that Ó Rathaille has James II's son, the Old Pretender, in mind in 'Maidin sul a smaoin Titan ...', an *aisling* which celebrates openly the restoration of 'the three kingdoms' through the splendid grouping of the hooded woman lighting three candles which blaze indescribably:

> Lasaid – sin trí coinnle go solas nach luadhaim
> Ar mhullach Chnuic aoird Fhírinne Conallach Ruaidh,
> Leanastar linn scaoth na mban
> gcochall go Tuamhain,
> Is fachtaim-se dhíobh díograis a n-oifige ar cuaird.[19]

Here is how the poet learns the significance of the three unearthly lights, as rendered by Edward, sixth Earl of Longford (1902–61):

> Then I caught pretty Aoibheall
> and asked her to say
> Why they lit their three candles
> o'er every bay
> 'Tis a light,' she replied, 'for a
> king that ere long
> Shall win back his Three
> Kingdoms and save them
> from wrong.'[20]

'*Maidin sul a smaoin Titan ...*', until the poet's dream dissolves, is a fantasy of hope and joy. Austin Clarke, in an exquisite paraphrase, has captured something of the poem's gossamer lightness:

> One day before Titan had
> lighted the way from his
> doorstep,
> I climbed to a hilltop silled by
> mist and, wherever I looked,
> were blue-hooded women who
> knew no envy:
> They came from a mound
> without sound through the
> grey of heather.[21]

Ó Rathaille's other great *aisling*, the breathtaking '*Gile na Gile*' (or 'Brightness of Brightness'), is one of the miracles of Irish literature – after its fashion as solitary and inexplicable as 'Kubla Khan'. Superficially, it is no more than a political allegory in a familiar mode. The poet in a dream meets a beautiful woman who symbolizes Ireland. She addresses him cryptically, flies, is followed by him to a fairy mansion, where both are imprisoned by a band of remotely demonic creatures. But the poet goes free, while she remains in the control of a sensual boor. While she is being disposed of to the boor, the poet upbraids her with unfaithfulness to her prince – the Old Pretender – and with a *slibire slímbhuartha* – 'an awkward, sorry churl'.[1] It would be absurd to interpret this poem solely in terms of modern psychology: thus we might see the lady's surrender to a masterful brute as an instance of the victory of sexual appetite over romantic love.

But I do not think it absurd to take cognizance of the piteously human pattern coexisting with the patent political allegory. The poet has seen his 'brightness of brightness' befouled, and must live to record the grand disillusion. As for the 'Brightness of Brightness' it is scarcely possible to render in English the description Ó Rathaille gives of this, the premier sky-woman of the *aisling* literature; the translator is James Clarence Mangan:

Gile na gile do chonnarc ar sligh in uaigness,	The Brightest of the Bright met me on my path so lonely;
Criostal an chriostail a goirm-roisc rinn-uaine,	The Crystal of all Crystals was her flashing dark-blue eye;
Binneas an bhinnis a friotal nár chíon-ghruamdha,	Melodious more than music was her spoken language only;
Deirge is finne do fionnadh 'na gríos-ghruadhnaib.[22]	And glorious were her cheeks, of a brilliant crimson dye.[23]

Lord Longford has been more successful, I think, in his version of the second stanza, which in the original begins, '*Caise na caise i ngach ruibe dá buidhe-chuachaibh* …'[24]

> *Curling of curling gold was in*
> *every hair of the heap;*
> *Thro' a world turned dusty and*
> *old would her locks in their*
> *lustre sweep,*
> *With a gleam that glittered as*
> *glass on the swell of her*
> *bosom full –*
> *High Heaven had brought it to*
> *pass that her bosom be*
> *beautiful.*[25]

The unfortunate 'heap' may be forgiven for the remarkable second line. Though the last line barely approximates to '*do geineadh ar ghineamhain dise san tír uach-traigh*',[26] which lends to Ó Rathaille's lady a supernatural dimension that has nothing to do with the otherworld of faery. It has something to do with 'I was set up from eternity, and of old, before the earth was made'.[27]

The *ceangal* or binding of the poem speaks of the lovely lady being without respite '*go bhfillid na leoin thar toinn*' – 'until the lions return from over the wave'. Ironically, any lions that came across the wave came some seventy years after Ó Rathaille's death: soldiers of revolutionary France stained with the blood of a king whose forefathers Ó Rathaille regarded as the natural allies of the Stuarts. And Ó Rathaille himself seems to have gone on an increasingly desolate path: 'that Dante of Munster', Daniel Corkery called him. And it might be said, without bathos, that his devotion to his Gaelic and Jacobite Beatrice, *la dolce guida* beckoning him ahead in Sliabh Luachra, was to bring him to the plight, where on the lip of the grave, it seems, he made the incomparable confessional poem that begins: '*Cabhair ní ghoirfead go gcuirtear mé i gcruinn-chomhrainn*'[28] ('I will not cry for help before I'm put into a narrow coffin'; the usual translation 'until I'm put' is an absurdity). Of that line Corkery has exclaimed, 'It seems to me we are hearing a voice that outLears Lear!'[29] He is right, up to a point. But there is *hysterica passio* in Ó Rathaille's blend of defiance and impassioned stoicism, in which one may hear the voice of an older tragic hero, the Philoctetes of Sophocles, or of another Shakespearean figure of archetypal doom – Timon of Athens:

> Then, Timon, presently prepare thy grave;
> Lie where the light foam of the sea may beat
> Thy grave-stone daily: make thine own epitaph,
> That death in me at others' lives may laugh.[30]

But it is also John Donne, I think, and sonnets such as 'Batter my heart, three-person'd God', and 'Death be not proud', that provoke a tingling in the blood comparable to the effect produced by Ó Rathaille's poem. It continues on its high level of disconsolation until, as it were, reaching 'port after storm':

Stadfadsa feasta, is gar dom éag gan mhoill,	I will stop now, a quick death is coming, since those fierce
Ó treascradh dragain Leamhan, Léin is Laoi;	men of the Laune and the Léin and the Lee have been
Rachadsa 'na bhfasc le searc na laoch don chill,	toppled. I will follow to the grave after the most beloved of heroes,
Na flatha fá raibh mo shean roimh éag do Chríost.[31]	princes under whom my forebears served before Christ's death.

Even a plain prose translation reverberates in the mind with the resonance of the highest verse. I am thinking of *Phèdre*: '*Soleil, je te viens voir pour la dernière fois*';

of the final Chorus in *Oedipus Rex*: 'Call no man happy until he is dead'; of Shakespeare's song: 'Fear no more the heat of the sun.'

The last line of Ó Rathaille's poem found its way into Yeats's poem 'The Curse of Cromwell', which appeared in *Last Poems* (1939):

> And there is an old beggar wandering in his pride –
> His fathers served their fathers before Christ was crucified.[32]

Yeats, of course, came to Ó Rathaille through his working association with Frank O'Connor.[33] But the spirit of Ó Rathaille, not merely a paraphrase of his words, shines through that section of 'The Municipal Gallery Revisited', which begins, 'My medieval knees lack health until they bend'.[34] Ó Rathaille was all too willing, perhaps, to bend the knee. But his verse also suggests that he was unwilling to bend it to upstarts, to the kind of louts he saw in possession of the Mac Carthy and Brown estates. The twin summits of his art, '*Gile na Gile*' and '*Cabhair ní Ghoirfead*', are marvellous paradigms of the poet in ecstasy and *in extremis*. They are also the desperate euphemism, and the passing bell, of a dying civilization. Ó Rathaille is a poet of the deluge.

Ireland and the Classical Tradition[1]

(The Irish Press, 2 December 1976)

Here's richness! Professor Stanford has written a book noble in conception, elegant in execution, and except for his few surprising omissions (surprising because
so near home and time) as comprehensive as any intelligent layman with
'smalle Latine and lesse Greeke' might wish. And in the year of the New Fiver*
when public and pundits are mocking at the image of Johannes Eriugena (i.e. 'born
in Ireland') Scottus (sic) the common man may be glad to know that Eriugena was
not surpassed as the first 'original' Irish philosopher until the advent of Berkeley
in the eighteenth century. The element of neo-Platonism in his work incurred
the displeasure of the Western Church four times, though his thought was derived
from St Augustine, and his later followers included Pope Sylvester II. When Gerard
Manley Hopkins came to UCD in 1884, as Professor of Greek, his views on neo-
Platonism and Eriugena were not popular in the prevalent Aristotelian atmosphere.
The wheel has come full circle, with valuable work from UCD from Professors J.J.
O'Meara[2] and Ludwig Bieler[3] on our most illustrious philosopher-punster. (A missed trick by W.B.S; he does not note that Professor O'Meara published an article
on Aristophanes and Beckett.)

As far back as the sixth century Pope Gregory the Great denounced the
classics for their immorality. In the ninth century Aldhelm in Britain warned a Saxon student who had spent some time in Ireland against the danger of studying the
classics. Yet in the sixth century St Columbanus refers to Horace, Virgil, Martial,
Juvenal, and the post-classical Statius, Ausonius and Claudian. He even knew at
least the name of Sappho. I have had occasion to read and sometimes in parallel
texts (as in the Leob editions) Juvenal and Martial. The influence of Dr Thomas
Bowdler survived long after his death.

Professor Stanford's survey of the influence of the classics on Irish thought
and imagination ranges from the 'first thousand years' almost to whatever 'classical' hogwash is shown on our screens. He is hyper-optimistic about the value of
package Greek holidays. I know only one other man of my generation in Dublin
who has visited Knossos, and I would remind Professor Stanford that Cacoyanis's
magnificent film version of The Trojan Woman closed after a week in Dublin, though
Fellini's Satyricon was successful. But then Petronius has more kicks than this piece

of Euripides mentioned. (Another missed trick: the late Edward Longford translated with his wife Christine, the whole of *Oresteia* of Aeschylus, done at the Gate in shortened form in the thirties and then published by Hodges Figgis; he also made versions of Euripides *The Bacchae* and of Sophocles's *Oedipus Rex*, in which Mc-Master[4] toured up and down the country to audiences some of whose grandparents could quote from the poetry of Eoghan Rua Ó Suilleabháin encrusted with classical references.)

Two Irishmen may be singled out in connection with the Minoan civilization of Crete: Robert Wood, whose writings on the putative Homeric sites helped the incredible Schliemann, and Sir William Ridgway, once Professor of Greek in Cork who took issue with Sir Arthur Evans, the excavator of Knossos. Wood may be described as the Irish pioneer of classical archaeology.

I can only skim scraps from W.B.S.'s book in a short review: that Thomas Leland, a distinguished exponent of Demosthenes, had among his pupils at TCD Burke (who inclined, however, to the Ciceronian ideal of oratory), Grattan, Flood and Philpot Curran, as well as Goldsmith, who later published popular classical histories, defended with vigour by Dr Johnson but scorned by Macaulay; that Swift used the classics as the political winds listed; that the Demosthenic and Ciceronian modes may have modelled the orations of Irish patriots. We may re-read Sullivan's *Speeches from the Dock* in the light of the Graeco-Roman tradition. I have not referred to Art, Architecture, Science, nor to Medicine. I have not mentioned Yeats, or Joyce, or Wilde. But you will find all those subjects, and those three writers, dealt with in a most entertainingly erudite book. It is most handsomely produced. But how in Zeus's name did '1720' escape as the date of *Gulliver's Travels*?

* The then new Irish £5 note, which had the image of Johannes Scottus Eriugena. [Ed.]

Jamesian Novelist[1]

(Hibernia, 7 October 1977)

Just four years ago I had the occasion to re-read the bulk of the Bowen canon, some six months after her death.[2] In a sense it was revisiting the glimpses of the moon, for I still had the orange Penguins, bought at a shilling a head, of some of her early novels: the third, fourth and fifth, *Friends and Relations* (1931), *To the North* (1932), and *The House in Paris* (1935). I tackled (the verb is correct) her last two novels, for the first time, *The Little Girls* (1964) and *Eva Trout* (1969), which left me as excitingly uneasy as they appear to have left Ms Glendinning. For they are closer to the worlds of Murdoch and Spark than they are to the last recognizably 'Bowenesque' novel, *A World of Love* (1955), which, alone with *The Last September* (1929), is set entirely in the Ballyhoura region of North Cork, the country of Sheehan's Doneraile, of Spenser's Kilcolman, and of happier memory, 'his gentle Mulla', the Awbeg.

But for Elizabeth Bowen, the country, chiefly, of her ancestral home, Bowen's Court, which was her beloved burden from the time she became its mistress in 1930 until she was forced to sell it in 1959, with the child-like belief that the house would be preserved by the new owner. It was levelled the following year. But not alone in fiction has it been preserved. Her book, *Bowen's Court* (1942), republished in 1964 with an elegiac Afterword of much beauty, is its monument and arguably her greatest achievement.

Ms Glendinning is not much concerned with critical evaluation of her subject: that is not her purpose. In her Foreword she asserts that 'she is to be spoken of in the same breath as Virginia Woolf ...', which seems to me to do Bowen a disservice, perhaps because I have never been able to subscribe to the Virginian cult. Woolf warned Bowen against the dangers of Henry James, but surely Bowen is the most successfully Jamesian novelist (*and* short story writer) of her epoch (it *was* an epoch: her first book, *Encounters*, came in 1923). It is true that when her first post-war novel, *The Heat of the Day*, appeared in 1949, some critics (and common readers) found the James stylistic influences – the inversions, the sinuosities – obtrusive. But although in later years she professed to find 'the more complicated books' of James beyond her, I am certain that she not so much learned but was assisted to perceive from books such as *What Maisie Knew* and *The Awkward Age*.

But it is Bowen the woman that Ms Glendinning is concerned with. She has, alas, to spend time on that ancient, boring chameleon question: how *Irish* was she? Well, the author might have said simply that racially she was, despite her Cromwellian ancestors, just as Irish as certain families of the Aran Islands who have both Spanish and Cromwellian ancestry. Certainly she recognizes the almost cliché Celtic elements in Bowen (her forefathers were of Welsh stock): the streak of wild-ness, the gaudiness (in her case personalized and disciplined), the sympathy with a non-Christian otherworld. She might have said more about certain eccentricities of her last years. There was madness in the Bowen blood. Her father was never quite right in the head from her own childhood years. A close connection was the Major Bowen-Colthurst who had Francis Sheehy-Skeffington shot. There must be more to be known about Elizabeth's reactions to the mental disorder and suicide of Virginia Woolf.

Ms Glendinning has a good deal to tell us about Bowen's private life, which yet remains tantalizing. In 1923 she married Alan Cameron, an educationalist who later held an administrative job in the BBC. He died in 1952. We are assured that in those thirty years she was never disloyal to him, though not, in the sexual sense, always faithful. There is a suggestion that the marriage was not consummated when in 1933 Elizabeth fell in love with a young man eight years her junior, whom she met at lunch in Oxford with Maurice Bowra. The affair lasted for three years, even after the lover, whose identity Ms Glendinning is at pains to conceal, had married and become a father (I think the careful reader will be able to outwit the biographer's discretion). The affair ended in 1936, when the lover went abroad. *The House in Paris* and *The Death of the Heart* were fed by this affair. Her wartime *amitié amoureuse* with Mr Charles Ritchie, later to become a very distinguished Canadian diplomat, lies back of *The Heart of the Day*. The amitié lasted until Elizabeth's death, from cancer, in 1973.

I wish I had space to discuss Ms Glendinning's admirable organization of Bowen's multi-layered social and literary activities; her successful coolness in face of the Anglo-Irish dimension argument; her lucid style which only rarely reads like a pastiche of Bowen's own.

A footnote, miniscule and poignant, for posterity: just four years ago, Father Brendan Wrixon drove me with a companion at the North Cork Writers' Festival, from Doneraile to Farahy churchyard, where 'Mrs Cameron' is buried. The com-panion was John B. Keane: I doubt he ever dreamed he would join Bowen as a Doctor of Dublin University.

Time Redeemed[1]

(Hibernia, 9 March 1978)

If anything sane emerges from the tanglewood of notes I have made on this shimmering, but not seldom opaque, book, I'll be blowed. Professor Donoghue[2] has never been a writer for sluggards, not is it uncharitable to state that he may take some quite legitimate pleasure in baffling those less well educated than himself. Whether his taste for high ground in the end militates against his effectiveness as a minister of the Word is another question.

Characteristically, his book has two epigraphs from sources the common reader would not usually juxtapose: Wordsworth's 'The Prelude' (1805) and Wallace Stevens's 'The Comedian as the Letter C'. It is from the latter quotation he takes his title. He might, with a sacrifice to elegance, have taken another description of 'man' from the same quotation: *'this nincompated pedagogue'*. For his subject, vast and demanding, is no less than the sacramental significance of the imagination in the life of Man.

Make no mistake about it. The catholicity of his sympathies, his grave and often poignant fairness, cannot disguise the fact that he is in heart and spirit a moralist: by which I mean one concerned with the effect on behaviour of all exercises of the intelligence (he might prefer 'mind'), of which the practice of literature is only one. In the opening essay, 'The Essential Power', in which he makes much (rightly, I believe) of Lionel Trilling, he would seem to make his position clear: 'If it comes to a choice between mind and that mindlessness which Trilling indicts, the fashionable subversion of knowledge and truth, then the choice is clear: I choose mind with all its limitations.' But 'imagination' can be preserved as the grander term.

The other six essays are investigations of various *kinds* of imagination. In the second essay he arrives at *'two rival positions on the imagination'*. This review allows me only a meagre paraphrase. The first position implies the Imagination as Creator (just as, traditionally, Man is the image of God). The second implies the Imagination as an agent determined by history and immediate societal conditions, and thus scarcely worthy of the name, as we have understood it, in various guises and emphases, from Plato to Wordsworth.

This is the position of the Structuralists about whom and their exegetes Professor Donoghue knows as much as anybody in these islands. Those whom he calls 'devotees of sensibility' (the slightly contemptuous phrase is, I think, aimed at self-indulgent apostles of Truth and Beauty: pinchbeck Keatsians) are unlikely even to have heard of Levi-Strauss or Roland Barthes, and just as unlikely to have read Mallarmé or Valéry or even Wallace Stevens, forever poised between the two 'positions'. If this reads as patronage, let me add that many of the names Professor Donoghue cites in this context I have not heard of myself.

As suggested, these opening essays are stiff going. But from then onwards we can enjoy the play of a well-stocked mind delighting in its own perceptions of startling congruities. Only the invincibly hostile would consider these perceptions indecorous. In a luminous study of Allen Tate, he can analogise details from *The Idiot* of Dostoevsky and *The Great Gatsby*. In 'The American Style of Failure', he brings together, almost punning on 'style', Henry James, Henry Adams, and again, Allen Tate. I must add the rider that, trusting too much to the intelligence of his readers, he does not care to distinguish between Tate's concept of 'symbolic imagination', and 'Symbolist' imagination, a very different thing. Dante, for example, is symbolic in Tate's understanding, but also of course literal.

In another essay we are charmed by clusters which can bring together, say, Pope, the Antonioni of *Blow Up* and Mr Philip Larkin; or, in opposition, the sentimental landscape poet Akenside and Nathaniel Hawthorne. In his study of *The Waste Land*, the shades of Longinus and Burke are bid be gone (though not with maledictions) when he writes 'Martyrdom is Eliot's favourite version of the Sublime.'

But for this reviewer the crown of the book is, fittingly, the last essay, 'Writing against Time': the colloquial style here to be taken literally. From the unlikely text of Shakespeare's *Henry VIII* – which he construes in terms of time which is linear and mundane (*tempus*) and *aevum* which is sempiternity, or, if you like, time redeemed, life as one damned thing after another made radiant and harmonious – he builds up the strongest possible indictment of our times. This is Donoghue at his best; reminding us that we have lost the Kingdom, the Power and the Glory.

But since he is human – never more so than in this essay – he must aver, 'The writers who touch us most deeply today are those who make something out of nothing: James, Kafka, Proust, Beckett, Eliot.' And I do not believe he would abate their power and glory, if only in lower case.

Heady Brew [1]

(Hibernia, 13 January 1978)

Professor Jeffares has been a dedicated Yeatsian since the publication in 1948 of *W. B. Yeats: Man and Poet,* which preceeded by a year Richard Ellmann's *Yeats: The Man and the Masks.* Both of these books were automatic reading for my generation. Dr Jeffares, apart from slighter works, has since published *A Commentary on the Collected Poems of W.B. Yeats* (1968) and, with A.S. Knowlan, *A Commentary on the Collected Plays* (1975). He was an obvious, though hardly the only, choice as presenter of this new volume in the Critical Heritage Series.

I approached it with some misgivings, because, plainly, volumes of this kind often have a stultifying effect when read from cover to cover, especially when the subject is Yeats, about whom one has been reading for thirty years. I must say flatly that this book, taken as a reviewer's gulp, is indigestible. But when one goes back and *sips* at it, as one might with an anthology of verse, there are rich and strange flavours. Here are some of them. Dowden of Trinity on Yeats at twenty: 'Willie Yeats is an interesting boy in the clouds - an interesting boy, whether he turn out much of a poet or not.' Wilde on *The Wanderings of Oisin and Other Poems* (1889): 'He does not rob of their stature the great heroes of Celtic mythology. He is very naive and very primitive, and speaks of his giants with the awe of a child ...' A letter from Robert Louis Stevenson about 'The Lake Isle of Innisfree', written in April 1894, shortly before his death. Lytton Strachey, at twenty-eight, on the first two volumes of the 1908 *Collected Works* : 'It is easy to imagine the kind of criticism which Mr Yeats would have received from eighteenth-century readers. Dr Johnson would have reserved for him his most annihilating commonsense, while Voltaire would have covered him with sparkling ridicule.' The brilliant and tragic Darrell Figgis in his book on Æ (1916): '... he and Æ were hailed as the leaders of a queer thing known as the Irish Literary Revival ... What was called the "Irish Literary Revival" was truly an English Literary Revival conducted by Irishmen.' (Odd that Corkery didn't root out that one).

I lay down the brew and when I take it up again find: Austin Clarke, at thirty-two, writing with full appreciation of *The Tower* (1928), a fugitive piece which must be of value to Clarkites as well as Yeatsians (there are two other uncollected pieces here by Clarke, on *A Full Moon in March* and *The Herne's Egg*); Denis Johnston on

Wheels and Butterflies (1934): 'It is well recognized that Mr Yeats, when he chooses, is one of the ablest politicians in Ireland and has on more than one occasion beaten the professionals to the ropes'; three important reviews of the notorious *Oxford Book of Modern Verse* (1936) which raised winds of chagrin in disparate regions, by the late John Hayward, John Sparrow, and H.A. Mason, the last from *Scrutiny*, suitably caustic about 'the Irish Brigade' (i.e. poets).

As I sip on (the image I fear is disintegrating) it becomes clear that, in fact, Professor Jeffares has done an excellent job in assembling this material from 1884 to the date of Auden's great elegy, which in its original form appeared in March 1939, less than two months after Yeats's death.

I have detected no major slips (specialists may be able to find minor), but Professor Jeffares may care to know that R.P. Blackmur has been dead since 1965.

Crystalline Prose[1]

(Hibernia, 22 May 1980)

This handsome volume gets off to a bad start with the very first sentence of anthropologist-photographer George Gmelch's Preface: 'This book contains fourteen essays written by J.M. Synge around the run (sic) of the century.' In fact it contains, in *In Wicklow*, seven titled essays (published separately from 1905 to 1908), in *West Kerry*, nine prose units without titles (some of which were published separately in 1907), and in *In Connemara* (originally *In the Congested Districts* in Vol. IV of *The Works of John M. Synge*, Maunsel, 1910), twelve titled essays originally commissioned by *The Manchester Guardian* and published, with illustrations by Jack B. Yeats, in 1907. 'Around the turn of the century' is a very loose phrase.

The glory of the book, shared with Synge's text, is in the fifty photographs, scenic and human, by Professor Gmelch. Synge himself, of course, was a camera enthusiast. One of the more memorable books in the spate that flowed in his centenary year, 1971, was *My Wallet of Photographs*, edited by Lilo Stephens. In *In West Kerry* we find him showing photographs of the Aran Islands and Wicklow to his hosts on the Great Blasket. In doing so, he comes across an old photograph of himself in the Luxembourg Gardens and one of the men whispers in Irish to one of the girls, pointing to the statues, 'Look at that ... in those countries they do have naked people standing about in their skins.' When Synge explains that the figures are marble, 'the little hostess' sighs, '*is deas an rud do bheith ag siubhal ins an domhain mór*'. This is an excellent example of the kind of epiphany with which these essays are replete.

Professor Gmelch has an introductory essay, perfunctory enough, '*J.M. Synge: Observer of Peasant Life*', the notes to which are badly jumbled. A second introductory essay, by Professor Ann Saddlemyer, despite its pretentious title, 'The Essays as Literature and Literary Sources', indicates usefully where in the essays we may look for the seminal material of the plays and, indeed, the poems. For instance, 'the happy inspiration' of Martin Doul in the last act of *The Well of the Saints*, 'Ah, a white beard's a grand thing on an old man ...', has its seed in the lamentation of an old man who had his white hair cut off in Kilmainham Jail, 'What use is an old man without his hair? A man has only his bloom like the trees; and what use is an old man without his hair?' That is from 'The Vagrants of Wicklow'.

It may be argued that Synge romanticized vagrants, gave them a factitious status. But then it could be argued that Dostoevsky romanticized murderers and lesser criminals. And no-one, unless with prejudice, will fail to recognize that, even today, much of what Synge wrote over seventy years ago about the Garden of Ireland has imaginative truth. Far better than Lamb and Addison and the other pre-scribed bores of my childhood; had we been given, for instance, the exquisite essay 'The People of the Glens', and learned about 'the three shadowy countries that are never forgotten in Wicklow – America (their El Dorado), the Union and the Madhouse'. The quality of Synge's prose has never, I suggest advisedly, been suffi-ciently appreciated in this country, overshadowed as we are by the shibboleths of an inherited educational system. Consider this from *In West Kerry*:

> The blueness of the sea and the hills from Carrantuohill to the Skelligs, the sin-gular loneliness of the hillside I was on, with a few choughs and gulls in sight only, had a splendour that was almost a grief in the mind.

As a writer of what Professor Saddlemyer calls 'essay journalism', Synge could have survived anywhere. He is superb about North Mayo, in what is inaccurately called *In Connemara*. What more vivid than his evocation of the market in the town-square of Belmullet:

> A little later there was another stir, and I saw a Chinaman wandering about, fol-lowed by a wondering crowd.

Synge's mind was instinct with the capacity for relishing the visible world. That is a clumsy way of saying that he was a seer. Only time and space stop me quoting more of his crystalline prose and citing his splendid humility. This lovely book should be read by everyone from ten upwards.

From the Abbey to Zozimus[1]

(Hibernia, 8 May 1980)

For this huge undertaking Professor Hogan has had three other professors as Advisory Editors, Zack Bowen, William J. Feeney and James Kilroy, and two Associate Editors, Mary Rose Callaghan and Richard Burnham. All six of this team contribute to the *Dictionary*, together with some fifty or so others of varying eminence (and competence). The result is a vastly entertaining and eccentric compilation. And the Editor-in-Chief himself, a noted servant of Irish literature, especially Irish drama, must be credited for much of the entertainment and some of the oddity, since by my count he is the largest contributor of entries, apart from his editorial matter, which consists of a Preface, an Introduction and an essay on 'Irish Writing in English'. He is to be commended for noting in the Preface the difficulty of compiling a *Dictionary of Irish Literature* that does not include writing in Irish, and points out that Seamus O'Neill has contributed 'a lengthy, specially commissioned critical and historical survey of writing in Irish, from the earliest times to the present day'. Gaelic scholars are the people to decide if Professor O'Neill be the best man to have made this survey. From my own limited knowledge, I am puzzled when he writes that Máirtín Ó Cadhain 'had little appreciation of form ...'

Professor Hogan's Introduction deserves a review to itself. He endeavours, with some wit and stylistic brilliance, to establish that 'The qualities that have formed the Irish writer are the qualities that have formed the Irish man.' They include 'Geography and Climate' – they effect 'a depressed elevation, a dull delight briefly shot through with instants of manic joy'; '*The Memory of the Dead*' – Irish politicians have often 'evoked the glorious past either for the admiration of a nobility that has come to be invested in [them] or for the admiration of heroism in the face of a yet un-redressed wrong'; '*The Land*' – is to the Irish man, 'the land was the ultimate glittering prize, to the Irish writer it has often seemed a curse'. Professor Hogan, of course, adumbrates other qualities. But I prefer to extract from his peroration a splendid confession of failure:

> One cannot write fairly or objectively about the country, for one slips unnoticed into the national rhetorical techniques of hyperbole and prevarication ... Nevertheless, one does what one can, and sometimes one does what one can-

not, but the significant point is that language as used by the Irish, even though it conceals more truth than it reveals, does also create. What it creates is literature, and that in abundance, and in literature truths can be found by those who seek them.

From this point on, a shortish review cannot cover the entire contents of the *Dictionary*, or even touch on omissions or desirable exclusions. Most welcome inclusions are a whole clutch of novelists of this century whose works are out of print: Shan F. Bullock, Darrell Figgis, Patrick MacGill, Gerald O'Donovan (for the record Patrick Kavanagh much admired the latter's *Father Ralph*), Eimer O'Duffy, Conal O'Riordan. But perhaps the non-specialist will be more interested in how fare some of the unquestionably eminent of this century. Richard M. Kain does Yeats proud. I am less happy about Zack Bowen's Joyce. What on earth does he mean by saying that Gogarty's 'urbanity and wit grace the character of Buck Mulligan in *Ulysses*'? Is he being ironic? And it is surely misleading to state that in 1929 the contributors to the symposium on *Work in Progress*, which I will call, for short, *Our Exagmination* ... were 'twelve outstanding men of letters of their day'. One of those men was, of course, Beckett. The Editor-in-Chief is excellent, suitably restrained, on the Master. But then Robert Hogan is excellent on all kinds of people, from the eighteenth-century Ennis child prodigy Thomas Dermody to Canon Sheehan. And even when damning without even the faintest of praise, he contrives to arouse interest. Thus, he begins his entry on John Keegan Casey, the young Fenian versifier: 'It is indeed easy to say that John Keegan Casey ... was a perfectly dreadful poet. Nevertheless, anyone capable of such a stirring ballad as "The Rising of The Moon" is worth some scrutiny.'

But now the time has come to take up the Editor-in-Chief's invitation to readers to bring to his attention any errors of fact they have noticed. I am not concerned with common misprints, nor do I claim that the following list is anything but a casual one.

It was John Broderick's second novel, *The Chameleons*, not his first, *The Pilgrimage*, which was re-issued as *The Fugitives*. Thomas Kinsella, in his sober piece on Austin Clarke, asserts that the first Mrs Clarke was Geraldine Cummins (the biographer of Edith Somerville). In fact it was Lia Cummins, a journalist and minimal poet. In an otherwise informed entry on Denis Devlin, Nora F. Lindstrom cites Gide, Villon and Éluard as the French poets Devlin most highly respected. But if Gide published verse it can only have been in his extreme youth, and I think I would have heard of it. Ms Lindstrom also appears to believe that pilgrims to Lough Derg go there to visit 'an Irish Abbey famous for centuries as a place of religious pilgrimage'. Indeed, she may even believe that Devlin's *Lough Derg* is a 'story' and not the record of an actual experience. Christine Longford went to Somerville College, Oxford, not Somerset College, which does not exist. That sad poet, Patrick MacDonogh, neglected in life and in death, has his name misspelt consistently 'MacDonagh' in the entry by the Editor-in-Chief, who, also, in the entry for Martin J. McHugh gives *A Minute's Walk*, instead of *A Minute's Wait*, as the name of his best-known play. The Resident Commissioner for Education who introduced Joseph O'Neill, another fine neglected novelist, into the Department of Education was William Starkie, not 'Starkey', and he was not O'Neill's 'former teacher' at the Queen's College, Galway, since when O'Neill was a student there, he was President. The same contributor, M. Kelly Lynch from Boston, believes that *Bluebeard,* a verse-play by O'Neill's wife, Mary Devenport O'Neill, was performed by Austin Clarke's Lyric Theatre Company in 1933, a manifest absurdity since that company was not founded until 1944. Anne Clissmann, who has written a book on Brian O'Nolan (Flann O'Brien/ Myles na Gopaleen), lists *The Insect Play* among his plays. But that is the name of a play by the Brothers Capek, which was adapted by Myles na Gopaleen under the title *Rhapsody in Stephen's Green* and done by Edwards-Mac Liammóir at the Gaiety in 1943.

All these errors, and others of greater or less importance, will no doubt be corrected in future editions (which it deserves) of this enormous undertaking. Also, some of the bibliographies might be reshaped. It is absurd, for instance, that Victoria Glendinning's *Life* (1977) should be omitted from the Elizabeth Bowen references.

Categorization[1]

(The Irish Press, 18 June 1981)

Categorization is one of the banes of otherwise estimable academic criticism: part of the mania for establishing one or more theses. So much of the present volume is, to my mind, admirable, that its title and editorial Introduction seem almost impertinent, pedagogical impositions on disparate materials. I prefer to describe the materials rather than question the validity of the 'genre' notion. It is fair though to note that Dr Schleifer is editor of the scholarly journal, *Genre*, associated with the University of Oklahoma. Apart from his Introduction, he contributes to this volume in abstruse, though not unilluminating, study of the autobiographical mode as practised by George Moore in *Hail and Farewell*. He is especially good on the significance of Moore's digressions. Yeats, by the way, was thirteen, not twelve, years younger than Moore, a pardonable slip. Less pardonable is to have Moore and Æ setting off, in *Salve,* for Newgate instead of Newgrange. (I concede that the error has comedic potential of the dusky kind.)

Edward Hirsch writes on Yeats as folklorist but clearly his essay was written before the publication of Mary Helen Thuende's *W. B. Yeats and Irish Folklore* (1980). Anthony Roche treats of the Other World theme as illustrated and enriched in Synge's *The Well of the Saints*, holding fast to the notion of that powerful morality's 'source' being the tale Synge heard in Aran of 'a woman of Sligo [who] had a son who was born blind'.

I am both impressed and irritated by Declan Kiberd's brilliant, but often wrong-headed, account of 'The Fall of the Stage Irishman'. He is exact, I think, when he writes about the Playboy riots: 'The protestors were convinced that they had witnessed a revival of the Stage Irishman ... but in reality the only Stage-Irish scenes had been enacted away from the stage amidst the uproar of the pit.' But in a lengthy footnote to his contention that Synge 'exploded forever the stage-myth of the fighting Irish', he finds it necessary to make a gratuitous sneer at the National Army who '*polish their superb hardware and mount displays of gymnastics*'. Closer to our own time he writes extremely well about Flann O'Brien and *An Beal Bocht*, but misleads the reader when he implies that what he calls O'Brien's 'greatest novel' was written after the change from 'Myles na gCopaleen' to 'Myles na Gopaleen.' That change came many years after 1941, when *An Beal Bocht* was first published, so there is no question of 'a return to his deepest self'. And I regret that so intelligent a man as Declan Kiberd should play to *les bien pensants*, by referring to Kavanagh, O'Brien and Behan as 'that doomed and drinksodden triumvirate'. He has also some extraordinary notions about Dublin's 'literary pubs.' But then so have many tourists.

Another Irishman, Terence Brown, writes less brilliantly, but more temperately, about the 'inadequacies' facing Irish writers 'After the Revival'. Dr Sean O'Faolain may be surprised (as I was) to find Dr Brown drawing parallels between his literary progress and that of Kavanagh. But it is refreshing to find Kavanagh being discussed, not as a magnificent eccentricity nor as a 'doomed and drink-sodden' musketeer, but as a serious and industrious writer.

There are two Joyce essays, both of high quality. Professor Jackson L. Cope writes of *Joyce and the City* (his *Waste Land*) in many contexts, including James Thomson's *The City of Dreadful Night*, George Gissing, Eliot and, above all of course, Dante. For myself, his most fruitful insights are into the function of the prophet, Elijah, both in *Dubliners* and *Ulysses*. His notation of the Dantesque echo in the opening sentence of the first story in *Dubliners*, 'The Sisters' – 'There was no hope for him this time' – prepares us for Professor Thomas F. Staley's masterly exegesis of the beginning paragraph of that most cryptic of Joyce's stories. Surprisingly this least showy of exegetes does not refer to a possible resonance in Father Flynn's 'third stroke' of Christ's third fall on the way to Calvary (there may be also a Petrine echo).

Professor Bernard Benstock analyses with great gusto the great eight-tiered opening sentence of the first volume of O'Casey's autobiography, *I Knock at the Door* (1939). So great has been his gusto, perhaps, that he consistently gives a wrong date for the publication of the final volume, *Sunset and Evening Star*: it is 1954, not 1955.

This spirited volume ends with a bang from Professor Hugh Kenner, who tells how Wake Forest University Press rejected a solicited Introduction to Thomas Kinsella's *Poems 1956–1973* and on what grounds. (He was, however, paid.) I am a little uncertain as to the ethics of Professor Kenner's 'anecdote' being printed, so close to the event. But his 'reflections' on Kinsella, and on post-Revival Irish poets in general, are certainly pregnant. And some people may be delighted by the notion of Kenner being put down for the sake of Kinsella. One would like to hear the latter's account of the affair.

The Startled Hare: Goldsmith as Literary Journalist and Compiler

(Goldsmith the Gentle Master, Ed. Sean Lucy)*

Given the traditional images of Goldsmith, derived chiefly from Scott and Thackeray, as a writer of delicate sentiment, gentle disposition and chaste humour, there is a minor irony in the circumstances of his apprenticeship, a very late one, as a literary journalist. Within a year of his arrival in London from Paris in August 1756, Goldsmith was teaching in an Academy for Boys in Peckham, run by a dissenting Minister, Rev. Thomas Milner. It was at this good man's table that Goldsmith met Ralph Griffiths, proprietor and editor-in-chief of *The Monthly Review*, founded in 1749. Now this journal could not have been launched at all were it not for the fortune that Griffiths made from the publication of a book called *The Memoirs of a Woman of Pleasure* by one John Cleland, better known nowadays under the title *Fanny Hill*.

It was this Ralph Griffiths who gave Goldsmith his *entrée* into letters, not as a mere hack but as a salaried member of *The Monthly Review*'s editorial staff. As we shall see, this auspicious relationship soon foundered. But at the age of twenty-eight Goldsmith *did* begin his literary career on a salary. From April 1757 Goldsmith worked regularly on the *Review* for about six months, when he surrendered his job. Why he did so is not clear. What matters is that he had served his time as a reviewer, and also, with dubious desirability, as an *extractor* from the works of acknowledged experts. This ability to make *précis* of specialist materials was to serve him well in his later years as a compiler. But that, as we shall see, was a mixed blessing.

After he had stopped work on *The Monthly Review* Goldsmith continued to accept commissions from Griffiths, and his unthinking acceptance of them was to cause him much annoyance, and eventually humiliation. By January 1759 Goldsmith was writing for Griffiths' rival, Tobias Smollett, the Scottish physician, and very considerable novelist, who edited *The Critical Review*. This infuriated Griffiths, already nettled by Goldsmith's transactions with the very superior publisher Robert Dodsley, who had brought out Young's *Night Thoughts,* Akenside's *Pleasures of Imagination,* Johnson's poem *London*, Thomas Gray's *Odes*, and other key works. It was to Dodsley that Goldsmith offered his first book, his *Enquiry into the Present State of Polite Learning*, which appeared in 1759.

Griffiths, by way of retaliation, threatened to sue Goldsmith on two grounds: non-payment of a tailor's bill which he, Griffiths, had endorsed, and non-return of four review-copies which he claimed were his and not Goldsmith's property. The affair blew over after Goldsmith had written a long, imploratory letter; not without dignity, but ample testimony of how in the 1760s, and for long after, a vindictive publisher could harass an improvident or unbusiness-like author. And, as we know, Goldsmith was all his life incurably feckless. It is not my business here to prove the psychology of this fecklessness, beyond suggesting that it was just another symptom of emotional immaturity. I would observe in passing that this immaturity may, in certain ways, have contributed to Goldsmith's special charm as an artist.

His correspondence from 1758 indicates that he was then already contemplating a series of letter-essays on the models of *Les Lettres Persanes* of Montesquieu (1721) and *Les Lettres Chinoises* of the Marquis d'Argens (1739). He was also, of course, steeped in the essays and journals of Marivaux. Marivaux had issued a series of *Feuilles* under the heading of *Le Spectateur Francais* (1720–24). On these Goldsmith was to draw heavily when he came to write his *Chinese Letters*. But before that, during the months October-November 1759, he produced eight numbers of a weekly called *The Bee: being Essays on the most interesting subjects*. These essays also depend on fruitful borrowing from Marivaux and others. Since, in general, they are unknown relative to the *Chinese Letters*, here from them is a sampling of Goldsmith's manner, which I would call nor English nor French, but rather Latin in the middle style, Horatian, in fact. In the fourth number he contemplates the success of rival journals, so much greater than that of his own:

> Their fame is diffused in a very wide circle, that of some as far as Islington, and some yet further still; while mine, I sincerely believe, has hardly travelled beyond the sound of Bow-bell; and while the works of others fly like unpinioned swans, I find my own move as heavily as a new-plucked goose.[1]

Of course, we must sense the gossamer mockery he is offering his rivals. They pride themselves on a circulation which, set against history and the world outside the coffeeshops, is as nugatory as Goldsmith's own.

No. 5 of *The Bee* contains an unfinished 'Reverie' in which the narrator meditates upon the perversity of critics who reserve their laurels for the mighty dead, who do not need them, and damn the living. Then, 'to eke out the page', as he jokes us, he presents us with his vision of several contemporaries aspiring to Immortality (in the literary sense). Space does not allow me to describe all these personages who wish to ascend to the courts of heaven by means of a vehicle called *the fame-machine*. (And, quite frivolously, I wonder if this vehicle were not in the sub-consciousness of H.G. Wells and E.M. Forster when they wrote their *The Time Machine* and *The Celestial Omnibus* respectively.) But we must take cognizance of one of the aspirants to *the fame-machine*. 'This was a very grave personage, who at some distance I took for one of the most reserved, and even disagreeable figures I had seen; but as he approached, his appearance improved, and when I could distinguish him thoroughly, I perceived that, in spite of the severity of his brow, he had one of the most good-natured countenances that could be imaged.'[2] This, of course, is Dr Johnson, whom Goldsmith had not yet met! Significantly, the author of *The Bee* represents Johnson as gaining access to *the fame-machine* not by virtue of his *magnum opus*, his *Dictionary*, but of what Johnson calls 'a mere trifle', in fact *The Rambler*, Johnson's collected bi-weekly essays from the years 1750–52. Goldsmith might sigh that *The Bee* had small sales, but he must have known that his genial references to Johnson and his essays would not go astray.

Towards the end of 1759 Goldsmith met John Newbery, a co-proprietor of *The Universal Chronicle*, to which Johnson was contributing his series under the name 'The Idler'. Newbery was launching a new daily, *The Public Ledger*. It was for this that Goldsmith proposed his series of *Chinese Letters*, which were published from January 1760 to August 1761. These 'letters' when collected were published in two volumes in 1762, as *The Citizen of the World*, Goldsmith's masterpiece in the field of occasional prose, as fine in kind as *The Vicar of Wakefield* and *She Stoops to Conquer*.

There was a time in this country when every child on secondary level was perforce familiar with one or more essays from *The Citizen*. Arguably, on a long-term basis, this fragmentary knowledge was better than total ignorance. But *The Citizen*, despite the circumstances of its composition – two essays a week over some twenty months – has claims to be considered as an artistic whole; a singular blend of convention and innovation illumined by fugitive gleams of personality, the elements of fantasy and whimsy grounded in first-hand experience of lower middle-class life in eighteenth-century London.

When I use the term 'convention' in this context, I have in mind chiefly the element of *chinoiserie*. Goldsmith was aware enough of fashion to cash in on the taste for the exotic in general and the Chinese in particular, which in earlier decades had taken root in France and almost simultaneously in England. But the *motif* of the expatriate, which is embodied on two different levels in the Chinese traveller Lien Chi Altangi and his friend the Man in Black, may be found earlier in *The Bee*. There an English traveller finds himself in Cracow, and writes to a friend:

> It is now seven years since I saw the face of a single creature who cared a farthing whether I was dead or alive. Secluded from all the comforts of confidence, friendship or society, I feel the solitude of a hermit, but not his ease.[3]

In 1759 it had, in fact, been seven years since Goldsmith left Ireland for Edinburgh. It does not do to forget that a collection like *The Citizen*, with its two displaced persons, Lien Chi and the Man in Black, is the work of a man himself, for better or worse, displaced. One might go further and say, a man who is *déclassé*, a younger son of minor Anglo-Irish gentry, passing between the salons and the pot-houses and the green rooms of an essentially alien city.

When, in effect, John Newbery pulled him out of hackery with the commission for the *Chinese Letters*, Goldsmith was lodging in a near-slum close to the Fleet Prison, called Green Arbour Court, a poignant and ridiculous name figuring the encroachment of city on country. His exact contemporary, Rev. Thomas Percy (of Percy's *Reliques*), once called on him there, and while they were talking, he records, 'a poor ragged little girl of very decent behaviour, entered, who, dropping a curtsie, said "My Mama sends her compliments, and begs the favour of you to lend her a chamber pot of coals"'.[4]

Here, surely, is a classic exemplum of genteel poverty, and there are others to be found in *The Citizen*. But as Goldsmith accompanies Lien Chi and the Man in Black on their walks and outings, we encounter instances of more frightening poverty. In Letter XXVI, during a country excursion, the friends come upon a spectacle which Goldsmith might as well have remembered from the midlands of Ireland or the streets of Dublin, as seen on the outskirts of London:

> A woman in rags, with one child in her arms, and another on her back, was attempting to sing ballads, but with such a mournful voice, that it was difficult to determine whether she was singing or crying.[5]

But it is in the depiction of a less naked poverty that Goldsmith excels, the kind of poverty from which Goldsmith himself was never quite immune. Hence, I think, his ability to treat with kindliness the absurdities of the pseudo man-about-town Ned Tibbs, in the bravery of whose pretensions there is something almost heroic. Tibbs, in Letter LIV, accosts the Man in Black (whose name, by the way, is revealed in full as 'William Drybone', perhaps an ironic syllabic equation to 'Oliver Goldsmith'), and Lien Chi describes the newcomer:

> His hat was pinched up with peculiar smartness; his looks were pale, thin and sharp; round his neck he wore a broad black ribbon, and in his bosom a buckle studded with glass; his hat was trimmed with tarnished twist; he wore by his side a sword with a black hilt, and his stockings of silk, though newly washed, were grown yellow by long service.[6]

These yellowed stockings I find almost as touching as the chamber pot of coals. We may smile at Tibbs here and elsewhere, but I do not think we can despise him. The distance between this gentle fun-poking and, say, Swift, is the distance between Horace and Juvenal. But there is, perhaps, a Swiftian note in Letter XC in which the Man in Black is discovered by Lien Chi playing the flute, and explains why. He has been first outraged and then plunged into melancholy by a book about 'thief-takers', or, as we might say, felon-setters.

This was an instance of such complicated guilt and hypocrisy, that I threw down the book in an agony of rage, and began to think with malice of all the human kind. I sat silent for some minutes, and soon perceiving the ticking of my watch beginning to grow noisy and troublesome, I quickly placed it out of hearing and strove to resume my serenity.

After having been further upset by the night watchman, and driven to listening for death-watches in the wainscot, he passes an irremediably miserable night.

Morning came, I sought for tranquillity in dissipation, sauntered from one place of public resort to another, but found myself disagreeable to my acquaintances and ridiculous to others. I tried at different times dancing, fencing, and riding, I solved geometrical problems, shaped tobacco-stoppers, wrote verses, and cut paper. At last I placed my affections on music, and find, that earnest employment if it cannot cure, at least will palliate every anxiety.[7]

The 'earnest employment' is playing the flute; surely a Swiftian image of man, tootling on the flute in the face of the cosmic Evil, but also, of course, of Goldsmith himself showing the back of his hand to bailiffs and editors champing at the bit for copy.

In that same year of 1762 when *The Citizen of the World* appeared, Goldsmith translated four-and-a-half (out of seven) volumes of Plutarch for Newbery, and wrote also a life of Richard Nash, the *arbiter elegantarum* of Bath. At the very beginning of the year, in *Lloyd's Evening Post*, he had published a series of five essays, under the title 'The Indigent Philosopher' borrowed from his beloved Marivaux. In the first of them, quite nakedly, he reveals the plight of the writer dependent on occasional work, or, as we might put it, the plight of the free-lance literary journalist:

For all this, as I said in the beginning, I expect to be paid; and this I dare aver, that the reader will remember my advice longer than I shall keep his money; for coin of all sizes has a surprising facility of slipping from me. Let the reader then only permit me to eat, and I will endeavour to increase his pleasures; his eatables and my philosophy will make a tolerable harmony together. A rich Fool, and an *Indigent Philosopher* are made for each other's support; they fit like ball and socket; but this I insist on, if the Public continue to keep me much longer in *indigence*, they shall see but very little more of my *philosophy*.[9]

Allowing for rhetoric, we may suppose then that it was 'indigence' which led Goldsmith into an agreement with Newbery to produce *A Survey of Experimental Philosophy*, a work which dogged him all his life and which was never completed. This was the first major step in his career as a popular science writer and also popular historian. It should be recalled that Goldsmith, at thirty-four, was not known as poet or novelist or dramatist. In the last decade of his life lay his two great poems, *The Traveller* (1764) and *The Deserted Village* (1770), his novel *The Vicar of Wakefield* (1766), and his two plays *The Good-Natured Man* (1768) and *She Stoops to Conquer* 1773). But these works were executed and published while intermittently he laboured at what may only be described as stylish hack work. I say 'stylish' because Oliver being the Goldsmith that he was, his fluvial narrative style never abandoned him. But let us examine some aspects of his work as an extractor or compiler. Between 1764 and 1774 he published four separate works on *English History*, the four in all making eight volumes. In addition to this mass of material there was the *Roman History* published in two volumes in 1769, followed in 1772 by *Dr Goldsmith's Roman History abridged by himself for the use of schools.* Posthumously published works included *The Grecian History*, and the eight volumes of *An History of the Earth and Animated Nature* which preoccupied Goldsmith for the last five years of his life. 'He is now writing a Natural History', announced Dr Johnson, 'and will make it as entertaining as a Persian tale.' But Boswell records Johnson in a different mood when the cultivated brewer Henry Thrale tried to humiliate Goldsmith by offering him the use of his stable in which to give a practical demonstration of a theory about horses and their reactions to the sight of blood:

> Nay, Sir, I would not have him prove it. If he is content to take his information from others, he may get through his book with little trouble, and without much endangering his reputation. But if he makes experiments for so comprehensive a book as his, there would be no end to them; his erroneous assertions would then fall upon himself and he might be blamed for not having made experiments as to every particular.[10]

For this vast compendium, Goldsmith had received, in 1769, an advance of four hundred guineas from the bookseller Thomas Davies; worth about ten times that in terms of today's purchasing power. For *The History of England from the Earliest Times to the Death of George II*, published in four volumes in 1771, he received the equivalent of about two thousand guineas. Given that Goldsmith's scientific and historical work involved no original research, but rather a capacity for ordering the facts of others in a lucid and graceful style, these were not contemptible sums. But they are representative only of what he could command after the *succés d'estime* of his poem *The Traveller,* at the end of 1764. Only six months before the publication of *The Traveller,* he received a mere twenty guineas (two hundred guineas in our currency) for *The History of England in a Series of Letters from a Nobleman to his Son.* He was already heavily in debt when his fortunes might seem to have changed. We should also take into account that, whereas he undertook his first book, *An Enquiry into the Present State of Polite Learning in Europe*, and all his creative work, without benefit or subsidy, his compilations were begun, usually, after he had received a substantial advance.

And the dream of financial security based on the achievement of grandiose schemes pursued him to the grave. Strange that this artist, whose finest work is in the mode of miniature, should think, almost from the beginning of his writing career in 1756, in terms of encyclopaedic projects, grand designs, the Bee aspiring to be the Bear, although he lacked even Johnson's minimal skill in the courtship of patronage.

In the winter of 1773–4, while still wrestling with *An History of the Earth and Animated Nature* (Davies, the original underwriter of the project had had to sell his interest in it to another publisher, John Nourse), Goldsmith dreamed up another grandiose scheme: no less than a *Universal Dictionary of the Arts and Sciences*, with Sir Joshua Reynolds, Dr Johnson, Edmund Burke, David Garrick, Charles Burney, and others, contributing under his own general editorship. Had it come to anything, this project might have lifted Goldsmith as compiler quite out of the category of hack, even superior hack. He would be co-ordinating the work of those whom he knew familiarly; not, as in the case of the *History of the Earth*, attempting to condense Buffon or over-construe Lucretius.

But it was too late. The booksellers were alarmed by the immensity of the project certainly, but also that it should be undertaken by 'a man with whose indolence of temper and method of procrastination they had long been acquainted'.[11] This is the language of Thomas Davies, who himself had suffered financially over *An History of the Earth*.

It may be asked how far conditions of authorship in his time contributed towards Goldsmith's costiveness as what nowadays we call 'a creative writer'. But we should recall that this term would not have been immediately comprehensible to, say, Johnson, who would not have understood an estimate of him based solely on his two great poems *London,* and *The Vanity of Human Wishes,* and his fable *Rasselas.* He would have commanded as much, perhaps more, attention by his *Dictionary* and his Edition of Shakespeare. There is no reason to believe that Goldsmith regarded his 'non-creative' work as so much pot-boiling, and there is no reason to believe that he regarded any of his works, original or contracted, as other than the legitimate fruits of his calling. A writer without inhibitions as to his own capacities and stamina, he took all sorts of knowledge as grist to his mill. When we consider Oliver Goldsmith in relation to his literary journalism and compilations, speculation as to what he would have achieved without the grind and the sweat is vanity. He himself would not have appreciated the notion; but perhaps the flowers of his art needed the often frenetic breaking of stony ground. The facts of his life, what we know of his heart and mind, which is little enough, suggest that, had he not been a hack, he would not have been the artist he became.

* *Goldsmith the Gentle Master,* Ed. Sean Lucy (Cork University Press 1984), pp. 26–37. (RTÉ/The Thomas Davis Lectures, in honour of the 250th anniversary of the birth of Oliver Goldsmith)

Ghost Writers[1]

(Hibernia, 17 January 1980)

At the moment of writing, I believe Henry James's *The Turn of the Screw* to be the world's greatest 'ghost' story, and James's forebears came from Cavan. Mr Tremayne (a pseudonym) might have tied in this fact with his thesis that the Irish and those of Irish extraction have a special affinity to the 'ghost' story and horror-fantasy. He censures, mildly, the great American super-naturalist, H.P. Lovecraft (a special favourite of Borges), for not pointing out that Charles Robert Maturin (1780–1824), Joseph Sheridan Le Fanu (1814–73), Fitz-James O'Brien (1828–62), Bram Stoker (1847–1912), M.P. Shiel (1865–1947) and Lord Dunsany (1878–1957), the writers represented in this book, had a common Irish nationality.

Since Claude Fierobe's massive study on *Maturin: L'Homme et L'Oeuvre* (Paris 1974), I can never pass St Peter's Church in Aungier's Street,[2] Dublin, without recalling that there, during the Lent of 1824, Maturin preached his *Five Sermons on the Errors of the Roman Catholic Church,* which I have long been meaning to read, if only (I might of course be edified) to detect any of the savage hatred for Papistry (and especially monasticism) which runs through his fictional masterpiece, *Melmoth the Wanderer* (1820), which Baudelaire hailed as *'la grande creation satanique du reverend Maturin'*. Mr Tremayne has extracted the fearsome Chapter Three of *Melmoth* to illustrate Maturin's lurid, labyrinthine imagination which, though it fed on many sources (including Goethe's *Faust, via* – according to M. Fierobe – Madame de Stael's *De l'Allemagne*), was ceaselessly inventive.

It is neither 'ironic' nor surprising, by the way, that Wilde chose 'Sebastian Melmoth' as his post-prison pseudonym. Maturin was his mother's uncle-in-law; his friends Robert Ross and More Adey wrote an anonymous preface to a new edition of the book in 1892, and he may have borrowed the portrait of John Melmoth for the controlling idea of *The Picture of Dorian Gray*. And in this very extract appears a classic Oscarism: 'Hypocrisy is said to be the homage that vice pays to virtue.' But possibly both nephew and grand-uncle hit independently on La Rochefoucauld's *'L'hypocrisie est un hommage que le vice rend a la vertue.'*

As with so much else, I owe my introduction to Le Fanu to the Longfords, Edward and Christine. I was fifteen when I saw Christine's adaptation of 'The Familiar', the story included here by Mr Tremayne, under the title *The Watcher*. She also dramatized Le Fanu's novel *Uncle Silas* in 1948. Edward had dramatized the vampire story 'Carmilla' in 1932. It was this story – collected in *In a Glass Darkly* in 1872 – that inspired Bram Stoker's *Dracula* (1897). Mr Tremayne includes Stoker's story 'The Burial of the Rats' (1895) which, while horrifying, does not strike me as being 'fantasy', unless we choose to pursue its Freudian inferences.

I confess that both Fitz-James O'Brien and M.P. Shiel are new to me. Curiously, while Mr Tremayne is at pains to emphasize the latter's anti-Semitism and general fascistic outlook, he says nothing of O'Brien's racism. On the first page of his remarkable *The Wondersmith* (1858), this Irishman in New York describes a run-down street in terms of 'the Hebraic taint of filth which it inherits from the ancestral thoroughfare' and it is 'slusky and greasy, as if it were twin brother of the Roman Ghetto'. Nonetheless, he likes it, 'though I have not a drop of Neopolitan blood in my veins'. A classic instance of Paddy in the States sneering at 'yids' and 'wops'. But he died from wounds received while fighting in the Union Army's Irish Brigade. *The Wondersmith*, while remarkable, owes much, I suspect, to E.T.A. Hoffmann, who discovered the fearfulness of dolls and automata. No doubt Mr Tremayne could have chosen a better instance of Shiel's work (as he could have of Stoker's), but an anthology must reflect personal taste. Certainly, for a neophyte, 'Xelucha', with its off-Pateresque prose and its curious learning, is intriguing. I like, too, the Jacobean relish for the profane lyricism of physical decay.

The two Dunsany pieces are completely devoid of the macabre: the first about a parable of the evils of progress, and the second a whimsy about ghostly cricketers.

The book, with its 'portraits' (but why confine Robert Ballagh's portrait of Le Fanu to the jacket?), its *intelligent* black-and-white drawings by Jeanette Dunne, and its general layout, is well-produced, except for the appalling number of misprints (or mis-spellings by a careless transcriber). Mr Tremayne was flirting with Nemesis when he rapped Brian Aldiss on his knuckles for writing 'Sheil' for 'Shiel'. He himself gives 'Rosetti' for 'Rossetti', and 'Van Vechtan' for 'Van Vechten' consistently, postdates Swift's death by two years, and graduates Stoker from Trinity at twenty-nine, instead of twenty-three . But he has done much service to his chosen writers and to the public for drawing its attention to them. He also provides some valuable follow-up material but, strangely, does not mention Charles Osborne's *The Bram Stoker Bedside Companion* (Gollancz, London 1973), which includes 'Dracula's Guest', an episode not published in the original fang-piece.

IV

POETRY IRELAND AND LITERARY
ERUDITION

Poetry Ireland Review Editorial 1

(The Poetry Ireland Review No. 1, Spring 1981)[1]

It is almost nineteen years since Liam Miller of The Dolmen Press and the poet James Liddy came to me and asked me if I would edit a magazine called *Poetry Ireland*, a title first coined by David Marcus in April 1948, then co-editor with Terence Smith of *Irish Writing*. David produced nineteen numbers of his *Poetry Ireland*, and then seven reduced numbers as supplements to *Irish Writing*, making twenty-six numbers in all. His successor as editor of *Irish Writing*, Sean J. White, produced two *Poetry Ireland* supplements, the last being in 1956.

So then in September 1962, with the assistance of James Liddy, James J. McAuley and Richard Weber, I produced the first issue of a new *Poetry Ireland*: of the contributors Austin Clarke, Patrick Kavanagh, Donagh MacDonagh and Leslie Daiken are dead. But I find to my gratification that from that first issue and the five that followed (the last being a double issue edited by John Montague from material assembled by me) the following appear in this first issue of *The Poetry Ireland Review*, without conscious planning by me: Seamus Heaney, Macdara Woods, Leland Bardwell, James Liddy, Paul Durcan, Lorna Reynolds, Monk Gibbon, Kevin Faller, John Montague, Michael Hartnett (but now in his departure from English, Mícheál Ó hAirtnéide) and speaking to us from beyond the grave, as it were, the late Austin Clarke – eleven in all. Of the remaining thirteen contributors,[2] some I had never even heard of when that last issue of *Poetry Ireland* appeared with the date Spring 1968 (in effect, it should have appeared in Autumn 1966 at the latest, but that was mainly my fault since just before then I left the country).[3]

Whatever, the presence of that eleven from what seems so very long ago gives to *The Poetry Ireland Review* (the brain-child of John F. Deane, who came to me as had Liam Miller and James Liddy in 1962) a kind of tenuous continuity with *Poetry Ireland*: that and Ruth Brandt's fabulous bird.

Poetry Ireland under my editorship did not publish verse in Irish, nor did it publish reviews; *The Poetry Ireland Review*, in the term of my editorship, willconsider verse in Irish and will publish reviews, although there are none in this issue. It will also welcome translations from any language. As for myself, my taste in verse is catholic and although the years cannot but have rubbed off on me certain predispositions, I think I know where I'm going.

Poetry Ireland Review Editorial 2

(The Poetry Ireland Review No. 2, Summer 1981)

The first issue of *PIR* has been, so I am told, a success, in so far as a magazine devoted to verse can ever be a success in this land. At a *Poetry Ireland* session held at St Enda's, Rathfarnham, on 12 June, at which Eavan Boland and Frank Ormsby were the readers, I was called upon to 'introduce' the *Review*: I affirmed my belief that editors, ideally, should neither be seen nor heard, since they were open to intimidation, contamination, and commination – or words to that effect. (The reading was graced by the presence of Nora Clarke, her husband's helpmate for forty-four years: *Pleasant, my Nora, on a May morning to drive* ... The only poets in the audience I identified were Richard Murphy and Gabriel Rosenstock.) Very serious-ly, literary editors, unless they are ruthless and *farouche*, are sitting ducks in a city where, for better or for worse, so many people aspire to write. That is one prob-lem. Another is that in Dublin, at least (but probably elsewhere as well) there is a bizarre notion that the publication of even the slimmest of volumes confers on the poet in question a regal status. The editor is thus on one side chivied by aspirants who avail of Dublin's notorious easiness of manner (which some might call bad manners) and, on the other, oppressed by awareness of all those waiting to be asked. For myself, I have to decide whom to ask and when: an editor of a 'little' magazine, even one as long in the tooth as myself, has eventually to eat humble pie. But, as indicated, there is a limit to solicitation.[4]

It will be noted that this issue does not contain biographical notes. I made the decision not to have them on the grounds that they consume valuable space. If any reader wants information about any poet he/she can either find it in a reference boo or write to me, including of course an S.A.E. And I might add that I could count on one hand the number of S.A.E.s I have received since I took on the job ... I suspect that some poor souls subconsciously do not wish to see again vers-es they fear may be rejected. And very few are willing to accept even the mildest criticism.

It is not, in my opinion, the business of an editor to proclaim the quality of his wares: although at St Enda's I felt justified in drawing attention to the importance in *PIR* 1 of Austin Clarke's *The Frenzy of Sweeny*, the play being in effect a paradigm of the poet's own life, and Seamus Heaney's 'The Names of the Hare', since it represents for him a wholly new direction. In this issue I find especially interesting Anthony Cronin's new direction,[5] and I am titillated by Frank Corcoran's German version of Gabriel Rosenstock's Gaelic *boutade*.[3] I hope others will join in the language game.

Poetry Ireland Review Editorial 3

(The Poetry Ireland Review No. 3, Winter 1981)

This issue of the *Review*, intended as a small tribute to the memory of Pádraic Colum, who was born in Longford on December 8, 1881, and died in Connecticut on January 11, 1972, may have an ancillary cultural reference. 1981 saw the publication of *An Biobla Naofa* and for a little while, but one hopes much more, attention was drawn to the great Protestant divine Bishop Bedell, whose old Testament in Irish was to appear in 1685, almost half-a-century after his death. Colum's *Kilmore*, the fifth of his Noh plays, which is printed for the first time in this issue, is as much a homage to Bedell as it is to Franciscan scribes, the Presbyterian insurgents of Ninety-Eight and the pioneer collector of traditional Irish airs, Edward Bunting. *Kilmore* has never been produced on stage, so far as I know, but was broadcast by RTÉ Radio in 1968 and repeated in 1971. It may, possibly, be Colum's last completed play. From a chat I had with him in the spring of 1966, sitting in St Stephen's Green, I know that he was then at work on it and attached much importance to its ecumenical significance, and the necessity for recognition by all communities of Bishop Bedell's work.

This was during or shortly after the Lantern Theatre's production of *The Challengers*, being three of his Noh plays, *Glendalough*, *Monasterboice* and *Cloughoughter*, linked by three matching preludes. The Pike Theatre had produced the first of the Noh plays, *Moytura*, during the Theatre Festival of 1963.

Even at that stage Pádraic Colum had been writing intermittently for the stage for some sixty years. He is best known of course for his three so-called 'Abbey' plays: *Broken Soil,* produced at the Molesworth Hall in 1903, after his anti-recruiting play, a one-acter, *The Saxon Shillin'*, had been rejected: As *The Fiddler's House*, produced first by the Theatre of Ireland in 1907 and not until 1919 at the Abbey), *The Land* (at the Abbey in 1905) and *Thomas Muskerry* (at the Abbey in 1910). But the early 'Abbey' plays and the late Noh plays are not the full extent of Colum's work for the theatre. From my own notes I glean the following: in 1912 he published a play on a Persian theme, *The Desert,* and in 1917 a new version as *Mogu the Wanderer*. This was produced at the Gate Theatre in 1931 as *Mogu of the Desert* (almost certainly this was a further revision). We know, too, that in 1910 he wrote a one-acter, *The Destruction of the Hostel*, for the boys of Pearse's St Enda's (published in *A Boy in Eirinn*, 1913); that in 1912 *Sinn Fein* published his Irish folk version of *The Second Shepherd's Play* from the Wakefield Cycle; that *the Irish Review* of 1912 published under the name of 'Walter Mennloch' and extract from a play called *The Empress*. But I can find no record in print of *The Grasshopper*, adapted with E. Washburn Freund from Hermann Keyserling, produced at the Abbey in 1922. He published *Balloon* in 1929, a full-length play. But where are his adaptation with Vladimir Orloff of Alexander Blok's *The Show-Booth* and his little miracle play, *The Miracle of the Corn*, which I saw presented in the late forties at the Abbey by Austin Clarke's Lyric Theatre Company? There must be much more ... Readers may well ask, 'why bother about Padraic Colum's work for the theatre'. The answer, as I see it, is simple: if he is worth our interest as a poet, then everything he wrote must interest us.

Pádraic Colum would have rejoiced over *An Duanaire, 1600–1900, Poems of the Dispossessed*, the joint work of Seán Ó Tuama and Thomas Kinsella, published in mid-1981. He would have welcomed the exquisite combination of textual scholarship and poetic sensibility. In this issue of the *Review* his *Kilmore* is followed by versions from the Irish of the seventh to the late twelfth or early thirteenth centuries by Thomas Kinsella: hints of what we may expect should *An Duanaire* be succeeeded by volumes dealing with the centuries before 1600.

Reference to Seán Ó Tuama, himself an original poet and dramatist (as well as being an erudite and quite unchauvinist critic of Gaelic literature), leads me to note the appearance of the sixth number of *Innti*, which began as a broadsheet at University College, Cork in 1970, appeared in a larger format in 1971, sputtered out as a booklet in 1973, and arose again in 1980 as a small book, and now with its third issue in that form, looks as if it has come to stay. *Innti*, edited by Michael Davitt,[6] Gabriel Rosenstock and Proinsias Ní Dhorchaí (two of whom were among the begetters in those blissful Corkonian days when Ó Ríordáin and Ó Riada were on call) carries a fervent notice of *An Duanaire* by Liam Ó Muirthile (another beget-ter) which ends, 'We are only beginning the process of repossession.' But of course its chief interest must be its eighteen poets (including Máirtín Ó Direáin, Máire Mhac an tSaoi and that formidable young lady Nuala Ní Dhomhnaill). I must, though, draw special attention to a comprehensive interview with Éoghan Ó Tuairisc: novelist, dramatist, and poet in English and Irish.[7] I am tempted to exceed this magazine's brief and quote Mr Ó Tuairisc on subjects other than verse. It may be legitimate to record that when in 1964 he published two books of verse on the same day: within a fortnight *Lux Aeterna*, in Irish, had gained him £400, and *The Weekend of Dermot and Grace* by the end of the year had brought in £12 ...

Tómás MacSíomóin was the subject interviewed in *Innti* 5: this is the place to apologize for the appearance of his name on the cover of *PIR 1* ... And I end thinking how Pádraic Colum must have felt when confronted with the gibberish served up as Roger Casement's most famous poem, 'In the Streets of Catania', in *The Irish Review* for September 1912.

Poetry Ireland Review Editorial 4

(The Poetry Ireland Review, No. 8, Autumn 1983)

A couple of issues ago I promised myself the pleasure of saying something about a new Papermac from Macmillan, W.B. Yeats's *Collected Plays*, a substantial volume which, if things were ordered properly, should have received much attention in our press: a cheap edition (Stg. £5.95) of the lifetime's work for the theatre of arguably the greatest poet in the English language since Milton. (This was the considered judgment of the late R.P. Blackmur, and I was gratified to hear it echoed the other day by Professor Augustine Martin, even in the trivial context of a radio interview.) This Papermac is an exact reproduction of the hardback Second Edition of *C.P.* (1952) which augmented the First Edition (1934). We have in all twenty-six plays, ranging from the first publication of *The Countess Cathleen* (1982) to the posthumously published *Purgatory*, and *The Death of Cuchulainn* (1939). When I write 'exact reproduction' I mean, of course, that the volume reproduces the eccentric unchronological order of the original: for instance, *On Baile's Strand* (1904) is placed *after* the 'heroic farce' *The Green Helmet* (1910), despite the fact that it is the first of the Cuchulainn plays.

But I would draw attention to the *variety* of the Yeatsian dramatic canon. Consider, to take samples, the differences in tone between the fairy-play *The Land of Heart's Desire* (1894) and the naturalistic prose-drama *The Words Upon the Window-Pane* (1934), between the Sophocles versions (1928 and 1934) and the surrealist fantasy *The Player Queen* (1922), between *Cathleen Ní Houlihan* (1902) the classic, perhaps the only durable dramatic utterance of Nationalism (I do not qualify this with 'Irish', my ears having been at time of writing much bludgeon-ed by politicians' references to 'the Irish people', as if their mandate could come from any other people), and *The Death of Cuchulainn* (1939) in which we have almost the paradox Nationalism having *died* in the Post Office, to be replaced by an artefact: *A statue's there to mark the place / By Oliver Sheppard done.* I might add that this, Yeats's last play, seems to me one of his greatest. I have been playing the game of choosing my six favourite Yeats plays (less than a quarter of the canon) and come up with the following: *The King's Threshold* (1904), *The Dreaming of the Bones* (1919), *The Player Queen* (1922), *The Words Upon the Window-Pane* (1934), *Purgatory* (1939) and *The Death of Cuchulainn* (1939). Perhaps some readers may care to play the game, which highlights the multiplicity of Yeats's theatrical genius.

With the eighth issue, I wind up my term as Editor ... I am conscious of the fact that my tastes, while not conservative, are certainly not catholic and accordingly some meritorious poets may have been turned away ... No doubt I have made many enemies, who have had the grace to remain silent (to my face). I have never been able to understand that editorial mentality which is untormented by doubts and regrets. Words alone may not be certain good, but they are the counters of human responses, ideally of wholly genuine human responses. The scruple-ridden editor may perhaps console himself with the reflection that most human responses are not genuine, being Pavlovian not Chekovian. Most words are spittle.

The foregoing apologia will have indicated why I am glad to lay down a responsibility and have it taken up by a poet young enough to be my son, Thomas McCarthy, Waterford-born but based in Cork. It is, by the way, wholly proper in the context of *Poetry Ireland* that after two years the *Review*'s centre should pass from Dublin to Cork. Two more years may see it in Galway or Belfast ...

Sam's Cross

(Cyphers 10, 1979)

The other day I came across a sentence William Carlos Williams wrote about Robert McAlmon: 'He has not chosen what he would and would not see.' To this text I append a saying of the eminent Islamic scholar and apologist of Notre-Dame de La Salette, Louis Massignon: '*Il n'est pas interdit de dire ce qu'on pense d'un cardinal.*'

Paul Durcan's third book (the first was *O Westport in the Light of Asia Minor*, 1975, the second *Teresa's Bar*, 1976) endorses my view of him as being among Irish poets the outstanding instance of what Alberti once aspired to be, *poeta de la calle*. There is scarcely a verse here whose matter might not be found or construed from the popular media, newspaper, radio or television, with the exception of the last lengthy (in XI sections) and ambitious poem, 'Love in a Grave', which I fancy he will some day rewrite: but see below. Mr Durcan might be called a satirist, but a distinctive kind. Folly and wickedness in high and low places he recognises and blasts, but while he gets his target, the more dominant impression than indignation is of sadness, and of disgust at the manifest *stupidity* of the forces of law and illegality, of order and disorder. This man from Westport and Dublin who lives in Cork really cares about his people. I instance in this connection (and the absurdly named 'Troubles') his verses on the Miami Showband massacre, the La Mon House explosions (the Catholic Archbishop of Armagh and *an Taoiseach agus a bhean* should read this) and, less successful by reason of the closing lines, 'The Minibus Massacre: On the Eve of the Epiphany'. Here we are concerned with the sad eye cast on recorded events. But beneath the skin of the immediate present there are comic and horrific nightmares and we have the terrible intuitions of 'Margaret Thatcher Joins the I.R.A.', 'Communist Cardinal Visits Dublin', and 'Bishop of Cork Murders His Wife': here there is at work an imagination which exults in its own ferocity, and can also be very funny. (The Bishop's wife, apparently, had prevented him watching Match of the Day.)

But Mr Durcan has another precious string almost unplayed in Irish verse since Austin Clarke died: the unsung private persons who make only, if they are lucky, the death notices. Some are memorable, welcome guests to the undying imaginative world that may be all some of us have: the Sapphic couple Nora and Hilda, Constance Purfield (*'I eat surgeon for breakfast, you know'*), Mr Morgan, Humphrey Creedon.

He honours finely some who made more than the death notices: Seamus
Murphy, Emmet Dalton, Mícheál Mac Liammóir (*'I dreamed a dream of Jean Cocteau /
Leaning against a wall in Killnamoe'*), Cearbhall Ó Dálaigh ('*Of the City Centre and the
Mountain-Pool'*) and David Thornley.

'Love in a Grave' is a long, partly autobiographical, reverie on two fine and private places: the grave and the bed of love, copulation and procreation, encasing the
story of a young gravedigger and a woman doctor. Here are some lines in calm lyric
mode, one of many modes in a tacky but immensely interesting poem:

> Come down to the sea, my love,
> across the limestone land;
> Let us walk, my love,
> with the limestone into the sea;
> I will wait, my love,
> with the limestone for the seawater
> To surge round your toes
> into its rock-duchies and
> its winkle kingdoms.

I have already indicated that 'Love in a Grave' may be Mr Durcan's *magnum opus*
to-date. I hope he will eliminate the shale for a new edition, in which some serious
misprints may also be corrected. I offer Mr Durcan a final text: '*I found myself guilty
of the crime of poetry upon London Bridge.*' That was Paul Valéry in 1896. Let Paul Durcan
plunge deep in criminality, act the blackguard in fact. We could be doing with one.

Book Reviews in *Poetry Ireland Review*

(The Poetry Ireland Review, Nos 2, 5 & 6)

Reductionist Poem, by Anthony Cronin. (Dublin 1980)
Ark of the North, by Paul Durcan. (Dublin 1982)
We Have Kept the Faith, by Francis Stuart (Dublin 1982)
RMS Titanic, by Anthony Cronin. (Dublin 1981)

41 Sonnets-Poems 82 by Anthony Cronin. (Dublin 1982)

Mr Cronin's book[1] is his first major work in verse since *Collected Poems 1950–1973* (Dublin, 1973), a long philosophical poem (644 lines as against the dubious 413 of *The Waste Land*). Odd as it may seem to the common reader, it is not always easy to be enthusiastic in a full-hearted way about the work of one's friends and contemporaries, but on this occasion I am compelled to say that I have been astonished (*'Etonne-moi, Antoine'*) and moved by this grave plea for the undoctored and unmanipulated normal in human existence. This is a poem of high seriousness and its burden is not in any way etiolated by parodic references to other writers, some of which are pointed out in the Notes. On the most obvious level the poem is an attack on those versions of Platonic idealism which in favour of a Republic (a synonym here for any organized collectivity) would crush 'A little republic of love'. I would need far more space to plumb the density of the poet's meditation and that delicacy of perception that distinguishes poetry from formal philosophical discourse in verse (e.g. Erasmus Darwin[2]). Apart from an implied parallel between the deceptions of neo-Platonism and the falsities of entertainment media (the latter brilliantly satirized in lines which take off, ironically, from a famous passage in the *Pisan Cantos*), there are autobiographical overtones which lend poignancy to the metaphysical stance (this last adjective is used, for all its inexactitude, in preference to the more categorical 'philosophical'): *'a part of him fiercely longs/ not only for love and money/ becoming in any case synonymous/ and a place at least equal in dignity/ to that of a B.B.C. producer/ or a visiting Irish one…'*.

When the time comes to write the history of Raven Arts, the researcher may, or should, be intrigued by some extra-literary aspects of the four books under review.[3] Mr Durcan's new book is a long poem written for Mr Stuart's eightieth birthday last April 28. Mr Durcan also introduces the new edition of Mr Cronin's long poem *R.M.S. Titanic*. Mr Cronin dedicated his *Reductionist Poem* (1980) to Mr Durcan and his novel, *Identity Papers*, to Mr Stuart. Mr Cronin also introduces the new expanded edition of Mr Stuart's *We Have Kept the Faith*. (The putative researcher might find that I myself am involved in these Alexandrine complexities: Mr Stuart dedicates one of his later poems, 'The Garden', to me and the curious may detect me in his last novel *The High Consistory*.[4] For no ostensible reason I am referred to by name in Mr Cronin's *Identity Papers*.)

An immediately relevant point in all this is that Mr Stuart is in his early eighties, Mr Cronin in his middle-fifties, and Mr Durcan in his late thirties, and that to my certain knowledge they have no connection with Finglas. If nothing else were needed, their association makes nonsense of a notion invented by the popular press and accepted, I know, by quite decent people: the notion of 'The Finglas Poets', a group of young working-class writers with revolutionary, even anti-social, ideas.[5] If Messrs Stuart, Cronin and Durcan are revolutionary, they are so in ways not to be programmed by people who wouldn't know an idea from an iced lolly, a passion from popcorn.

The foregoing is by no means an oblique apologia for all the productions of the Raven Arts Press, though the present four are certainly worthy. Mr Durcan's poem for Mr Stuart reminds me obscurely of a half-forgotten phrase from Novalis: that we are nearest to death when we dream that we dream. Its taking-off point may have been Mr Stuart's Berlin lyric of 1944, 'Ireland' (contained in the extended section of *We Have Kept the Faith*) which he refers to explicitly, and which ends:

> *Steeped with your few lost lights in the long Atlantic dark*
> *Sea birds shelter, our shelter and our ark.*

The 'ark' of Mr Durcan's narrator or *persona* is the Belfast-Dublin train and his first companion will be an Egyptian or Islamic-type girl who will leave the train at Drogheda. Her Egyptian origin is stated explicitly, but I make the qualification since in their initially silent communion he asks,

> *Do you remember Dr Riordan in Tripoli?*
> *Not even the waves could keep up with his laughter*

The Tripoli in question is the Libyan capital and I know that Dr Riordan is a real person,[6] known both to Mr Durcan and myself and, come to think of it, Mr Cronin. (The family must be kept together.) It is quite fortuitous knowledge on my part that leads me to the conclusion that *Ark of the North* may be, in part, a collage of private memoranda as distinct from identifiable literary allusions. Of the latter is that one to Mr Stuart's lyric. Before what may be a metaphor for the climax of sexual congress, the fall of the guillotine, the *persona's* 'last thoughts' include:

> *That in the year of my birth there was a man in Berlin*
> *Who, in the pitiless floodwaters of war*

> *In the unbunging of black holes in the yellowgreen grass*
> *Among the rooftops floating skywards*
> *Into the Tiergarten and Kottbusser Tor,*
> *Like Dmitry Shostakovich marooned in Stalingrad,*
> *Scored a poem – composed a lyric*
> *Known as Ireland 1944.*

Mr Durcan was in fact born in 1944 and Mr Stuart was then in Berlin. And I recall that one of the more alert of our journalists, himself a writer of fiction, could not see the relevance of *Ark of the North* to Mr Stuart ... The latter's presence may be sensed behind even the deplorable Steward of the Turf Club of Ireland who enters the carriage at Drogheda after the Arab girl has left. In their hilariously idiotic interchange, only a comment of the *persona* has any sense: 'Horses are breathtaking' – an observation incomprehensible to the Steward, but not, in any sense, including Maupassant's *pincement au coeur* to a lover of of the track like Mr Stuart.

I have said enough to suggest that Mr Durcan's poem is richly allusive, ironic and plangent, and well worth a little homework. It is also an imaginative gloss on the work of Francis Stuart: death, the Madonna, Venus, imprisonment, the drama of the track, are all there.

Mr Stuart's earliest poems, while palpably Yeatsian, have considerable interest in relation to his novels: some of them, addressed to a *prima ballerina* have already been reprinted as part of the text of the great *Black List,* Section H[7] (1971). The later poems, written from about 1944 to 1980, are much more enigmatic, crabbed in style, and often with a streak of self-deprecatory humour quite absent from the pre-War fiction though quietly in evidence in *Black List* and its three successors. This little collection, containing verses written as early as 1919 and as recently as 1980, makes an exquisitely appropriate pendant to the chain of novels from 1931 to 1981.

In his afterword to this new edition of *R.M.S. Titanic*, Mr Cronin tells us that the British film *A Night to Remember*, with Kenneth More (who died earlier in 1982) portraying Mr Lightoller, Third Officer of the *Titanic*, 'was the immediate inspiration of the poem'. By a singular coincidence, as I got down to reading the poem again, I was about to turn off the TV when the B.B.C. flashed *A Night to Remember* as part of a tribute to Kenneth More. One wonders if that excellent actor ever knew he had helped to inspire so fine a poem. For, after over twenty years, very fine it is: a meditation of high seriousness on the philosophic (and emblematic) significance of a great natural disaster. Mr Cronin does not see this disaster as being out of history, a particular night to remember, but rather a paradigm in the human conjugation. If there be a weakness in his exposition of the paradigm it is in the less than implicit suggestion that in extremity the well-heeled must of necessity be of baser metal than the down-at-heel:

> *The screaming rich sucked under*
> *And the poor cry in that icy darkness*
> *One last time.*

The Dives-Lazarus dichotomy will not hold. On the other hand, Mr Cronin's audacious choice of a Liverpool Rowton House from which to brood on the disaster, coupled with a West of Ireland landscape, urine with ozone, makes for exciting richness in the paradigm.

The first ten of Mr Cronin's *Sonnet-Poems* appeared as a group originally in *The Poetry Ireland Review* (Summer, 1981), though in a different sequence, and with some few variants. At the time I recognized that this was an expansion of the Cronin imaginative territory: the scapes ranged from Cambridgshire and the rise of the manorial system to the suburban wartime cinema and the psychic domination of heroes like Gable. Clearly we were not being asked to sit back and have an agrreable poetic browse. Only once before had I felt compelled to telephone enthusiasm to a contributor and that was in 1962 when I was editing the second series of *Poetry Ireland* and, ironically, the poet was Austin Clarke,[8] a poet with whom Mr Cronin has never shown much sympathy. Again ironically, this new book is as densely allusive, as luminously bookish as anything Clarke ever produced. While perhaps only less than a fifth of the *Sonnet-Poems* have appeared, it would be presumptuous to pontificate on their ultimate thrust. But it is clear that Mr Cronin is engaged in an exploration of the roots and branches of contemporary civilizations and it is not too much to say that he has set himself a task of Poundian dimensions. And, like Pound, he requires in his reader, at the very least, a well-stocked mind. To exemplify, there are few of us at home with the German Jewish Francophile poet Heinrich Heine at the same time as the writings of James Connolly and Alice Stopford Green, with Scott and Stevenson at the same time as Wilde and Ernest Dowson. Quotation rather than exposition may best serve, at this point of time, to illustrate what I find exciting in this new magisterial Cronin. Here is the last of the sonnet-poems in the present sequence:

> *Off boulevards which flame in blue and red,*
> *Colour of brimstone, where the coaches come,*
> *Holiday coloured, orange pink and yellow,*
> *Discharging senior citizens to enjoy*
> *At a place Lautrec and an eager La Gouloue*
> *Had made a legend in a rosier time*
> *Some hours of sanitized and distant strip,*
> *Down darker streets are found by the more daring*
> *Privileges which were once a great lord's prize.*
> *The faces cold or pert, some beautiful,*
> *And not much marked by this impersonal traffic,*
> *Many which, given other circumstance,*

> *To gaze on the high cheek and hollow eyes*
> *Might haunt a true romantic all his days.*

Perhaps it is only the true romantic that can fathom the splendours and miseries, not alone of courtesans, but of civilizations. Let us hope Mr Cronin will complete his high endeavour, and be thankful for what so far he has done.

Private Passion

(New Hibernia, January 1986)

Just over twenty years ago an Irish poetry critic, (and still) one of the more literate of that select band, took me to task for my 'indiscriminate' inclusion of certain
very young poets in a magazine I was editing[1] One of those poets was Paul Durcan.
I take a little pride in having had the gumption to publish him, and am more than
than a little ashamed that I risked only a fragment.[2]

Happily, in the interim I have had three opportunities to acclaim my supposed
ugly-duckling: on the publications of *Sam's Cross* (1978), *Ark of the North* (1982) and
The Selected Paul Durcan (1982). In my review of the first (in *Cyphers*) I found it apposite to refer to, among others, William Carlos Williams, Rafael Alberti, Austin
Clarke and Paul Valéry. Among the 'others' was the Islamic scholar and apologist of
Our Lady of La Salette, Louis Massignon, who wrote once: 'It is not forbidden to
say what one thinks of a cardinal.' This perfectly orthodox proposition has a peculiar relevance to many of the poems in Mr Durcan's new collection[3] which, more
than one might hope for, compensates for a noticeable slackness – even a measure
of slap-dashery – in his last volume, published ion 1983, *Jumping the Train Tracks with
Angela*.

This new book is divided into two parts: the first consisting of poems about
certain drolleries and obsenities in Irish private and public lives, and the second
about a particular private life, Mr Durcan's own. Many of the poems in the first
part will offend people who abide by the reverse of Massignon's dictum quoted
above, for Mr Durcan's critique of episcopal obsessions is couched in grotesquely
satirical terms. Two poems in the critique are also very funny, highlighting through
the reports of a far from sober newscaster just how absurd eminent ecclesiastics can
sound when they climb upon their hobbyhorses. (Lacking the courage of Mr
Durcan, I am being circumspect, deliberately, about the subjects of these 'reports'.)
But of course Mr Durcan is not obsessed by clerical poppycock alone.

I would link four poems as an indictment of the well-heeled bourgeoisie: 'The
Haulier's Wife Meets Jesus on the Road Near Moone', which reads somewhat like
an episode in a novel by Mr Francis Stuart; 'The National Gallery Restaurant', in
which one of the mohair [suit] brigade protests at 'being looked at by persons in
pictures' on his way to eat; 'Catholic Father Prays for His Daughter's Abortion',

whose title explains its subject, as immediate as a popular RTE radio programme; 'Bird-Watcher on Pigeon House Road', Mr Durcan's astonishing gloss on the domestic respectability of a heroin dealer.

The eighteen poems in the second part of the book deal directly or allusively with the poet's idyllic courtship and marriage and the shipwreck of that marriage, after fifteen years, in 1984. Durcanites will recall that in his first full collection, *O Westport in the Light of Asia Minor* (1975), he has two poems, 'Nessa' and 'Hymn to Nessa'. The first poem in the second part is 'Hymn to a Broken Marriage', beginning, *'Dear Nessa – Now that our marriage is over'*. The extraordinary feature of this poem and of many of those that follow is that while the marriage may, in fact, be what people call 'broken', it continues to exist, metaphysically, in the consciousness of the poet, and thus in his poems. But while many of these poems re-create stages in the marriage – chiefly while the couple lived in various parts of London and in Cork city – there are others in which the poet plays out crises in festive (?)[4] situations. These include 'The Jewish Bride', and the title poem, 'The Berlin Wall Café'. From the first I take:

> *A Jewish Bride who has survived the death camp,*
> *Free at last of my swastika eyes*
> *Staring at you from across spiked dinner plates*
> *Or from out of the bunker of a TV armchair;*
> *Free of the glare off my Gestapo voice; ...*

More accessible are poems like 'Around the Corner from Francis Bacon', and 'Windfall, 8 Parnell Hill, Cork', stages in the idyll. The fragmentation of the idyll is figured in 'Cleaning Ashtrays' – *'Now Julietless, how Romeo pines for all those days and nights / Cleaning ashtrays – cleaning ashtrays for his only Juliet.'*

Paul Durcan has always been an excitingly unpredictable poet. But nothing he had hitherto written prepared me for his confrontation with 'the eternity of his loss'.

Dánta, le Caitlín Maude (1963-82)[1]

(Cyphers 23, 1985)

Caitlín, singer and actress, but pre-eminently poet, died of cancer on 6 June 1982, aged forty-one. She published no book. Indeed her published work was relatively scanty over a period of almost twenty years (1963–82). She was better known, per-haps, as a singer in the *sean-nós* and had achieved a *succès d'estime* in Máiréad Ní Ghráda's play *An Triail* presented at the Damer Hall during the Theatre Festival of 1964. But even if over nearly two decades she published only twenty-four poems, such was their impact that those who cared about such matters would inevitably list her among the leading writers in Irish. And now Mr Ciarán Ó Coigligh has assem-bled for us fifty-two poems, meaning that we have twenty-eight 'new' pieces.

She was twenty-two when in *Comhar* she burst upon us with seven poems of quite extraordinarily disparate content and vision. Máire Mhac an tSaoi before her and Nuala Ní Dhomhnaill after her have shown that women writers of verse in Irish can, like their peers in English, transcend the demeaning and discriminatory label of 'poetess'. No-one in his or her right mind would describe as 'poetess' Emily Brontë or Emily Dickinson or Sylvia Plath. Those first published poems of Caitlín established her immediately as not being a 'poetess'. 'Entreaty' *(Impí)* reverses the roles of Diarmaid and Gráinne and has the woman pleading for an asexual rela-tionship (there is nothing about what we call so glibly 'platonic friendship' to be found in Plato). Astonishingly it was followed by 'Concerto', an impressionistic depiction of sexual ecstasy: *'surge and frenzy / of joy and wonder / stifling and drown-ing / till pleasure explodes / and dies away / in a long-drawn lament ...'*.

Those poems of ascetic and sensual love were followed by (for so young a poet) a mature reflection on the whole unsatisfactory business and frustration of artistic making, 'Spasm' *(Treall)*: *But God I'm Tired!* And then came 'Let Us Pray' *(Guímis)*, which might have been written by Charles Péguy: *'Christ / show your fair counte-nance / again amongst the people / do not renege ... do not renege / however deserved the renegal.'* Clearly this girl from Ros Muc was, potentially, a major religious poet. Yet another facet of her vision was seen in 'The Flowers' *(Na Blátha)*: *Flowers are not flowers / but the source of beauty and torment.* In 'Congratulation' *(Comhghairdeachas)* we found that rare and lovely thing in verse: an index to an unspoken private life, lines from the secret scriptures of intensely personal pain. We will never know the occasion of the hurt recorded in 'Congratulation', any more than that which lies behind the first of the 'new' poems, 'To a former friend' (*D'Iarcara*): '*I can't help thinking / friend, / it was a good thing / you were only a friend.*'

Nineteen-sixty-three and the first published poems set the compass for Caitlín's verse. She would write of God and religion, of sex and the private life, more especially the shades of love and friendship. Later we learnt of her kinship with the physical world and her poignant feeling for her country. 'My Affinities' (*Mo Dháimh*) is almost shocking in its disavowal of the human: '*My affinity is with bog* ... *They baptised me / They put a bib around me / But my care was for moss and mud.*' That same year, 1968, she gave us two Irelands, the misshapen creature of 'Botch' (*Liobar*) and the ideal of 'The Mother' (*An Mháthair*). One thing that may be said about the botch is that it is pure, '*Pure, I say, pure / As pure as crystal* ... *You wouldn't be ashamed to put it under / the priest's breakfast / Or, the Sign of the Cross on us! / the Holy Communion.*'

Strangely, Mr Ó Coigligh in his commentary seems to miss the ferocious irony in these lines, for this spectacular purity is attributed to a country which has already been described as 'dead'. But there is that other Ireland, Caitlín's, the reverse of Pearse's 'Mise Éire', since she is eternally young and beautiful and has not been betrayed by her children. Yet it is likely (though it does not occur to Mr Ó Coigligh) that there is a measure of irony in this image of the lovely young mother with her strapping sons and laughing maidens from the heart of Éamon de Valéra.

Caitlín had many ironic skills, as for instance in the group of five 'new' poems which deals with poets and poetry. In one of them a company director's typist goes sick and he has to do his own typing: '*the letters / so disgusted him / that he tore them up / and wrote a poem* ... *a while later / he left his job / his home / his wife / and his family / ... and now / he is a poet / ... poor man*'. In the poem beginning 'It's time to write the last poem' (*Tá sé in am an dán deiridh a scríobh*) there is more than irony, something like sheer fun as she lists the options for the 'last poem', '*dán tourists*', for instance, tourists '*who bring tropical diseases / and money / who give bad thoughts to the bishop / who has to write an additional sermon for his diocese / to clear his conscience*'.

That kind of almost surreal fun may be seen also in the *amhrán bréagach* – 'lying' poem or song – which Caitlín wrote for a visit by Scottish Gaelic poets to Ros Muc in March 1977: *I rose up one morning and saw a great wonder: / Jack Lynch on Cnoc Mordán driving cattle / Liam Cosgrave on an ass, on his way to collect the dole, / And Ryan (Ritchie) to his heart's content begging with a cap.* The fun here is bitter. Mr Ó Coigligh reminds us that Caitlín once said, on a television programme, 'when I think of politicians, I think of shysters' (*chaimiléirí*).

She published only three poems in 1969: 'The White Leaf' (*An Bhileog Bhán*), a love-poem based on an outrageously rococo *concetto*; 'Vietnam Love Song', a mock callous celebration of sexual love above the atrocities of war – '*we could have stayed on the field of slaughter / but the sorrowful faces of the soldiers / made us laugh / and we chose a soft place by the river*'; – and the Joycean 'Advice' (*Comhairle*): '*my poems /*

where is your proper aloofness/ what's this loose talk/ with every stranger?'

To the period immediately after her marriage to Cathal Ó Luain on 27 December 1969 may belong the 'new' poem 'To My Love' (*Do Mo Ghrá*): *'an intricate fresh wood/ our love/ in this narrow habitation/ – a couple of rooms/ it is the whole world – the softness of its leafage/ the shelter of its branches/ even in the darkness/ escorted us through the thorny places'.* Granted a case of dangerously mixed metaphors, those few words, *'cúpla seomara/ is é an saol Fodhlach é',* are wonderfully effective as an image of young marital love.

Curiously, what appears to have been a long period of poetic sterility (some four years?) was heralded in 1971 by 'Poems and Fleas (Lice Really)' (*Dánta agus Dreamcaidí – Míola dáiríre*), which ends: *'today there are those/ who would comb the hair from my head/ in search of a poem/ and they don't get even a louse'.* This extraordinary poem about the sensations of a child under the operation of a tooth-comb, and the elimination and destruction of the vermin as they fall on the spread-out newspaper (shades of Rimbaud and *Chercheuses de Poux*) is perhaps the best illustration of Caitlín's absolute rejection of the genteel, but we might also consider in that context 'Snow 1968', where she speaks of the dungheap (*aoiligh*) as being 'piss and cowshit' (*fual is bualtrach*) no less dear to snow than the bishop's grave, the guards' patrol-car or 'that new suit of yours'.

It is in the latter part of the book that we find the bulk of the 'new' poems, including those she wrote in the six months before her death. Here also are the four poems that appeared originally in *Cyphers*, one in 1976 and three, the last she was to see in print, in 1980–81. The very last of these, 'Dead Alive' (*Marbh Beo*) gives the date of its publication, Winter 1981 in *Cyphers 16*. Already a dying woman, she inveighs against 'false life' (*beatha bréagach*): *'The house begins at music/ with the thrumming of the false life,/ life itself a stump,/ its shadow moving.'*

Mr Ó Coigligh consigns nine poems to the period 30 December 1981 to 6 June 1982. The poems are without titles. That beginning *Between the Family Rosary and the thirty acres* is about one of those outsiders or misfits for whom Caitlín had an especial tenderness, a woman who *like Christ took the lonely way* for all that she lacked the protection of 'neighbourly respect' (*meas comharsan*), 'the praise of friends' (*moladh na gcarad*) or 'the oil of the sacraments' (*ola na sacraiméid*). The little black bird in the poem with that opening (*An tÉinín Dubh*) might well be equated with Caitlín herself: *'The little black bird/ looked down/ on the destruction,/ the destruction of her own life/ of her gaiety/ and her broken wings beside …'.* 'Patients' Congress' (*Comhdháil na nOthar*) distinguishes between possible curable disease and irremediable metaphysical an-guish. There are two poems with Joycean overtones: 'Watch that passionate man', and 'Is there one who understands me?' The first is a clear advocacy of the passionate heart and a contemptuous rejection of the spirit that would make a 'quick calculation' (*comhaireamh pras*) of 'the cost of a kiss' (*costas póige*). The second does not have an obvious link with its title, a line from *Finnegans Wake*. It must for the time being remain cryptic, but I surmise that this is a political verse: *Let their portion be left/ to cats and eunuchs* – who are the cats and eunuchs? The penultimate poem, 'Consider' (*Sílstean*), is a tranquil acceptance of the 'thorn' or the 'jaggedness' (*spiacán*) of life, ordained by both the pagan world and Christ: '*the sharp touch/ the hard game/ are the fate of the individual/ – that or an ease that is not ease*'. The passionate yet frugal soul will not settle for 'ease' (*eascaíocht*).

Mr Ó Coigligh has served Caitlín well, even if his critical commentary is at times otiose. He can at times be positively helpful in the reading of a poet who is seldom 'easy': obliquity and inference are native to her. And that in the face of so much passion. In 1970 Máirtín Ó Direáin published a poem (in *Crainn is Cairde*) addressed to '*Caitlín Maude upon having heard her read her poem*'. I take leave to render it into rough English:

> *In my mind*
> *You are not man nor woman*
> *As you say your poem –*
> *If saying be the right word –*
> *But a being of the sea's kin;*
> *Its blue and its green*
> *Contending in your eyes*
> *As you let loose astray your feeling*
> *In a spring-tide of words:*
> *Do you despise pen*
> *Or paper as instrument,*
> *The time your poem comes*
> *Scalding from your brimming heart.*

Ah, how I wish I had known that heart better, and envy those who did.

John Jordan
Bloomsday, 1985

Shaw, Wilde, Synge and Yeats: Ideas, Epigrams, Blackberries and Chassis

(from Part IV of The Irish Mind: Exploring Intellectual Traditions)[1]

With certain notable exceptions, Irish drama is not distinguished by its originality of thought. It may of course be properly argued that it is not the business of the drama in any case to embody originality of thought, philosophical, metaphysical, ethical or otherwise, that the theatre of Jean-Paul Sartre is diminished rather than enriched in its effectiveness by the overtones of his philosophy and that the same holds true of the Christian existentialist Gabriel Marcel and his theatre. There are some who would argue that the theatre of Bernard Shaw is vitiated by 'ideas'; that, for example, the 'Don Juan in Hell' section of Act III of *Man and Superman* is a violation of the play's comedic structure.[2] There are also some artless or fatuous enough to believe that Yeats's penultimate play *Purgatory* (1938), perhaps his most perfect, could have been written had he eschewed his notions about reincarnation and the memories of the dead.[3] Quite rightly, critics, academic and otherwise, have hailed three Irishmen, George Farquhar, Oliver Goldsmith, and Richard Brinsley Sheridan, as the chief ornaments of eighteenth-century stage comedy.[4] But it is not possible to speak about the philosophical background of these brilliant men, for it does not exist. And they wrote almost exclusively for the London stage. In that context, they may be said to have a common mentality; the émigré mentality, not at all to be confused with the casts of mind that led Joyce first to Paris in 1902 and later to Trieste in 1904, and Beckett finally to Paris in 1938. Even in pre-Union days London was Mecca. After the Union, it was not only Mecca but Moscow (in the Chekhovian sense) for gifted young Irish dramatists-to-be, like Oscar Wilde and his junior by two years, Bernard Shaw, neither of them particularly concerned with Irish woes.[5]

Almost everywhere we turn during the first decade of the 'Irish dramatic movement' (to use Una Ellis-Fermor's terminology)[6] we run into the monitory intellectual shade of Henrik Ibsen. It was of course Shaw, through his criticism, and William Archer, through his translations, that brought the name of Ibsen before the public in these islands. In 1891 Shaw published a small book called *The Quintessence of Ibsenism*.[7] It was a fruit of his association with the Fabian Society which he had joined immediately after its foundation in 1884.[8] In the spring of 1890 the society planned a series of papers 'under the general heading of Socialism in Contemporary Literature'. Shaw consented to 'take Ibsen'. By his own account his lecture might have lain fallow were it not for the 'frantic newspaper controversy' that followed upon the first London performances of, successively, *Rosmersholm / Ghosts,* and *Hedda Gabler.* Shaw stepped in to clear the air with his little book. Thus, before ever any play of his was staged, Shaw was identified with his own coinage: Ibsenism.[9] His first play produced was *Widowers' Houses* in 1892. He tells us in the preface to the *First Volume of Plays:Pleasant and Unpleasant* (1898) how it came to be written. Originally he and William Archer had set out in 1885 to write a play in collaboration. But their aims diverged and Shaw was left with two acts of an unfinished play which he set aside, only to complete seven years later, when a native work was required for J.T. Grein's Independent Theatre, founded specifically for the purpose of proclaiming the New Theatre. *Widowers' Houses* may seem tame nowadays, but, irrefutably, it has an Ibsenite theme: the stripping of illusion and self-deception, in this case those of the young doctor, Harry Trench. But in the original preface to *Widowers' Houses* (1893) Shaw was careful to point out that there were respectable native sources for many of the ideas in his play that critics detected as Norwegian importations.[10] We must of course always be careful about the absolute truth of Shaw's disavowals. In this connection the preface to *Major Barbara* (1905) is of crucial importance and merits extensive quotation, if only because of the light that it throws on a slightly earlier play, *Man and Superman,* written between 1901 and 1903. 'Schopenhauer wrote a splenetic essay which, as it is neither polite nor profound, was probably intended to knock this nonsense on the head.' (The 'nonsense' was all aspects of the male romantic convention about women.) 'A sentence – denouncing the idolised form as ugly – has been largely quoted' (Schopenhauer, in the essay 'On Women', in *Parega* [1851], referred to them as 'that undersized, narrow-shouldered, broad-hipped, and short-legged race', and 'the number two of the human race'.)[11] Shaw goes on: 'The English critics have read that sentence, and I must here affirm with as much gentleness as the implication will bear, that it has yet to be proved that they have dipped any deeper. At all events, whenever an English playwright presents a young and marriageable woman as being anything but a romantic heroine, he is disposed of without further thought, as an echo of Schopenhauer.' In what for Shaw is something uncharacteristically close to a *cri du coeur*, he complains, 'My own case is a specially hard one, because, when I implore the critics who are obsessed with the Schopenhauerian formula to remember that playwrights, like sculptors, study their figures from life, not from philosophic essays, they reply passionately that I am not a playwright and that my stage figures do not live.' And he tells us that long before he ever read a word of Schopenhauer, the socialist revival of the 1880s had brought him into contact with Ernest Belfort Bax, an English socialist and philosophic essayist, 'whose handling of modern feminism would provoke romantic protests from Schopenhauer himself, or even Strindberg'.[12]

In the same preface, Shaw disavows the direct influence of Nietzsche in *Man and Superman*. Here some of his statements are harder to take than his disavowal of Schopenhauer in favour of Ernest Belfort Bax. 'I first heard the name of Nietzsche from a German mathematician, Miss Borchardt, who had read my 'Quintessence of Ibsen' [*sic*], and told me that she saw what I had been reading: namely, Nietzsche's *Jenseits von Gut ünd Bose (Beyond Good and Evil*, 1886). Which I protest I had never seen, and could not have read with any comfort, for want of the necessary German, if I had seen it.'[13]

Shaw may here be pulling our legs. A modern philosopher, R.J. Hollingdale, tells us that by the end of 1889, Nietzsche's philosophy was 'available to anyone who could read and reach a bookshop'.[14]

Shaw, however, cannot deny that he has borrowed the word *Ubermensch* (Superman) from Nietzsche, but in relation to *Major Barbara* is constrained to deny that Nietzsche was the first to put forward the 'objection to Christianity as a pernicious slave-morality'. Just as he claims to have been made familiar with Schopenhauerian notions before he had ever heard of that philosopher, so the Nietzschean view of Christianity 'was familiar to me, before I ever heard of Nietzsche'. And he cites a Captain Wilson, inventor of the term 'Crosstianity', to distinguish the retrograde element in Christendom, and the Scottish philosophic historian Stuart-Glennie, both of whom he had encountered thirty years earlier, shortly after he had arrived in London.[15]

But one must turn now to *Man and Superman*, which Professor Turco has described as 'the first of Shaw's efforts to bear the unmistakeable stamp of a major work by a major writer'.[16]

It is in this play that Shaw coined the expression 'the life force' as a motive power behind the universe. Critics of an earlier period may be forgiven for equating this with the *élan vital* of Henri Bergson, who used it in his *Creative Evolution*. But Bergson's book was published in 1907, four years after *Man and Superman*.[17]

In his glittering 'Epistle Dedicatory' to A.B. Walkley, Shaw, as perhaps nowhere else, gives us an account of his personal predilections in literature (and painting and music): 'Bunyan, Blake, Hogarth and Turner (these four apart and above all the English classics), Goethe, Shelley, Schopenhauer, Wagner, Ibsen, Morris, Tolstoy, and Nietzsche are among the writers whose peculiar sense of the world I recognize as more or less akin to my own.'[18]

And he arrives at an outrageous synthesis: 'Bunyan's perception that Righteousness is filthy rags, his scorn for Mr Legality in the village of Morality, his defiance of the Church as the supplanter of religion, his insistence on courage as the virtue of virtues, his estimate of the career of the conventionally respectable

and sensible Worldly Wiseman as no better at bottom than the life and death of
Mr Badman: all this expressed by Bunyan in terms of a tinker's theology, is what
Nietzsche has expressed in terms of post-Darwin, post-Schopenhauer philosophy;
Wagner in terms of polytheistic mythology; and Ibsen in terms of mid-nineteenth
century Parisian dramaturgy.'[19] One does not think, usually, of Bunyan as a man of
'ideas': yet perhaps there is a touch of him in the silenced priest Keegan in Shaw's
only full-length play set entirely in Ireland, *John Bull's Other Island* (1904). 'For four
wicked centuries the world has dreamed this foolish dream of efficiency; and the
end is not yet, but the end will come.'[20] Many years later in the Preface to *Back to
Methusaleh* (1921) Shaw was to return to the importance in his mental world of
John Bunyan: when he first began to write for the stage, 'Nietzsche ... was supposed to have been the first man to whom it had occurred that mere morality and
legality and urbanity lead nowhere, as if Bunyan had never written Badman. Schopenhauer was credited with the distinction between the Covenant of Grace and the
Covenant of Works...'[21]

   In this brief discussion of Shaw's ideas, I have come only as far as 1905 and
I have not touched upon English influences like Samuel Butler, author of the
Victorian classic *The Way of All Flesh*, and *Erewhon*. It will have been seen that Shaw,
while admitting to intense admiration for Schopenhauer, Nietzsche and Ibsen, was
at pains to stress that he came to them intellectually prepared, in a mental state of
grace, so to speak. It so happens that the present writer does not believe that
knowledge of Shaw's intellectual background is a pre-requisite to the enjoyment of
his plays in the theatre. And in print we have always the assistance of of those cogent
and ebullient prefaces ... Perhaps the last words may be left to an unlikely advo-
cate, Jorge Luis Borges:

> The collective and civic problems of his early works will lose their interest, or
> have lost it already; the jokes in the Pleasant Plays (*sic.*) run the risk of becom-
> ing, some day, no less uncomfortable than those of Shakespeare ... the ideas
> declared in his prologues (prefaces?) and his eloquent tirades will be found in
> Schopenhauer and Samuel Butler; but Lavinia, Blanco Posnet, Keegan, Shotover,
> Richard Dudgeon and, above all, Julius Caesar, surpass any character imagined
> by the art of our time. If we think of (Paul Valéry's) Monsieur Teste alongside
> them, or Nietzsche's histrionic Zarathustra, we can only perceive with astonish-
> ment and even outrage the primacy of Shaw ... The biography of Bernard Shaw
> by Frank Harris contains an admirable letter by the former ... 'I understand
> everything and everyone and I am nothing and no one'. From this nothingness
> (so comparable to that of God before creating the world, so comparable to that
> primordial divinity which another Irishman, Johannes Scottus Eriugena, called
> *Nihil*), Bernard Shaw educed almost innumerable persons or dramatis personae:
> the most ephemeral of these is, I suspect, that G.B.S. who represented him in
> public and who lavished in the newspaper columns so many facile witticisms ...

> The work of Shaw ... leaves one with a flavour of liberation, the flavour of the
> stoic doctrines and the flavour of the sagas.

And to his references to Schopenhauer and Butler, Borges appends a dazzling
footnote: 'In *Man and Superman* we read that hell is not a penal establishment but
rather a state dead sinners elect for reasons of intimate affinity, just as the blessed
do with heaven; the treatise, *De Coelo et Inferno*, by Swedenborg, published in 1758,
expounds the same doctrine.'[22] The encyclopaedic Borges has given us a formidable conspectus of the 'Irish mind': from Eriugena to Shaw.

II

Earlier in the year that Shaw inaugurated a native Ibsenite drama with *Widowers'*
Houses (1892), Oscar Wilde had his first great London success on the stage with
Lady Windermere's Fan. There will be more to say about this and Wilde's other comedies later in this essay, but it is first necessary to go back a decade and investigate
what ideologies, if any, preoccupied the younger Wilde. His mother, of course, had
been 'Speranza' of *The Nation*, author of the inflammatory article in 1848 which led
to the suppression of the magazine.[23] Such nationalist feeling as Wilde possessed
came from her. The only substantial evidence of attachment to nationalism as such
is to be found in records of his American lecture tour in 1882, just a decade before
the three glorious years that preceeded the débâcle of 1895. For instance in Chic-
ago on February 10, 1882 he is reported as saying: 'Ireland is the Niobe among nations. The noblest of materials for a great nation were there wrecked by the folly of
England.'[24] More important is the lecture he gave in San Francisco on April 5, on
'The Irish poets of '48', part of which has been included by Mr Montgomery Hyde.
'As regards the men of '48, I look on their work with peculiar reverence and love,
for I was indeed trained by my mother to love and reverence them as a Catholic child
is the saints of the calendar.' Whether this be sincere or no, one cannot help noting
the familiarity of the sentiments, which might have come from any humble Catholic
nationalist: the equation of patriotism and religious fervour is an excessively common Irish trope. He goes on to pay tribute to William Smith O'Brien, John Mitchel
and Charles Gavan Duffy, and of course to his mother. And he certainly knew his
Irish-American audience when he came out with this splendid fustian:

> Indeed the poetic genius of the Celtic race never flags or wearies. It is as sweet
> by the groves of California as by the groves of Ireland, as strong in foreign lands
> as in the land that gave it birth. And indeed I do not know anything more won-
> derful, or more characteristic of the Celtic genius, than the quick artistic spirit
> in which we adapted ourselves to the English tongue. The Saxon took our lands
> from us and left them desolate – we took their language and added new beau-
> ties to it.[25]

And while Wilde was spouting these callow nationalist sentiments for a fat fee, we may remember his junior by two years plunging into his twelve-year career as a socialist orator for no fees at all, just about the same time.[26]

The juxtaposition may be fruitful, since it highlights two Dublin geniuses at the inception of their careers, and reminds us that while Wilde's rhetorical nationalism blossomed and wilted very quickly, Shaw's, after the turn of the century, was to manifest itself in many modes, not least in *John Bull's Other Island*, both play and preface, albeit of a kind the natives did not know.

In 1880 Wilde had written his first play: *Vera, or The Nihilists*. The American actor-manageress Marie Prescott put it on in New York in August 1883 and it was a total failure. But of interest is Wilde's own attitude to what was currently the red-hot subject of nihilism. He wrote to Marie Prescott:

> ... I have tried to express within the limits of art that Titan cry of the peoples for liberty, which in the Europe of our day is threatening thrones, and making governments unstable from Spain to Russia and from north to southern seas. It deals with no theories of government, but with men and women simply; and modern nihilistic Russia ... is merely the fiery and fervent background in front of which the persons of my dream live and love.[27]

Vera must be set aside as a work of art: but it has a curiosity value as evidence of Wilde's interest, in his twenties, in political heterodoxy, going hand in hand with his rebellion against artistic orthodoxy. We may even see in this interest in nihilism (or anarchy) a pointer towards the remarkable essay he was to publish in February 1891, 'The Soul of Man Under Socialism'. This is the text, some fourteen-thousand words, which entitles Wilde to consideration as a serious political thinker, whether it be in the context of socialism, anarchy or individualism. At time of publication, the Tory *Spectator* commentated: 'The article, if serious, would be thoroughly unhealthy, but it leaves on us the impression of being written merely to startle and to excite talk.' According to Robert Ross it was suggested by an address on Fabian socialism given some months before by Bernard Shaw at which Wilde spoke.[28] Possibly because of the unlikely authorship, it was to attain widespread circulation: when in 1908 Robert Ross was honoured at a dinner on the occasion of the first collected edition of Wilde's writings, he could inform the audience that there were Chinese and Russian translations of 'The Soul of Man Under Socialism', on sale in the bazaars of Nijni Novgorod.[29] Eight years later, in the course of defending Wilde against an attack by Alfred Douglas in his *Oscar Wilde and Myself* (1914), the German critic Ernst Bendz wrote: 'I fancy there is just a chance that, when all the unexhilarating lucubrations of a hundred well-meaning Sidney Webbs are long dead and forgotten, 'The Soul of Man' will still be remembered and read, not for its magic of words only, but because, after another century or two has completed its course, poor incorrigible humanity will still be as hopefully yearning for and struggling towards those fortunate shores that Wilde has presented to us with intuitive and ideal truth.'[30] This, I believe, has been so far the best-formulated emotional reaction to 'The Soul of Man'. A doctrinaire socialist reaction may be found in a letter written by the inferior American novelist Upton Sinclair to Frank Harris about the latter's biography of Wilde: 'There is an essay of Wilde's which is extensively circulated in pamphlet form – 'The Soul of Man Under Socialism'. You do not mention it. We ought to know about it. Was it a youthful aberration? It is so utterly out of key with the rest of his early work. I, of course, would like to believe that it was an expression of his true self, before leisure-class society corrupted him.'[31] This seems to me a cogent testimony to the conviction communicated in Wilde's essay, its fundamental gravity.

But 'The Soul of Man Under Socialism' may be viewed at its most significant from the points of view of both aesthetics and politics when we consider its importance for another great Dubliner, James Joyce, an importance carefully documentd by Dominic Manganiello.[32] 'If the only indication Joyce ever gave of a political outlook was with reference to Tucker,[33] he found the most complete expression of the anarchistic ideal for artists in Oscar Wilde's "The Soul of Man Under Socialism".'[34] In 1909 Joyce considered Wilde's essay sufficiently important to warrant translation into Italian.[35] As Professor Manganiello suggests, 'It may be argued that Wilde is speaking of socialism, not anarchism, but as Hesketh Pearson points out, Wilde's whole trend of thought was antagonistic to the Webb-Shavian deification of the State.'[36] Wilde is recorded as having in the 1890s in Paris declared himself to be an anarchist.[37] There is then the famous passage in *De Profundis*: 'I hope to live long enough, and to produce work of such a character that I will be able at the end of my days to say "Yes. This is just where the artistic life leads a man". Two of the most perfect lives I have come across in my own experience are the lives of Verlaine and of Prince Kropotkin: both of them men who passed years in prison; the first, the one Christian poet since Dante; the other a man with the soul of the beautiful white Christ that seems coming out of Russia.'[38] Wilde certainly had known Verlaine,[39] and 'in my own experience' suggests that he had known Kropotkin, possibly through William Morris, who may even have introduced Kropotkin into *News from Nowhere* which was published in 1890, just before 'The Soul of Man Under Socialism'.[40] Kropotkin was to praise Morris's book as 'perhaps the most thoroughly and deeply anarchistic conception of future society that has ever been written'.[41] But 'Kropotkin viewed anarchism as a species of socialism and he, along with Bakunin and Proudhon, considered himself a socialist'.[42] The fact that Wilde's essay followed so closely after Morris's book does not mean that we need entertain the possibility, given striking similarities in content, that Wilde dashed off his essay post-haste; almost certainly he would have read Morris's fantasy when it appeared earlier in serial form in *The Commonweal*, the weekly journal of the Socialist League which Morris had helped to found in 1884 after leaving the Social Democratic Foundations.[43] But if there are similarities in thought between *News from Nowhere* and Wilde's essay, it must not be forgotten that Morris's book is a utopian romance in form, while Wilde encapsules his reflections on socialism in the essay form as he had himself individualized it: conversational though elaborately mannered, epigrammatic and ironic. A few instances will suffice to illustrate Wilde's method. Having considered the evils of the system as it stands and the efforts by humanitarians to alleviate them, he concludes, 'Charity creates a multitude of sins.'[44] In a catherine-wheel of pseudo paradoxes he demolishes received opinion of the unprivileged:

> The virtues of the poor may be readily admitted and are much to be regretted ... the best among the poor are never grateful. They are ungrateful, discontented, disobedient and rebellious. They are quite right to be so... Disobedience, in the eyes of anyone who has read history, is man's original virtue... As for the virtuous poor, one can pity them, of course, but one cannot possibly admire them.[45]

And so in a tone of voice easily recognizable as the tone used by Lord Henry Wotton in *The Picture of Dorian Gray* just about the same time, and to be used in the next four years by Lord Darlington in *Lady Windermere's Fan*, by Lord Illingworth in *A Woman of No Importance*, by Lord Goring in *An Ideal Husband*, and by Algernon Moncrieff in *The Importance of Being Earnest*, Wilde arrives at his devastating conclusion about the 'virtuous' poor:

> They have made private terms with the enemy and sold their birthright for very bad pottage. They must also be extraordinarily stupid. I can quite understand a man accepting laws that protect private property, and admit of its accumulation, as long as he himself is able under these conditions to realize some form of beautiful and harmonious life. But it is almost incredible to me how a man whose life is marred and made hideous by such laws can possibly acquiesce in their continuance.[46]

Wilde is working up, enlisting on the way the precepts of Christ, often perhaps interpreted idiosyncratically, towards his notion of individualism. And it is to be attained through socialism. 'As a natural result the state must give up all idea of government.'[47] Wilde's description of the forms of despotism and his general exposition of the necessity for non-government probably influenced Joyce.[48] Wilde distinguished three kinds of 'despot': 'the Prince' who tyrannizes over the body, 'the Pope' who tyrannizes over [the] soul, and 'the People' that tyrannizes over body and soul alike. 'Wilde made explicit what is only implicit in Joyce.'[49]

Wilde's essay concludes with a utopian vision:

> The new individualism, for whose service socialism, whether it wills or not, is working, will be perfect harmony. It will be what the Greeks sought for, but could not, except in thought, realise completely because they had slaves, and fed them; it will be what the Renaissance sought for, but could not realize com-

pletely except in Art, because they had slaves and starved them. It will be complete, and through it each man will attain to his perfection. The new Individualism is the new Hellenism.[50]

'The Soul of Man Under Socialism' was not, of course, the 'youthful aberration' supposed by Upton Sinclair: Wilde was just past thirty-six when he wrote it.
But it does seem initially an unlikely work coming from him. It is only when reading passages such as those quoted above about the 'virtuous' poor, 'anarchic' statements even today, in the West or anywhere else, that one realizes how much of the
wit in the four West End comedies is 'anarchic'. Those exquisite young noblemen
(all of course projections of Wilde himself) do represent a threat to the *status quo*:
they are anarchists in that laughingly they postulate overturning the values of the
polite society in which they move.

In February 1893 *Salomé* appeared, simultaneously in Wilde's original French
and in the English version by Lord Alfred Douglas. This 'Tragedy in One Act' is written, as Professor Kevin Sullivan has pointed out, in 'that curious jewelled style, vivid
and obscure at once, full of argot and archaisms ... which characterized the 'poiso-
nous book' (the *A Rebours* of J.K. Huysmans) that so fascinated Dorian Gray.[51] The
importance of *Salomé*, apart from the fact that it was to provide a libretto for an
opera by Richard Strauss (in 1905), may have been sociological rather than literary
or dramatic: the Lord Chamberlain refused it a performing licence and further high-
lighted the absurdity of British theatrical censorship.[52] It can only have been
coincidence that fourteen years later another Dublin dramatist, John Millington
Synge, should have spoken so disparagingly about Huysmans.

III

For their first season in May 1899 the Irish Literary Theatre gave W.B. Yeats's *The
Countess Cathleen* and Martyn's *The Heather Field*. By a curious coincidence, in
Ireland at that stage, only the Catholic landowner Martyn (1859–1924) and the
Catholic undergraduate James Joyce, who would publish an article the following
year on Ibsen's last play, *When We Dead Awake*, in the prestigious *Fortnightly Review*,
were declared Ibsenites. In October 1901, on the occasion of the Irish Literary
Theatre's third and last season, which presented Yeats's and George Moore's
Diarmuid and Grania and Douglas Hyde's one-act *Casadh an tSúgáin*, Joyce wrote an
article, published in pamphlet form, 'The Day of the Rabblement', in which he
denounced the Irish Literary Theatre as 'the property of the rabblement of the most
belated race in Europe'.[53] He considered the programme a surrender to 'the
trolls', almost a direct insult to 'the old master who is dying in Christiania'.[54] The
three giants of the Abbey Theatre's first quarter century, Yeats, Synge and O'Casey,
were to be unaffected in their practice by 'the old master'.[55] Synge, indeed, is

openly hostile to Ibsen. This is on the evidence of two Prefaces, the first to *The Playboy of the Western World* dated 21 January 1907 (just before the play's first production) and the second to *The Tinker's Wedding*, dated 2 December 1907. (This play however was written originally 'about the time I was working at *Riders to the Sea* and *In the Shadow of the Glen*', which would be circa 1902–03.)[56] The Preface to *The Playboy* scarcely needs quoting, but it may be possible to gloss some of its contents with a rather different emphasis than usual. In itself the Preface is a fine, resonant piece of prose, characterized though by those noble, almost hieratic, generalizations to be found unlimitedly in Yeats. The sombre rhythms of the prose may lull the sympathetic reader into acceptance of beautiful half-truths. 'It is probable that when the Elizabethan dramatist took his ink-horn and sat down to his work, he used many phrases that he had just heard, as he sat down at dinner, from his mother or his children.'[57] This romanticized picture of the Elizabethan dramatist at work is not convincing: a working dramatist like Shakespeare or Ben Jonson, not to mention roisterers like Marlowe or Greene, are unlikely to have worked in the circumstances of easy domesticity evoked by Synge. Even if they did, there is no valid analogy with what Synge goes on to tell us. 'In Ireland those of us who know the people have the same privilege. When I was writing [In] *The Shadow of the Glen*, some years ago, I got more aid than any learning could have given me from a chink in the floor of the old Wicklow house where I was staying, that let me hear what was being said by the servant girls in the kitchen.'[58] This reader has no inclination to sneer at the inevitable image of Synge on his hunkers with his ear to the ground. But there is a world of difference between the putative Elizabethan after-dinner playwright and the turn-of-the-nineteenth-century eavesdropper. His next point is valid in a limited way: 'In countries where the imagination of the people, and the language they use, is rich and living, it is possible for a writer to be rich and copious in his words, and at the same time to give the reality, which is the root of all poetry, in a comprehensive and natural form.'[59] But its validity is sapped when he goes on: 'In the modern literature of towns, however, richness is found only in sonnets, or in one or two elaborate books that are far away from the profound and common interests of life. We have, on one side, Mallarmé and Huysmans producing this literature; and on the other, Ibsen and Zola dealing with reality in joyless and pallid works.'[60] That imposing phrase, 'the profound and common interests of life', means virtually nothing unless Synge is proposing the intolerable doctrine that only among peasants with a rich folk-speech can the texture of the human condition be found in its authenticity, and that there is no way in which the artist can render that texture by subtle, oblique, or glancing means. By reducing Mallarmé (the most esoteric instance in modern European poetry he could find) he is reducing the whole Symbolist movement in poetry, which of course embraced the work of his friend, mentor and senior by only six years, W.B. Yeats. Further generalizations, however high-sounding, are quite as vulnerable. 'On the stage one must have reality, and one must have joy; and that is why the intellectual modern drama has failed...'[61]

One is reluctant to say it, but only a strangely provincial or obsessed mind could conceive of Ibsen, Chekhov, Strindberg, or indeed Shaw as early as 1907, as having 'failed'. 'In a good play every speech should be as fully flavoured as a nut or an apple...'[62] To which some critics might reply that if that indisputable masterpiece *The Playboy* has a weakness, it is in its 'over-flavouring', its surplus of nuts and apples.

In the Preface to *The Tinker's Wedding,* dated some ten months later, Synge is even more intransigent about 'the intellectual modern drama'. 'We should not go to the theatre', he pronounces, 'as we go to a chemist's or a dram-shop, but as we go to a dinner where the food we need is taken with pleasure and excitement. This was nearly always so in Spain, England and France when the drama was at its richest – the infancy and decay of the drama tend to be didactic – but in these days the playhouse is too often stocked with the drugs of many seedy problems...'[63] The alert reader must ask what the problems of *Hamlet*, of the *Phèdre* of Racine, or the Cipriano of Calderón in *El Magico Prodigioso* are, if not 'seedy', if 'seedy' implies issues of good and evil and delving into the 'foul rag and bone shop of the heart'. He may also ask whether *Oedipus Rex* represents the 'decay' of Greek drama and if it be 'didactic' or not. Just how short-sighted Synge could be may be seen in a further passage: 'The drama, like the symphony, does not teach or prove anything. Analysts with their problems, and teachers with their systems, are soon as old-fashioned as the pharmacopoeia of Galen – look at Ibsen and the Germans – but the best plays of Ben Johnson and Moliére can no more go out of fashion than the blackberries on the hedges.'[64]

Even as I write, the Abbey Theatre is preparing a production of Ibsen's *A Doll's House*, now over a century old: in 1879 Ibsen achieved what was in effect the true glory of Ibsenism, 'the writing of a major serious play in simple prose, employing characters who were not Kings and Princesses, nor even Capulets and Montagues, but ordinary people called Mr and Mrs, such as might live next door'.[65]

The curious anomaly in Synge's attitude to Ibsen is that his own plays should have provoked initially audience and journalistic reactions not dissimilar from those provoked by the first London productions of Ibsen. As Mícheál Ó hAodha has pointed out, Nora in *In the Shadow of the Glen* (which outraged nationalists, including Arthur Griffith, who was widely read enough to know better, and Maud Gonne, who outside Ireland had clearly been sexually emancipated in the fullest sense) 'is a more modern woman than Ibsen's Nora in *A Doll's House*'.[66] One could go further and say that if we clear our minds of nuts, apples, blackberries and the like, Pegeen Mike in *The Playboy* is in respects as Ibsenite (or even Schopenhauerian!) as Ann Whitefield in *Man and Superman*, which preceded Synge's play by a few years. There is no question but that she makes the running, initially, in the relationship with Christy Mahon. In her father's house she is the dominant figure and, in so far as she can be in her particular circumstances, she is an emancipated woman, scorning male strictures and subservience to clerical ordinance. And in the splendid assertiveness of Synge's Deirdre (in the unfinished *Deirdre of the Sorrows*) we may find traces (they are to be found of course in the Irish original of the tale) of, of all possible heroines, Ibsen's Hedda Gabler.

'The drama, like the symphony, does not teach or prove anything.' In so far as Synge's theatre is conspicuously a-political, this statement holds true. At a time when nationalism, in varying shades of green, some dashed with socialistic red, and some with ecclesiastical purple, was very much on display in the market-place and dram-shops, in numerous short-lived periodicals and in the activities of The Gaelic Athletic Association founded in 1884, and The Gaelic League founded in 1893, Synge held aloof. So far as he was concerned, Yeats's *Cathleen Ni Houlihan* might never have been staged in 1902, the year before his own first play *In the Shadow of the Glen* ruffled nationalist susceptibilities.

IV

'The old master' does crop up in relation to Sean O'Casey, still, arguably, the greatest of the dramatists cradled by the Abbey after Synge, but, in complete contrast to him, one who did not stand aloof from contemporary movements in politics. But the acknowledgment of Ibsen occurs only when Boyle, the self-styled 'Captain' of *Juno and the Paycock* (1924), comes upon a volume of Ibsen being read by his daughter Mary: 'three stories, *The Doll's House, Ghosts,* an' *The Wild Duck* – buks only fit for chiselurs!' This Ibsen reference makes for more than an ironic joke: it is significant that Ibsen should be considered an essential part of the self-education of an ardent girl trade unionist from the slums of the Dublin of the 1920s.[67] There is more than ample documentation in the six volumes of his *Autobiography* (1939–54) and the volumes so far published of his *Letters* to establish, outside the texts of his plays, that O'Casey from an early age was a socialist-communist.[68] Jack Lindsay has singled out his resignation in October 1914 from the secretaryship of the Irish Citizen Army as a turning point: clearly, the subsequent alliance of the Army with the Irish Volunteers was something that was foreseen by O'Casey. He was committed to the working-class cause, but was not willing to take part in what was essentially a middle-class revolution, the Rising of Easter 1916.[69]

O'Casey's first three major plays, *The Shadow of a Gunman* (1923), *Juno and the Paycock* (1924) and *The Plough and the Stars* (1926), were written extraordinarily close to the periods they imaginatively portray. Even in Ireland these periods tend to be confused in the minds of younger generations. The first deals with an episode during the Black and Tan stage of the War of Independence (1919–21); the second with events during the Civil War (1922–3); while the third goes furthest back in

time, to the events of Easter Week 1916. The title of this last play refers to the flag
of the Irish Citizen Army, the labour leader James Connolly's relatively tiny army of
workers. Seán O'Faoláin has described O'Casey's early plays as 'an exactly true
statement of the Irish revolution whose flag should be, not tricolour, but the plough
and the stars of the labouring classes'. But, he continues, a labouring class did not
come to power. It was, in the event, as O'Casey recognized, a petit-bourgeois revolution, and as Seán O'Faoláin put it, 'The upshot of it was the [un]holy alliance
between Church, the new businessman, and the politicians.'[70] Whereas for O'Casey,
'My sympathies were always with the rags and tatters that sheltered the tenement –
living temples of the Holy Ghost.'.[71]

There is no overt socialist critique in *The Shadow*: beyond perhaps the implication of moral inadequacy in the poet Donal Davoren, who quotes Shelley and paraphrases Shaw, but whose conduct in the face of arrest and possible death is no better or worse than that of the pedlar Seamus Shields (who quotes Shakespeare read-
ily: perhaps poet and pedlar are aspects of two kinds of Irishman. Davoren is a sentimental socialist, Shields a superstitious and reactionary Catholic, for all his drol-
lery). *Juno*, we can see now, quite clearly embodies a critique of economic conditions and their consequences for the dignity of human beings. The heroism of 'Juno'
Boyle is patent. She is the eternal slum mother, compounded of Erda and Anna
Livia. Less patent are the incorrigible selfishness and moral coarseness of her
'Paycock' husband, for the eminently good reason that he makes us laugh. The characters in *Juno* are not ever aware, of course, that they are actors on a world stage.
But Boyle's famous curtain line, 'I'm telling you … Joxer … th' whole worl's …
in a terr … ible state o'…chassis', must be seen as more than the cliché lamentation of a drunk. Given what has gone before, the revelation of Mary Boyle's pregnancy and the puritanical reaction of Boyle (and of her brother Johnny), Johnny's
abduction by Irregulars (Anti-Treatyites) with the appalling inquiry as a prelude to
murder, 'Have you your beads?' (this, so far as I know, never disturbs Irish audiences, long conditioned to the conjunction of violence and religious devotion), and
the general disintegration of the Boyle family, that last line stands out as a ferocious
indictment of a world where human dignity counts for nothing.

The comedic characters in *The Plough* are, perhaps, more salvageable than those
in *Juno*. But the play is as much a depiction of chaos, of 'chassis'. Act II, set in a pub,
perhaps gives us the fullest index to maelstrom. Wonderful and desperately human
wrangling goes on, while outside a speaker gives us extracts from Pearse's oration
at the grave of O'Donovan Rossa and also from an article he published in *Spark*, [in]
December 1915, called 'Peace and the Gael'. O'Casey culled from it the passage in
which Pearse declares, 'The old heart of the earth needed to be warmed with the
red blood of the battle fields … Such august homage was never offered to God as
this: the homage of millions of lives given gladly for love of country.'[72] That state-

ment, since it explicitly equates death in war 'for love of country' with 'homage' to
the Almighty, is perhaps more crucial to Act II's overall significance than the
passages from the Rossa speech. The Speaker's rhetoric and the several mini-wars
of words in the pub (including that between the half-baked Marxist, the Young
Covey, and the old-style nationalist Uncle Peter) make for an ironic counterpoint:
dialogue and situation constitute O'Casey's first major pacifist statement. With
hindsight we can see that it was on the cards that O'Casey would write an out-and-
out anti-play: which he did with *The Silver Tassie* (1928). While some of the characters in *The Plough* exhibit a kind of flawed nobility under stress – Fluther Good,
Bessie Burgess – there is no nobility evident in *The Tassie* where even maternal, let
alone conjugal, love is unmasked in the fairy light of separation allowances. Part of
the harsh sadness of the physical and consequent spiritual mutilation of the hero
Harry Heegan arises from the fact that he has confronted the actuality of war and
returned to a society in which civilians, in whom the springs of imaginative imagination have long since dried, if ever they existed, are now cocooned in their private fantasies, locked in themselves, and so, by the ethic of O'Casey, humanly half-
dead, less alive in fact than Harry; who is paralysed from the waist down.[73]
Although O'Casey in *The Silver Tassie* has broadened his expositional technique (by
way of the expressionistic Act II which employs chant, repetition of catch-lines, and
other devices of the period), he maintains the method of the earlier so-called 'naturalistic plays', achieving his effects by the juxtaposition of the grave and the
farcical, the clownish and the heroic. And in all four mentioned [plays] the message
is clearly pacifist: war, of any kind, entails the destruction of the innocent and the
possible corruption of the living, and as much moral poltroonery and spiritual
meanness as it does occasional grandeur of conduct.

It is not until *The Star Turns Red* (1940) that we find O'Casey as explicitly a
propagandist of Marxist revolution. This is one of the more difficult of the later
plays since, inevitably, its reception will be coloured by the political orientations of
[its] audience, or reader. In it O'Casey strives to create a massive allegory which
embraces his thinking on the Dublin [Lockout] Strike of 1913, the 1917 Russian
Revolution and the Spanish Civil War. While at times the play is cumbersome, even
jejune, its cumulative effect is powerful, leading up to the apocalyptic climax when
the Star of Bethlehem turns red, literally, and the revolution begins just as the fatuous lord mayor and his wife are preparing for a Christmas Eve reception for local
notabilities, while somewhere off-stage the poor are being entertained to tea (dis-
pensed from a giant watering can, with another such can 'of beautiful boiling water
... to stretch out the lovely tea').[74]

Although *The Star Turns Red* is as close as any Irish dramatist ever came to an explicitly communist play, the very fact that it is set during the last hours of Christmas
Eve has immense qualificatory significance. Clearly O'Casey has a vision, however

muddled, of a synthesis between communism and Christianity. His position might be summed up as follows: basically communism is more Christian than institutional Christianity, and the message of pristine Christianity is revolutionary. The expansion of the International is the expansion of the Kingdom of God on Earth: a naïve concept, perhaps, but so far as I know O'Casey is the only dramatist in the English-speaking theatre to explore its theatrical possibilities.

I have touched on only about a third of O'Casey's dramatic output: *Red Roses for Me* (1942), for instance, might be examined as a socialist play, as indeed might *Within the Gates* (1933). But no sane reading of O'Casey can gainsay that he is of an ideological piece, while contriving to remain always different in his successive attempts to strip the comic mask he has himself imposed on apathy and the petrifaction of true feeling. Like all the greatest Irish dramatists he is concerned with authenticity of feeling: like Shaw, who had so much heart (as may be seen in *Heartbreak House* and *Saint Joan*, for instance) for all that his mind might be crackling with Schopenhauer's *The World as Will and Understanding*, and Nietzsche's *Thus Spake Zarathustra;* like Synge, caught up in his stark yet fantastic isolationist dream; like Wilde, even, of whom it might be argued that the spangled epigrams were his defensive ammunition against the kind of world he rejected in 'The Soul of Man Under Socialism'.

The two most famous Irish dramatists since the Second World War, indeed since O'Casey, have been Samuel Beckett and Brendan Behan, two very dissimilar manifestations of the Irish mind in the theatre. Beckett's *Waiting for Godot* appeared first in French in 1953 and has been followed by a numerous string of pieces for stage and radio; in both French and English originals. He who was once a nine-days' wonder, according to some, is now a classic, probing ever more minutely into the feeling of *being*, and paring away ever more scrupulously at his findings. When we grow impatient with the more extreme instances of Beckett's investigation of being, let us remember how much he has given us of pity, if not of terror, by way of plangent, almost Virgilian, shorthand dialogue, if not of the rhetorics which are the especial glory of Shaw, Synge and O'Casey. Shaw, of course, was scarcely palatable sustenance in a country that has managed only two internationally recognized philosophers, with some thousand years between them, the old Eriugena on our five-pound notes, and George Berkeley. His only heirs as a disputative dramatist have been Denis Johnston (born 1901), Conor Cruise O'Brien (born 1917) and Brian Friel (born 1929).[75] Synge's only heir of platinum quality has been the Kerry folk dramatist, George Fitzmaurice (1877–1963).[76] Fitzmaurice, though, is no trailer after Synge. His folk idiom is unmistakably his own and his imagination giddy and acerb.

Brendan Behan (1923–64) must stand or fall on the strength of *The Quare Fellow* (1954) and *The Hostage* (1958). He may be said to have been influenced by O'Casey in his commingling of clownery and pathos: both owe much to the tradition of Dion Boucicault (as indeed does Shaw in such a play as *The Devil's Disciple*). For all their palpable faults, Behan's two plays are almost frantically alive, beakers of the tears and vomit and guffaws of an outsize personality with a just barely shielded soft centre.

It is worth noting that in the living theatre, as distinct from the study and the lecture-hall, Irish dramatists may survive this century on the strength of a comparatively small body of work, if we reckon from the 1890s: *The Importance of Being Earnest,* from Wilde; *The Playboy* from Synge (and *Riders to the Sea*); *Purgatory,* and *The Words Upon the Windowpane,* from Yeats; two or three pieces from O'Casey; *Waiting for Godot* ... A respectable enough collection. But, if put beside *The Collected Poems* of Yeats, and the *Ulysses* of Joyce, and a body of fiction embracing the best of O'Flaherty, O'Faolain, and Stuart and Flann O'Brien ... Dare it be questioned that it is in the theatre that the Irish mind best expresses itself? Is it a preposterous notion to consider how our theatre might have developed had Swift written for the stage? And it may well be that the Irish are a race of actors, producing instant theatre in the process of stravaiging from the cradle to the grave.

A Worthy Quartet

(Poetry Ireland Review, Autumn 1987)

Poems 1956–1986, James Simmons. (Gallery/Bloodaxe)
The Journey and other Poems, Eavan Boland. (Carcanet/Arlen House)
At the Protestant Museum, Hugh Maxton. (Dolmen)
Letters to the Hinterland, Roy McFadden. (Dedalus)

In 1978 The Blackstaff Press published *The Selected James Simmons* with an erudite and succinct introduction by Edna Longley, which in this new book has been extended by two pages, to cover additional material: Selections from *Constantly Singing* (1980) and from *From the Irish* (1985), and five new, uncollected, poems. The last of these, and the last poem in the book, 'Explorations in the Arts', suggests that Simmons (born 1933) is moving towards more than half-acceptance of the Modernist School as developed by Pound and Eliot. 'Old Tom and Ezra' are certainly disparaged, but largely because they were 'industrial complexes' carved out to 'tower in academe': '*Entrepreneurs, they bossed/and forced fashions that gave them power/Writers like Edward Thomas, Hardy, Frost/ didn't leave industries behind them. No,/ they left a land conserved where things still grow.*'

The complexity of Simmons' present attitude to the neo-fascist aristocratic (as he sees them, if only to ruffle complacent acceptance) 'frigid crazy pair' may be indicated by the counter-compliment, '*Well they weren't pathetic./ God knows, they were both bright and energetic*'.

Frankly, Simmons' earlier reductions of the greatest of the so-called 'Modernists' whose centenaries are upon us, do not convince me in their sincerity: I sense mischief provoked by indignation in the face of uncritical admiration. But we may forget that the younger Eliot's cool response to Milton, later mitigated, was also a move against a monolithic reverence for an enthroned demi-god. To go back a decade in the canon, Simmons' redactions of Eliot and Pound affect me less than his 'John Donne' in *Judy Garland and the Cold War* (1976). When he attributes, with considerable wit, Donne's ordination to his '*faking a hot lust for the Holy Ghost!*', unlikely as it may seem, Simmons appears not to have read Donne's *Sermons*, or his other prose devotional works. Also from *Judy Garland,* we have 'For Thomas Moore', which I incline to appreciate more than when I first read it. For years I was put off

Moore by Patrick Kavanagh. Now I concur with Simmons that he wrote 'marvellous songs'. From *Judy Garland* also comes his 'Ode to Walter Allen', a splendid celebration of the departed-from-Coleraine Professor of English who was also a novelist, a poet and a critic. I met him once in a pub in Oxford with the then Secretary
to the Delegates of the Clarendon Press, Dan Davin. I cannot help feeling that Simmons, through affection, may have rendered Allen as a *persona,* a little more testily
glamourous than life.

It is well known that James Simmons is an *aficionado*, an informed one, of Jazz.
In *The Long Summer Still to Come* (1973) he celebrates his involvement with the great
exponents of jazz, with the poem 'Didn't He Ramble', dedicated to Michael Longley. Few will credit that almost all the names he cites are familiar to me. I first heard
of Count Basie from Professor Anthony Hughes when we were at the Christian
Brothers' primary school in Donore Avenue, c. 1941. Sidnet (*sic.*) Bechet was performing at *La Rose Rouge* in Paris in 1949, though I never saw him or heard him (in
person). The epigraph to the poem is by a relative of Jelly Roll Morton. Even a
'popular' poet like Simmons needs *some* annotation if he is to be savoured. Some of
the poet's best (and most poignant) work comes in his early books: *Ballad of a
Marriage* (1966).

The title-poem leads to the tough and exquisite couplet, '*no families wave, no
organs play /this long and gradual wedding day*'; and *Late but in Earnest* (1967), in which
one of the saddest poems is 'Lot's Wife', in which the biblical story is astonishingly convincing. But I must return to the last two volumes. In *Constantly Singing* he
explores, but does not exploit, the break-up of his twenty-year-old marriage:
'Meditations in Time of Divorce', if read superficially, might suggest that the husband was a bored sensualist. Read with attention, the pain of the separation is
patent and drastic, and in 'After Eden' there is a palpable generosity of spirit: '*His
last glimpse is of her standing / in faded chiffon nightwear, humble, beautiful / like a dark
harvest etching …*'

I have wondered for years whether Eavan Boland, 'schooled in London and
New York' had acquired enough Irish in TCD to translate Aogán Ó Rathaille: this in
admiration for her version of one of his poems which she called 'A Time of
Change'. A similar wonderment, magnified, besets me faced with Simmons' 'The
Old Woman of Portrush', modelled after the Middle Irish 'Old Woman of Beare',
and 'Lament for a Dead Policeman' after the the eighteenth-century Irish 'Lament
for Art O' Leary': did Simmons acquire Irish in his years at the New University of
Ulster? Whether he did or not, these are, to my eye and ear, magnificent poems. I
have to quote, as it is written, part of the Ulster Catholic policeman's Protestant
Widow's lament:

> *My dearest honey,*
> *at our home tonight*
> *what can I answer*

Francis and wee Tom
when they ask for Daddy?
I wiped the blood
from our front door
with lukewarm water
and Fairy Liquid.
Your gore I swabbed,
darling, as you would
have done, my true one.

This is not, of course, translation, but it exposes for our appreciation, in my case tremulous, an astonishing gift for the fruitful adaptation of classic models.

I have come full circle. There is much in the work of James Simmons that is whimsical, small-boyish, arch, even when he is treating sexual matters, as there is much that is gravely humorous, adult, compassionate. But it seems to me that his work since 1980 as represented here is profoundly serious. If he continues in, say, the mood of 'Exploration in the Arts', or rather explores its crevices and niches, the time will have passed when Simmons is regarded by some as an ageing *enfant terrible*; the dazzle is becoming a sustained and impassioned glow.

Eavan Boland has produced her fifth book of verse at the age of forty-two. Child of an international diplomat and a painter who studied the Post Expressionists, she is quoted by Brendan Kennelly as having announced (not later than 1978) that she carries 'an aversion to the whole of British culture'. From six to twelve she was educated by London nuns which, maybe, accounts for her aversion, not strongly noticeable in her verse. I cannot find offhand references to British painters; in her book *Nightfeed* (1982) there are poems involving Van Eyck, Ingres, Degas and Renoir.

In *The Journey,* Boland is at her most mature and least affectedly winsome to-date. From the beginning the book is sterling, from her memories of herself aged nine intruding into her mother's London studio, to her bitter lunge at Pearse's 'Mise Eire', to her Chardin model '*edged in reflected light / `hardened by / the need to be ordinary*', and to much more. From the varied imaginative opulence, I recall on the spot her perception of '*the oral song / avid as superstition / layered like an amber in / the wreck of language / and the remnants of a nation*', of her schoolgirl reading of the Sixth Book of the *Aeneid*, '*the Styx, the* damned, *the pity and / the improvised poetic of imprisoned meanings*', and how she interpreted a drawing by Renoir called 'Girlhood'. All the poems so far mentioned occur in Part 1 of *The Journey,* which is the title of the 24-quatrain poem that opens Part II. *Aeneid* VI (clearly a favoured Boland text) provides the epigraph for this almost surreal nighmare in which Sappho conducts the poet to the Underworld. 'The Journey' has its 'Envoi'. I take it the muse of 'Envoi' is expected to illuminate the apocryphal: '*If she will not bless the ordinary / if she will not sanctify the common / then here I am and here I stay and then am I / the most miserable of women.'*

The Journey ends with 'The Glass King', from the story of the exquisite lunatic King of France, Charles VI, and his placid wife in 1385, Isabella of Bavaria. It and its predecessor, 'The Woman Takes Her Revenge on the Moon' remind me just a little (which may shock E.B.) of Edith Sitwell at the peak of her pre-religious period. The weakest poems in the *The Journey* seem to be 'An Irish Childhood in England: 1951', and 'Fond Memory'. I do not question their authenticity. I do question the success of their re-creation of thirty-year-old experience. But the failures on the journey are insignificant compared to the luminous successes.

'Hugh Maxton' is also W.J. McCormack, literary historian and biographer of J. Sheridan Le Fanu. He is forty this year. The 'Protestant Museum' of the title of his latest book of verse is the Lutheran museum in Budapest, where he spent a winter in 1983. As we have seen from his six other slim volumes, Maxton's verse tends to be almost dogmatically terse and tense. But this does not mean that it is also numb emotionally. Read, or sipped, with care, Maxton's little book (dedicated to John Montague) has a flavour of Kafka. I find the Czech in the title-poem, but also in 'Mount Nebo' and 'Epitaph for J.K.'. As I read him, Maxton links the Insurrection of 1798 (in 'Mount Nebo') with the abortive Hungarian revolution of 1956. In Gorey in '98, Captain John Hunter Gowan *'captain in the yeomanry / hunter of men from the law / tables a bowl of punch / and stirs with the accusing / finger a gift for his girls'*. In 'At the Protestant Museum' the second last orison is: *'Pray for the soul of Hunter Gowan who a week prior to the late insurrection cut with his sword the finger off a papish to whisk his punch, as true huntsmen do with the fox's brush'*. The conclusion of the poem is unostentatiously heretical where orthodox Christians are concerned: *'Pray for the soul of Christ in whom all things begin'*. 'J.K.', who died in 1975, was, it seems, Maxton's uncle: the elegy *'prompted by John Byrne / of Glenealy'* is of formidable strength and pathos, almost in defiance of Maxton's deliberate low key. His epigraphs, by the way, are from Nietzsche, MacNeice, Dante (translated by Seamus Heaney), and Theodor Adorno (in the original German).

The Belfast poet Roy McFadden will be sixty-six next November. The word 'Hinterland' of his title occurs, I estimate, in four different poems: 'The Colonel' (*'He stayed with childhood, in the hinterland'*); 'Shop Soil' (*'Headstrong chrysanthemums / Unbending merchandise / you say address a hinterland'*); 'The Girl' (*'A figure hearkening from the hinterland'*). 'Hinterland' is repeated in 'The Astoria', the last poem in the book. Clearly from its five usages it carries a metaphysical, as well as a physical, connotation. And the poems that embody it are among the more successful in the book, like 'The Astoria', *'succinctly gone'*; *'In your mind / Circle and Stalls line up / To join old greenery / Vegetating in the hinterland / Where yesterday perhaps is still today.'*

Hinterland is perhaps a located area of Belfast: it is also a province of the spirit with paradoxical quintessences. McFadden's Belfast is of quite out-of-ordinary subtlety in its tones and in its people: Mr Kershaw, the Colonel, the girl whose *'alice-blue dress was stained / with the grass of that last summer'*, and whom he sees again '*after thirty years/ of burnt-out summers*', the schoolboy-fight between Kernaghan and Maginess which turns into rehearsal for the '*acts of war*', the professional poetry reader who has turned verse into a commercial commodity, his paying audience '*Drugged by the monotone/ The trudging traffic of his images/ A substitute for summer in the blood*'. McFadden's point is clear: poetry which is a substitution, rather than an illumination, a revelation, a radiance even emerging from twisted, ugly, matter, is sanative rather than comfortably consolatory. The poem I like best in the new McFadden is 'Welsh Funeral: Carnmoney', perhaps because of its last verse: '*Ambivalent citizen/ reluctant patriot/ I thought of Ballinderry in the Spring/ When Samuel Ferguson mourned Thomas Davis, and/ Quickened like leaves to his greenfinger song; / And said: Tom Davies will recruit the daffodil*'. There is a quite notable fancy in the idea of the Welsh singer enlisting the daffodil – for what?

Simmons (whose *Poems 1956–1986* has been chosen by *Poetry Ireland* for the Choice subscribers – after I had completed the present *Review* and before submitting it) seems to me to have risen to his zenith in his last two books. Perhaps foolishly, I suspect that he distrusts formal success; hence his nose-thumbing at Eliot. It will be interesting to see how he reacts to Eliot's centenary next year. Boland achieved kudos for her verse when she was barely twenty-three. Twenty years later she has justified her apparent detachment from poetic cliques and her dangerous attachment to bringing up babies. Maxton (McCormack) has published seven volumes, etiolated but increasingly passionate, despite his almost manneristic adhesion to compression and substatement. McFadden, at the moment, appears to be enjoying a winter renaissance: the fruits are palpable but flawed. In all, a quartet worthy of respect and lauds.

Acid Joy

(New Hibernia, March 1986)

Climbing the Light by Pearse Hutchinson. (Gallery Press, November 1985)

This is the poet's fifth collection in English. From the previous four collections he garnered his *Selected Poems* (1980), a book which received only a little of the serious attention it deserved. I have no qualms about quoting Douglas Sealy, when he wrote about that volume in *The Poetry Ireland Review*: 'the fifty-one poems gathered here whose wide embrace attempts to take in all sad, suffering, absurd humanity, with the exception of the tyrannical, the cruel, the bigoted, and the close-minded and the hard-hearted'. It is many years since the arbiter of Southern American elegancies, the late John Crowe Ransome, made a plea for the restoration of respect for 'substantive', as distinct from 'formal', values in poetry. In short, he wanted us to establish the gravity of a poet's material. I think that Sealy on Hutchinson had something of that in mind.

In the event (not altogether unlikely) that some people may be coming un-initiated to Hutchinson's verse, I had better say that he is the most eccentric of all the living Irish poets; eccentric as we might apply the word to the author of *The Anatomy of Melancholy* or Sir Thomas Browne, full of curious learning and esoteric locutions. His verse reflects the fact that he is a genuine polyglot. He, of course, knows Irish (in which he published a collection, *Faoístín Bhacach,* in 1968),[1] Castilian, and Catalan (from which he translated a selection of the poet Josep Carner, in 1962). He is proficient in French and Italian (I have not seen his Italian versions of Old Irish poetry with Melita Cataldi, published in 1982) and has more than a smattering of German, Dutch, Swedish and Portuguese (from a medieval dialect of the latter he has translated *Friend Songs,*[2] in 1970).

Hutchinson's obsession with the reality of words and the human history they encapsule, reminds me of Gautier's famous (and arrogant) pronouncement, 'I am a man for whom the external world exists.' For Hutchinson, all words, in whatever language, but more intensely in minority tongues like Irish and Catalan, *exist.*[3]

In that context a key poem in the new book is 'Dream', where the sleeper puggled (P.H., do you know that word?) with word lust, searches in Ó Donaill's

Irish-English Dictionary when he should be looking in De Bhaldraithe's *English-Irish Dictionary*, which he cannot find. The missing dictionary acquires an almost sexual significance: at least signifies the loss of some potency, creative or emotional.

Those minority tongues, Irish and Catalan, inspire pith and passion in many of the poems in the new book. 'Manifest Destiny', the best Irish verse satire since the death of Austin Clarke (and I am well aware of Paul Durcan's work in the field), owes much to the variant meanings of *póirín*: small potato, jackstone, stone-crop. The farce of Ballyporeen[6] and the Jackstone Cowboy is evoked in the harsh light of our subservience to the Great Powers, more particularly the White House:

> *But for all this glory to come to pass*
> *we must work night and day*
> *might and main*
> *to ensure*
> *that every future incumbent of the White House*
> *can, with cross-channel help,*
> *trace his glorious descent back*
> *to one or other manifest destiny village in the ould sod.*

Hutchinson's flail does not spare the mere Irish. '*It is of course just possible/ that some Chicano, Black, or Jew/ might throw a bleeding-heart spanner in the works.*' But never mind: '*the Limerick pogrom/ and the Sack of Baltimore might yield/ some helpful hints...*'

Catalonia and the Catalans, Hutchinson's first ingrained love in his thirty-five-year-old relationship with Spain, inspire several poems, notably 'She Made Her False Name Real', about Catalan repression of the Jews of Mallorca in the fourteenth century in the wake of peasant revolt against the authorities. The Jews, traditional scapegoats, were compelled to 'convert' and change their Yiddish names. '*A change of name's a trivial thing/ it only leads to centuries of bitterness*'. The poem celebrates one old woman who refused, initially, to accept disinheritance of her race and religion: 'she made the name the Christians forced upon her Jewish and real and Christian beyond their burning'. Five centuries later, Hutchinson chooses a Catalan martyr, one Ripoll, not burnt but hung, above their cardboard flames in Valencia in 1826, as '*a dogmatizing heretic and perverter of youth*'. His last words were '*I believe in God*', in Catalan.

Lest I give an impression of a superior didactic poet with linguistic and ethnological preoccupations, I must say that some of the finest poems here are deeply and personally poignant, in particular 'Miracles' and 'Findrum', which create two of the faces of love, and the long 'The Kid on the Mountain', from which the book gets its title, an autobiographical poem which has moved me more than any of its kind by an Irish poet since the canal sonnets of Kavanagh, and Clarke's 'The Loss of Strength'. A few lines might give the tone of the poem, by a poet not easily quotable since his verse owes much to what Herbert Read used call 'organic form':

> Remember at thirty-four (was that still beauty and pain?)
> crossing the Pyrenaen frontier breaking bread together,
> for the first time together in that beloved country,
> the good strong Spanish bread that needs no butter —

Climbing the Light reveals, naturally, an older Hutchinson: earlier rumbustious-ness has given way to an acid kind of joy.

Literary Erudition

(New Hibernia, May 1987)

A Letter to Peachtree and Nine Other Stories by Benedict Kiely. (Gollancz, London 1987)

Benedict Kiely will be sixty-eight next August[1]. His first book, *Counties of Contention: A Study of the Origins and Implications of the Partition of Ireland*, was published in 1945, when he was twenty-six. In 1946 he published his first novel, *Land Without Stars*, and in 1947 his study of *The Works and Days of William Carleton* (1794–1869), *Poor Scholar*. Since 1946 nine novels have appeared, of which the last two, *Proxopera* (1977) and *Nothing Happens in Carmincross* (1985), seem to me to be the most powerful and most poignant of his achievements in the form.

The first of them was dramatized by Peter Luke, but the piece was reckoned a failure when directed at The Gate by Hilton Edwards for the [Dublin] Theatre Festival of 1978. I question whether the alleged failure was so grievous: whether or no, it did not dislocate my impression of a subterranean hostility to the purity of motive inherent in *Proxopera*. That book might, quite properly, be styled a long short story. Mr Kiely's virtuosity as a short story writer emerged as late, in book form, as 1963, with the seventeen stories of *A Journey to the Seven Streams*. This was followed in 1973 by the dozen stories of *A Ball of Malt and Madame Butterfly*, and in 1978 by the ten stories of *A Cow in the House*.

It seems to me that the ten stories of *A Letter to Peachtree*, while they retain familiar Kiely chords of whimsicality, genial cynicism, tenderness for all landscapes luxuriant or arid, and a regard for his fellow humans that some (including Tom Paulin) may dismiss as sentimental, mark collectively a leap forward. He has touched the limits of obliquity.

There is the extraordinary 'Secondary Top', where the secondary schoolteacher Fineen O'Driscoll, who plays darts with the lads in the local pub, is the subject of a visitation, on moral grounds, by two officials from the Department of Education, the narrator, and his boss, Mr Dale, who is more interested in fishing in rivers, than in fishing out the peccadilloes of slightly wild schoolteachers. Indeed, neither the local police nor (which is slightly surprising) the local clergy are avid for the dislodgement of little, bright, winsome, Fineen. It is never made explicit that Fineen interferes with his pupils, but the first letter of complaint to the

Department had come from 'Worried Mother'. How the problem is resolved is humane and humorous and just a shade sad: the adult is not seldom the victim of the adolescent.

The title story, 'A Letter to Peachtree' — a street in Atlanta — is a tower of discreet strength. The narrator is an Irish-American scholar who is writing a dissertation on the fiction of the late Brinsley MacNamara (the pseudonym of John Weldon),[2] chiefly his novel *The Valley of the Squinting Windows,* which, in 1918, was burned publicly by indignant parishioners (abetted by the parish priest) of his hometown, Delvin, Co. Westmeath. But 'A Letter' is set in Dublin in 1945 or '46, after the publication of Brinsley's volume of stories, *Some Curious People,* eighteen years before his death, and there is an engaging snapshot of him in the Abbey Bar, long since extinct, and where in 1948 I first met B.K. (introduced to him by Pearse Hutchinson).

It is just possible I may have also encountered some of the newspapermen with whom the narrator travels eighty miles from Dublin to see a scandalous play by 'a French jailbird' (who could only be Jean Genet). Whatever they finally see appears to be no Genet, but the seventeenth-century John Ford's *'Tis a Pity She's a Whore.* (Does B.K. know that Austin Clarke's M.A. thesis was written on John Ford? If he does, he would surely have included an allusion in a story rich in literary references, Irish, English, and American, from Gerald Griffin to Sinclair Lewis and Sherwood Anderson.)

I have said enough, but not all, about B.K.'s easy and humorous erudition. Even at the risk of showing off, I must note also in 'Your Left Foot Is Crazy' the superb use he makes of Carleton's novel *Farndorougha, the Miser* (1839), which he read as a boy in serial form in the *Ulster Herald,* and the character Buckramback; in 'The Jeweller's Boy' the provincial journalist Eddy O'Neill's urbane discourse, to the boy of the title, on journalism as practised by O. Henry, Shaw, and Chesterton; in 'The Python' the transformation of 'three blooming American belles into three Boccaccio heroines', one of whom, Fiametta, 'talked of St Exupery and Kafka and wonders, God bless the girl's digestion, what effect Schopenhauer and Kierkegaard had on Kafka', and the evocation of the consumptive Cork poet and inventive translator from the Irish, J.J. Callanan (1795–1829).[3]

B.K.'s display of international literary erudition is not an affectation. I have laid emphasis on it because some critics have neglected it, through ignorance or quiet malice.[4]

Chapter and Verse[1]

(Krino, Spring 1987)[2]

Mr Paulin, who is thirty-eight this year and lectures in English at the University of Nottingham, became known in the Republic of Ireland not as the accomplished if deceptively prosaic poet that he is, but as the author of the first *Field Day* pamphlet, 'A New Look at the Language Question', in which he adroitly registers his distaste for the prose of the late F.S.L. Lyons, Owen Dudley Edwards, Benedict Kiely and Frank Delaney, the last-named accused of having infected 'southern Irish writers' with his 'saccharine gabbiness'. The pamphlet, published in 1983, revealed Paulin (he will not object, I believe, to being surnamed) as erudite, most serious-minded, and puritanically conscientious. I found myself reacting in a parochial Catholic way that shocked me. My first, exploratory, reading of the Introduction to Paulin's anthology of political verse also made me feel alien, unIrish, uneducated; I will try to compress my reactions to my first reading of the Introduction with my more measured reactions to it in re-reading.

Paulin initially makes a trenchant attack upon the 'close-reading' of poetry. He describes as 'Manicheans' those who 'dismiss as mere politics' everything outside the 'garden of pure perfect forms' that is Art. He makes a devastating but unconvincing attack on the 'close readers': 'The practitioner of close reading agrees with Henry Ford that history is bunk and enforces that belief with a series of fallacies ... these supposedly fallacious ways of reading literature are designed to hinder the reader who believes that there is often a relationship between art and politics, rather than a clear-cut opposition between formal garden and contingent scrap-heap.' The first poet mentioned by Paulin in his discourse on poets who write about 'political reality' is Burns, described as a 'radical republican', who nonetheless 'could combine a dedicated egalitarianism with a pride in the House of Stuart that was both personal and national'. Burns is singled out as 'one of the most notable victims of the aristocratic, hierarchical, conservative tradition which Arnold and T.S. Eliot have floated as the major cultural hegemony in these islands'. While granting that Eliot offered 'a strategic defence of Burns's verse', Paulin denounces as 'a major act of cultural desecration' Eliot's 'subversion of Milton's reputation'. Eliot, abetted by F.R. Leavis and the *Scrutiny* critics, the New Critics and 'that reactionary theologian, C.S. Lewis' (Lewis wrote about theological matters, but never,

so far as I know, claimed the status of theologian), 'was able to rewrite English literary history and almost obliterate the Protestant prophetic tradition'. Paulin,
quite trenchantly, indicates in that last sentence, his primary literary loyalty (I do
not know if it is also the basis of whatever religious belief he may hold). Immediately after he counts himself among 'those of us who still revere Milton as the
greatest English poet and the most dedicated servant of English liberty'. The first
of these judgments, while questionable (even when we take it for granted he is
excluding the dramatic verse of Shakespeare), is permissible, the second is unquestionably dubious. Paulin appears to be taking it for granted that the Church of
Rome and the Church of England are not to be considered worthy of 'English liberty'. Paulin's antagonism to the Church of England (and the Church of Rome by
extension) boils over when he writes, 'Together, Arnold and Eliot ensured that the
magic of monarchy and superstition permeated English literary criticism and education like a syrupy drug.' That phrase 'the magic of monarchy and superstition', if
'papacy' were substituted for 'monarchy', would not sound strange from the mouth
of Rev. Ian Paisley. And Paulin is surely flogging a dead horse when he writes that
'in time it may be generally acknowledged that Milton is no more a non-political
writer than Joyce was – or Dante, or Virgil'. That is a smart but shallow sentence.
The 'politics' of Joyce were of a kind and quality utterly different from those of
either Dante or Virgil. Nor do I credit that anyone today even remotely acquainted
with Milton's work would maintain that it is 'non-political'.

On the third page of his Introduction, Paulin becomes decidedly more convincing. He hails *Paradise Lost* and Dryden's *Absalom and Achitophel* as 'the two greatest political poems in English' and 'works of the committed imagination'. Milton,
'the most dedicated servant of English liberty', was also 'a republican, a regicide,
the official propagandist of the English parliament', while Dryden became 'a monarchist and a Tory after the Restoration'. Paulin does not mention that Dryden became a Roman Catholic and remained one after the ascent to the throne in 1688 of
William of Orange. He says of Milton and Dryden: 'their political beliefs are fundamental to their poems and our reading is enriched by a knowledge of those
beliefs and an understanding of the social experience which helped to form them.
(I say "helped" because in the end we accede to a political position by an act of faith
– Milton's essential faith was love of liberty, Dryden's love of order)'. From Milton
and Dryden, he makes a brilliant leap to the dilemmas of poets of the last sixty
years in Eastern Europe. 'In the Western democracies it is still possible for many
readers ... to share the view ... that poets are gifted with an ability to hold themselves above history ... However, in some societies – particularly totalitarian ones
– history is a more or less inescapable condition.' He instances Zbigniew Herbert
(b.1924: five poems translated from the Polish) and Tadenz Rózewicz (b.1921: two
from the Polish) and Miroslav Holub (b.1923: one from the Polish) as exemplars of
'ironic gravity and absence of hope'. He goes on to consider the different fates of

two Russian co-evals, Mandelstam (1891–1938: four translations) and Pasternak (1890–1960: Robert Lowell's masterly translation of *Hamlet in Russia, A Soliloquy*). Mandelstam died in the Gulag, Pasternak survived the Stalinist purges but contrived to leave a body of cryptically plaintive but seemingly resigned verse. Pasternak's case brings him to an important point in his definition of what are for him political poems. They do not 'necessarily make an ideological statement. They can instead embody a general historical awareness – an observation of the rain – rather than offering a specific attitude to state affairs'. Paulin returns from the contemporary Russians to Dryden, whose *Absalom and Achitophel* he described as being, politically, 'a brilliant dirty trick, an inspired piece of black propaganda', but, aesthetically, 'a great masterpiece'. Paulin takes it for granted that the Whig leader was quite justified in opposing the accession of James Stuart, Duke of York, who happened to be a Catholic. Somewhat abruptly, Paulin leaps forward again: some instances of Yeats's political stratagems are given. The couplet '*Did that play of mine send out / Certain men the English shot?*', from 'The Man and the Echo' in *Last Poems* (1936–39), Paulin takes as a confession of 'the poet's impurity, his responsibility for political violence'. The poem 'Easter 1916', dated 25 September 1916, was privately printed in 1917 for some of Yeats's friends. It was not published commercially until 1921 in the volume *Michael Robartes and the Dancer*. Conor Cruise O'Brien, in his by no means fulsome essay, 'Passion and Cunning: Politics of Yeats' (in A. Norman Jeffares and K.G.W. Cross [eds], *In Excited Reverie* [1965]), has one magnanimous statement to make: 'By the time when "Easter 1916" and "The Rose Tree" were published, in the autumn of 1920, the pot had boiled over. The Black and Tan terror was now at its height throughout Ireland. To publish these poems in this context was a political act and a bold one: probably the boldest of Yeats's career.'

But Paulin is not prepared to accept the boldness of Yeats's act. He even suggests that the Labour-orientated *New Statesman* was the *safest* outlet for 'Easter 1916', since the magazine was engaged in a campaign against the British government's campaign of 'official terrorism'. 'A statement which might have isolated and exposed Yeats in the autumn of 1916 now helped to consolidate links between British socialists and Irish nationalists.' If so, the links were frail an short-lived. Paulin castigates Yeats's 'self-confessed circus-act which appears to have fooled many spectators into believing the poet was somehow above the vulgarities of politics'. And he 'would guess that Samuel Beckett had the great ringmaster in mind when he created Pozzo in *Waiting for Godot*'. Paulin, clearly, has little more affection for Yeats than he has for Eliot, although he includes eight poems, as against an extract from Eliot's 'Little Gidding' (Section III). Ezra Pound, the friend of Yeats and Eliot, and quite definitely a luminous poet despite his crack-brained Fascism, has not even a reference in Paulin's anthology.

Paulin, with what never appears to be ostentatious erudition, sketches the seven traditions he adjudges to have contributed to the history of political verse in English. Thus one wonders why the publishers did not demur when the editor included translations from Irish (*Fear Dorcha Ó Mealláin*, translated by Thomas Kinsella and Egan O'Rahilly – why the anglicization of the second Gaelic poet's name? – translated by Eavan Boland and by Frank O'Connor); Italian (Dante's portrait of Ugolino in the *Inferno*, translated by Seamus Heaney); German (Goethe and Heine, translated by Paulin; Brecht, translated by an unknown; Enzenburger, b.1929, translated by Michael Hamburger); Polish (I have referred to these translations above); Russian (apart from those already mentioned, two women poets Tsvetayeva and Anna Akhmatova and the suicide Mayakovsky, all translated by Paulin); Spanish (Neruda, translation of the Chilean master by the American poet Robert Bly); French (André Chénier, translated by Paulin, and Rimbaud translated by the late Robert Lowell).

The seven traditions receive tell-tale spatial treatment. The 'Popular' gets less than three pages; the 'Monarchist' less than five', the 'Puritan-Republican' twelve; the 'Irish' a little more than three; the 'Scottish' three; the 'American' a little more than three; the 'Anti-Political' two pages. About 'The Popular Tradition' Paulin has some surprising comments. 'It shapes itself in anonymous ballads, popular songs, broadsheets, nursery rhymes like *Gunpowder Plot Day*' and – this I find engaging – 'its visceral energies can be felt in both Kipling and Yeats'. How visceral? 'This rich proletarian tradition looks to the prelapsarian Adam and Eve as ideal images of a just society...' In the sixteen-forties the Leveller, John Lilburne, the ascribed author of *Vox Plebis* wrote, 'For as God created every man free in Adam: so by nature are all alike freemen born.' Paulin traces 'the image of free Adam', with a side-kick at Episcopalians – why not Roman Catholics? – who regard such an image 'pejoratively', through Milton and Marvell to Arthur Hugh Clough (1819–61). Paulin very justly hails 'The Fallen Elm', 'a bitter and tender elegy' by John Clare (1793–1864) 'which seems to rise up from a vast, anonymous historical experience'. Paulin links Clare's elegy with the activities of an organization few Irishmen will have heard of, the United English, who like the United Irishmen looked to French Republican aid 'to free this Contray'. The oath of the United English has been recorded in the spelling of an Irish accent. Paulin unexpectedly introduces Browning's 'The Lost Leader', in which the 'lithe dactylic rhythms are shared by many Irish rebel songs'. The Lost Leader, of course, was William Wordsworth who accepted the laureateship in April 1843. The speaker of the poem sees the acceptance as a betrayal of the working-classes. Paulin might have made the point that the first line, 'Just for a handful of silver he left us', links Wordsworth with Judas and those he 'left' with the disciples of Christ.

After Browning, Paulin finds that 'the popular verse' tradition in political poetry weakened, until now the tradition is best represented by 'pop' poet John Cooper Clarke (b.1948) and the younger West Indian (Paulin or his researchers fail to say from which island), Linton Kwesi Johnson (b. 1952). At the end of 'The Popular Tradition', Paulin is severe about Ted Hughes (who compiled a magnificent if methodically eccentric anthology, *The Rattle Bag*, with Seamus Heaney, Paulin's fellow *Field Day* director). He writes, 'The student of Ted Hughes's poetry will notice that it draws strongly on a popular vernacular, but his recent acceptance of the laureateship suggests that he has been co-opted by the rival monarchist tradition.' Goodness gracious me. Paulin stops short of accusing Hughes of leaving 'us' for a handful of silver. In 'The Monarchist Tradition', Paulin hails Spenser as a 'Protestant prophet' and alleges that his 'mystic patriotism, belief in social hierarchy and reverence for institutions 'sprung out from English race', which characterize monarchism' (and which also characterize *The Faerie Queene*) are not his true colouring. In looking forward to the 'new Hierusalem' and identifying the English as God's 'chosen people' he is anticipating the 'radical Protestant beliefs' held later by Milton. Paulin reminds us that Milton believed 'our sage and serious poet Spenser' to have been fully committed to the puritan cause. It is many years since I heard the UCD specialist in Langland, the late Father T.P. Dunning, describe (off the platform) Spenser as 'a cur'. I confess to having been shocked, but Paulin's brief account of Spenser might lead many to think of him as an Elizabethan time-server.

Paulin cites Shakespeare's 'conservative pessimism' as belonging to 'the opposing tradition' of Spenser and Milton which we must, I suppose, call 'liberal optimism'. Paulin allows for Shakespeare's 'populist anger' in Sonnet 66, '*Tired with all these, for restful death I cry*', and includes it alongside two excerpts from *Coriolanus*, which Eliot described as Shakespeare's 'most assured artistic success', but which Paulin describes as anti-populist. Given Paulin's by now entrenched commitments to revolutionary puritanism, the fact also that he admits 'it would require a large and separate anthology to give a comprehensive account of Shakespeare's political vision', I cannot see why Paulin included any Shakespeare at all. And his description of him as 'a conservative pessimist' *pur et simple* suggests that Paulin is baiting the naive and the gullible among his readers.

Characteristically, Paulin then attempts to establish Gerard Manley Hopkins in the Monarchist Tradition. Certainly, Hopkins was loyal to Victoria as a British citizen, loyal to the Church as a member of the Society of Jesus, but I cannot grasp Paulin's contention that he saw 'the working class as occupying a fixed position in the divine social design – it is a lowly member of the body politic and leads a bestial, mindless existence, careless of the "lacklevel" or inegalitarian nature of society'. Without mentioning the fact, he returns to another convert to the Roman Church, Dryden, since *Absalom and Achitophel*, like 'Tom's Garland' of Hopkins, answers Milton's 'radical vision, his belief in the free individual conscience'. Paulin's recurring vindications of Milton as the apostle of 'the free individual conscience' suggest that 'conscience' has no function in the intellectual and spiritual lives of those born into hierarchical Churches, whether they stay in them or not.

This is a form of bigotry no more or less distasteful than Christian presumption of evil in genuine agnostics or atheists. Paulin is on more solid ground when he detects the 'paternalist strain within English conservatism' which informs Ben Jonson's 'To Penshurst', hostile to, among other things, 'mercantile capitalism and recent money'. Paulin finds 'this anarchistic disdain for *the* cash-nexus' in the opening section of Tennyson's 'Maud' and 'it is an influential strand in Yeats's social thought'. Given Paulin's declared preferences, he has a remarkably cogent passage linking Yeats with the Elizabethan-Jacobean Ben Jonson and the early and late Augustans, Dryden and Pope: like them Yeats 'has a horror of the destruction of culture by the rough beasts of egalitarianism'. We have met the phrase 'conservative pessimist' in connection with Shakespeare. It is used again in connection with the translator of Ecclesiastes in the King James Bible, and, surprisingly, in connection with Eliot's 'Little Gidding' it is used not disdainfully. In that poem he imagines a cultural consensus where the English people are at last united 'in the strife which divided them'. Charles I – the beaten, broken 'king at nightfall' – combines in Eliot's historical memory with '*one who died blind and quiet*' and that unnamed figure is the poet whose reputation Eliot did so much to maim. The regicide Milton is here allowed a ghostly presence in the canon as the ancient wounds are healed by 'Eliot's sacramental vision'. Paulin admires the poignancy of Eliot's 'salving lines' and whatever our political stance, 'it is impossible not to admire his achievement in writing this type of religious and patriotic verse'. But Eliot is still in the corner. Admiration for 'Little Gidding' 'ought not to make us collude with Eliot's displacement of the major tradition of English political verse and we must be alert to the Burkean or High Anglican conspiracy which has so distorted literary history'.

In 'The Puritan-Republican Tradition' Paulin repairs the mischief he attributes to the influence of Eliot, and he does so brilliantly and with missionary ardour. He admires the puritan imagination which reads the Bible 'in a directly personal manner' so that Psalm 114 in the Authorized Version 'is a song of freedom that exults in the litheness of a released vernacular'. For Milton, Stuart absolutism, which Jonson helped to beautify, was 'a sojourn in Egypt where a "people of strange language" oppressed God's chosen people, the English'. We are asked to consider that Milton is echoing St John in his sonnet defending his treatises on divorce. Like Cromwell, he believed in 'the free way' not 'the formal'. He is therefore opposed to 'a classic hierarchy'. Yeats in his senate speech on divorce invoked the rights of Irish Protestants 'won by the labours of Milton and other great men'. Paulin allies Shaw with Yeats in this 'resolute Anglo-Irish tradition' and might mislead those who are not Irish, and of course Irish Catholics, into believing that the Church of Ireland looks benevolently on divorce. I wish also that Paulin had given chapter for his contention that this 'resolute Anglo-Irish tradition, paradoxically finds its most complete aesthetic summation in Joyce's superbly "catholic" imagination'. What Paulin has to say about Milton's world-view is intensely interesting. Since he regards

Paradise Lost as 'the greatest poem in the English language' that is not surprising. What puzzles a non-Protestant like myself is his contention that 'Theology and politics fuse completely in the Protestant imagination and it is essential that we read Milton in that knowledge, hard as Protestant hermeneutics are to convey in an England which appears have forgotten its remarkable history.' Reading Paulin on Milton, one almost forgets the existence of Luther, Calvin, Zwingli, of all the great 'protestors' against Rome. England itself is impugned for its slackness in adherence to Miltonism. Paulin glosses the Archangel Michael's speeches in Book XII with quotations from the *Second Epistle of St Peter* and *Revelations*. Protestant frustration is attested by the closing passages of *Samson Agonistes* and the conclusion of Yeats's 'In Memory of Eva Gore-Booth and Con Markievicz'. Clearly, Paulin is Milton's Evangelist. Paulin's reverence for Milton indeed creates the illusion of him being the essential Protestant, a dangerous ploy when we remember his attachment to Cromwell, whose campaigns in Ireland may not have been quite as atrocious as they were recounted when I went to school, but whose name is still anathema to those who have heard of it (fewer these days I suspect).

It is a relief to turn from Paulin on Milton to Paulin on Andrew Marvell, whom he makes sound much more interesting. He is especially good on 'Upon Appleton House' which, in its fantasy, is anti-Roman Catholic, rather than actively propagandist for the Milton-Cromwell Second Reformation. Paulin also gives us Marvell's 'The Mower Against Gardens', which might have been written by a monarchist cavalier. Marvell's 'An Horation Ode upon Cromwell's Return from Ireland', while it certainly offers a heroic image of Cromwell, offers an almost saintly image of Charles I awaiting the axe on 'the tragic scaffold'. Paulin passes over the 'Ode' and so does not have to explain away Marvell's calm and poignant lines about Charles, which picture his exit from mortality as almost saintly:

> He nothing common did or mean
> Upon that memorable scene:
> But with his keener eye
> The axe's edge did try:
> Nor called the gods with vulgar spite
> To vindicate his helpless right,
> But bowed his comely head,
> Down, as upon a bed.

Paulin manages to include Gray's 'Elegy' *in* 'The Puritan-Republican Tradition' because of its 'compassion for the rural poor'. Such a placing strikes me as eccentric: Paulin *likes* the 'Elegy'; therefore it must be assimilated to the tradition with which he has most sympathy. Blake's 'entire canon', with 'its firm biblical foundations and Miltonic vision', is 'a member of the popular tradition'. We have now come to the point where it appears that for Paulin, 'the popular tradition' and 'the

Puritan-Republican tradition', if not synonymous, tend to dovetail. Although
Paulin has hailed Browning's indictment of Wordsworth as 'The Lost Leader', he
quotes copiously from the second version of 'The Prelude' (1850). (There is also
one extract from the original version of 1805.) Paulin's strict joy is occasionally
relaxed by the inclusion of an unexpected extract, such as the noble invocation of
the 'Genius of Burke'. However, referring to the sonnet 'Great men have been among
us', Paulin finds that Wordsworth 'presents himself sternly in the line of succession'
to those 'who called Milton friend'. From Wordsworth, Paulin passes to Clough, 'a
shamefully neglected poet who was closely interested in British, Irish, European
and American poets'. Clough was in his early thirties when radically committed in
1848, 'that year of revolutions', and 1849. Brief discussion of Clough affords Paulin
another opportunity to douse Arnold, Clough's friend. Although Clough 'later
became an embittered reactionary', Paulin, with commendable honesty, says that
'It is an ambition of this anthology to redeem Clough from the neglect which his
work has suffered', but also 'to suggest his links with Auden in a tradition of upper-
middle-class radicalism and sympathy with "the old democratic fervour" '. Paulin is
warm about the earlier Auden, although there is a pejorative note when he
describes that poet as 'crossing over' to 'the monarchist or Anglo-Catholic tradition' and makes the sweeping, almost damning, statement that 'The Puritan-
Republican tradition ends in England with the early Auden though some critics
would claim that its inheritor is Tony Harrison.' (Harrison, b. 1937 is represented
by 'On Not Being Milton'.) 'A tragic impoverishment' is how Paulin describes 'the
diminution of this tradition'. One is mildly surprised when he appends, 'so too is
the attenuation of the rival monarchist tradition'. After lack-lustre references to
Philip Larkin (1922–1985) and Geoffrey Hill (b. 1932), represented as laudatores
temporis acti, he concludes: 'Sadly, it would seem that political verse is virtually a
lost art in England now.' Clearly he is grieved that the conservative literary puritan', Donald Davie (b. 1922), joined the Church of England and supported 'the
reactionary Anglicanism' of a periodical, Poetry Nation Review, I have not seen.

When Paulin comes to 'The Irish Tradition' he is entertaining but eccentric.
Aogán Ó Rathaille is described not only as 'an adherent of the Jacobite order', but
'an exponent of a distinctive type of Irish snobbery which we can variously detect in
Wilde, Synge and Yeats'. Paulin's use of 'snobbery' is self-defeating, since it exposes
him himself to the charge of 'snobbery', a proletarian disdain for those poets who
have indicated attachment to the medieval order. However, both 'The Irish Jacobite
and the Irish rebel traditions of political verse are opposed by a populist Orange tradition which believes in hierarchy and deference – a deference to the new Williamite
order which can be combined with hostility to England.' He cites lines from the
anonymous (and admirable) ballad 'The Orange Lily' to illustrate 'that aggressive
feeling of cultural inferiority which still afflicts the loyalist imagination'. In Yeats,

Paulin finds that his magisterial aristocratic style' in his later verse 'delights in certain intent cadences drawn from the ballad traditions of both protestant and catholic
culture'. Paulin finds a formal echo of Yeats's 'The Fisherman' in Seamus Heaney's
'Casualty' from *FieldWork* (1976) and also a spiritual repossession of Yeats's concern
in 'The Fisherman' to find an audience of 'my own race'. Paulin is especially warm
about Heaney, born the year of Yeats's death, 1939. He has written the most succinct summation of Heaney's unique position among Ulster Catholic poets: 'his
warmly inclusive vision has always rejected those nets of class, religion and ethnici-
ty which Stephen Dedalus describes in *A Portrait of the Artist* ... we must also recog-
nise the manner in which Heaney's work rises out of the post-partition Ulster
Catholic community, out of a rural society which has always felt itself trapped within the modern concrete of the State of Northern Ireland'. The last sentence in this
context is important and poignant, scarcely to be grasped by professed admirers of
Heaney in the Republic who read him as an up-to-date traditional nationalist: 'To
oppose the historic legitimacy of that state (Northern Ireland) and at the same time
refuse the simplicities of traditional nationalism is to initiate certain imaginative pos-
itives and offer a gracious and level trust.' Paulin treats Paul Muldoon (b. 1951)
almost as cordially as Heaney. He posits a Northern vision 'which lies beyond a self-
regarding, emotional Irish nationalism and an equally self-regarding British complacency, and in their very different manners both Heaney and Muldoon give that possibility a strict and definite shape'. He concludes with a trenchant statement that
must have irked many good souls: 'Only nationalists, whether British or Irish, claim
monopoly of "truth".'

In 'The Scottish Tradition' Paulin maintains again that, fundamentally, Burns
was not a Jacobite, despite evidence of 'Charlie, He's My Darling' and counters that
evidence with Burns's 'The Tree of Liberty' in which the French Revolution is
hailed as the exemplar for a similar upheaval in Britain. Paulin very sensibly recognizes in Hugh MacDiarmid (1892–1978) the apparent paradox of Marxist interna-
tionalism and commitment to MacDiarmid's Scottish nationalism. He sees
MacDiarmid's 'In Memoriam James Joyce' as a brilliant indictment of 'that strain of
Anglican whimsy and antiquarian eccentricity in English culture', and he hails 'his
parody of Arnoldian judgement'. And he praises also MacDiarmid's indictment of
'that tedious moralism which is such a dominant force in English literary criticism
and which is so careless of formal beauty'. Paulin seems unaware that his own
critical standards are not devoid of 'moralism', admittedly of a lively kind. He finds
in Douglas Dunn (b. 1942), as in MacDiarmid, 'a rigorously Calvinist tendency
which expresses itself in his angry disciplined attack on Sir Walter Scott for turning *our country round upon its name/And time*' (from 'Green Breeks'). To my mind,
Dunn's poem is not absolutely anti-Scott, for it ends with the presumption of mag-
nanimity in the not-altogether *kitsch* and 'mendacious' poet-novelist: *'Be not amused,*

Scott. Go and give him thanks / He let you patronize his "lower ranks" / Go, talk to him, and tell him who you are / Face to face, at last / Scott; and kiss his scar.' Astonishingly, the proposed encounter in eternity between Scott and '*Green Breeks*' reminds me of Eliot's juxtaposition of Charles I and Milton *'folded in a single party'* in 'Little Gidding'. Paulin disposes, surprisingly, of 'The American Tradition' in political verse in about three-and-a-half pages. It strikes me that he has in this case restricted his range of choice by narrowing his definition of 'political'. He does not, incidentally, include anything by Philip Frenau, whom he describes as 'the first American political poet', but tells us that his 'George the Third's Soliloquy' is echoed in 'George III', a luminous and ironic poem by Robert Lowell (1917–77) which sees the shade of George in a modern clown of 'tragic buffoonery', Richard Nixon.

Paulin hails Whitman's free verse 'for its Jeffersonian populist confidence in republican democracy'. 'One's-Self I Sing', Paulin describes as speaking 'for the pleasure-loving side of the puritan imagination'; this statement requires considerable glossing for readers who have not been taught that 'the puritan imagination' is 'pleasure-loving'. Paulin's inclusion of Robert Frost's 'Mending Wall' is a little puzzling; but it is a political poem in the sense that the neighbour conducts his life on the basis of proverbial sayings like 'Good fences make good neighbours'. More space is given to Robinson Jeffers (who made an inexplicable appearance in John Montague's *The Faber Book of Irish Verse*, 1974) whose 'spartan conservatism' is, not surprisingly, admired by a poet and critic who believes Milton to be the greatest English poet in the classic canon, although he would flinch at the adjective 'conservative' applied to Milton. However, perhaps Jeffers's kind of conservatism is not orthodox; in 'Shine, Republic', he writes, *'The love of freedom / has been the quality of Western man'*. Later he writes, *'For the Greeks the love of beauty, for Rome of ruling, for the / present age the passionate love of discovery / But in one noble passion we are one; and Washington, Luther / Tacitus, Aeschylus, one kind of man.'* The spartan element emerges when Jeffers addresses America: *'You were not born / to prosperity, you were born to love freedom'*. Jeffers 'is a critical analyst of American freedom'. With unexpected enthusiasm Paulin salutes the American 'Jane Austen incognita', Elizabeth Bishop (1911–79), who obliquely criticizes Jeffers's analysis in her account of Trollope's visit to Washington during the Civil War. The descendant of New York State Tories, Elizabeth Bishop 'is silently amused at the vulgarities of democracy, and offended by the thuggish, gimcrack recency of the country's neoclassical capital'. Like her friend Robert Lowell, Bishop is 'a social critic who believes in original sin, not primal innocence'. But both Lowell and Bishop give way to the Blues singers – 'they are the most authentic American political poets and their work challenges the more comfortable written tradition'.

Paulin's conclusion to his Introduction is, in a sense, a self-challenge. Poems tthat adopt anti-political attitudes are essentially conservative, it may be argued, but 'such an absolutist reading usually wrongs the sacral moments of being which this type of poetry can offer'. Paulin reckons that Derek Mahon's 'A Disused Shed in Co. Wexford' has 'sacral moments of being', as does Marvell's verse and Southey's 'The Battle of Blenheim', which is both 'an anti-war ballad' and a 'humanist vision of historical suffering'. Such poems spring from a 'condition of supremely unillusioned quietism'. Beckett's characters and many Russian and East European poets occupy 'that bare drained landscape'. These Eastern European poets are not, finally, 'anti-political': 'In confronting a sealed, utterly fixed reality the East European imagination designs a form of anti-poetry or survivor's art. It proffers a basic ration of the Word, like a piece of bread and chocolate in wartime.'

I have put down my objections to Paulin's anthology and to certain of his statements in the Introduction. But although I cannot fathom his presentation of Milton as a puritan liberal humanist and his acceptance of him as a celebrator of regicide, nor his reluctant admiration of Eliot, nor indeed his quasi-fascist omission of the supposed fascist Ezra Pound (who certainly paid for his 'war-crimes'), I must record my perhaps perverse pleasure in Paulin's combination of scholarship, wilfulness, unabashed prejudice, and admirably toned prose. For the record, his most admirable critiques are of Marvell and Elizabeth Bishop. And Paulin's own three volumes of verse should be read in the chiaroscuro of his Introduction.

Notes

LETTERS TO LEO PAVIA AND JAMES AGATE

1. This letter from the fourteen-year-old John Jordan to Leo Pavia, assistant to the then famous English drama critic, James Agate, is the first published by Agate in the nine-volume series of his autobiographical diaries, *Ego* (London 1935–48), though it was not the first written by John Jordan to Agate and his assistant. James Evershed Agate (1877–1947), critic, essayist novelist and diarist, was born in Pendleton, Lancashire, near Manchester, the son of a cotton manufacturer's agent. He was regarded by some as the writer from Manchester who had conquered London in the 'man from the Provinces' manner of Arnold Bennett and J.B. Priestley (though his father, Charles, came originally from Horsham in Sussex; while his mother, Eulalie Julia Young, was a Yorkshire-woman who studied piano under a pupil of Chopin, and spoke fluent French). While still a child, Agate ran away from home to see the great actor Macready.

    From 1907 he was the theatre critic of the *Manchester Guardian*; during the First World War he was a captain in the Army Service Corps (Cavalry) in France; he wrote *Lines of Communication* in 1917, and a year later a book of essays on the theatre entitled *Buzz! Buzz!* He succeeded to a post once held by George Bernard Shaw when in 1921 he became the theatre critic for *The Saturday Review*. He wrote three novels, *Responsibility* (1919), *Blessed are the Rich* (1924), and *Gemel in London* (1928). He was the drama critic of *The Sunday Times* from 1923 to 1947, and of the BBC from 1925 to 1932. By an odd coincidence he died on the same day of June as did John Jordan, the 6th, though forty-one years earlier.

2. Published in *Ego* 7 (London 1944), pp. 306–07.
3. John Jordan was born in Dublin on 8 April 1930 (d. 6 June 1988).
4. On page 309 of *Ego* 7, Agate notes that his 'accounts' of his writing for *The Sunday Times*, *Daily Express*, *Tatler*, *Ego* 7, *Noblesse Oblige* and 'odd articles' show that in 1944 he wrote approximately 316,000 words. He calculated that from September 1921 to December 1939 he wrote a total of 5,000,000 words; and that up until the end of 1944 he wrote 6,480,000 words.

THIRD EGO LETTER

1. From *Ego* 8 (London 1947), pp. 67–8.

FOURTH EGO LETTER

1. Op. cit. pp. 92–3.
2. Noel Coward-isms.
3. Charlotte Payne-Townshend, a cousin of Edith Somerville.

SIXTH EGO LETTER

1. Home of Hilton Edwards and his partner Micheál Mac Liammóir, founding directors of the Gate Theatre.
2. Mr Jordan, of course, soon rectified this omission: he got to know the Longfords well, firstly at the Gate Theatre (which Lord Longford as a director leased from the Edwards-Mac Liammóir Company for six months of each year from 1936) and later socially and as a near neighbour. Christine, Lady Longford (*née* Trew), and her husband, Edward Arthur Henry Pakenham, 6th Earl of Longford, had their Dublin town house in Leinster Road, literally around the corner from the Jordans in Park View Avenue. It is one of this editor's regrets that as a young man he declined an invitation from John Jordan to accompany him to tea at the Longfords' home.
3. J(ames) E(vershed) Agate.

SEVENTH EGO LETTER

1. A play on dialogue from Synge's *Riders to the Sea*.
2. This is a droll and veiled reference to the fact that a greyhound stadium had been opened near the Jordan home in Harold's Cross.
3. This is quite a hilarious fancy on the part of Agate: one can hardly imagine anyone less like an 'Irish navvy' than John Jordan.

EIGHTH EGO LETTER

1. At the news of Leo Pavia's death.
2. Op. cit. pp. 243–4.

NINTH EGO LETTER

1. Op. cit. pp. 181–2
2. It appears that he must have read Agate's books in the public library, probably in Rathmines, at the bottom of Leinster Road, which is a main thoroughfare off Park View Avenue, his home.

TENTH EGO LETTER

1. *Ego 9* (London 1946), pp. 181–2.

ELEVENTH EGO LETTER

1. Op. cit. pp. 10—11.
2. Rathmines Public Library: see Endnote 2 in Ninth Ego Letter above.

TWELFTH EGO LETTER

1. Ego 9 (London 1948), p. 321.
2. John Jordan was a few weeks short of his seventeenth birthday (on 8 April) when he wrote this letter to James Agate, the last one reproduced and published in *Ego 9* (London 1948).

DUBLIN'S JOYCE

1. Hugh Kenner, *Dublin's Joyce* (London and Bloomington Indiana 1955).

JOYCE: ONE OF THE BOYS

1. Richard Ellmann, *James Joyce* (New York and Oxford 1959).
2. This date, 15 January 1941, is the date of Joyce's burial, rather than that of his death, which occurred at 2.15 a.m. on Monday, 13 January 1941. In the original publication of this review in *Hibernia*, typographical errors rendered the date of 15 January as 1951, and Fluntern was misspelt as Fluntem.

JOYCE WITHOUT FEARS: A PERSONAL JOURNEY

1. John Ryan (ed.), *A Bash in the Tunnel: James Joyce by the Irish* (Brighton and London 1970).
2. There are, also, Charles Duff's *James Joyce and the Plain Reader* (London 1932), and L.A.G. Strong's *The Sacred River* (London 1947/9).
3. Maurice Harmon (ed.), *The Celtic Master* (Dublin 1969), p. 7. This is the first scholarly book about Joyce to be published in Ireland.
4. James Joyce, *Dubliners* (Modern Library 1954), p. 9.
5. Which used to stand at Lower Great Georges' Street in Dublin.
6. Residual elements of this attitude, unfortunately, survive among some members of the staff there, as this editor recently experienced, ironically while attempting to get photocopies of some of Mr Jordan's typescripts and newspaper cuttings held by the National Library.
7. Ellsworth Mason and Richard Ellmann (eds), *The Critical Writings of James Joyce* (New York 1964), p. 228.
8. Richard Ellmann, *James Joyce* (New York 1959), p. 35.
9. *A Portrait of the Artist As a Young Man* (New York 1964).
10. In fact, up to ten years or less before John Jordan wrote this essay, the Brothers in Synge Street still remained 'Chesterbelloc', and many of them were still 'good souls with a taste for the Leather'.

11. *The Lawless Roads* (London 1947), p. 10.

12. This editor may well have been the said 'informant'.

13. James Joyce, *Ulysses*, Bodley Head edn, Fourth Impression (London 1964), pp. 142–3. (Presumably the John Lane Bodley Head of London, 4th Impression of the 1962 reset edition rather than a Random House edition.)

14. Numbers 84 and 86 St Stephen's Green.

15. See above, note 6.

16. Ed. cit. p. 189.

17. Since the death of her husband, the Earl of Longford, in 1961, Christine, Countess of Longford. Their home has been razed by building speculators. It is a regret of this editor that he did not take up an invitation from Mr Jordan in the early 1970s to accompany him to tea with Christine Longford at her home in Leinster Road.

18. Patrick Swift (1928–83) was a friend of John Jordan since their schooldays at Synge Street, CBS. He studied in Italy, and lived in Paris and London, where he edited the literary magazine *X*. He settled in the Algarve in the 1960s. Along with the poet David Wright he wrote three books on Portuguese regions. Swift painted a portrait of Patrick Kavanagh and of Jordan (see frontispiece). The IMMA at the Royal Hospital in Dublin staged a retrospective of his paintings in the early 1990s. See John Jordan's magnificent poem to Swift, 'Second Letter to P.S.', in *The Collected Poems* (Dublin 1991), pp. 51–2.

19. James Joyce, *Finnegans Wake,* 3rd edn (London 1964), p. 215.

20. There are other references such as this one among John Jordan's papers about the time in 1969 when he accepted 'an amicable settlement' from UCD, and retired from academe.

21. *Finnegans Wake* (London 1964), p. 627.

22. *Ulysses* (Bodley Head new edition, London 1962), p. 6.

23. Ibid. p. 8. Robert Martin Adams has pointed out that the epigram is based on one of Wilde's in 'The Decay of Lying'. See *Surface and Symbol* (New York 1967).

24. Ibid. p. 24.

25. See C.P. Curran, *James Joyce Remembered* (London 1968).

26. Federico Garcia Lorca, 'Somnambule Ballad', trans Stephen Spender and J.L. Gili, ed. cit., 1943. [This is as stated by Jordan.]

27. Harry Blamires, *The Bloomsday Book* (London 1966), p. 69, makes the curious error of writing 'He wanders down Grafton Street'.

28. Alas, not any longer.

29. It has changed even further since the year of which I am writing, 1947.

30. Ed. cit. p. 234.

31. Lyster died in 1922, the year of *Ulysses*.

32. I read *Axël* the following summer in H.P.R. Finberg's translation: The copy was lent to me by a lady who claimed to have been an intimate of Gogarty. I learned years later that Christine Longford had met her husband in H.P.R. Finberg's rooms at Oxford. So the wheel had come full circle to a point years before my birth.

33. 'The Circus Animals' Desertion', W.B. Yeats, *Collected Poems* (London 1961) p. 392.

34. *François Villon* (London 1945)

35. *Le Figaro Littéraire*, 2 mai 1959 (interview with Georges Adam).

LEOPOLD BLOOM: *ULYSSES*

1. The original typescript of this piece is marked at its head, *'Reader: Ronnie Walsh'*, indicating that this script was prepared by John Jordan for broadcast by RTÉ Radio. The date of composition seems to have been 1977. See, also, 'Untitled Lecture on Leopold Bloom ...', part of the John Jordan Papers held by The National Library of Ireland, Collection List No. 45, 35, 056/8 (4).

JOYCE'S TRIESTENE LIBRARY

1. Richard Ellmann, *The Consciousness of Joyce* (London 1977).

STAN WAS NO 'MUTE INGLORIOUS JOYCE'

1. George Harris Healey, *The Dublin Diary of Stanislaus Joyce* (London 1962).
2. It seems clear from this first-hand account, from other contemporaneous accounts, and even from Tuohy's portrait of a bewildered and aged John Stanislaus Joyce, that 'Pappie' Joyce suffered from the condition of alcoholism, a condition that may also have affected his celebrated son, James, which may account for the more sympathetic attitude shown by James towards his father.
3. *Sprightly Running* by John Wain (London 1962)
4. John Jordan himself, of course, *was* 'a scholarship boy' at Oxford in the fifties.

OSCAR WILDE

1. MS marked at head 'c. 1960', with a related letter signed 'Jim' on notepaper of Department of English, University College Dublin.
2. Hail Mary, full of grace.
3. Here, the MS has a gloss in the margin stating, 'Written ten years ago', i.e. c. 1950.
4. This remark, and others in the text, suggest that this piece was written to be delivered as a talk, either in public or in a radio broadcast.
5. See also, 'Life is a Limitation', following a review in *Hibernia* (26 July 1979, vol. 43, No. 29) of Rupert Hart-Davis (ed.), *The Selected Letters of Oscar Wilde* (Oxford 1979).

ONE OF THE SADDEST BOOKS EVER TO COME OUT OF IRELAND / UNTITLED ESSAY ON FLANN O'BRIEN

1. Flann O'Brien, *At Swim-Two-Birds* (London 1960).
2. Since this review by John Jordan of *At Swim-Two-Birds*, and probably because its re-publication was a success, *An Beal Bocht* was translated into English as *The Poor Mouth*, in 1964.
3. That is, as Myles na Gopaleen, aka 'Myles of the Little Horses'.

FLANN O'BRIEN: AN UNTITLED ESSAY

1. At an International Symposium on Flann O'Brien, according to another MS folio among the John Jordan Papers.
2. Brian O'Nolan, or Brian Ó Nualláin (1911–66).
3. John Jordan spent the summer of 1962 recovering from pulmonary tuberculosis in in the James Connolly Memorial Hospital, resident, as he put it himself, in 'a grianán of Noel Browne's'.
4. See Anthony Cronin, *Dead as Doornails* (Dublin 1975/Mullingar 1987); also, John Ryan, *Remembering How We Stood* (Dublin 1987). This latter reminiscence of literary life in Dublin in the fifties and sixties was inevitably dubbed by a wit in McDaid's as, 'Remembering How We Staggered'.

FOR AVILA WITH LOVE

1. This is a reference to St Teresa of Avila's status as a Doctor of the Church. It does not refer to the other Mother Teresa, of Calcutta, the Albanian nun born Gonxha Agnes Bojaxhiu (1910–97) in Skopje, who for some years was a Loreto Sister in Dublin before she went to Calcutta to help the poor there, where she founded the Missionaries of Charity. This latter Mother Teresa was beatified in October 2003.

THE IRISH NOVELISTS

1. Review, in *Studies*, of Thomas Flanagan, *The Irish Novelists (1800–1850)* (New York, London and Oxford 1959).
2. Ibid.

POETRY IRELAND

1. I am grateful to Mr David Marcus and Mr Liam Miller for information.
2. This is the editorial in the first, revived, issue of *Poetry Ireland*, Autumn 1962.

REPORT ON THOMAS KINSELLA

1. Written circa 1962–3, possibly for the Editorial Board of *Poetry Ireland*, newly formed, or else for the Department of English at University College, Dublin.
2. Nor have I read recent writing on Kinsella.
3. *Poems and Translations* (New York 1961), pp. 2–4.
4. Ibid. p. 14, ibid. p. 31.
5. The first in *Downstream* (Dublin and Oxford 1962) p. 20; the second in *P&T* [*Poems and Translations*], p. 36 and *Downstream*, p. 13; and the last in *P&T*, p. 51 and *D.* [*Downstream*], p. 22.

THREE FACES OF IRELAND

1. Money from these Bond Drives in America (de Valera himself went on fundraising drives there in 1927 and 1929) was used later by de Valera to set up *The Irish Press* newspaper company, the financial control of which by members of the de Valera family
became a controversial issue when the company collapsed in 1995 and it was revealed
that a separate *Irish Press* share-holding entity had been set up in the United States by the
time *The Irish Press* had been launched in September 1931.
2. The Irish-language monthly magazine founded in 1948 under the auspices of The
Gaelic League (Conradh na Gaeilge).
3. The trials of leading Nazi leaders of the Third Reich, conducted by the Allies after the
Second World War.
4. A topic that had begun to exercise the minds of politicians and academics in Ireland by
1962.

A TESTIMONY: SOME IRISH VERSE IN ENGLISH SINCE 1945

1. I have also excluded some fine Northern Ireland poets – John Hewitt, Roy McFadden,
Maurice James Craig – because I am less familiar with their work as a whole. I admire
particularly some early poems of McFadden.
2. My further views on Patrick Kavanagh may be found in 'Mr Kavanagh's Progress', in
Studies (Autumn 1960).
3. Pearse Hutchinson's collected translations, entitled *Done into English*, were published in
November 2003, in Dublin. His *Collected Poems* was published in Dublin in 2002.
4. Pearse Hutchinson's *Tongue Without Hands* was published in 1963.
5. Kinsella's fullest collection to-date is *Poems and Translations* (New York 1961) and Montague's is *Poisoned Lands* (London 1961). (Kinsella's *Collected Poems* 1956–94 was published by Oxford University Press in 1996; Montague's *Collected Poems* was published by
Gallery Press in October 1995.)

OFF THE BARRICADE: A NOTE ON THREE IRISH POETS

1. *Poems and Translations* has been awarded the Art Council's £250 prize for the best book
of poetry published in English during 1961 by an Irish-born writer.
2. The Dolmen Press.
3. I mean, of course, Irish poets in English, and I exclude from this generalization such
poets as Graves, MacNeice and Day-Lewis, who cut their teeth poetically out of Ireland.
4. When I reviewed *Moralities* briefly in 1960, I said I did not know what was meant in this
poem by 'thigh-scales'. This was an instance of remarkable stupidity, for I myself knew
well the 'sea-rock' and the slippery clinging weed of the coast south of Dublin. I owe
Mr Kinsella an apology.
5. This poem's title echoes the title of a 1959 French New-Wave film called *Hiroshima,
Mon Amour* directed by Alain Resnais and based on a screenplay by Marguerite Duras,
adapted from her novel of the name.

ON D.H. LAWRENCE

1. Apparently the manuscript of a talk given by John Jordan in 1960.

SEAN O'CASEY (1880–1980)

1. These dates, of course are not the birth and death dates of O'Casey, but the span covered in this essay. O'Casey's own dates are 1880–1964.

THE PASSIONATE AUTODIDACT: THE IMPORTANCE OF *LITERA SCRIPTA* FOR SEAN O'CASEY

1. *I Knock at the Door* (1939), in *Autobiographies* (2 vols, London 1963), I, 175. *Autobiographies* is hereafter cited as *A*.

2. Denis Johnston runs him close. See *The Dramatic Works of Denis Johnston* (3 vols, Gerards Cross: Colin Smythe 1977/1979).

3. *A*, II, 165. See J. Hartley Manners, *Peg o' My Heart* (New York 1912). The play was first produced in 1913.

4. *A*, I, 195–6. Cf. David Krause, ed., *The Dolmen Boucicault* (Dublin 1963), pp. 181–2.

5. Jack Lindsay, 'Sean O'Casey as a Socialist Artist', in Ronald Ailing (ed.), *Sean O'Casey Modern Judgements* (London 1969), p. 202.

6. *A*, I, 356. See John Ruskin, *The Crown of Wild Olive* (Orpington Kent 1882), pp. 90–1.

7. *A*, I, 293. Cf. Anthony Butler, 'Town Talk', *Evening Herald*, 22 July 1975.

8. *Purgatory*, in W.B. Yeats, *Collected Plays* (London 1963), p. 681.

9. Joseph Hone, *W.B. Yeats*, 1865–1939 (London 1962), p. 249.

10. Brenna Katz Clarke and Harold Ferrar, *The Dublin Drama League 1919–41* (Dublin 1979), pp. 22–31. Sean O'Casey attended, [Gabriel] Fallon estimates, about 60 percent of the Drama League's plays (p. 16).

11. Ronald Ayling & Michael J. Durkan, *Sean O'Casey: A Bibliography* (London/Basingstoke 1978), p. 7.

12. *Collected Plays*, 4 vols (London 1949–64), I, 93. Hereafter cited as *CP*.

13. *CP*, I, 96, 101, 105, 156.

14. *CP*, I, 23. *Elizabeth, or, the Exiles of Siberia*, a novel by Marie Cottin, was first published in Paris in 1806, the first Dublin edition (a translation) appearing in 1811. It went through many editions up to the 1890s. Maurice Harmon describes it as 'that kind of sentimental novel in which heroines of extraordinary virtue undergo the most unlikely hazards and are then rewarded by marriage, money, happiness and position'. See Harmon's article, 'Didja ever rade Elizabeth, or Th' Exile o' Sibayria?' in *Era*, 3 (n.d.), 34–8. The quotation is from p. 34.

15. André Boné, *William Carleton, romancier irlandais* (1794–1869) (Paris: Publications de la Sorbonne 1978), p. 129.

16. Ruth Dudley Edwards, *Patrick Pearse: The Triumph of Failure* (London 1979), p. 245.

17. For space considerations I have omitted all the one-act plays, of which there are eight extant. See Ayling and Durkan, *Sean O'Casey: A Bibliography* (Washington 1978).

18. *Within the Gates* (London 1933), p. 55
19. *CP*, III, 157–8. Cf. A, I, 355–6
20. Probably an illusion to Alfred Noyes's *Voltaire* (London 1936). Noyes, a convert to the Catholic Church, displeased the Holy Office.
21. 'The Haunted Inkbottle', in *The James Joyce Quarterly*, VIII (no. 1, Fall, 1970), p. 86. See also Christopher Murray, 'Two More Allusions in Cock-a-Doodle Dandy', in *The Sean O'Casey Review*, IV (no. 1, Fall 1977), 6–18.
22. *The Bishop's Bonfire* (London 1955), p. 53.
23. *Complete Plays with Prefaces,* 6 vols (New York 1963), III, p. 380.
24. See P.A. Sheehan, *Under the Cedars and the Stars* (Dublin 1903).
25. *The Drums of Father Ned* (London 1960), p. 34.
26. Ibid, p. 92. Cf. James Joyce, *Ulysses* (London 1962), p. 42.
27. Ibid, p. 95. Cf. T.S. Eliot, 'The Hollow Men', in *Complete Poems and Plays* (New York 1962), p. 59.
28. *Behind the Green Curtains, Figuro in the Night, The Moon Shines on Kylenamoe* (London 1961), p. 28.
29. *Figuro*, p. 99.

DUBLIN'S PROMETHUS-AUTOLYCUS

1. David Krause (ed.) *The Letters of Sean O'Casey, Vol. II, 1942–54* (London 1981).
2. An interesting aside on the matter of Kavanagh's birth-date, which for quite some time was surrounded by a fog of confusion: Kavanagh told the researcher for *Who's Who* that he was born in 1905, taking a year off his age (presumably for some egotistical notion). Because this went into print, the incorrect date of 1905 was given as his birth-date when the stone support for his 'seat' on the bank of the Grand Canal at Baggot Street, Dublin, was chiselled for the inscription. The author Sr Una Agnew reminded me of this fact recently at the centenary commemoration for the poet at the seat.

MURDER IN THE CATHEDRAL

1. This remark by John Jordan was ecumenical before ecumenism was in any way popular in Ireland. In 1949, Irish government ministers of the Costello administration refused to enter St Patrick's Cathedral for the funeral of the Irish President, Dr Douglas Hyde, who was a member of the Church of Ireland. Government ministers attending the funeral waited outside the cathedral for the Service to end, as Austin Clarke put it in his poem 'Burial of an Irish President', '... *In Government cars, hiding / Around the corner*'. See 'Austin Clarke', in this volume.

JOTTINGS ON THE USE OF THE GRAIL MOTIF IN T.S. ELIOT'S *THE WASTE LAND*

1. Jessie Laidlay Weston, *From Ritual to Romance*, Chap. VIII, 'The Medicine Man' (reprint, New York 1957), p. 108.

2. Jessie Laidlay Weston, *The Romance Cycle of Charlemagne and his Peers* (London 1905), p. 44.

3. This episodic impression may be due to Pound's editing, which is supposed to have reduced the length of the poem by half.

4. Similar criticism of modern life was heard in many quarters during the 1920s and 1930s; visual comment through the medium of the cinema is to be seen in René Clair's *Le Million* and *A nous la liberté*, Chaplin's *Modern Times*, and more recently in Jacques Tati's *Mon Uncle*.

5. The parody of Pope's *Rape of the Lock* is obvious, but perhaps we should also remember that it was a common belief that synthetic perfume was made from the urine of a horse. The truth of this belief is hard to determine, but, as a hypothesis, it has a perverse attraction and seems horribly likely.

6. The lust of the rape of Philomel mirrors that in the room. The cry of the nightingale – Jug jug jug, etc. – is very close to 'jig-jig' and may be a bourdon to the seduction episode. Of course, the nightingale always sings in Eliot's poetry when there is any suggestion of infertility, cf. 'The nightingale is singing near the Convent of the Sacred Heart'.

7. Cf. the washing of the feet in the Grail legend.

8. There is one intriguing motif that recurs throughout the poem and which is not due to the influence of Miss Weston. This is the use of the adjective 'red': (ll. 25–6) 'There is shadow under this red rock' ('Come in under the shadow of this red rock') (l. 270) Red sails (ll. 282–3) 'A gilded shell Red and gold' (l. 322) 'After the torchlight red on sweaty faces' (l. 344). But red sullen faces sneer and snarl Red is a dominant colour motif in all the extant Grail romances, but its significance is not obvious, e.g. Red Knight. It is possible that Eliot has retained a memory that those belonging to the tower of the dead in *The Aeneid* wore red, or has been influenced by the glowing red walls of the city of Dis (Dante, *Inferno*, VIII, 67), or may have remembered that Siva, god of the dead in the Veda, is called Rudia, ie. red (Miss Weston seems to have overlooked this). However, it is strange that any of these influences should be so strong when Eliot is using so much Grail or pseudo-Grail material which itself incorporates this motif. Failing any influences from Miss Weston, can we postulate another unknown or unacknowledged source? A.C.L. Browne, *Origins of the Grail Legend* (New York 1943), details a Celtic, and more particularly an Irish, source for the Grail legend, one which interprets 'red' as being the colour for death, and reveals a symbolism in the Grail legend, which would place Camelot on the border of the land of the dead (fairyland?) and would make the Grail quest a trip to fairyland. The possibility of an influence on Eliot from a Celtic source is fascinating; perhaps the mention of the red rock in the description of the house of Donn, Irish king of the dead, is fortuitous, but it is remarkable when juxtaposed with ll. 25–6 of *The Waste Land*: 'Teach Duinn dámaig, dun Congaile (House of Donn rich in hosts, fortresss of battle) Carrach rúadfáebrach ráthaigthe (Red-cornered rock of security) Ráith r′″g fri lán lir féthaigthe (Royal city on the smooth sea, coach of a boar) Fail nir, net gr′″phe grádaigthe' (Nest of a griffin of high rank) *Ir. Texte*, III, I, p. 22. The Irishness of this use of 'red' is confirmed in a note by Alfred Nutt in D. MacInnes, *Folk and Hero Tales*, pp. 475–7, where he indicates the rivalry common in Irish folk tales between the hero and a red or red-haired villain.

   The following summary of an episode from the eighth-century *Togail Bruidne Da*

Derga is also interesting: 'King Conaire is journeying to his death at the Bruiden Da Derga', 'Hostel of the Two Reds', and he sees before him three horsemen riding towards the hostel. 'Three red frocks had they, and three red mantles; three red bucklers they bore, and three red spears were in their hands, three red steads they bestrode, and three red heads of hair were on them. Red were they all, both body and hair and raiment, both steeds and men.' King Conaire says that it is a 'geis' (taboo) for him to allow the three reds to go before him 'do thig Deirg' – to the house of Red. Three times he sends his son to try to overtake them and persuade them to turn back. The boy cannot approach them nearer than a spear's length, however much he lashes his horse. At his third attempt one of the riders calls back to him: 'Weary are the horses which we ride. We ride the horses of Donn Detscorach from the elf mounds. Though we are alive we are dead' (translation by W. Stokes, *Rev. celt.* XXII, 1901). Chrétien de Troyes constantly uses a similar motif: In Erec the giant Mabonagrain is clad in red, in the Lancelot the seneschal of Meleagant wears red, in Yvain we find Esclados li ros, and in Percival the 'vermaus chevaliers de la forest de Quinqueroi'. The motif also occurs in *Parzival*, 181, 11f. However, in no case is the significance obvious. Elizabeth Drew (*T.S. Eliot*: The *Design of his Poetry*, Chap V [New York 1949] p. 69) has noticed Eliot's use of the motif, but seems at a loss to explain it: 'The redness of the rock remains rather baffling. May it be a reference to the Mount of Purgatory reddened by the setting sun in Canto 111 of the *Purgatorio*?' This may be so, but as Cleanth Brooks has remarked: 'May it be that Eliot has not revealed all the cards in his hand?'

9. D.E.S. Maxwell, *The Poetry of T.S. Eliot* (London 1952), states: 'Hieronymo's mad againe' stands by itself and is not, I think, in *The Spanish Tragedy*, but is an invention of Eliot's. In fact the sub-title of the original edition of the play is 'Old Hieronymo's mad againe'.

10. I must plead guilty to the same sin as Miss Weston, since I am unable to put my hand on the source. It is mentioned somewhere in '*The Use of English*', but where? Eliot's imitations and parodies seem endless, cf. 'Macaverty the Mystery Cat', based on Kipling.

Bibliography: Cleanth Brooks, 'The Waste Land: An Analysis', in B. Rajan (ed.), *T.S. Eliot* (London 1947). A.C.L. Browne, *The Origin of the Grail Legend* (New York 1943). Elizabeth Drew, *T.S.Eliot: The Design of his Poetry* (New York 1949). Northrop Frye, *T.S. Eliot* (London 1963). D.E.S. Maxwell, *The Poetry of T.S. Eliot* (London 1952). Jessie Laidlay Weston, *From Ritual to Romance* (reprint, New York 1957). Jessie Laidlay Weston, *The Romance Cycle of Charlemagne and his Peers* (London 1905).

OTHELLO

1. From the time of the Second World War onwards, the Edwards-Mac Liammóir Company normally resident at the Gate Theatre in Dublin took seasons at the Gaiety Theatre, to facilitate a residency by the other Gate Company, Longford Productions, at the home theatre in the Gate.

2. The role of Othello in this 1962 production was to have been played by the great actor-director Anew McMaster (1894–1962) until he fell ill and shortly afterwards died.

LONG DAY'S JOURNEY INTO NIGHT

1. This review was just one of five which Jordan wrote for the November 1962 issue of *Hibernia*. It was not unusual for him to cover nearly all of the plays in the annual Dublin Theatre Festival for one or more issues of *Hibernia*, for much of the 1960s and 1970s. In the December 1960 issue, for instance, he reviewed John Ervine's *The Lady of Belmont* [q.v.], Eugene O'Neill's *A Moon for the Misbegotten*, Brendan Behan's *The Hostage* [q.v.], and noticed J.M. Synge's *In the Shadow of the Glen*, as well as a play by the journalist Anthony Butler.

2. See John Jordan's pieces on Beckett in this volume, especially 'Man's Last Dignity'.

LEST WE FORGET

1. The books in question are: John Ryan's *Remembering How We Stood* (Dublin 1975); and Anthony Cronin's *Dead As Doornails* (Dublin 1976).

2. An ironic understatement: The house in question, on Leinster Road, was a Big House, as it was the townhouse in Dublin of Edward Packenham, Lord Longford, and his wife Christine, the playwright, whose theatrical company, Longford Productions, had a six-month's tenancy per year at The Gate Theatre, Dublin.

3. P[atrick] J. Bourke (1883–1932), the actor-manager, playwright and pioneer filmmaker, who was originally attached to the Queen's Theatre, was the head of the family that also ran a theatrical outfitters' shop on Dame Street near the Olympia Theatre.

4. The Catacombs were a 'warren of basement rooms beneath a Georgian house' at number 13 Fitzwilliam Place, Dublin 2, used as an 'after-hours' drinking den by the habituées of certain bars off Grafton Street, particularly McDaid's and The Bailey. Among the 'regulars' who turned up there and sometimes stayed the night were Brendan Behan, Gainor Crist (caricatured by J.P. Donleavy as 'Sebastian Dangerfield'), the poet and biographer Tony Cronin, as well as the author of *The Ginger Man*, J.P. Donleavy, the poets Pearse Hutchinson and Patrick Kavanagh, A.K. O'Donoghue ('O'Keefe' in *The Ginger Man*) and, on occasion, John Jordan and the Pike Theatre directors Alan Simpson and Carolyn Swift. The caretaker of the 'den' was a somewhat eccentric Englishman, Dickie Wyeman, whose propensity to call his male friend, an army officer, 'faithful heart' caused Brendan Behan to dub the officer 'the sacred heart'. See Michael O'Sullivan, *Brendan Behan: A Life* (Dublin 1997).

5. Séamus de Búrca (1912-), son of P.J. Bourke and nephew of Peadar Kearney. His dramatic works include an adaptation of Charles Kickham's *Knocknagow*, also the play *Thomas Davis* (1948) and *The End of Mrs Oblong* (1968). See 'A Bourke/De Búrca Double Number', *Journal of Irish Literature*, 2 & 3 (1984), which contains an interview. [Ed.]

6. Séamus de Burca, *Dear Eva*. Published by P.J. Bourke (Dublin 1977).

MORE ABOUT BRENDAN

1. Ulick O'Connor, *Brendan Behan* (London 1970).

2. Brendan Behan, *Hold Your Hour and Have Another* (London 1963).

THE QUARE FELLOW

1. *The Complete Plays of Brendan Behan*. Introduction by Alan Simpson (London 1978).

THE HAEMORRHAGE

1. Gainor Crist, an American ex-serviceman who served in the U.S. Navy, and like J.P. Donleavy (who caricatured him in an infamous Rabelaisan portrait) studied at Trinity College, Dublin, on a G.I. Bill grant, and frequented the 'literary' bars off Grafton Street, such as McDaid's and The Bailey, and frequented 'the Catacombs', a subterranean, rather louche drinking haunt in the basement of a Georgian house at Fitzwilliam Place, Dublin. He was from Dayton, Ohio, the son of a physician who accompanied Admiral Byrd to the South Pole. He left Dublin in 1951 to live in Spain with his second wife, Pamela. On a sea voyage to the Canary Islands in the mid-sixties he went on a drinking binge with the captain, took ill and died. He is buried in Santa Cruz.
2. John Jordan, *Blood and Stations* (Dublin 1976).
3. Brendan Behan and Seán O'Sullivan (the artist).
4. Pamela O'Malley, born 12 July 1929, who originally came from Limerick and was a relative of the late Donough O'Malley, the Irish Minister for Education. She was the second wife of Gainor Crist, whom she married in Gibralter. She has lived in Madrid for many years. She was imprisoned twice by the Franco regime because of her left-wing political activities and ardent espousal of trades union campaigns. A long-time teacher, she was decorated by the post-Franco government for her contribution to education in Spain. She died in Madrid on 12 February 2006.
5. The poet, who was a friend of John Jordan since their schooldays at Synge Street, CBS, Dublin, in the 1940s.
6. The then-infant son of Sebastian Ryan and 'Sammy' Sheridan Ryan, one of two Godchildren of John Jordan, the other being Catherine McFadden.
7. *The Ginger Man*, J.P. Donleavy's 1955 novel, in which the eponymous anti-hero, Sebastian Dangerfield, is 'a crude and grossly exaggerated distortion of a character allegedly based on Gainor Crist' (in John Jordan's words to the present editor).

MR KAVANAGH'S PROGRESS

1. Such an interpretation, based on faded tales of twenty years ago, has been offered recently (24 July 1960) by Mr Micheál Mac Liammóir in *The Sunday Times*.
2. Longmans (Dublin 1960).
3. Of course, the revised version from *Kitty Stobling* has become the standard version: the original version from *Nimbus* is unknown now to most people.
4. Such hard-headed, unsentimental criticism as this does not seem to have affected the friendly relations between Jordan and Kavanagh: in fact, their friendship grew considerable during the remainder of Kavanagh's lifetime (despite misleading urban legends of vehement 'slagging' in McDaid's pub).

OBITUARY FOR PATRICK KAVANAGH

1. Thursday, 30 November 1967.
2. He was knocked down by a car in a road accident in Dublin and died in St Vincent's Hospital on 6 May 1966. MacBryde, an artist from Scotland who became an *habitué* of McDaid's and other Dublin pubs, in the mid-sixties had shared a house at 136 Upper Leeson Street with Patrick Kavanagh, Frank Henry, a retired schoolteacher, and Dr Richard (Dickie) Riordan, author of *45 Days in a Greek Cooler*, who was Kavanagh's friend and physician and best man at his wedding to Katherine Barry Moloney the following year. (Cf. Antoinette Quinn, *Patrick Kavanagh: A Biography* (Dublin 2001).
3. At this time, John Jordan was a Visiting Professor of English at St John's, Newfoundland, on secondment from his post as lecturer in English at UCD.
4. Often in McDaid's pub in Harry Street.
5. Harold Wilson's Labour government in Britain.
6. A reference to the fact that Patrick Kavanagh had had his left lung removed in an operation to treat lung cancer at the Rialto Hospital (now St James's Hospital) Dublin on 31 March 1955.
7. St John's, Newfoundland.
8. The novelist and columnist Brian O'Nolan (Brian Ó Nualláin/aka Flann O'Brien), whose masterpiece, *The Third Policeman*, was not published until 1967, a year after he died of cancer in Dublin.
9. Probably a reference to Paul Durcan.

FROM A SMALL TOWNLAND IN MONAGHAN

1. Patrick Kavanagh, *The Green Fool* (London 1971). Originally published by Michael Joseph in 1938, it was the subject of a libel action by Gogarty: in the offending passage Kavanagh wrote that when visiting Gogarty's house in Ely Place he had mistaken the 'white-robed Maid' who had answered the door 'for his wife – or mistress' (cf. Antoinette Quinn, *Patrick Kavanagh, A Biography* (Dublin 2001), pp. 112–14.
2. This writer can verify that some, but not all, of his neighbours were afraid that 'he would put you in a book'.

TO KILL A MOCKINGBIRD

1. Dr Richard Riordan, one-time Registrar at The Meath Hospital, Dublin, friend and personal physician to Patrick Kavanagh.
2. They saw each other nearly every day in McDaid's pub in Harry Street or, in the last couple of years of Kavanagh's life, in The Bailey bar in Duke Street, Dublin; until John Jordan went as a Visiting Professor of English to The Memorial University, St John's, Newfoundland in summer of 1967.
3. Trinity College, Dublin, aka Dublin University.
4. University College, Dublin, a constituent college of The National University of Ireland. The so-called New Liberals in question are thought to include two professors of history,

said to be Theo Moody (TCD) and T. Desmond Williams (UCD).

5. Thomas Doyle, S.C. The solicitor was Rory O'Connor, of the firm James O'Connor and Sons, 34 Upper Ormond Quay, Dublin.

6. The authorship of this 'Profile' attack in *The Leader* on Kavanagh has never been conclusively established, but it is now thought that the diplomat-poet Valentin Iremonger (1918–91) 'had a hand in it'. Another suspect is the aforementioned historian from UCD, T. Desmond Williams. See Antoinette Quinn's *Patrick Kavanagh: A Biography* (Dublin 2001), pp. 314–16, pp. 328–9, and pp. 337–42.

7. Even as late in his life as the autumn of 1966, recalling the events of *The Leader* trial caused considerable anguish to Patrick Kavanagh, as this editor can attest. Coming upon my copy of *Envoy*, which contained a reference to the trial in a 'Diary' piece written by himself, caused the poet to fly into a rage in The Bailey bar in Dublin.

8. John Mulcahy.

9. It continued to trouble and sadden John Jordan, who knew the leading figures in the academic world in Dublin, until his own death in 1988.

SACRED KEEPER

1. John Montague confirmed recently (30 July 2004), at a talk that he gave in Inniskeen on 'Kavanagh's Dublin Circle', that he was indeed the person who edited the 1964 *Collected Poems* of Patrick Kavanagh, although he said that he himself hardly regarded that book as a proper *Collected Poems*, since Kavanagh handed in a manuscript/typescript of only 100 pages and did not include among those pages any excerpt from *The Great Hunger*. Montague also revealed that the publishers had first considered asking John Jordan to edit Kavanagh's poems, but had changed their mind when it was pointed out (by a person or persons unknown) that Kavanagh and Jordan met together regularly in McDaid's pub, and therefore secrecy as to the editing could not be maintained. Why there should be secrecy remains a mystery!

2. Much more recently, in a talk he gave at Trinity College, Dublin on 22 July 2004, the eighty-eight-year-old Dr Peter Kavanagh revisited this whole sorry ground, making reference to his role in publishing some of his brother's work. *The Irish Times* reported that he said at this talk in Trinity that he had collected 'a heap' of pages of manuscripts and typescripts, and 'revised, edited and published' what he regarded as 'the canon of Patrick Kavanagh's work'. According to this newspaper report, he claimed that Patrick's widow and legal heir, Katherine Moloney Kavanagh 'never demonstrated to me any interest in the publication of Patrick's work': Dr Kavanagh then went on to criticize her for suing him over the ownership of the copyright to her husband's work. This litigation was ruled on by the High Court in Dublin (and subsequently on appeal) in favour of Katherine Kavanagh. (See *The Irish Times*, Friday, 23 July 2004.) In a follow-up interview by Patsy McGarry in *The Irish Times* on 9 August 2004, Dr Kavanagh sweepingly dismissed the merits of virtually every Irish poet (including W.B. Yeats and Seamus Heaney) except his brother, Patrick. He again complained 'about a legal problem that means his books, which include a biography of his brother, are unavailable in Ireland'. Apparently, he did not explain the reasons why this 'legal problem' arose, or

acknowledge the legal rights of Katherine Moloney Kavanagh as Patrick's widow, and the rights as vested in the Trustees of her Estate.

HOPKINS ANNOTATED

1. Review in *Irish Independent* of Donald McChesney, *A Hopkins Commentary* (London 1969).
2. *Poems of Gerard Manley Hopkins* (Oxford 1918).
3. See also, 'Turbulent Poet', a review by John Jordan in *Hibernia*, 14 September 1978, of Paddy Kitchen, *Gerard Manley Hopkins* (London 1978).

OBLOMOV

1. As the expresssion indicates, this piece was delivered as a talk that was broadcast as part of the RTÉ series 'Rich and Strange' on 10 July 1973.

AUSTIN CLARKE

1. Patrick Kavanagh having died in 1967.
2. Where John Jordan later wrote his own fine verse, 'A Guest of the Dean's', after Clarke's *Mnemosyne Lay in Dust,* with, as it were, the shade of Dean Jonathan Swift looking over both men's shoulders.
3. Where John Jordan spent some time recovering from a minor stroke in 1986.
4. How prescient this remark, given present-day (2006) circumstances in Iraq.

THE CLARKE CANON

1. Review of G. Craig Tapping, *Austin Clarke: A Study of his Writings* (Dublin 1981). See also *Austin Clarke, Theodore de Banville, and Yeats,* in *Poetry Ireland Newsletter No. 16*, March 1980. A copy of the *Newsletter* was inscribed by John Jordan, 'For Augustine Martin, with best wishes, John Jordan'.
2. This editor can verify this statement: Mr Jordan, until illness began to affect him about 1986, had a prodigious memory which seemed, at times, almost photographic.
3. This is quite extraordinary, since it is extremely difficult for anyone born since the Second World War, to understand what precisely was deemed so objectionable in *The Sun Dances at Easter.*
4. Since this was written, another study of Clarke's writings has been done, see Maurice Harmon, *Austin Clarke: A Critical Introduction* (Dublin 1990).

THE IRISH DIMENSION

1. Joseph Ronsley (ed.), *Myth and Reality in Irish Literature* (Wilfrid Laurier University Press, USA 1978).
2. Presumably the Irish playwright and novelist, Thomas (Tom) Kilroy (b. 1934), author of *The Death and Resurrection of Mr Roche*, and *Talbot's Box*, and *The Big Chapel*.

3. A lecturer in English at UCD.

4. This name, misprinted and illegible in *Hibernia*, is clearly that of the chairperson.

KATE O'BRIEN: FIRST LADY OF IRISH LETTERS

1. 'While not a great success' is a relative term: in fact, the play could be said to have been quite reasonably successful, as its first run in London lasted three months. It gave her the confidence in her ability to become a full-time writer.

2. It also won the James Tate Black Prize that year.

3. Books were being banned in Ireland at this time for reasons that appear inexplicable, even ludicrous, today. The heroine of the title in *Mary Lavelle* is portrayed as she becomes sexually active.

4. This novel examines the spiritual development of a nun and is a subtly feminist book.

5. Since the mid-eighties seven of Kate O'Brien's works have been re-published, more recently by Virago Press of London, in their *Modern Classics* series: *Without My Cloak, Mary Lavelle, The Ante Room, That Lady, The Land of Spices, Farewell Spain, The Last of Summer.*

6. The plot of *That Lady* concerns the conflict between Aña de Mendoza and Philip II of Spain, and celebrates individual resistance to despotic power.

7. See Lorna Reynolds, *Kate O'Brien* (1987); Adele M. Dalsimer, *Kate O'Brien: A Critical Study* (Dublin 1990); and Eibhear Walshe (ed.), *Ordinary People Dancing: Essays on Kate O'Brien* (Cork 1993). Eibhear Walshe's biography, *Kate O'Brien: A Writing Life* (Irish Academic Press, Dublin), appeared in March 2006.

KATE O'BRIEN (*The Stony Thursday Book*)

1. John Jordan wrote his own tribute in the form of a short lyric verse called 'Without Her Cloak' that he published in his last slim volume, *With Whom Did I Share the Crystal?*

> The last time we met (Mild May before the year you plunged into strong waters) You said, "They were very good to me." So in walled Avila of unspeakable Térèsa I recalled you to the manager of the Hotel Jardín. It was the Feast of the Assumption. A useful cliché that same high Castilian courtesy. Fortuitously of course the argent is real. When I told him you were dead (Dead, though you walk beside me, cloaked, ribald, vulnerable) His dark mild eyes crinkled. The argent real was in his threnody: La pobre Mees Katie – twice.
>
> Vallodolid, 21 August 1977

KATE O'BRIEN (*New Hibernia*)

1. Jordan won a National University of Ireland Travelling Studentship in the autumn of 1952, and in 1953 he became a postgraduate scholar at Pembroke College, Oxford, where he chaired the Arts Committee, was President of the Johnson Society and acted with the players of the OUDS.

2. The venue for three-day 'silent' Retreats for pupils from the CBS Secondary School, Synge Street, for many years in the 1940s, 50s and 60s (as this editor recalls).

3. See 'K. O'B', in *The Stony Thursday Book 3* [q.v.].

CHATELAINE OF AN AGE

1. Daniel J. Murphy (ed.), *The Journals of Lady Gregory Vol. 1: 1916–26* (Colin Smythe, 1978).

MAN'S LAST DIGNITY

1. Samuel Beckett, *Play* (London 1964).

AMOR FATI SIVE CONTEMPTUS MUNDI

1. Out of print. But see Lloyd Frankenberg (ed.), *James Stephens: A Selection* (London 1962), pp. 163–74.
2. Cf. Dante, *Inferno,* Calderon, *El Purgatorio de San Patricio.*
3. Brian Coffey (ed.), The *Collected Poems of Denis Devlin* (Dublin 1964), p. 35.
4. Peter Kavanagh (ed.), *November Haggard* (New York 1971), p. 117.
5. J.M. Synge, *The Plays and Poems of J.M. Synge* (London 1963).
6. *Ulysses* (London 1962), p. 8.
7. Op cit. pp. 134–5.
8. *Mercier*, p. 49.
9. *Ulysses*, ed. cit. p. 393.
10. Op cit. p. 139.
11. *The Hard Life* (1961), pp. 147–8.
12. Samuel Beckett, *Murphy* (1938, 2nd ed. 1969,), p. 183.
13. Op cit. p. 187.
14. *Ulysses*, p. 8.
14. See *Mercier*, p. 56.
15. *The Plays and the Poems of J.M. Synge,* p. 37.
16. *The Aran Islands* (1907, reprinted 1961), p. 58.
17. *The Islandman*, trs. Robin Flower (1937, reprinted 1978), p. 147. In failing to take account of literature in Modern Irish, this essay is off-side.
18. *Essay in Aid of a Grammar of Assent* (1870, reprinted 1955), p. 79.

NEW POETRY

1. *Irish Independent*, 19 November 1977, p. 7.

PILGRIMAGES

1. A colleague of John Jordan's in the Department of English at UCD in the sixties.
2. So called as he was Rector of the Irish College at Salamanca, before becoming P.P. of Inniskeen, where is buried in the same graveyard as Patrick Kavanagh – near the entrance.

YOUNGER POET

1. *Door into the Dark* (London 1969). This review is the one to which John Jordan refers in his second notice of the same book in the same paper, 'Heaney Re-visited', which appeared on 26 July 1969.

HEANEY REVISITED

1. This review in the *Irish Independent* on 26 July 1969 gave the wrong book title, citing *Death of a Naturalist* as the title under review. But this piece is self-evidently a notice of Seamus Heaney's second collection, *Door into the Dark*, not of his first, *Death of a Naturalist*, which appeared three years earlier in 1966.

DEORAÍOCHT, LE PÁDRAIC Ó CONAIRE (1882–1928)

1. John Jordan (ed.), *The Pleasures of Gaelic Literature* (Cork 1977).

J'AI LU TOUS LES LIVRES

1. Guillaume-Albert-Wladimir-Alexandre-Apollinaire Kostrowitzky, was born in Rome on 26 August 1880, the 'illegitimate' son of Mlle. Olga de Kostrowitzky, a Polish adventuress of 'noble' birth, and Francesco Flugi d'Aspermont, an officer in the Bourbon army.
2. See also the review by John Jordan in *Hibernia* (November 1979) entitled 'Merde and All', of *Louis-Ferdinand Céline* by Merlin Thomas (London 1979), for comment on Céline's *Voyage au bout de la nuit.*

PERFECT THOUGHTS

1. This is a review of James R. Lawler (ed.), *Paul Valéry: An Anthology* (London 1978).

FRANCIS STUART'S SPIRITUAL JOURNEY

1. *The Irish Press* book review, 29 April 1972. *Black List, Section H*, Francis Stuart's latest novel was published [1971] by the Southern Illinois University Press at $10.00. Today, on the author's seventieth birthday, John Jordan discusses the book and its background.
2. See, *Things to Live For* (from) W. J. McCormack (ed.), *A Festschrift For Francis Stuart on His Seventieth Birthday, MCMLXXXII* (Dublin 1972) pp. 19–23.

THINGS TO LIVE FOR

1. *A Festschrift for Francis Stuart on His Seventieth Birthday, MCMLXXII.*
2. See John Jordan's poem, 'A Paella for Drivellers', in his *Collected Poems* (Dublin 1991), pp. 109–12, in which he writes: '*For my heroes are people I fear to fight for, / Jews, Sephardic*

and Ashkenazy, / Palestine refugees, disloyal Kurds, / The world's great galaxy of Nansens, / God's chosen miserable ...'

3. For a number of years immediately after the end of the Second World War, Germany was divided into four Zones occupied by the troops of the three Western allies (Britain, France and the USA) and the Soviet Union.

SMALL AND THREATENED PLACES

1. Francis Stuart, *Memorial* (London 1973).

THE PATRIOT GAME

1. William Molyneaux, *The Case of Ireland Stated* (Dublin 1977); and Jonathan Swift, *A Dialogue in Hybernian Stile & Irish Eloquence*, ed. Alan Bliss (Dublin 1977).
2. *A Dialogue ...* op. cit.
3. Aodh Mac Gabhráin (Mac Shamhradháin) (Hugh McGauran), poet and scholar, born c 1715 in Glengole, Co. Cavan. He belonged to the Ó Neachtain group of scholars. Credited also with the composition of 'Achasán an Mharcaigh', a scatological verse.
4. See, also, 'For Creeshes Sake', a review in *Hibernia*, 7 February 1980, of *Spoken English in Ireland 1600–1740* by Alan Bliss (Dublin 1980).

PAINED AND FREE

1. Peter Steele, *Jonathan Swift: Preacher and Jester* (Dublin 1979).
2. Clive T. Probyn (ed.), *The Art of Jonathan Swift* (London 1979.)

AODHAGÁN Ó RATHAILLE

1. *The Pleasures of Gaelic Poetry*, ed. Seán Mac Réamoinn (London 1982), pp. 81–91.
2. Tomás Ó Crohan, *The Islandman,* trans. Robin Flower (Dublin and London 1937).
3. John Montague (ed.), *The Faber Book of Irish Verse* (London 1974), p. 30.
4. See Seán Ó Tuama, *Filí faoi Sceimhle* (Dublin 1978), pp. 87–124, for a full discussion of Ó Rathaille, the MacCarthys and the Browns.
5. On the Bardic Schools, see Douglas Hyde, *A Literary History of Ireland*, Chapter XIX (1899, new edition, 1967).
6. *Dánta Aodhagáin Uí Rathaille*, eds P.S. Dinneen and Tadhg O'Donoghue (2nd edition, 1911), p. xxxii.
7. *An Duinníneach* (Dublin 1958), p. 318.
8. Ó Tuama, *op. cit.* p. 94.
9. Ibid. p. 95.
10. Ibid. p. 95.
11. *Dánta, op. cit.* p. 26.
12. Ibid. p. 27.
13. *Faber Book of Irish Verse*, op. cit. p. 144.

14. *Dánta, op. cit.* p. 28.
15. Ibid. p. 30.
16. *Kings, Lords and Commons* (1959), p. 102.
17. *Dánta, op. cit.* p. 31.
18. Ó Tuama, *op. cit.* p. 164.
19. *Dánta, op. cit.,* p. 22.
20. *The Dove and the Castle* (Dublin 1946), p. 174.
21. *Collected Poems* (1974), p. 229.
22. *Dánta, op. cit.* p. 21.
23. Ibid, p. 18.
24. *Dánta, op. cit.* p. 18.
25. *The Dove and the Castle.*
26. *Dánta,* p. 114.
27. *Proverbs,* 8, xxiii.
28. *Dánta, op. cit.* p. *14*
29. The Hidden Ireland, *op. cit.* p. 179
30. IV. 3. 380–3.
31. *Dánta, op. cit.* p. 116
32. *Collected Poems (*2nd edition, 1950), p. 350.
33. Cf. *Kings, Lords and Commons, op. cit.* pp. v and 109.
34. *Collected Poems, op. cit.* p. 369.

IRELAND AND THE CLASSICAL TRADITION

1. W.B. Stanford, *Ireland and the Classical Tradition* (Rowman & Littlefield, 1976; republished Dublin 1998).
2. John J. O'Meara (1915–2003), born in Eyrecourt, Co. Galway, educated at UCD and Oxford University, he trained for the priesthood and for the Jesuit Order, before being laicized. Professsor of Latin at UCD, he wrote on St Augustine, *The Young Augustine* (Dublin 1954); translated John Scottus Eriugena's *Periphyseon* (On Nature), edited a Latin version of *The Voyage of St Brendan*, and wrote an autobiographical memoir, *The Singing Masters* (The Lilliput Press, Dublin 1990).
3. UCD history don in the 1960s.
4. Anew McMaster (1894–1962), the noted actor/director, who founded a Shakespearean touring company, first in England and after the Second World War, which toured as a fit-up company in Ireland.

JAMESIAN NOVELIST

1. Review of Victoria Glendinning, *Elizabeth Bowen: Portrait of a Writer* (London 1977.)
2. Elizabeth (Dorothea Cole) Bowen (1899–1973), novelist and short story writer, author of *The Last September* (1929), *Death of the Heart* (1938), and *The Heat of the Day* (1949), was born in Dublin into a family of Welsh extraction that had settled in Cork in the seventeenth century.

TIME REDEEMED

1. Denis Donoghue, *The Sovereign Ghost: Studies in Imagination* (London 1978).
2. The noted academic literary critic, who holds the Henry James Chair of English and American Letters at New York University, was one of John Jordan's colleagues at UCD in the 1960s.

HEADY BREW

1. A. Norman Jeffares (ed.), *W.B. Yeats: The Critical Heritage* (London 1977).

CRYSTALLINE PROSE

1. Review of J.M. Synge, *In Wicklow, West Kerry and Connemara* (Dublin 1980).

FROM THE ABBEY TO ZOZIMUS

1. *Dictionary of Irish Literature*. Editor-in-Chief: Robert Hogan (Dublin 1980). A revised, expanded, two-volume second edition was published by Greenwood Press (Westport, Connecticut, USA) in January 1997.

CATEGORIZATION

1. Review in *The Irish Press* of Ronald Schleifer (ed.), *The Genres of the Irish Literary Revival* (Dublin 1981).

THE STARTLED HARE

1. *Collected Works,* five vols, ed. Arthur Friedman (Oxford 1966), I, p. 415.
2. *Works*, I, p. 447.
3. *Works,* I, p. 370.
4. Quoted by John Ginger, *The Notable Man* (London 1977), p. 122.
5. *Works,* II, p. 111.
6. *Works*, II, p. 226.
7. *Works,* II, p. 367–8
8. *Works,* III, p. 183.
9. Boswell, *Life,* ed. G.B.Hill, II, p. 232.
10. Quoted by Ginger, *op.cit.* p. 348.

GHOST WRITERS

1. Peter Tremayne (ed.), *Irish Masters of Fantasy* (Dublin 1980).
2. No longer a church, now converted to commercial purposes.

POETRY IRELAND REVIEW EDITORIALS 1, 2, 3 & 4

1. The first eight issues of the revived *Poetry Ireland* magazine in the 1980s were edited by John Jordan, from Spring 1981 to Autumn 1983.
2. The remaining thirteen contributors to the first issue of *The Poetry Ireland Review* were: Padraig J. Daly, Gerald Dawe, Peter Fallon, Maurice Farley, Sean Lucy, Hugh Mc-Fadden, Hayden Murphy, Richard Murphy, Eiléan Ní Chuilleanáin, Gearóid O'Brien, Cyril Ó Céirín, Hugh O'Donnell, and Francis Stuart.
3. To take up the post of Associate Professor of English at The Memorial University, St John's, Newfoundland.
4. One of the poets from whom John Jordan *did* solicit verses at this time was Thomas Kinsella: I was in his presence when he made a phone-call to Kinsella seeking a contribution, which came for *PIR* 3; a sequence *from* the Irish of *Anon.* seventh century/ninth to tenth century/eleventh century, entitled 'The Boyhood of Christ', 'Cold Weather', 'I Bring You News', 'Eve Am I', and 'Oisin'.
5. 'Ten Sonnet Poems', pp. 5–10.
6. Died, suddenly, aged fifty-five, on 19 June 2005.
7. See also *L'Attaque*, by Éoghan Ó Tuairisc, in *Hibernia*, May 1962, and 'The West's Awake', a review by John Jordan of *L'Attaque*, in *The Irish Press*, 21 Lunasa 1980.

BOOK REVIEWS IN *POETRY IRELAND REVIEW*

1. *Reductionist Poem* (1981). Reviewed in *PIR* 2.
2. Erasmus Darwin (1731–1802), the physician, poet, philosopher, grandfather of Charles Darwin – not Desiderius Erasmus, the Dutch humanist of early Renaissance fame.
3. *Ark of the North, We Have Kept the Faith, R.M.S. Titanic,* and *41 Sonnets.* All reviewed in *PIR* Numbers 5 & 6, double issue, pp. 63–7.
4. (1981) Mr Stuart and Mr Jordan had been friends for many years (see 'Things to Live For' – from *A Festschrift For Francis Stuart*; and 'Francis Stuart's Spiritual Odyssey' [q.v.]. John Jordan was one of the small number of guests invited by Francis Stuart to attend his marriage to the artist Finola Graham in Dublin in 1987.
5. This urban legend may have arisen because the publisher/editor of Raven Arts Press, the writer Dermot Bolger (b. 1959), was born in Finglas and seen by some middle-class journalists as a kind of 'working-class hero', though it is a moot point whether he is in fact working-class, or lower middle-class.
6. Dr Richard Riordan, one-time Medical Registrar at the Meath Hospital, Dublin, poet, friend of Patrick Kavanagh and best man at the Monaghan poet's marriage to Katherine Barry Moloney at The Church of the Three Patrons, Rathgar Road, Dublin in 1967.
7. See 'Francis Stuart's Spiritual Odyssey' (q.v.).
8. The poem by Austin Clarke that caused John Jordan to 'telephone enthusiasm' was 'The Song of the Books', which he published in the magazine *Poetry Ireland No.1*, Autumn 1962.

PRIVATE PASSION

1. *Poetry Ireland* (1963–8).
2. Paul Durcan's poem 'Actually' was published by John Jordan in *Poetry Ireland 3*, Spring 1964. 'One of the Uneven Numbers' appeared in *Poetry Ireland no. 4*, Summer 1964. Among the other (then) young poets published in this series of *PI.* were: Christy Brown (*My Left Foot*), Seamus Heaney, Michael Harnett (*sic.*), Derek Mahon and Macdara Woods.
3. *The Berlin Wall Café* (Belfast 1985).
4. This word is difficult to decipher in the printed version of the original review.

DÁNTA, LE CAITLÍN MAUDE

1. *Dánta*, le Caitlín Maude. Ciarán Ó Coigligh a chuir in eagar (Dublin 1985). Caitlín Maude (1941–82), poet, actress and singer, was born in Casla, Conamara, and worked as a teacher in Ireland and in London. Her recording of sean-nós singing, *Caitlín*, was produced by Gael-Linn in 1975. She co-wrote a play with the dual-language poet Micheál Ó hArtnéide/Michael Hartnett called *An Lasair Choille*, and also wrote some short fiction and articles.

SHAW, WILDE, SYNGE AND YEATS

1. Richard Kearney (ed.), *The Irish Mind: Exploring Intellectual Traditions* (Dublin 1985), pp. 209–25.
2. Alfred Turco, Jr, *Shaw's Moral Vision* (New York 1978), p. 150.
3. v. Peter Ure, 1963, *Yeats the Playwright*, Ch. 5, *passim*.
4. The author omits Congreve, since contrary to popular opinion, he was not Irish-born.
5. This will be qualified later.
6. Una Ellis-Fermor, *The Irish Dramatic Movement* (London 1939).
7. A revised and enlarged edition appeared in 1912, with a section covering Ibsen's plays after 1891.
8. Stanley Weintraub (ed.), *Shaw: An Autobiography 1856–98* (1962, reprinted New York 1969/70), p. 132.
9. *Ibid.* p. 236.
10. *The Complete Prefaces of Bernard Shaw* (London 1965), pp. 704–45.
11. Frederick Copleston, *Arthur Schopenhauer, Philosopher of Pessimism*, 2nd ed. (London 1975), pp. 39–40.
12. Bernard Shaw, 1962, *Complete Plays with Prefaces*, 6 vols (New York 1962), vol. 1, pp. 302–03.
13. *Ibid.* p. 303.
14. *Nietzsche: The Man and his Philosophy* (Baton Rouge, 1965), p. 302.
15. *Op. cit.* pp. 303–05.
16. Turco (1976), *op. cit.* p. 145.
17. *Ibid.* p. 160.

18. B. Shaw, 1962, *op. cit.* vol. 3, p. 507. By an uncharacteristic slip, Shaw includes Turner and Hogarth among 'the writers'. The inclusion of Wagner is dubious, if justifiable.

19. *Ibid.* p. 511.

20. *John Bull's Other Island* was written in 1904 'at the request of Mr William Butler Yeats as a contribution to the repertory of the Irish Literary Theatre … The play was at that time beyond the resources of the new Abbey Theatre … There was another reason for changing the destination of *John Bull's Other Island* … It was uncongenial to the spirit of the neo-Gaelic movement which is bent on creating a new Ireland after its own ideal, whereas my play is a very uncompromising presentment of the real old Ireland.' B. Shaw, 1962, *op. cit.* vol. 2, p. 443. Shaw wrote only one other play, the one-act *O'Flaherty V.C.,* which is set wholly in Ireland. Act 1 of Part 4 of *Back to Methusaleh* (1921) is set in the Burren.

21. B. Shaw, *Complete Plays*, vol. 2 (1962), p. x.

22. Jorge Luis Borges, *Labyrinths: Selected Stories and Other Writings*, eds Donald A. Yates and James E. Irby (New York 1964). 'A Note on (towards) Bernard Shaw', collected in Jorge Luis Borges, *Otras Inquisiciones* (Buenos Aires 1952).

23. H. Montgomery Hyde, *Oscar Wilde* (New York 1976), p. 5.

24. Lloyd Lewis and Henry Justin Smith, *Oscar Wilde Discovers America* (New York 1936), p. 168.

25. Hyde, 1976, *op. cit.* pp. 68–9.

26. *Autobiography*, pp. 116–17.

27. Hyde (1976), *op. cit.* p. 89.

28. *Ibid.*, p. 125.

29. *Ibid.*, p. 381.

30. Karl Beckson (ed.), *Oscar Wilde: The Critical Heritage* (London 1970), p. 372.

31. *Ibid.*, p. 392.

32. Dominic Manganiello, *Joyce's Politics* (London 1980).

33. Benjamin Tucker, *Instead of a Book, by a Man Too Busy to Write One* (New York 1893).

34. Manganiello, *op. cit.* pp. 219–20.

35. *Ibid.* p. 220.

36. *Ibid.* p. 220.

37. George Woodcock, *Anarchism* (London 1975), p. 30.

38. *De Profundis*, in Rupert Hart-Davis (ed.), *The Selected Letters of Oscar Wilde* (New York 1979), p. 216.

39. Hyde, 1976, *op. cit.* pp. 83–4.

40. James W. Hulse, *A Study of Revolutionaries in London* (Oxford 1970), p. 99.

41. *Ibid.* p. 99.

42. Manganiello, *op. cit.* p. 220.

43. Michael Wilding, *Political Fictions* (London 1980), p. 48.

44. 'The Soul of Man Under Socialism', in G.F. Maine (ed.), *The Works of Oscar Wilde* (London 1961), p. 1018.

45. *Ibid.* p. 1020.

46. *Ibid.* p. 1026.

47. Manganiello, *op. cit.* p. 221.

48. Ed. G.F. Maine, 1961, *op. cit.* p. 1038.

49. Manganiello, *op. cit.* p. 221.

50. Ed. G.F. Maine, 1961, *op. cit.* p. 1043.

51. *Oscar Wilde* (Columbia Essays on Modern Writers), 1972, p. 21.

52. Hyde, 1976, *op. cit.* p. 140.

53. Ellsworth Mason & Richard Ellmann, *The Critical Writings of James Joyce* (New York 1964), p. 70.

54. *Ibid.* p. 72.

55. But his influence was to be found in the so-called Cork Realists, Lennox Robinson (1886–1958) and T.C. Murray (1873–1959) and, we are told, the mysterious R.J. Ray.

56. T.R. Henn (ed.), *The Plays and Poems of J.M. Synge* (London 1963), p. 108.

57. *Ibid.* p. 174.

58. *Ibid.*

59. *Ibid.*

60. *Ibid.*

61. *Ibid.* pp. 174–5.

62. *Ibid.* p. 175.

63. *Ibid.* p. 108.

64. *Ibid.*

65. Michael Meyer, *Henrik Ibsen: The Making of a Dramatist 1828–64* (London 1967), p. 24.

66. *Theatre in Ireland* (1974), p. 48.

67. Sean O'Casey, *Collected Plays*, 4 vols (London 1963, originally 1949), vol. 1, p. 23.

68. Collected in two volumes as *Autobiographies*, 1963. See *The Letters of Sean O'Casey*, ed. David Krause (London and New York 1975), vol. 1, 1910–41; 1980, vol. 2, 1942–54.

69. 'Sean O'Casey as a Socialist Artist', in Ronald Ayling (ed.), *Sean O'Casey: Modern Judgements* (London 1969), p. 192.

70. 'Ireland after Yeats', in *The Bell,* vol. 18, No. 2 (summer 1953), pp. 37–48.

71. *Letters*, vol. 1, p. 131 (to *Irish Statesman*, 7 February 1925).

72. Cf. John Jordan, spring 1980, 'The Passionate Autodidact: The Importance of Litera Scripta for Sean O'Casey', in *Irish University Review*, vol. 10, no. 1, pp. 70–1.

73. John Jordan, 'Illusion and Actuality in the Later O'Casey', *Modern Judgements, op. cit.* pp. 146–7.

74. *Collected Plays*, vol. 2, p. 333.

75. See for instance Denis Johnston (1931), *The Moon in the Yellow River*; Conor Cruise O'Brien (1969), *Murderous Angels;* Brian Friel (1981), *Faith Healer.*

76. See *The Plays of George Fitzmaurice*, 3 vols (Dublin 1967–70).

ACID JOY

1. Since this review was written, Pearse Hutchinson has published other verse in Irish: his second full collection *as Gaeilge* was *Le Cead na Gréine* (An Clóchomar Tta, 1989); *The Soul that Kissed the Body* (1990) is a selection of his own translations from his poetry in Irish (see ' "Rus in Urbe": Cómhrá le Pearse Hutchinson', *Innti, II* (1988).

2. *Cantigas d'Amigo* – the amorous song-poems by the Galician and Portuguese troubadors of the thirteenth and fourteenth centuries.

3. Gallery Press published Pearse Hutchinson's own choice of his collected translations, entitled *Done into English*, at the end of November 2003. *Plus ça change, plus c'est la même chose* ... none of the broadsheet Irish newspapers (including *The Irish Times*) has yet reviewed this book, the distillation of a lifetime's work of translation by a major Irish poet.

4. The village in Tipperary where some enterprising local historian/genealogist/entrepreneur discovered 'Irish roots' for US President Ronald Reagan in the presidential election year of 1984.

LITERARY ERUDITION

1. As this book is being edited in August 2005, Ben Kiely was preparing to celebrate his eighty-sixth birthday.

2. Brinsley MacNamara (1890–1963), novelist and playwright, the son of a schoolmaster in Delvin Co. Westmeath, was an actor with the Abbey Theatre Company. He is best known for his first novel, *The Valley of the Squinting Windows*, which caused a furore when it was published in 1918, resulting in a boycott of his father's school and subsequent litigation involving neighbours. See Padraic O'Farrell, *The Burning of Brinsley MacNamara* (The Lilliput Press, Dublin 1990).

3. Jeremiah J. Callanan (1795–1829), poet and translator, born into a medical family at Ballinhassig, Co. Cork. He studied for the priesthood at Maynooth Seminary, but left before ordination and then studied at TCD. He became a member of the literary circle in Cork that included Thomas Crofton Croker and John Windele. He translated from the Irish and gathered folklore. He lived for a time in Lisbon. He is the author of *The Recluse of Inchydoney* (1830), and *The Poems of J.J. Callanan* (Cork 1847–61).

4. In his Critic's Choice for 1978 in *Hibernia* magazine, John Jordan selected Ben Kiely's book *All the Way to Bantry Bay*, and said of it: 'Benedict Kiely gives the bedizened slut and silk of the kind [sic] that is our island [race of people] a fresh run.' See *Hibernia*, 21 December 1978, p. 34.

CHAPTER AND VERSE

1. Tom Paulin (ed.), *The Faber Book of Political Verse* (London 1986).

2. This essay also appeared in Gerald Dawe and Jonathan Williams (eds), *Krino 1986–96: An Anthology of Modern Irish Writing* (Dublin 1996), pp. 342–53.

Index

D

E

F

Fielding, Henry 92
Fierobe, Claude 328
Figgis, Darrell 312, 317
Finberg, H.P.R. 4
Fitzgerald, Jim 14
Fitzmaurice, George 27, 216, 368
Fitz-Simon, Christopher 204
Flanagan, Thomas (Prof.) 6, 90
Flood, Henry 91, 307
Flower, Robin 20, 254, 294
Folio 3
Fontaine, Jean de la 279
Ford, Henry 380
Ford, John 25, 139, 379
Forster, E.M. 323
Fra Angelico (Guido di Pietro) 65, 145
Francis of Assisi (St) 290
Franck, Cesar 84
Franco, Francisco (Generalissimo) 13,
   229, 236, 237
Frazer, James George (Sir) 152
Frenau, Philip 389
Freud, Sigmund 158
Freund, E. Washburn 337
Friedman, Arthur 22
Friel, Brian 13, 27, 368
Frost, Robert 204, 205, 389, 370
Frye, Northrop 11
Fussell, Paul 296

G

Gaffney, M.H. (O.P.) 132
Gallagher, Patrick 3
Galvin, Patrick 132
Gardiner, Helen 6
Garnier, Robert 278
Garrick, David 327
Garrity, Devin A. 102
Gate Theatre 3, 4, 5, 6, 24, 31, 136, 163,
   307, 336, 378
Gautier, Theophile 9, 279, 375
Geertz, Clifford 249
Genet, Jean 249, 379

Giacosa, Giuseppe 139
Gibbon, Monk 331
Gide, André 90, 279, 281, 288, 317
Gilbert, W.S. 168
Gili, J.H. 42
Ginger, John 22
Gissing, George 320
Glendinning, Victoria 22, 308–9, 318
Glob, P.V. 266
Glover, Samuel 90
Gmelch, George 314
Goethe, Johann Wolfgang von 44, 328,
   356, 383
Gogarty, Oliver St John 4, 14, 42, 52, 56,
   59, 82, 122, 135–6, 139, 146, 195, 199,
   258, 317
Gogol, Nikolai 9, 208
Goldsmith, Oliver 11, 90, 138, 145, 193,
   204–5, 260, 307, 321–7, 354
Goncharov, Ivan 9, 81, 208–9, 212
Gonne, Iseult 283–4
Gonne, Maud 215, 241, 286, 296, 364
Gore-Booth, Eva 386
Gorman, Herbert 34, 38
Gosse, Edmund 214
Gowan, John Hunter 373
Gower, G. 236
Graham, Finola 23
Grattan, Henry 91, 293, 307
Graves, Robert 7, 102
Gray, Thomas 68–74, 137–8, 144–5, 321,
   328, 387
Greacen, Robert 102, 110
Green, Julien 286
Greene, David H. (Prof.) 149, 219
Greene, Graham 13, 30, 40, 45, 127, 220
Greene, Robert 44, 363
Gregory the Great (Pope) 306
Gregory, Augusta (Lady) 14, 130, 135,
   139, 150, 241, 242
Gregory, Robert 4, 6, 12, 44, 74, 76–7,
   102, 108, 110, 142, 145, 192, 204, 207,
   242, 283, 317
Grein, J.T. 355

Grey, Zane 136
Griffin, Gerald 79, 90, 93, 141, 379
Griffith, Arthur 56, 28, 135, 139, 364
Griffiths, Ralph 321, 322
Grotowski, Jerry 248
Gualli, Eamon 162
Guerin, Eugenie 286
Guerin, Maurice de 286
Guillén, Jorge 282
Guillet, Pernette Due 278

H

Hackett, Frances 55, 237
Hamburger, Michael 383
Hamlet 6, 36, 45, 145, 147, 156, 158,
    161, 206, 364, 382
Handke, Peter 248
Hardy, Thomas 135, 258, 370
Harmon, Maurice 3, 8, 16, 37
Harris, Frank 357, 360
Harrison, Tony 387
Hart-Davis, Rupert 5, 26, 76–7
Harte, Denis 10
Hartley, Anthony 278, 279
Hartnett, Michael 7, 222–4, 256, 258,
    331
Harvey, Francis 259
Hawthorne, Nathaniel 311
Haydn, Franz Joseph 30
Hayman, Ronald 248
Hayward, John 313
Healey, George Harris 57–8
Heaney, Seamus 7, 15, 19, 24, 264–8,
    331, 335, 373, 383–4, 388
Heath-Stubbs, John 60
Heidegger, Martin 291
Heine, Heinrich 383
Henley, William Ernest 168
Henn, T.R. 26, 254
Henry VIII (King) 137, 311
Henry, Frank 12, 14
Henry, O. 379

Herbert, George 202, 206, 261
Herbert, Zbigniew 381
Hewitt, John 7, 240, 241, 259
Hibernia 3, 7, 8, 10–13, 15–16, 19, 23,
    34, 36, 55, 57, 62, 76, 79, 82, 87, 98,
    102, 122, 151, 158, 160–2, 164–5, 167,
    169, 171, 197–9, 213, 219, 227, 231,
    236, 241, 244, 247, 278, 281, 285, 293,
    295, 308, 310, 312, 314, 316, 328, 348,
    375, 378
Hickey, Patrick 279
Higgins, F.R. 107, 183, 213
Hill, Geoffrey 387
Hinsley, Arthur Cardinal 149
Hitchcock, Alfred 131
Hobbes, Thomas 75
Hoffman, E.T.A. 329
Hogan, Jeremiah J. 4
Hogan, Robert (Prof.) 22, 145, 316–17
Hogarth, William 25, 356
Hollingdale, R.J. 356
Holub, Miroslav 382
Homer 32
Hone, Joseph 8
Hone, Nathaniel 145
Hopkins, Gerard Manley 6, 16, 202,
    206–7, 306, 384–5
Horace (Quintus Horatius Flaccus) 279,
    306, 324
Horniman, Annie 150
Houlihan, Con 248
Hudson, W.H. 135
Hughes, Anthony (Prof.) 371
Hughes, Ted 384
Hugo, Victor 138, 279
Huizinga, Johan 296
Hulse, James W. 26
Hutchinson, Pearse 3, 5, 7, 9, 12, 13, 14,
    27, 107–8, 116, 168, 175–7, 214, 257,
    375–9
Huxley, Aldous 118, 136
Huysmans, Joris Karl 69, 287, 362–3
Hyde, Douglas 88, 287–8

N

T